Discovering Computers 2007

A GATEWAY TO INFORMATION

Web Enhanced — BRIEF

Discovering Computers

2007

A GATEWAY TO INFORMATION

Web Enhanced — BRIEF

Gary B. Shelly
Thomas J. Cashman
Misty E. Vermaat

Contributing Authors

Jeffrey J. Quasney

Susan L. Sebok

Jeffrey J. Webb

THOMSON COURSE TECHNOLOGY
25 THOMSON PLACE
BOSTON MA 02210

SHELLY
CASHMAN
SERIES®

Australia • Canada • Denmark • Japan • Mexico • New Zealand • Philippines • Puerto Rico • Singapore
South Africa • Spain • United Kingdom • United States

THOMSON

COURSE TECHNOLOGY

Discovering Computers 2007:
A Gateway to Information, Web Enhanced
Brief

Gary B. Shelly

Thomas J. Cashman

Misty E. Vermaat

Executive Editor:
Alexandra Arnold

Series Consulting Editor:
Jim Quasney

Product Manager:
Reed Cotter

Associate Product Manager:
Heather Hawkins

Editorial Assistant:
Klenda Martinez

Marketing Manager:
Dana Merk

Marketing Coordinator/Copywriter:
Melissa Marcoux

Print Buyer:
Justin Palmeiro

**Thomson Course Technology
Production Contact:**
Pamela Elizian

Researcher:
F. William Vermaat

Development Editor:
Lyn Markowicz

Proofreader:
Nancy Lamm

Final Reader:
Kim Kosmatka

Management Services:
Pre-Press Company, Inc.

Interior Designer:
Pre-Press Company, Inc.

Cover Image:
Pre-Press Company, Inc.

Illustrator:
Pre-Press Company, Inc.

Compositor:
Pre-Press Company, Inc.

Printer:
Banta Menasha

Discovering Computers *2007*

A GATEWAY TO INFORMATION Web Enhanced — BRIEF

Contents

CHAPTER 4

The Components of the System Unit 182

CHAPTER 5

Input 232

Special Feature
PERSONAL MOBILE DEVICES

CHAPTER 6
Output

Special Feature
DIGITAL IMAGING AND VIDEO TECHNOLOGY

CHAPTER 7
Storage

Discover Computers
and make concepts real with . . .

Online Companion

Use the Online Companion at scsite.com/dc2007 to bring unparalleled currency to the learning experience. Access additional information about important topics and make use of online learning games, practice tests, and additional reinforcement. Gain access to this dynamic site through CoursePort, Thomson Course Technology's login page.

Learn How To

Apply the concepts presented in the chapter to every day life with these hands-on activities. See the Learn How To activities in action with new videos on the Online Companion.

Ethics and Issues

Ethics and Issues boxes raise controversial, computer-related topics of the day, challenging readers to closely consider general concerns of computers in society.

Case Studies

Exercise your mind and construct creative solutions to the thought-provoking case studies presented in each chapter. The Case Study exercises are constructed for class discussion, independent research, or examination in a team environment.

practical, hands-on elements.

High-Tech Talk

The High-Tech Talk article at the end of each chapter expands on a topic covered in the chapter and presents a more technical discussion.

Career Corner

Each chapter ends with a Career Corner feature that introduces a computer-career opportunity relating to a topic covered in the chapter.

Companies on the Cutting Edge

Everyone who interacts with computers should be aware of the key computer-related companies. Each chapter profiles two of these key companies.

Technology Trailblazers

The Technology Trailblazers section in each chapter offers a glimpse into the life and times of the more famous leaders of the computer industry.

Discover Computers
and make concepts real with . . .

Web Link

Obtain current information and a different perspective about key terms and concepts by visiting the Web addresses in the Web Links found in the margins throughout the book.

Looking Ahead

The Looking Ahead boxes offer a glimpse at the latest advances in computer technology that will be available, usually within five years.

FAQ

FAQ (frequently asked questions) boxes offer common questions and answers about subjects related to the topic at hand.

Learn It Online

The Learn It Online exercises, which include online videos, practice tests, interactive labs, learning games, and Web-based activities offer a wealth of online reinforcement.

interactive Web elements.

Web Research

Each Web Research exercise references an element in the book, requires follow-up research on the Web, and suggests writing a short article or presenting the findings of the research to the class.

Quiz Yourself

Three Quiz Yourself boxes per chapter help ensure retention by reinforcing sections of the chapter material, rather than waiting for the end of the chapter to test. Use the answers in Appendix B for a quick check of the answers, and take additional these quizzes on the Web for interactivity and easy use.

Primary and Secondary Key Terms

Before taking a test, use the Key Terms page as a checklist of terms to know. In the text, primary key terms appear in bold font and secondary key terms appear in italic font. Visit a Key Terms page on the Web and click any term for additional information.

Discover Computers
and make concepts real with . . .

Picture Yourself

Picture yourself using the concepts presented in each chapter. This section at the beginning of each chapter is intended to bridge the gap between the chapter-specific material and everyday life using computers.

Chapter Objectives and Table of Contents

Before reading the chapter, carefully read through the Objectives and Contents to discover knowledge that will be gleaned from chapter.

Step Figures

Each chapter includes numerous step figures that present the more complex computer concepts using a step-by-step pedagogy.

Checkpoint

Use these three pages of label-the-figure, multiple choice, true/false, matching, and short answer exercises to reinforce understanding of the topics presented in the chapter.

Initial Chapter Figure

Carefully study the first figure in each chapter because it provides an easy-to-follow overview of the major purpose of the chapter.

pedagogical elements.

Chapter Review

Use the two-page Chapter Review before taking an examination to ensure familiarity with the computer concepts presented. This section includes each objective, followed by a one- or two-paragraph summary. Visit a Chapter Review page on the Online Companion, and click the Audio button to listen to the Chapter Review.

Special Features

Eight special features following Chapters 1, 2, 5, 6, and 8 encompass topics from the history of computers, to what's hot on the Web, to a buyer's guide, to the latest in new technology.

Preface

The Shelly Cashman Series® offers the finest textbooks in computer education. We are proud of the fact that the previous eleven editions of this textbook have been the most widely used in computer education. With each new edition of the book, we have implemented significant improvements based on current computer trends and comments made by instructors and students. *Discovering Computers 2007* continues with the innovation, quality, and reliability you have come to expect from the Shelly Cashman Series.

In *Discovering Computers 2007: A Gateway to Information*, you will find an educationally sound, highly visual, and easy-to-follow pedagogy that presents an in-depth treatment of introductory computer subjects. Students will finish the course with a solid understanding of computers, how to use computers, and how to access information on the World Wide Web.

OBJECTIVES OF THIS TEXTBOOK

Discovering Computers 2007: A Gateway to Information, Brief is intended for use as a stand-alone textbook or in combination with an applications, Internet, or programming textbook in a one-quarter or one-semester introductory computer course. No experience with computers is assumed. The objectives of this book are to:

- Present the most-up-to-date technology in an ever-changing discipline
- Give students an in-depth understanding of why computers are essential components in business and society
- Teach the fundamentals of computers and computer nomenclature, particularly with respect to personal computer hardware and software, and the World Wide Web
- Present the material in a visually appealing and exciting manner that motivates students to learn
- Assist students in planning a career
- Provide exercises and lab assignments that allow students to interact with a computer and learn by actually using the computer and the World Wide Web
- Present strategies for purchasing a desktop computer, a notebook computer, a Tablet PC, and a personal mobile device
- Offer alternative learning techniques and reinforcement via the Web
- Offer distance-education providers a textbook with a meaningful and exercise-rich Online Companion

DISTINGUISHING FEATURES

To date, more than six million students have learned about computers using a *Discovering Computers* textbook. With the additional World Wide Web integration and interactivity, streaming up-to-date audio and video, extraordinary step-by-step visual drawings and photographs, unparalleled currency, and the Shelly and Cashman touch, this book will make your computer concepts course exciting and dynamic. Distinguishing features of the Shelly Cashman Series *Discovering Computers* books include:

A Proven Pedagogy
Careful explanations of complex concepts, educationally-sound elements, and reinforcement highlight this proven method of presentation.

A Visually Appealing Book that Maintains Student Interest

The latest technology, pictures, drawings, and text are combined artfully to produce a visually appealing and easy-to-understand book. Many of the figures include a step-by-step presentation (see page 196), which simplifies the more complex computer concepts. Pictures and drawings reflect the latest trends in computer technology. This combination of pictures, step-by-step drawings, and easy-to-read text layout sets the standard for computer textbook design.

Latest Technologies and Terms

The technologies and terms your students see in this book are those they will encounter when they start using computers. Only the latest application software is shown throughout the book. New topics and terms include blog, developer, podcast, gaming desktop computer, Media Center PC, ultra personal computer (uPC), game console, digital audio player, wiki, content aggregator, RSS 2.0 (Really Simple Syndication), Atom, podcast, blogger, professional photo editing software, document management software, blog software, blogware, Centrino, multicore processor, FireWire hub, Viiv technology, gaming keyboard, control pad, Click Wheel, gamepad, retinal scanner, earphones, headphones, contrast ratio, earbuds, longitudinal recording, perpendicular recording, HD-DVD disc, UMD, adware, Document Explorer, Virtual Folders, Windows Vista, and Windows XP Professional x64 Edition.

World Wide Web Enhanced

This book uses the World Wide Web as a major supplement. The purpose of integrating the World Wide Web into the book is to (1) offer students additional information and currency on important topics; (2) use its interactive capabilities to offer creative reinforcement and online quizzes; (3) make available alternative learning techniques with Web-based learning games, practice tests, and interactive labs; (4) underscore the relevance of the World Wide Web as a basic information tool that can be used in all facets of society; (5) introduce students to doing research on the Web; and (6) offer instructors the opportunity to organize and administer their traditional campus-based or distance-education-based courses on the Web using WebCT, Blackboard, or MyCourse 2.1. This textbook, however, does not depend on Web access to be used successfully. The Web access adds to the already complete treatment of topics within the book.

Extensive End-of-Chapter Materials

A notable strength of the *Discovering Computers* textbooks is the extensive student activities at the end of each chapter. Well-structured student activities can make the difference between students merely participating in a class and students retaining the information they learn. The activities in the *Discovering Computers 2007* books include: Chapter Review, Key Terms, Checkpoint, Learn It Online, Learn How To, Web Research, and Case Studies.

ORGANIZATION OF THIS TEXTBOOK

Discovering Computers 2007: A Gateway to Information, Brief provides a thorough introduction to computers. The material is divided into eight chapters, five special features, three appendices, and a glossary/index.

Chapter 1 – Introduction to Computers   In Chapter 1, students are introduced to basic computer concepts, such as what a computer is, how it works, and what makes it a powerful tool.

Special Feature – Timeline 2007 Milestones in Computer History   In this special feature, students learn about the major computer technology developments during the past 66 years.

Chapter 2 – The Internet and World Wide Web   In Chapter 2, students learn about the Internet, World Wide Web, browsers, e-mail, FTP, and instant messaging.

Special Feature – Making Use of the Web   In this special feature, more than 150 popular up-to-date Web sites are listed and described. Basic searching techniques also are introduced.

Chapter 3 – Application Software   In Chapter 3, students are introduced to a variety of business software, graphics and multimedia software, home/personal/educational software, and communications software.

Chapter 4 – The Components of the System Unit   In Chapter 4, students are introduced to the components of the system unit; how memory stores data, instructions, and information; and how the system unit executes an instruction.

Chapter 5 – Input   Chapter 5 describes the various techniques of input and commonly used input devices.

Special Feature – Personal Mobile Devices   In this special feature, students receive a detailed presentation of personal mobile device operating systems, built-in personal mobile device software, personal mobile device application software, and how to obtain and install personal mobile device software. Also included is a personal mobile device buyer's guide.

Chapter 6 – Output   Chapter 6 describes the various methods of output and commonly used output devices.

Special Feature – Digital Imaging and Video Technology   In this special feature, students are introduced to using a personal computer, digital camera, and video camera to manipulate photographs and video.

Chapter 7 – Storage   In Chapter 7, students learn about various storage media and storage devices.

Chapter 8 – Operating Systems and Utility Programs   In Chapter 8, students learn about a variety of stand-alone operating systems, network operating systems, and embedded operating systems.

Special Feature – Buyer's Guide 2007: How to Purchase a Personal Computer   In this special feature, students are introduced to purchasing a desktop computer, notebook computer, and Tablet PC.

Appendix A – Coding Schemes and Number Systems   Appendix A presents the ASCII, EBCDIC, and Unicode coding schemes.

Appendix B – Quiz Yourself Answers   Appendix B provides the answers for the Quiz Yourself questions in the text.

Appendix C – Computer Acronyms   Appendix C summarizes the computer acronyms discussed in the book.

Glossary/Index   The Glossary/Index includes a definition and page references for every key term presented in the book.

SHELLY CASHMAN SERIES INSTRUCTOR RESOURCES

The Shelly Cashman Series is dedicated to providing you with all of the tools you need to make your class a success. Information on all supplementary materials is available through your Course Technology representative or by calling one of the following telephone numbers: Colleges and Universities, 1-800-648-7450; High Schools, 1-800-824-5179; Private Career Colleges, 1-800-477-3692 ; Canada, 1-800-268-2222; Corporations with IT Training Centers, 1-800-477-3692; and Government Agencies, Health-Care Organizations, and Correctional Facilities, 1-800-477-3692.

Instructor Resources CD-ROM

The Instructor Resources CD-ROM includes both teaching and testing aids. The contents of each item on the Instructor Resources CD-ROM (ISBN 1-4188-5957-5) are described below.

Instructors Manual   The Instructor's Manual is made up of Microsoft Word files, which include detailed lesson plans with page number references, lecture notes, classroom activities, discussion topics, and projects to assign.

Syllabus   Sample syllabi, which can be customized easily to a course, are included. The syllabi cover policies, class and lab assignments and exams, and procedural information.

Figure Files   Illustrations for every figure in the textbook are available in electronic form. Use this ancillary to present a slide show in lecture or to print transparencies for use in lecture with an overhead projector. If you have a personal computer and LCD device, this ancillary can be an effective tool for presenting lectures.

Solutions to Exercises   Solutions are included for all end-of-chapter exercises.

Test Bank & Test Engine   The ExamView test bank includes 220 questions for every chapter (50 multiple-choice, 100 true/false, and 70 completion) with page number references, and when appropriate, figure references. Each question also is identified by objective and type of term (primary or secondary). The test bank comes with a copy of the test engine, ExamView, the ultimate tool for your objective-based testing needs.

Printed Test Bank   A Microsoft Word version of the test bank you can print also is included.

Test Out/Final Exam   Use this objective-based test to test students out of your course, or use it as a final examination. A master answer sheet is included.

Pretest/Posttest   Use these carefully prepared tests at the beginning and the end of the semester to measure student progress. A master answer sheet is included.

Data Files for Students   All the files that are required by students to complete the exercises are included. You can distribute the files on the Instructor Resources CD-ROM to your students over a network, or you can have them follow the instructions on the inside back cover of this book to obtain a copy of the Data Disk.

Course Presenter

Course Presenter (ISBN 1-4188-5958-3) is a one-click-per-slide presentation system on CD-ROM that provides PowerPoint slides for every subject in each chapter. Use this presentation system to give interesting, well-organized, and knowledge-based lectures. Several up-to-date G4TechTV computer-related video clips are available for optional presentation. Course Presenter provides consistent coverage for multiple lecturers.

Student Edition Labs

More than thirty Web-based interactive labs will help your students master hundreds of computer concepts including input and output devices, file management and desktop applications, computer privacy, virus protection, and much more. Featuring up-to-the-minute content, eye-popping graphics, and rich animation, the highly interactive Student Edition Labs offer students an alternative way to learn through dynamic observation, step-by-step practice, and challenging review questions. Access the free Student Edition Labs from the *Discovering Computers 2007* Online Companion at scsite.com/dc2007 or see the Student Edition Lab exercises on the Learn It Online pages at the end of each chapter.

Online Content

Course Technology offers textbook-based content for Blackboard, WebCT, and MyCourse 2.1.

BlackBoard and WebCT As the leading provider of IT content for the Blackboard and WebCT platforms, Course Technology delivers rich content that enhances your textbook to give your students a unique learning experience.

MyCoure 2.1 MyCourse 2.1 is Course Technology's powerful online course management and content delivery system. MyCourse 2.1 allows nontechnical users to create, customize, and deliver Web-based courses; post content and assignments; manage student enrollment; administer exams; track results in the online grade book; and more.

SUPPLEMENTS

Two supplements can be used in combination with this textbook.

SAM Computer Concepts

Add the power of assessment and detailed reporting to your Student Edition Lab assignments with SAM Computer Concepts.

SAM (Skills Assessment Manager) Computer Concepts helps you energize your training assignments by allowing students to learn and quiz on important computer skills in an active, hands-on environment. By adding SAM Computer Concepts to your curriculum, you can:

- Reinforce your students' knowledge of key computer concepts with hands-on application exercises.
- Allow your students to "learn by listening," with rich audio in their computer concepts labs.
- Build computer concepts exams from a test bank of more than 50,000 objective-based questions or create your own test questions.
- Schedule your students' computer concepts training and testing assignments with powerful administrative tools.
- Track student exam grades and training progress using more than one dozen student and classroom reports.

Study Guide

This highly popular *Study Guide* (ISBN 1-4188-4371-7) includes a variety of activities that help students recall, review, and master introductory computer concepts. The *Study Guide* complements the end-of-chapter material with a guided chapter outline; a self-test consisting of true/false, multiple-choice, short answer, fill-in, and matching questions; an entertaining puzzle; and other challenging exercises.

SHELLY CASHMAN SERIES – TRADITIONALLY BOUND TEXTBOOKS

The Shelly Cashman Series presents the following computer subjects in a variety of traditionally bound textbooks. For more information, see your Course Technology representative or call 1-800-648-7450. For Shelly Cashman Series information, visit Shelly Cashman Online at scseries.com

	COMPUTERS
Computers	Discovering Computers 2007: A Gateway to Information, Complete
	Discovering Computers 2007: A Gateway to Information, Introductory
	Discovering Computers 2007: A Gateway to Information, Brief
	Discovering Computers: Fundamentals, Third Edition
	Teachers Discovering Computers: Integrating Technology in the Classroom, Fourth Edition
	Essential Introduction to Computers, Sixth Edition (40-page)

	WINDOWS APPLICATIONS
Microsoft Office	Microsoft Office 2003: Essential Concepts and Techniques, Second Edition (5 projects)
	Microsoft Office 2003: Brief Concepts and Techniques, Second Edition (9 projects)
	Microsoft Office 2003: Introductory Concepts and Techniques, Second Edition (15 projects)
	Microsoft Office 2003: Introductory Concepts and Techniques, Premium Edition (15 projects)
	Microsoft Office 2003: Advanced Concepts and Techniques (12 projects)
	Microsoft Office 2003: Post Advanced Concepts and Techniques (11 projects)
	Microsoft Office XP: Essential Concepts and Techniques (5 projects)
	Microsoft Office XP: Brief Concepts and Techniques (9 projects)
	Microsoft Office XP: Introductory Concepts and Techniques, Windows XP Edition (15 projects)
	Microsoft Office XP: Introductory Concepts and Techniques, Enhanced Edition (15 projects)
	Microsoft Office XP: Advanced Concepts and Techniques (11 projects)
	Microsoft Office XP: Post Advanced Concepts and Techniques (11 projects)
Integration	Teachers Discovering and Integrating Microsoft Office: Essential Concepts and Techniques, Second Edition
	Integrating Microsoft Office XP Applications and the World Wide Web: Essential Concepts and Techniques
PIM	Microsoft Outlook 2002: Essential Concepts and Techniques • Microsoft Office Outlook 2003: Introductory Concepts and Techniques
Microsoft Works	Microsoft Works 6: Complete Concepts and Techniques[1] • Microsoft Works 2000: Complete Concepts and Techniques[1]
Microsoft Windows	Microsoft Windows XP: Comprehensive Concepts and Techniques[2] Service Pak 2 Edition
	Microsoft Windows XP: Brief Concepts and Techniques
	Microsoft Windows 2000: Comprehensive Concepts and Techniques[2]
	Microsoft Windows 2000: Brief Concepts and Techniques
	Microsoft Windows 98: Comprehensive Concepts and Techniques[2]
	Microsoft Windows 98: Essential Concepts and Techniques
	Introduction to Microsoft Windows NT Workstation 4
Notebook Organizer	Microsoft Office OneNote 2003: Introductory Concepts and Techniques
Word Processing	Microsoft Office Word 2003: Comprehensive Concepts and Techniques, CourseCard Edition[2] • Microsoft Word 2002: Comprehensive Concepts and Techniques[2]
Spreadsheets	Microsoft Office Excel 2003: Comprehensive Concepts and Techniques, CourseCard Edition[2] • Microsoft Excel 2002: Comprehensive Concepts and Techniques[2]
Database	Microsoft Office Access 2003: Comprehensive Concepts and Techniques, CourseCard Edition[2] • Microsoft Access 2002: Comprehensive Concepts and Techniques[2]
Presentation Graphics	Microsoft Office PowerPoint 2003: Comprehensive Concepts and Techniques, CourseCard Edition[2] • Microsoft PowerPoint 2002: Comprehensive Concepts and Techniques[2] • Microsoft Producer 2003: Essential Concepts and Techniques
Desktop Publishing	Microsoft Office Publisher 2003: Comprehensive Concepts and Techniques[2] • Microsoft Publisher 2002: Comprehensive Concepts and Techniques[1]

	PROGRAMMING
Programming	Microsoft Visual Basic .NET: Comprehensive Concepts and Techniques[2] • Microsoft Visual Basic 6: Complete Concepts and Techniques[1] • Java Programming: Comprehensive Concepts and Techniques, Third Edition[2] • Structured COBOL Programming, Second Edition • Understanding and Troubleshooting Your PC • Programming Fundamentals Using Microsoft Visual Basic .NET

	INTERNET
Concepts	Discovering the Internet: Brief Concepts and Techniques, Second Edition • Discovering the Internet: Complete Concepts and Techniques, Second Edition
Browser	Microsoft Internet Explorer 6: Introductory Concepts and Techniques, Windows XP Edition • Microsoft Internet Explorer 5: An Introduction • Netscape Navigator 6: An Introduction • Introduction to the World Wide Web • Mozilla Firefox: Introductory Concepts and Techniques
Web Page Creation	Web Design: Introductory Concepts and Techniques, Second Edition • HTML: Comprehensive Concepts and Techniques, Third Edition[2] • Microsoft Office FrontPage 2003: Comprehensive Concepts and Techniques, CourseCard Edition[2] • Microsoft FrontPage 2002: Comprehensive Concepts and Techniques[2] • Microsoft FrontPage 2002: Essential Concepts and Techniques • JavaScript: Complete Concepts and Techniques, Second Edition[1] • Macromedia Dreamweaver MX 2004: Comprehensive Concepts and Techniques[2]

	SYSTEMS ANALYSIS
Systems Analysis	Systems Analysis and Design, Sixth Edition

	DATA COMMUNICATIONS
Data Communications	Business Data Communications: Introductory Concepts and Techniques, Fourth Edition

[1]Also available as an Introductory Edition, which is a shortened version of the complete book, [2]Also available as an Introductory Edition and as a Complete Edition, which are shortened versions of the comprehensive book.

Discovering
Computers
2007
A GATEWAY TO INFORMATION

CHAPTER ONE

Introduction to Computers

Picture Yourself in a Computer Class

While waiting for the instructor to begin her first lecture, you hear several classmates announce they will be meeting at the local coffeehouse to talk about homework and form study groups. Many of them sound nervous and anxious about this Introduction to Computers class. As they talk, you think about your experiences with computers. You had a beginning programming class in high school. You use the Internet regularly to chat with friends. With your digital camera, you take pictures and e-mail them to family members. No study groups for you.

During the lecture, the instructor reads several computer advertisements to the class. The ads use computer terms and acronyms you have never heard, like bus, SDRAM, USB flash drive, TFT, media player, SCSI, HT Technology, Bluetooth, Ethernet, firewall, NIC, and Wi-Fi. Now, *you* get a bit nervous and anxious. When she finishes reading, the instructor tells the class not to worry if some or most of the words in the ads are unfamiliar. "As we work through this course together," she says, "you will learn everything you need to know to buy a computer." While walking out the classroom door, you ask your friend, "What time is everyone meeting at the coffeehouse? I want to get in one of those study groups."

Read Chapter 1 to become familiar with some of the terms mentioned in the advertisement, discover practical uses of computers, and set a foundation for your further learning throughout this book.

After completing this chapter, you will be able to:

1. Recognize the importance of computer literacy
2. Define the term, computer
3. Identify the components of a computer
4. Discuss the advantages and disadvantages of using computers
5. Recognize the purpose of a network
6. Discuss the uses of the Internet and World Wide Web
7. Distinguish between system software and application software
8. Describe the categories of computers
9. Identify the elements of an information system
10. Describe the various types of computer users
11. Discuss various computer applications in society

CONTENTS

A WORLD OF COMPUTERS

Computers are everywhere: at work, at school, and at home. Many daily activities either involve the use of or depend on information from a computer. As shown in Figure 1-1, people use all types and sizes of computers for a variety of reasons and in a range of places. Some computers sit on top of a desk or on the floor; others are small enough to carry.

Computers are a primary means of communication for billions of people. People use computers to correspond with businesses, employees with other employees and customers, students with teachers, and family members with friends and other family members. In addition to corresponding via text messages, people use computers to send each other pictures, diagrams, drawings, music, and videos.

Through computers, society has instant access to information from around the globe. Local and national news, weather reports, sports scores, airline schedules, telephone directories, maps and directions, job listings, credit reports, and countless forms of educational material always are accessible. From the computer, you can meet new friends, share photographs and videos, shop, fill prescriptions, file taxes, or take a course.

At home or while on the road, people use computers to manage schedules, balance checkbooks, pay bills, track personal income and expenses, transfer funds, and buy or sell stocks. Banks place automated teller machines (ATMs) all over the world, making it easy for customers to deposit or withdraw funds at anytime. At the grocery store, a computer tracks purchases, calculates the amount of money due, and often

FIGURE 1-1   People use computers in their daily activities.

generates coupons customized to buying patterns. Vehicles include onboard navigation systems that provide directions, call for emergency services, and track the vehicle if it is stolen.

In the workplace, employees use computers to create correspondence such as e-mail messages, memos, and letters; calculate payroll; track inventory; and generate invoices. Some applications such as automotive design and weather forecasting use computers to perform complex mathematical calculations. At school, teachers use computers to assist with classroom instruction. Students complete assignments and do research on computers in lab rooms and at home.

People also spend hours of leisure time using a computer. They play games, listen to music, watch videos and movies, read books and magazines, research genealogy, compose music and videos, retouch photographs, and plan vacations.

As technology continues to advance, computers are becoming more a part of everyday life. Thus, many people believe that computer literacy is vital to success in today's world. **Computer literacy** involves having a knowledge and understanding of computers and their uses.

This book presents the knowledge you need to be computer literate. As you read this first chapter, keep in mind it is an overview. Many of the terms and concepts introduced in this chapter will be discussed in more depth later in the book.

WHAT IS A COMPUTER?

A **computer** is an electronic device, operating under the control of instructions stored in its own memory, that can accept data, process the data according to specified rules, produce results, and store the results for future use.

Data and Information

Computers process data into information. **Data** is a collection of unprocessed items, which can include text, numbers, images, audio, and video. **Information** conveys meaning and is useful to people.

As shown in Figure 1-2, for example, computers process several data items to print information in the form of a payroll check.

FAQ 1-1

Is data a singular or plural word?

The word data is plural for datum. With respect to computers, however, it is accepted and common practice to use the word data in both the singular and plural context. For more information, visit scsite.com/dc2007/ch1/faq and then click Data.

An **FAQ** (frequently asked question) helps you find answers to commonly asked questions. Web sites often post an FAQ section, and each chapter in this book includes FAQ boxes related to topics in the text.

Information Processing Cycle

Computers process data (input) into information (output). A computer often holds data, information, and instructions in storage for future use. *Instructions* are the steps that tell the computer how to perform a particular task. Some people refer to the series of input, process, output, and storage activities as the *information processing cycle*.

Most computers today can communicate with other computers. As a result, communications also has become an essential element of the information processing cycle.

DATA

28 Hours
Hammond, IN 46323
$12.50 per hour
Kayla Robertson
1192 Reeder Road

PROCESSES

- Multiplies hourly pay rate by hours to determine gross pay (350.00)
- Organizes data
- Computes payroll taxes (49.00)
- Subtracts payroll taxes from gross pay to determine net pay (301.00)

678911

Date: June 17, 2007 $ 301.00   Dollars

Joan Smith
President

Maple Construction
421 Cedar Road
Hammond, IN 46323

pay to the order of Kayla Robertson

Three Hundred One and 00/100

:788340374934: 14 12 77 43 2

Memo   00678911

INFORMATION

FIGURE 1-2 A computer processes data into information. In this simplified example, the employee's name and address, hourly pay rate, and hours worked all represent data. The computer processes the data to produce the payroll check (information).

THE COMPONENTS OF A COMPUTER

A computer contains many electric, electronic, and mechanical components known as **hardware**. These components include input devices, output devices, a system unit, storage devices, and communications devices. Figure 1-3 shows some common computer hardware components.

Input Devices

An **input device** is any hardware component that allows you to enter data and instructions into a computer. Six widely used input devices are the keyboard, mouse, microphone, scanner, digital camera, and PC video camera (Figure 1-3).

A computer keyboard contains keys you press to enter data into the computer. A mouse is a small handheld device. With the mouse, you control movement of a small symbol on the screen, called the pointer, and you make selections from the screen.

A microphone allows a user to speak into the computer to enter data and instructions. A scanner converts printed material (such as text and pictures) into a form the computer can use.

With a digital camera, you take pictures and then transfer the photographed images to the computer or printer instead of storing the images on traditional film. A PC video camera is a digital video camera that allows users to create a movie or take still photographs electronically.

WEB LINK 1-1

Input Devices

For more information, visit scsite.com/dc2007/ch1/weblink and then click Input Devices.

FIGURE 1-3 Common computer hardware components include a keyboard, mouse, microphone, scanner, digital camera, PC video camera, printer, monitor, speakers, system unit, internal disk drives, external hard disk, USB flash drive, card reader/writer, and modem.

Output Devices

An **output device** is any hardware component that conveys information to one or more people. Three commonly used output devices are a printer, a monitor, and speakers (Figure 1-3 on the previous page).

A printer produces text and graphics on a physical medium such as paper. A monitor displays text, graphics, and videos on a screen. Speakers allow you to hear music, voice, and other audio (sounds).

System Unit

The **system unit** is a case that contains the electronic components of the computer that are used to process data (Figure 1-3). The circuitry of the system unit usually is part of or is connected to a circuit board called the motherboard.

Two main components on the motherboard are the processor and memory. The *processor* is the electronic component that interprets and carries out the basic instructions that operate the computer. *Memory* consists of electronic components that store instructions waiting to be executed and data needed by those instructions. Although some forms of memory are permanent, most memory keeps data and instructions temporarily, which means its contents are erased when the computer is shut off.

FAQ 1-2

What is a CPU?

The processor. Most people in the computer industry use the terms *CPU* (*central processing unit*) and processor to mean the same. For more information, visit scsite.com/dc2007/ch1/faq and then click CPU.

Storage Devices

Storage holds data, instructions, and information for future use. For example, computers can store hundreds or millions of customer names and addresses. Storage holds these items permanently.

A computer keeps data, instructions, and information on **storage media**. Examples of storage media are floppy disks, Zip disks, USB flash drives, hard disks, CDs, DVDs,

and memory cards. A **storage device** records (writes) and/or retrieves (reads) items to and from storage media. Drives and readers/writers, which are types of storage devices (Figure 1-3), accept a specific kind of storage media. For example, a CD drive (storage device) accepts a CD (storage media). Storage devices often function as a source of input because they transfer items from storage to memory.

A floppy disk consists of a thin, circular, flexible disk enclosed in a square-shaped plastic shell that is inserted in and removed from a floppy disk drive. A typical floppy disk stores up to about 1.4 million characters. A Zip disk looks similar to a floppy disk but has much greater storage capabilities — up to about 750 million characters. You insert Zip disks in and remove them from Zip drives.

A USB flash drive is a portable storage device that has much more storage capacity than a floppy disk but is small and lightweight enough to be transported on a keychain or in a pocket (Figure 1-3). You plug a USB flash drive in a special, easily accessible opening on the computer.

A hard disk provides much greater storage capacity than a floppy disk, Zip disk, or USB flash drive. The average hard disk can hold more than 100 billion characters. Hard disks are enclosed in an airtight, sealed case. Although some are external or removable, most are housed inside the system unit (Figure 1-4).

FIGURE 1-4   Hard disks are self-contained devices. The hard disk shown here must be installed in the system unit before it can be used.

A compact disc is a flat, round, portable metal disc with a plastic coating. One type of compact disc is a CD-ROM, which you can access using most CD and DVD drives (Figure 1-5). Another type of compact disc is a DVD-ROM, some of which have enough storage capacity to store two full-length movies. To use a DVD-ROM, you need a DVD drive.

Some portable devices, such as digital cameras, use memory cards as the storage media. You then can transfer the stored items, such as electronic photographs, from the memory card to a computer or printer using a card reader/writer (Figure 1-3 on page 7).

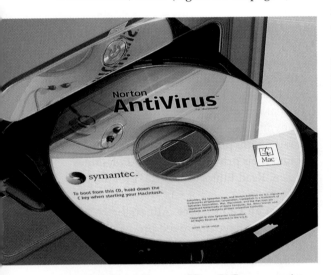

FIGURE 1-5 To use a CD or DVD, you need a CD or DVD drive.

Communications Devices

A **communications device** is a hardware component that enables a computer to send (transmit) and receive data, instructions, and information to and from one or more computers. A widely used communications device is a modem (Figure 1-3).

Communications occur over cables, telephone lines, cellular radio networks, satellites, and other transmission media. Some transmission media, such as satellites and cellular radio networks, are wireless, which means they have no physical lines or wires.

ADVANTAGES AND DISADVANTAGES OF USING COMPUTERS

Society has reaped many benefits from using computers. Both business and home users can make well-informed decisions because they have instant access to information from anywhere in the world. A **user** is anyone who communicates with a computer or utilizes the information it generates. Students, another type of user, have more tools to assist them in the learning process. Read Looking Ahead 1-1 for a look at the next generation of benefits from using computers.

LOOKING AHEAD 1-1

Medical Breakthroughs with Computer Implants, Devices

The battle to curb obesity eventually may be won with an implantable stomach device. This technology, called a gastric stimulator, would zap the stomach or nerves with electric current, in much the same way a cardiac pacemaker stimulates the heart, to boost metabolism or regulate appetite signals.

Another possible surgery will involve implanting miniature computers or computer components in the body to help it perform basic functions. A processor, for example, could help release hormones. A brain computer interface may monitor and treat diseases, such as epilepsy and depression, that affect brain activity. A body-scanning machine will evaluate patients' pain when they cannot communicate.

In addition, robotic legs strapped to the body can assist people such as firefighters and soldiers who must bear heavy loads for extended periods of time. For more information, visit scsite.com/dc2007/ch1/looking and then click Processor Implants.

ADVANTAGES OF USING COMPUTERS   Benefits of computers are possible because computers have the advantages of speed, reliability, consistency, storage, and communications.

- **Speed**: Computer operations occur through electronic circuits. When data, instructions, and information flow along these circuits, they travel at incredibly fast speeds. Many computers process billions or trillions of operations in a single second. Processing involves computing (adding, subtracting, multiplying, dividing), sorting (e.g., alphabetizing), organizing, formatting, checking spelling and grammar, charting, displaying pictures, recording audio clips, playing music, and showing a movie. For a more technical discussion about how computers process data, read the High-Tech Talk article on page 38.
- **Reliability**: The electronic components in modern computers are dependable and reliable because they rarely break or fail.
- **Consistency**: Given the same input and processes, a computer will produce the same results — consistently. Computers generate error-free results, provided the input is correct and the instructions work. A computing phrase — known as *garbage in, garbage out* — points out that the accuracy of a computer's output depends on the accuracy of the input. For example, if you do not use the flash on a digital camera when indoors, the resulting pictures that are displayed on the computer screen may be unusable because they are too dark.
- **Storage**: A computer can transfer data quickly from storage to memory, process it, and then store it again for future use. Many computers store enormous amounts of data and make this data available for processing anytime it is needed.
- **Communications**: Most computers today can communicate with other computers, often wirelessly. Computers with this capability can share any of the four information processing cycle operations — input, process, output, and storage — with another computer or a user.

DISADVANTAGES OF USING COMPUTERS   Some disadvantages of computers relate to the violation of privacy, the impact on the labor force, health risks, and the impact on the environment.

- **Violation of Privacy**: Nearly every life event is stored in a computer somewhere…in medical records, credit reports, tax records, etc. It is crucial that personal and confidential records be protected properly. In many instances, where these records were not properly protected, individuals have found their privacy violated and identities stolen. Read Ethics & Issues 1-1 for a related discussion.
- **Impact on Labor Force**: Although computers have improved productivity in many ways and created an entire industry with hundreds of thousands of new jobs, the skills of millions of employees have been replaced by computers. Thus, it is crucial that workers keep their education up-to-date. A separate impact on the labor force is that some companies are outsourcing jobs to foreign countries instead of keeping their homeland labor force employed.

ETHICS & ISSUES 1-1

Who Is Responsible for Identity Theft?

Using e-mail and other techniques on the Internet, scam artists are employing a technique known as phishing to try to steal your personal information, such as credit card numbers, banking information, and passwords. For example, an e-mail message may appear to be a request from your credit card company to verify your Social Security number and online banking password. Instead, the information you submit ends up in the hands of the scammer, who then uses the information to access your accounts, apply for credit in your name, or sell and trade the information with other criminals. Sadly, the result often is identity theft. Consumer advocates often blame credit card companies and credit bureaus for lax security standards. Meanwhile, the companies blame consumers for being too gullible and forthcoming with private information. Both sides blame the government for poor privacy laws and light punishments for identity thieves. But while the arguments go on, law enforcement agencies bear the brunt of the problem by spending hundreds of millions of dollars responding to complaints and finding and processing the criminals. Under current laws, who is responsible for Internet identity theft? Why? Should laws be changed to stop it or should consumers change behavior? What is an appropriate punishment for identity thieves? Given the international nature of the Internet, how can foreign identity thieves be handled?

- **Health Risks**: Prolonged or improper computer use can lead to injuries or disorders of the hands, wrists, elbows, eyes, neck, and back. Computer users can protect themselves from these health risks through proper workplace design, good posture while at the computer, and appropriately spaced work breaks.
- **Impact on Environment**: Computer manufacturing processes and computer waste are depleting natural resources and polluting the environment. The amount of resources required to manufacture a personal computer equals that of a mid-sized car. When computers are discarded in landfills, they release toxic materials and potentially dangerous levels of lead, mercury, and flame retardants. Strategies that can help protect the environment include recycling, regulating manufacturing processes, extending the life of computers, and immediately donating replaced computers.

Test your knowledge of pages 4 through 11 in Quiz Yourself 1-1.

QUIZ YOURSELF 1-1

Instructions: Find the true statement below. Then, rewrite the remaining false statements so they are true.

1. A computer is a motorized device that processes output into input.

2. A storage device records (reads) and/or retrieves (writes) items to and from storage media.

3. An output device is any hardware component that allows you to enter data and instructions into a computer.

4. Computer literacy involves having a knowledge and understanding of computers and their uses.

5. Computers have the disadvantages of fast speeds, high failure rates, producing consistent results, storing small amounts of data, and communicating with others.

6. Three commonly used input devices are a printer, a monitor, and speakers.

Quiz Yourself Online: To further check your knowledge of computer literacy, computers and their components, and the advantages and disadvantages of computers, visit scsite.com/dc2007/ch1/quiz and then click Objectives 1 – 4.

NETWORKS AND THE INTERNET

A **network** is a collection of computers and devices connected together via communications devices and transmission media. When a computer connects to a network, it is **online**.

Networks allow computers to share *resources*, such as hardware, software, data, and information. Sharing resources saves time and money. In many networks, one or more computers act as a server. The server controls access to the resources on a network. The other computers on the network, each called a client or workstation, request resources from the server (Figure 1-6). The major differences between the server and client computers are that the server ordinarily has more power, more storage space, and expanded communications capabilities.

Many homes and most businesses and schools network their computers and devices. Home networks usually are small, existing within a single structure, and often are wireless. Business and school networks can be small, such as in a room or building, or widespread, connecting computers across a city, country, or the globe. The world's largest computer network is the Internet.

FIGURE 1-6 A server manages the resources on a network, and clients access the resources on the server. This network enables three separate computers to share the same printer, one wirelessly.

The Internet

The **Internet** is a worldwide collection of networks that connects millions of businesses, government agencies, educational institutions, and individuals (Figure 1-7).

More than one billion people around the world use the Internet daily for a variety of reasons, including the following:

- Communicate with and meet other people
- Access a wealth of information, news, and research findings
- Shop for goods and services
- Bank and invest
- Take a class
- Access sources of entertainment and leisure, such as online games, music, videos, books, and magazines
- Download music
- Share information

Figure 1-8 shows examples in each of these areas.

People connect to the Internet to exchange information with others around the world. E-mail allows you to send messages to other users. With instant messaging, you can have a live conversation with another connected user.

In a chat room, you can communicate with multiple users at the same time — much like a group discussion.

Businesses, called access providers, offer users and companies access to the Internet free or for a fee. By subscribing to an access provider, you can use your computer and a communications device, such as a modem, to connect to the many services of the Internet.

The Web, short for World Wide Web, is one of the more popular services on the Internet. Think of the Web as a global library of information available to anyone connected to the Internet. The **Web** contains billions of documents called Web pages. A **Web page** can contain text, graphics, audio, and video. The eight screens shown in Figure 1-8 are examples of Web pages. Web pages often have built-in connections, or links, to other documents, graphics, other Web pages, or Web sites. A Web site is a collection of related Web pages. Some Web sites allow users to access music that can be downloaded, or transferred to storage media in a computer or digital audio player, and then listen to the music through speakers, headphones, or earphones.

WEB LINK 1-4

The Internet

For more information, visit scsite.com/dc2007/ch1/weblink and then click Internet.

FIGURE 1-7
The Internet is the largest computer network, connecting millions of computers around the world.

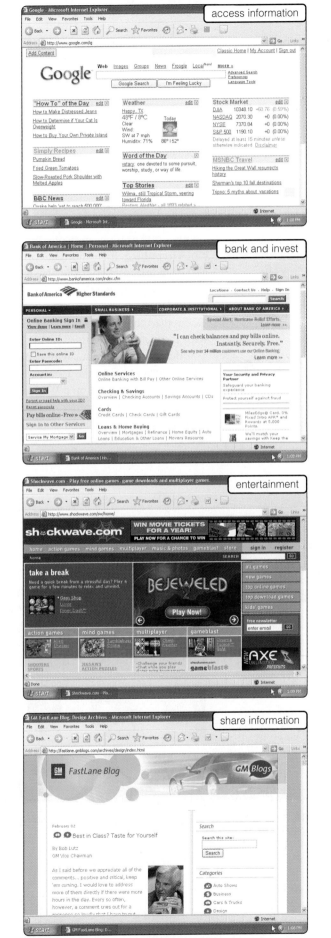

FIGURE 1-8 Users access the Internet for a variety of reasons.

In addition to accessing and using information on the Web, many people use the Web as a means to share personal information, photographs, videos, or artwork with the world. Anyone can create a Web page and then make it available, or *publish* it, on the Internet for others to see (read Ethics & Issues 1-2 for a related discussion). A **photo sharing community,** for example, is a Web site that allows users to create an online photo album and store their electronic photographs (Figure 1-9). Some Web sites provide publishing services free.

Hundreds of thousands of people today use blogs to publish their thoughts on the Web. A *blog* is an informal Web site consisting of time-stamped articles in a diary or journal format, usually listed in reverse chronological order. As others read the articles in a blog, they reply with their own thoughts.

Podcasts are a popular way people verbally share information on the Web. A *podcast* is recorded audio stored on a Web site that can be downloaded to a computer or a portable digital audio player such as an iPod. At a convenient time and location, the user listens to the downloaded podcast.

WEB LINK 1-5

Blogs

For more information, visit scsite.com/dc2007/ch1/weblink and then click Blogs.

FAQ 1-3

What do consumers buy on the Internet?

A recent survey found that online consumers spend the most on clothing, as shown in the chart below. For more information, visit scsite.com/dc2007/ch1/faq and then click Internet Purchases.

FIGURE 1-9 This user posts pictures to a photo sharing community, which allows others to view, print, or download the pictures.

ETHICS & ISSUES 1-2

Who Is Responsible for the Accuracy of Web Pages?

Since the dawn of the Web, some groups have used Web sites to try to convince people that the Holocaust in World War II did not occur. Using fake research papers and authoritative looking Web pages, these groups hope to revise history to their liking. In response, other groups have created Web sites to counter those claims and provide evidence of the truth. Many people think that anything in print is true, even what they read on the Web. Yet, authors with a wide range of expertise, authority, motives, and biases create Web pages. Web pages can be as accurate as the most scholarly journal, or no truer than the most disreputable supermarket tabloid. The Web makes it easy to obtain information, but Web page readers must make an extra effort to determine the quality of that information. In evaluating a Web page, experts suggest that you consider such factors as the purpose, scope, sponsor, timeliness, presentation, author, and permanence of the page. Ultimately, who is responsible for the accuracy of information on the Web? Why? What factors are most important in evaluating the accuracy of a Web page? Why? Should people be held accountable for what they publish on the Web? If so, by whom?

COMPUTER SOFTWARE

Software, also called a **program**, consists of a series of instructions that tells the computer what to do and how to do it.

You interact with a program through its user interface. The user interface controls how you enter data and instructions and how information is displayed on the screen. Software today often has a graphical user interface. With a **graphical user interface** (**GUI** pronounced gooey), you interact with the software using text, graphics, and visual images such as icons (Figure 1-10). An *icon* is a miniature image that represents a program, an instruction, or some other object. You can use the mouse to select icons that perform operations such as starting a program.

The two categories of software are system software and application software. The following sections describe these categories of software.

System Software

System software consists of the programs that control or maintain the operations of the computer and its devices. System software serves as the interface between the user, the application software, and the computer's hardware. Two types of system software are the operating system and utility programs.

OPERATING SYSTEM An *operating system* is a set of programs that coordinates all the activities among computer hardware devices. It provides a means for users to communicate with the computer and other software. Many of today's computers use Windows XP, which is one of Microsoft's operating systems (Figure 1-10).

When a user starts a computer, portions of the operating system load into memory from the computer's hard disk. It remains in memory while the computer is on.

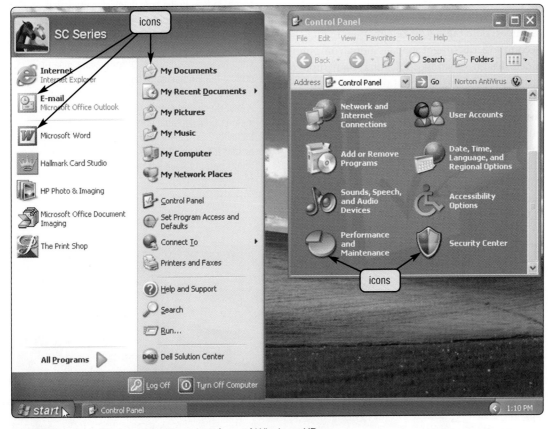

FIGURE 1-10 The graphical user interface of Windows XP.

UTILITY PROGRAM A *utility program* allows a user to perform maintenance-type tasks usually related to managing a computer, its devices, or its programs. Most operating systems include several utility programs for managing disk drives, printers, and other devices. You also can buy utility programs that allow you to perform additional computer management functions.

Application Software

Application software consists of programs designed to make users more productive and/or assist them with personal tasks. A widely used type of application software related to communications is a Web browser, which allows users with an Internet connection to access and view Web pages. Other popular application software includes word processing software, spreadsheet software, database software, and presentation graphics software.

Many other types of application software exist that enable users to perform a variety of tasks. These include personal information management, note taking, project management, accounting, document management, computer-aided design, desktop publishing, paint/image editing, audio and video editing, multimedia authoring, Web page authoring, personal finance, legal, tax preparation, home design/landscaping, education, reference, and entertainment (e.g., games or simulations, etc.). As shown in Figure 1-11, you can purchase application software from a store that sells computer products. Read Ethics & Issues 1-3 for a related discussion.

ETHICS & ISSUES 1-3

Is Computer Gaming More Good than Bad?

Grand Theft Auto: San Andreas is one of today's most popular computer games. In the game, players advance through the mafia by conveying secret packages, following alleged snitches, and planting car bombs. Since its release, shoppers have bought millions of copies of Grand Theft Auto. Purchasers praise the game's vivid graphics, edgy characters, and wide range of allowable behaviors. Recently, the game was found to contain hidden adult content accessible by using a special code. Some parents and politicians condemn the game's explicit violence and the rewards it gives players for participating in illegal acts. They fear that games like Grand Theft Auto eventually could lead to antisocial or criminal behavior. Even worse, critics fear that the game's popularity may influence future developers of computer games aimed at younger children. Despite the fears, research has shown that playing violent games has no impact on behavior or increased crime. In fact, in the time in which gaming has become popular, violent crime has decreased by 50 percent in America. Some researchers and parents note the positive aspects of gaming, such as increased dexterity for players, use of critical thinking skills to solve problems in games, meeting goals, and following rules. What impact, if any, do violent computer games or games that include unacceptable acts have on individual behavior? On balance, is computer gaming good or bad for people? Why? What other motivations might parents have who limit their children's computer gaming?

FIGURE 1-11 Stores that sell computer products have shelves stocked with software for sale.

Installing and Running Programs

The instructions in a program are stored on storage media such as a hard disk or compact disc. When purchasing software from a computer store, you typically receive a box that includes a CD(s) or DVD(s) that contains the program. You also may receive a manual or printed instructions explaining how to install and use the software.

Installing is the process of setting up software to work with the computer, printer, and other hardware components. When you buy a computer, it usually has some software preinstalled on its hard disk. This enables you to use the computer the first time you turn it on. To begin installing additional software from a CD or DVD, insert the program disc in a CD or DVD drive. The computer then copies all or part of the program from the disc to the computer's hard disk.

Once software is installed, you can use, or **run**, it. When you instruct the computer to run an installed program, the computer *loads* it, which means the program is copied from storage to memory. Once in memory, the computer can carry out, or *execute*, the instructions in the program. Figure 1-12 illustrates the steps that occur when a user installs and runs a greeting card program.

FAQ 1-4

Which spelling is correct, disk or disc?

Both are correct, depending on usage. When referring to CD, DVD, and other *optical* (laser) storage, computer professionals typically use the term, disc. The term, disk, normally refers to floppy disks, Zip disks, hard disks, and other nonoptical storage media. For more information, visit scsite.com/dc2007/ch1/faq and then click Disk or Disc.

FIGURE 1-12 INSTALLING AND RUNNING A COMPUTER PROGRAM

Step 1: INSTALL
When you insert a greeting card program disc in the CD drive for the first time, the computer begins the procedure of installing the greeting card program on the hard disk.

CD-ROM

Step 2: RUN
Once installed, you can instruct the computer to run the greeting card program. The computer transfers instructions from the hard disk to memory.

instructions transfer to memory

Step 3: USE
The greeting card program executes. Using this program, you can create custom greeting cards.

Software Development

A *programmer*, sometimes called a *developer*, is someone who develops software or writes the instructions that direct the computer to process data into information. When writing instructions, a programmer must be sure the program works properly so the computer generates the desired results. Complex programs can require thousands to millions of instructions.

Programmers use a programming language or program development tool to create computer programs. Popular programming languages include C++, Java, JavaScript, Visual C# 2005, and Visual Basic 2005. Figure 1-13 shows some of the instructions a programmer may write to create a Web application.

FIGURE 1-13 The top figure illustrates some of the instructions a programmer writes in JavaScript to create the Web application shown in the bottom figure.

Test your knowledge of pages 11 through 18 in Quiz Yourself 1-2.

QUIZ YOURSELF 1-2

Instructions: Find the true statement below. Then, rewrite the remaining false statements so they are true.

1. A resource is a collection of computers and devices connected together via communications devices and transmission media.

2. Installing is the process of setting up software to work with the computer, printer, and other hardware components.

3. Popular system software includes Web browsers, word processing software, spreadsheet software, database software, and presentation graphics software.

4. The Internet is one of the more popular services on the Web.

5. Two types of application software are the operating system and utility programs.

Quiz Yourself Online: To further check your knowledge of networks, the Internet and Web, and system software versus application software, visit scsite.com/dc2007/ch1/quiz and then click Objectives 5 – 7.

CATEGORIES OF COMPUTERS

Industry experts typically classify computers in seven categories: personal computers, mobile computers and mobile devices, game consoles, servers, mainframes, supercomputers, and embedded computers. A computer's size, speed, processing power, and price determine the category it best fits. Due to rapidly changing technology, however, the distinction among categories is not always clear-cut. Still, many people refer to these categories when discussing computers.

Figure 1-14 summarizes the seven categories of computers. The following pages discuss computers and devices that fall in each category.

CATEGORIES OF COMPUTERS

Category	Physical Size	Number of Simultaneously Connected Users	General Price Range
Personal computers (desktop)	Fits on a desk	Usually one (can be more if networked)	Several hundred to several thousand dollars
Mobile computers and mobile devices	Fits on your lap or in your hand	Usually one	Less than a hundred dollars to several thousand dollars
Game consoles	Small box or handheld device	One to several	Several hundred dollars or less
Servers	Small cabinet	Two to thousands	Several hundred to a million dollars
Mainframes	Partial room to a full room of equipment	Hundreds to thousands	$300,000 to several million dollars
Supercomputers	Full room of equipment	Hundreds to thousands	$500,000 to several billion dollars
Embedded computers	Miniature	Usually one	Embedded in the price of the product

FIGURE 1-14 This table summarizes some of the differences among the categories of computers. These should be considered general guidelines only because of rapid changes in technology.

PERSONAL COMPUTERS

A **personal computer** is a computer that can perform all of its input, processing, output, and storage activities by itself. A personal computer contains a processor, memory, and one or more input, output, and storage devices.

Two popular styles of personal computers are the PC (Figure 1-15) and the Apple (Figure 1-16). The term, *PC-compatible*, refers to any personal computer based on the original IBM personal computer design. Companies such as Dell, Gateway, Hewlett-Packard, and Toshiba sell PC-compatible computers. PC and PC-compatible computers have processors with different architectures than processors in Apple computers. These two types of computers also use different operating systems. PC and PC-compatible computers usually use a Windows operating system. Apple computers use a Macintosh operating system (Mac OS).

Two types of personal computers are desktop computers and notebook computers. The next section discusses desktop personal computers. Notebook computers are discussed in the mobile computers section.

WEB LINK 1-7

Personal Computers
For more information, visit scsite.com/dc2007/ch1/weblink and then click Personal Computers.

FIGURE 1-15 The PC and compatible computers usually use a Windows operating system.

FIGURE 1-16 Apple computers, such as the iMac, use a Macintosh operating system.

FAQ 1-5

How many PCs have been sold worldwide?

One billion PCs were sold during their first 25 years on the market. Experts predict that the next billion PCs will be sold between 2000 and 2008, a mere eight-year period. For more information, visit scsite.com/dc2007/ch1/faq and then click PC Sales.

Desktop Computers

A **desktop computer** is designed so the system unit, input devices, output devices, and any other devices fit entirely on or under a desk or table (Figures 1-15 and 1-16 on the previous page). In many models, the system unit is a tall and narrow *tower*, which can sit on the floor vertically — if desktop space is limited.

Some desktop computers function as a server on a network. Others, such as a gaming desktop computer and Media Center PC, target a specific audience. The *gaming desktop computer* offers high-quality audio, video, and graphics with optimal performance for sophisticated single-user and networked or Internet multi-player games. A *Media Center PC* is a home entertainment desktop computer that provides a means of accessing television programs, radio broadcasts, photographs, and videos, as well as basic computing capabilities. These high-end computers cost much more than the basic desktop computer.

Another expensive, powerful desktop computer is the workstation, which is geared for work that requires intense calculations and graphics capabilities. An architect uses a workstation to design buildings and homes. A graphic artist uses a workstation to create computer-animated special effects for full-length motion pictures and video games.

FAQ 1-6

Does the term, workstation, have two meanings?

Yes. In the computer industry, a *workstation* can be a high-powered computer or a client computer on a network. For more information, visit scsite.com/dc2007/ch1/faq and then click Workstation.

MOBILE COMPUTERS AND MOBILE DEVICES

A **mobile computer** is a personal computer you can carry from place to place. Similarly, a **mobile device** is a computing device small enough to hold in your hand.

The most popular type of mobile computer is the notebook computer. The following sections discuss the notebook computer and widely used mobile devices.

Notebook Computers

A **notebook computer**, also called a **laptop computer**, is a portable, personal computer designed to fit on your lap. Notebook computers are thin and lightweight, yet they can be as powerful as the average desktop computer. Notebook computers are more expensive than desktop computers with equal capabilities.

On a typical notebook computer, the keyboard is on top of the system unit, and the monitor attaches to the system unit with hinges (Figure 1-17). These computers weigh on average between 2.5 and 9 pounds, which allows users easily to transport the computers from place to place. Most notebook computers can operate on batteries or a power supply or both.

display

CD or DVD drive

hinge

keyboard

FIGURE 1-17   On a typical notebook computer, the keyboard is on top of the system unit, and the display attaches to the system unit with hinges.

TABLET PC Resembling a letter-sized slate, the **Tablet PC** is a special type of notebook computer that allows you to write or draw on the screen using a digital pen (Figure 1-18). With a *digital pen*, users write or draw by pressing the pen on the screen, and issue instructions to the Tablet PC by tapping on the screen. For users who prefer typing instead of handwriting, some Tablet PC designs have an attached keyboard; others allow you to connect a separate keyboard to the device. Tablet PCs also support voice input so users can enter text and issue instructions by speaking into the computer.

Tablet PCs are useful especially for taking notes in lectures, at meetings, conferences, and other forums where the standard notebook computer is not practical. With a cost of about $1,000 or more, some users may find Tablet PCs more appropriate for their needs than traditional notebook computers.

digital pen

FIGURE 1-18
A Tablet PC combines the features of a traditional notebook computer with the simplicity of pencil and paper.

Mobile Devices

Mobile devices, which are small enough to carry in a pocket, usually do not have disk drives. Instead, these devices store programs and data permanently on special memory inside the system unit or on small storage media such as memory cards. You often can connect a mobile device to a personal computer to exchange information between the computer and the mobile device.

Some mobile devices are **Internet-enabled**, meaning they can connect to the Internet wirelessly. With an Internet-enabled device,

users can chat, send e-mail and instant messages, and access the Web.

Three popular types of mobile devices are handheld computers, PDAs, and smart phones. Some combination mobile devices also are available, for example, a PDA/smart phone.

HANDHELD COMPUTER A **handheld computer**, sometimes referred to as an *ultra personal computer* (*uPC*) or a *handtop computer*, is a computer small enough to fit in one hand (Figure 1-19). Because of their reduced size, the screens on handheld computers are small. Many handheld computers communicate wirelessly with other devices or computers and also include a digital pen or stylus for input. Similar to a digital pen, a *stylus* is a small metal or plastic device that looks like a ballpoint pen but uses pressure instead of ink to write, draw, or make selections.

Some handheld computers have specialized keyboards. Many handheld computers are industry-specific and serve the needs of mobile employees, such as meter readers and parcel delivery people, whose jobs require them to move from place to place.

stylus

FIGURE 1-19
This OQO handheld computer is a full PC that fits in your hand and weighs less than one pound.

PDA The PDA is one of the more popular lightweight mobile devices in use today. A **PDA** (*personal digital assistant*) provides personal organizer functions such as a calendar, an appointment book, an address book, a calculator, and a notepad (Figure 1-20). Most PDAs also offer a variety of other application software such as word processing, spreadsheet, personal finance, and games.

The primary input device of a PDA is a stylus. Some PDAs do have a built-in miniature keyboard. If you prefer to type on a PDA that does not have a keyboard, you can insert the PDA in a special separate keyboard. Some PDAs also support voice input and have built-in cameras.

Many PDAs are Internet-enabled so users can check e-mail and access the Web. Some also provide telephone capabilities. Because of all the added features, increasingly more people are replacing their pocket-sized appointment books with PDAs.

stylus

FIGURE 1-20
PDAs provide personal information management functions as well as Internet access and telephone capabilities.

FAQ 1-7

Do PDAs have industry-specific applications?

Yes. Restaurant servers use PDAs to record customer orders and transmit them to the kitchen. Doctors use PDAs to access patients' records, view laboratory results, and transmit prescriptions to the pharmacy. Law enforcement officials use PDAs to run background checks and issue tickets. For more information, visit scsite.com/dc2007/ch1/faq and then click PDAs.

SMART PHONE Offering the convenience of one-handed operation, a **smart phone** is an Internet-enabled telephone that usually also provides PDA capabilities. In addition to basic telephone capabilities, a smart phone allows you to send and receive e-mail messages and access the Web. Higher-priced models have color screens, play music, and include built-in cameras so you can share photographs or videos with others as soon as you capture the image (Figure 1-21).

As smart phones and PDAs continue a trend of offering similar functions, it is becoming increasingly difficult to differentiate between the two devices. This trend, known as *convergence*, has led manufacturers to refer to PDAs and smart phones simply as *handhelds*. Some factors that affect a consumer's purchasing decision include the device's size, screen size, and capabilities of available software.

GAME CONSOLES

A **game console** is a mobile computing device designed for single-player or multiplayer video games (Figure 1-22). Standard game consoles use a handheld controller(s) as an input device(s); a television screen as an output device; and hard disks, CDs, DVDs, and/or memory cards for storage. Weighing on average between five and nine pounds, the compact size of game consoles makes them easy to use at home, in the car, in a hotel, in a camper, or any location that has an electrical outlet. Two popular models are Microsoft's Xbox 360 and Sony's PlayStation 3.

A handheld game console is small enough to fit in one hand, making it more portable than the standard game console. With the handheld game console, the controls, screen, and speakers are built into the device. Because of their reduced size, the screens are small — three to four inches. Some models use cartridges to store games; others use a miniature type of CD or DVD. Many handheld game consoles can communicate wirelessly with other similar consoles for multiplayer gaming. Two popular models are Nintendo's Game Boy Micro and Sony's PlayStation Portable (PSP).

In addition to gaming, many console models allow users to listen to music, watch movies, and connect to the Internet. Game consoles cost a few hundred dollars or less.

WEB LINK 1-8

Game Consoles

For more information, visit scsite.com/dc2007/ch1/weblink and then click Game Consoles.

FIGURE 1-21 In addition to basic telephone functionality, smart phones allow you to check e-mail, access the Web, listen to music, and share photos and videos.

game console

handheld game console

FIGURE 1-22
Game consoles provide hours of video game entertainment.

SERVERS

A **server** controls access to the hardware, software, and other resources on a network and provides a centralized storage area for programs, data, and information (Figure 1-23). Servers can support from two to several thousand connected computers at the same time.

In many cases, one server accesses data, information, and programs on another server. In other cases, people use personal computers or terminals to access data, information, and programs on a server. A terminal is a device with a monitor, keyboard, and memory.

FIGURE 1-23
A server controls access to resources on a network.

MAINFRAMES

A **mainframe** is a large, expensive, powerful computer that can handle hundreds or thousands of connected users simultaneously (Figure 1-24). Mainframes store tremendous amounts of data, instructions, and information. Most major corporations use mainframes for business activities. With mainframes, large businesses are able to bill millions of customers, prepare payroll for thousands of employees, and manage thousands of items in inventory. One study reported that mainframes process more than 83 percent of transactions around the world.

Mainframes also can act as servers in a network environment. Servers and other mainframes can access data and information from a mainframe. People also can access programs on the mainframe using terminals or personal computers.

FIGURE 1-24
Mainframe computers can handle thousands of connected computers and process millions of instructions per second.

SUPERCOMPUTERS

A **supercomputer** is the fastest, most powerful computer — and the most expensive (Figure 1-25). The fastest supercomputers are capable of processing more than 100 trillion instructions in a single second. With weights that exceed 100 tons, these computers can store more than 20,000 times the data and information of an average desktop computer.

Applications requiring complex, sophisticated mathematical calculations use supercomputers. Large-scale simulations and applications in medicine, aerospace, automotive design, online banking, weather forecasting, nuclear energy research, and petroleum exploration use a supercomputer.

FIGURE 1-25 This supercomputer simulates various environmental occurrences such as global climate changes, pollution, and earthquakes.

EMBEDDED COMPUTERS

An **embedded computer** is a special-purpose computer that functions as a component in a larger product. Embedded computers are everywhere — at home, in your car, and at work. The following list identifies a variety of everyday products that contain embedded computers.

- Consumer Electronics: mobile and digital telephones, digital televisions, cameras, video recorders, DVD players and recorders, answering machines
- Home Automation Devices and Appliances: thermostats, sprinkling systems, security monitoring systems, microwave ovens, washing machines
- Automobiles: antilock brakes, engine control modules, airbag controller, cruise control

- Process Controllers and Robotics: remote monitoring systems, power monitors, machine controllers, medical devices
- Computer Devices and Office Machines: keyboards, printers, faxes, copiers

Because embedded computers are components in larger products, they usually are small and have limited hardware. These computers perform various functions, depending on the requirements of the product in which they reside. Embedded computers in printers, for example, monitor the amount of paper in the tray, check the ink or toner level, signal if a paper jam has occurred, and so on. Figure 1-26 shows some of the many embedded computers in cars.

Adaptive cruise control systems detect if cars in front of you are too close and, if necessary, adjust the vehicle's throttle, may apply brakes, and/or sound an alarm.

Advanced airbag systems have crash-severity sensors that determine the appropriate level to inflate the airbag, reducing the chance of airbag injury in low-speed accidents.

Tire pressure monitoring systems send warning signals if tire pressure is insufficient.

Cars equipped with wireless communications capabilities, called *telematics*, include such features as navigation systems and Internet access.

Drive-by-wire systems sense pressure on the gas pedal and communicate electronically to the engine how much and how fast to accelerate.

FIGURE 1-26   Some of the embedded computers designed to improve your safety, security, and performance in today's automobiles.

ELEMENTS OF AN INFORMATION SYSTEM

To be valuable, information must be accurate, organized, timely, accessible, useful, and cost-effective to produce. Generating information from a computer requires the following five elements:

- Hardware
- Software
- Data
- People
- Procedures

Together, these elements (hardware, software, data, people, and procedures) comprise an *information system*. Figure 1-27 shows how each of the elements of an information system in a large business might interact.

The hardware must be reliable and capable of handling the expected workload. The software must be developed carefully and tested thoroughly. The data entered into the computer must be accurate.

Most companies with mid-sized and large computers have an IT (information technology) department. Staff in the IT department should be skilled and up-to-date on the latest technology. IT staff also should train users so they understand how to use the computer properly. Today's users also work closely with IT staff in the development of computer applications that relate to their areas of work.

Finally, all the IT applications should have readily available documented procedures that address operating the computer and using its applications.

FIGURE 1-27 HOW THE ELEMENTS OF AN INFORMATION SYSTEM IN A LARGE BUSINESS MIGHT INTERACT

Step 1:
IT staff (people) develop procedures for processing time cards (data).

Step 2:
Employees (people) in the payroll department use a program (software) to enter the time cards (data) in the computer.

Step 3:
The computer (hardware) performs calculations required to process the payroll and stores the results on storage media such as a hard disk (hardware).

Step 4:
Paychecks (information) print on a corporate printer (hardware).

EXAMPLES OF COMPUTER USAGE

Every day, people around the world rely on different types of computers for a variety of applications. To illustrate the range of uses for computers, this section takes you on a visual and narrative tour of five categories of users:

- Home user
- Small office/home office (SOHO) user
- Mobile user
- Power user
- Large business user

The following pages discuss the types of hardware and software required by each category of user.

Home User

In an increasing number of homes, the computer no longer is a convenience. Instead, it is a basic necessity. Each family member, or **home user**, spends time on the computer for different reasons that include budgeting and personal financial management, Web access, communications, and entertainment (Figure 1-28).

FIGURE 1-28a (personal financial management)

FIGURE 1-28b (Web access)

FIGURE 1-28c (communications)

FIGURE 1-28d (entertainment)

FIGURE 1-28 The home user spends time on a computer for a variety of reasons.

On the Internet, home users access a huge amount of information, take college classes, pay bills, manage investments, shop, listen to the radio, watch movies, read books, play games, file taxes, book airline reservations, and make telephone calls. They also communicate with others around the world through e-mail, blogs, instant messaging, and chat rooms using personal computers, PDAs, and smart phones. With a digital camera, home users take photographs and then send the electronic images to others (Figure 1-29). Using a PC video camera, which costs less than $100, home users easily have live video calls with friends, family members, and others. Read Ethics & Issues 1-4 for a related discussion.

Many home users have a portable digital audio player, so they can download music or podcasts, and listen to the music and/or audio at a later time through earphones attached to the player. They also usually have one or more game consoles to play video games individually or with friends and family members.

Today's homes also typically have one or more desktop computers. Many home users network multiple desktop computers throughout the house, often wirelessly. These small networks allow family members to share an Internet connection and a printer.

To meet their needs, home users have a variety of software. They type letters, homework assignments, and other documents with word processing software. Personal finance software helps the home user with personal finances, investments, and family budgets. Other software assists with preparing taxes, keeping a household inventory, and setting up maintenance schedules.

Reference software, such as encyclopedias, medical dictionaries, or a road atlas, provides valuable information for everyone in the family. With entertainment software, the home user can play games, compose music, research genealogy, or create greeting cards. Educational software helps adults learn to speak a foreign language and youngsters to read, write, count, and spell.

FIGURE 1-29 Home users take and view photographs on a digital camera.

FAQ 1-8

Can I listen to an audio CD on my computer?

Yes, in most cases. Simply insert the CD in the computer's CD or DVD drive. Within a few seconds, you should hear music from the computer's speakers or in your headphones or earphones. If no music plays, it is possible you need to run a program that starts the audio CD. For more information, visit csite.com/dc2007/ch1/faq and then click Audio CDs.

ETHICS & ISSUES 1-4

Does Internet Dating Really Work?

Once, people met dates through family and friends, work, or community, religious, and recreational activities. These social networks sometimes resulted in a perfect match, but often, time constraints, the limited pool of participants, and infrequent meetings made it difficult to find a potential partner. Today, many people are turning to another resource — Internet dating, also called online dating or e-dating. Internet dating is a half-billion dollar industry, and the market for these services has grown almost 40 percent in the past year. Internet dating service members supply information about their appearance, interests, and personalities and then search the service for people they might like to meet. The services are easy to use, have a large range of participants, allow relationships to develop at a comfortable pace, and usually offer advanced options such as live chat, voice mail, and computer matchmaking. On the other hand, in an Internet dating service it can be difficult to judge the truthfulness of the profiles of other members or the claims made in live chat or e-mail. Although introductory memberships often are free, many services require substantial fees for extended benefits. Are Internet dating services worth it? Why or why not? How is Internet dating changing the way people meet? If you used an Internet dating service, what precautions might you take to protect yourself from deceptive acts of other members?

Small Office/Home Office User

Computers assist small business and home office users in managing their resources effectively. A **small office/home office** (*SOHO*) includes any company with fewer than 50 employees, as well as the self-employed who work from home. Small offices include local law practices, accounting firms, travel agencies, and florists. SOHO users typically have a desktop computer to perform some or all of their duties. Many also have PDAs or smart phones to manage appointments and contact information.

SOHO users access the Internet — often wirelessly — to look up information such as addresses, directions (Figure 1-30a), postal codes, flights, and package shipping rates or to make telephone calls. Nearly all SOHO users communicate with others through e-mail.

Many are entering the *e-commerce* arena and conduct business on the Web. Their Web sites advertise products and services and may provide a means for taking orders. Small business Web sites sometimes use a *Web cam*, which is a video camera that displays its output on a Web page. A Web cam allows SOHO users to show the world a live view of some aspect of their business.

To save money on hardware and software, small offices often network their computers. For example, the small office connects one printer to a network for all employees to share.

SOHO users often have basic business software such as word processing and spreadsheet software to assist with document preparation and finances (Figure 1-30b). They are likely to use other industry-specific types of software. A candy shop, for example, will have software that allows for taking orders and payments, updating inventory, and paying vendors.

FIGURE 1-30a   (Web access)

FIGURE 1-30b   (spreadsheet program)

FIGURE 1-30   People with a home office and employees in small offices typically use a personal computer for some or all of their duties.

Mobile User

Today, businesses and schools are expanding to serve people across the country and around the world. Thus, increasingly more employees and students are **mobile users**, who work on a computer while away from a main office or school (Figure 1-31). Examples of mobile users are sales representatives, real estate agents, insurance agents, meter readers, package delivery people, journalists, consultants, and students.

Mobile users often have a notebook computer, Internet-enabled PDA, or smart phone. With these computers and devices, the mobile user connects to other computers on a network or the Internet, often wirelessly accessing services such as e-mail and the Web. Mobile users can transfer information between their mobile device and another computer, such as one at the main office or school.

The mobile user works with basic business software such as word processing and spread-sheet software. With presentation graphics software, the mobile user can create and deliver presentations to a large audience by connecting a mobile computer or device to a video projector that displays the presentation on a full screen. Many scaled-down programs are available for mobile devices such as PDAs and smart phones.

FIGURE 1-31 Mobile users have notebook computers, Tablet PCs, PDAs, and smart phones so they can work, do homework, send messages, or connect to the Internet while away from a wired connection.

Power User

Another category of user, called a **power user**, requires the capabilities of a workstation or other type of powerful computer (Figure 1-32). Examples of power users include engineers, scientists, architects, desktop publishers, and graphic artists. Power users often work with *multimedia*, combining text, graphics, audio, and video into one application. These users need computers with extremely fast processors because of the nature of their work.

The power user's workstation contains industry-specific software. For example, engineers and architects use software to draft and design floor plans, mechanical assemblies, or vehicles. A desktop publisher uses software to prepare marketing literature such as newsletters, brochures, and annual reports. A geologist uses software to study the earth's surface. This software usually is expensive because of its specialized design.

Power users exist in all types of businesses. Some work at home. Their computers typically have network connections and Internet access.

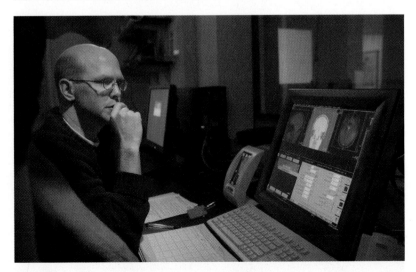

FIGURE 1-32 This scientist uses a powerful computer to study brain imaging.

Large Business User

A large business has hundreds or thousands of employees or customers that work in or do business with offices across a region, the country, or the world. Each employee or customer who uses a computer in the large business is a **large business user** (Figure 1-33).

Many large companies use the words, *enterprise computing*, to refer to the huge network of computers that meets their diverse computing needs. The network facilitates communications among employees at all locations. Users access the network of servers or mainframes through desktop computers, mobile computers, PDAs, and smart phones.

Large businesses use computers and the computer network to process high volumes of transactions in a single day. Although they may differ in size and in the products or services offered, all generally use computers for basic business activities. For example, they bill millions of customers, prepare payroll for thousands of employees, and manage thousands of items in inventory. Some large businesses use blogs to open communications among employees, customers, and/or vendors.

Large businesses typically have e-commerce Web sites, allowing customers and vendors to conduct business online. The Web site also showcases products, services, and other company information. Customers, vendors, and other interested parties can access this information on the Web. Once an order is placed, computers update inventory records to reflect goods sold and goods purchased.

The marketing department in a large business uses desktop publishing software to prepare marketing literature. The accounting department uses software for accounts receivable, accounts payable, billing, general ledger, and payroll activities.

The employees in the *information technology (IT) department* keep the computers and the network running. They also determine when and if the company requires new hardware or software.

Large business users work with word processing, spreadsheet, database, and presentation graphics software. They also may use calendar programs to post their schedules on the network. And, they might use PDAs or smart phones to maintain contact information. E-mail and Web browsers enable communications among employees, vendors, and customers.

Some large businesses place kiosks in public locations. A *kiosk* is a freestanding computer, usually with a touch screen (Figure 1-34).

Many employees of large businesses telecommute. **Telecommuting** is a work arrangement in which employees work away from a company's standard workplace and often communicate with the office through the computer. Employees who telecommute have flexible work schedules so they can combine work and personal responsibilities, such as child care.

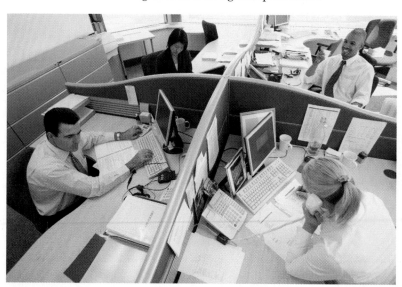

FIGURE 1-33 A large business can have hundreds or thousands of users in offices across a region, the country, or the world.

FIGURE 1-34 Airline travelers check in using this self-service kiosk.

Putting It All Together

The previous pages discussed the hardware and software requirements for the home user, small office/home office user, mobile user, power user, and large business user. The table in Figure 1-35 summarizes these requirements.

CATEGORIES OF USERS

User	Hardware	Software
HOME	• Desktop or notebook computer • PDA or smart phone • Game consoles	• Business (e.g., word processing) • Personal information manager • Personal finance, online banking, tax preparation • Web browser • E-mail, blogging, instant messaging, and chat rooms • Internet telephone calls • Photo editing • Reference (e.g., encyclopedias, medical dictionaries, road atlas) • Entertainment (e.g., games, music composition, greeting cards) • Educational (e.g., tutorials, children's math and reading software)
SMALL OFFICE/ HOME OFFICE	• Desktop computer • PDA or smart phone • Shared network printer	• Business (e.g., word processing, spreadsheet, database) • Personal information manager • Company specific (e.g., accounting, legal reference) • Network management • Web browser • E-mail • Internet telephone calls
MOBILE	• Notebook computer equipped with a wireless modem, or a Tablet PC • Video projector • PDA or smart phone	• Business (e.g., word processing, spreadsheet, note taking, presentation graphics) • Personal information manager • Web browser • E-mail
POWER	• Workstation or other powerful computer with multimedia capabilities • PDA or smart phone	• Desktop publishing • Multimedia authoring • Computer-aided design • Photo, audio, and video editing • Personal information manager • Web browser • E-mail
LARGE BUSINESS	• Server or mainframe • Desktop or notebook computer • Industry-specific handheld computer • PDA or smart phone • Kiosk	• Business (e.g., word processing, spreadsheet, database, presentation graphics) • Personal information manager • Accounting • Network management • Web browser • E-mail • Blogging

FIGURE 1-35 Today, computers are used by millions of people for work tasks, school assignments, and leisure activities. Different computer users require different kinds of hardware and software to meet their needs effectively.

COMPUTER APPLICATIONS IN SOCIETY

The computer has changed society today as much as the industrial revolution changed society in the eighteenth and nineteenth centuries.

People interact directly with computers in fields such as education, finance, government, health care, science, publishing, travel, and manufacturing. In addition, they can reap the benefits from breakthroughs and advances in these fields. The following pages describe how computers have made a difference in people's interactions with these disciplines. Read Looking Ahead 1-2 for a look at the next generation of computer applications in society.

LOOKING AHEAD 1-2

Robots Perform Mundane Tasks, Entertain

Playwright Karel Capek created the name, robot, for his humanoid machines that turned against their creators. Today, mobile, intelligent robots perform tasks typically reserved for humans in a $5 billion global market.

Each day, the iRobot Roomba self-propelled vacuum cleans homes, and the da Vinci Surgical System's robotic hands drill through bones and make incisions. Sony's home robot, QRIO, responds to voices and faces, displays emotions, and walks and dances fluidly.

Tomorrow's practical and versatile robots will serve a variety of personal and industrial needs. By 2010, the expected $17 billion market should include products to care for senior citizens, transport people in major cities, and perform hundreds of thousands of mobile utility jobs, such as picking up and delivering items. For more information, visit scsite.com/dc2007/ch1/looking and then click Robots.

Education

Education is the process of acquiring knowledge. In the traditional model, people learn from other people such as parents, teachers, and employers. Many forms of printed material such as books and manuals are used as learning tools. Today, educators also are turning to computers to assist with education (Figure 1-36).

Many schools and companies equip labs and classrooms with computers. Some schools require students to have a notebook computer or PDA to access the school's network or Internet wirelessly. To promote education by computer, many vendors offer substantial student discounts on software.

Sometimes, the delivery of education occurs at one place while the learning occurs at other locations. For example, students can take a class on the Web. Some classes are blended; that is, part of the learning occurs in a classroom and the other part occurs on the Web. More than 70 percent of colleges offer some type of distance learning classes. A few even offer entire degrees online.

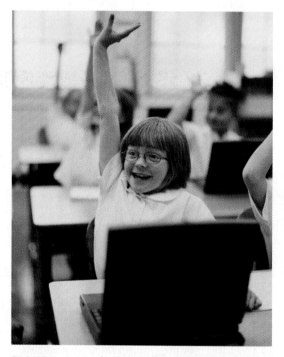

FIGURE 1-36 In some schools, students have notebook computers on their desks during classroom lectures.

Finance

Many people and companies use computers to help manage their finances. Some use finance software to balance checkbooks, pay bills, track personal income and expenses, manage investments, and evaluate financial plans. This software usually includes a variety of online services. For example, computer users can track investments and do online banking. With **online banking**, users access account balances, pay bills, and copy monthly transactions from the bank's computer right into their personal computers.

Many financial institutions' Web sites also offer online banking (Figure 1-37). When using a Web site instead of finance software on your computer, all your account information is stored on the bank's computer. The advantage is you can access your financial records from anywhere in the world.

FIGURE 1-37   Many financial institutions' Web sites offer online banking.

Investors often use **online investing** to buy and sell stocks and bonds — without using a broker. With online investing, the transaction fee for each trade usually is much less than when trading through a broker.

Government

A government provides society with direction by making and administering policies. To provide citizens with up-to-date information, most government offices have Web sites. People in the United States access government Web sites to file taxes, apply for permits and licenses, pay parking tickets, buy stamps, report crimes, apply for financial aid, and renew vehicle registrations and driver's licenses.

Employees of government agencies use computers as part of their daily routine. North American 911 call centers use computers to dispatch calls for fire, police, and medical assistance. Military and other agency officials use the U.S. Department of Homeland Security's network of information about domestic security threats to help protect against terrorist attacks. Law enforcement officers have online access to the FBI's National Crime Information Center (NCIC) in police cars that have rugged notebook computers and fingerprint scanners or through PDAs (Figure 1-38). The NCIC contains more than 52 million missing persons and criminal records, including names, fingerprints, parole/probation records, mug shots, and other information.

FIGURE 1-38   Law enforcement officials have in-vehicle computers and PDAs to access emergency, missing person, and criminal records in computer networks in local, state, and federal agencies.

Health Care

Nearly every area of health care uses computers. Whether you are visiting a family doctor for a regular checkup, having lab work or an outpatient test, or being rushed in for emergency surgery, the medical staff around you will be using computers for various purposes:

- Hospitals and doctors use computers to maintain patient records.
- Computers monitor patients' vital signs in hospital rooms and at home.
- Computers and computerized devices assist doctors, nurses, and technicians with medical tests (Figure 1-39).
- Doctors use the Web and medical software to assist with researching and diagnosing health conditions.
- Doctors use e-mail to correspond with patients.
- Pharmacists use computers to file insurance claims.
- Surgeons implant computerized devices, such as pacemakers, that allow patients to live longer.

- Surgeons use computer-controlled devices to provide them with greater precision during operations, such as for laser eye surgery and robot-assisted heart surgery.

Many Web sites provide up-to-date medical, fitness, nutrition, or exercise information. These Web sites also maintain lists of doctors and dentists to help you find the one that suits your needs. They have chat rooms, so you can talk to others diagnosed with similar conditions. Some Web sites even allow you to order prescriptions online.

An exciting development in health care is telemedicine, which is a form of long-distance health care. Through *telemedicine*, health-care professionals in separate locations conduct live conferences on the computer. For example, a doctor at one location can have a conference with a doctor at another location to discuss a bone X-ray. Live images of each doctor, along with the X-ray, are displayed on each doctor's computer.

Science

All branches of science, from biology to astronomy to meteorology, use computers to assist them with collecting, analyzing, and modeling data. Scientists also use the Internet to communicate with colleagues around the world.

Breakthroughs in surgery, medicine, and treatments often result from scientists' use of computers. Tiny computers now imitate functions of the central nervous system, retina of the eye, and cochlea of the ear. A cochlear implant allows a deaf person to listen. Electrodes implanted in the brain stop tremors associated with Parkinson's disease. Cameras small enough to swallow — sometimes called a camera pill — take pictures inside your body to detect polyps, cancer, and other abnormalities (Figure 1-40).

A *neural network* is a system that attempts to imitate the behavior of the human brain. Scientists create neural networks by connecting thousands of processors together much like the neurons in the brain are connected. The capability of a personal computer to recognize spoken words is a direct result of scientific experimentation with neural networks.

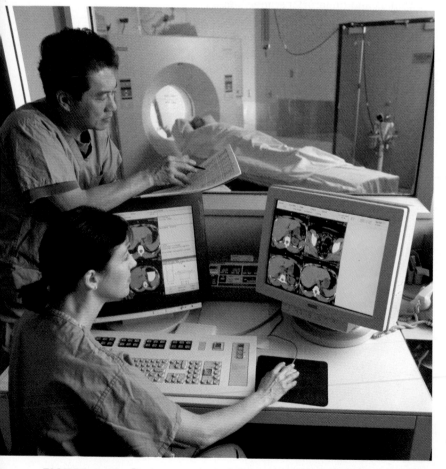

FIGURE 1-39   Doctors, nurses, technicians, and other medical staff use computers while performing tests on patients.

FIGURE 1-40　HOW A CAMERA PILL WORKS

Step 1:
A patient swallows a tiny capsule that contains a miniature disposable camera, lights, a transmitter, and batteries. The camera is positioned at the clear end of the capsule.

Step 3:
The doctor transfers the data on the recording device to a computer so it can be processed and analyzed.

Step 2:
As the capsule moves through the inside of the patient's body, the camera snaps about 50,000 pictures, which are transmitted to a recording device worn as a belt on the patient's waist.

Publishing

Publishing is the process of making works available to the public. These works include books, magazines, newspapers, music, film, and video. Special software assists graphic designers in developing pages that include text, graphics, and photographs; artists in composing and enhancing songs; filmmakers in creating and editing film; and journalists and mobile users in capturing and modifying video clips.

Many publishers make their works available online (Figure 1-41). Some Web sites allow you to copy the work, such as a book or music, to your desktop computer, handheld computer, PDA, or smart phone.

FIGURE 1-41　Many magazine and newspaper publishers make the content of their publications available online.

Travel

Whether traveling by car or airplane, your goal is to arrive safely at your destination. As you make the journey, you may interact with some of the latest technology.

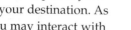

WEB LINK 1-11

Onboard Navigation Systems

For more information, visit scsite.com/dc2007/ch1/weblink and then click Onboard Navigation Systems.

Vehicles manufactured today often include some type of onboard navigation system. Many airlines now provide online access, allowing passengers to connect their mobile computer or device to the Internet (Figure 1-42). Some airlines even provide passengers with Internet-enabled devices during flights.

In preparing for a trip, you may need to reserve a car, hotel, or flight. Many Web sites offer these services to the public. For example, you can order airline tickets on the Web. If you plan to drive somewhere and are unsure of the road to take to your destination, you can print directions and a map from the Web.

FAQ 1-9

Do home users book travel on the Web?

Yes, it is estimated that nearly 22 percent ($53 billion) of the travel industry's revenues stem from leisure travel bookings. As shown in the chart, computer users of all ages visit travel agency Web sites. For more information, visit scsite.com/dc2007/ch1/faq and then click Travel Bookings.

Online Travel Agency Use
(by Age)

55+ 22%
18–24 11%
25–34 19%
45–54 23%
35–44 25%

Source: The ClickZ Network

Manufacturing

Computer-aided manufacturing (*CAM*) refers to the use of computers to assist with manufacturing processes such as fabrication and assembly. Industries use CAM to reduce product development costs, shorten a product's time to market, and stay ahead of the competition.

Often, robots carry out processes in a CAM environment. CAM is used by a variety of industries, including oil drilling, power generation, food production, and automobile manufacturing. Automobile plants, for example, have an entire line of industrial robots that assemble a car (Figure 1-43).

Special computers on the shop floor record actual labor, material, machine, and computer time used to manufacture a particular product. The computers process this data and automatically update inventory, production, payroll, and accounting records on the company's network.

FIGURE 1-43 Automotive factories use industrial robots to weld car bodies.

FIGURE 1-42 Airlines today offer inflight Internet connections to passengers.

Test your knowledge of pages 18 through 36 in Quiz Yourself 1-3.

QUIZ YOURSELF 1-3

Instructions: Find the true statement below. Then, rewrite the remaining false statements so they are true.

1. A desktop computer is a portable, personal computer designed to fit on your lap.

2. A personal computer contains a processor, memory, and one or more input, output, and storage devices.

3. Each large business user spends time on the computer for different reasons that include budgeting and personal financial management, Web access, communications, and entertainment.

4. A home user requires the capabilities of a workstation or other powerful computer.

5. Mainframes are the fastest, most powerful computers — and the most expensive.

6. The elements of an information system are hardware, e-mail, data, people, and the Internet.

7. With embedded computers, users access account balances, pay bills, and copy monthly transactions from the bank's computer right into their personal computers.

Quiz Yourself Online: To further check your knowledge of categories of computers, information system elements, computer users, and computer applications in society, visit scsite.com/dc2007/ch1/quiz and then click Objectives 8 – 11.

CHAPTER SUMMARY

Chapter 1 introduced you to basic computer concepts such as what a computer is, how it works, and its advantages and disadvantages. You learned about the components of a computer. Next, the chapter discussed networks, the Internet, and computer software. The many different categories of computers, computer users, and computer applications in society also were presented.

This chapter is an overview. Many of the terms and concepts introduced will be discussed further in later chapters. For a history of hardware and software developments, read the Timeline 2007 that follows this chapter.

Personal Computer Salesperson

When you decide to buy or upgrade a personal computer, the most important person with whom you interact probably will be a personal computer salesperson. This individual will be a valuable resource to you in providing the information and expertise you need to select a computer that meets your requirements.

Computer manufacturers and retailers that sell several types of personal computers need competent salespeople. A *personal computer salesperson* must be computer literate and have a specific knowledge of the computers he or she sells. The salesperson also must have a working knowledge of computer peripherals (printers, scanners, cameras, etc.). In addition, a successful salesperson has a friendly, outgoing personality that helps customers feel comfortable. Through open-ended questions, the salesperson can determine a customer's needs and level of experience. With this information, the salesperson can choose the best computer for the customer and explain the features of the computer in language the customer will understand. Most computer salespeople also can recommend a qualified installer for your computer or qualified service technician.

Computer salespeople typically have at least a high school diploma. Before reaching the sales floor, however, salespeople usually complete extensive company training programs. These programs often consist of self-directed, self-paced Web-training classes. Most salespeople also participate in training updates, often on a monthly basis.

Personal computer salespeople generally earn a guaranteed amount plus a commission for each sale. A computer salesperson can earn about $45,000 a year. Top salespeople can be among a company's more highly compensated employees, earning in excess of $85,000. For more information, visit scsite.com/dc2007/ch1/careers and then click Personal Computer Salesperson.

High-Tech Talk

ANALOG VERSUS DIGITAL:
MAKING THE CONVERSION

Data is processed in one of two ways: analog or digital. People generally process *analog* data — that is, continuous wave patterns. The sight and sound of a traveling subway car transmits to your eyes and ears as light and sound waves, or smooth up-and-down patterns (Figure 1-44a). A computer, by contrast, is *digital*, which means computers process data in two discrete states: positive (on, or 1) and non-positive (off, or 0) as shown in Figure 1-44b. The 1 and 0 represent the two digits used by the binary number system. While this system is at the heart of digital computing, binary digital impulses appear as long strings of 1s and 0s.

If sound and light waves are analog and a computer is digital, how does a computer record audio clips, play music, or show a movie? How can a digital computer use an analog telephone line to dial up to access the Internet?

The key lies in analog-to-digital and digital-to-analog conversions. For example, the computer's sound card allows you to record sounds and playback sounds. The sound card performs these conversions to record a digital audio clip of your analog voice. The sound card connects to the microphone, which is an analog input source. The diaphragm in the microphone converts the analog sound waves into an analog electrical signal. This signal flows to the sound card's *analog-to-digital converter (ADC)*, which converts the signal into digital data. The digital data flows to the *digital signal processor (DSP)*, compressing the data to save space. Finally, the compressed data is stored in an audio file format.

To play a recorded sound, the computer reverses the process. The processor retrieves and sends the digital data to the DSP to be decompressed. The DSP sends the decompressed digital data to the sound card's *digital-to-analog converter (DAC)*, which converts the digital data back to an analog voltage for output via a speaker or headset. In other words, a DAC takes that long binary number string of 1s and 0s and turns it into an electronic signal that the sound output devices can decode and use.

Similarly, a video card allows you to record a video or play a movie on a DVD. A camera and microphone capture and send the analog picture and sound signals to a video card. The video card's ADC converts the signals into digital data. The digital data is compressed and saved in a file format such as AVI (audio/video interleave) or MPEG (Moving Picture Experts Group). When playing a movie, the computer decompresses and separates the video and audio data. It then sends the signals to the video card's DAC. The DAC translates the digital data into analog signals and sends them to the monitor and speakers, where they are displayed as your movie.

The modem in a computer also links the analog and digital worlds. When using a dial-up modem, the computer does not transmit digital data directly across analog telephone lines. Instead, the modem converts the computer's digital signals to analog signals (called *modulation*) to be sent over telephone lines. When the analog signal reaches its destination, another modem recreates the original digital signal (*demodulation*). This allows the receiving computer to process the data. The next time you dial up using a modem, pick up the telephone. The loud, screeching noise you hear is the sound of digital data after being converted to analog sound waves. For more information, visit scsite.com/dc2007/ch1/tech and then click Analog versus Digital.

FIGURE 1-44a   (analog signal)

FIGURE 1-44b   (digital signal)

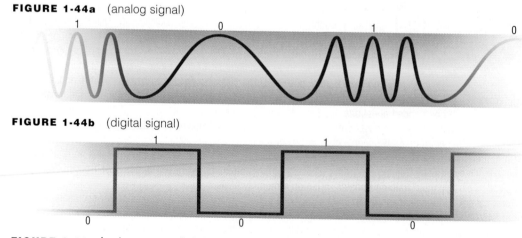

FIGURE 1-44   Analog versus digital signals.

Companies on the Cutting Edge

DELL
COMPUTERS YOUR WAY

As a leading manufacturer of personal computers, *Dell* prides itself on its direct approach to computer sales. Founded by Michael Dell in 1984, the company deals openly with customers, one at a time. This direct approach eliminates retailers that add cost and time to the ordering process.

Dell uses the Internet to enhance the advantages of direct marketing and hosts one of the world's largest volume e-commerce Web sites. Customers can configure and price computers, order systems, and track their orders online.

In response to the U.S. Environmental Protection Agency's estimate that 250 million computers will be discarded from 2002 to 2007, Dell began an aggressive campaign to increase the amount of computer equipment it recycles by 50 percent. For more information, visit scsite.com/dc2007/ch1/companies and then click Dell.

APPLE COMPUTER
INTRODUCING INNOVATIVE TECHNOLOGIES

Millions of computer users in more than 120 countries loyally use *Apple Computer's* hardware and software with a passion usually reserved for sports teams and musical groups.

Steven Jobs and Stephen Wozniak founded Apple in 1976 when they marketed the Apple I, a circuit board they had developed in Jobs's garage. In 1977, Apple Computer incorporated and introduced the Apple II, the first mass-marketed personal computer. Apple introduced the Macintosh product line in 1984, which featured a graphical user interface.

Under Jobs's direction as CEO, Apple introduced the iMac, the iBook, the Power Mac G5, the iPod digital audio player, and Mac OS X. Strong demand for the iPod Mini helped boost the company's earnings. Product sales jumped after Apple introduced its pay-per-download iTunes online music store in 2003. For more information, visit scsite.com/dc2007/ch1/companies and then click Apple Computer.

Technology Trailblazers

BILL GATES
MICROSOFT'S FOUNDER

Bill Gates, the founder and chief software architect of Microsoft Corporation, suggests that college students should learn how to learn by getting the best education they can. Because he is considered by many as the most powerful person in the computing industry, it might be wise to listen to him.

Gates learned to program computers when he was 13. Early in his career, he developed the BASIC programming language for the MITS Altair, one of the first microcomputers. He founded Microsoft in 1975 with Paul Allen, and five years later, they provided the first operating system, called MS-DOS, for the IBM PC. Today, Microsoft's Windows and Office products dominate the software market.

Gates consistently has been placed at the top of *Forbes'* World's Richest People list, with assets of more than $46 billion. For more information, visit scsite.com/dc2007/ch1/people and then click Bill Gates.

ANNE MULCAHY
XEROX CEO

Color printing and consulting services are the two areas where the Xerox Corporation can make a difference, according to *Anne Mulcahy*, the company's CEO and chairman of the board. She should know the nature of the business, having started her career with the Stamford, Connecticut-based corporation more than 30 years ago as a field sales representative.

One of Mulcahy's first decisions after landing the top job in 2001 was eliminating the corporation's tagline, "The Document Company." She believes the company's name, standing solo, speaks for itself in the printing, copying, and services worlds. Her decisions to revamp the company have revolved around Xerox's roots of innovation and customer care. Mulcahy believes it is essential to adapt to the world's changing technology, but the adaptations need a foundation in the basic principles that made Xerox a household word. For more information, visit scsite.com/dc2007/ch1/people and then click Anne Mulcahy.

Chapter Review

The Chapter Review section summarizes the concepts presented in this chapter. To listen to the audio version of this Chapter Review, visit scsite.com/dc2007/ch1/review. To obtain help from other students regarding any subject in this chapter, visit scsite.com/dc2007/ch1/forum and post your thoughts or questions.

① Why Is Computer Literacy Important? **Computer literacy** involves having knowledge and understanding of computers and their uses. As computers become more a part of everyday life, many people believe that computer literacy is vital to success.

② What Is a Computer? A **computer** is an electronic device, operating under the control of instructions stored in its own memory, that can accept data, process the data according to specified rules, produce results, and store the results for future use.

③ What Are the Components of a Computer? The electric, electronic, and mechanical components of a computer, or **hardware**, include input devices, output devices, a system unit, storage devices, and communications devices. An **input device** allows you to enter data or instructions into a computer. An **output device** conveys information to one or more people. The **system unit** is a case that contains the electronic components of a computer that are used to process data. A **storage device** records and/or retrieves items to and from **storage media**. A **communications device** enables a computer to send and receive data, instructions, and information to and from one or more computers.

④ What Are the Advantages and Disadvantages of Using Computers? Computers have the advantages of speed, reliability, consistency, storage, and communications. They perform operations at incredibly fast speeds, are dependable and reliable, consistently generate error-free results, can store enormous amounts of data, and can share processing with other computers. Disadvantages of computers relate to the violation of privacy, the impact on the labor force, health risks, and the impact on the environment.

> Visit scsite.com/dc2007/ch1/quiz or click the Quiz Yourself button. Click Objectives 1 – 4.

⑤ What Is the Purpose of a Network? A **network** is a collection of computers and devices connected together via communications devices and transmission media. Networks allow computers to share *resources*, such as hardware, software, data, and information.

⑥ How Are the Internet and World Wide Web Used? The **Internet** is a worldwide collection of networks that connects millions of businesses, government agencies, educational institutions, and individuals. People use the Internet to communicate with and meet other people, access news and information, shop for goods and services, bank and invest, take classes, for entertainment and leisure, download music, and share information. The **Web**, short for World Wide Web, is a global library of documents containing information that is available to anyone connected to the Internet.

⑦ How Is System Software Different from Application Software? **Software**, also called a **program**, is a series of instructions that tells the computer what to do and how to do it. **System software** consists of the programs that control or maintain the operations of a computer and its devices. Two types of system software are the *operating system*, which coordinates activities among computer hardware devices, and *utility programs*, which perform maintenance-type tasks usually related to a computer, its devices, or its programs. **Application software** consists of programs that perform specific tasks for users. Popular application software includes Web browsers, word processing software, spreadsheet software, database software, and presentation graphics software.

> Visit scsite.com/dc2007/ch1/quiz or click the Quiz Yourself button. Click Objectives 5 – 7.

Chapter Review

⑧ What Are the Categories of Computers? Industry experts typically classify computers in seven categories: personal computers, mobile computers and mobile devices, game consoles, servers, mainframes, supercomputers, and embedded computers. A **personal computer** is a computer that can perform all of its input, processing, output, and storage activities by itself. A **mobile computer** is a personal computer that you can carry from place to place, and a **mobile device** is a computing device small enough to hold in your hand. A **game console** is a mobile computing device designed for single-player or multiplayer video games. A **server** controls access to the hardware, software, and other resources on a network and provides a centralized storage area for programs, data, and information. A **mainframe** is a large, expensive, powerful computer that can handle hundreds or thousands of connected users simultaneously and can store tremendous amounts of data, instructions, and information. A **supercomputer** is the fastest, most powerful, and most expensive computer and is used for applications requiring complex, sophisticated mathematical calculations. An **embedded computer** is a special-purpose computer that functions as a computer in a larger product.

⑨ What Are the Elements of an Information System? An *information system* combines hardware, software, data, people, and procedures to produce timely and useful information. People in an *information technology (IT) department* develop procedures for processing data. Following these procedures, people use hardware and software to enter the data into a computer. Software processes the data and directs the computer hardware to store changes on storage media and produce information in a desired form.

⑩ What Are the Types of Computer Users? Computer users can be separated into five categories: home users, small office/home office users, mobile users, large business users, and power users. A **home user** is a family member who uses a computer for a variety of reasons, such as budgeting and personal financial management, Web access, communications, and entertainment. A **small office/home office** (*SOHO*) user is a small company or self-employed individual who works from home. SOHO users access the Internet to look up information and use basic business software and sometimes industry-specific software. **Mobile users** are employees and students who work on a computer while away from a main office or school. A **power user** uses a workstation or other powerful computer to work with industry-specific software. Power users exist in all types of businesses. A **large business user** works in a company with many employees and uses a computer and computer network to process high volumes of transactions.

⑪ What Computer Applications Are Used in Society? People interact directly with computers in fields such as education, finance, government, health care, science, publishing, travel, and manufacturing. In education, students use computers and software to assist with learning or take distance learning classes. In finance, people use computers for **online banking** and **online investing**. Government offices have Web sites to provide citizens with up-to-date information, and government employees use computers as part of their daily routines. In health care, computers are used to maintain patient records, monitor patients, assist with medical tests and research, correspond with patients, file insurance claims, provide greater precision during operations, and as implants. All branches of science use computers to assist with collecting, analyzing, and modeling data and to communicate with colleagues around the world. Publishers use computers to assist in designing pages and make the content of their works available online. Many vehicles use some type of online navigation system to help people travel more quickly and safely. Manufacturers use **computer-aided manufacturing** (*CAM*) to assist with the manufacturing process.

Visit scsite.com/dc2007/ch1/quiz or click the Quiz Yourself button. Click Objectives 8 – 11.

Key Terms

You should know the Primary Terms and be familiar with the Secondary Terms. Use the list below to help focus your study. To further enhance your understanding of the Key Terms in this chapter, visit scsite.com/dc2007/ch1/terms. See an example of and a definition for each term, and access current and additional information about the term from the Web.

Primary Terms

(shown in bold-black characters in the chapter)

application software (16)
communications device (9)
computer (6)
computer literacy (5)
computer-aided manufacturing (36)
data (6)
desktop computer (20)
embedded computer (24)
FAQ (6)
game console (22)
graphical user interface (GUI) (15)
handheld computer (21)
hardware (7)
home user (26)
information (6)
input device (7)
installing (17)
Internet (12)
Internet-enabled (21)
laptop computer (20)
large business user (30)
mainframe (23)
mobile computer (20)
mobile device (20)
mobile users (29)
network (11)
notebook computer (20)
online (11)
online banking (32)

online investing (33)
output device (8)
PDA (21)
personal computer (19)
photo sharing community (14)
power user (29)
program (15)
run (17)
server (23)
small office/home office (28)
smart phone (22)
software (15)
storage device (8)
storage media (8)
supercomputer (23)
system software (15)
system unit (8)
Tablet PC (21)
telecommuting (30)
user (9)
Web (12)
Web page (12)

Secondary Terms

(shown in italic characters in the chapter)

blog (14)
CAM (36)
convergence (22)
developer (18)
digital pen (21)
e-commerce (28)
enterprise computing (30)
execute (17)
gaming desktop computer (20)
garbage in, garbage out (10)
handhelds (22)
handtop computer (21)
icon (15)
information processing cycle (6)
information system (25)
information technology (IT) department (30)
instructions (6)
kiosk (30)
loads (17)
Media Center PC (20)
memory (8)
multimedia (29)
neural network (34)
operating system (15)
PC-compatible (19)
personal digital assistant (21)
podcast (14)
processor (8)
programmer (18)

publish (14)
resources (11)
SOHO (28)
stylus (21)
telematics (24)
telemedicine (34)
tower (20)
ultra personal computer (uPC) (21)
utility program (16)
Web cam (28)

Checkpoint

Use the Checkpoint exercises to check your knowledge level of the chapter. The Beyond the Book exercises will help broaden your understanding of the concepts presented in this chapter. To complete the Checkpoint exercises interactively, visit scsite.com/dc2007/ch1/check.

Label the Figure

Identify these common computer hardware components.

a. card reader/writer (storage)

b. CD/DVD drive (storage)

c. digital camera (input)

d. floppy disk drive (storage)

e. internal hard disk drive (storage)

f. keyboard (input)

g. microphone (input)

h. modem (communications)

i. monitor (output)

j. mouse (input)

k. PC video camera (input)

l. printer (output)

m. scanner (input)

n. speaker (output)

o. system unit (processor, memory, storage)

p. USB flash drive (storage)

q. external hard disk (storage)

True/False

Mark T for True and F for False. (See page numbers in parentheses.)

_____ 1. Many people believe that computer literacy is vital to success in today's world. (5)

_____ 2. Hardware consists of a series of instructions that tells the computer what to do and how to do it. (7)

_____ 3. The circuitry of the system unit usually is part of or is connected to a circuit board called the server. (8)

_____ 4. The computing phrase, garbage in, garbage out, points out that the accuracy of a computer's output depends on the accuracy of the input. (10)

_____ 5. A network is a collection of computers and devices connected together via communications devices and transmission media. (11)

_____ 6. Businesses, called access providers, offer users and companies access to the Internet free or for a fee. (12)

_____ 7. System software serves as the interface between the user, the application software, and the computer's hardware. (15)

_____ 8. Handheld computers never have keyboards. (21)

_____ 9. An information system consists of hardware, software, networks, and procedures. (25)

_____ 10. Home users type letters, homework assignments, and other documents with personal finance software. (27)

_____ 11. With online investing, the transaction fee for each trade usually is much more than when trading through a broker. (33)

Discovering Computers 2007
A Gateway to Information

Checkpoint

Multiple Choice   Select the best answer. (See page numbers in parentheses.)

1. Computer literacy involves having a knowledge and understanding of _____. (5)
   a. computer programming
   b. computers and their uses
   c. computer repair
   d. all of the above

2. A computer can _____. (6)
   a. accept data
   b. process data according to specified rules
   c. produce and store results
   d. all of the above

3. The series of input, process, output, and storage sometimes is referred to as the _____ cycle. (6)
   a. information processing
   b. computer programming
   c. data entering
   d. Web browsing

4. Commonly used _____ devices are a keyboard, a mouse, and a microphone. (7)
   a. input
   b. storage
   c. output
   d. mobile

5. A disadvantage of computers is that _____. (10)
   a. computer operations occur at very slow speeds
   b. the components in computers are undependable
   c. prolonged computer use can lead to injuries
   d. most computers cannot communicate

6. A _____ controls access to the resources on a network. (11)
   a. server
   b. workstation
   c. client
   d. tower

7. _____ can be thought of as a library of information available to anyone connected to the Internet. (12)
   a. The Web
   b. E-mail
   c. Instant messaging
   d. A blog

8. Two types of _____ are desktop computers and notebook computers. (19)
   a. embedded computers
   b. supercomputers
   c. servers
   d. personal computers

9. A _____ is a special type of notebook computer that is useful for taking notes in lectures, at meetings, and other forums where the standard notebook computer is not practical. (21)
   a. smart phone
   b. Tablet PC
   c. game console
   d. PDA

10. A _____ is a mobile computing device designed for single-player or multiplayer video games. (22)
    a. Media Center PC
    b. gaming desktop computer
    c. game console
    d. mobile device

11. An information system should have readily available documented _____ that address(es) operating the computer and using its applications. (25)
    a. hardware
    b. procedures
    c. software
    d. data

12. Examples of the _____ category of computer users include engineers, scientists, architects, desktop publishers, and graphic artists. (29)
    a. mobile user
    b. large business user
    c. power user
    d. small office/home office user

13. When using _____, users access account balances, pay bills, and copy monthly transactions from a bank's computer right to their personal computers. (32)
    a. e-commerce
    b. personal finance software
    c. online banking
    d. accounting software

14. _____ is a system that attempts to imitate the behavior of the human brain. (34)
    a. Telemedicine
    b. A neural network
    c. E-commerce
    d. A kiosk

Checkpoint

 Matching   Match the terms with their definitions. (See page numbers in parentheses.)

_____ 1. processor (8)
_____ 2. memory (8)
_____ 3. publish (14)
_____ 4. install (17)
_____ 5. execute (17)
_____ 6. stylus (21)
_____ 7. game console (22)
_____ 8. Web cam (28)
_____ 9. multimedia (29)
_____ 10. kiosk (30)

a. stores instructions waiting to be executed and the data needed
b. carry out the instructions in a computer program
c. set up software to work with a computer and other hardware components
d. combines text, graphics, audio, and video into one application
e. video camera that displays its output on a Web page
f. collection of computers and devices connected together
g. mobile device that can connect to the Internet wirelessly
h. metal or plastic device that uses pressure to write, draw, or make selections
i. freestanding computer, usually with a touch screen
j. mobile computing device designed for single-player or multiplayer video games
k. interprets and carries out basic instructions that operate a computer
l. make a Web page available on the Internet for others to see

Short Answer   Write a brief answer to each of the following questions.

1. How is data different from information? _____ What is the information processing cycle? _____
2. How is hardware different from software? _____ What is a programmer? _____
3. Why do people use the Web? _____ What can be contained on a Web page? _____
4. What are seven categories of computers? _____ What determines how a computer is categorized? _____
5. What is telecommuting? _____ Why do people telecommute? _____

Beyond the Book   Read the following book elements, learn more about each using the Web, and then write a brief report.

1. Ethics & Issues — Who Is Responsible for Identity Theft? (10), Who Is Responsible for the Accuracy of Web Pages? (14), Is Computer Gaming More Good than Bad? (16), Does Internet Dating Really Work? (27)

2. Career Corner — Personal Computer Salesperson (37)

3. Companies on the Cutting Edge — Dell or Apple Computer (39)

4. FAQs (6, 8, 14, 17, 20, 22, 27, 36)

5. High-Tech Talk — Analog versus Digital: Making the Conversion (38)

6. Looking Ahead — Medical Breakthroughs with Computer Implants, Devices (9) or Robots Perform Mundane Tasks, Entertain (32)

7. Making Use of the Web — Fun and Entertainment (116)

8. Picture Yourself in a Computer Class (2)

9. Technology Trailblazers — Bill Gates or Anne Mulcahy (39)

10. Timeline 2007 (52)

11. Web Links (7, 8, 9, 12, 14, 16, 19, 22, 26, 36)

Learn It Online

Use the Learn It Online exercises to reinforce your understanding of the chapter concepts. To access the Learn It Online exercises, visit scsite.com/dc2007/ch1/learn.

(1) At the Movies — Walking the PC Pioneer Trail

To view the Walking the PC Pioneer Trail movie, click the number 1 button. Locate your video and click the corresponding High-Speed or Dial-Up link, depending on your Internet connection. Watch the movie and then complete the exercise by answering the question that follows. Many of the pioneers of the technology industry in the United States established their businesses in Silicon Valley. What explanation can you offer for why the founders of these companies all set up shop in this area?

(2) At the Movies — Black Viper's Windows XP Tips

To view the Black Viper's Windows XP Tips movie, click the number 2 button. Locate your video and click the corresponding High-Speed or Dial-Up link, depending on your Internet connection. Watch the movie and then complete the exercise by answering the question that follows. Windows XP is a large and powerful program that often runs many applications that you will never use. These programs require a lot of resources that can be used by other programs. Which of these programs would you turn off to make your computer run more efficiently and faster?

(3) Student Edition Labs — Using Input Devices

Click the number 3 button. A new browser window will open, displaying the Student Edition Labs (screen shown in the figure below). Follow the on-screen instructions to complete the Using Input Devices Lab. When finished, click the Exit button. If required, submit your results to your instructor.

(4) Student Edition Labs — Using Windows

Click the number 4 button. A new browser window will open, displaying the Student Edition Labs. Follow the on-screen instructions to complete the Using Windows Lab. When finished, click the Exit button. If required, submit your results to your instructor.

(5) Practice Test

Click the number 5 button. Answer each question. When completed, enter your name and click the Grade Test button to submit the quiz for grading. Make a note of any missed questions. If required, submit your score to your instructor.

Learn It Online

6 Who Wants To Be a Computer Genius²?

Click the number 6 button to find out if you are a computer genius. Directions about how to play the game will be displayed. When you are ready to play, click the Play button. Submit your score to your instructor.

7 Wheel of Terms

Click the number 7 button to reinforce important terms you learned in this chapter by playing the Shelly Cashman Series version of this popular game. Directions about how to play the game will be displayed. When you are ready to play, click the Play button. Submit your score to your instructor.

8 DC Track and Field

Click the number 8 button to use what you have learned in this chapter to compete against other students in three track and field events. Directions about how to play the game will be displayed. When you are ready to play, click the start first event button. If required, submit your score to your instructor.

9 You're Hired!

Click the number 9 button to use what you have learned in this chapter to embark on the path to a career in computers. Directions about how to play the game will be displayed. When you are ready to play, click the begin game button. If required, submit your score to your instructor.

10 Crossword Puzzle Challenge

Click the number 10 button. Complete the puzzle to reinforce skills you learned in this chapter. Directions about how to play the game will be displayed. When you are ready to play, click the Play button. Submit the completed puzzle to your instructor.

11 Lab Exercises

Click the number 11 button. When the Lab Exercises menu appears, click the exercise assigned by your instructor. A new browser window will open. Follow the on-screen instructions to complete the exercise. When finished, click the Exit button. If required, submit your results to your instructor.

12 Learn the Web

No matter how much computer experience you have, navigating the Web for the first time can be intimidating. How do you get started? Click the number 12 button and click the links to discover how you can find out everything you want to know about the Internet.

13 Chapter Discussion Forum

Select an objective from this chapter on page 3 about which you would like more information. Click the number 13 button and post a short message listing a meaningful message title accompanied by one or more questions concerning the selected objective. In two days, return to the threaded discussion by clicking the number 13 button. Submit to your instructor your original message and at least one response to your message.

14 Google Maps

Click the number 14 button to learn how to locate businesses in your area, view a location's surroundings via satellite, and find directions from one location to another. Print a copy of the Google Maps page and then step through the exercise. If required, submit your results to your instructor.

Learn How To

Use the Learn How To activities to learn fundamental skills when using a computer and accompanying technology. Complete the exercises and submit them to your instructor. To see a video of a Learn How To activity, visit scsite.com/dc2007/ch1/howto.

LEARN HOW TO 1: Start and Close an Application

An application accomplishes tasks on a computer. You can start any application by using the Start button.

Complete these steps to start the Web browser application called Internet Explorer:
1. Click the Start button (🔳 start) at the left of the Windows taskbar on the bottom of the screen. *The Start menu is displayed.*
2. Point to All Programs on the Start menu. *The All Programs submenu appears (Figure 1-45).*
3. Click the program name, Internet Explorer, on the All Programs submenu. *The Internet Explorer browser window opens (Figure 1-46).*

An item on the All Programs submenu might have a small right arrow next to it. When this occurs, point to the item and another submenu will appear. Click the application name on this submenu to start the application. Some application names might appear on the Start menu

FIGURE 1-45

FIGURE 1-46

itself. If so, click any of these names to start the corresponding application.

Below the line on the left side of the Start menu, Windows displays the names of the applications recently opened on the computer. You can start any of these applications by clicking the name of the application.

To close an application, click the Close button (🔳) in the upper-right corner of the window. If you have created but not saved a document, Windows will ask if you want to save the document. If you do not want to save it, click the No button in the displayed dialog box. If you want to save it, refer to Learn How To number 1 in Chapter 3 on page 178.

Exercise

1. Using the Start button, start the application named WordPad found on the Accessories submenu of the All Programs submenu. WordPad is a word processing application. Type the following: `To start an application, click the application name on the All Programs submenu` and then type your name. Click the Print button (🖨) on the toolbar. Submit the printout to your instructor.
2. Close the WordPad application. If you are asked if you want to save changes to the document, click the No button. Start the WordPad application again, type some new text, and then close the WordPad application. When the dialog box is displayed, click the Cancel button. What happened? Now, close the WordPad window without saving the document. Submit your answer to your instructor.

Learn How To

3. Using the Start button, start the e-mail program on the computer. What is the name of the e-mail program? In the program window, what menu names are displayed on the menu bar at the top of the window? Close the e-mail program. Submit your answers to your instructor.

LEARN HOW TO 2: Use the Discovering Computers 2007 Online Companion (scsite.com/dc2007)

The Discovering Computers 2007 Online Companion provides a variety of activities and exercises. To use the site, you first must register and establish a user name and password. Perform the following steps to register:
1. Start the Web browser.
2. Type scsite.com/dc2007 in the Address box of the Web browser. Press the ENTER key.
3. When the registration page is displayed, click the New User Registration link.
4. Follow the on-screen instructions to complete registration.

When you first type a Web address to display a page from the dc2007 site, you must enter your user name and password to gain access to the site. When you are done using the site, close the browser so no one else can visit the site with your user name and password.

Exercise
1. Start the Web browser on your computer.
2. Type scsite.com/dc2007/ch1/howto in the Address box of the browser and then press the ENTER key.
3. If the registration page is displayed and you have not yet registered, complete the steps above. If you are registered, enter your user name and password, and then click the Enter button.
4. Navigate to the Chapter 1 home page.
5. Visit each of the Exercises Web pages (Case Studies, Chapter Review, Checkpoint, Key Terms, Learn How To, Learn It Online, and Web Research). Use the navigation bar on the left of the screen to display these pages.
6. Click the browser's Close button to close the application.
7. Write a report that describes the use of each of the Exercises pages you visited. Which page do you think will prove the most valuable to you when using the book and the Web site? Why? Which will be the least useful? Why? Submit your report to your instructor.

LEARN HOW TO 3: Find Out About Your Computer

By following these steps, you can find out about your computer:
1. Click the Start button on the Windows XP taskbar.
2. Point to All Programs on the Start menu, point to Accessories on the All Programs submenu, and then point to System Tools on the Accessories submenu.
3. Click System Information on the System Tools submenu. Windows displays a system summary in the right side of the window, and an index of categories in the left side of the window (Figure 1-47).

To determine more information about your computer, click any of the plus signs in the left side of the window. Then, click the item about which you want more information.

FIGURE 1-47

Exercise
1. Submit the answers to the following questions about your computer:
   a. What type of operating system (OS Name) is in use?
   b. What company manufactured the computer?
   c. How much RAM (physical memory) is on the computer?
   d. How much data can you store on the C: drive?
   e. What is the name of a CD or DVD drive found on the computer?

Web Research

Use the Internet-based Web Research exercises to broaden your understanding of the concepts presented in this chapter. Visit scsite.com/dc2007/ch1/research to obtain more information pertaining to each exercise. To discuss any of the Web Research exercises in this chapter with other students, post your thoughts or questions at scsite.com/dc2007/ch1/forum.

(1) Scavenger Hunt Use one of the <u>search engines</u> listed in Figure 2-10 in Chapter 2 on page 78 or your own favorite search engine to find the answers to the questions below. Copy and paste the Web address from the Web page where you found the answer. Some questions may have more than one answer. If required, submit your answers to your instructor. (1) What are three accredited online colleges or universities that offer a bachelor's degree in computer information technology? (2) Two National Science Foundation (NSF) programs were established in 1997 to interconnect 50 university and scientific computing sites. What colleges host these two sites? What were the locations of the five original NSF-financed supercomputer centers? (3) Personal finance software helps you balance your checkbook and manage your finances. What is the name of a popular personal finance software program? (4) What is the name of the first spreadsheet program? (5) A programming language developed by the U.S. Department of Defense was named to honor a famous woman mathematician. What is the name of this programming language?

(2) Search Sleuth Visit the <u>Google Web site</u> (google.com) and then click the About Google link at the bottom of the page. Using your word processing program, answer the following questions and then, if required, submit your answers to your instructor. (1) Below Our Company, click Corporate Info. Who are the founders of Google? (2) Click the Technology link on the left side of the page. Provide a summary on the steps Google takes to complete a query. (3) Click your browser's Back button twice or press the BACKSPACE key two times to return to the About Google page. Below Our Search, click the Google Web Search Features link. How is Google including books in its search results? What are some of Google's newest features? What weather information is available? (4) Click your browser's Back button two times to return to the Google home page. In the Google Search text box, type `computer` and click the Google Search button. Approximately how many hits resulted? Do any definitions appear? If so, list the definitions. How much time did it take to complete the search? (5) In the Google Search text box, type `personal computer` and click the Search button. Compare this to your earlier search. Are there more or fewer hits? How much time did it take to complete the second search? (6) Click one of the resulting personal computer links and review the information. Write a 50-word summary. Using the information contained within the Web site, do you think you have sufficient knowledge to purchase a computer intelligently?

(3) Newsgroups One of the more popular topics for <u>newsgroups</u> is the Internet. Find three newsgroups, such as those listed in CyberFiber (cyberfiber.com/internet.htm) or Google Groups, that discuss an aspect of the Internet. Read the newsgroup postings and post a reply to one message. Summarize three topics under discussion and your reply to a message.

(4) Journaling Respond to your readings in this chapter by writing at least one page about your reactions, evaluations, and reflections about computer usage in your school. For example, how many students have high-speed <u>Internet</u> access at home or in on-campus housing? Are students without this Internet access at a disadvantage for completing homework assignments and research papers? Do electronic materials in the classroom get students more engaged in learning? You also can write about the new terms you learned by reading this chapter. If required, submit your journal to your instructor.

(5) Ethics in Action The Internet has increased the ease with which students can plagiarize material for research paper assignments. Teachers are using online services, such as Turnitin.com, to help detect plagiarized papers and to help students understand how to cite sources correctly. Visit the <u>Turnitin site</u> (turnitin.com) and then write a summary of how this service is used. How prevalent is plagiarism on your campus? What action should an instructor take when a student submits a plagiarized paper? If required, submit your summary to your instructor.

Case Studies

Use the Case Studies to apply the concepts presented in the chapter to real-world situations. Visit scsite.com/dc2007/ch1/cases to obtain more information pertaining to each exercise. To discuss the Case Studies in this chapter with other students, visit scsite.com/dc2007/ch1/forum and post your thoughts or questions.

CASE STUDY 1 — Class Discussion   You are the assistant parts manager for a local car dealership. Your dealership sells cars from two different manufacturers. Your responsibilities include checking inventory, obtaining pricing and picking up parts from local auto parts stores, and performing miscellaneous tasks at the dealership. Eventually, you would like to be promoted to parts manager. The owner has just purchased a new computer for the parts department. He has told you that, in order to be promoted, you must become proficient in the use of computers and **computer software**. Review the computer courses offered at your school. Prepare a list of courses that you feel would help you acquire the computer proficiency required for you to be promoted. Draft a letter to the owner detailing your course choices and explaining why each course would be beneficial. Be prepared to discuss your findings.

CASE STUDY 2 — Class Discussion   You are a member of your local school district's board of education. Over the past year, the number of computers purchased by the district increased by 85 percent, while the supply of library books declined by almost 10 percent. School officials claim that computers extend learning opportunities and develop the **computer literacy** needed in today's technological world. Yet, some parents are complaining that computer purchases represent frivolous, status-seeking spending. Notebook computers are purchased for teachers, while textbooks and library books are too old, too worn, and too scarce. Use the Web and/or print media to learn how computers are being used in schools. As a school board member, draft a proposal recommending the percentage of the instructional materials budget that should be spent on computers versus the percentage that should be spent on library books and textbooks. Note the factors that influenced your decision. Be prepared to discuss your recommendations.

CASE STUDY 3 — Research   Computers are everywhere. Watching television, driving a car, using a charge card, even ordering fast food all involve computers, not to mention browsing the Web on your personal computer. Your car computer is an **embedded computer** that can be described as special-purpose, because it only accepts specific input and performs limited functions. Your personal computer, on the other hand, is general-purpose, meaning it accepts a wide range of input and can perform a variety of tasks. For one day, make a list of each computer you encounter (be careful not to limit yourself just to the computers you see). How is the computer used? Is the computer special-purpose or general-purpose? Why? How was the task the computer performs accomplished before computers? Write a brief report or use PowerPoint to create a presentation and share your findings.

CASE STUDY 4 — Research   You are an assistant manager at a local computer store. Your manager suspects that for cultural, financial, or societal reasons, certain groups of people are more likely to buy computers than others. To increase the impact of the store's promotions, your manager has asked you to discover if computers are purchased by individuals from a broad spectrum, or if a certain type exists that represents most **computer buyers**. Use the Web and/or print media to learn more about the demographics of computer buyers. What gender are most buyers? In what age range do they fall? What seems to be the typical educational level? What is the approximate average income of a typical buyer? Do buyers tend to share any other characteristics? If you discover any trends, what reasons might be behind the results? Write a brief report or use PowerPoint to create a presentation and share your findings.

CASE STUDY 5 — Team Challenge   People use computers in a variety of fields, including education, finance, government, health care, science, publishing, travel, and manufacturing. Although the way people use computers varies, each use of a computer involves **computer hardware**, computer software, and normally some type of communications capability over networks, such as the Internet. Form a three-member team and choose a field in which you all are interested. Using the Web and/or print media, assign one member of your team to investigate hardware used in the field, another member to investigate software used in the field, and the third member to investigate communications capabilities used in the field. After your investigation, characterize a hypothetical business or organization in the field. Based on your investigation, prepare a report that recommends specific hardware, software, and networking capabilities that would be best for the business or organization; explain your recommendations in the report.

Special Feature

scsite.com/dc2007/ch1/timeline

Timeline 2007

MILESTONES IN COMPUTER HISTORY

Dr. John V. Atanasoff and Clifford Berry design and build the first electronic digital computer. Their machine, the Atanasoff-Berry-Computer, or ABC, provides the foundation for advances in electronic digital computers.

John von Neumann in front of the electronic computer built at the Institute for Advanced Study. This computer and its von Neumann architecture served as the prototype for subsequent stored program computers worldwide.

William Shockley, John Bardeen, and Walter Brattain invent the transfer resistance device, eventually called the transistor. The transistor would revolutionize computers, proving much more reliable than vacuum tubes.

1937   **1943**   **1945**   **1946**   **1947**   **1951**

Dr. John W. Mauchly and J. Presper Eckert, Jr. complete work on the first large-scale electronic, general-purpose digital computer. The ENIAC (Electronic Numerical Integrator And Computer) weighs 30 tons, contains 18,000 vacuum tubes, occupies a 30 × 50 foot space, and consumes 160 kilowatts of power. The first time it is turned on, lights dim in an entire section of Philadelphia.

The first commercially available electronic digital computer, the UNIVAC I (UNIVersal Automatic Computer), is introduced by Remington Rand. Public awareness of computers increases when the UNIVAC I, after analyzing only five percent of the popular vote, correctly predicts that Dwight D. Eisenhower will win the presidential election.

During World War II, British scientist Alan Turing designs the Colossus, an electronic computer created for the military to break German codes. The computer's existence is kept secret until the 1970s.

Dr. Grace Hopper considers the concept of reusable software in her paper, "The Education of a Computer." The paper describes how to program a computer with symbolic notation instead of the detailed machine language that had been used.

The IBM 305 RAMAC system is the first to use magnetic disk for external storage. The system provides storage capacity similar to magnetic tape that previously was used, but offers the advantage of semi-random access capability.

More than 200 programming languages have been created.

IBM introduces two smaller, desk-sized computers: the IBM 1401 for business and the IBM 1620 for scientists. The IBM 1620 initially is called the CADET, but IBM drops the name when campus wags claim it is an acronym for, Can't Add, Doesn't Even Try.

Fortran (FORmula TRANslation), an efficient, easy-to-use programming language, is introduced by John Backus.

1952　1953　1957　1958　1959　1960

The IBM model 650 is one of the first widely used computers. Originally planning to produce only 50 machines, the system is so successful that eventually IBM manufactures more than 1,000. With the IBM 700 series of machines, the company will dominate the mainframe market for the next decade.

Core memory, developed in the early 1950s, provides much larger storage capacity than vacuum tube memory.

Jack Kilby of Texas Instruments invents the integrated circuit, which lays the foundation for high-speed computers and large-capacity memories. Computers built with transistors mark the beginning of the second generation of computer hardware.

COBOL, a high-level business application language, is developed by a committee headed by Dr. Grace Hopper. COBOL uses English-like phrases and runs on most business computers, making it one of the more widely used programming languages.

Dr. John Kemeny of Dartmouth leads the development of the BASIC programming language. BASIC will be widely used on personal computers.

Computer Science Corporation becomes the first software company listed on the New York Stock Exchange.

Under pressure from the industry, IBM announces that some of its software will be priced separately from the computer hardware. This unbundling allows software firms to emerge in the industry.

Digital Equipment Corporation (DEC) introduces the first minicomputer, the PDP-8. The machine is used extensively as an interface for time-sharing systems.

In a letter to the editor titled, "GO TO Statements Considered Harmful," Dr. Edsger Dijsktra introduces the concept of structured programming, developing standards for constructing computer programs.

The ARPANET network, a predecessor of the Internet, is established.

1964 **1965** **1968** **1969** **1970**

The number of computers has grown to 18,000. Third-generation computers, with their controlling circuitry stored on chips, are introduced. The IBM System/360 computer is the first family of compatible machines, merging science and business lines.

Alan Shugart at IBM demonstrates the first regular use of an 8-inch floppy (magnetic storage) disk.

Fourth-generation computers, built with chips that use LSI (large-scale integration) arrive. While the chips used in 1965 contained as many as 1,000 circuits, the LSI chip contains as many as 15,000.

IBM introduces the term word processing for the first time with its Magnetic Tape/Selectric Typewriter (MT/ST). The MT/ST was the first reusable storage medium that allowed typed material to be edited without having to retype the document.

MITS, Inc. advertises one of the first microcomputers, the Altair. Named for the destination in an episode of *Star Trek*, the Altair is sold in kits for less than $400. Although initially it has no keyboard, no monitor, no permanent memory, and no software, 4,000 orders are taken within the first three months.

VisiCalc, a spreadsheet program written by Bob Frankston and Dan Bricklin, is introduced. Originally written to run on Apple II computers, VisiCalc will be seen as the most important reason for the acceptance of personal computers in the business world.

The IBM PC is introduced, signaling IBM's entrance into the personal computer marketplace. The IBM PC quickly garners the largest share of the personal computer market and becomes the personal computer of choice in business.

Ethernet, the first local area network (LAN), is developed at Xerox PARC (Palo Alto Research Center) by Robert Metcalf. The LAN allows computers to communicate and share software, data, and peripherals. Initially designed to link minicomputers, Ethernet will be extended to personal computers.

The first public online information services, CompuServe and the Source, are founded.

| 1971 | 1975 | 1976 | 1979 | 1980 | 1981 |

IBM offers Microsoft Corporation cofounder, Bill Gates, the opportunity to develop the operating system for the soon-to-be announced IBM personal computer. With the development of MS-DOS, Microsoft achieves tremendous growth and success.

Dr. Ted Hoff of Intel Corporation develops a microprocessor, or microprogrammable computer chip, the Intel 4004.

Steve Jobs and Steve Wozniak build the first Apple computer. A subsequent version, the Apple II, is an immediate success. Adopted by elementary schools, high schools, and colleges, for many students, the Apple II is their first contact with the world of computers.

The first computer virus, Elk Cloner, is spread via Apple II floppy disks, which contained the operating system. A short rhyme would appear on the screen when the user pressed Reset after the 50th boot of an infected disk.

Alan Shugart presents the Winchester hard drive, revolutionizing storage for personal computers.

Special Feature

scsite.com/dc2007/ch1/timeline

3.275 Million

3,275,000 personal computers are sold, almost 3,000,000 more than in 1981.

Apple introduces the Macintosh computer, which incorporates a unique, easy-to-learn, graphical user interface.

COMPAQ

Compaq, Inc. is founded to develop and market IBM-compatible PCs.

Microsoft

Microsoft has public stock offering and raises approximately $61 million. Within 20 years, Microsoft's stock is worth nearly $350 billion or 5,735 times the amount raised in the initial public stock offering.

Hayes introduces the 300 bps smart modem. The modem is an immediate success.

Hewlett-Packard announces the first LaserJet printer for personal computers.

1982   **1983**   **1984**   **1986**   **1988**

Instead of choosing a person for its annual award, *TIME* magazine names the computer Machine of the Year for 1982, acknowledging the impact of computers on society.

Lotus Development Corporation is founded. Its spreadsheet software, Lotus 1-2-3, which combines spreadsheet, graphics, and database programs in one package, becomes the best-selling program for IBM personal computers.

Microsoft surpasses Lotus Development Corporation to become the world's top software vendor.

While working at CERN, Switzerland, Tim Berners-Lee invents an Internet-based hypermedia enterprise for information sharing. Berners-Lee will call this innovation the World Wide Web.

World Wide Web Consortium releases standards that describe a framework for linking documents on different computers.

Several companies introduce computers using the Pentium processor from Intel. The Pentium chip is the successor to the Intel 486 processor. It contains 3.1 million transistors and is capable of performing 112,000,000 instructions per second.

Microsoft releases Microsoft Office 3 Professional, the first version of Microsoft Office.

1989   **1991**   **1992**   **1993**

The Intel 486 becomes the world's first 1,000,000 transistor microprocessor. It crams 1.2 million transistors on a .4" x .6" sliver of silicon and executes 15,000,000 instructions per second — four times as fast as its predecessor, the 80386 chip.

Microsoft releases Windows 3.1, the latest version of its Windows operating system. Windows 3.1 offers improvements such as TrueType fonts, multimedia capability, and object linking and embedding (OLE). In two months, 3,000,000 copies of Windows 3.1 are sold.

The White House launches its Web site, which includes an interactive citizens' handbook and White House history and tours.

Special Feature

scsite.com/dc2007/ch1/timeline

U.S. Robotics introduces PalmPilot, a handheld personal organizer. The PalmPilot's user friendliness and low price make it a standout next to more expensive personal digital assistants (PDAs).

Jim Clark and Marc Andreessen found Netscape and launch Netscape Navigator 1.0, a browser for the World Wide Web.

Sun Microsystems launches Java, an object-oriented programming language that allows users to write one application for a variety of computer platforms. Java becomes one of the hotter Internet technologies.

Microsoft Windows NT Server

Microsoft releases Windows NT 4.0, an operating system for client-server networks. Windows NT's management tools and wizards make it easier for developers to build and deploy business applications.

1994　　1995　　1996

Linux

Linus Torvalds creates the Linux kernel, a UNIX-like operating system that he releases free across the Internet for further enhancement by other programmers.

Microsoft Windows 95 Upgrade
for users of Windows

Microsoft releases Windows 95, a major upgrade to its Windows operating system. Windows 95 consists of more than 10,000,000 lines of computer instructions developed by 300 person-years of effort. More than 50,000 individuals and companies test the software before it is released.

1/3　2/3

Two out of three employees in the United States have access to a personal computer, and one out of every three homes has a personal computer. Fifty million personal computers are sold worldwide and more than 250,000,000 are in use.

Apple and Microsoft sign a joint technology development agreement. Microsoft buys $150,000,000 of Apple stock.

More than 10,000,000 people take up telecommuting, which is the capability of working at home and communicating with an office via computer. Increasingly more firms embrace telecommuting to help increase productivity, reduce absenteeism, and provide greater job satisfaction.

Apple Computer introduces the iMac, the next version of its popular Macintosh computer. The iMac abandons such conventional features as a floppy disk drive but wins customers with its futuristic design, see-through case, and easy setup. Consumer demand outstrips Apple's production capabilities, and some vendors are forced to begin waiting lists.

DVD, the next generation of optical disc storage technology, is introduced. DVD can store computer, audio, and video data in a single format, with the capability of producing near-studio quality. By year's end, 500,000 DVD players are shipped worldwide.

1997

1998

Intel introduces the Pentium II processor with 7.5 million transistors. The new processor, which incorporates MMX technology, processes video, audio, and graphics data more efficiently and supports applications such as movie editing, gaming, and more.

E-commerce, or electronic commerce — the marketing of goods and services over the Internet — booms. Companies such as Dell, E*TRADE, and Amazon.com spur online shopping, allowing buyers to obtain everything from hardware and software to financial and travel services, insurance, automobiles, books, and more.

Microsoft releases Internet Explorer 4.0 and seizes a key place in the Internet arena. This new Web browser is greeted with tremendous customer demand.

Microsoft ships Windows 98, an upgrade to Windows 95. Windows 98 offers improved Internet access, better system performance, and support for a new generation of hardware and software. In six months, more than 10,000,000 copies of Windows 98 are sold worldwide.

Fifty million users are connected to the Internet and World Wide Web.

Governments and businesses frantically work to make their computers Y2K (Year 2000) compliant, spending more than $500 billion worldwide. Y2K non-compliant computers cannot distinguish whether 01/01/00 refers to 1900 or 2000, and thus may operate using a wrong date. This Y2K bug can affect any application that relies on computer chips, such as ATMs, airplanes, energy companies, and the telephone system. In the end, the Y2K bug turned out not to be a problem.

Shawn Fanning, 19, and his company, Napster, turn the music industry upside down by developing software that allows computer users to swap music files with one another without going through a centralized file server. The Recording Industry of America, on behalf of five media companies, sues Napster for copyright infringement and wins.

U.S. District Judge Thomas Penfield Jackson rules in the antitrust lawsuit brought by the Department of Justice and 19 states that Microsoft used its monopoly power to stifle competition.

1999

2000

Microsoft introduces Office 2000, its premier productivity suite, offering new tools for users to create content and save it directly to a Web site without any file conversion or special steps.

E-commerce achieves mainstream acceptance. Annual e-commerce sales exceed $100 billion, and Internet advertising expenditures reach more than $5 billion.

Open Source Code software, such as the Linux operating system and the Apache Web server created by unpaid volunteers, begin to gain wide acceptance among computer users.

Dot-com companies (Internet based) go out of business at a record pace — nearly one per day — as financial investors withhold funding due to the companies' unprofitability.

Microsoft ships Windows 2000 and Windows Me. Windows 2000 offers improved behind-the-scene security and reliability. Windows Me is designed for home users and lets them edit home movies, share digital photos, index music, and create a home network.

Intel unveils its Pentium 4 chip with clock speeds starting at 1.4 GHz. The Pentium 4 includes 42 million transistors, nearly twice as many contained on its predecessor, the Pentium III.

Microsoft releases major operating system updates with Windows XP for the desktop and servers, and Pocket PC 2002 for handheld computers. Windows XP is significantly more reliable than previous versions, features a 32-bit computing architecture, and offers a new look and feel. Pocket PC 2002 offers the handheld computer user a familiar Windows interface and consistent functionality.

According to the U.S. Department of Commerce, Internet traffic is doubling every 100 days, resulting in an annual growth rate of more than 700 percent. It has taken radio and television 30 years and 15 years, respectively, to reach 60 million people. The Internet has achieved the same audience base in 3 years.

2000

2001

Microsoft introduces Office XP, the next version of the world's leading suite of productivity software. Features include speech and handwriting recognition, smart tags, and task panes.

Telemedicine uses satellite technology and videoconferencing to broadcast consultations and to perform distant surgeries. Robots are used for complex and precise tasks. Computer-aided surgery uses virtual reality to assist with training and planning procedures.

Avid readers enjoy e-books, which are digital texts read on compact computer screens. E-books can hold the equivalent of 10 traditional books containing text and graphics. Readers can search, highlight text, and add notes.

After several years of negligible sales, the Tablet PC is reintroduced as the next-generation mobile PC. The lightweight device, the size of a three-ring notebook, is ideal for people on the go.

Wireless computers and devices, such as keyboards, mouse devices, home networks, and public Internet access points become commonplace. Latest operating systems include support for both the Wi-Fi (wireless fidelity) and Bluetooth standards. Wireless capabilities are standard on many PDAs and Tablet PCs.

Digital video cameras, DVD writers, easy-to-use video editing software, and improvements in storage capabilities allow the average computer user to create Hollywood-like videos with introductions, conclusions, scenes rearranged, music, and voice-over.

2002

2003

Microsoft launches its .NET strategy, which is a new environment for developing and running software applications featuring ease of development of Web-based services.

Microsoft ships Office 2003, the latest version of its flagship Office suite. More than 400 million people in 175 nations and 70 languages are using a version of Office.

DVD writers begin to replace CD writers (CD-RW). DVDs can store up to eight times as much data as CDs. Uses include storing home movies, music, photos, and backups.

Intel ships its revamped Pentium 4 chip with the 0.13 micron processor and Hyper-Threading (HT) Technology, operating at speeds of 3.06 GHz. This new development eventually will enable processors with a billion transistors to operate at 20 GHz.

In an attempt to maintain their current business model of selling songs, the Recording Industry Association of American (RIAA) files over 250 lawsuits against individual computer users who offer copyrighted music over peer-to-peer networks.

Flat-panel LCD monitors overtake bulky CRT monitors as the popular choice of computer users. Although flat-panel LCD monitors cost more, they offer several advantages including physical size, weight, true display size, better power consumption, and no radiation emission.

Companies such as RealNetworks, Microsoft, Sony, and Wal-Mart stake out turf in the online music store business started by Apple Computer. In the previous year, Apple's iTunes Music Store Web site sold nearly 20 million songs for 99 cents each.

USB flash drives, which are small enough to fit on a key chain but can store up to 4 billion characters, become a cost-effective way to trans-port data and information from one computer to another.

2004

Linux, the open-source operating system, makes major inroads into the server market as a viable alternative to Microsoft Windows, Sun's Solaris, and the UNIX operating systems.

Linux

Major retailers begin requiring suppliers to include radio frequency identification (RFID) tags or microchips with antennas, which can be as small as 1/3 of a millimeter across, in the goods they sell. When a transponder receives a certain radio query, it responds by transmitting its unique ID code. Besides carrying out the functions of the bar code, RFIDs may eventually eliminate long checkout lines.

GERRY WEBER

Apple Computer introduces the sleek iMac G5. The new computer's display device contains the system unit.

106 million, or 53 percent, of the 200 million online population in America accesses the Internet via speedy broadband.

Special Feature

scsite.com/dc2007/ch1/timeline

Microsoft
Windows XP
Media Center Edition 2005

Microsoft unveils Windows XP Media Center Edition 2005. This operating system allows users to access the routine capabilities of a Windows XP-based PC while focusing on delivering media content such as music, digital photography, movies, and television.

Spyware Pharming
Spam Phishing
Spim Spit

Spam, spyware, phishing, pharming, spim, and spit take center stage, along with viruses, as major nuisances to the 801 million computer users worldwide.

The Mozilla Foundation, the creator of the free open source Firefox browser, claims to have captured 10 percent of the browser market, primarily at the expense of Microsoft's Internet Explorer (IE) browser.

Blogging
Podcasting

Blogging and podcasting become mainstream methods for distributing information via the Web.

iPod
the
Video-Pod

Apple releases the latest version of its popular pocket-sized iPod audio player. First it played songs, then photos, then podcasts, and now, in addition, up to 150 hours of music videos and TV shows on a 2.5" color display.

2005

The smart phone overtakes the PDA as the personal mobile device of choice. A smart phone offers the user a cellular phone, full personal information management and e-mail functionality, a Web browser, instant message capabilities, and even the ability to listen to music, play video and games, and take pictures with its built-in camera.

Xbox360

Microsoft introduces Visual Studio 2005. The product includes Visual Basic, Visual C#, Visual J#, Visual C++, and SQL Server. Microsoft also releases a Visual Studio 2005 Express Edition for hobbyists, students, and nonprofessionals.

Microsoft releases the Xbox 360, its latest game console. Features include the capability to play music, display photos, and network with computers and other Xbox games.

Microsoft
Visual Studio 2005

Sony launches its PlayStation 3 and Nintendo launches its Revolution. Sony won the previous numbers games with worldwide sales of 90 million PlayStation 2 consoles to Microsoft's 24 million Xbox consoles and Nintendo's 21 million GameCube consoles.

IBM produces the fastest supercomputer called Blue Gene/L. It can perform approximately 28 trillion calculations in the time it takes you to blink your eye, or about one-tenth of a second. The Blue Gene/L primarily is used to explore hydrodynamics, quantum chemistry, molecular dynamics, climate modeling, and financial modeling.

Municipalities across the United States begin deploying low-cost, high-speed, broadband wireless connectivity to all points within their jurisdiction. Citizens access the Internet at broadband speeds using wireless desktop computers, notebook computers or handheld devices to connect to Wi-Fi access points. Some municipalities see the deployment of wireless networks as a way to bridge the digital divide.

Microsoft releases the latest version of its flagship Office suite. New features include the most significant update to the user interface in more than a decade and the capability to save documents in XML and PDF formats.

2006

Microsoft ships the latest version of its widely used operating system, Windows Vista™. Windows Vista focuses on greatly improving security, deployment, manageability, and performance. Included with Windows Vista is a new version of the world's most popular Web browser, Internet Explorer 7. New features of the browser include advancements in security and enhanced browsing for end users.

Apple begins selling Macintosh computers with Intel microprocessors.

An IBM virtual supercomputer project, called the World Community Grid, links nearly 100,000 personal computers worldwide. The grid, designed to accommodate up to 10 million computers, is made up of personal computers whose owners volunteered their use when the computers otherwise would be sitting idle. The supercomputer is used to create a scientific database available to researchers around the world. The next project for this powerful grid is to maintain an up-to-date HIV/AIDS database as the virus evolves into drug-resistant forms.

CHAPTER TWO

The Internet and World Wide Web

Picture Yourself Instant Messaging

While eating popcorn and waiting for the movie to begin, you hear an alarm. Did you forget to turn off your smart phone? You look at the phone and notice that a friend is sending you an instant message from his home computer. With a few minutes until the lights dim in the theater, you open the message. At that moment, a chorus of your friends' voices singing "Happy Birthday" loudly plays through the phone while the same words appear on the phone's screen. Quickly, you turn off the phone's sound and look around — hoping no one heard. No such luck. Nearly everyone in the theater found it quite amusing.

With the phone's sound turned off, you press some buttons to reply to the instant message, thanking your musical friends for their greeting. Your friend replies that he just bought a PC video camera and wanted to try sending a video instant message over his high-speed Internet line. Everyone gathered at his house to sing and send you the message. After conversing for a few minutes, you punch in CU later on the phone and set your online status to Away — so everyone knows you will be unavailable. Then, you press another button to display the Cubs score and the weather report. Next, you decide to check e-mail messages. The movie is starting . . . time to disconnect from the Internet.

To learn how technology allows you access to your friends, sports scores, weather reports, and e-mail, read Chapter 2 and discover features of the Internet and World Wide Web.

After completing this chapter, you will be able to:

1. Discuss the history of the Internet
2. Explain how to access and connect to the Internet
3. Analyze an IP address
4. Identify the components of a Web address
5. Explain the purpose of a Web browser
6. Search for information on the Web
7. Describe the types of Web sites
8. Recognize how Web pages use graphics, animation, audio, video, virtual reality, and plug-ins
9. Identify the steps required for Web publishing
10. Describe the types of e-commerce
11. Explain how e-mail, FTP, newsgroups and message boards, mailing lists, chat rooms, instant messaging, and Internet telephony work
12. Identify the rules of netiquette

CONTENTS

THE INTERNET

One of the major reasons business, home, and other users purchase computers is for Internet access. Through the Internet, society has access to global information and instant communications. Further, access to the Internet can occur anytime from a computer anywhere: at home, at work, at school, in a restaurant, on an airplane, and even at the beach.

The **Internet**, also called the *Net*, is a worldwide collection of networks that links millions of businesses, government agencies, educational institutions, and individuals. Each of the networks on the Internet provides resources that add to the abundance of goods, services, and information accessible via the Internet.

Today, more than one billion users around the world access a variety of services on the Internet, some of which are shown in Figure 2-1. The World Wide Web and e-mail are two of the more widely used Internet services. Other services include FTP (File Transfer Protocol), newsgroups, chat rooms, instant messaging, and Internet telephony. To enhance your understanding of these services, the chapter begins by discussing the history of the Internet and how the Internet works and then explains each of these services.

FIGURE 2-1a (Web)

FIGURE 2-1c (FTP – File Transfer Protocol)

FIGURE 2-1b (e-mail)

FIGURE 2-1 People around the world use a variety of Internet services in daily activities. Internet services allow users to access the Web, send e-mail messages, transfer documents and photographs, post messages, chat with a group, or have a private conversation with an online friend(s) or family member(s).

HISTORY OF THE INTERNET

The Internet has its roots in a networking project started by the Pentagon's *Advanced Research Projects Agency* (*ARPA*), an agency of the U.S. Department of Defense. ARPA's goal was to build a network that (1) allowed scientists at different physical locations to share information and work together on military and scientific projects and (2) could function even if part of the network were disabled or destroyed by a disaster such as a nuclear attack. That network, called *ARPANET*, became functional in September 1969, linking scientific and academic researchers across the United States.

The original ARPANET consisted of four main computers, one each located at the University of California at Los Angeles, the University of California at Santa Barbara, the Stanford Research Institute, and the University of Utah. Each computer served as a host on the network. A *host*, more commonly known today as a server, is any computer that provides services and connections to other computers on a network. Hosts often use high-speed communications to transfer data and messages over a network.

As researchers and others realized the great benefit of using ARPANET's e-mail to share data and information, ARPANET underwent phenomenal growth. By 1984, ARPANET had more than 1,000 individual computers linked as hosts. Today, more than 350 million hosts connect to the Internet.

Some organizations connected entire networks to ARPANET to take advantage of the high-speed communications it offered. In 1986, the

FIGURE 2-1d   (newsgroup)

FIGURE 2-1f   (instant messaging)

FIGURE 2-1e   (chat)

FIGURE 2-1g
(Internet telephony)

National Science Foundation (NSF) connected its huge network of five supercomputer centers, called *NSFnet*, to ARPANET. This configuration of complex networks and hosts became known as the Internet.

Until 1995, NSFnet handled the bulk of the communications activity, or **traffic**, on the Internet. In 1995, NSFnet terminated its network on the Internet and resumed its status as a research network.

Today, the Internet consists of many local, regional, national, and international networks. Numerous corporations, commercial firms, and other companies provide networks to handle the Internet traffic. Both public and private organizations own networks on the Internet. These networks, along with telephone companies, cable and satellite companies, and the government, all contribute toward the internal structure of the Internet. Read Looking Ahead 2-1 for a look at the next generation of the Internet.

Even as the Internet grows, it remains a public, cooperative, and independent network. Each organization on the Internet is responsible only for maintaining its own network. No single person, company, institution, or government agency controls or owns the Internet. The *World Wide Web Consortium* (*W3C*), however, oversees research and sets standards and guidelines for many areas of the Internet. The mission of the W3C is to contribute to the growth of the Web. Nearly 400 organizations from around the world are members of the W3C. They advise, define standards, and address other issues.

HOW THE INTERNET WORKS

Data sent over the Internet travels via networks and communications media owned and operated by many companies. The following sections present various ways to connect to these networks on the Internet.

Connecting to the Internet

Employees and students often connect to the Internet through a business or school network. In this case, the computers usually are part of a network that connects to an Internet access provider through a high-speed connection line leased from a telephone company.

Some homes use dial-up access to connect to the Internet. **Dial-up access** takes place when the modem in your computer uses a standard telephone line to connect to the Internet. This type of access is an easy and inexpensive way for users to connect to the Internet. A dial-up connection, however, is slow-speed technology.

Many home and small business users are opting for higher-speed *broadband* Internet connections through DSL, cable television networks, radio signals, or satellite.
- **DSL** (*digital subscriber line*) is a technology that provides high-speed Internet connections using regular copper telephone lines.
- A **cable modem** allows access to high-speed Internet services through the cable television network.
- *Fixed wireless* high-speed Internet connections use a dish-shaped antenna on your house or business to communicate with a tower location via radio signals.
- A *satellite modem* communicates with a satellite dish to provide high-speed Internet connections via satellite.

In most cases, broadband Internet access is always on. That is, it is connected to the Internet the entire time the computer is running. With dial-up access, by contrast, you must establish the connection to the Internet. Usually a modem dials the telephone number to the Internet access provider.

Mobile users access the Internet using a variety of technologies. Most hotels and airports provide dial-up or broadband Internet connections. Wireless Internet access technologies, such as through radio networks, allow mobile users to connect easily to the Internet with notebook computers, Tablet PCs, PDAs, and smart

LOOKING AHEAD 2-1

Internet Speeds into the Future

The Internet of the future will be much larger and faster. According to some Internet experts, in the next 20 years, Web surfers will be able to browse more than 250 million Web sites.

This increase in volume will be based, in part, on *Internet2*. This not-for-profit project connects more than 206 educational and 60 research institutions via a high-speed private network. When used solely as a research tool, Internet2 applications process massive amounts of data, such as linking observatories atop Hawaii's tallest mountains and video conferences from 20 remote sites across the world.

Recently, the recording industry charged scores of college students with copyright infringement for trading millions of copyrighted songs through Internet2 privileged access. For more information, visit scsite.com/dc2007/ch2/looking and then click Internet2.

phones while away from a telephone, cable, or other wired connection. Many public locations, such as airports, hotels, schools, shopping malls, and coffee shops, are *hot spots* that provide wireless Internet connections to users with mobile computers or devices.

Access Providers

An **access provider** is a business that provides individuals and companies access to the Internet free or for a fee. The most common fee arrangement for an individual Internet account is a fixed amount, usually about $10 to $25 per month for dial-up, $15 to $40 for DSL, $20 to $45 for cable, $35 to $70 for fixed wireless, and $60 to $99 for satellite. For this fee, many providers offer unlimited Internet access. Others specify a set number of access hours per month. With the latter arrangement, the provider charges extra for each hour of connection time that exceeds an allotted number of access hours. To attract more customers, some access providers also offer Web publishing services. Web publishing is discussed later in the chapter.

Users access the Internet through regional or national ISPs, online service providers, and wireless Internet service providers (Figure 2-2).

FIGURE 2-2 Common ways to access the Internet are through a regional or national Internet service provider, an online service provider, or a wireless Internet service provider.

An **ISP** (**Internet service provider**) is a regional or national access provider. A *regional ISP* usually provides Internet access to a specific geographic area. A *national ISP* is a business that provides Internet access in cities and towns nationwide. For dial-up access, some national ISPs provide both local and toll-free telephone numbers. Due to their larger size, national ISPs usually offer more services and have a larger technical support staff than regional ISPs. Examples of national ISPs are AT&T Worldnet Service and EarthLink.

In addition to providing Internet access, an **online service provider** (**OSP**) also has many members-only features. These features include special content and services such as news, weather, legal information, financial data, hardware and software guides, games, travel guides, e-mail, photo communities, online calendars, and instant messaging. Some even have their own built-in Web browser. The fees for using an OSP sometimes are slightly higher than fees for an ISP. The two more popular OSPs are AOL (America Online) and MSN (Microsoft Network). AOL differs from many OSPs in that it provides gateway functionality to the Internet, meaning it regulates the Internet services to which members have access.

With dial-up Internet access, the telephone number you dial connects you to an access point on the Internet, called a *point of presence* (*POP*). When selecting an ISP or OSP, ensure it provides at least one local POP telephone number. Otherwise, long-distance telephone charges will apply for the time you connect to the Internet.

A **wireless Internet service provider** (*WISP*) is a company that provides wireless Internet access to computers with wireless modems or access devices or to Internet-enabled mobile computers or devices. Internet-enabled mobile devices include PDAs and smart phones. An antenna on or built into the computer or device typically sends signals through the airwaves to communicate with a wireless Internet service provider. Some examples of wireless Internet service providers include Boingo Wireless, Cingular Wireless, T-Mobile, and Verizon Wireless.

How Data Travels the Internet

Computers connected to the Internet work together to transfer data and information around the world using servers and clients. On the Internet, your computer is a client that can access data, information, and services on a variety of servers.

The inner structure of the Internet works much like a transportation system. Just as interstate highways connect major cities and carry the bulk of the automotive traffic across the country, several main transmission media carry the heaviest amount of traffic on the Internet. These major carriers of network traffic are known collectively as the *Internet backbone*.

In the United States, the transmission media that make up the Internet backbone exchange data at several different major cities across the country. That is, they transfer data from one network to another until it reaches its final destination (Figure 2-3).

FIGURE 2-3 HOW A HOME USER'S DATA MIGHT TRAVEL THE INTERNET USING A CABLE MODEM CONNECTION

Step 1:
You initiate an action to request data from the Internet. For example, you request to display a Web page on your computer screen.

Step 2:
A cable modem transfers the computer's digital signals to the cable television line in your house.

Step 3:
Your request (digital signals) travels through cable television lines to a central cable system, which is shared by up to 500 homes in a neighborhood.

Step 4:
The central cable system sends your request over high-speed fiber-optic lines to the cable operator, who often also is the ISP.

Step 5:
The ISP routes your request through the Internet backbone to the destination server (in this example, the server that contains the requested Web site).

Step 6:
The server retrieves the requested Web page and sends it back through the Internet backbone to your computer.

Internet Addresses

The Internet relies on an addressing system much like the postal service to send data to a computer at a specific destination. An **IP address**, short for *Internet Protocol address*, is a number that uniquely identifies each computer or device connected to the Internet. The IP address usually consists of four groups of numbers, each separated by a period. The number in each group is between 0 and 255. For example, the numbers 216.239.39.99 are an IP address. In general, the first portion of each IP address identifies the network and the last portion identifies the specific computer.

These all-numeric IP addresses are difficult to remember and use. Thus, the Internet supports the use of a text name that represents one or more IP addresses. A **domain name** is the text version of an IP address. Figure 2-4 shows

an IP address and its associated domain name. As with an IP address, the components of a domain name are separated by periods.

In Figure 2-4, the com portion of the domain name is called the top-level domain. Every domain name contains a *top-level domain*, which identifies the type of organization associated with the domain. *Dot-com* is the term sometimes used to describe organizations with a top-level domain of com.

| IP address | → | 216.239.39.99 |
| Domain name | → | www.google.com |

top-level domain

FIGURE 2-4 The IP address and domain name for the Google Web site.

The group that assigns and controls top-level domains is the *Internet Corporation for Assigned Names and Numbers (ICANN* pronounced EYE-can). Figure 2-5 lists some top-level domains. For international Web sites outside the United States, the top-level domain also ends with a two-letter country code, such as au for Australia or fr for France. For example, www.philips.com.au is the domain name for Philips Australia.

The *domain name system (DNS)* is the method that the Internet uses to store domain names and their corresponding IP addresses. When you specify a domain name, a **DNS server** translates the domain name to its associated IP address so data can be routed to the correct computer. A DNS server is an Internet server that usually is associated with an Internet access provider.

For a more technical discussion about Internet addresses, read the High-Tech Talk article on page 102.

EXAMPLES OF TOP-LEVEL DOMAINS

Original Top-Level Domains	Type of Domain
com	Commercial organizations, businesses, and companies
edu	Educational institutions
gov	Goverment agencies
mil	Military organizations
net	Network provider
org	Nonprofit organizations
Newer Top-Level Domains	**Type of Domain**
museum	Accredited museums
biz	Businesses of all sizes
info	Businesses, organizations, or individuals providing general information
name	Individuals or families
pro	Certified professionals such as doctors, lawyers, and accountants
aero	Aviation community members
coop	Business cooperatives such as credit unions and rural electric co-ops
Proposed Top-Level Domains	**Type of Domain**
asia	Businesses that originate in Asian countries
cat	Catalan cultural community
jobs	Employment or human resource businesses
mail	Registries to control spam (Internet junk mail)
mobi	Delivery and management of mobile Internet services
post	Postal service
tel	Internet communications
travel	Travel industry
xxx	Adult content

FIGURE 2-5 With the dramatic growth of the Internet during the last few years, the Internet Corporation for Assigned Names and Numbers (ICANN) recently adopted seven new top-level domains and is evaluating nine additional TLDs.

FAQ 2-4

How does a person or company get a domain name?

For top-level domains of biz, com, info, name, net, and org, you register for a domain name from a *registrar*, which is an organization that sells and manages domain names. In addition to determining prices and policies for domain name registration, a registrar may offer additional services such as Web site hosting. For more information, visit scsite.com/dc2007/ch2/faq and then click Registrar.

Test your knowledge of pages 68 through 74 in Quiz Yourself 2-1.

QUIZ YOURSELF 2-1

Instructions: Find the true statement below. Then, rewrite the remaining false statements so they are true.

1. An access provider is a business that provides individuals and companies access to the Internet free or for a fee.

2. A WISP is a number that uniquely identifies each computer or device connected to the Internet.

3. An IP address, such as www.google.com, is the text version of a domain name.

4. Dial-up access takes place when the modem in your computer uses the cable television network to connect to the Internet.

5. The World Wide Web Consortium (W3C) oversees research and owns the Internet.

Quiz Yourself Online: To further check your knowledge of Internet history, accessing and connecting to the Internet, and Internet addresses, visit scsite.com/dc2007/ch2/quiz and then click Objectives 1 – 3.

THE WORLD WIDE WEB

Although many people use the terms World Wide Web and Internet interchangeably, the World Wide Web actually is a service of the Internet. While the Internet was developed in the late 1960s, the World Wide Web emerged nearly three decades later — in the early 1990s. Since then, it has grown phenomenally to become one of the more widely used Internet services.

The **World Wide Web** (*WWW*), or **Web**, consists of a worldwide collection of electronic documents. Each electronic document on the Web is called a **Web page**, which can contain text, graphics, audio (sound), and video. Additionally, Web pages usually have built-in connections to other documents.

Some Web pages are static (fixed); others are dynamic (changing). Visitors to a *static Web page* all see the same content. With a *dynamic Web page*, by contrast, visitors can customize some or all of the viewed content such as desired stock quotes, weather for a region, or ticket availability for flights.

A **Web site** is a collection of related Web pages and associated items, such as documents and pictures, stored on a Web server. A **Web server** is a computer that delivers requested Web pages to your computer. The same Web server can store multiple Web sites. For example, many access providers grant their subscribers free storage space on a Web server for personal or company Web sites.

The following pages discuss how to browse the Web, use a Web address, search for information on the Web, and recognize types of Web sites. Also discussed are multimedia on the Web and Web publishing.

Browsing the Web

A **Web browser**, or **browser**, is application software that allows users to access and view Web pages. To browse the Web, you need a computer that is connected to the Internet and that has a Web browser. The more widely used Web browsers for personal computers are Internet Explorer, Netscape, Mozilla, Firefox, Opera, and Safari.

With an Internet connection established, you start a Web browser. The browser retrieves and displays a starting Web page, sometimes called the browser's home page. Figure 2-6 shows how a Web browser displays a home page. The initial home page that is displayed

FIGURE 2-6   HOW A WEB BROWSER DISPLAYS A HOME PAGE

Step 1:
Click the Web browser program name to start the Web browser software.

Step 2:
Behind the scenes, the Web browser looks up its home page setting. For illustration purposes only, the screen below shows the home page setting is msn.com.

Step 3:
The Web browser communicates with a server maintained by your Internet access provider. The server translates the domain name of the home page to an IP address and then sends the IP address to your computer.

Step 4:
The Web browser uses the IP address to contact the Web server associated with the home page and then requests the home page from the server. The Web server sends the home page to the Web browser, which formats the page for display on your screen.

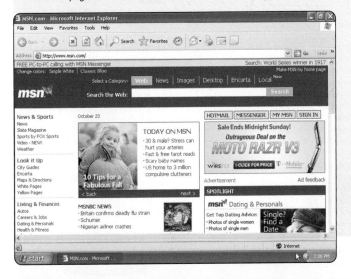

is one selected by your Web browser. You can change your browser's home page at anytime.

The more common usage of the term, **home page**, refers to the first page that a Web site displays. Similar to a book cover or a table of contents for a Web site, the home page provides information about the Web site's purpose and content. Often it provides connections to other documents, Web pages, or Web sites. Many Web sites allow you to personalize the home page so it contains areas of interest to you.

Internet-enabled mobile devices such as PDAs and smart phones use a special type of browser, called a *microbrowser*, which is designed for their small screens and limited computing power. Many Web sites design Web pages specifically for display on a microbrowser (Figure 2-7).

For a computer or mobile device to display a Web page, the page must be downloaded. **Downloading** is the process of a computer receiving information, such as a Web page, from a server on the Internet. While a browser downloads a Web page, it typically displays an animated logo or icon in the top-right corner of the browser window. The animation stops when the download is complete.

Depending on the speed of your Internet connection and the amount of graphics involved, a Web page download can take from a few seconds to several minutes. To speed up the display of Web pages, most Web browsers allow users to turn off the graphics and other multimedia elements.

FIGURE 2-7 Sample microbrowser screens.

Web Addresses

A Web page has a unique address, called a **URL** (*Uniform Resource Locator*) or **Web address**. For example, the home page for The Weather Channel Web site has http://www.weather.com as its Web address. A Web browser retrieves a Web page using its Web address.

If you know the Web address of a Web page, you can type it in the Address box at the top of the browser window. For example, if you type the Web address http://www.weather.com/maps/activity/skinprotection/index_large.html in the Address box and then press the ENTER key, the browser downloads and displays the Web page shown in Figure 2-8.

A Web address consists of a protocol, domain name, and sometimes the path to a specific Web page or location on a Web page. Many Web page addresses begin with http://. The *http*, which stands for *Hypertext Transfer Protocol*, is a set of rules that defines how pages transfer on the Internet. The first portion of the domain name identifies the type of Internet server. For example, www indicates a Web server.

To help minimize errors, most browsers and Web sites do not require the http:// and www portions of the Web address. For example, typing weather.com/maps/activity/skinprotection/index_large.html, instead of the entire address, still accesses the Web site. If you enter an incorrect Web address, a list of similar addresses from which you can select may be displayed in the browser window. Many Web sites also allow users to eliminate the .htm or .html from the Web page name.

When you enter the Web address, http://www.weather.com/maps/activity/skinprotection/index_large.html in the Web browser, it sends a request to the Web server that contains the weather.com Web site. The server then retrieves the Web page named index_large.html in the maps/activity/skinprotection/ path and delivers it to your browser, which then displays the Web page on the screen.

When you enter a Web address in a browser, you request, or *pull*, information from a Web server. Some Web servers also can *push* content to your computer at regular intervals or whenever updates are made to the site. For example, some Web servers provide the capability of displaying current sporting event scores or weather reports on your computer screen.

For information about useful Web sites and their associated Web addresses, read the Making Use of the Web feature that follows this chapter.

protocol   domain name   path   Web page name

http://www.weather.com/maps/activity/skinprotection/index_large.html

FAQ 2-5

How many Web pages does the average user visit in a month?

More than one thousand. This and other interesting average Web usage statistics are in the table below. For more information, visit scsite.com/ dc2007/ch2/faq and then click Web User Statistics.

Web pages visited per month	1,036 pages
Web pages visited per Internet session	34 pages
Time spent surfing per Internet session	51 minutes
Time spent viewing a single Web page	46 seconds
Source: The ClickZ Network	

FIGURE 2-8   After entering the Web address http://www.weather.com/maps/activity/ skinprotection/index_large.html in the Address box, this Web page at The Weather Channel Web site is displayed.

Navigating Web Pages

Most Web pages contain links. A **link**, short for *hyperlink*, is a built-in connection to another related Web page or part of a Web page. Links allow you to obtain information in a nonlinear way. That is, instead of accessing topics in a specified order, you move directly to a topic of interest. Branching from one related topic to another in a nonlinear fashion is what makes links so powerful. Some people use the phrase, **surfing the Web**, to refer to the activity of using links to explore the Web.

On the Web, a link can be text or an image. Text links may be underlined and/or displayed in a color different from other text on the Web page. Pointing to, or positioning the pointer on, a link on the screen typically changes the shape of the pointer to a small hand with a pointing index finger. The Web page shown in Figure 2-9 contains a variety of link types, with the pointer on one of the links.

Each link on a Web page corresponds to another Web address. To activate a link, you *click* it, that is, point to the link and then press the left mouse button. Clicking a link causes the Web page associated with the link to be displayed on the screen. The linked object

might be on the same Web page, a different Web page at the same Web site, or a separate Web page at a different Web site in another city or country. To remind you visually that you have clicked a link, a text link often changes color after you click it.

WEB LINK 2-2

Web Addresses

For more information, visit scsite.com/ dc2007/ch2/weblink and then click Web Addresses.

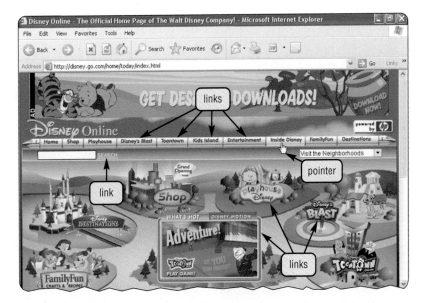

FIGURE 2-9   This Web page contains various types of links: text that is underlined, text in a different color, and images.

Searching for Information on the Web

The Web is a global resource of information. One primary use of the Web is to search for specific information, including text, graphics, audio, and video. The first step in successful searching is to identify the main idea or concept in the topic about which you are seeking information. Determine any synonyms, alternate spellings, or variant word forms for the topic. Then, use a search tool to locate the information.

The two most commonly used search tools are subject directories and search engines. A **subject directory** classifies Web pages in an organized set of categories, such as sports or shopping, and related subcategories. A **search engine** is a program that finds Web sites and Web pages.

Some Web sites offer the functionality of both a subject directory and a search engine. Yahoo! and Google, for example, are widely used search engines that also provide a subject directory. To use Yahoo! or Google, you enter the Web address (yahoo.com or google.com) in the Address box in a browser window. The table in Figure 2-10 lists the

Web addresses of several popular general-purpose subject directories and search engines.

SUBJECT DIRECTORIES A subject directory provides categorized lists of links arranged by subject. Figure 2-11 shows how to use Yahoo!'s

WIDELY USED SEARCH TOOLS

Search Tool	Web Address	Subject Directory	Search Engine
A9.com	a9.com		X
AlltheWeb	alltheweb.com		X
Alta Vista	altavista.com	X	X
AOL Search	search.aol.com		X
Ask Jeeves	ask.com	X	X
Dogpile	dogpile.com		X
Excite	excite.com	X	X
Gigablast	gigablast.com	X	X
Google	google.com	X	X
HotBot	hotbot.com		X
LookSmart	looksmart.com	X	X
Lycos	lycos.com	X	X
MSN Search	search.msn.com	X	X
Netscape Search	search.netscape.com	X	X
Open Directory Project	dmoz.org	X	X
Overture	overture.com		X
Teoma	teoma.com		X
WebCrawler	webcrawler.com		X
Yahoo!	yahoo.com	X	X

FIGURE 2-10   Many subject directories and search engines allow searching about any topic on the Web.

FIGURE 2-11   HOW TO USE A SUBJECT DIRECTORY

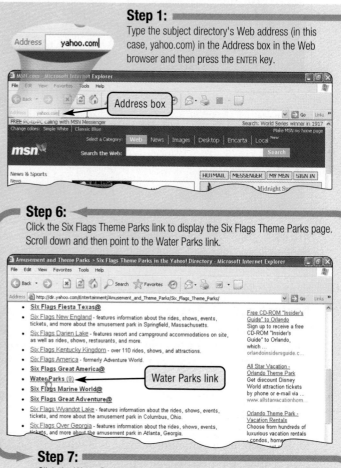

Step 1:
Type the subject directory's Web address (in this case, yahoo.com) in the Address box in the Web browser and then press the ENTER key.

Address box

Step 6:
Click the Six Flags Theme Parks link to display the Six Flags Theme Parks page. Scroll down and then point to the Water Parks link.

Water Parks link

Step 7:
Click the Water Parks link to display the Six Flags Water Parks page. Scroll down to the SITE LISTINGS area, if necessary, and then point to the Six Flags Hurricane Harbor Los Angeles link.

SITE LISTINGS area

Six Flags Hurricane Harbor Los Angeles link

subject directory to search for information about Six Flags Hurricane Harbor Los Angeles. As shown in the figure, you locate a particular topic by clicking links through different levels, moving from the general to the specific. Each time you click a category link, the subject directory displays a list of subcategory links, from which you again choose. You continue in this fashion until the search tool displays a list of Web pages about the desired topic.

The major problem with a subject directory is deciding which categories to choose as you work through the menus of links presented.

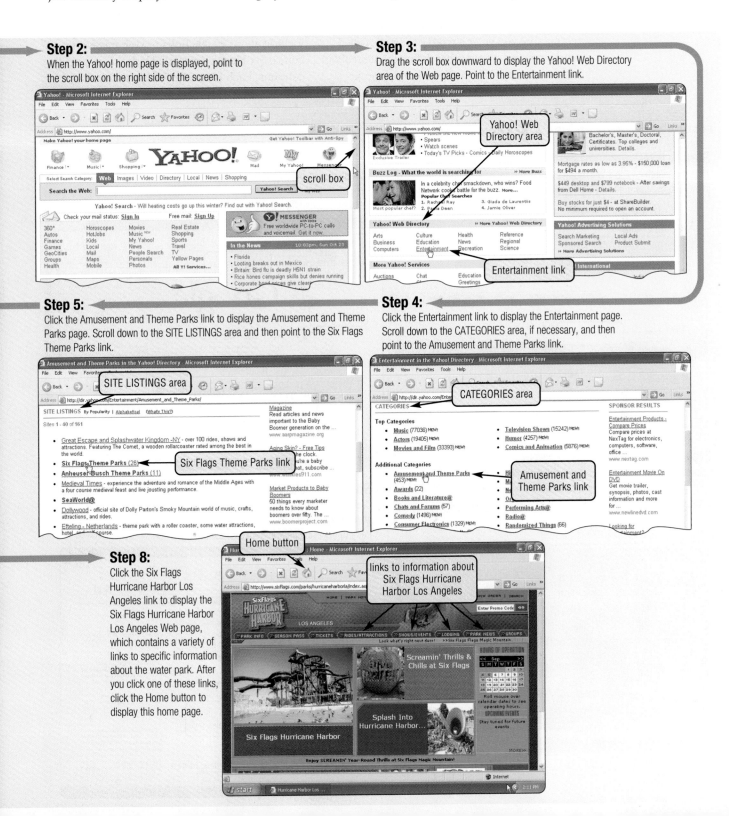

Step 2:
When the Yahoo! home page is displayed, point to the scroll box on the right side of the screen.

Step 3:
Drag the scroll box downward to display the Yahoo! Web Directory area of the Web page. Point to the Entertainment link.

Step 5:
Click the Amusement and Theme Parks link to display the Amusement and Theme Parks page. Scroll down to the SITE LISTINGS area and then point to the Six Flags Theme Parks link.

Step 4:
Click the Entertainment link to display the Entertainment page. Scroll down to the CATEGORIES area, if necessary, and then point to the Amusement and Theme Parks link.

Step 8:
Click the Six Flags Hurricane Harbor Los Angeles link to display the Six Flags Hurricane Harbor Los Angeles Web page, which contains a variety of links to specific information about the water park. After you click one of these links, click the Home button to display this home page.

SEARCH ENGINES A search engine is particularly helpful in locating Web pages about certain topics or in locating specific Web pages for which you do not know the exact Web address. Thousands of search engines are available. Some are general and perform searches on any topic; others are restricted to certain subjects, such as finding people, job hunting, or locating real estate.

Instead of clicking through links, search engines require that you enter a word or phrase, called **search text** or *keywords*, that define the item about which you want information. Search engines often respond with results that include thousands of links to Web pages, many of which may have little or no bearing on the information you are seeking. You can eliminate the superfluous pages by carefully crafting a keyword that limits the search.

Figure 2-12 shows how to use the Google search engine to search for the phrase, Six Flags Hurricane Harbor Los Angeles coupons. The results of the search, called *hits*, shown in Step 3 include about 90,000 links to Web pages that reference Six Flags Hurricane Harbor Los Angeles coupons. Each hit in the list has a link that, when clicked, displays an associated Web site

FIGURE 2-12 HOW TO USE A SEARCH ENGINE

Step 1:
Type the search engine's Web address (in this case, google.com) in the Address box in the Web browser and then press the ENTER key.

Step 2:
When the Google home page is displayed, type `Six Flags Hurricane Harbor Los Angeles coupons` as the search text and then point to the Google Search button.

Step 4:
Click the Hurricane Harbor Los Angeles link to display a Web page with information about how to obtain discount tickets.

Step 3:
Click the Google Search button. When the results of the search are displayed, scroll through the links and read the descriptions. Point to the Hurricane Harbor Los Angeles link.

or Web page. Most search engines sequence the hits based on how close the words in the search text are to one another in the Web page titles and their descriptions. Thus, the first few links probably contain more relevant information.

If you enter a phrase with spaces between the words in the search text, most search engines display results (hits) that include all of the words, except for common words (e.g., to, the, and). The table in Figure 2-13 lists some common operators you can include in your search text to refine your search. Other techniques you can use to improve your Web searches include the following:

- Use specific nouns and put the most important terms first in the search text.
- List all possible spellings, for example, email, e-mail.
- Before using a search engine, read its Help information.

- If the search is unsuccessful with one search engine, try another.

Many search engines use a program called a *spider* to build and maintain lists of words found on Web sites. When you enter search text, the search engine scans this prebuilt list for hits. The more sophisticated the search engine combined with precise search criteria, the more rapid the response and effective the search.

In addition to searching for Web pages, many search engines allow you to search for images, news articles, and local businesses. Read Looking Ahead 2-2 for a look at the next generation of searching techniques.

FAQ 2-6

Who uses Google to search the Web?

People all around the world use Google to conduct more than 250 million searches per day. Google has been accessed in many languages including English, German, Japanese, Spanish, French, Chinese, and Dutch. For more information, visit scsite.com/dc2007/ch2/faq and then click Google Facts.

SEARCH ENGINE OPERATORS

Operator	Description	Examples	Explanation
Space or +	Use the space or plus operator (+) when you want search results to display hits that include specific words.	art + music art music	Results have both words art and music — in any order.
OR	Use the OR operator when you want search results to display hits that include only one word from a list.	dog OR puppy	Results have either the word dog or puppy.
		dog OR puppy OR canine	Results have the word dog or puppy or canine.
-	Use the minus operator (-) when you want to exclude a word from your search results.	automobile -convertible	Results include automobile but do not include convertible.
" "	Use the quotation marks operator when you want to search for an exact phrase in a certain order.	"19th century literature"	Results include only hits that have the exact phrase, 19th century literature.
*	Use the asterisk operator (*) when you want search results to substitute characters in place of the asterisk.	writer*	Results include any word that begins with writer (e.g., writer, writers, writer's).

FIGURE 2-13   Use search engine operators to help refine a search.

LOOKING AHEAD 2-2

3-D Search Engines Get the Picture

Conventional search engines, such as Google, use words to find information. But what happens when a computer user needs to locate a wing nut or camshaft based on a particular shape, not part number or model? The 3-D search engines being developed would help people who work with patterns and contours search for images. These search engines presently are being created to assist designers and engineers at large industrial companies with millions of inventoried parts, but university researchers predict image searches will be common on the Internet within 15 years.

Other search engines of the future will customize the results based on the researcher's background, include a voice interface, and use a thesaurus to keep a query in context. For more information, visit scsite.com/dc2007/ch2/looking and then click Search Engines.

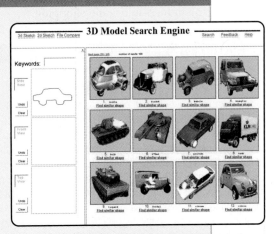

Types of Web Sites

Eleven types of Web sites are portal, news, informational, business/marketing, educational, entertainment, advocacy, blog, wiki, content aggregator, and personal (Figure 2-14). Many Web sites fall in more than one of these categories. The following pages discuss each of these types of Web sites.

PORTAL A **portal** is a Web site that offers a variety of Internet services from a single, convenient location (Figure 2-14a). Most portals offer the following free services: search engine and/or subject directory; news; sports and weather; free Web publishing services; reference tools such as yellow pages, stock quotes, and maps; shopping malls and auctions; and e-mail and other forms of online communications. Companies often create their own portals for use by employees, vendors, and customers.

Many portals have Web communities. A **Web community** is a Web site that joins a specific group of people with similar interests or relationships. These communities may offer online photo albums, chat rooms, and other services to facilitate communications among members.

When you connect to the Internet, the first Web page that is displayed often is a portal. Popular portals include AltaVista, AOL, Excite, GO.com, HotBot, LookSmart, Lycos, MSN, NBCi, Netscape, and Yahoo!. You may notice that many of these portals are popular search engines or subject directories. Some also are Internet access providers.

A *wireless portal* is a portal designed for Internet-enabled mobile devices. Wireless portals attempt to provide all information a wireless user might require. These portals offer services geared to the mobile user such as search engines, news, stock quotes, weather, maps, e-mail, calendar, instant messaging, and shopping.

NEWS A news Web site contains newsworthy material including stories and articles relating to current events, life, money, sports, and the weather (Figure 2-14b). Many magazines and newspapers sponsor Web sites that provide summaries of printed articles, as well as articles not included in the printed versions. Newspapers and television and radio stations are some of the media that maintain news Web sites.

INFORMATIONAL An informational Web site contains factual information (Figure 2-14c). Many United States government agencies have informational Web sites providing information such as census data, tax codes, and the congressional budget. Other organizations provide information such as public transportation schedules and published research findings.

BUSINESS/MARKETING A business/marketing Web site contains content that promotes or sells products or services (Figure 2-14d). Nearly every business has a business/marketing Web site. Allstate Insurance Company, Dell Inc., General Motors Corporation, Kraft Foods Inc., and Walt Disney Company all have business/marketing Web sites. Many of these companies also allow you to purchase their products or services online.

EDUCATIONAL An educational Web site offers exciting, challenging avenues for formal and informal teaching and learning (Figure 2-14e). On the Web, you can learn how airplanes fly or how to cook a meal. For a more structured learning experience, companies provide online training to employees; and colleges offer online classes and degrees (read Ethics & Issues 2-1 for a related discussion). Instructors often use the Web to enhance classroom teaching by publishing course materials, grades, and other pertinent class information.

ETHICS & ISSUES 2-1

Is the Internet as Good as the Classroom?

College can be a rewarding experience, both personally and professionally. Some people, however, do not have the opportunity, time, or money needed to attend a traditional college. Many schools address this problem with online classes, also called Internet courses. Online classes allow students to learn whenever and wherever they can access a course's Web page, often for less cost than traditional tuitions. A student might be able to complete an entire degree program without ever physically attending a class. Many online classes present material using captivating simulations, real-life case studies, and interactive tools. And, online classes seem to work — one research report found that online students learn as well as or better than their classroom-based counterparts. Yet, even the best online classes lack some of the most important features of the bricks-and-mortar campus experience, such as casual talks with professors, informal study groups in the dorm, or enthusiastic discussions in the campus coffee shop. What are the most important advantages and disadvantages of online classes? Why? Does a degree earned online have the same value as a traditional degree? Why? Does the answer depend more on the college or on the course of study? What type of course is best, and least, suited for online classes? Why?

FIGURE 2-14b (news)

FIGURE 2-14a (portal)

FIGURE 2-14c (informational)

FIGURE 2-14e (educational)

FIGURE 2-14d (business/marketing)

FIGURE 2-14f (entertainment)

FIGURE 2-14h (blog)

FIGURE 2-14g (advocacy)

FIGURE 2-14i (wiki)

FIGURE 2-14j (content aggregator)

FIGURE 2-14k (personal)

FIGURE 2-14 Types of Web sites.

ENTERTAINMENT An entertainment Web site offers an interactive and engaging environment (Figure 2-14f on the previous page). Popular entertainment Web sites offer music, videos, sports, games, ongoing Web episodes, sweepstakes, chats, and more. Sophisticated entertainment Web sites often partner with other technologies. For example, you can cast your vote about a topic on a television show.

ADVOCACY An advocacy Web site contains content that describes a cause, opinion, or idea (Figure 2-14g). The purpose of an advocacy Web site is to convince the reader of the validity of the cause, opinion, or idea. These Web sites usually present views of a particular group or association. Sponsors of advocacy Web sites include the Democratic National Committee, the Republican National Committee, the Society for the Prevention of Cruelty to Animals, and the Society to Protect Human Rights.

BLOG A **blog**, short for *Weblog*, is an informal Web site consisting of time-stamped articles, or posts, in a diary or journal format, usually listed in reverse chronological order (Figure 2-14h). Blogs reflect the interests, opinions, and personalities of the author, called the *blogger*, and sometimes site visitors. According to a Web tracking company, more than 500,000 posts appear on blogs each day. Businesses use blogs to communicate with employees, customers, and vendors. Blogs at school provide a means for teachers to collaborate with other teachers and students. Home users also use blogs to share aspects of their personal life with family, friends, and others.

WIKI A **wiki** is a collaborative Web site that allows users to add to, modify, or delete the Web site content via their Web browser. Most wikis are open to modification by the general public. Wikis usually collect recent edits on a Web page so someone can review them for accuracy. The difference between a wiki and a blog is that users cannot modify original posts made by the blogger. A popular wiki is Wikipedia, a free Web encyclopedia (Figure 2-14i).

WEB LINK 2-3

Wiki
For more information, visit scsite.com/dc2007/ch2/weblink and then click Wiki.

CONTENT AGGREGATOR A *content aggregator* is a business that gathers and organizes Web content and then distributes, or feeds, the content to subscribers for free or a fee. Examples of distributed content include news, music, video, and pictures. Subscribers select content in which they are interested. Whenever this content changes, it is downloaded automatically (pushed) to the subscriber's computer or mobile device.

RSS 2.0, which stands for *Really Simple Syndication*, is a specification that content aggregators use to distribute content to subscribers (Figure 2-14j). *Atom* is another specification sometimes used by content aggregators to distribute content.

PERSONAL A private individual or family not usually associated with any organization may maintain a personal Web site or just a single Web page (Figure 2-14k). People publish personal Web pages for a variety of reasons. Some are job hunting. Others simply want to share life experiences with the world.

Evaluating a Web Site

Do not assume that information presented on the Web is correct or accurate. Any person, company, or organization can publish a Web page on the Internet. No one oversees the content of these Web pages. Figure 2-15 lists guidelines for assessing the value of a Web site or Web page before relying on its content.

GUIDELINES FOR EVALUATING THE VALUE OF A WEB SITE

Evaluation Criteria	Reliable Web Sites
Affiliation	A reputable institution should support the Web site without bias in the information.
Audience	The Web site should be written at an appropriate level.
Authority	The Web site should list the author and the appropriate credentials.
Content	The Web site should be well organized and the links should work.
Currency	The information on the Web page should be current.
Design	The pages at the Web site should download quickly and be visually pleasing and easy to navigate.
Objectivity	The Web site should contain little advertising and be free of preconceptions.

FIGURE 2-15 Criteria for evaluating a Web site's content.

Multimedia on the Web

Most Web pages include more than just formatted text and links. The more exciting Web pages use multimedia. **Multimedia** refers to any application that combines text with graphics, animation, audio, video, and/or virtual reality. Multimedia brings a Web page to life, increases the types of information available on the Web, expands the Web's potential uses, and makes the Internet a more entertaining place to explore. Multimedia Web pages often require proper hardware and software and take more time to download because they contain large graphics files and video or audio clips.

The sections that follow discuss how the Web uses graphics, animation, audio, video, and virtual reality.

more compressed the file, the smaller the image and the lower the quality. The goal with JPEG graphics is to reach a balance between image quality and file size.

GIF (pronounced jiff) graphics also use compression techniques to reduce file sizes. The GIF format works best for images that have only a few distinct colors. The newer *PNG* (pronounced ping) graphics format improves upon the GIF format, and thus may eventually replace the GIF format.

The BMP and TIFF formats listed in Figure 2-17 may require special viewer software, and they have larger file sizes. Thus, these formats are not used on the Web as frequently as JPEG, GIF, and PNG formats.

FAQ 2-7

What is a file?

A *file* is a unit of storage. When you want the computer to store items (e.g., data, information, programs, graphics, audio clips, or video clips), it places them in files on storage media such as a hard disk. File sizes vary depending on items being stored. For example, graphics files usually consume more storage space than data files. For more information, visit scsite.com/dc2007/ch2/faq and then click Files.

GRAPHICS   A **graphic**, or *graphical image*, is a digital representation of nontext information such as a drawing, chart, or photograph. Today, many Web pages use colorful graphical designs and images to convey messages (Figure 2-16).

The Web contains countless images about a variety of subjects. You can download many of these images at no cost and use them for non-commercial purposes. Recall that downloading is the process of transferring an object from the Web to your computer. For example, you can insert images into greeting cards, announcements, and other documents.

Of the graphics formats that exist on the Web (Figure 2-17), the two more common are JPEG and GIF formats. *JPEG* (pronounced JAY-peg) is a format that compresses graphics to reduce their file size, which means the file takes up less storage space. Smaller file sizes result in faster downloading of Web pages because small files transmit faster than large files. The

FIGURE 2-16   This Web page uses colorful graphical designs and images to convey its messages.

GRAPHICS FORMATS USED ON THE WEB

Abbreviation	Name
BMP	Bit Map
GIF	Graphics Interchange Format
JPEG	Joint Photographic Experts Group
PNG	Portable Network Graphics
TIFF	Tagged Image File Format

FIGURE 2-17   The Web uses graphics file formats for images.

Some Web sites use thumbnails on their pages because graphics can be time-consuming to display. A *thumbnail* is a small version of a larger graphic. You usually can click a thumbnail to display a larger image (Figure 2-18).

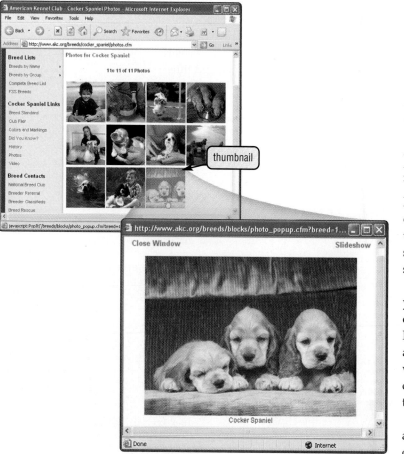

FIGURE 2-18   Clicking the thumbnail in the top screen displays a larger image in a separate window.

ANIMATION   Many Web pages use **animation**, which is the appearance of motion created by displaying a series of still images in sequence. Animation can make Web pages more visually interesting or draw attention to important information or links. For example, text that animates by scrolling across the screen can serve as a ticker to display stock updates, news, sports scores, weather, or other information. Web-based games often use animation.

Web page developers add animation to Web pages using a variety of techniques. Web page authoring programs, such as Macromedia Flash, enable Web site developers to combine animation and interactivity in Web pages. Developers unfamiliar with Web page authoring programs can create an *animated GIF*, which combines several GIF images in a single GIF file.

AUDIO   On the Web, you can listen to audio clips and live audio. **Audio** includes music, speech, or any other sound.

Simple applications on the Web consist of individual audio files available for downloading to a computer. Once downloaded, you can play (listen to) the contents of these files. Some common Web audio file formats are listed in Figure 2-19. Audio files are compressed to reduce their file sizes. For example, the **MP3** format reduces an audio file to about one-tenth its original size, while preserving much of the original quality of the sound.

Some music publishers have Web sites that allow users to download sample tracks free to persuade them to buy the entire CD. Other Web sites allow a user to purchase and download an entire CD of music tracks to the hard disk (Figure 2-20). Keep in mind that it is legal to download copyrighted music only if the song's copyright holder has granted permission for users to download and play the song.

To listen to an audio file on your computer, you need special software called a **player**. Most current operating systems contain a player. Popular players include iTunes, RealPlayer, and Windows Media Player. If your player will not play a particular audio format, you can download the necessary player free from the Web.

Some applications on the Web use streaming audio. **Streaming** is the process of transferring data in a continuous and even flow. Streaming allows users to access and use a file while it is transmitting. For example, *streaming audio* enables you to listen to music as it downloads to your computer. Many radio and television stations use streaming audio to broadcast music, interviews, talk shows, sporting events, music videos, news, live concerts, and other segments.

Podcasting is another popular method of distributing audio. A *podcast* is recorded audio, usually an MP3 file, stored on a Web site that can be downloaded to a computer or a portable digital audio player such as an iPod. Examples of podcasts include music, radio shows, news stories, classroom lectures, political messages, and television commentaries. Podcasters register their podcasts with content aggregators. Subscribers select podcast feeds they want to be downloaded automatically whenever they connect. Some Web sites, such as podcast.net, specialize in podcast distribution. Others, such as National Public Radio, have incorporated a podcast component in their existing Web site.

AUDIO WEB FILE FORMATS

Audio File Format	Description
AA	Audible Audio (commonly used for downloadable e-books)
AAC	Advanced Audio Coding
AIFF	Audio Interchange File Format
ASF	Advanced Streaming (or Systems) Format (part of Windows Media framework)
MP3	Moving Pictures Experts Group Audio Layer 3 (MPEG-3)
WAV	Windows waveform
WMA	Windows Media Audio (part of Windows Media framework)
RA	RealAudio sound file (supported by RealPlayer)
QT	QuickTime audio, video, or 3-D animation (included with Mac OS, also available separately)

FIGURE 2-19 Popular Web audio file formats.

FIGURE 2-20 HOW TO PURCHASE AND DOWNLOAD MUSIC

Step 1:
Display the music Web site on the screen. Search for, select, and pay for the music you want to purchase from the music Web site.

Step 2:
Download the music from the Web site's server to your computer's hard disk.

Step 3a:
Listen to the music from your computer's hard disk.

Step 3b: Download music from your computer's hard disk to a portable digital audio player. Listen to the music through headphones attached to the digital audio player.

VIDEO Video consists of full-motion images that are played back at various speeds. Most video also has accompanying audio. Instead of turning on the television, you can use the Internet to watch live and/or prerecorded coverage of your favorite programs (Figure 2-21) or enjoy a live performance of your favorite vocalist.

Simple video applications on the Web consist of individual video files, such as movie or television clips, that you must download completely before you can play them on the computer. Video files often are compressed because they are quite large in size. These clips also are quite short in length, usually less than 10 minutes, because they can take a long time to download. The *Moving Pictures Experts Group* *(MPEG)* defines a popular video compression standard, a widely used one called *MPEG-4*.

As with streaming audio, *streaming video* allows you to view longer or live video

images as they download to your computer. Widely used standards supported by most Web browsers for transmitting streaming video data on the Internet are AVI (Audio Video Interleaved), QuickTime, Windows Media Format, and RealVideo. Like RealAudio, RealVideo is supported by RealPlayer.

VIRTUAL REALITY Virtual reality (VR) is the use of computers to simulate a real or imagined environment that appears as a three-dimensional (3-D) space. On the Web, VR involves the display of 3-D images that users explore and manipulate interactively (Figure 2-22).

Using special VR software, a Web developer creates an entire 3-D Web site that contains infinite space and depth, called a *VR world*. A VR world, for example, might show a room with furniture. Users walk through such a VR room by moving an input device forward, backward, or to the side.

Games often use VR. Many practical applications of VR also exist. Science educators create VR models of molecules, organisms, and other structures for students to examine. Companies use VR to showcase products or create advertisements. Architects create VR models of buildings and rooms so clients can see how a completed construction project will look before it is built.

FIGURE 2-21 A video of passengers having fun on a theme park ride.

mouse pointer

FIGURE 2-22 Web site visitors use VR to see the inside of Grand Central Station in New York. As you move the mouse pointer, you see different views inside the station.

PLUG-INS   Most Web browsers have the capability of displaying basic multimedia elements on a Web page. Sometimes, a browser might need an additional program, called a plug-in. A **plug-in** is a program that extends the capability of a browser. You can download many plug-ins at no cost from various Web sites (Figure 2-23). Some plug-ins run on all sizes of personal computers and mobile devices. Others have special versions for mobile devices.

Web Publishing

Before the World Wide Web, the means to share opinions and ideas with others easily and inexpensively was limited to the media, classroom, work, or social environments. Generating an advertisement or publication that could reach a massive audience required much expense. Today, businesses and individuals convey information to millions of people by creating their own Web pages. The content of the Web pages ranges from new stories to product information to blogs.

POPULAR PLUG-IN APPLICATIONS

Plug-In Application	Description	Web Address
Acrobat Reader	View, navigate, and print Portable Document Format (PDF) files — documents formatted to look just as they look in print	adobe.com
Flash Player	View dazzling graphics and animation, hear outstanding sound and music, display Web pages across an entire screen	macromedia.com
QuickTime	View animation, music, audio, video, and VR panoramas and objects directly in a Web page	apple.com
RealPlayer	Listen to live and on-demand near-CD-quality audio and newscast-quality video; stream audio and video content for faster viewing; play MP3 files; create music CDs	real.com
Shockwave Player	Experience dynamic interactive multimedia, 3-D graphics, and streaming audio	macromedia.com
Windows Media Player	Listen to live and on-demand audio; play or edit WMA and MP3 files; burn CDs, watch DVD movies	microsoft.com

FIGURE 2-23 Most plug-ins can be downloaded free from the Web.

WEB LINK 2-4

Plug-Ins

For more information, visit scsite.com/ dc2007/ch2/weblink and then click Plug-Ins.

Web publishing is the development and maintenance of Web pages. To develop a Web page, you do not have to be a computer programmer. For the small business or home user, Web publishing is fairly easy as long as you have the proper tools. The five major steps to Web publishing are as follows: (1) plan a Web site, (2) analyze and design a Web site, (3) create a Web site, (4) deploy a Web site, and (5) maintain a Web site. Figure 2-24 illustrates these steps with respect to a personal Web site.

FIGURE 2-24   HOW TO PUBLISH YOUR RESUME ON THE WEB

Step 1:
Plan a Web site.
Think about issues that could affect the design of the Web site.

Step 2:
Analyze and design a Web site. Design the layout of the elements of the Web site.

Step 3:
Create a Web site. Use word processing software or Web page authoring software to create the Web site.

Step 4:
Deploy a Web site. Save the Web site on a Web server.

Step 5:
Maintain a Web site.
Visit your Web site regularly to be sure it is working and current.

Test your knowledge of pages 75 through 91 in Quiz Yourself 2-2.

QUIZ YOURSELF 2-2

Instructions: Find the true statement below. Then, rewrite the remaining false statements so they are true.

1. A blog is a Web site that uses a regularly updated journal format to reflect the interests, opinions, and personalities of the author and sometimes site visitors.

2. A Web browser classifies Web pages in an organized set of categories, such as sports or shopping, and related subcategories.

3. Audio and video files are downloaded to reduce their file sizes.

4. Popular portals include iTunes, RealPlayer, and Windows Media Player.

5. The more widely used search engines for personal computers are Internet Explorer, Netscape, Mozilla, Firefox, Opera, and Safari.

6. To develop a Web page, you have to be a computer programmer.

7. To improve your Web searches, use general nouns and put the least important terms first in the search text.

Quiz Yourself Online: To further check your knowledge of Web addresses, Web browsers, searching, types of Web sites, elements of a Web page, and Web publishing, visit scsite.com/dc2007/ch2/quiz and then click Objectives 4 – 9.

E-COMMERCE

E-commerce, short for *electronic commerce*, is a business transaction that occurs over an electronic network such as the Internet. Anyone with access to a computer, an Internet connection, and a means to pay for purchased goods or services can participate in e-commerce (Figure 2-25).

In the past, e-commerce transactions were conducted primarily using desktop computers. Today, many mobile computers and devices, such as PDAs and smart phones, also access the Web wirelessly. Some people use the term *m-commerce* (mobile commerce) to identify e-commerce that takes place using mobile devices.

Popular uses of e-commerce by consumers include shopping, investing, and banking. Users can purchase just about any product or service on the Web. Some examples include flowers, books, computers, prescription drugs, music, movies, cars, airline tickets, and concert tickets. Through online investing, individuals buy and sell stocks or bonds without using a broker.

Three different types of e-commerce are business-to-consumer, consumer-to-consumer, and business-to-business. *Business-to-consumer (B2C) e-commerce* consists of the sale of goods

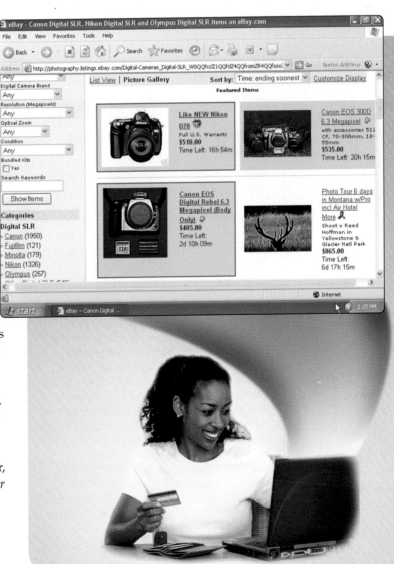

FIGURE 2-25 E-commerce activities include shopping for goods at an online auction, such as eBay.

and services to the general public. For example, Dell has a B2C Web site. Instead of visiting a computer store to purchase a computer, customers can order one that meets their specifications directly from the Dell Web site.

A customer (consumer) visits an online business through an **electronic storefront**, which contains product descriptions, graphics, and a shopping cart. The **shopping cart** allows the customer to collect purchases. When ready to complete the sale, the customer enters personal data and the method of payment, preferably through a secure Internet connection (read Ethics & Issues 2-2 for a related discussion).

Instead of purchasing from a business, consumers can purchase from each other. For example, with an **online auction**, users bid on an item being sold by someone else. The highest bidder at the end of the bidding period purchases the item. *Consumer-to-consumer (C2C) e-commerce* occurs when one consumer sells directly to another, such as in an online auction. eBay is one of the more popular online auction Web sites.

Most e-commerce, though, actually takes place between businesses, which is called *business-to-business (B2B) e-commerce*. Businesses often provide goods and services to other businesses, such as online advertising, recruiting, credit, sales, market research, technical support, and training. For example, some MasterCard and Visa credit card companies provide corporations with Web-based purchasing, tracking, and transaction downloading capabilities.

WEB LINK 2-5

E-Commerce

For more information, visit scsite.com/dc2007/ch2/weblink and then click E-Commerce.

FAQ 2-8

How popular is online shopping?

Researchers predict that e-commerce sales will grow at a steady rate of 19 percent per year until at least 2008. At that time, online shopping will account for approximately 10 percent of all retail sales in the United States, or 63 million households. For more information, visit scsite.com/dc2007/ch2/faq and then click Online Shopping.

ETHICS & ISSUES 2-2

Should All Sales on the Internet Be Taxed?

The Supreme Court has ruled that merchants can charge state and local sales taxes only when they have a physical presence, such as a store or office building, where the purchase is made. Because Internet merchants often do not have a physical presence in a buyer's state, online purchases often are sales tax free. One study predicts that by 2011 Internet sales will cost state and local governments more than $54 billion in sales tax revenues, forcing them either to raise taxes or cut services. In response, many states have enacted "use" taxes that require residents to report, and pay sales tax on, items purchased on the Internet but used at home. Even a use tax, though, does not address other problems. The sales-tax-free status of some Internet purchases also may have a negative impact on local businesses that must charge sales tax and on lower-income families who are less likely to make purchases on the Internet. Yet, many feel any tax on e-commerce is unmanageable (forcing merchants to adjust to varying sales tax rates) and unjustified. Should sales taxes be applied to Internet purchases? Why? Is a use tax a viable alternative? Why or why not? How else can the problems of taxing, or not taxing, Internet purchases be addressed?

OTHER INTERNET SERVICES

The Web is only one of the many services on the Internet. The Web and other Internet services have changed the way we communicate. We can send e-mail messages to the president, have a discussion with experts about the stock market, chat with someone in another country about genealogy, and talk about homework assignments with classmates via instant messages. Many times, these communications take place completely in writing — without the parties ever meeting each other.

At home, work, and school, people use computers and Internet-enabled mobile devices so they always have instant access to e-mail, FTP (File Transfer Protocol), newsgroups and message boards, mailing lists, chat rooms, instant messaging, and Internet telephony. The following pages discuss each of these Internet services.

E-Mail

E-mail (short for *electronic mail*) is the transmission of messages and files via a computer network. E-mail was one of the original services on the Internet, enabling scientists and researchers working on government-sponsored projects to communicate with colleagues at other locations. Today, e-mail is a primary communications method for both personal and business use.

You use an **e-mail program** to create, send, receive, forward, store, print, and delete e-mail messages. Outlook and Outlook Express are two popular e-mail programs. The steps in Figure 2-26 illustrate how to send an e-mail message using Outlook. The message can be simple text or can include an attachment such as a word processing document, a graphic, an audio clip, or a video clip.

FIGURE 2-26   HOW TO SEND AN E-MAIL MESSAGE

Step 1:
Start an e-mail program and point to the New Mail Message button.

Step 2:
Click the New Mail Message button to display the Message window.

Step 3:
Enter the recipient's e-mail address, the subject, and the message in the Message window.

Step 4:
Click the Insert File button to attach a JPEG file containing a picture to the message. Click the Send button to send the message.

Step 5:
When Carly receives the e-mail message, she opens the JPEG file to view the picture.

Internet access providers typically supply an e-mail program as a standard part of their Internet access services. Some Web sites, such as MSN Hotmail and Yahoo!, provide free e-mail services. To use these Web-based e-mail programs, you connect to the Web site and set up an e-mail account, which typically includes an e-mail address and a password. Read Ethics & Issues 2-3 for a related discussion.

Just as you address a letter when using the postal system, you must address an e-mail message with the e-mail address of your intended recipient. Likewise, when someone sends you a message, they must have your e-mail address. An **e-mail address** is a combination of a user name and a domain name that identifies a user so he or she can receive Internet e-mail (Figure 2-27).

A **user name** is a unique combination of characters, such as letters of the alphabet and/or numbers, that identifies a specific user. Your user name must be different from the other user names in the same domain. For example, a user named Carly Martinez whose server has a domain name of scsite.com might want to select CMartinez as her user name. If scsite.com already has a CMartinez (for Carlos Martinez), Carly will have to select a different user name, such as carlymartinez or carly_martinez.

Sometimes, companies decide user names for employees. In many cases, however, users select their own user names, often selecting a nickname or any other combination of characters for their user name. Many users select a combination of their first and last names so others can remember it easily.

In an Internet e-mail address, an @ (pronounced at) symbol separates the user name from the domain name. Your service provider supplies the domain name. Using the example in Figure 2-27, a possible e-mail address for Carly Martinez would be carlymartinez@scsite.com, which would be read as follows: Carly Martinez at s c site dot com. Most e-mail programs allow you to create an **address book**, which contains a list of names and e-mail addresses.

When you send an e-mail message, an outgoing mail server that is operated by your Internet access provider determines how to route the message through the Internet and then sends the message. *SMTP (simple mail transfer protocol)* is a communications protocol used by some outgoing mail servers.

ETHICS & ISSUES 2-3

E-Mail: Irritant or Liberator?

E-mail is one of the more popular services on the Internet. Worldwide, more than 230 million people send and receive e-mail messages. E-mail makes business managers more productive by allowing them to share information, ideas, and opinions easily. But ironically, this easy sharing also can make managers less productive. Every day, managers wade through rivers of e-mail messages. Some of the messages are important, but many are copies of messages sent to others, notes on minor matters, or observations once shared in brief telephone calls or on walks to the water cooler. Most messages expect a quick reply, so hours can be spent dealing with e-mail. The constant flow of e-mail steals the time and interrupts the concentration needed for everyday work activities. Even worse, as managers become accustomed to the brief, rapid thinking demanded for e-mail, they can become unused to the creative, contemplative, persistent thought processes required for complex projects. Managers use a variety of measures to dam the flood of e-mail, including limiting the amount of time spent on messages, having colleagues telephone when they send important messages, and using filtering software to prioritize messages. What is the best way to deal with e-mail? Why? In terms of productivity, how can a company maximize the advantages of e-mail and minimize the disadvantages?

carlymartinez@scsite.com

FIGURE 2-27 An e-mail address is a combination of a user name and a domain name.

As you receive e-mail messages, an incoming mail server — also operated by your Internet access provider — holds the messages in your mailbox until you use your e-mail program to retrieve them. *POP3*, the latest version of POP (*Post Office Protocol*), is a communications protocol used by some incoming mail servers. Most e-mail programs have a mail notification alert that informs you via a message or sound when you receive new mail. Figure 2-28 illustrates how an e-mail message may travel from a sender to a receiver.

WEB LINK 2-6

E-Mail
For more information, visit scsite.com/dc2007/ch2/weblink and then click E-Mail.

FAQ 2-9

Can my computer get a virus through e-mail?

Yes. A *virus* is a computer program that can damage files and the operating system. One way that virus authors attempt to spread a virus is by sending virus-infected e-mail attachments. If you receive an e-mail attachment, you should use an antivirus program to verify that it is virus free.

For more information, read the High-Tech Talk article on page 168, the section about viruses and antivirus programs in Chapter 8, and visit scsite.com/dc2007/ch2/faq and then click Viruses.

FIGURE 2-28   HOW AN E-MAIL MESSAGE MAY TRAVEL FROM A SENDER TO A RECEIVER

Internet service provider's outgoing mail server

Step 1:
Using e-mail software, you create and send a message.

Step 2:
Your software contacts software on your service provider's outgoing mail server.

outgoing mail server

Step 3:
Software on the outgoing mail server determines the best route for the data and sends the message, which travels along Internet routers to the recipient's incoming mail server.

Internet service provider's incoming mail server

Step 4:
When the recipient uses e-mail software to check for e-mail messages, the message transfers from the incoming mail server to the recipient's computer.

Internet router

Internet router

FTP

FTP (*File Transfer Protocol*) is an Internet standard that permits file uploading and downloading (transferring) with other computers on the Internet. Uploading is the opposite of downloading; that is, **uploading** is the process of transferring documents, graphics, and other objects from your computer to a server on the Internet. Web page authors, for example, often use FTP to upload their Web pages to a Web server.

Many operating systems include FTP capabilities (Figure 2-29). If yours does not, you can download FTP programs from the Web, usually for a small fee.

An *FTP server* is a computer that allows users to upload and/or download files using FTP. An FTP site is a collection of files including text, graphics, audio clips, video clips, and program files that reside on an FTP server. Many FTP sites have *anonymous FTP*, whereby anyone can transfer some, if not all, available

files. Some FTP sites restrict file transfers to those who have authorized accounts (user names and passwords) on the FTP server.

Large files on FTP sites often are compressed to reduce storage space and download time. Before you can use a compressed (zipped) file, you must uncompress (unzip) it. Chapter 8 discusses utilities that zip and unzip files.

Newsgroups and Message Boards

A **newsgroup** is an online area in which users have written discussions about a particular subject (Figure 2-30). To participate in a discussion, a user sends a message to the newsgroup, and other users in the newsgroup read and reply to the message. The entire collection of Internet newsgroups is called *Usenet*, which contains tens of thousands of newsgroups about a multitude of topics. Some major topic areas include news, recreation, society, business, science, and computers.

A computer that stores and distributes newsgroup messages is called a *news server*. Many universities, corporations, Internet access providers, and other large organizations have a news server. Some newsgroups require you to enter a user name and password to participate in the discussion. Only authorized members can use this type of newsgroup. For example, a newsgroup for students taking a college course may require a user name and password to access the newsgroup. This ensures that only students in the course participate in the discussion.

To participate in a newsgroup, typically you use a program called a *newsreader*. Outlook Express includes a newsreader. You also can download newsreaders free or for a fee on the Web. Instead of using your own newsreader, some Web sites that sponsor newsgroups have a built-in newsreader. A newsreader enables you to access a newsgroup to read previously entered messages, called *articles*. You can *post*, or add, articles of your own. The newsreader also keeps track of which articles you have and have not read.

Newsgroup members frequently post articles as a reply to another article — either to

FIGURE 2-29a (FTP site being added to My Network Places folder)

FIGURE 2-29b (FTP site link is displayed in My Network Places folder)

FIGURE 2-29 Many operating systems, such as Windows XP, have built-in FTP capabilities.

FIGURE 2-30 Users in a newsgroup read and reply to other users' messages.

answer a question or to comment on material in the original article. These replies may cause the author of the original article, or others, to post additional articles related to the original article. A *thread* or *threaded discussion* consists of the original article and all subsequent related replies. A thread can be short-lived or continue for some time, depending on the nature of the topic and the interest of the participants.

Using a newsreader, you can search for newsgroups discussing a particular subject such as a type of musical instrument, brand of sports equipment, or employment opportunities. If you like the discussion in a particular newsgroup, you can *subscribe* to it, which means its location is saved in your newsreader for easy future access.

In some newsgroups, posted articles are sent to a moderator instead of immediately displaying on the newsgroup. The *moderator* reviews the contents of the article and then posts it, if appropriate. With a *moderated newsgroup*, the moderator decides if the article is relevant to the discussion. The moderator may choose to edit or discard inappropriate articles. For this reason, the content of a moderated newsgroup is considered more valuable.

A popular Web-based type of discussion group that does not require a newsreader is a **message board**. Many Web sites use message boards instead of newsgroups because they are easier to use.

Mailing Lists

A **mailing list** is a group of e-mail names and addresses given a single name. When a message is sent to a mailing list, every person on the list receives a copy of the message in his or her mailbox. To add your e-mail name and address to a mailing list, you **subscribe** to it (Figure 2-31). To remove your name, you **unsubscribe** from the mailing list. Some mailing lists are called *LISTSERVs*, named after a popular mailing list program.

FIGURE 2-31 When you join a mailing list, you and all others on the mailing list receive e-mail messages from the Web site.

WEB LINK 2-9

Mailing Lists

For more information, visit scsite.com/ dc2007/ch2/weblink and then click Mailing Lists.

Thousands of mailing lists exist about a variety of topics in areas of entertainment, business, computers, society, culture, health, recreation, and education. To locate a mailing list dealing with a particular topic, search for the keywords, mailing list or LISTSERV, in a search engine. Many vendors use mailing lists to communicate with their customer base.

Chat Rooms

A **chat** is a real-time typed conversation that takes place on a computer. **Real time** means that you and the people with whom you are conversing are online at the same time. A **chat room** is a location on an Internet server that permits users to chat with each other. Anyone in the chat room can participate in the conversation, which usually is specific to a particular topic.

As you type on your keyboard, a line of characters and symbols is displayed on the computer screen. Others connected to the same chat room server also see what you have typed (Figure 2-32). Some chat rooms support voice chats and video chats, in which people hear or see each other as they chat.

WEB LINK 2-10

Chat Rooms

For more information, visit scsite.com/ dc2007/ch2/weblink and then click Chat Rooms.

To start a chat session, you connect to a chat server through a program called a *chat client*. Today's browsers usually include a chat client. If yours does not, you can download a chat client from the Web. Some Web sites allow users to conduct chats without a chat client.

Once you have installed a chat client, you can create or join a conversation on the chat server to which you are connected. The chat room should indicate the discussion topic. The person who creates a chat room acts as the operator and has responsibility for monitoring the conversation and disconnecting anyone who becomes disruptive. Operator status can be shared or transferred to someone else.

Instant Messaging

Instant messaging (**IM**) is a real-time Internet communications service that notifies you when one or more people are online and then allows you to exchange messages or files or join a private chat room with them. Some IM services support voice and video conversations (Figure 2-33). Many IM services also can alert you to information such as calendar appointments, stock quotes, weather, or sports scores. They also allow you to send pictures or other documents to a recipient. For IM to work, both parties must be online at the same time. Also, the receiver of a message must be willing to accept messages.

People use IM on all types of computers, including desktop computers and mobile computers and devices, such as smart phones. To use IM, you may have to install *instant messenger* software on the computer or device you plan to use. Some operating systems, such as Windows XP, include an instant messenger. No standards currently exist for IM. To ensure successful communications, all individuals on the contact list need to use the same or a compatible instant messenger.

FIGURE 2-32 As you type, the words and symbols you enter are displayed on the computer screens of other people in the same chat room.

FIGURE 2-33 AN EXAMPLE OF INSTANT MESSAGING

Step 1:
Log in to the IM server.

Step 2:
The server determines if any of your established friends, family, or coworkers, called *buddies*, are online.

IM server

Step 3:
You send instant messages, voice, and/or video communications to an online buddy.

Step 4:
Your instant message, voice, and/or video travels through a messaging server and then to the online buddy's computer.

Step 5:
Your online buddy replies.

messaging server

Internet Telephony

Internet telephony, also called *Voice over IP* (Internet Protocol), enables users to speak to other users over the Internet using their desktop computer, mobile computer, or mobile device. That is, Internet telephony uses the Internet (instead of the public switched telephone network) to connect a calling party to one or more local or long-distance called parties.

To place an Internet telephone call, you need a high-speed Internet connection (e.g., via DSL or cable modem); Internet telephone service; a microphone or telephone, depending on the Internet telephone service; and Internet telephone software or a telephone adapter, depending on the Internet telephone service. Calls to other parties with the same Internet telephone service often are free, while calls that connect to the telephone network typically cost about $13 to $25 per month.

WEB LINK 2-11

Internet Telephony
For more information, visit scsite.com/ dc2007/ch2/weblink and then click Internet Telephony.

As you speak in a microphone or telephone connected to your computer, the Internet telephone software and the computer's sound card or the telephone adapter convert your spoken words (analog signals) to digital signals and then transmit the digitized audio over the Internet to the called parties. Software and equipment at the receiving end reverse the process so the receiving parties can hear what you have said. Figure 2-34 illustrates a user's equipment configuration for Internet telephony.

FAQ 2-10

How popular is Internet telephony?

Vonage, a leader in Internet telephony services, recently indicated that it is growing by 15,000 new subscribers each week. For more information, visit scsite.com/dc2007/ch2/faq and then click Internet Telephony.

Internet

cable/DSL modem

telephone adapter

personal computer

telephone

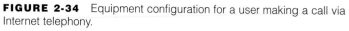

FIGURE 2-34 Equipment configuration for a user making a call via Internet telephony.

NETIQUETTE

Netiquette, which is short for Internet etiquette, is the code of acceptable behaviors users should follow while on the Internet; that is, it is the conduct expected of individuals while online. Netiquette includes rules for all aspects of the Internet, including the World Wide Web, e-mail, FTP, newsgroups and message boards, chat rooms, and instant messaging. Figure 2-35 outlines some of the rules of netiquette.

NETIQUETTE

Golden Rule: Treat others as you would like them to treat you.

1. In e-mail, newsgroups, and chat rooms:
   - Keep messages brief. Use proper grammar, spelling, and punctuation.
   - Be careful when using sarcasm and humor, as it might be misinterpreted.
   - Be polite. Avoid offensive language.
   - Read the message before you send it.
   - Use meaningful subject lines.
   - Avoid sending or posting *flames*, which are abusive or insulting messages. Do not participate in *flame wars*, which are exchanges of flames.
   - Avoid sending spam, which is the Internet's version of junk mail. *Spam* is an unsolicited e-mail message or newsgroup posting sent to many recipients or newsgroups at once.
   - Do not use all capital letters, which is the equivalent of SHOUTING!
   - Use **emoticons** to express emotion. Popular emoticons include

:)	Smile	:\	Undecided
:(	Frown	:o	Surprised
:l	Indifference		

   - Use abbreviations and acronyms for phrases:

BTW	by the way
FYI	for your information
FWIW	for what it's worth
IMHO	in my humble opinion
TTFN	ta ta for now
TYVM	thank you very much

   - Clearly identify a *spoiler*, which is a message that reveals a solution to a game or ending to a movie or program.
2. Read the *FAQ* (frequently asked questions), if one exists. Many newsgroups and Web pages have an FAQ.
3. Do not assume material is accurate or up-to-date. Be forgiving of other's mistakes.
4. Never read someone's private e-mail.

FIGURE 2-35 Some of the rules of netiquette.

Test your knowledge of pages 91 through 100 in Quiz Yourself 2-3.

QUIZ YOURSELF 2-3

Instructions: Find the true statement below. Then, rewrite the remaining false statements so they are true.

1. A chat room is a location on an Internet server that permits users to chat with each other.
2. An e-mail address is a combination of a user name and an e-mail program that identifies a user so he or she can receive Internet e-mail.
3. Business-to-consumer e-commerce occurs when one consumer sells directly to another, such as in an online auction.
4. FTP is an Internet standard that permits file reading and writing with other computers on the Internet.
5. Spam uses the Internet (instead of the public switched telephone network) to connect a calling party to one or more called parties.
6. Netiquette is the code of unacceptable behaviors while on the Internet.
7. On a newsgroup, a subscription consists of the original article and all subsequent related replies.

Quiz Yourself Online: To further check your knowledge of e-commerce, e-mail, FTP, newsgroups and message boards, mailing lists, chat rooms, instant messaging, Internet telephony, and netiquette, visit scsite.com/dc2007/ch2/quiz and then click Objectives 10 – 12.

CHAPTER SUMMARY

This chapter presented the history and structure of the Internet. It discussed the World Wide Web at length, including topics such as browsing, navigating, searching, Web publishing, and e-commerce (read Ethics & Issues 2-4 for a related discussion). It also introduced other services available on the Internet, such as e-mail, FTP, newsgroups and message boards, chat rooms, instant messaging, and Internet telephony. Finally, the chapter listed rules of netiquette.

ETHICS & ISSUES 2-4

Should Companies Be Able to Track Your Online Habits?

When you visit a Web site that includes an advertisement, someone probably is recording the fact that you visited that Web site and viewed the advertisement with your browser. Over time, companies that specialize in tracking who views which online advertisements can amass an enormous amount of information about your online Web surfing habits. This collection of information is considered to be part of your online profile. One company claims that through the use of advertisements on Web pages, it can track well over one billion Web page views per day. Through tracking the Web sites a user visits, the products they buy, and the articles they read, a company may attempt to profile the visitor's beliefs, associations, and habits. Although a user may think he or she is anonymous while navigating the Web, the company can attempt through various means to link the user's true identity with the user's online profile. The company can sell online profiles, with or without the user's true identity, to other advertisers or organizations. Should organizations be allowed to track your Web surfing habits? Why or why not? Should organizations be allowed to associate your real identity with your online identity and profit from the information? Should companies give you the option of not being tracked? What are the benefits and dangers of online tracking?

CAREER CORNER

Web Developer

If you are looking for a job working with the latest Internet technology, then Web developer could be the career for you. A *Web developer* analyzes, designs, develops, implements, and supports Web applications and functionality. Specialized programming skills required include HTML, JavaScript, Java, Perl, C++, and VBScript. Developers also may need multimedia knowledge, including Adobe Photoshop, Macromedia Flash, and Macromedia Director. Developers must be aware of emerging technologies and know how they can be used to enhance a Web presence.

A Web developer must be able to appreciate a client's needs, recognize the technologies involved to meet those needs, and explain those technologies to the client. For example, if the client is a large corporation seeking to set up an online store, a Web developer must understand e-commerce and be able to explain requirements, probable costs, and possible outcomes in a way the client can understand.

Educational requirements vary from company to company and can range from a high school education to a four-year degree. Many companies place heavy emphasis on certifications. Two of the more popular certifications are available through the International Webmasters Association (IWA) and the World Organization of Webmasters (WOW). A wide salary range exists — from $35,000 to $70,000 — depending on educational background and location. For more information, visit scsite.com/dc2007/ch2/careers and then click Web Developer.

High-Tech Talk

A COMPUTER'S INTERNET PROTOCOL (IP) ADDRESS

Every computer on the Internet has a unique address, called an IP address, that distinguishes it from other computers on the Internet. An IP address has two parts that identify a specific computer: one part to identify the network where that computer resides and a second part to pinpoint the specific computer or host within that network.

A typical IP address — such as 216.239.39.99 — has four groups of numbers that range from 0 through 255. This form of the IP address sometimes is called a *dotted decimal number* or *dotted quad.* The four groups of numbers in the dotted quad are called octets, because they each have 8 bits when viewed in binary form for a total of 32 bits in the IP address. For instance, the binary form of 216.239.39.99 is 11011000.11101111.00101001.01100011 (Figure 2-36). For more information about how the binary system works, see Appendix A.

domain name → www.google.com

identifies the network | identifies the specific computer

IP address → 216.239.39.99

IP address in binary form → 11011000 | 11101111 | 00101001 | 01100011

first octet | second octet | third octet | fourth octet

FIGURE 2-36
Components of an IP address.

Because each of the 8 bits can be 1 or 0, the total possible combinations per octet are 2^8, or 256. Combining the four octets of an IP address provides a possible 2^{32} or 4,294,967,296 unique values. The actual number of available addresses is about 3 billion, because some values are reserved for special use and are, therefore, off limits.

To request data such as a Web page from a computer on the Internet, you need only an IP address. For instance, if you type the Web address, http://216.239.39.99, your browser will display the home page on the machine hosting the Google Web site. Of course, remembering one IP address out of billions is a little overwhelming — so you probably would just type the domain name, www.google.com, in your browser. Your browser then contacts a domain name server (DNS) to resolve the human-readable domain name into a machine-readable IP address. Each domain name server houses a simple database that maps domain names to IP addresses. The DNS would resolve the human-readable domain name, www.google.com, into a machine-readable IP address, 216.239.39.99.

Domain names are helpful because they are easier for people to remember than IP addresses. You can learn more about a domain using the whois form at the Network Solutions Web site (www.netsol.com and then click the whois link). If you type a domain name, such as google.com, the form displays the registration information for that domain, including its IP address.

Like all other computers, your computer must have an IP address to connect to the Internet or another computer that has an IP address. Servers generally have *static IP addresses,* because they usually are connected to the Internet and their IP addresses do not change often. When you connect to the Internet using your home computer, you most likely are using a temporary or *dynamic IP address.* Your access provider uses the *Dynamic Host Configuration Protocol (DHCP)* to assign your computer a temporary dynamic IP address from a pool of IP addresses. The dynamic IP address is unique only for that session. Once you disconnect, the DHCP server puts that IP address back in the IP address pool so it can assign it to the next requesting computer. Even if you immediately reconnect, the DHCP server might not assign you the same IP address. Using DHCP and dynamic IP addresses means an Internet service provider needs only one IP address for each modem it supports, rather than one for each of its millions of customers.

Billions of IP addresses sounds like a lot. But, because so many computers connected to the Internet need unique IP addresses, a growing shortage of IP addresses exists. A new IP addressing scheme, called *IPv6* or *IPng (IP Next Generation)* will lengthen IP addresses from 32 bits to 128 bits and increase the number of available IP addresses to a whopping 3.4×10^{38}, or 340,000,000,000,000,000,000,000,000,000,000,000,000.

Do you want to know the IP address currently assigned to your computer?

- With Windows 2000/XP, click the Start button on the taskbar and then click Run. Type `cmd` to open the MS-DOS window. Type `ipconfig` and then press the ENTER key.

- With Windows 98, click the Start button on the taskbar and then click Run. Type `winipcfg` and then press the ENTER key.

If you are using an older version of AOL, the IP address might read 0.0.0.0 because AOL uses a proprietary method to assign IP addresses. For more information, visit scsite.com/dc2007/ch2/tech and then click IP Addresses.

Companies on the Cutting Edge

GOOGLE
POPULAR SEARCH ENGINE

The founders of *Google*, the leading Internet search engine, state that their mission is to organize the world's information. Every day, their Web site handles hundreds of millions of queries for information. In seconds, it can locate specific phrases and terms on four billion Web pages by using more than 10,000 connected computers.

Sergey Brin and Larry Page launched Google in 1998 in a friend's garage. The name is derived from "googol," which is the name of the number 1 followed by 100 zeros. Nearly 4,200 employees work for the Mountain View, California, corporation worldwide. In 2005, the company expanded its multilingual search capabilities by partnering with the most-visited Spanish-language Web site, Univision.com. For more information, visit scsite.com/dc2007/ch2/companies and then click Google.

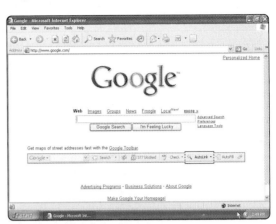

YAHOO!
POPULAR WEB PORTAL

Yahoo!, the first navigational portal to the Web, began as a hobby for Jerry Yang and David Filo when they were doctoral candidates in electrical engineering at Stanford University. They started creating and organizing lists of their favorite Web sites in 1994. The following year, they shared their creation, named Yahoo!, with fellow students and then released their product to the Internet community.

Yahoo! is an acronym for Yet Another Hierarchical Officious Oracle. What makes Yahoo! unique is that staff members build the directory by assuming the role of a typical Web researcher. Yahoo! is recognized for its breadth of features; in 2005, it added an audio search service that lets users preview an individual song or artist from 16 different services and a job search engine found at HotJobs.com. For more information, visit scsite.com/dc2007/ch2/companies and then click Yahoo!.

Technology Trailblazers

TIM BERNERS-LEE
CREATOR OF THE WORLD WIDE WEB

The World Wide Web (WWW) has become one of the more widely used Internet services, and its roots are based on *Tim Berners-Lee's* work. Berners-Lee is credited with creating the first Web server, browser, and URL addresses.

He developed his ideas in 1989 while working at CERN, the European Particle Physics Laboratory in Geneva, Switzerland, and based his work on a program he had written for his own use to track random associations. Today, he works quietly in academia as director of the World Wide Web Consortium (W3C) at the Massachusetts Institute of Technology.

In 2005, Berners-Lee told the British Broadcasting Corporation (BBC) that he is pleased to see that blogging is becoming a creative medium that resembles his original idea of the World Wide Web. For more information, visit scsite.com/dc2007/ch2/people and then click Tim Berners-Lee.

MEG WHITMAN
EBAY PRESIDENT AND CEO

Meg Whitman joined eBay in 1998 and has been instrumental in helping the company become the world's largest online marketplace. Before that time, she was an executive for the Keds Division of the Stride Rite Corporation and general manager of Hasbro Inc.'s Preschool Division. She then served as president and CEO of Florists Transworld Delivery (FTD).

She credits her success to listening to the loyal eBay community, and she occasionally answers their e-mails personally. She holds degrees in economics from Princeton University and management from the Harvard Business School.

More than 100 million people worldwide were part of the eBay community in 2005, and Whitman is looking to expand the marketplace, especially in China. She predicts the number of Chinese users will surpass the number of American users by 2009. For more information, visit scsite.com/dc2007/ch2/people and then click Meg Whitman.

Chapter Review

The Chapter Review section summarizes the concepts presented in this chapter. To listen to the audio version of this Chapter Review, visit scsite.com/dc2007/ch2/review. To obtain help from other students regarding any subject in this chapter, visit scsite.com/dc2007/ch2/forum and post your thoughts or questions.

(1) **What Is the History of the Internet?**   The **Internet** is a worldwide collection of networks that links millions of businesses, government agencies, educational institutions, and individuals. The Internet has its roots in *ARPANET*, a network started in 1969 to link researchers across the United States. In 1986, the National Science Foundation connected its huge network, called *NSFnet*, to ARPANET, creating a configuration of complex networks and hosts that became known as the Internet.

(2) **How Can You Access and Connect to the Internet?**   Employees and students often connect to the Internet through a business or school network. The networks usually use a high-speed line leased from a telephone company. Some home and small businesses connect to the Internet with **dial-up access**, which uses a modem in the computer and a standard telephone line. Many home and small business users opt for higher-speed *broadband* connections, such as DSL, cable television networks, radio signals, or satellite. **DSL** provides Internet connections using regular copper telephone lines. A **cable modem** allows access to Internet services through the cable television network. *Fixed wireless* connections use a dish-shaped antenna to communicate via radio signals. A *satellite modem* communicates with a satellite dish. An **access provider** is a business that provides access to the Internet free or for a fee. An **ISP** (**Internet service provider**) is a regional or national access provider. An **online service provider** (**OSP**) provides Internet access in addition to members-only features. A **wireless Internet service provider** *(WISP)* provides wireless Internet access to users with wireless modems or Internet-enabled mobile devices.

(3) **What Is an IP Address?**   An **IP address** (*Internet Protocol address*) is a number that uniquely identifies each computer or device connected to the Internet. The Internet relies on IP addresses to send data to computers at specific locations. A **domain name** is the text version of an IP address.

> Visit scsite.com/dc2007/ch2/quiz or click the Quiz Yourself button. Click Objectives 1 – 3.

(4) **What Are the Components of a Web Address?**   The **World Wide Web** (*WWW*), or **Web**, consists of a worldwide collection of electronic documents. Each electronic document is called a **Web page**. A **URL** (*Uniform Resource Locator*), or **Web address**, is a unique address for a Web page. A Web address consists of a protocol, a domain name, and sometimes the path to a specific Web page or location on a Web page.

(5) **What Is the Purpose of a Web Browser?**   A **Web browser**, or **browser**, is application software that allows users to access and view Web pages. When you type a Web address in the Address box of a browser window, a computer called a **Web server** delivers the requested Web page to your computer. Most Web pages contain links. A **link** is a built-in connection that, when clicked, displays a related Web page or part of a Web page.

(6) **How Can You Search for Information on the Web?**   Two commonly used search tools are subject directories and search engines. A **subject directory** classifies Web pages in an organized set of categories. By clicking links, you move through categories to display a list of Web pages about a desired topic. A **search engine** is a program that finds Web sites and Web pages. To use a search engine, you enter a word or phrase, called **search text**, that defines the item about which you want information. The search engine displays a list of *hits*. When clicked, each hit displays an associated Web site or Web page.

Chapter Review

(7) What Are the Types of Web Sites?   A **portal** is a Web site that offers a variety of Internet services from a single location. A news Web site contains newsworthy material. An informational Web site contains factual information. A business/marketing Web site promotes or sells products or services. An educational Web site offers avenues for teaching and learning. An entertainment Web site provides an interactive and engaging environment. An advocacy Web site describes a cause, opinion, or idea. A **blog** is an informal Web site consisting of time-stamped articles, or posts, in a diary or journal format, usually listed in reverse chronological order. A **wiki** is a collaborative Web site that allows users to add to, modify, or delete the Web site content via their Web browser. A *content aggregator* is a business that gathers and organizes Web content and then distributes, or feeds, the content to subscribers for free or a fee. A personal Web site is maintained by a private individual or family.

(8) How Do Web Pages Use Graphics, Animation, Audio, Video, Virtual Reality, and Plug-Ins?
Some Web pages use **multimedia**, which combines text with graphics, animation, audio, video, and/or virtual reality. A **graphic** is a digital representation of nontext information such as a drawing or photograph. **Animation** is the appearance of motion created by displaying a series of still images. **Audio** includes music, speech, or any other sound. **Video** consists of full-motion images. **Virtual reality (VR)** is the use of computers to simulate an environment that appears as three-dimensional space. A **plug-in** is a program that extends a browser's capability to display multimedia elements.

(9) What Are the Steps Required for Web Publishing?   Web publishing is the development and maintenance of Web pages. The five major steps to Web publishing are: (1) plan a Web site, (2) analyze and design a Web site, (3) create a Web site, (4) deploy a Web site, and (5) maintain a Web site.

connect
Visit scsite.com/dc2007/ch2/quiz or click the Quiz Yourself button. Click Objectives 4 – 9.

(10) What Are the Types of E-Commerce?   **E-commerce**, short for *electronic commerce*, is a business transaction that occurs over an electronic network such as the Internet. *Business-to-consumer (B2C) e-commerce* consists of the sale of goods and services to the general public. *Consumer-to-consumer (C2C) e-commerce* occurs when one consumer sells directly to another, such as an **online auction**. *Business-to-business (B2B) e-commerce* takes place between businesses that exchange goods and services.

(11) How Do E-Mail, FTP, Newsgroups and Message Boards, Mailing Lists, Chat Rooms, Instant Messaging, and Internet Telephony Work?   **E-mail** (short for *electronic mail*) is the transmission of messages and files via a computer network. **FTP** (*File Transfer Protocol*) is an Internet standard that permits file **uploading** and **downloading** with other computers. A **newsgroup** is an online area in which users have written discussions. A **message board** is a Web-based type of discussion group that is easier to use than a newsgroup. A **mailing list** is a group of e-mail names and addresses given a single name, so that everyone on the list receives a message sent to the list. A **chat room** is a location on an Internet server that permits users to conduct real-time typed conversations. **Instant messaging (IM)** is a real-time Internet communications service that notifies you when one or more people are online. **Internet telephony** enables users to speak over the Internet using a computer or mobile device.

(12) What Are the Rules of Netiquette?   **Netiquette**, which is short for Internet etiquette, is the code of acceptable behaviors users should follow while on the Internet. Netiquette rules include: keep messages short, be polite, avoid sending *flames* or *spam*, use **emoticons** and acronyms, read the *FAQ*, do not assume material is accurate or up-to-date, and never read someone's private e-mail.

connect
Visit scsite.com/dc2007/ch2/quiz or click the Quiz Yourself button. Click Objectives 10 – 12.

Key Terms

You should know the Primary Terms and be familiar with the Secondary Terms. Use the list below to help focus your study. To further enhance your understanding of the Key Terms in this chapter, visit scsite.com/dc2007/ch2/terms. See an example of and a definition for each term, and access current and additional information about the term from the Web.

Primary Terms

(shown in bold-black characters in the chapter)

access provider (71)
address book (94)
animation (86)
audio (86)
blog (84)
browser (75)
cable modem (70)
chat (98)
chat room (98)
dial-up access (70)
DNS server (74)
domain name (73)
downloading (76)
DSL (70)
e-commerce (91)
electronic storefront (92)
e-mail (92)
e-mail address (94)
e-mail program (93)
emoticons (100)
FTP (96)
graphic (85)
home page (76)
instant messaging (IM) (98)
Internet (68)
Internet telephony (99)
IP address (73)
ISP (Internet service provider) (72)
link (77)
mailing list (97)
message board (97)
MP3 (86)
multimedia (85)
netiquette (100)

newsgroup (96)
online auction (92)
online service provider (OSP) (72)
player (86)
plug-in (89)
portal (82)
real time (98)
RSS 2.0 (84)
search engine (78)
search text (80)
shopping cart (92)
streaming (86)
subject directory (78)
subscribe (97)
surfing the Web (77)
traffic (70)
unsubscribe (97)
uploading (96)
URL (76)
user name (94)
video (88)
virtual reality (VR) (88)
Web (75)
Web address (76)
Web browser (75)
Web community (82)
Web page (75)
Web publishing (90)
Web server (75)
Web site (75)
wiki (84)
wireless Internet service provider (72)
World Wide Web (75)

Secondary Terms

(shown in italic characters in the chapter)

Advanced Research Projects Agency (ARPA) (69)
animated GIF (86)
anonymous FTP (96)
ARPANET (69)
articles (96)
Atom (84)
blogger (84)
broadband (70)
business-to-business (B2B) e-commerce (92)
business-to-consumer (B2C) e-commerce (91)
chat client (98)
click (77)
consumer-to-consumer (C2C) e-commerce (92)
content aggregator (84)
digital subscriber line (70)
domain name system (DNS) (74)
dot-com (73)
dynamic Web page (75)
electronic commerce (91)
electronic mail (92)
FAQ (100)
File Transfer Protocol (96)
fixed wireless (70)
flame wars (100)
flames (100)
FTP server (96)
GIF (85)
graphical image (85)
hits (80)
host (69)
hot spots (71)
http (76)
hyperlink (77)
Hypertext Transfer Protocol (76)
instant messenger (98)
Internet backbone (72)
Internet Corporation for Assigned Names and Numbers (ICANN) (74)
Internet Protocol address (73)
JPEG (85)
keywords (80)
LISTSERVs (97)

m-commerce (91)
microbrowser (76)
moderated newsgroup (97)
moderator (97)
Moving Pictures Experts Group (MPEG) (88)
MPEG-4 (88)
national ISP (72)
Net (68)
news server (96)
newsreader (96)
NSFnet (70)
PNG (85)
podcast (86)
point of presence (POP) (72)
POP3 (95)
post (96)
Post Office Protocol (95)
pull (76)
push (76)
Really Simple Syndication (84)
regional ISP (72)
satellite modem (70)
SMTP (simple mail transfer protocol) (94)
spam (100)
spider (81)
spoiler (100)
static Web page (75)
streaming audio (86)
streaming video (88)
subscribe (97)
thread (97)
threaded discussion (97)
thumbnail (86)
top-level domain (73)
Uniform Resource Locator (76)
Usenet (96)
Voice over IP (99)
VR world (88)
Weblog (84)
wireless portal (82)
WISP (72)
World Wide Web Consortium (W3C) (70)
WWW (75)

Checkpoint

Use the Checkpoint exercises to check your knowledge level of the chapter. The Beyond the Book exercises will help broaden your understanding of the concepts presented in this chapter. To complete the Checkpoint exercises interactively, visit scsite.com/dc2007/ch2/check.

Label the Figure

Identify the types of Web sites.

a. advocacy

b. blog

c. business/marketing

d. content aggregator

e. educational

f. entertainment

g. informational

h. news

i. personal

j. portal

k. wiki

True/False

Mark T for True and F for False. (See page numbers in parentheses.)

_____ 1. A single government agency owns and controls the Internet. (70)

_____ 2. DSL is a technology that provides high-speed Internet connections over the cable television network. (70)

_____ 3. In general, the first portion of each IP address identifies the specific computer and the last portion identifies the network. (73)

_____ 4. Most current browsers and Web sites require the http:// and www portions of a Web address. (76)

_____ 5. Pointing to, or positioning the pointer on, a link on a Web page typically changes the shape of the pointer to a small hand with a pointing index finger. (77)

_____ 6. A major problem with a subject directory is deciding which categories to choose as you work through the menus of links presented. (79)

_____ 7. The purpose of an informational Web site is to convince the reader of the validity of a cause, opinion, or idea. (84)

_____ 8. A podcast is a collaborative Web site that allows users to add to, modify, or delete the Web site content via their Web browser. (86)

_____ 9. To develop a Web page, you do not have to be a computer programmer. (90)

_____ 10. An online auction is an example of business-to-consumer (B2C) e-commerce. (92)

_____ 11. A chat room is a location on an Internet server that permits users to chat with each other. (98)

_____ 12. A flame is an unsolicited e-mail message or newsgroup posting sent to many recipients or newsgroups at once. (100)

Checkpoint

 Multiple Choice Select the best answer. (See page numbers in parentheses.)

1. The Internet has its roots in _____, which was a networking project started by an agency of the U.S. Department of Defense. (69)
   a. ICANN
   b. NSFnet
   c. WISP
   d. ARPANET

2. Many public locations are _____ that provide wireless Internet connections to users with mobile computers or devices. (71)
   a. hot spots
   b. ISPs
   c. Weblogs
   d. chat clients

3. As with an IP address, the components of a domain name are separated by _____. (73)
   a. commas
   b. periods
   c. colons
   d. semicolons

4. Many Web page addresses begin with _____, which stands for a set of rules that defines how pages transfer on the Internet. (76)
   a. W3C   b. http
   c. hits   d. pop

5. Some people use the phrase, _____, to refer to the activity of using links to explore the Web. (77)
   a. surfing the Web
   b. weaving the Net
   c. navigating the Net
   d. bringing in the Net

6. All of the following techniques can be used to improve Web searches except _____. (81)
   a. list all possible spellings
   b. read a search engine's Help information
   c. use general nouns and put the most important terms last
   d. if a search is unsuccessful, try another search engine

7. A(n) _____ is a business that gathers and organizes Web content and then distributes, or feeds, the content to subscribers for free or a fee. (84)
   a. WISP
   b. ISP
   c. content aggregator
   d. blogger

8. A _____ is recorded audio stored on a Web site that can be downloaded to a computer or a portable digital audio player. (86)
   a. blog
   b. wiki
   c. portal
   d. podcast

9. _____ is the process of transferring data in a continuous and even flow, allowing users to access and use a file while it is transmitting. (86)
   a. Streaming
   b. Linking
   c. Surfing
   d. Clicking

10. _____ is not a step in Web publishing. (90)
    a. Planning a Web site
    b. Deploying a Web site
    c. Creating a Web site
    d. Moderating a Web site

11. At a consumer-to-consumer (C2C) Web site, a(n) _____ allows users to purchase from other consumers. (92)
    a. news server
    b. online auction
    c. wireless portal
    d. shopping cart

12. In an e-mail address, a _____ is a unique combination of characters that identifies a specific user. (94)
    a. domain name
    b. URL
    c. user name
    d. dot com

13. The _____ standard permits uploading and downloading of files on the Internet. (96)
    a. FTP
    b. newsgroup
    c. message board
    d. LISTSERV

14. Use _____, such as :) for smile and :(for frown, to express emotions in e-mail, newsgroups, and chat rooms. (100)
    a. flames
    b. spam
    c. spoilers
    d. emoticons

Checkpoint

Matching   Match the terms with their definitions. (See page numbers in parentheses.)

_____ 1. traffic (70)

_____ 2. home page (76)

_____ 3. link (77)

_____ 4. spider (81)

_____ 5. RSS 2.0 (84)

_____ 6. MP3 (86)

_____ 7. player (86)

_____ 8. plug-in (89)

_____ 9. m-commerce (91)

_____ 10. address book (94)

a. first page that a Web site displays

b. program that extends the capability of a browser

c. specification used by content aggregators to distribute content

d. software used to listen to an audio file on a computer

e. bulk of communications activity on the Internet

f. built-in connection to a related Web page or part of a Web page

g. format that reduces an audio file to about one-tenth its original size

h. term used to identify e-commerce that takes place using mobile devices

i. contains a list of names and e-mail addresses

j. copy a program from storage to memory

k. browser designed for the small screens and limited power of PDAs and smart phones

l. program used to build and maintain lists of words found on Web sites

Short Answer   Write a brief answer to each of the following questions.

1. How is a regional ISP different from a national ISP? _____ How is an ISP different from a WISP? _____

2. How is a static Web page different from a dynamic Web page? _____ What is a Web site? _____

3. What are the differences between blogs, wikis, and podcasts? _____ When might you use each? _____

4. What three graphics formats are used frequently on the Web? _____ How are they different? _____

5. What is a threaded discussion? _____ What is a moderated newsgroup? _____

Beyond the Book   Read the following book elements, learn more about each using the Web, and then write a brief report.

1. Ethics & Issues — Is the Internet as Good as the Classroom? (82), Should All Sales on the Internet Be Taxed? (92), E-Mail: Irritant or Liberator? (94), or Should Companies Be Able to Track Your Online Habits? (101)

2. Career Corner — Web Developer (101)

3. Companies on the Cutting Edge — Google or Yahoo! (103)

4. FAQs (71, 72, 74, 77, 81, 85, 92, 95, 100)

5. High-Tech Talk — A Computer's Internet Protocol (IP) Address (102)

6. Looking Ahead — Internet Speeds into the Future (70) or 3-D Search Engines Get the Picture (81)

7. Making Use of the Web — Travel (118)

8. Picture Yourself Instant Messaging (66)

9. Technology Trailblazers — Tim Berners-Lee or Meg Whitman (103)

10. Web Links (72, 77, 84, 89, 92, 95, 96, 97, 98, 99)

Learn It Online

Use the Learn It Online exercises to reinforce your understanding of the chapter concepts. To access the Learn It Online exercises, visit scsite.com/dc2007/ch2/learn.

① At the Movies — Google Search Secrets

To view the Google Search Secrets movie, click the number 1 button. Locate your video and click the corresponding High-Speed or Dial-Up link, depending on your Internet connection. Watch the movie and then complete the exercise by answering the question that follows. Using the Internet to gather information can seem daunting. The introduction of powerful search engines has enhanced the Internet research experience. Properly utilizing a search engine can benefit almost any project. How might you go about using Google to search for information for a research paper?

② At the Movies — Instant Message from Anywhere

To view the Instant Message from Anywhere movie, click the number 2 button. Locate your video and click the corresponding High-Speed or Dial-Up link, depending on your Internet connection. Watch the movie, and then complete the exercise by answering the question that follows. Instant messaging (IM) is a fun way to stay in touch with your friends, but until now it has been limited to use on the computer. New technology developments have cut the wires, and now you can take IM on the road. What are some of the limitations of wireless instant messaging?

③ Student Edition Labs — Connecting to the Internet

Click the number 3 button. A new browser window will open, displaying the Student Edition Labs. Follow the on-screen instructions to complete the Connecting to the Internet Lab. When finished, click the Exit button. If required, submit your results to your instructor.

④ Student Edition Labs — Getting the Most out of the Internet

Click the number 4 button. A new browser window will open, displaying the Student Edition Labs. Follow the on-screen instructions to complete the Getting the Most out of the Internet Lab. When finished, click the Exit button. If required, submit your results to your instructor.

⑤ Student Edition Labs — E-mail

Click the number 5 button. A new browser window will open, displaying the Student Edition Labs. Follow the on-screen instructions to complete the E-mail Lab. When finished, click the Exit button. If required, submit your results to your instructor.

⑥ Practice Test

Click the number 6 button. Answer each question. When completed, enter your name and click the Grade Test button to submit the quiz for grading. Make a note of any missed questions. If required, submit your score to your instructor.

⑦ Who Wants To Be a Computer Genius²?

Click the number 7 button to find out if you are a computer genius. Directions about how to play the game will be displayed. When you are ready to play, click the Play button. Submit your score to your instructor.

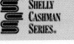
Learn It Online

⑧ Wheel of Terms

Click the number 8 button to reinforce important terms you learned in this chapter by playing the Shelly Cashman Series version of this popular game. Directions about how to play the game will be displayed. When you are ready to play, click the Play button. Submit your score to your instructor.

⑨ DC Track and Field

Click the number 9 button to use what you have learned in this chapter to compete against other students in three track and field events. Directions about how to play the game will be displayed. When you are ready to play, click the start first event button. If required, submit your score to your instructor.

⑩ You're Hired!

Click the number 10 button to use what you have learned in this chapter to embark on the path to a career in computers. Directions about how to play the game will be displayed. When you are ready to play, click the begin game button. If required, submit your score to your instructor.

⑪ Crossword Puzzle Challenge

Click the number 11 button. Complete the puzzle to reinforce skills you learned in this chapter. Directions about how to play the game will be displayed. When you are ready to play, click the Play button. Submit the completed puzzle to your instructor.

⑫ Lab Exercises

Click the number 12 button. When the Lab Exercises menu appears, click the exercise assigned by your instructor. A new browser window will open. Follow the on-screen instructions to complete the exercise. When finished, click the Exit button. If required, submit your results to your instructor.

⑬ In the News

In her book, *Caught in the Net*, Kimberly S. Young contends that the Internet can be addictive. Young's methodology and conclusions have been questioned by several critics, but Young remains resolute. She points out that at one time, no one admitted to the existence of alcoholism. Click the number 13 button and read a news article about the impact of Internet use on human behavior. What effect did the Internet have? Why? In your opinion, is the Internet's influence positive or negative? Why?

⑭ Chapter Discussion Forum

Select an objective from this chapter on page 67 about which you would like more information. Click the number 14 button and post a short message listing a meaningful message title accompanied by one or more questions concerning the selected objective. In two days, return to the threaded discussion by clicking the number 14 button. Submit to your instructor your original message and at least one response to your message.

⑮ Google Earth

Click the number 15 button to download Google Earth. Once you have downloaded Google Earth, use it to fly to your home, school, Grand Canyon, Baghdad, Paris, and Moscow. At each location, use the buttons to change the view. Print a copy of the map showing your school, handwrite on the map the school's elevation, and submit the map to your instructor.

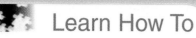
Learn How To

Use the Learn How To activities to learn fundamental skills when using a computer and accompanying technology. Complete the exercises and submit them to your instructor. To see a video of a Learn How To activity, visit scsite.com/dc2007/ch2/howto.

LEARN HOW TO 1: Change a Web Browser's Home Page

When you start a Web browser, a Web page is displayed. You can change the page that appears when you start a Web browser or when you click the Home button on the browser toolbar by completing the following steps:

1. With the browser running, click Tools on the menu bar and then click Internet Options on the Tools menu. *The Internet Options dialog box is displayed (Figure 2-37).*
2. If necessary, in the Home page area in the General sheet, select the Web address in the Address box.
3. Type the Web address of the page you want to display both when you start the browser and when you click the Home button.
4. Click the OK button in the Internet Options dialog box.

When you start the browser or click the Home button on the browser toolbar, the selected Web page will be displayed.

FIGURE 2-37

Exercise

1. Start your Web browser. Write down the address of the browser's current home page. Then, change the browser's home page to www.cnn.com. Close the browser.
2. Start your Web browser. What is the lead story on cnn.com? Use links on the page to view several stories. Which story do you find most interesting? Click the Home button on the browser toolbar. What happened? Submit these answers to your instructor.
3. Change the browser's home page to your school's home page. Click the Home button on the browser toolbar. Click the Calendar or Events link, and then locate two campus events of which you were unaware. Report these two campus events to your instructor.
4. Change the browser's home page back to the address you wrote down in Step 1.

LEARN HOW TO 2: Create and Use Your Own Weblog (Blog)

A Weblog, commonly referred to as a blog, can contain any information you wish to place in it. Originally, blogs consisted of Web addresses, so that an individual or group with a specific interest could direct others to useful places on the Web. Today, blogs contain addresses, thoughts, diaries, and anything else a person or group wants to share.

Once you have created a blog, you can update it. A variety of services are available on the Web to help you create and maintain your blog. One widely used service is called Blogger. To create a blog using Blogger, complete the following steps:

1. Start your Web browser, type `www.blogger.com` in the Address box, and then press the ENTER key. *The Blogger home page is displayed (Figure 2-38).*
2. Click the CREATE YOUR BLOG NOW arrow on the Blogger home page.
3. Enter the data required on the Create an account page. Your user name and password will allow you to change and manage your blog. Your Display name is the name that will be shown on the blog as the author of the material on the blog. Many people use their own names, but others use pseudonyms as their "pen names" so they are not readily identifiable.
4. Click the Continue arrow and then enter your Blog title and Blog address. These are the names and addresses everyone will use to view your blog. By default, the blog is stored and maintained on the blogspot server.
5. Click the Continue arrow. *The Choose a template screen is displayed.*
6. Choose a template for your blog and then click the Continue arrow.

Learn How To

7. Your blog will be created for you. When you see the Your blog has been created screen, click the Start posting arrow.
8. From the screen that is displayed, you can post items for your blog, specify settings, change the template, and view your blog.
9. When you have posted all your information, click the Sign out button at the top right of the screen. You will be logged out.
10. To edit your blog and add or change information on it, visit the Blogger home page and sign in by entering your user name and password. You will be able to post to your blog.
11. Others can view your blog by entering its address in the browser's Address box and then pressing the ENTER key.

Exercise

1. Start your Web browser and visit www.blogger.com. Click the TAKE A QUICK TOUR button and go through all the screens that explain about a blog. What did you learn that you did not know? What type of blog do you find most compelling — a group or an individual blog? Why? Turn in your answers to your instructor.
2. Optional: Create your own blog. Carefully name it and begin your posts at this time. What is your blog name and address? What is its primary purpose? Is it an individual or group blog? Write a paragraph containing the answers to these questions and any other information you feel is pertinent. Turn in this paragraph to your instructor.

FIGURE 2-38

LEARN HOW TO 3: Bid and Buy a Product from eBay

Online auctions have grown to be a favorite shopping space for many people. A leading online auction Web site is eBay. To submit a bid for an item on eBay, complete the following steps:

1. Type www.ebay.com in the Address box of your browser. Press the ENTER key. *The eBay home page is displayed (Figure 2-39).*
2. Pick an item you find interesting and on which you might bid.
3. Enter your item in the What are you looking for text box and then click the Find It button.
4. Scroll through the page to see the available items.
5. To bid on an item, click the Place Bid button.
6. Enter the amount of your bid. Click the Continue button.
7. You must be registered to bid on eBay. If you are registered, enter your eBay User ID and Password and then click the Submit button. If not, click the Register button and follow the instructions.
8. After registering, you will confirm your bid and receive notification about your bid.
9. You will be notified by e-mail if you won the bid. If so, you will arrange with the seller for payment and shipment.

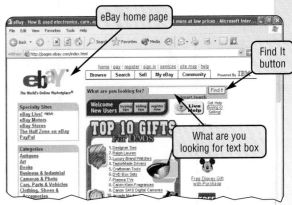

FIGURE 2-39

The eBay Web site contains reminders that when you bid on an item, you are entering into a contract to purchase the item if you are the successful bidder. Bidding on eBay is serious business.

Exercise

1. Start your browser and display the eBay home page.
2. In the What are you looking for text box, enter the name of an upcoming sporting event you would like to attend followed by the word, tickets. For example, enter Super Bowl tickets. Click the Search button.
3. Did you find available tickets? Were there more tickets available than you expected, or fewer? Are the bid prices reasonable or ridiculous? How many bids were made for all the tickets? How much time is left to bid? What items did you find that you were not expecting? Submit answers to these questions to your instructor.
4. Enter an item of your choice in the What are you looking for text box. If you feel so inclined, bid on an item. Do you think this manner of buying goods is valuable? Why? Will you visit eBay again? Why? Submit answers to these questions to your instructor.

Web Research

Use the Internet-based Web Research exercises to broaden your understanding of the concepts presented in this chapter. Visit scsite.com/dc2007/ch2/research to obtain more information pertaining to each exercise. To discuss any of the Web Research exercises in this chapter with other students, post your thoughts or questions at scsite.com/dc2007/ch2/forum.

① Scavenger Hunt Use one of the <u>search engines</u> listed in Figure 2-10 in Chapter 2 on page 78 or your own favorite search engine to find the answers to the questions below. Copy and paste the Web address from the Web page where you found the answer. Some questions may have more than one answer. If required, submit your answers to your instructor. (1) Microsoft Internet Explorer and Netscape Navigator are the two more popular Web browsers. What is the name of the first graphical Web browser? (2) What cable company was established in 1858 to carry instantaneous communications across the ocean that would eventually be used for Internet communications? (3) What American president in 1957 created both the interstate highway system and the Advanced Research Projects Agency (ARPA)? (4) Where is the location of Microsoft's headquarters? (5) How many Web pages is Google currently searching?

② Search Sleuth The Internet has provided the opportunity to access encyclopedias online. One of the more comprehensive encyclopedia research sites is **Encyclopedia.com**. Visit this Web site and then use your word processing program to answer the following questions. Then, if required, submit your answers to your instructor. (1) The site's home page lists the top five searches for the day. What are today's top five searches? Click one of these links. What magazines and newspapers contain information about this topic? (2) Type "World Wide Web" as the keyword in the Search text box. How many articles discussing the World Wide Web are found on the Encyclopedia.com Web site? (3) In the search results list, click the first link. What is the definition of the World Wide Web according to the first sentence of the article? Who is the American computer consultant who promoted the idea of linking documents via hypertext during the 1960s? What words are hyperlinks within this article? (5) Type multimedia as the keyword in the Search text box. In the search results list, click the multimedia link. What hardware typically is required to work with multimedia according to this article? What are some optional hardware devices? (6) Type "personal computer" as the keyword in the Search text box. Click one of the personal computer links, review the material, and, if required, submit to your instructor a 50-word summary of the information you read.

③ Newsgroups One of the more popular topics for <u>newsgroups</u> is netiquette. Read the information Borland Software Corporation (info.borland.com/newsgroups/netiquette.html) provides on general newsgroup conduct. Then find three newsgroups, such as those listed in CyberFiber (cyberfiber.com/internet.htm) or Google Groups, that discuss this topic. Read the information and then summarize the advice provided.

④ Journaling Respond to your readings in this chapter by writing at least one page about your reactions, evaluations, and reflections about using the <u>Internet</u>. For example, how many e-mail messages do you send and receive daily? How many Web pages do you visit each month? Have you shopped online? Have your instructors required you to access the Internet for class projects? Which search engines have you used? You also can write about the new terms you learned by reading this chapter. If required, submit your journal to your instructor.

⑤ Ethics in Action <u>Web cams</u> are video cameras that display their output on a Web page. The feasibility of installing Web cams in 47,000 locations susceptible to terrorist threats, such as nuclear and chemical plants, national airports, and gas storage facilities, is being explored. Citizens would monitor the cameras and report suspicious activity. Critics of this proposal state that the constant surveillance is an invasion of privacy. Visit the USHomeGuard Web site (ushomeguard.org) and then write a summary of the citizen corps' roles in this project. Then locate other Web sites that oppose this plan and summarize their views. If required, submit your summary to your instructor.

Case Studies

Use the Case Studies to apply the concepts presented in the chapter to real-world situations. Visit scsite.com/dc2007/ch2/cases to obtain more information pertaining to each exercise. To discuss the Case Studies in this chapter with other students, visit scsite.com/dc2007/ch2/forum and post your thoughts or questions.

CASE STUDY 1 — Class Discussion The owner of Deuce Investments, where you are employed part-time as a stock-research analyst, recently attended a one-day continuing education course for small businesses at the local community college. The title of the course was *Ten Reasons Why Your Company Needs the Internet to Compete in Today's Business Environment*. She now feels that the Internet might be useful as an investment-research tool, and she has asked you to investigate the costs associated with making the Internet available for use in the company during business hours. Examine the types of <u>access providers</u> available in your community, the monthly cost, and other significant factors that might influence her decision. Draft a memo to the owner summarizing your recommendations. Be prepared to discuss your recommendations in class.

CASE STUDY 2 — Class Discussion Many retailers, such as Sports Authority, Barnes and Noble, and Toys R Us, are <u>brick-and-click businesses</u>. That is, they allow customers to conduct complete transactions at a physical location as well as online at a Web site. Choose a local brick-and-click business in which you have shopped at the physical location and visit the Web site of the business. Compare the type, availability, and cost (include tax and shipping) of products or services available. Prepare a report that summarizes the advantages and disadvantages of dealing with the physical location versus the Web site of a brick-and-click business. Would you rather shop at the physical location or at the Web site? Why? Does the answer depend on the business, the product, or some other factor? Be prepared to share your findings in class.

CASE STUDY 3 — Research This chapter lists eleven types of Web sites: <u>portal</u>, news, informational, business/marketing, educational, entertainment, advocacy, blog, wiki, content aggregator, and personal. Use the Internet to find at least one example of each type of Web site. For each Web site, identify the Web address, the multimedia elements used, the purpose of the Web site, and the type of Web site. Explain why you classified each site as you did. Then, keeping in mind the purpose of each Web site, rank the sites in terms of their effectiveness. Write a brief report or use PowerPoint to create a presentation and share your findings with your class.

CASE STUDY 4 — Research <u>The Internet</u> has had a tremendous impact on business. For some businesses, that influence has not been positive. For example, surveys suggest that as a growing number of people order products online, traditional brick-and-mortar businesses are seeing fewer customers. Use the Web and/or print media to learn more about businesses that have been affected negatively by the Internet. What effect has the Internet had? How can the business compete with the Internet? How has the Internet changed business in positive ways? Write a brief report or use PowerPoint to create a presentation and share your findings with your class.

CASE STUDY 5 — Team Challenge Mr. Steve Sandberg is vice president of operations for a major luxury hotel chain. He and three of his associates want to start a new chain of discount hotels called Sleepy Hollow. They have made a plan that includes opening hotels initially in Chicago, St. Louis, Denver, and Houston. They plan to offer comfortable rooms, high-speed Internet access, and continental breakfast. Besides offering reservations over the telephone, they want to develop a Web site that will allow customers to negotiate a nightly rate as their check-in time approaches. Form a three-member team and assist Mr. Sandberg in evaluating existing major hotel Web sites by listing the advantages and disadvantages of each. Assign each member the task of evaluating three of the following hotel chains: Marriot, Hilton, Holiday Inn, Ramada, Super 8, Motel 6, Days Inn, Fairfield Inn, and Radisson. Make sure every hotel chain listed is assigned to at least one team member. Have each member print the <u>home page</u> of the hotel chain he or she is assigned. In evaluating the Web sites, each member should pay particular attention to the following areas: (1) design of Web site, (2) ease of use, (3) reservations, (4) awards programs, (5) specials, (6) online Help, (7) about the hotel, and (8) contact the hotel. Meet with your team to share each member's findings and then write a final report or create a PowerPoint presentation that summarizes the team's conclusions and ranks the sites in terms of their effectiveness.

Special Feature

Making Use of the Web

Awealth of information is available on the World Wide Web. The riches are yours if you know where to find this material. Locating useful Web sites may be profitable for your educational and professional careers, as the resources may help you research class assignments and make your life more fulfilling and manageable.

Because the World Wide Web does not have an organizational structure to assist you in locating reliable material, you need additional resources to guide you in searching. To help you find useful Web sites, this Special Feature describes specific information about a variety of Web pages, and it includes tables of Web addresses, so you can get started. The material is organized in several areas of interest.

AREAS OF INTEREST	
Fun and Entertainment	Learning
Travel	Science
Finance	Environment
Resources	Health
Blogs	Research
Government	Careers
Shopping and Auctions	Arts and Literature
Weather, Sports, and News	

Web Exercises at the end of each category will reinforce the material and help you discover Web sites that may add a treasure trove of knowledge to your life.

Fun and Entertainment
THAT'S ENTERTAINMENT

Rock 'n' Roll on the Web

Consumers place great significance on buying entertainment products for fun and recreation. Nearly 10 percent of the United States's economy is spent on attending concerts and buying DVDs, CDs, reading materials, sporting goods, and toys.

Many Web sites supplement our cravings for fun and entertainment. For example, you can see and hear the musicians inducted into the Rock and Roll Hall of Fame and Museum (Figure 1). If you need an update on your favorite reality-based television program or a preview of an upcoming movie, E! Online and Entertainment Tonight provide the latest features on television and movie stars. The Internet Movie Database contains credits and reviews of more than 60,000 titles.

Watch the surfers riding the waves in Hawaii and romp with pandas at the San Diego Zoo. Web cams, which are video cameras that display their output on Web pages, take armchair travelers across the world for views of natural attractions, historical monuments, colleges, and cities. Many Web sites featuring Web cams are listed in the table in Figure 2.

FUN AND ENTERTAINMENT WEB SITES

Web Cams	URL
AfriCam Virtual Game Reserve	africam.com
Discovery Channel Cams	dsc.discovery.com/cams/cams.html
EarthCam — Webcam Network	earthcam.com
Iowa State Insect Zoo Live Camera	zoocam.ent.iastate.edu
Panda Cam San Diego Zoo	sandiegozoo.org/zoo/ex_panda_station.html
The Automated Astrophysical Site-Testing Observatory (AASTO) (South Pole)	www.phys.unsw.edu.au/southpolediaries/webcam.html
CamVista.com	camvista.com
Wild Birds Unlimited Bird FeederCam	wbu.com/feedercam_home.htm
Surfrider Surf Report	surfrider.org/earth.asp
WorldLIVE	worldlive.cz/en/webcams
Entertainment	**URL**
AMG All Music Guide	allmusic.com
E! Online	eonline.com
ETonline	et.tv.yahoo.com
Entertainment Weekly's EW.com	ew.com/ew
MSN Entertainment	entertainment.msn.com
Old Time Radio (OTR) — Radio Days: A Soundbite History	otr.com
Rock and Roll Hall of Fame and Museum	rockhall.com
The Internet Movie Database (IMDb)	imdb.com
World Radio Network (WRN)	wrn.org

For more information about fun and entertainment Web sites, visit scsite.com/dc2007/ch2/web.

FIGURE 1 Visitors exploring the Rock and Roll Hall of Fame and Museum Web site will find history, exhibitions, programs, and the names and particulars of the latest inductees.

FIGURE 2 When you visit Web sites offering fun and entertainment resources, you can be both amused and informed.

FUN AND ENTERTAINMENT WEB EXERCISES

1 Visit the WorldLIVE site listed in Figure 2. View two of the Web cams closest to your hometown, and describe the scenes. Then, visit the Discovery Channel Cams Web site and view two of the animal cams in the Featured Cams. What do you observe? Visit another Web site listed in Figure 2 and describe the view. What are the benefits of having Web cams at these locations throughout the world?

2 What are your favorite movies? Use The Internet Movie Database Web site listed in Figure 2 to search for information about two of these films, and write a brief description of the biographies of the major stars and director for each movie. Then, visit one of the entertainment Web sites and describe three of the featured stories. At the Rock and Roll Hall of Fame and Museum Web site, view the information about Elvis and one of your favorite musicians. Write a paragraph describing the information available about these rock stars.

Travel
GET PACKING!

Explore the World without Leaving Home

When you are ready to arrange your next travel adventure or just want to explore destination possibilities, the Internet provides ample resources to set your plans in motion.

To discover exactly where your destination is on this planet, cartography Web sites, including MapQuest (Figure 3), Maps.com, and Rand McNally, allow you to pinpoint your destination. View your exact destination using satellite imagery with Google Earth and MSN Virtual Earth.

Some good starting places are general travel Web sites such as Expedia Travel, Cheap Tickets, and Travelocity, which is owned by the electronic booking service travel agents use. These all-encompassing Web sites, including those in Figure 4, have tools to help you find the lowest prices and details on flights, car rentals, cruises, and hotels.

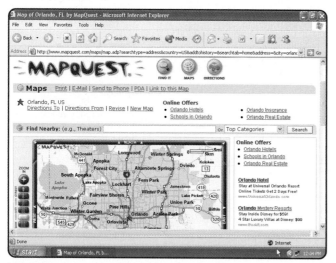

FIGURE 3 MapQuest provides directions, traffic reports, maps, and more.

TRAVEL WEB SITES

General Travel	URL
Cheap Tickets	cheaptickets.com
Expedia Travel	expedia.com
Orbitz	orbitz.com
Travelocity	travelocity.com
Cartography	**URL**
Google Maps	maps.google.com
MapQuest	mapquest.com
Maps.com	maps.com
MSN Virtual Earth	virtualearth.com
Rand McNally	randmcnally.com
Travel and City Guides	**URL**
World's Largest Cities	greatestcities.com
Frommers.com	frommers.com
For more information about travel Web sites, visit scsite.com/dc2007/ch2/web.	

FIGURE 4 These travel resources Web sites offer travel information to exciting destinations throughout the world.

TRAVEL WEB EXERCISES

1 Visit one of the cartography Web sites listed in Figure 4 and obtain the directions from your campus to one of these destinations: the White House in Washington, D.C.; Elvis's home in Memphis, Tennessee; Walt Disney World in Orlando, Florida; or the Grand Old Opry in Nashville, Tennessee. How many miles is it to your destination? What is the estimated driving time? Use Google Maps or MSN Virtual Earth to view an actual satellite photograph of your destination. Then, visit one of the general travel Web sites listed in the table and plan a flight from the nearest major airport to one of the four destinations for the week after finals and a return trip one week later. What is the lowest economy coach fare for this round-trip flight? What airline, flight numbers, and departure and arrival times did you select?

2 Visit one of the travel and city guides Web sites listed in Figure 4, and choose a destination for a getaway this coming weekend. Write a one-page paper giving details about this location, such as popular hotels and lodging, expected weather, population, local colleges and universities, parks and recreation, ancient and modern history, and tours. Include a map or satellite photograph of this place. Why did you select this destination? How would you travel there and back? What is the breakdown of expected costs for this weekend, including travel expenditures, meals, lodging, and tickets to events and activities? What URLs did you use to complete this exercise?

Finance
MONEY MATTERS

Cashing In on Financial Advice

You can manage your money with advice from financial Web sites that offer online banking, tax help, personal finance, and small business and commercial services.

If you do not have a personal banker or a financial planner, consider a Web adviser to guide your investment decisions. The Motley Fool (Figure 5) provides commentary and education on investing strategies, financial news, and taxes.

If you are ready to ride the ups and downs of the NASDAQ and the Dow, an abundance of Web sites listed in Figure 6, including Reuters and Morningstar.com, can help you pick companies that fit your interests and financial needs.

Claiming to be the fastest, easiest tax publication on the planet, the Internal Revenue Service Web site contains procedures for filing tax appeals and contains IRS forms, publications, and legal regulations.

FIGURE 5 The Motley Fool Web site contains strategies and news stories related to personal financing and investing.

FINANCE WEB SITES

Advice and Education	URL
Bankrate.com	bankrate.com
LendingTree	lendingtree.com
Loan.com	loan.com
MSN Money	moneycentral.msn.com
The Motley Fool	fool.com
Wells Fargo	wellsfargo.com
Yahoo! Finance	finance.yahoo.com
Stock Market	**URL**
E*TRADE Financial	us.etrade.com
Financial Engines	financialengines.com
Reuters	www.investor.reuters.com
Harris*direct*	harrisdirect.com
Merrill Lynch Direct	mldirect.ml.com
Morningstar.com	morningstar.com
The Vanguard Group	vanguard.com
Taxes	**URL**
H&R Block	hrblock.com
Internal Revenue Service	irs.gov

For more information about finance Web sites, visit scsite.com/ dc2007/ch2/web.

FIGURE 6 Financial resources Web sites offer general information, stock market analyses, and tax advice, as well as guidance and money-saving tips.

FINANCE WEB EXERCISES

1 Visit three advice and education Web sites listed in Figure 6 and read their top business world reports. Write a paragraph about each, summarizing these stories. Which stocks or mutual funds do these Web sites predict as being sound investments today? What are the current market indexes for the DJIA (Dow Jones Industrial Average), S&P 500, and NASDAQ, and how do these figures compare with the previous day's numbers?

2 Using two of the stock market Web sites listed in Figure 6, search for information about Microsoft, Adobe Systems, and one other software vendor. Write a paragraph about each of these stocks describing the revenues, net incomes, total assets for the previous year, current stock price per share, highest and lowest prices of each stock during the past year, and other relevant investment information.

Resources
LOOK IT UP

Web Resources Ease Computer Concerns

From dictionaries and encyclopedias to online technical support, the Web is filled with a plethora of resources to answer your computer questions.

Keep up with the latest developments by viewing online dictionaries and encyclopedias that add to their collections of computer and product terms on a regular basis. Shopping for a new computer can be a daunting experience, but many online guides, including PCWorld.com (Figure 7), can help you select the components that best fit your needs and budget.

If you are not confident in your ability to solve a problem alone, turn to online technical support. Web sites, such as those shown in Figure 8, often provide streaming how-to video lessons, tutorials, and real-time chats with experienced technicians. Hardware and software reviews, price comparisons, shareware, technical questions and answers, and breaking technology news are found on comprehensive portals.

FIGURE 7 Buying and upgrading a computer is simplified with helpful Web sites such as PCWorld.com.

RESOURCES WEB SITES

Dictionaries and Encyclopedias	URL
CDT's Guide to Online Privacy	cdt.org/privacy/guide/terms
ComputerUser High-Tech Dictionary	computeruser.com/resources/dictionary
TechWeb: The Business Technology Network	www.techweb.com/encyclopedia
Webopedia: Online Computer Dictionary for Computer and Internet Terms and Definitions	webopedia.com
whatis?com	whatis.com

Computer Shopping Guides	URL
A Computer Guide: Reviews on Software and Hardware	acomputerguide.com/www/
The CPU Scorecard	cpuscorecard.com
The Online Computer Buying Guide	grohol.com/computers
TechBargains.com	techbargains.com
Tom's Hardware Guide	tomshardware.com
Viewz Desktop Computer Buying Guide	viewz.com/shoppingguide/compbuy.shtml
ZDNet Shopper	shopper-zdnet.com.com

Upgrading Guides	URL
CNET Shopper.com	shopper.cnet.com
eHow	ehow.com
Focus on Macs	macs.about.com
PCWorld.com	pcworld.com/howto
Upgrade Source	upgradesource.com

Online Technical Support	URL
Dux Computer Digest	duxcw.com
MSN Tech & Gadgets	computingcentral.msn.com
PC911	pcnineoneone.com
PC Pitstop	pcpitstop.com

Technical and Consumer Information	URL
CNET.com	cnet.com
CompInfo — The Computer Information Center	www.compinfo-center.com
NewsHub	newshub.com
PC Today	pctoday.com
Wired News	wirednews.com
ZDNet	zdnet.com

For more information about resources Web sites, visit scsite.com/dc2007/ch2/web.

FIGURE 8 A variety of Web resources can provide information about buying, repairing, and upgrading computers.

RESOURCES WEB EXERCISES

1 Visit the dictionaries and encyclopedias Web sites listed in Figure 8. Search these resources for five terms. Create a table with two columns: one for the cyberterm and one for the Web definition. Then, create a second table listing five recently added or updated words and their definitions on these Web sites. Next, visit two of the listed computer shopping guides Web sites to choose the components you would buy if you were building a customized desktop computer and notebook computer. Create a table for both computers, listing the computer manufacturer, processor model name or number and manufacturer, clock speed, RAM, cache, number of expansion slots, and number of bays.

2 Visit three upgrading guides Web sites listed in Figure 8. Write a paragraph describing available advice for buying a motherboard. Describe the strengths and weaknesses of these Web sites, focusing on such criteria as clarity of instructions, thoroughness, and ease of navigation. Would you use these Web sites as a resource to troubleshoot computer problems? Then, view two technical and consumer information Web sites listed in the table and write a paragraph about each one, describing the top two news stories of the day.

Blogs
EXPRESS YOURSELF

Blogosphere Growing Swiftly

Internet users are feeling the need to publish their views, and they are finding Weblogs, or blogs for short, the ideal vehicle. The blogosphere began as an easy way for individuals to express their opinions on the Web. Today, this communication vehicle has become a powerful tool, for individuals, groups, and corporations are using blogs to promote their ideas and advertise their products.

Bloggers generally update their Web sites frequently to reflect their views. Their posts range from a paragraph to an entire essay and often contain links to other Web sites. The more popular blogs discuss politics, lifestyles, and technology.

Corporate blogs, such as The GM FastLane Blog (Figure 9), discuss all aspects of the company's products, whereas all-encompassing blogs, such as the Metafilter Community Weblog and others in Figure 10, are designed to keep general readers entertained and informed.

Blogs are affecting the manner in which people communicate, and some experts predict they will one day become our primary method of sharing information.

BLOGS WEB SITES

BLOG	URL
A List Apart	alistapart.com
Bloglines Top Links	bloglines.com/toplinks
Boing Boing: A Directory of Wonderful Things	boingboing.net
Davenetics* Politics + Media + Musings	davenetics.com
Geek News Central	geeknewscentral.com
GM FastLane Blog	fastlane.gmblogs.com
kottke.org: home of fine hypertext products	kottke.org
Metafilter Community Weblog	metafilter.com
Scripting News	scripting.com

For more information about blogs Web sites, visit scsite.com/dc2007/ch2/web.

FIGURE 10 These blogs offer information about technology, news, politics, and entertainment.

BLOGS WEB EXERCISES

1 Visit one of the blog Web sites listed in Figure 10 that provides lists of the more popular blogs. Select three links from the lists and visit the specific blogs. Make a table listing the blog name, its purpose, the author, its audience, and advertisers, if any, who sponsor the blog.

2 Many Internet users read the technology blogs to keep abreast of the latest developments. Visit two technology blogs listed in Figure 10 and write a paragraph describing the top story in each blog. Read the posted comments, if any. Then, write another paragraph describing two other stories found on these blogs that cover material you have discussed in this course. Write a third paragraph discussing which one is more interesting to you. Would you add reading blogs to your list of Internet activities? Why or why not?

FIGURE 9 General Motors' executives share their insights by posting to the GM FastLane Blog.

Government
STAMP OF APPROVAL

Making a Federal Case for Useful Information

When it is time to buy stamps to mail your correspondence, you no longer need to wait in long lines at your local post office. The U.S. Postal Service has authorized several corporations to sell stamps online.

You can recognize U.S. Government Web sites on the Internet by their .gov top-level domain abbreviation. For example, The Library of Congress Web site is lcweb.loc.gov, as shown in Figure 11. Government and military Web sites offer a wide range of information, and some of the more popular sites are listed in Figure 12. The Time Service Department Web site will provide you with the correct time. If you are looking for a federal document, FedWorld lists thousands of documents distributed by the government on its Web site. For access to the names of your congressional representatives, visit the extensive Hieros Gamos Web site.

GOVERNMENT RESOURCES WEB SITES

Postage	URL
Endicia	endicia.com
Pitney Bowes	pb.com
Stamps.com	stamps.com

Government	URL
FedWorld	www.fedworld.gov
Hieros Gamos — Law and Legal Research Center	hg.org
NARA — United States National Archives and Records Administration	archives.gov
National Agricultural Library	nal.usda.gov
The Library of Congress	lcweb.loc.gov
THOMAS Legislative Information	thomas.loc.gov
Time Service Department	tycho.usno.navy.mil
United States Department of Education	ed.gov
United States Department of the Treasury	www.treas.gov
United States Government Printing Office	www.access.gpo.gov
United States National Library of Medicine	nlm.nih.gov
United States Patent and Trademark Office	www.uspto.gov
USAJOBS	usajobs.opm.gov
White House	whitehouse.gov

For more information about government Web sites, visit scsite.com/dc2007/ch2/web.

FIGURE 12 These Web sites offer information about buying U.S.-approved postage online and researching federal agencies.

FIGURE 11 The Library of Congress Web site contains more than 119 million items written in 470 languages.

GOVERNMENT WEB EXERCISES

1. View the three postage Web sites listed in Figure 12. Compare and contrast the available services on each one. Consider postage cost, necessary equipment, shipping services, security techniques, and tracking capability. Explain why you would or would not like to use this service.

2. Visit the Hieros Gamos Web site listed in Figure 12. What are the names, addresses, and telephone numbers of your two state senators and your local congressional representative? On what committees do they serve? Who is the chief justice of the Supreme Court, and what has been this justice's opinion on two recently decided cases? Who are the members of the president's cabinet? Then, visit two other Web sites listed in Figure 12. Write a paragraph about each Web site describing its content and features.

Shopping and Auctions
BARGAINS GALORE

Let Your Mouse Do Your Shopping

From groceries to clothing to computers, you can buy just about everything you need with just a few clicks of your mouse. Electronic retailers (e-tailers) are cashing in on cybershoppers' purchases. Books, computer software and hardware, and music are the hottest commodities.

The two categories of Internet shopping Web sites are those with physical counterparts, such as Wal-Mart and Best Buy, and those with only a Web presence, such as Amazon.com. Popular Web shopping sites are listed in Figure 13.

Another method of shopping for the items you need, and maybe some you really do not need, is to visit auction Web sites, including those listed in Figure 13. Categories include antiques and collectibles, automotive, computers, electronics, music, sports, sports cards and memorabilia,

and toys. Online auction Web sites can offer unusual items, including *Star Wars* props and memorabilia and a round of golf with Tiger Woods. eBay (Figure 14) is one of thousands of Internet auction Web sites and is the world's largest personal online trading community.

FIGURE 14 eBay is one of the world's more popular auction Web sites.

SHOPPING AND AUCTIONS WEB SITES

Auctions	URL
eBay®	ebay.com
MusicHotBid	musichotbid.com
Sothebys	sothebys.com
Yahoo! Shopping Auctions	auctions.yahoo.com
Books and Music	**URL**
Amazon.com	amazon.com
Barnes & Noble.com	bn.com
Tower Records	towerrecords.com
Computers and Electronics	**URL**
Crutchfield	crutchfield.com
BestBuy	bestbuy.com
Buy.com	buy.com
Miscellaneous	**URL**
drugstore.com	drugstore.com
Froogle	froogle.com
Sharper Image	sharperimage.com
Walmart.com	walmart.com

For more information about shopping and auctions Web sites, visit scsite.com/dc2007/ch2/web.

FIGURE 13 Making online purchases can help ease the burden of driving to and fighting the crowds in local malls.

SHOPPING AND AUCTIONS WEB EXERCISES

1 Visit two of the computers and electronics and two of the miscellaneous Web sites listed in Figure 14. Write a paragraph describing the features these Web sites offer compared with the same offerings from stores. In another paragraph, describe any disadvantages of shopping at these Web sites instead of actually visiting a store. Then, describe their policies for returning unwanted merchandise and for handling complaints.

2 Using one of the auction Web sites listed in Figure 14, search for two objects pertaining to your hobbies. For example, if you are a baseball fan, you can search for a complete set of Topps cards. If you are a car buff, search for your dream car. Describe these two items. How many people have bid on these items? Who are the sellers? What are the opening and current bids?

Weather, Sports, and News
WHAT'S NEWS?

Weather, Sports, and News Web Sites Score Big Hits

Rain or sun? Hot or cold? Weather is the leading online news item, with at least 10,000 Web sites devoted to this field. More than 20 million people view The Weather Channel Web site (Figure 15) each month.

Baseball may be the national pastime, but sports aficionados yearn for everything from auto racing to cricket. The Internet has more than one million pages of multimedia sports news, entertainment, and merchandise.

The Internet has emerged as a major source for news, with one-third of Americans going online at least once a week and 15 percent going online daily for reports of major news events. Many of these viewers are using Really Simple Syndication (RSS) technology to be notified when new stories about their favorite topics are available on the Internet. Popular weather, sports, and news Web sites are listed in Figure 16.

FIGURE 15 Local, national, and international weather conditions and details about breaking weather stories are available on The Weather Channel Web pages.

WEATHER, SPORTS, AND NEWS WEB SITES

Weather	URL
Infoplease Weather	infoplease.com/weather.html
Intellicast.com	intellicast.com
National Weather Service	www.crh.noaa.gov
STORMFAX	stormfax.com
The Weather Channel	weather.com
WX.com	wx.com

Sports	URL
CBS SportsLine.com	cbs.sportsline.com
ESPN.com	espn.com
NCAAsports.com	ncaasports.com
OFFICIAL WEBSITE OF THE OLYMPIC MOVEMENT	olympic.org
SIRC — A World of Sport Information	sirc.ca
Sporting News Radio	radio.sportingnews.com

News	URL
MSNBC	msnbc.com
NYPOST.COM	nypost.com
onlinenewspapers.com	onlinenewspapers.com
Privacy.org	privacy.org
SiliconValley.com	siliconvalley.com
Starting Page Best News Sites	startingpage.com/html/news.html
USATODAY.com	usatoday.com
washingtonpost.com	washingtonpost.com

For more information about weather, sports, and news Web sites, visit scsite.com/dc2007/ch2/web.

FIGURE 16 Keep informed about the latest weather, sports, and news events with these Web sites.

WEATHER, SPORTS, AND NEWS EXERCISES

 Visit two of the sports Web sites in the table and write a paragraph describing the content these Web sites provide concerning your favorite sport. Visit Google.com and then search for stories about this sport team or athlete. Then, create a customized news page with stories about your sports interests. Include RSS feeds to get regularly updated summaries on this subject.

Visit the onlinenewspapers.com and Starting Page Best News Sites Web sites listed in Figure 16 and select two newspapers from each site. Write a paragraph describing the top national news story featured in each of these four Web pages. Then, write another paragraph describing the top international news story displayed at each Web site. In the third paragraph, discuss which of the four Web sites is the most interesting in terms of story selection, photographs, and Web page design.

Learning
YEARN TO LEARN

Discover New Worlds Online

While you may believe your education ends when you finally graduate from college, learning is a lifelong process. For example, enhancing your culinary skills can be a rewarding endeavor. No matter if you are a gourmet chef or a weekend cook, you will be cooking in style with the help of online resources, including those listed in Figure 17.

LEARNING WEB SITES

Cooking	URL
Betty Crocker	bettycrocker.com
recipecenter.com	recipecenter.com
Internet	**URL**
Learn the Net	learnthenet.com
Search Engine Watch	searchenginewatch.com
Wiredguide	wiredguide.com
Technology and Science	**URL**
HowStuffWorks	howstuffworks.com
ScienceMaster	sciencemaster.com
General Learning	**URL**
Bartleby.com: Great Books Online	bartleby.com
Blue Web'n	www.kn.pacbell.com/wired/bluewebn
MSN Encarta	encarta.msn.com

For more information about learning Web sites, visit scsite.com/dc2007/ch2/web.

FIGURE 17 The information gleaned from these Web sites can help you learn about many aspects of our existence.

If you would rather sit in front of the computer than stand in front of the stove, you can increase your technological knowledge by visiting several Web sites with tutorials on building your own Web sites, the latest news about the Internet, and resources for visually impaired users.

Have you ever wondered how the Global Positioning System (GPS) works? Take a look at the ScienceMaster site to find details. You might be interested in finding out about how your car's catalytic converter reduces pollution or how the Electoral College functions. Marshall Brain's HowStuffWorks Web site (Figure 18) is filled with articles and animations.

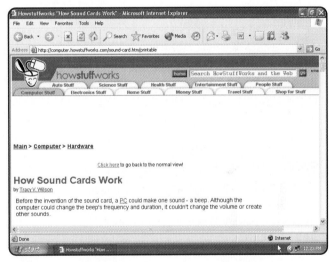

FIGURE 18 The HowStuffWorks Web site provides easy-to-understand information about technology and other facets of our lives.

LEARNING WEB EXERCISES

1 Visit one of the cooking Web sites listed in Figure 17 and find two recipes or cooking tips that you can use when preparing your next meal. Write a paragraph about each one, summarizing your discoveries. What are the advantages and disadvantages of accessing these Web sites on the new Web appliances that might someday be in your kitchen?

2 Using one of the technology and science Web sites and one of the other Web sites listed in Figure 17, search for information about communications and networks. Write a paragraph about your findings. Then, review the material in the general learning Web sites listed in Figure 18, and write a paragraph describing the content on each Web site that is pertinent to your major.

Science
$$E = MC^2$$

Rocket Science on the Web

For some people, space exploration is a hobby. Building and launching model rockets allow these scientists to participate in exploring the great frontier of space. For others, space exploration is their life. Numerous Web sites, including those in Figure 19, provide in-depth information about the universe.

SCIENCE WEB SITES

Periodicals	URL
Astronomy.com	astronomy.com
Archaeology Magazine	archaeology.org
NewScientist.com	newscientist.com
OceanLink	oceanlink.island.net
Science Magazine	sciencemag.org
Scientific American.com	sciam.com
Resources	**URL**
National Science Foundation (NSF)	nsf.gov
Science.gov: FirstGov for Science	science.gov
SOFWeb	www.sofweb.vic.edu.au
Science Community	**URL**
American Scientist, The Magazine of Sigma Xi, The Scientific Research Society	amsci.org
Federation of American Scientists	fas.org
NASA	www.nasa.gov
Sigma Xi, The Scientific Research Society	sigmaxi.org

For more information about science Web sites, visit scsite.com/dc2007/ch2/web.

FIGURE 19 Resources available on the Internet offer a wide range of subjects for enthusiasts who want to delve into familiar and unknown territories in the world of science.

NASA's Astronaut Flight Lounge Web site contains information about rockets, the space shuttle, the International Space Station, space transportation, and communications. Other science resources explore space-related questions about astronomy, physics, the earth sciences, microgravity, and robotics.

Rockets and space are not the only areas to explore in the world of science. Where can you find the latest pictures taken with the Hubble Space Telescope? Do you know which cities experienced an earthquake today? Have you ever wondered what a 3-D model of the amino acid glutamine looks like? You can find the answers to these questions and many others through the Librarians' Internet Index (lii.org) shown in Figure 20.

FIGURE 20 Numerous science resources are organized clearly in the Librarians' Internet Index.

SCIENCE WEB EXERCISES

1. Visit the NASA Web site listed in the table in Figure 19. View the links about spacecraft, the universe, or tracking satellites and spacecraft, and then write a summary of your findings.

2. Visit the Librarians' Internet Index shown in Figure 20. Click the Science, Computers, & Technology link and then click the Inventions topic. View the Web site for the Greatest Engineering Achievements of the Twentieth Century. Pick two achievements, read their history, and write a paragraph summarizing each of these accomplishments. Then, view two of the science Web sites listed in Figure 19 and write a paragraph about each of these Web sites describing the information each contains.

Environment
THE FATE OF THE ENVIRONMENT

Protecting the Planet's Ecosystem

From the rain forests of Africa to the marine life in the Pacific Ocean, the fragile ecosystem is under extreme stress. Many environmental groups have developed Internet sites, including those listed in Figure 21, in attempts to educate worldwide populations and to increase resource conservation.

ENVIRONMENT WEB SITES

NAME	URL
Central African Regional Program for the Environment (CARPE)	carpe.umd.edu
Earthjustice	www.earthjustice.org
EarthTrends: The Environmental Information Portal	earthtrends.wri.org
Environmental Defense	edf.org
Environmental Sites on the Internet	www.ima.kth.se/im/envsite/envsite.htm
EPA AirData — Access to Air Pollution Data	epa.gov/air/data
Global Environmental Resources	rochesterenvironment.com/global_resources.htm
GreenNet	www.gn.apc.org
New American Dream	newdream.org
The Virtual Library of Ecology & Biodiversity	conbio.org/vl
USGS Acid rain data and reports	bqs.usgs.gov/acidrain
UWM Environmental Health, Safety & Risk Management	www.uwm.edu/Dept/EHSRM/EHSLINKS

For more information about environment Web sites, visit scsite.com/dc2007/ch2/web.

FIGURE 21 Environment Web sites provide vast resources for ecological data and action groups.

On an international scale, the Environmental Sites on the Internet Web page developed by the Royal Institute of Technology in Stockholm, Sweden, has been rated as one of the better ecological Web sites. Its comprehensive listing of environmental concerns range from aquatic ecology to wetlands.

The U.S. federal government has a number of Web sites devoted to specific environmental concerns. For example, the U.S. Environmental Protection Agency (EPA) provides pollution data, including ozone levels and air pollutants, for specific areas. Its AirData Web site, shown in Figure 22, displays air pollution emissions and monitoring data from the entire United States and is the world's most extensive collection of air pollution data.

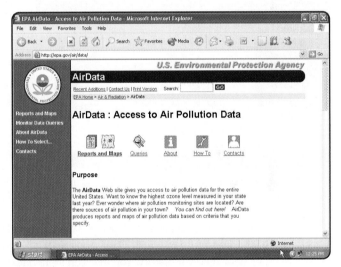

FIGURE 22 A visit to the EPA AirData Web site, with its extensive database, can assist you in checking your community's ozone and air pollutant levels.

ENVIRONMENT WEB EXERCISES

1 The New American Dream Web site encourages consumers to reduce the amount of junk mail sent to their homes. Using the table in Figure 21, visit the Web site and write a paragraph stating how many trees are leveled each year to provide paper for these mailings, how many garbage trucks are needed to haul this waste, and other statistics. Read the letters that you can use to eliminate your name from bulk mail lists. To whom would you mail these letters? How long does it take to stop these unsolicited letters?

2 Visit the EPA AirData Web site. What is the highest ozone level recorded in your state this past year? Where are the nearest air pollution monitoring Web sites, and what are their levels? Where are the nearest sources of air pollution? Read two reports about two different topics, such as acid rain and air quality, and summarize their findings. Include information about who sponsored the research, who conducted the studies, when the data was collected, and the impact of this pollution on the atmosphere, water, forests, and human health. Whom would you contact for further information regarding the data and studies?

Health
NO PAIN, ALL GAIN

Store Personal Health Records Online

More than 70 million consumers use the Internet yearly to search for health information, so using the Web to store personal medical data is a natural extension of the Internet's capabilities. Internet health services and portals are available online to store your personal health history, including prescriptions, lab test results, doctor visits, allergies, and immunizations. Web sites such as WebMD (Figure 23) are free to consumers.

FIGURE 23 You can store health records for you and your family in the WebMD database.

In minutes, you can register with a health Web site by choosing a user name and password. Then, you create a record to enter your medical history. You also can store data for your emergency contacts, primary care physicians,

specialists, blood type, cholesterol levels, blood pressure, and insurance plan. No matter where you are in the world, you and medical personnel can obtain records via the Internet or fax machine. Some popular online health database management systems are shown in Figure 24.

HEALTH WEB SITES

Medical History	URL
Aetna InteliHealth	intelihealth.com
GlobalMedic	globalmedic.com
PersonalMD	personalmd.com
WebMD Health	my.webmd.com/my_health_record

General Health	URL
Centers for Disease Control and Prevention	www.cdc.gov/
familydoctor.org	familydoctor.org
healthfinder	www.healthfinder.gov
Medical Library Association Consumer and Patient Health Information Section (CAPHIS)	caphis.mlanet.org/consumer
MedlinePlus	medlineplus.gov
PE Central	pecentral.org/websites/healthsites.html
www.health.gov	health.gov

For more information about health Web sites, visit scsite.com/dc2007/ch2/web.

FIGURE 24 These health Web sites allow you to organize your medical information and store it in an online database and also obtain information about a variety of medical conditions and treatments.

HEALTH WEB EXERCISES

1 Access one of the health Web sites listed in Figure 24. Register yourself or a family member, and then enter the full health history. Create an emergency medical card if the Web site provides the card option. Submit this record and emergency card to your instructor.

2 Visit three of the health Web sites listed in Figure 24. Describe the features of each. Which of the three is the most user-friendly? Why? Describe the privacy policies of these three Web sites. Submit your analysis of these Web sites to your instructor.

Research
SEARCH AND YE SHALL FIND

Info on the Web

A 2004 Web Usability survey conducted by the Nielsen Norman Group found that 88 percent of people log onto a computer and then use a search engine as their first action. Search engines require users to type words and phrases that characterize the information being sought. Yahoo! (Figure 25), Google, and AltaVista are some of the more popular search engines. The key to effective searching on the Web is composing search queries that narrow the search results and place the most relevant Web sites at the top of the results list.

Subject directories are collections of related Web sites. Yahoo! and LookSmart have two of the more comprehensive subject directories on the Web. Their organized lists often are called trees because a few main categories, such as Entertainment, Computing, Lifestyle, and Work, branch out to more specific subtopics. Popular subject directories and search engines are listed in Figure 26.

RESEARCH WEB SITES

Search Engines	URL
A9.com	a9.com
AlltheWeb	alltheweb.com
AOL Search	search.aol.com
Gigablast	gigablast.com
HotBot	hotbot.com
Internet Archive Wayback Machine	archive.org
Overture	overture.com
WebCrawler	webcrawler.com
Subject Directories and Search Engines	**URL**
Alta Vista	altavista.com
Ask Jeeves	askjeeves.com
Excite	excite.com
Google	google.com
MSN Search	search.msn.com
Yahoo!	yahoo.com

For more information about research Web sites, visit scsite.com/ dc2007/ch2/web.

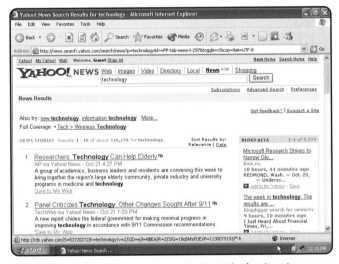

FIGURE 25 The Yahoo! News search results for the phrase, technology, lists more than 116,000 stories.

FIGURE 26 Web users can find information by using search engines and subject directories.

RESEARCH WEB EXERCISES

1 Use two of the search engines listed in Figure 26 to find three Web sites that review the latest digital cameras from Sony and Kodak. Make a table listing the search engines, Web site names, and the cameras' model numbers, suggested retail price, megapixels, memory, and features.

2 If money were no object, virtually everyone would have an exquisite car. On the other hand, drivers need a practical vehicle to drive around town daily. Use one of the subject directories listed in Figure 26 to research your dream car and another directory to research your practical car. Write a paragraph about each car describing the particular subject directory tree you used, the manufacturer's suggested retail price (MSRP) of the car, standard and optional equipment, engine size, miles per gallon, and safety features. Visit the Internet Archive Wayback Machine Web site to obtain information about previous models of this vehicle.

Careers
IN SEARCH OF THE PERFECT JOB

Web Helps Career Hunt

While your teachers give you valuable training to prepare you for a career, they rarely teach you how to begin that career. You can broaden your horizons by searching the Internet for career information and job openings.

First, examine some of the job search Web sites. These resources list thousands of openings in hundreds of fields, companies, and locations. For example, the Monster Web site, shown in Figure 27, allows you to choose a broad job area, narrow your search to specific fields within that area, and then search for specific salary ranges, locations, and job functions.

When a company contacts you for an interview, learn as much about it and the industry as possible before the interview. Many of the Web sites listed in Figure 28 include detailed company profiles and links to their corporate Web sites.

FIGURE 27 Monster's global online network connects companies with career-minded individuals.

CAREER WEB SITES

Job Search	URL
BestJobsUSA.com	bestjobsusa.com
CareerBuilder	careerbuilder.com
CareerNet	careernet.com
College Grad Job Hunter	collegegrad.com
Cytiva	careerexchange.com
EmploymentGuide.com	employmentguide.com
Job.com	job.com
JobBankUSA.com	jobbankusa.com
JobWeb.com	www.jobweb.com
Monster	monster.com
Spherion	spherion.com
USAJOBS	usajobs.opm.gov
VolunteerMatch	volunteermatch.org
Yahoo!.HotJobs.com	hotjobs.com
Company/Industry Information	**URL**
Career ResourceCenter.com	resourcecenter.com
Forbes.com	forbes.com/careers
FORTUNE	fortune.com
Hoover's	hoovers.com
Occupational Outlook Handbook	stats.bls.gov/oco

For more information about career Web sites, visit scsite.com/dc2007/ch2/web.

FIGURE 28 Career Web sites provide a variety of job openings and information about major companies worldwide.

CAREERS WEB EXERCISES

1 Use two of the job search Web sites listed in Figure 28 to find three companies with job openings in your field. Make a table listing the Web site name, position available, description, salary, location, desired education, and desired experience.

2 It is a good idea to acquire information before graduation about the industry in which you would like to work. Are you interested in the automotive manufacturing industry, the restaurant service industry, or the financial industry? Use two of the company/industry information Web sites listed in Figure 28 to research a particular career related to your major. Write a paragraph naming the Web sites and the specific information you found, such as the nature of the work, recommended training and qualifications, employment outlook, and earnings. Then, use two other Web sites to profile three companies with positions available in this field. Write a paragraph about each of these companies, describing the headquarters' location, sales and earnings for the previous year, total number of employees, working conditions, perks, and competitors.

Arts and Literature
FIND SOME CULTURE

Get Ready to Read, Paint, and Dance

Brush up your knowledge of Shakespeare, grab a canvas, and put on your dancing shoes. Visual arts and literature Web sites, including those in Figure 29, are about to sweep you off your cyberfeet.

ARTS AND LITERATURE WEB SITES

Arts	URL
Access Place Arts	accessplace.com/arts.htm
Art News — absolutearts.com	absolutearts.com
GalleryGuide.com	galleryguide.com
Louvre Museum	louvre.fr
Montreal Museum of Fine Arts	mmfa.qc.ca
The Children's Museum of Indianapolis	childrensmuseum.org
The Getty	getty.edu
The New York Times: Arts	nytimes.com/pages/arts/index.html
Virtual Library museums pages (VLmp)	vlmp.museophile.com
Literature	**URL**
Bartleby.com	bartleby.com
Bibliomania	bibliomania.com
Electronic Literature Directory	directory.wordcircuits.com
Fantastic Fiction	fantasticfiction.co.uk
Project Gutenberg	promo.net/pg
shakespeare.com	shakespeare.com
The Modern Library eBook List	randomhouse.com/modernlibrary/ebookslist.html

For more information about arts and literature Web sites, visit scsite.com/dc2007/ch2/web.

FIGURE 29 Discover culture throughout the world by visiting these arts and literature Web sites.

The full text of hundreds of books is available online from the Bibliomania and Project Gutenberg Web sites. Shakespeare.com provides in-depth reviews and news of the world's most famous playwright and his works. The Bartleby.com Web site features biographies, definitions, quotations, dictionaries, and indexes.

When you are ready to absorb more culture, you can turn to various art Web sites. Many museums have images of their collections online. Among them are the Getty Museum in Los Angeles (Figure 30), the Montreal Museum of Fine Arts, and the Louvre Museum in Paris.

Access Place Arts and The New York Times Web sites focus on the arts and humanities and provide fascinating glimpses into the worlds of dance, music, performance, cinema, and other topics pertaining to creative expression.

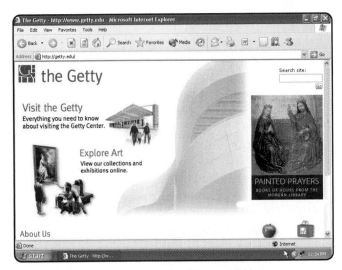

FIGURE 30 Permanent and temporary exhibitions, educational activities, and a bookstore are featured on the Getty Museum Web site.

ARTS AND LITERATURE WEB EXERCISES

 Visit The Modern Library eBook List Web site listed in Figure 29 and view one book in the 20th CENTURY NOVELS, 19th CENTURY NOVELS, BRITISH LITERATURE, and HISTORY sections. Create a table with columns for the book name, author, cost, online store, local store, and description. Then, read the excerpt from each of the four books and write a paragraph describing which of these four books is the most interesting to you. What are the advantages and disadvantages of reading classic literature electronically?

2 Using the arts Web sites listed in Figure 29, search for three temporary exhibitions in galleries throughout the world. Describe the venues, the artists, and the works. What permanent collections are found in these museums? Some people shop for gifts in the museums' stores. View and describe three items for sale.

CHAPTER THREE

Application Software

Picture Yourself Using Software

As your biology instructor reviews for the upcoming test, you use note taking software and a digital pen to mark important points in your electronic notes. Then, you write "Professor Jenson said that this is going to be on the test." At the end of class, you start the appointment calendar software in your PDA and record the date of the test.

Later that day, when you open your e-mail program to check messages, you see a message from a friend asking what he missed in biology class. You type a reply to his message, attach a copy of your electronic lecture notes to the message, and then click the Send button.

Time to start composing your philosophy paper about Socrates. You use the research feature of your word processing program to learn about this ancient Greek philosopher and then write the paper — being sure to cite all sources. While writing the paper, your personal finance software alerts you that it is time to download transaction information from the bank's computer to your computer. With this service, your computerized checkbook balance always is up-to-date. Ready for a break, you fire up the train simulator program and experience the thrill of driving a train.

Read Chapter 3 to learn more about note taking software, PDA application software, e-mail programs, word processing software, personal finance software, and entertainment software, and discover many other types of application software.

After completing this chapter, you will be able to:

1. Identify the categories of application software

2. Explain ways software is distributed

3. Explain how to work with application software

4. Identify the key features of widely used business programs

5. Identify the key features of widely used graphics and multimedia programs

6. Identify the key features of widely used home, personal, and educational programs

7. Identify the types of application software used in communications

8. Describe the function of several utility programs

9. Discuss the advantages of using application software on the Web

10. Describe the learning aids available for application software

CONTENTS

APPLICATION SOFTWARE

With the proper software, a computer is a valuable tool. Software allows users to create letters, memos, reports, and other documents; design Web pages and diagrams; draw and alter images; record and enhance audio and video clips; prepare and file taxes; play single player or multiplayer games; compose e-mail messages and instant messages; and much more. To accomplish these and many other tasks, users work with application software. **Application software** consists of programs designed to make users more productive and/or assist them with personal tasks. Application software has a variety of uses:

1. To make business activities more efficient
2. To assist with graphics and multimedia projects
3. To support home, personal, and educational tasks
4. To facilitate communications

The table in Figure 3-1 categorizes popular types of application software by their general use. Although many types of communications software exist, the ones listed in Figure 3-1 are application software oriented. Utility programs, which are not a category of application software, are widely used to manage and protect computer resources. Successful use of application software generally requires the use of one or more of the utility programs identified in Figure 3-1.

As you become familiar with application software, it is likely you will use software from more than one of the categories in Figure 3-1. The four categories are not mutually exclusive. Software listed in one category may be used in other categories. For example, e-mail and Web browser programs, which are categorized as communications software, often are used for business or personal reasons.

Application software is available in a variety of forms: packaged, custom, open source, shareware, freeware, and public domain.

- **Packaged software** is mass-produced, copyrighted retail software that meets the needs of a wide variety of users, not just a single user or company. Word processing and spreadsheet software are examples of packaged software. Packaged software is available in retail stores or on the Web.

CATEGORIES OF APPLICATION SOFTWARE

① Business	② Graphics and Multimedia	③ Home/Personal/Educational
• Word Processing • Spreadsheet • Database • Presentation Graphics • Note Taking • Personal Information Manager (PIM) • PDA Business Software • Software Suite (e.g., word processing, spreadsheet, presentation graphics, PIM) • Project Management • Accounting • Document Management • Enterprise Computing Software	• Computer-Aided Design (CAD) • Desktop Publishing (for the Professional) • Paint/Image Editing (for the Professional) • Photo Editing (for the Professional) • Video and Audio Editing (for the Professional) • Multimedia Authoring • Web Page Authoring	• Software Suite (for Personal Use) (e.g., word processing, spreadsheet, database) • Personal Finance • Legal • Tax Preparation • Desktop Publishing (for Personal Use) • Paint/Image Editing (for Personal Use) • Photo Editing • Clip Art/Image Gallery • Video and Audio Editing (for Personal Use) • Home Design/Landscaping • Reference • Educational • Entertainment

④ ← **Communications** →

• E-Mail • Newsgroup/Message Board	• FTP • Chat Room	• Web Browser • Instant Messaging	• Video Conferencing/Telephone Calls • Blogging

← **Popular Utility Programs** →

• Antivirus • File Compression	• Personal Firewall • Backup	• Spyware Remover • CD/DVD Burning	• Internet Filters • Personal Computer Maintenance	• File Manager

FIGURE 3-1 The four major categories of popular application software are outlined in this table. Communications software often is bundled with other application or system software. Also identified in the table are widely used utility programs.

- **Custom software** performs functions specific to a business or industry. Sometimes a company cannot find packaged software that meets its unique requirements. In this case, the company may use programmers to develop tailor-made custom software, which usually costs more than packaged software.

- **Open source software** is software provided for use, modification, and redistribution. This software has no restrictions from the copyright holder regarding modification of the software's internal instructions and redistribution of the software. Open source software usually can be downloaded from the Internet, sometimes at no cost.

- **Shareware** is copyrighted software that is distributed at no cost for a trial period. To use a shareware program beyond that period, you send payment to the program developer. Shareware developers trust users to send payment if software use extends beyond the stated trial period. In some cases, a scaled-down version of the software is distributed free, and payment entitles the user to the fully functional product.

- **Freeware** is copyrighted software provided at no cost by an individual or a company that retains all rights to the software. Thus, programmers typically cannot incorporate freeware in applications they intend to sell. The word, free, in freeware indicates the software has no charge.

- **Public-domain software** has been donated for public use and has no copyright restrictions. Anyone can copy or distribute public-domain software to others at no cost.

Thousands of shareware, freeware, and public-domain programs are available on the Internet for users to download. Examples include communications programs, graphics programs, and games. These programs usually have fewer capabilities than retail programs.

After you purchase or download software, you install it. During installation, the program may ask you to register and/or activate the software. Registering the software is optional and usually involves submitting your name and other personal information to the software manufacturer or developer. Registering the software often entitles you to product support. *Product activation* is a technique that some software manufacturers use to ensure the software is not installed on more computers than legally licensed. Usually, the software does not function or has limited functionality until you activate it via the Internet or telephone. Thus, activation is a required process for programs requesting it.

The Role of System Software

System software serves as the interface between the user, the application software, and the computer's hardware (Figure 3-2). To use application software, such as a word processing program, your computer must be running system software — specifically, an operating system. Three popular personal computer operating systems are Windows XP, Linux, and Mac OS X.

Each time you start a computer, the operating system is *loaded* (copied) from the computer's hard disk into memory. Once the operating system is loaded, it coordinates all the activities of the computer. This includes starting application software and transferring data among input and output devices and memory. While the computer is running, the operating system remains in memory.

Application Software

System Software

FIGURE 3-2 A user does not communicate directly with the computer hardware. Instead, system software is the interface between the user, the application software, and the hardware. For example, when a user instructs the application software to print, the application software sends the print instruction to the system software, which in turn sends the print instruction to the hardware.

Working with Application Software

To use application software, you must instruct the operating system to start the program. The steps in Figure 3-3 illustrate how to start and interact with the Paint program. The following paragraphs explain the steps in Figure 3-3.

Personal computer operating systems often use the concept of a desktop to make the computer easier to use. The **desktop** is an on-screen work area that has a graphical user interface (Read Looking Ahead 3-1 for a look at the next generation of user interfaces). Step 1 of Figure 3-3 shows icons, a button, and a pointer on the Windows XP desktop. An **icon** is a small image displayed on the screen that represents a program, a document, or some other object. A **button** is a graphical element that you activate to cause a specific action to take place. One way to activate a button is to click it. To **click** a button on the screen requires moving the pointer to the button and then pressing and releasing a button on the mouse (usually the left mouse button). The **pointer** is a small symbol displayed on the screen that moves as you move the mouse. Common pointer shapes are an I-beam (I), a block arrow ($\lessgtr$), and a pointing hand ($\textcircled{\uparrow}$).

The Windows XP desktop contains a Start button on the lower-left corner of the taskbar.

FIGURE 3-3   HOW TO START AN APPLICATION

Step 1:
When you turn on a PC-compatible computer, Windows XP loads into memory and displays the desktop on the screen.

Step 2:
Click the Start button on the Windows taskbar, point to All Programs on the Start menu, point to Accessories on the All Programs submenu, and then point to Paint on the Accessories submenu.

Step 3:
Click Paint. The Paint window is displayed on the desktop.

Step 4:
Instruct the Paint program to open a file that is stored on the hard disk.

Step 5:
Instruct the Paint program to print the picture. When the Print dialog box is displayed, click the Print button.

When you click the Start button, the Start menu is displayed on the desktop. A **menu** contains a list of commands from which you make selections. A **command** is an instruction that causes a program to perform a specific action.

The arrowhead symbol at the right edge of some menu commands indicates a submenu of additional commands is available. A *submenu* is a menu that is displayed when you point to a command on a previous menu. As illustrated in Step 2 of Figure 3-3, when you click the Start button and point to the All Programs command on the Start menu, the All Programs submenu is displayed. Pointing to the Accessories command on the All Programs submenu displays the Accessories submenu.

To start a program, you can click its program name on a menu or submenu. This action instructs the operating system to start the application, which means the program's instructions load from a storage medium (such as a hard disk) into memory. For example, when you click Paint on the Accessories submenu, Windows loads the Paint program instructions from the computer's hard disk into memory.

Once loaded into memory, the program is displayed in a window on the desktop (Step 3 of Figure 3-3). A **window** is a rectangular area of the screen that displays data and information. The top of a window has a **title bar**, which is a horizontal space that contains the window's name.

With the program loaded, you can create a new file or open an existing one. A *file* is a named collection of stored data, instructions, or information. A file can contain text, images, audio, and video. To distinguish among various files, each file has a file name. A *file name* is a unique combination of letters of the alphabet, numbers, and other characters that identifies a file. The title bar of the document window usually displays a document's file name. Step 4 of Figure 3-3 shows the contents of the file, Horseback Riding, displaying in the Paint window. The file contains an image photographed with a digital camera.

In some cases, when you instruct a program to perform an activity such as printing, the program displays a dialog box. A *dialog box* is a window that provides information, presents available options, or requests a response. Dialog boxes, such as the one shown in Step 5 of Figure 3-3, often contain option buttons, text boxes, check boxes, and command buttons. Clicking the Print button in the dialog box instructs the computer to print the picture.

Test your knowledge of pages 134 through 137 in Quiz Yourself 3-1.

FAQ 3-1

Will a document print like it looks on a screen?

Yes, because most application software is *WYSIWYG* (*what you see is what you get*). The software embeds invisible codes around the text and graphics, which instructs the computer how to present the information. For more information, visit scsite.com/dc2007/ch3/faq and then click WYSIWYG.

QUIZ YOURSELF 3-1

Instructions: Find the true statement below. Then, rewrite the remaining false statements so they are true.

1. Application software is used to make business activities more efficient; assist with graphics and multimedia projects; support home, personal, and educational tasks; and facilitate communications.

2. Public-domain software is mass-produced, copyrighted retail software that meets the needs of a wide variety of users, not just a single user or company.

3. To use system software, your computer must be running application software.

4. When an application is started, the program's instructions load from memory into a storage medium.

Quiz Yourself Online: To further check your knowledge of application software categories, ways software is distributed, and working with application software, visit scsite.com/dc2007/ch3/quiz and then click Objectives 1 – 3.

LOOKING AHEAD 3-1

User Interfaces of the Future

Most computers today use a graphical user interface. Next-generation user interfaces will be more natural and human-centric, meaning they will enable people to interact with a computer using human-like communication methods. Developments in this area include gesture recognition, 3-D interfaces, and neural interfaces.

With gesture recognition, the computer will detect human motions. Computers with this type of user interface will have the capability of recognizing sign language, reading lips, tracking facial movements, and following eye gazes.

Imagine rotating a window or object to read its flipside, switching from a desktop view to a panoramic view, or tacking sticky notes right on a Web screen. All these scenarios will be possible with the upcoming 3-D user interfaces.

Neural interfaces may help quadriplegic people gain independence with everyday activities, such as maneuvering wheelchairs and typing. These systems use a tiny chip with sensors implanted on the brain and external computers that convert brainwaves into output signals the person can control. For more information, visit scsite.com/dc2007/ch3/looking and then click User Interfaces.

BUSINESS SOFTWARE

Business software is application software that assists people in becoming more effective and efficient while performing their daily business activities. Business software includes programs such as word processing, spreadsheet, database, presentation graphics, note taking, personal information manager software, PDA business software, software suites, project management, accounting, document management, and enterprise computing software. Figure 3-4 lists popular programs for each of these categories.

The following sections discuss the features and functions of business software. Word processing and spreadsheet software have a heavier emphasis because of their predominant use.

Word Processing Software

Word processing software is one of the more widely used types of application software. **Word processing software**, sometimes called a *word processor*, allows users to create and manipulate documents containing mostly text and sometimes graphics (Figure 3-5). Millions of people use word processing software every day to develop documents such as letters, memos, reports, fax cover sheets, mailing labels, newsletters, and Web pages.

Word processing software has many features to make documents look professional and visually appealing. Some of these features include the capability of changing the shape and size of characters, changing the color of characters, and organizing text in newspaper-style columns. When using colors for characters, however, they will print as black or gray unless you have a color printer.

Most word processing software allows users to incorporate many types of graphical images in documents. One popular type of graphical image is clip art. **Clip art** is a collection of

POPULAR BUSINESS PROGRAMS

Application Software	Manufacturer	Program Name
Word Processing	Microsoft	Word
	Sun	StarOffice Writer
	Corel	WordPerfect
Spreadsheet	Microsoft	Excel
	Sun	StarOffice Calc
	Corel	Quattro Pro
Database	Microsoft	Access
	Sun	StarOffice Base
	Corel	Paradox
	Microsoft	Visual FoxPro
	Oracle	Oracle Database
	MySQL AB	MySQL
Presentation Graphics	Microsoft	PowerPoint
	Sun	StarOffice Impress
	Corel	Presentations
Note Taking	Microsoft	OneNote
	Agilix	GoBinder
	Corel	Grafigo
Personal Information Manager (PIM)	Microsoft	Outlook
	IBM	Lotus Organizer
	Palm	Desktop
PDA Business Software	CNetX	Pocket SlideShow
	Microsoft	Pocket Word Pocket Excel Pocket Outlook
	PalmOne	VersaMail
	Ultrasoft	Money

Application Software	Manufacturer	Program Name
Software Suite (for the Professional)	Microsoft	Office Office for Mac
	Sun	StarOffice Office Suite
	Corel	WordPerfect Office
	IBM	Lotus SmartSuite
Project Management	Microsoft	Project
	Primavera	SureTrak Project Manager
Accounting	Intuit	QuickBooks
	Sage Software	Peachtree Accounting
Document Management	Adobe	Acrobat
	Enfocus	PitStop
	ScanSoft	PDF Converter PaperPort
Enterprise Computing Software	Oracle	PeopleSoft Enterprise Human Resources
	Best Software	Sage MAS 500
	MSC Software	MSC.SimManager
	Oracle	Oracle Manufacturing
	SAP	mySAP Customer Relationship Management
	NetSuite	NetERP
	Apropos Technology	Apropos Enterprise Edition

FIGURE 3-4   Popular business software.

drawings, diagrams, maps, and photographs that you can insert in documents. In Figure 3-5, a user inserted a clip art image of an alarm clock in the document. Word processing software usually includes public-domain clip art. You can find additional public-domain and proprietary images on the Web or purchase them on CD or DVD.

All word processing software provides at least some basic capabilities to help users create and modify documents. Defining the size of the paper on which to print and specifying the *margins* — that is, the portion of the page outside the main body of text, including the top, the bottom, and both sides of the paper — are examples of some of these capabilities. If you type text that extends beyond the right page margin, the word processing software automatically positions text at the beginning of the next line. This feature, called *wordwrap*, allows users to type words in a paragraph continually without pressing the ENTER key at the end of each line. When you modify paper size or margins, the word processing software automatically rewraps text so it fits in the adjusted paper size and margins.

As you type more lines of text than can be displayed on the screen, the top portion of the document moves upward, or scrolls, off the screen. *Scrolling* is the process of moving different portions of the document on the screen into view.

A major advantage of using word processing software is that users easily can change what they have written. For example, a user can insert, delete, or rearrange words, sentences, paragraphs, or entire sections. The find, or *search*, feature allows you to locate all occurrences of a certain character, word, or phrase. This feature, in combination with the *replace* feature, allows you to substitute existing characters or words with new ones.

Word processing software includes a *spelling checker*, which reviews the spelling of individual words, sections of a document, or the entire document. The spelling checker compares the words in the document with an electronic dictionary that is part of the word processing software. You can customize the

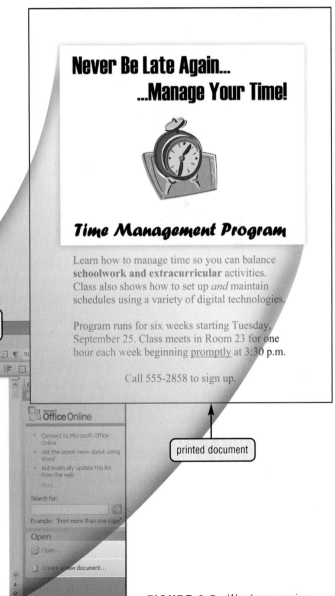

FIGURE 3-5 Word processing software enables users to create professional and visually appealing documents.

WEB LINK 3-1

Word Processing Software

For more information, visit scsite.com/dc2007/ch3/weblink and then click Word Processing Software.

electronic dictionary by adding words such as companies, streets, cities, and personal names, so the software can check the spelling of those words too.

Another benefit of word processing software is the capability to insert headers and footers in a document. A *header* is text that appears at the top of each page, and a *footer* is text that appears at the bottom of each page. Page numbers, company names, report titles, and dates are examples of items often included in headers and footers.

In addition to these basic capabilities, most current word processing programs provide numerous additional features, which are listed in the table in Figure 3-6.

ADDITIONAL WORD PROCESSING FEATURES

AutoCorrect	As you type words, the AutoCorrect feature corrects common spelling errors. AutoCorrect also corrects capitalization mistakes.
AutoFormat	As you type, the AutoFormat feature automatically applies formatting to the text. For example, it automatically numbers a list or converts a Web address to a hyperlink.
Collaboration	Collaboration includes discussions and online meetings. Discussions allow multiple users to enter comments in a document and read and reply to each other's comments. Through an online meeting, users share documents with others in real time and view changes as they are being made.
Columns	Most word processing software can arrange text in two or more columns to look like a newspaper or magazine. The text from the bottom of one column automatically flows to the top of the next column.
Grammar Checker	The grammar checker proofreads documents for grammar, writing style, sentence structure errors, and reading statistics.
Ink Input	Supports input from a digital pen. Word processing software that supports ink input incorporates user's handwritten text and drawings in a word processing document. Ink input is popular on Tablet PCs.
Macros	A *macro* is a sequence of keystrokes and instructions that a user records and saves. When you want to execute the same series of instructions, execute the macro instead.
Mail Merge	Creates form letters, mailing labels, and envelopes.
Reading Layout	For those users who prefer reading on the screen, reading layout increases the readability and legibility of an on-screen document by hiding unnecessary toolbars, increasing the size of displayed characters, and providing navigation tools.
Research	Some word processing software allows you to search through various forms of online and Internet reference information — based on selected text in a document. Research services available include a thesaurus, English and bilingual dictionaries, encyclopedias, and Web sites that provide information such as stock quotes, news articles, and company profiles.
Smart Tags	*Smart tags* automatically appear on the screen when you perform a certain action. For example, typing an address causes a smart tag to appear. Clicking this smart tag provides options to display a map of the address or driving directions to or from the address.
Tables	Tables organize information into rows and columns. In addition to evenly spaced rows and columns, some word processing programs allow you to draw tables of any size or shape.
Templates	A *template* is a document that contains the formatting necessary for a specific document type. Templates usually exist for memos, fax cover sheets, and letters. In addition to templates provided with the software, users have access to many online templates through the manufacturer's Web site.
Thesaurus	With a thesaurus, a user looks up a synonym (word with the same meaning) for a word in a document.
Tracking Changes	If multiple users work with a document, the word processing software highlights or color-codes changes made by various users.
Voice Recognition	With some word processing programs, users can speak into the computer's microphone and watch the spoken words appear on the screen as they talk. With these programs, users edit and format the document by speaking or spelling an instruction.
Web Page Development	Most word processing software allows users to create, edit, format, and convert documents to be displayed on the World Wide Web.

FIGURE 3-6   Many additional features are included with word processing software.

Developing a Document

With application software, such as word processing, users create, edit, format, save, and print documents. During the process of developing a document, users likely will switch back and forth among all of these activities.

When you **create** a document, you enter text or numbers, insert graphical images, and perform other tasks using an input device such as a keyboard, mouse, microphone, or digital pen. If you are using Microsoft Word to design an announcement, for example, you are creating a document.

To **edit** a document means to make changes to its existing content. Common editing tasks include inserting, deleting, cutting, copying, and pasting. Inserting text involves adding text to a document. Deleting text means that you are removing text or other content. Cutting is the process of removing a portion of the document and storing it in a temporary storage location, sometimes called a *clipboard*. A clipboard also contains items that you copy (duplicate) in a document. *Pasting* is the process of transferring an item from a clipboard to a specific location in a document. Read Ethics & Issues 3-1 for a related discussion.

When users **format** a document, they change its appearance. Formatting is important because the overall look of a document significantly can affect its ability to communicate clearly. Examples of formatting tasks are changing the font, font size, or font style of text.

A **font** is a name assigned to a specific design of characters. Two basic types of fonts are serif and sans serif. A *serif font* has short decorative lines at the upper and lower ends of the characters. Sans means without. Thus, a *sans serif font* does not have the short decorative lines at the upper and lower ends of the characters. Times New Roman is an example of a serif font. Arial is an example of a sans serif font.

Font size indicates the size of the characters in a particular font. Font size is gauged by a measurement system called points. A single *point* is about 1/72 of an inch in height. The text you are reading in this book is about 10 point. Thus, each character is about 5/36 (10/72) of an inch in height. A *font style* adds emphasis to a font. Bold, italic, and underline are examples of font styles. Figure 3-7 illustrates fonts, font sizes, and font styles.

ETHICS & ISSUES 3-1

How Should Schools Deal with Internet Plagiarism?

A high school teacher failed 28 students for plagiarizing, or copying, material from the Internet. When parents complained, the school board passed the students, and the teacher resigned. Plagiarism is not new, but word processing software and the Internet make it easier than ever. Students can use term paper Web sites to copy complete papers on a variety of topics. According to one survey, half of those who responded said that cheating does not or may not matter in the long run. Students who plagiarize blame peer pressure, classroom competition, the "busy work" nature of some assignments, and the permissive attitude that pervades the Internet. Teachers have several tools to catch plagiarists, including a variety of Internet-based services that compare suspected papers to papers found on the Internet and produce an originality report highlighting text that may have been copied. Some instructors, however, are reluctant to investigate the integrity of a student's work and possibly ruin an academic career, but more and more schools require instructors to do such checking using paid services to check papers. How should educators deal with plagiarism? Should a school's response to plagiarism depend on such factors as the material copied, the assignment for which it was copied, or the reason it was copied? Why or why not?

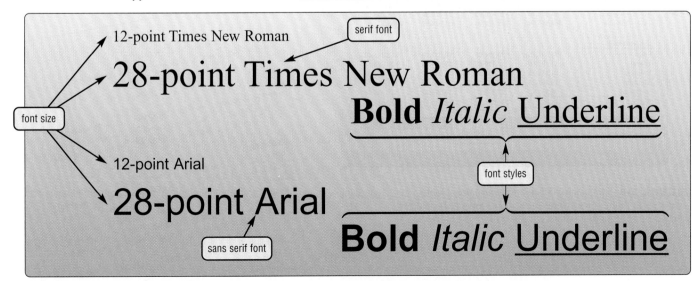

FIGURE 3-7   The Times New Roman and Arial fonts are shown in two font sizes and a variety of font styles.

During the process of creating, editing, and formatting a document, the computer holds it in memory. To keep the document for future use requires that you save it. When you **save** a document, the computer transfers the document from memory to a storage medium such as a USB flash drive, hard disk, or CD. Once saved, a document is stored permanently as a file on the storage medium.

When you **print** a document, the computer places the contents of the document on paper or some other medium. One of the benefits of word processing software is the ability to print the same document many times, with each copy looking just like the first. Instead of printing a document and physically distributing it, some users e-mail the document to others on a network such as the Internet.

Spreadsheet Software

Spreadsheet software is another widely used type of application software. **Spreadsheet software** allows users to organize data in rows and columns and perform calculations on the data. These rows and columns collectively are called a *worksheet*. For years, people used paper to organize data and perform calculations by hand. In an electronic worksheet, you organize data in the same manner, and the computer performs the calculations more quickly and accurately (Figure 3-8). Because of spreadsheet software's logical approach to organizing data, many people use this software to organize and present nonfinancial data, as well as financial data.

As with word processing software, most spreadsheet software has basic features to help users create, edit, and format worksheets. Spreadsheet software also incorporates many of the features found in word processing software such as macros, checking spelling, changing fonts and font sizes, adding colors, tracking changes, recognizing voice input, inserting audio and video clips, providing research capabilities, recognizing handwritten text and drawings, and creating Web pages from existing spreadsheet documents.

The following sections describe the features of most spreadsheet programs.

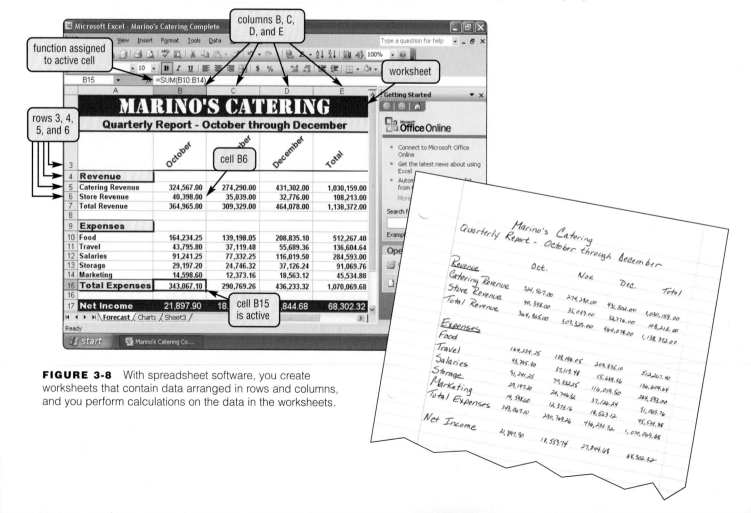

FIGURE 3-8   With spreadsheet software, you create worksheets that contain data arranged in rows and columns, and you perform calculations on the data in the worksheets.

SPREADSHEET ORGANIZATION A spreadsheet file is similar to a notebook with up to 255 related individual worksheets. Data is organized vertically in columns and horizontally in rows on each worksheet (Figure 3-8). Each worksheet typically has 256 columns and 65,536 rows. One or more letters identify each column, and a number identifies each row. The column letters begin with A and end with IV. The row numbers begin with 1 and end with 65,536. Only a small fraction of these columns and rows are displayed on the screen at one time. Scrolling through the worksheet displays different parts of it on the screen.

A *cell* is the intersection of a column and row. Each worksheet has more than 16 million (256 × 65,536) cells in which you can enter data. The spreadsheet software identifies cells by the column and row in which they are located. For example, the intersection of column B and row 6 is referred to as cell B6. As shown in Figure 3-8, cell B6 contains the number, 40,398.00, which represents the store revenue for October.

Cells may contain three types of data: labels, values, and formulas. The text, or *label*, entered in a cell identifies the worksheet data and helps organize the worksheet. Using descriptive labels, such as Total Revenue and Total Expenses, helps make a worksheet more meaningful.

CALCULATIONS Many of the worksheet cells shown in Figure 3-8 contain a number, called a *value*, that can be used in a calculation. Other cells, however, contain formulas that generate values. A *formula* performs calculations on the data in the worksheet and displays the resulting value in a cell, usually the cell containing the formula. When creating a worksheet, you can enter your own formulas.

In many spreadsheet programs, you begin a formula with an equal sign, a plus sign, or a minus sign. Next, you enter the formula, separating cell references (e.g., B10) with operators. Common operators are + for addition, − for subtraction, * for multiplication, and / for division. In Figure 3-8, for example, cell B15 could contain the formula =B10+B11+B12+B13+B14, which would add together (sum) the contents of cells B10, B11, B12, B13, and B14. That is, this formula calculates the total expenses for October. A more efficient way to sum the contents of cells, however, is to use a special type of formula, called a function.

A *function* is a predefined formula that performs common calculations such as adding the values in a group of cells or generating a value such as the time or date. For example, instead of using the formula =B10+B11+B12+B13+B14 to calculate the total expenses for October, you could use the SUM function. This function requires you to identify the starting cell and the ending cell in a group to be summed, separating these two cell references with a colon. For example, the function =SUM(B10:B14) instructs the spreadsheet program to add all of the numbers in cells B10 through B14. Figure 3-9 lists functions commonly included in spreadsheet programs.

SPREADSHEET FUNCTIONS

Financial	
FV (rate, number of periods, payment)	Calculates the future value of an investment
NPV (rate, range)	Calculates the net present value of an investment
PMT (rate, number of periods, present value)	Calculates the periodic payment for an annuity
PV (rate, number of periods, payment)	Calculates the present value of an investment
RATE (number of periods, payment, present value)	Calculates the periodic interest rate of an annuity
Date and Time	
DATE	Returns the current date
NOW	Returns the current date and time
TIME	Returns the current time
Mathematical	
ABS (number)	Returns the absolute value of a number
INT (number)	Rounds a number down to the nearest integer
LN (number)	Calculates the natural logarithm of a number
LOG (number, base)	Calculates the logarithm of a number to a specified base
ROUND (number, number of digits)	Rounds a number to a specified number of digits
SQRT (number)	Calculates the square root of a number
SUM (range)	Calculates the total of a range of numbers
Statistical	
AVERAGE (range)	Calculates the average value of a range of numbers
COUNT (range)	Counts how many cells in the range have numeric entries
MAX (range)	Returns the maximum value in a range
MIN (range)	Returns the minimum value in a range
STDEV (range)	Calculates the standard deviation of a range of numbers
Logical	
IF (logical test, value if true, value if false)	Performs a test and returns one value if the result of the test is true and another value if the result is false

FIGURE 3-9 Functions typically found in spreadsheet software.

RECALCULATION   One of the more powerful features of spreadsheet software is its capability of recalculating the rest of the worksheet when data in a worksheet changes. When you enter a new value to change data in a cell, any value affected by the change is updated automatically and instantaneously. In Figure 3-8 on page 142, for example, if you change the store revenue for October from 40,398.00 to 45,398.00, the total revenue in cell B7 automatically changes from 364,965.00 to 369,965.00.

Spreadsheet software's capability of recalculating data also makes it a valuable budgeting, forecasting, and decision making tool. Most spreadsheet software includes a *what-if analysis* feature, where you change certain values in a spreadsheet to reveal the effects of those changes.

CHARTING   Another standard feature of spreadsheet software is *charting*, which depicts the data in graphical form. A visual representation of data through charts often makes it easier for users to see at a glance the relationship among the numbers.

Three popular chart types are line charts, column charts, and pie charts. Figure 3-10 shows examples of these charts that were plotted from the data in Figure 3-8. A *line chart* shows a trend during a period of time, as indicated by a rising or falling line. For example, a line chart could show the total expenses for the three months. A *column chart*, also called a *bar chart*, displays bars of various lengths to show the relationship of data. The bars can be horizontal, vertical, or stacked on top of one another. For example, a column chart might show the total monthly expenses, with each bar representing a different category of expense. A *pie chart*, which has the shape of a round pie cut into slices, shows the relationship of parts to a whole. For example, you might use a pie chart to show the percentage each expense category contributed to the total expenses.

Charts, as well as any other part of a workbook, can be linked to or embedded in a word processing document.

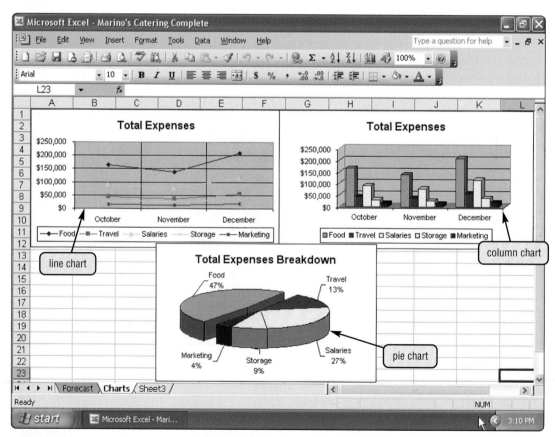

FIGURE 3-10   Three basic types of charts provided with spreadsheet software are line charts, column charts, and pie charts. The charts shown here were created from the data in the worksheet in Figure 3-8.

Database Software

A **database** is a collection of data organized in a manner that allows access, retrieval, and use of that data. In a manual database, you might record data on paper and store it in a filing cabinet. With a computerized database, such as the one shown in Figure 3-11, the computer stores the data in an electronic format on a storage medium such as a hard disk.

Database software is application software that allows users to create, access, and manage a database. Using database software, you can add, change, and delete data in a database; sort and retrieve data from the database; and create forms and reports using the data in the database.

With most popular personal computer database programs, a database consists of a collection of tables, organized in rows and columns. Each row, called a *record*, contains data about a given person, product, object, or event. Each column, called a *field*, contains a specific category of data within a record.

The Store database shown in Figure 3-11 consists of two tables: an Item table and a

Supplier table. The Item table contains ten records (rows), each storing data about one item. The item data is grouped into six fields (columns): Item Code, Description, On Hand, Cost, Selling Price, and Supplier Code. The On Hand field, for instance, contains the quantity on hand in inventory. The Item and Supplier tables relate to one another through a common field, Supplier Code.

Users run queries to retrieve data. A *query* is a request for specific data from the database. For example, a query might request products that are low on hand. Database software can take the results of a query and present it in a window on the screen or send it to the printer.

FAQ 3-3

How big is the largest database?

According to a recent survey, the world's largest database holds 29 trillion characters. In the next few years, the size of the largest database is expected to exceed 5 quadrillion characters. For more information, visit scsite.com/dc2007/ch3/faq and then click Enterprise Databases.

FIGURE 3-11 This database contains two tables: one for the items and one for the suppliers. The Item table has 10 records and 6 fields; the Supplier table has 4 records and 7 fields.

Presentation Graphics Software

Presentation graphics software is application software that allows users to create visual aids for presentations to communicate ideas, messages, and other information to a group. The presentations can be viewed as slides, sometimes called a *slide show*, that are displayed on a large monitor or on a projection screen (Figure 3-12).

Presentation graphics software typically provides a variety of predefined presentation formats that define complementary colors for backgrounds, text, and graphical accents on the slides. This software also provides a variety of layouts for each individual slide such as a title slide, a two-column slide, and a slide with clip art, a picture (Figure 3-13), a chart, a table, or animation. In addition, you can enhance any text, charts, and graphical images on a slide with 3-D and other special effects such as shading, shadows, and textures.

When building a presentation, users can set the slide timing so the presentation automatically displays the next slide after a preset delay. Presentation graphics software allows you to apply special effects to the transition between slides. One slide, for example, might fade away as the next slide is displayed.

To help organize the presentation, you can view thumbnail versions of all the slides in slide sorter view. *Slide sorter view* presents a screen view similar to how 35mm slides look on a photographer's light table. The slide sorter allows users to arrange the slides in any order.

Presentation graphics software typically includes a clip gallery that provides images, pictures, video clips, and audio clips to enhance multimedia presentations. Users with an artistic ability can create their own graphics using paint/image editing software (discussed later in the chapter) and then *import* (bring in) the graphics into the slide. Some audio and video editing programs, such as Producer, work with presentation graphics software, providing users with an easy means to record and insert video, music, and audio commentary in a presentation.

Presentation graphics software incorporates some of the features found in word processing software such as checking spelling, formatting, recognizing voice input, providing research capabilities, recognizing handwritten text and drawings, and creating Web pages from existing slide shows.

WEB LINK 3-3

Presentation Graphics Software

For more information, visit scsite.com/dc2007/ch3/weblink and then click Presentation Graphics Software.

FIGURE 3-12   This presentation created with presentation graphics software consists of five slides.

FIGURE 3-13 In presentation graphics software, users can change the design and layout of any slide in a presentation.

Note Taking Software

Note taking software is application software that enables users to enter typed text, handwritten comments, drawings, or sketches anywhere on a page and then save the page as part of a notebook (Figure 3-14). The software can convert handwritten comments to typed text or store the notes in handwritten form. Users also can include audio recordings as part of their notes.

Once the notes are captured (entered and saved), users easily can organize them, reuse them, and share them. This software allows users to search through saved notes for specific text. It even can search through an entire notebook. Users also can flag important notes with color, highlights, and shapes.

On a desktop or notebook computer, users enter notes primarily via the keyboard or microphone. On a Tablet PC, however, the primary input device is a digital pen. Users find note taking software convenient during meetings, class lectures, conferences, in libraries, and other settings that previously required a pencil and tablet of paper for recording thoughts and discussions.

Note taking software incorporates many of the features found in word processing software such as checking spelling, changing fonts and font sizes, adding colors, recognizing voice input, inserting audio and video clips, and providing research capabilities.

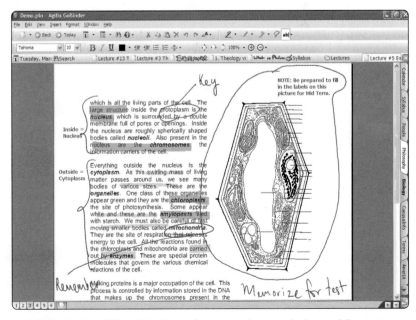

FIGURE 3-14 With note taking software, students and other mobile users can handwrite notes, draw sketches, and type text.

Personal Information Manager Software

A **personal information manager** (**PIM**) is application software that includes an appointment calendar, address book, notepad, and other features to help users organize personal information. With a PIM, you can take information previously tracked in a weekly or daily calendar, and organize and store it on your computer. The appointment calendar allows you to schedule activities for a particular day and time. With the address book, you can enter and maintain names, addresses, telephone numbers, and e-mail addresses of customers, coworkers, family members, and friends. You can use the notepad to record ideas, reminders, and other important information.

Most PDAs and many smart phones today include, among many other features, PIM functionality. Using a PDA or smart phone, you can synchronize, or coordinate, information so that both the PDA or smart phone and the computer have the latest version of the information. Some PDAs and smart phones synchronize with the computer wirelessly. With others, you connect the PDA or smart phone to the computer with a cable, or you insert the device in a cradle, which has a cable that plugs in the computer (Figure 3-15).

FIGURE 3-15 With most PDAs and smart phones, you can synchronize or transfer information from the device to a desktop computer, so the updated important information always is available.

PDA Business Software

In addition to PIM software, a huge variety of business software is available for PDAs. Although some PDAs have software built in, most have the capability of accessing software on miniature storage media such as memory cards. Business software for PDAs allows users to create documents and worksheets, manage databases and lists, create slide shows, take notes, manage budgets and finances, view and edit photographs, read electronic books, plan travel routes, compose and read e-mail messages, send instant messages, and browse the Web. For additional information about software for PDAs, read the Personal Mobile Devices feature that follows Chapter 5.

Software Suite

A **software suite** is a collection of individual programs sold as a single package. Business software suites typically include, at a minimum, the following programs: word processing, spreadsheet, e-mail, and presentation graphics. Two of the more widely used software suites are Microsoft Office and Sun StarOffice.

Software suites offer two major advantages: lower cost and ease of use. Buying a collection of programs in a software suite usually costs significantly less than purchasing them individually. Software suites provide ease of use because the programs in a software suite normally use a similar interface and share features such as clip art and spelling checker. For example, once you learn how to print using the software suite's word processing program, you can apply the same skill to the spreadsheet and presentation graphics programs in the software suite.

FAQ 3-4

What is the difference between Microsoft Office and Microsoft Office System?

Microsoft Office is a suite of core desktop business programs. Office is available in a variety of editions, each of which includes at least Word, Excel, and Outlook. *Microsoft Office System* is a portfolio of programs and services that are tightly integrated yet available for purchase as separate entities. In addition to Microsoft Office, other products in the Microsoft Office System include OneNote, InfoPath, Visio, FrontPage, and Project. For more information, visit scsite.com/dc2007/ch3/faq and then click Microsoft Office System.

Project Management Software

Project management software allows a user to plan, schedule, track, and analyze the events, resources, and costs of a project (Figure 3-16). Project management software helps users manage project variables, allowing them to complete a project on time and within budget. An engineer, for example, might use project management software to manage new product development to schedule product screening, market evaluation, technical product evaluation, and manufacturing processes.

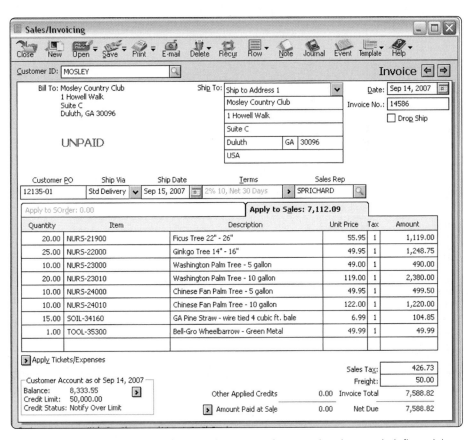

FIGURE 3-16 Project management software allows you to track, control, and manage the events, resources, and costs of a project.

Accounting Software

Accounting software helps companies record and report their financial transactions (Figure 3-17). With accounting software, business users perform accounting activities related to the general ledger, accounts receivable, accounts payable, purchasing, invoicing, and payroll functions. Accounting software also enables users to write and print checks, track checking account activity, and update and reconcile balances on demand.

Newer accounting software supports online credit checks, billing, direct deposit, and payroll services. Some accounting software offers more complex features such as job costing and estimating, time tracking, multiple company reporting, foreign currency reporting, and forecasting the amount of raw materials needed for products. The cost of accounting software for small businesses ranges from less than one hundred to several thousand dollars. Accounting software for large businesses can cost several hundred thousand dollars.

FIGURE 3-17 Accounting software helps companies record and report their financial transactions.

Document Management Software

Document management software provides a means for sharing, distributing, and searching through documents by converting them into a format that can be viewed by any user (Figure 3-18). The converted document, which mirrors the original document's appearance, can be viewed and printed without the software that created the original document. A popular file format used by document management software to save converted documents is *PDF* (Portable Document Format), developed by Adobe Systems. To view and print a PDF file, you need Acrobat Reader software, which can be downloaded free from Adobe's Web site.

Many businesses use document management software to share and distribute company brochures, literature, and other documents electronically. Home users distribute fliers, announcements, and graphics electronically. Some document management software allows users to edit and add comments to the converted document.

WEB LINK 3-4

Document Management Software

For more information, visit scsite.com/dc2007/ch3/weblink and then click Document Management Software.

FIGURE 3-18 Adobe Acrobat allows users to create and edit PDF files.

Enterprise Computing Software

A large organization, commonly referred to as an enterprise, requires special computing solutions because of its size and large geographic distribution. A typical enterprise consists of a wide variety of departments, centers, and divisions — collectively known as functional units. Nearly every enterprise has the following functional units: human resources, accounting and finance, engineering or product development, manufacturing, marketing, sales, distribution, customer service, and information technology. Each of these functional units has specialized software requirements, as outlined below.

- Human resources software manages employee information such as benefits, personal information, performance evaluations, training, and vacation time.
- Accounting software manages everyday transactions, such as sales and payments to suppliers. Financial software helps managers budget, forecast, and analyze.
  - Engineering or product development software allows engineers to develop plans for new products and test their product designs.
  - Manufacturing software assists in the assembly process, as well as in scheduling and managing the inventory of parts and products.
  - Marketing software allows marketing personnel to create marketing campaigns and track their effectiveness.
  - Sales software enables the sales force to manage contacts, schedule meetings, log customer interactions, manage product information, and take customer orders.
  - Distribution software analyzes and tracks inventory and manages product shipping status.
  - Customer service software manages the day-to-day interactions with customers, such as telephone calls, e-mail messages, Web interactions, and instant messaging sessions.
  - Information technology staff use a variety of software to maintain and secure the hardware and software in an enterprise.

GRAPHICS AND MULTIMEDIA SOFTWARE

In addition to business software, many people work with software designed specifically for their field of work. Power users such as engineers, architects, desktop publishers, and graphic artists often use sophisticated software that allows them to work with graphics and multimedia. This software includes computer-aided design, desktop publishing, paint/image editing, photo editing, video and audio editing, multimedia authoring, and Web page authoring. Figure 3-19 lists some popular programs in each of these categories, specifically designed for professional or more technically astute users. These programs often cost several hundred dollars or more. Many of these programs incorporate user-friendly interfaces and/or have scaled-down versions, making it possible for the home and small business users to create documents using these programs. The following sections discuss the features and functions of graphics and multimedia software.

POPULAR GRAPHICS AND MULTIMEDIA SOFTWARE

Application Software	Manufacturer	Program Name
Computer-Aided Design (CAD)	Autodesk	AutoCAD
	Quality Plans	Chief Architect
	Microsoft	Visio
Desktop Publishing (for the Professional)	Adobe	InDesign
	Corel	Ventura
	Quark	QuarkXPress
Paint/Image Editing (for the Professional)	Adobe	Illustrator
	Corel	Painter
	Macromedia	FreeHand
Photo Editing (for the Professional)	Adobe	Photoshop
	Extensis	Photo Imaging Suite
Video and Audio Editing (for the Professional)	Adobe	Audition
		Encore DVD
		Premiere Pro
	Cakewalk	SONAR
	Sony	ACID Pro
	Ulead	MediaStudio Pro
		DVD Workshop
Multimedia Authoring	SumTotal Systems	ToolBook Instructor
	Macromedia	Authorware
		Director
Web Page Authoring	Adobe	GoLive
	Lotus	FastSite
	Macromedia	Dreamweaver
		Fireworks
		Flash
	Microsoft	FrontPage

FIGURE 3-19 Popular graphics and multimedia programs — for the professional.

Computer-Aided Design

Computer-aided design (CAD) software is a sophisticated type of application software that assists a professional user in creating engineering, architectural, and scientific designs. For example, engineers create design plans for airplanes and security systems. Architects design building structures and floor plans (Figure 3-20). Scientists design drawings of molecular structures.

CAD software eliminates the laborious manual drafting that design processes can require. Three-dimensional CAD programs allow designers to rotate designs of 3-D objects to view them from any angle. Some CAD software even can generate material lists for building designs.

FIGURE 3-20 Architects use CAD software to create building designs.

Desktop Publishing Software (for the Professional)

Desktop publishing (DTP) software enables professional designers to create sophisticated documents that contain text, graphics, and many colors. Professional DTP software is ideal for the production of high-quality color documents such as textbooks, corporate newsletters, marketing literature (Figure 3-21), product catalogs, and annual reports. Today's DTP software allows designers to convert a color document into a format for use on the World Wide Web.

Although many word processing programs have some of the capabilities of DTP software, professional designers and graphic artists use DTP software because it supports page layout. *Page layout* is the process of arranging text and graphics in a document on a page-by-page basis. DTP software includes color libraries to assist in color selections for text and graphics. A *color library* is a standard set of colors used by designers and printers to ensure that colors will print exactly as specified. Designers and graphic artists can print finished publications on a color printer, take them to a professional printer, or post them on the Web.

Paint/Image Editing Software (for the Professional)

Graphic artists, multimedia professionals, technical illustrators, and desktop publishers use paint software and image editing software to create and modify graphical images such as those used in DTP documents and Web pages. **Paint software**, also called *illustration software*, allows users to draw pictures, shapes, and other graphical images with various on-screen tools such as a pen, brush, eyedropper, and paint bucket (Figure 3-22). **Image editing software** provides the capabilities of paint software and also includes the capability to enhance and modify existing images and pictures. Modifications can include adjusting or enhancing image colors, and adding special effects such as shadows and glows.

FIGURE 3-22   With paint software, artists can create and modify any type of graphical image.

Photo Editing Software (for the Professional)

Professional photo editing software is a type of image editing software that allows photographers, videographers, engineers, scientists, and other high-volume digital photo users to edit and customize digital photographs (Figure 3-23). Professional photo editing software allows users to save images in a wide variety of file formats. With professional photo editing software, users can retouch photos, crop images, remove red-eye, change image shapes, color-correct images, straighten images, remove or rearrange objects in a photo, and apply filters. Read Ethics & Issues 3-2 for a related discussion.

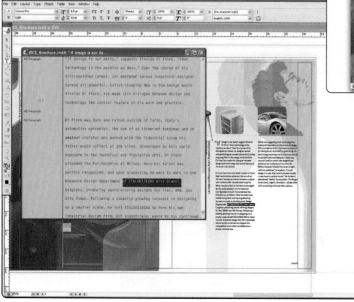

FIGURE 3-21   Professional designers and graphic artists use DTP software to produce sophisticated publications such as marketing literature.

FIGURE 3-23 With professional photo editing software, users can edit and customize digital photographs.

ETHICS & ISSUES 3-2

Altering Digital Photographs — Art or Fraud?

A *Los Angeles Times* photographer combined two digital photographs of the Iraq war, taken minutes apart, to create a single picture that appeared on the newspaper's front page. The photographer merged the photos to improve the composition, but when the source of the picture became known, the newspaper fired the photographer, citing a policy that forbids altering the content of news photos. Many commercial artists, photojournalists, and creators of cartoons, book covers, and billboards use photo editing software to alter photographs. With this software, an artist can convert photographs to a digital form that can be colorized, stretched, squeezed, texturized, or otherwise altered. The National Press Photographers Association, however, has expressed reservations about digital altering and endorses the following: "As [photo] journalists we believe the guiding principle of our profession is accuracy; therefore, we believe it is wrong to alter the content of a photograph in any way … that deceives the public." Yet, some insist that the extent to which a photo "deceives the public" is in the eye of the beholder. Is it ethical to alter digital photographs? Why or why not? Does the answer depend on the reason for the alteration, the extent of the alteration, or some other factor? If some alteration is accepted, can photographic integrity still be guaranteed? Why or why not?

Video and Audio Editing Software (for the Professional)

Video editing software (Figure 3-24) allows professionals to modify a segment of a video, called a clip. For example, users can reduce the length of a video clip, reorder a series of clips, or add special effects such as words that move horizontally across the screen.

Video editing software typically includes audio editing capabilities. **Audio editing software** lets users modify audio clips and produce studio-quality soundtracks. Audio editing software usually includes *filters*, which are designed to enhance audio quality. For example, a filter might remove a distracting background noise from the audio clip.

FIGURE 3-24 With video editing software, users modify video images.

Multimedia Authoring Software

Multimedia authoring software allows users to combine text, graphics, audio, video, and animation in an interactive application (Figure 3-25). With this software, users control the placement of text and images and the duration of sounds, video, and animation. Once created, multimedia presentations often take the form of interactive computer-based presentations or Web-based presentations designed to facilitate learning, demonstrate product functionality, and elicit direct-user participation. Training centers, educational institutions, and online magazine publishers all use multimedia authoring software to develop interactive applications. These applications may be available on a CD or DVD, over a local area network, or via the Internet.

FAQ 3-5

How do I know which program to buy?

Many companies offer downloadable *trial versions* of their software that allow you to use the software free for a limited time. Try a few. Read computer magazines and Web sites for reviews of various products. For more information, visit scsite.com/dc2007/ch3/faq and then click Trial Versions.

Web Page Authoring Software

Web page authoring software helps users of all skill levels create Web pages that include graphical images, video, audio, animation, and other special effects with interactive content (Figure 3-26). In addition, many Web page authoring programs allow users to organize, manage, and maintain Web sites.

Application software, such as Word and Excel, often includes Web page authoring features. This allows home users to create basic Web pages using application software they already own. For more sophisticated Web pages, users work with Web page authoring software. Many Web page developers also use multimedia authoring software along with, or instead of, Web page authoring software for Web page development.

FIGURE 3-25 Multimedia authoring software allows you to create dynamic presentations that include text, graphics, video, sound, and animation.

FIGURE 3-26 With Web page authoring software, users create sophisticated Web pages.

Test your knowledge of pages 138 through 154 in Quiz Yourself 3-2.

QUIZ YOURSELF 3-2

Instructions: Find the true statement below. Then, rewrite the remaining false statements so they are true.

1. Audio editing software typically includes video editing capabilities.
2. Enterprise computing software provides the capabilities of paint software and also includes the capability to modify existing images.
3. Millions of people use spreadsheet software every day to develop documents such as letters, memos, reports, fax cover sheets, mailing labels, newsletters, and Web pages.
4. Professional accounting software is ideal for the production of high-quality color documents such as textbooks, corporate newsletters, marketing literature, product catalogs, and annual reports.
5. Spreadsheet software is application software that allows users to create visual aids for presentations to communicate ideas, messages, and other information to a group.
6. Two of the more widely used CAD programs are Microsoft Office and Sun StarOffice.
7. Web page authoring software helps users of all skill levels create Web pages.

Quiz Yourself Online: To further check your knowledge of types and features of business programs and graphics/multimedia programs, visit scsite.com/dc2007/ch3/quiz and then click Objectives 4 – 5.

SOFTWARE FOR HOME, PERSONAL, AND EDUCATIONAL USE

A large amount of application software is designed specifically for home, personal, and educational use. Most of the programs in this category are relatively inexpensive, often priced less than $100 and sometimes free. Figure 3-27 lists popular programs for many of these categories. The following sections discuss the features and functions of this application software.

POPULAR SOFTWARE PROGRAMS FOR HOME/PERSONAL/EDUCATIONAL USE

Application Software	Manufacturer	Program Name
Software Suite (for Personal Use)	Microsoft	Works
	Sun	OpenOffice.org
Personal Finance	Intuit	Quicken
	Microsoft	Money
Legal	Broderbund	Family Lawyer
	Cosmi	Perfect Attorney
	H&R Block	Kiplinger's Home & Business Attorney
		Kiplinger's WILLPower
	Nolo	Quicken Legal Business
		Quicken WillMaker
Tax Preparation	2nd Story Software	TaxACT
	H&R Block	TaxCut
	Intuit	TurboTax
Desktop Publishing (for Personal Use)	Broderbund	The Print Shop
		PrintMaster
	Microsoft	Publisher
Paint/Image Editing (for Personal Use)	Corel	CorelDRAW
		Paint Shop Pro
	Sun	StarOffice Draw
	The GIMP Team	The Gimp

Application Software	Manufacturer	Program Name
Photo Editing (for Personal Use)	Adobe	Photoshop Elements
	Corel	Paint Shop Photo Album
	Dell	Picture Studio
	Microsoft	Digital Image Photo Story
	Roxio	PhotoSuite
	Ulead	PhotoImpact Photo Express
Clip Art/Image Gallery	Broderbund	ClickArt
	Nova Development	Art Explosion
Video and Audio Editing (for Personal Use)	Microsoft	Movie Maker Producer for PowerPoint
	Pinnacle Systems	Studio MovieBox
	Roxio	VideoWave
	Ulead	VideoStudio
Home Design/ Landscaping	Broderbund	3D Home Architect
	Quality Plans	Home Designer
	ValuSoft	LandDesigner
Reference	Learning Company	American Heritage Talking Dictionary
	Microsoft	Encarta Streets & Trips
	Rand McNally	StreetFinder TripMaker

FIGURE 3-27 Many popular software programs are available for home, personal, and educational use.

Software Suite (for Personal Use)

A software suite (for personal use) combines application software such as word processing, spreadsheet, database, and other programs in a single, easy-to-use package. Many computer vendors install a software suite for personal use, such as Microsoft Works, on new computers sold to home users.

As mentioned earlier, the programs in a software suite use a similar interface and share some common features. The programs in software suites for personal use typically are available only through the software suite; that is, you cannot purchase them individually. These programs may not have all the capabilities of business application software. For many home users, however, the capabilities of software suites for personal use more than meet their needs.

Personal Finance Software

Personal finance software is a simplified accounting program that helps home users and small office/home office users balance their checkbooks, pay bills, track personal income and expenses (Figure 3-28), set up budgets, manage home inventory, track investments, and evaluate financial plans. Personal finance software helps determine where, and for what purpose, you are spending money so you can manage your finances. Reports can summarize transactions by category (such as dining), by payee (such as the electric company), or by time (such as the last two months). Financial planning features include analyzing home and personal loans, preparing income taxes, and managing retirement savings.

Most of these personal finance programs also offer a variety of online services, which require access to the Internet. For example, users can track investments online, compare insurance rates from leading insurance companies, and bank online. **Online banking** offers access to account balances, provides bill paying services, and allows you to download monthly transactions and statements from the Web directly to your computer.

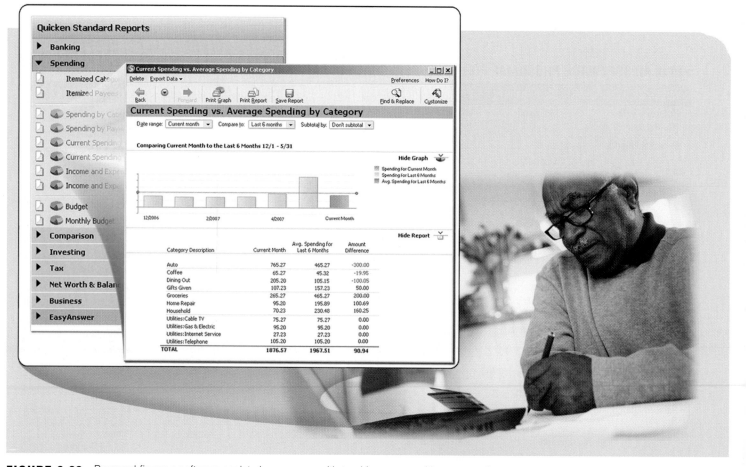

FIGURE 3-28 Personal finance software assists home users with tracking personal income and expenses.

FAQ 3-6

How many people bank online?

Currently, about 40 million people bank online. By 2010, this number is expected to grow to 50 million. The chart below depicts popular online banking activities. For more information, visit scsite.com/dc2007/ch3/faq and then click Online Banking.

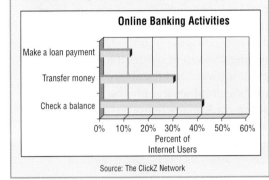

Online Banking Activities

Source: The ClickZ Network

Legal Software

Legal software assists in the preparation of legal documents and provides legal information to individuals, families, and small businesses (Figure 3-29). Legal software provides standard contracts and documents associated with buying, selling, and renting property; estate planning; marriage and divorce; and preparing a will or living trust. By answering a series of questions or completing a form, the legal software tailors the legal document to specific needs.

Once the legal document is created, you can file the paperwork with the appropriate agency, court, or office; or take the document to your attorney for his or her review and signature. Before using one of these software programs to create a document, you may want to check with your local bar association for its legality.

Tax Preparation Software

Tax preparation software is used to guide individuals, families, or small businesses through the process of filing federal taxes (Figure 3-30). These programs forecast tax liability and offer money-saving tax tips, designed to lower your tax bill. After you answer a series of questions and complete basic forms, the software creates and analyzes your tax forms to search for potential errors and deduction opportunities. Once the forms are complete, you can print any necessary paperwork, and then they are ready for filing.

WEB LINK 3-5

Tax Preparation Software

For more information, visit scsite.com/dc2007/ch3/weblink and then click Tax Preparation Software.

FAQ 3-7

Can I file my taxes online?

Yes, many taxpayers *e-file*, or use tax software and/or tax preparation Web sites to file federal and state returns electronically. With tax professionals available to answer questions in a chat room or via e-mail, many taxpayers find this service easy-to-use and relatively inexpensive. The IRS hopes that 80 percent of taxpayers will e-file their taxes by 2007. For more information, visit scsite.com/dc2007/ch3/faq and then click E-Filing Taxes.

FIGURE 3-29 Legal software provides legal information to individuals, families, and small businesses and assists in record keeping and the preparation of legal documents.

FIGURE 3-30 Tax preparation software guides individuals, families, or small businesses through the process of filing federal taxes.

Desktop Publishing Software (for Personal Use)

Instead of using professional DTP software (as discussed earlier in this chapter), many home and small business users work with simpler, easy-to-understand DTP software designed for smaller-scale desktop publishing projects (Figure 3-31). **Personal DTP software** helps home and small business users create newsletters, brochures, advertisements, post-cards, greeting cards, letterhead, business cards, banners, calendars, logos, and Web pages.

Personal DTP programs provide hundreds of thousands of graphical images. You also can import (bring in) your own digital photographs into the documents. These programs typically guide you through the development of a document by asking a series of questions, offering numerous predefined layouts, and providing standard text you can add to documents. Then, you can print a finished publication on a color printer or post it on the Web.

Many personal DTP programs also include paint/image editing software and photo editing software.

Paint/Image Editing Software (for Personal Use)

Personal paint/image editing software provides an easy-to-use interface, usually with more simplified capabilities than its professional counterpart, including functions tailored to meet the needs of the home and small business user.

As with the professional versions, personal paint software includes various simplified tools that allow you to draw pictures, shapes, and other images (Figure 3-32). Personal image editing software provides the capabilities of paint software and the ability to modify existing graphics and photos. These products also include many templates to assist you in adding an image to documents such as greeting cards, banners, calendars, signs, labels, business cards, and letterhead.

FAQ 3-8

How do pictures get in the computer from a digital camera?

Most digital cameras save pictures on miniature storage media, such as a memory card. By inserting the memory card in a card reader/writer in or attached to the computer, users can access images the same way they access files on a disk drive. With some cameras, pictures also can transfer along a cable that connects the camera to the computer. For more information, visit scsite.com/dc2007/ch3/faq and then click Digital Imaging.

FIGURE 3-31 With Publisher, home and small business users can create professional-looking publications such as this flyer with tear-offs.

FIGURE 3-32 Home users can purchase affordable paint/image editing programs that enable them to draw images.

Photo Editing Software

Instead of professional photo editing software, many home and small business users work with easier-to-use personal photo editing software. **Personal photo editing software** allows users to edit digital photographs by removing red-eye, erasing blemishes, restoring aged photos, adding special effects (Figure 3-33), or creating electronic photo albums. When you purchase a digital camera, it usually includes photo editing software. You can print edited photographs on labels, calendars, business cards, and banners; or post them on a Web page. Some photo editing software allows users to send digital photographs to an online print service, which will deliver high-resolution printed images through the postal service. Many online print services have a photo community where users can post photographs on the Web for others to view.

FIGURE 3-33 Personal photo editing software enables home users to edit digital photographs.

Clip Art/Image Gallery

Application software often includes a **clip art/image gallery**, which is a collection of clip art and photographs. Some applications have links to additional clips available on the Web. You also can purchase clip art/image gallery software that contains hundreds of thousands of images (Figure 3-34).

In addition to clip art, many clip art/image galleries provide fonts, animations, sounds, video clips, and audio clips. You can use the images, fonts, and other items from the clip art/image gallery in all types of documents, including word processing, desktop publishing, spreadsheet, and presentation graphics.

FIGURE 3-34 Clip art/image gallery software contains hundreds of thousands of images.

WEB LINK 3-7

Microsoft Office Clip Art

For more information, visit scsite.com/dc2007/ch3/weblink and then click Microsoft Office Clip Art.

Video and Audio Editing Software (for Personal Use)

Many home users work with easy-to-use video and audio editing software, which is much simpler to use than its professional counterpart, for small-scale movie making projects (Figure 3-35). With these programs, home users can edit home movies, add music or other sounds to the video, and share their movies on the Web. Some operating systems include video editing and audio editing software.

FIGURE 3-35 With personal video and audio editing software, home users can edit their home movies.

Home Design/Landscaping Software

Homeowners or potential homeowners can use **home design/landscaping software** to assist them with the design, remodeling, or improvement of a home, deck, or landscape (Figure 3-36). Home design/landscaping software includes hundreds of predrawn plans that you can customize to meet your needs. Once designed, many home design/ landscaping programs print a materials list outlining costs and quantities for the entire project.

FIGURE 3-36 Home design/landscaping software can help you design or remodel a home, deck, or landscape.

Reference and Educational Software

Reference software provides valuable and thorough information for all individuals (Figure 3-37). Popular reference software includes encyclopedias, dictionaries, health/ medical guides, and travel directories.

Educational software is software that teaches a particular skill. Educational software exists for just about any subject, from learning how to type to learning how to cook. Preschool to high-school learners use educational software to assist them with subjects such as reading and math or to prepare them for class or college entry exams. Educational software often includes games and other content to make the learning experience more fun.

Many educational programs use a computer-based training approach. **Computer-based training** (CBT), also called computer-aided instruction (CAI), is a type of education in which students learn by using and completing exercises with instructional software. CBT typically consists of self-directed, self-paced instruction about a topic. Beginning athletes, for example, use CBT programs to learn the intricacies of baseball, football, soccer, tennis, and golf. The military and airlines use CBT simulations to train pilots to fly in various conditions and environments. Schools use CBT to teach students math, language, and software skills.

Entertainment Software

Entertainment software for personal computers includes interactive games, videos, and other programs designed to support a hobby or provide amusement and enjoyment. For example, you might use entertainment software to play games (Figure 3-38), make a family tree, listen to music, or fly an aircraft.

FIGURE 3-38 Entertainment software can provide hours of recreation.

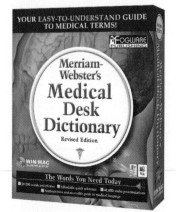

FIGURE 3-37 This reference dictionary gives text definitions and audio pronunciations of medical terms.

APPLICATION SOFTWARE FOR COMMUNICATIONS

One of the main reasons people use computers is to communicate and share information with others. Some communications software is considered system software because it works with hardware and transmission media.

Other communications software makes users more productive and/or assists them with personal tasks, and thus, is considered application software. Chapter 2 presented a variety of application software for communications, which is summarized in the table in Figure 3-39. Read Ethics & Issues 3-3 for a related discussion.

APPLICATION SOFTWARE FOR COMMUNICATIONS

E-Mail
- Messages and files sent via a network such as the Internet
- Requires an e-mail program
  - Integrated in many software suites and operating systems
  - Available free at portals on the Web
  - Included with paid Internet access service
  - Can be purchased separately from retailers

FTP
- Method of uploading and downloading files with other computers on the Internet
- Download may require an FTP program; upload usually requires an FTP program
  - Integrated in some operating systems
  - Available for download on the Web for a small fee
  - Can be purchased separately from retailers

Web Browser
- Allows users to access and view Web pages on the Internet
- Requires a Web browser program
  - Integrated in some operating systems
  - Available for download on the Web free or for a fee

Video Conferencing/Telephone Calls
- Meeting/conversation between geographically separated people who use a network such as the Internet to transmit video/audio
- Requires a microphone, speakers, and sometimes a video camera attached to your computer
- Requires video conferencing software

Newsgroup/Message Board
- Online area where users have written discussions
- Newsgroup may require a newsreader program
  - Integrated in some operating systems, e-mail programs, and Web browsers; built into some Web sites
  - Available for download on the Web, usually at no cost
  - Included with some paid Internet access services

Chat Room
- Real-time, online typed conversation
- Requires chat client software
  - Integrated in some operating systems, e-mail programs, and Web browsers
  - Available for download on the Web, usually at no cost
  - Included with some paid Internet access services
  - Built into some Web sites

Instant Messaging
- Real-time exchange of messages, files, audio, and/or video with another online user
- Requires instant messenger software
  - Integrated in some operating systems
  - Available for download on the Web, usually at no cost
  - Included with some paid Internet access services

Blogging
- Time-stamped articles, or posts, in a diary or journal format, usually listed in reverse chronological order
- Blogger needs *blog software*, or *blogware*, to create/maintain blog
  - Some Web sites do not require installation of blog software

FIGURE 3-39   A summary of application software for home and business communications.

ETHICS & ISSUES 3-3

Should Companies Monitor Employees' E-Mail?

According to one survey, more than 42 percent of all companies monitor (after transmission) or intercept (during transmission) employees' e-mail. Employers can use software to find automatically personal or offensive e-mail messages that have been sent or received, and intercept and filter messages while they are being sent or received. Companies monitor e-mail to improve productivity, increase security, reduce misconduct, and control liability risks. Few laws regulate employee monitoring, and courts have given employers a great deal of leeway in watching work on company-owned computers. In one case, an employee's termination for using her office e-mail system to complain about her boss was upheld, even though the company allowed e-mail use for personal communications. The court decreed that the employee's messages were inappropriate for workplace communications. Executives have not escaped scrutiny, either. Prominent leaders, such as Bill Gates, have had e-mail messages they sent used against them in court. Many employees believe that monitoring software violates their privacy rights. State laws usually favor the privacy of the employee, while federal laws tend to favor the employer's right to read employees' e-mail messages. To reduce employee anxiety about monitoring e-mail and to follow some state laws, legal experts suggest that companies publish written policies and accept employee feedback, provide clear descriptions of acceptable and unacceptable behavior, respect employee needs and time, and establish a balance between security and privacy. Should companies monitor or intercept employees' e-mail? Why or why not? How can a company balance workplace security and productivity with employee privacy? If a company monitors e-mail use, what guidelines should be followed to maintain worker morale? Why? Is intercepting and filtering e-mail more offensive than monitoring e-mail? Why?

POPULAR UTILITY PROGRAMS

Utility programs are considered system software because they assist a user with controlling or maintaining the operation of a computer, its devices, or its software. Some utility programs are included with the operating system, and others are available as stand-alone programs.

Utility programs typically offer features that provide an environment conducive to successful use of application software. One of the more important utility programs protects a computer against viruses. A computer *virus* is a potentially damaging computer program that affects, or infects, a computer negatively by altering the way the computer works without the user's knowledge or permission. For a technical discussion about viruses, read the High-Tech Talk article on page 168.

Other features of utility programs include protecting a computer against unauthorized intrusions; removing spyware from a computer; filtering e-mail messages, Web content, and advertisements; managing files and disks; compressing files; backing up; burning (recording on) a CD or DVD; and maintaining a personal computer. The table in Figure 3-40 briefly describes several utility programs. Chapter 8 discusses them in more depth.

FAQ 3-9

How much does a computer virus attack cost a company?

A recent survey found that it typically costs an enterprise about $10,000 to recover from a computer virus attack. When the virus attacks multiple servers, however, the costs can exceed $100,000. For more information, visit scsite.com/dc2007/ch3/faq and then click Computer Virus Attacks.

WIDELY USED UTILITY PROGRAMS

Utility Program	Description
Antivirus Program	An *antivirus program* protects a computer against viruses by identifying and removing any computer viruses found in memory, on storage media, or in incoming files.
Personal Firewall	A *personal firewall* detects and protects a personal computer from unauthorized intrusions.
Spyware Remover	A *spyware remover* detects and deletes spyware on your computer.
Internet Filters • Anti-Spam Program	An *anti-spam program* attempts to remove spam (Internet junk mail) before it reaches your e-mail inbox.
• Web Filter	A *Web filter* restricts access to specified Web sites.
• Pop-Up Blocker	A *pop-up blocker* stops advertisements from displaying on Web pages and disables pop-up windows.
File Manager	A *file manager* provides functions related to file and disk management.
File Compression	A *file compression utility* shrinks the size of a file(s), so the file takes up less storage space than the original file.
Backup	A *backup utility* allows users to copy selected files or an entire hard disk to another storage medium.
CD/DVD Burning	A *CD/DVD burner* writes text, graphics, audio, and video files on a recordable or rewritable CD or DVD.
Personal Computer Maintenance	A *personal computer maintenance utility* identifies and fixes operating system problems, detects and repairs disk problems, and includes the capability of improving a computer's performance.

FIGURE 3-40 A summary of widely used utility programs.

APPLICATION SOFTWARE ON THE WEB

As discussed earlier in this chapter, users can purchase application software from a software vendor, retail store, or Web-based business. Users typically install purchased application software on a computer before they run it. Installed software has two disadvantages: (1) it requires disk space on your computer, and (2) it can be costly to upgrade as vendors release new versions. As an alternative, some users opt to access Web applications.

A **Web application** is application software that exists on a Web site. Users access Web applications anywhere from any computer or device, as long as it has an Internet connection (read Looking Ahead 3-2 for a look at the next generation of Web access). Web applications usually store users' data and information on their servers. For this reason, users concerned with data security may shy away from this option.

Some Web sites provide free access to the application. For example, one site creates a map and driving directions when a user enters a starting and destination point (Figure 3-41). Other Web sites allow you to use the program free and pay a fee when a certain action occurs. For example, you can prepare your tax return free using TurboTax for the Web, but if you elect to print it or file it electronically, you pay a minimal fee.

LOOKING AHEAD 3-2

Driving Down the Web Highway

Analysts predict you will access the Internet from practically everywhere: home, office, airport, grocery store, and the local coffee shop. Why not from your car?

As it sits in your garage, your car's computer could connect to your home computer and then relay information about fluid levels and the amount of gas in the tank. It could notify you when the oil needs to be changed and when the tires should be rotated. You even could start the car remotely on chilly days by pressing a button on your notebook computer as you eat your breakfast cereal at the kitchen table.

Automobile manufacturers are touting their cyber cars of the future equipped with Internet access. They are planning in-dash screens with continuous information about traffic, weather forecasts, and restaurant guides. Their plans also call for having the Internet access disconnect when the vehicle is in motion so that drivers do not attempt to drive and surf the Web simultaneously. For more information, visit scsite.com/dc2007/ch3/looking and then click Cyber Cars.

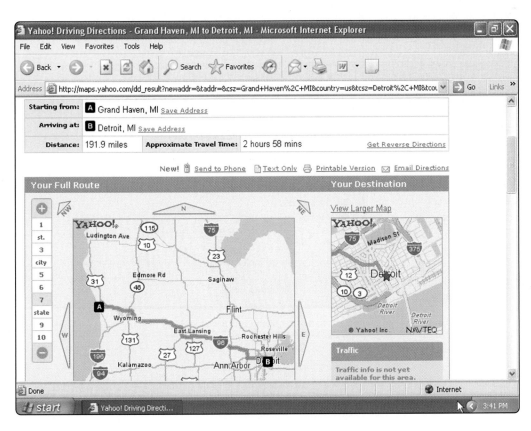

FIGURE 3-41 This Web site creates a map and provides directions when you enter a starting and destination point.

Application Service Providers

Storing and maintaining programs can be a costly investment for businesses. Thus, some have elected to outsource one or more facets of their information technology (IT) needs to an application service provider. An *application service provider* (*ASP*) is a third-party organization that manages and distributes software and services on the Web. That is, instead of installing the software on your computer, you run the programs from the Internet.

The five categories of ASPs are:

1. *Enterprise ASP*: customizes and delivers high-end business applications, such as finance and database
2. *Local/Regional ASP*: offers a variety of software applications to a specific geographic region
3. *Specialist ASP*: delivers applications to meet a specific business need, such as human resources or project management
4. *Vertical Market ASP*: provides applications for a particular industry, such as construction, health care, or retail
5. *Volume Business ASP*: supplies prepackaged applications, such as accounting, to businesses

A variety of payment schemes are available. Some rent use of the application on a monthly basis or charge based on the number of user accesses. Others charge a one-time fee.

LEARNING AIDS AND SUPPORT TOOLS FOR APPLICATION SOFTWARE

Learning how to use application software effectively involves time and practice. To assist in the learning process, many programs provide online Help, Web-based Help, wizards, and templates.

Online Help is the electronic equivalent of a user manual (Figure 3-42a). It usually is integrated in a program. In most programs, a function key or a button on the screen starts the Help feature. When using a program, you can use the Help feature to ask a question or access the Help topics in subject or alphabetical order.

Most online Help also links to Web sites that offer *Web-based Help*, which provides updates and more comprehensive resources to respond to technical issues about software (Figure 3-42b). Some Web sites contain chat rooms, in which a user can talk directly with a technical support

FIGURE 3-42a (online Help)

FIGURE 3-42 Many programs include online Help, Web-based Help, and templates. *(continued)*

FIGURE 3-42b (Web-based Help)

FIGURE 3-42c (template)

FIGURE 3-42 Many programs include online Help, Web-based Help, and templates. *(continued)*

person or join a conversation with other users who may be able to answer questions or solve problems.

A *wizard* is an automated assistant that helps a user complete a task by asking questions and then automatically performing actions based on the responses. A *template* is a document that contains the formatting necessary for a specific document type (Figure 3-42c). Many software applications include wizards and templates. For example, word processing software uses wizards for creating charts and documents and contains templates for memorandums, meeting agendas, fax cover sheets, flyers, letters, and resumes. Spreadsheet software includes wizards for creating charts and building functions and templates for invoices and purchase orders.

If you want to learn more about a particular program from a printed manual, many books are available to help you learn to use the features of personal computer programs. These books typically are available in bookstores and software stores (Figure 3-43).

Many colleges and schools provide training on several of the applications discussed in this chapter. For more information, contact your local school for a list of class offerings.

FIGURE 3-43 Bookstores often sell trade books to help you learn to use the features of personal computer application software.

Web-Based Training

Web-based training (*WBT*) is a type of CBT (computer-based training) that uses Internet technology and consists of application software on the Web. Similar to CBT, WBT typically consists of self-directed, self-paced instruction about a topic. WBT is popular in business, industry, and schools for teaching new skills or enhancing existing skills of employees, teachers, or students. When using a WBT product, students actively become involved in the learning process instead of remaining passive recipients of information.

Many Web sites offer WBT to the general public (Figure 3-44). Such training covers a wide range of topics, from how to change a flat tire to creating documents in Word. Many of these Web sites are free. Others require registration and payment to take the complete Web-based course.

WBT often is combined with other materials for distance learning courses.

Distance learning (**DL**) is the delivery of education at one location while the learning takes place at other locations. DL courses provide time, distance, and place advantages for students who live far from a college campus or work full time. These courses enable students to attend class from anywhere in the world and at times that fit their schedules. Many national and international companies offer DL training. These training courses eliminate the costs of airfare, hotels, and meals for centralized training sessions.

WBT companies often specialize in providing instructors with the tools for preparation, distribution, and management of DL courses. These tools enable instructors to create rich, educational Web-based training sites and allow the students to interact with a powerful Web learning environment. Through the training site, students can check their progress, take practice tests, search for topics, send e-mail messages, and participate in discussions and chats.

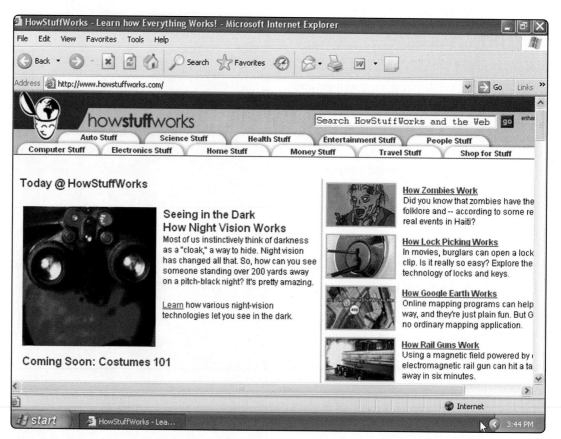

FIGURE 3-44 At the HowStuffWorks Web-based training site, you can learn how computers, autos, electronics, and many other products work.

Test your knowledge of pages 155 through 166 in Quiz Yourself 3-3.

QUIZ YOURSELF 3-3

Instructions: Find the true statement below. Then, rewrite the remaining false statements so they are true.

1. An anti-spam program protects a computer against viruses by identifying and removing any computer viruses found in memory, on storage media, or in incoming files.
2. Computer-based training is a type of Web-based training that uses Internet technology and consists of application software on the Web.
3. E-mail and Web browsers are examples of communications software that are considered application software.
4. Legal software is a simplified accounting program that helps home users and small office/home office users balance their checkbooks, pay bills, track investments, and evaluate financial plans.
5. Personal DTP software is a popular type of image editing software that allows users to edit digital photographs.

Quiz Yourself Online: To further check your knowledge of types and features of home, personal, educational, and communications programs, utility programs, Web applications, and software learning aids, visit scsite.com/dc2007/ch3/quiz and then click Objectives 6 – 10.

CHAPTER SUMMARY

This chapter illustrated how to start and use application software. It then presented an overview of a variety of business software, graphics and multimedia software, home/personal/educational software, and communications software (read Ethics & Issues 3-4 for a related discussion).

The chapter also described widely used utility programs and identified various Web applications. Finally, learning aids and support tools for application software were presented.

ETHICS & ISSUES 3-4

Copying Software — A Computer Crime!

Usually, when you buy software, you legally can make one copy of the software for backup purposes. Despite the law, many people make multiple copies, either to share or to sell. In a recent survey, more than 50 percent of students and 25 percent of instructors admitted that they had illegally copied, or would illegally copy, software. Microsoft, a leading software manufacturer, estimates that almost 25 percent of software in the United States has been copied illegally. Among small businesses, the rate may be even higher. The Business Software Alliance, an industry trade association, believes that 40 percent of small U.S. businesses use illegally copied software. Illegally copied software costs the software industry more than $13 billion a year in lost revenues, and the law allows fines up to $150,000 for each illegal copy of software. People and companies copy software illegally for a variety of reasons, insisting that software prices are too high, software often is copied for educational or other altruistic purposes, copied software makes people more productive, no restrictions should be placed on the use of software after it is purchased, and everyone copies software. What should be the penalty for copying software? Why? Can you counter the reasons people give for copying software illegally? How? Would you copy software illegally? Why or why not?

Help Desk Specialist

A Help Desk specialist position is an entryway into the information technology (IT) field. A *Help Desk specialist* deals with problems in hardware, software, or communications systems. Job requirements may include the following: solve procedural and software questions both in person and over the telephone, develop and maintain Help Desk operations manuals, and assist in training new Help Desk personnel.

Usually, a Help Desk specialist must be knowledgeable about the major programs in use. Entry-level positions primarily involve answering calls from people with questions. Other positions provide additional assistance and assume further responsibilities, often demanding greater knowledge and problem-solving skills that can lead to more advanced IT positions. This job is ideal for people who must work irregular hours, because many companies need support people to work evenings, weekends, or part-time.

Educational requirements are less stringent than they are for other jobs in the computer field. In some cases, a high school diploma is sufficient. Advancement requires a minimum of a two-year degree, while management generally requires a bachelor's degree in IT or a related field. Certification is another way Help Desk specialists can increase their attractiveness in the marketplace. Entry-level salaries range from $37,000 to $60,000 per year. Managers range from $49,500 to $90,000. For more information, visit scsite.com/dc2007/ch3/careers and then click Help Desk Specialist.

High-Tech Talk

COMPUTER VIRUSES:
DELIVERY, INFECTION, AND AVOIDANCE

Bagle. Spudrag. Netsky. Qweasy. Like the common cold, virtually countless variations of computer viruses exist. Unlike the biological viruses that cause the common cold, people create computer viruses. To create a virus, an unscrupulous programmer must code and then test the virus code to ensure the virus can replicate itself, conceal itself, monitor for certain events, and then deliver its *payload* — the destructive event or prank the virus was created to deliver. Despite the many variations of viruses, most have two phases to their execution: infection and delivery.

To start the infection phase, the virus must be activated. Today, the most common way viruses spread is by people running infected programs disguised as e-mail attachments. During the infection phase, viruses typically perform three actions:

1. First, a virus replicates by attaching itself to program files. A *macro virus* hides in the macro language of an application, such as Word. A *boot sector virus* targets the master boot record and executes when the computer boots up. A *file virus* attaches itself to program files. The file virus, Win32.Hatred, for example, replicates by first infecting Windows executable files for the Calculator, Notepad, Help, and other programs on the hard disk. The virus then scans the computer to locate .exe files on other drives and stores this information in the system registry. The next time an infected file is run, the virus reads the registry and continues infecting another drive.

2. Viruses also conceal themselves to avoid detection. A *stealth virus* disguises itself by hiding in fake code sections, which it inserts within working code in a file. A *polymorphic virus* actually changes its code as it infects computers. Win32.Hatred uses both concealment techniques. The virus writes itself to the last file section, while modifying the file header to hide the increased file size. It also scrambles and encrypts the virus code as it infects files.

3. Finally, viruses watch for a certain condition or event and activate when that condition or event occurs. The event might be booting up the computer or hitting a date on the system clock. A *logic bomb* activates when it detects a specific condition (say, a name deleted from the employee list). A *time bomb* is a logic bomb that activates on a particular date or time. Win32.Hatred, for instance, unleashes its destruction when the computer clock hits the seventh day of any month. If the triggering condition does not exist, the virus simply replicates.

During the delivery phase, the virus unleashes its payload, which might be a harmless prank that displays a silly message — or it might be destructive, corrupting or deleting data and files. When Win32.Hatred triggers, it displays the author's message and then covers the screen with black dots. The virus also deletes several antivirus files as it infects the system. The most dangerous viruses do not have an obvious payload, instead they quietly modify files. A virus, for example, could randomly change numbers in an inventory program or introduce delays to slow a computer.

Other kinds of electronic annoyances exist in addition to viruses. While often called viruses, worms and Trojan horse applications actually are part of a broader category called *malicious-logic programs*.

- A *worm*, such as the CodeRed or Sircam worm, resides in active memory and replicates itself over a network to infect machines, using up the system resources and possibly shutting the system down.

- A *Trojan horse* is a destructive program disguised as a real application, such as a screen saver. When a user runs a seemingly innocent program, a Trojan horse hiding inside can capture information, such as user names and passwords, from your system or open up a backdoor that allows a hacker remotely to control your computer. Unlike viruses, Trojan horses do not replicate themselves.

As with the common cold, every computer user is susceptible to a computer virus. In 1995, the chance that a virus would infect your computer was 1 in 1,000; by 2004, the odds were only 1 in 7. Even with better antivirus software, viruses are tough to avoid, as deceitful programmers craft new electronic maladies to infect your computer. Figure 3-45 lists steps you can follow to protect your computer from a virus infection. For more information, visit scsite.com/dc2007/ch3/tech and then click Computer Viruses.

STEPS TO VIRUS PROTECTION

1. Install the latest Windows updates.
2. Purchase a good antivirus program.
3. After installing an antivirus program, scan your entire computer to be sure your system is clean.
4. Update your antivirus definitions regularly.
5. Be suspicious of any and all unsolicited e-mail attachments.
6. Stay informed about viruses and virus hoaxes.
7. Install a personal firewall program.
8. Download software only if you are sure the Web site is legitimate.
9. Avoid as best you can visiting unscrupulous Web sites.

FIGURE 3-45 Guidelines to keep your computer virus free.

Companies on the Cutting Edge

ADOBE SYSTEMS
DIGITAL IMAGING LEADER

Practically every image seen on a computer and in print has been shaped by software developed by *Adobe Systems, Inc.* The company, based in San Jose, California, is one of the world's largest application software corporations and is committed to helping people communicate effectively.

Adobe Photoshop and Photoshop Album have set the industry standard for digital imaging and digital video software, while Creative Suite is used for design and publishing. The company's Portable Document Format (PDF) and Adobe Reader are used to share documents among users electronically. More than 600 million copies of the free Adobe Reader have been downloaded in 26 languages.

In 2005, Adobe entered into an agreement to acquire Macromedia, which develops such Web page authoring software as Flash MX and Dreamweaver MX. For more information, visit scsite.com/dc2007/ch3/companies and then click Adobe.

MICROSOFT
REALIZING POTENTIAL WITH BUSINESS SOFTWARE

Microsoft's mission is "to enable people and businesses throughout the world to realize their potential." As the largest software company in the world, *Microsoft* has indeed helped computer users in every field reach their goals.

When Microsoft was incorporated in 1975, the company had three programmers, one product, and revenues of $16,000. Thirty years later, the company employs more than 57,000 people, produces scores of software titles with Office and Windows leading the industry, and has annual revenue of more than $36 billion.

The company's recent efforts have focused on security issues, with up to 35 percent of the research and development budget being spent preventing malicious software from getting onto computers, and promoting its Media Center, an entertainment hub designed for the living room. For more information, visit scsite.com/dc2007/ch3/companies and then click Microsoft.

Technology Trailblazers

DAN BRICKLIN
VISICALC DEVELOPER

When *Dan Bricklin* was enrolled at the Harvard Business School in the 1970s, he often used his calculator to determine the effect of changing one value on a balance sheet. He recognized the need to develop a program that would perform a series of calculations automatically when the first number was entered.

He named his creation VisiCalc, short for Visible Calculator. He and a friend formed a company called Software Arts and programmed the VisiCalc prototype using Apple Basic on an Apple II computer. The small program was the first piece of application software that provided a reason for businesses to buy Apple computers. It laid the foundation for the development of other spreadsheets and included many of the features found in today's spreadsheet software.

He currently is president of Software Garden, Inc., a company he founded in 1985, where he does software product development and consulting. For more information, visit scsite.com/dc2007/ch3/people and then click Dan Bricklin.

MASAYOSHI SON
SOFTBANK PRESIDENT AND CEO

Many students carry photographs of family and friends in their wallets and book bags. As a 16-year-old student in the 1970s, *Masayoshi Son* carried a picture of a microchip. He predicted that the microchip was going to change people's lives, and he wanted to be part of that trend.

While majoring in economics at the University of California, Berkeley, he earned his first million dollars by importing arcade games from Japan to the campus, developing new computer games, and selling a patent for a multilingual pocket translator to Sharp Corporation.

At age 23 he founded Softbank, which is Japan's second-largest broadband Internet service and telephone provider. He also is chairman of Yahoo! Japan. Today, he is one of the world's wealthiest entrepreneurs. For more information, visit scsite.com/dc2007/ch3/people and then click Masayoshi Son.

Chapter Review

The Chapter Review section summarizes the concepts presented in this chapter. To listen to the audio version of this Chapter Review, visit scsite.com/dc2007/ch3/review. To obtain help from other students regarding any subject in this chapter, visit scsite.com/dc2007/ch3/forum and post your thoughts or questions.

(1)   What Are the Categories of Application Software?   **Application software** consists of programs designed to make users more productive and/or assist them with personal tasks. The major categories of application software are business software; graphics and multimedia software; home, personal, and educational software; and communications software.

(2)   How Is Software Distributed?   Application software is available in a variety of forms. **Packaged software** is mass-produced, copyrighted retail software that meets the needs of a variety of users. **Custom software** performs functions specific to a business or industry. **Open source software** is provided for use, modification, and redistribution. **Shareware** is copyrighted software that is distributed free for a trial period. **Freeware** is copyrighted software provided at no cost by an individual or a company that retains all rights to the software. **Public-domain software** is free software donated for public use and has no copyright restrictions.

(3)   How Do You Work with Application Software?   Personal computer operating systems often use the concept of a **desktop**, which is an on-screen work area that has a graphical user interface. To start an application in Windows XP, move the **pointer** to the Start **button** in the corner of the desktop and **click** the Start button by pressing and releasing a button on the mouse. Then, click the program name on the Start **menu** or on the *submenu* that displays when you point to a **command**. Once loaded into memory, the program is displayed in a **window** on the desktop.

Visit scsite.com/dc2007/ch3/quiz or click the Quiz Yourself button. Click Objectives 1 – 3.

(4)   What Are the Key Features of Widely Used Business Programs?   **Business software** assists people in becoming more effective and efficient while performing daily business activities. Business software includes the following programs. **Word processing software** allows users to **create** a document by entering text and inserting graphical images, **edit** the document by making changes, and **format** the document by altering its appearance. **Spreadsheet software** allows users to organize data in rows and columns, perform calculations, recalculate when data changes, and chart the data. **Database software** allows users to create a **database**, which is a collection of data organized to allow access, retrieval, and use of that data. **Presentation graphics software** allows users to create a *slide show* that is displayed on a monitor or projection screen. **Note taking software** enables users to enter typed text, handwritten comments, drawings, or sketches on a page and then save the page as part of a notebook. A **personal information manager (PIM)** is software that includes features to help users organize personal information. A **software suite** is a collection of individual programs sold as a single package. **Project management software** allows users to plan, schedule, track, and analyze a project. **Accounting software** helps companies record and report their financial transactions. **Document management software** provides a means for sharing, distributing, and searching through documents by converting them into a format that can be viewed by any user.

(5)   What Are the Key Features of Widely Used Graphics and Multimedia Programs?   Graphics and multimedia software includes the following programs. **Computer-aided design (CAD) software** assists in creating engineering, architectural, and scientific designs. **Desktop publishing (DTP) software** enables professional designers to create sophisticated documents that contain text, graphics, and colors. **Paint software** lets users draw graphical images with various on-screen tools. **Image editing software** provides the capabilities of paint software and includes the capability to modify existing images. **Professional photo editing software** is a type of image editing software that allows

Visit scsite.com/dc2007/ch3/quiz or click the Quiz Yourself button. Click Objectives 4 – 5.

Chapter Review

photographers, videographers, engineers, scientists, and other high-volume digital photo users to edit and customize digital photographs. **Video editing software** allows professionals to modify segments of a video. **Audio editing software** lets users modify audio clips and produce studio-quality soundtracks. **Multimedia authoring software** allows users to combine text, graphics, audio, video, and animation into an interactive application. **Web page authoring software** helps users create Web pages that include graphical images, video, audio, animation, and other special effects.

⑥ What Are the Key Features of Widely Used Home, Personal, and Educational Programs?
Software for home, personal, and educational use includes the following applications. A software suite (for personal use) combines application software such as word processing, spreadsheet, and database into a single package. **Personal finance software** is an accounting program that helps users balance their checkbooks, pay bills, track income and expenses, track investments, and evaluate financial plans. **Legal software** assists in the preparation of legal documents. **Tax preparation software** guides users through filing federal taxes. **Personal DTP software** helps users create newsletters, brochures, advertisements, greeting and business cards, logos, and Web pages. **Personal paint/image editing software** provides an easy-to-use interface with functions tailored to meet the needs of home and small business users. **Personal photo editing software** is a type of image editing software used to edit digital photographs. Application software often includes a **clip art/image gallery**, which is a collection of clip art and photographs. **Home design/landscaping software** assists with the design, remodeling, or improvement of a home or landscape. **Educational software** teaches a particular skill. **Reference software** provides valuable and thorough information for all individuals. **Entertainment software** includes interactive games, videos, and other programs to support hobbies or provide amusement.

⑦ What Are the Types of Application Software Used in Communications?   Application software for communications includes e-mail programs to transmit messages via a network; FTP programs to upload and download files on the Internet; Web browsers to access and view Web pages; video conferencing/telephone call software for meetings or conversations on a network; newsreader/message board programs that allow online written discussions; chat room software to have real-time, online typed conversations; instant messaging software for real-time exchange of messages or files; and *blog software*, or *blogware*, to create and maintain a blog.

⑧ What Are the Functions of Utility Programs?   Utility programs support the successful use of application software. An *antivirus program* protects a computer against a computer *virus*, which is a potentially damaging computer program. A *personal firewall* detects and protects a personal computer from unauthorized intrusions. A *spyware remover* detects and deletes spyware. An *anti-spam program* removes spam (Internet junk mail). A *Web filter* restricts access to specified Web sites. A *pop-up blocker* disables pop-up windows. A *file manager* provides functions related to file and disk management. A *file compression utility* shrinks the size of a file. A *backup utility* allows users to copy selected files or an entire hard disk to another storage medium. A *personal computer maintenance utility* fixes operating system and disk problems.

⑨ What Are the Advantages of Using Application Software on the Web?   A Web **application** is application software that exists on a Web site. Web applications require less disk space on a computer than installed software and are less costly to upgrade. An *application service provider (ASP)* is a third-party organization that manages and distributes software and services on the Web.

⑩ What Learning Aids Are Available for Application Software?   To assist in the learning process, many programs offer Help features. **Online Help** is the electronic equivalent of a user manual. Most online Help links to *Web-based help*, which provides updates and more comprehensive resources. A *wizard* is an automated assistant that helps users complete a task by asking questions and then performing actions based on the responses. A *template* is a document that contains the formatting necessary for a specific document type.

Visit scsite.com/dc2007/ch3/quiz or click the Quiz Yourself button. Click Objectives 6 – 10.

Quizzes and
Learning Games

Computer Genius
Crossword Puzzle
DC Track and Field
Practice Test
Quiz Yourself
Wheel of Terms
You're Hired!

Exercises

Case Studies
Chapter Review
Checkpoint
▶ Key Terms
Learn How To
Learn It Online
Web Research

Beyond the Book

Career Corner
Companies
FAQs
High-Tech Talk
Looking Ahead
Making Use of
the Web
Trailblazers
Web Links

Features

Chapter Forum
Install Computer
Lab Exercises
Maintain Computer
Tech News
Timeline 2007

Key Terms

You should know the Primary Terms and be familiar with the Secondary Terms. Use the list below to help focus your study. To further enhance your understanding of the Key Terms in this chapter, visit scsite.com/dc2007/ch3/terms. See an example of and a definition for each term, and access current and additional information about the term from the Web.

Primary Terms

(shown in bold-black characters in the chapter)

accounting software (149)
application software (134)
audio editing software (153)
business software (138)
button (136)
click (136)
clip art (138)
clip art/image gallery (159)
command (137)
computer-aided design (CAD) software (151)
computer-based training (CBT) (160)
create (141)
custom software (135)
database (145)
database software (145)
desktop (136)
desktop publishing (DTP) software (152)
distance learning (DL) (166)
document management software (150)
edit (141)
educational software (160)
entertainment software (160)
font (141)
font size (141)
format (141)
freeware (135)
home design/ landscaping software (160)
icon (136)
image editing software (152)
legal software (157)
menu (137)
multimedia authoring software (154)

note taking software (147)
online banking (156)
online Help (164)
open source software (135)
packaged software (134)
paint software (152)
personal DTP software (158)
personal finance software (156)
personal information manager (PIM) (148)
personal paint/image editing software (158)
personal photo editing software (159)
pointer (136)
presentation graphics software (146)
print (142)
professional photo editing software (152)
project management software (149)
public-domain software (135)
reference software (160)
save (142)
shareware (135)
software suite (148)
spreadsheet software (142)
tax preparation software (157)
title bar (137)
video editing software (153)
Web application (163)
Web page authoring software (154)
Web-based training (166)
window (137)
word processing software (138)

Secondary Terms

(shown in italic characters in the chapter)

anti-spam program (162)
antivirus program (162)
application service provider (ASP) (164)
backup utility (162)
bar chart (144)
blog software (161)
blogware (161)
CD/DVD burner (162)
cell (143)
charting (144)
clipboard (141)
color library (152)
column chart (144)
dialog box (137)
enterprise ASP (164)
field (145)
file (137)
file compression utility (162)
file manager (162)
file name (137)
filters (153)
font style (141)
footer (140)
formula (143)
function (143)
header (140)
illustration software (152)
import (146)
label (143)
line chart (144)
loaded (135)
local/regional ASP (164)
margins (139)
page layout (152)
pasting (141)

PDF (150)
personal computer maintenance utility (162)
personal firewall (162)
pie chart (144)
point (141)
pop-up blocker (162)
product activation (135)
query (145)
record (145)
replace (139)
sans serif font (141)
scrolling (139)
search (139)
serif font (141)
slide show (146)
slide sorter view (146)
specialist ASP (164)
spelling checker (139)
spyware remover (162)
submenu (137)
system software (135)
template (165)
value (143)
vertical market ASP (164)
virus (162)
volume business ASP (164)
WBT (166)
Web-based Help (164)
Web filter (162)
what-if analysis (144)
wizard (165)
word processor (138)
wordwrap (139)
worksheet (142)

Checkpoint

Use the Checkpoint exercises to check your knowledge level of the chapter. The Beyond the Book exercises will help broaden your understanding of the concepts presented in this chapter. To complete the Checkpoint exercises interactively, visit scsite.com/dc2007/ch3/check.

Label the Figure

Identify these elements in the Windows XP graphical user interface.

a. Accessories command

b. Accessories submenu

c. All Programs command

d. All Programs submenu

e. Start button

f. Start menu

g. Paint command

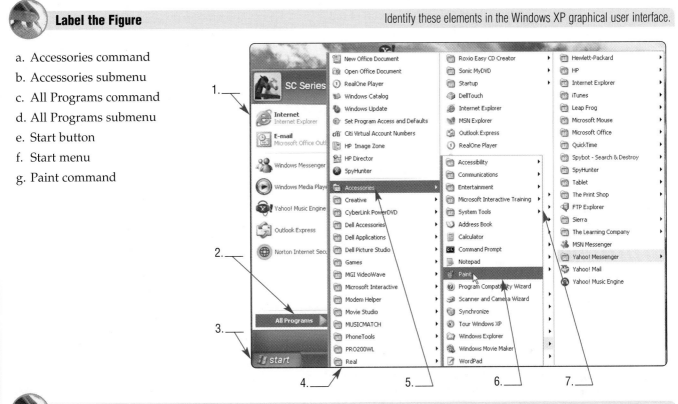

True/False

Mark T for True and F for False. (See page numbers in parentheses.)

_____ 1. The four categories of application software are mutually exclusive. (134)

_____ 2. Programmers cannot incorporate freeware in applications they intend to sell. (135)

_____ 3. To click a button on the screen requires moving the pointer away from the button and then pressing and holding down a button on the mouse (usually the right mouse button). (136)

_____ 4. A menu is an instruction that causes a program to perform a specific action. (137)

_____ 5. A font is a name assigned to a specific design of characters. (141)

_____ 6. Many graphics and multimedia programs have user-friendly interfaces and scaled-down versions, making it possible for the home and small business user to create documents using these programs. (151)

_____ 7. Professional photo editing software is a type of image editing software that allows photographers, videographers, engineers, scientists, and other high-volume digital photo users to edit and customize digital photographs. (153)

_____ 8. Legal software assists in the preparation of legal documents and provides legal information to individuals, families, and small businesses. (157)

_____ 9. Personal DTP programs never include paint/image editing software or photo editing software. (158)

_____ 10. Some communications software is considered system software because it works with hardware and transmission media. (161)

_____ 11. Utility programs are considered application software because they make users more productive or assist with personal tasks. (162)

_____ 12. Web applications store users' data and information on their servers, so users concerned with data security may shy away from this option. (163)

Checkpoint

 Multiple Choice

Select the best answer. (See page numbers in parentheses.)

1. _____ has no restrictions from the copyright holder regarding modification of the software's internal instructions and redistribution of the software. (135)
   a. Packaged software
   b. Custom software
   c. Open source software
   d. Shareware

2. In a document window, the _____ usually displays a document's file name. (137)
   a. status bar   b. title bar
   c. menu   d. dialog box

3. In word processing, pasting is the process of _____. (141)
   a. moving different portions of the document on the screen into view
   b. transferring an item from the clipboard to a specific location in a document
   c. locating all occurrences of a certain character, word, or phrase
   d. removing a portion of a document and storing it in a temporary storage location

4. Most spreadsheet software includes a what-if analysis feature, where you _____. (144)
   a. depict the data in a spreadsheet in graphical form
   b. enter labels to identify worksheet data and organize the worksheet
   c. review the spelling of individual words and sections of a worksheet
   d. change values in a spreadsheet to identify the effects of those changes

5. With database software, users can run a _____, which is a request for specific data from the database. (145)
   a. record   b. function
   c. query   d. field

6. Users find _____ software convenient during meetings, class lectures, and other settings that previously required a pencil and paper for recording thoughts and discussions. (147)
   a. word processing   b. database
   c. note taking   d. accounting

7. _____ software provides a means for sharing, distributing, and searching through documents by converting them into a format that can be viewed by any user. (150)
   a. Database
   b. Document management
   c. Portable Document Format
   d. Word processing

8. DTP software supports page layout, which is the process of _____. (152)
   a. creating engineering, architectural, and scientific designs
   b. arranging text and graphics in a document on a page-by-page basis
   c. enhancing and modifying existing images and pictures
   d. standardizing the colors on a page used by designers and printers

9. _____ helps home users determine where, and for what purpose, they are spending money. (156)
   a. Legal software
   b. Personal DTP software
   c. Personal finance software
   d. Tax preparation software

10. _____ is a collection of clip art and photographs. (159)
    a. Professional photo editing software
    b. Personal photo editing software
    c. Clip art/image gallery
    d. Entertainment software

11. A(n) _____, which can be used to upload and download files with other computers and on the Internet, is integrated in some operating systems. (161)
    a. FTP program   b. Web browser
    c. e-mail program   d. chat client

12. A(n) _____ restricts access to specified Web sites. (162)
    a. anti-spam program b. Web filter
    c. spyware remover   d. antivirus program

13. An enterprise ASP _____. (164)
    a. supplies packaged applications
    b. provides applications for a particular industry
    c. customizes and delivers high-end business applications
    d. offers a variety of software applications to specific regions

14. _____ is the electronic equivalent of a user manual. (164)
    a. Online Help (OH)
    b. Software wizards (SW)
    c. Online banking (OB)
    d. Distance learning (DL)

Checkpoint

Matching

Match the terms with their definitions. (See page numbers in parentheses.)

_____ 1. icon (136)

_____ 2. button (136)

_____ 3. window (137)

_____ 4. clip art (138)

_____ 5. cell (143)

_____ 6. slide sorter view (146)

_____ 7. document management software (150)

_____ 8. PDF (150)

_____ 9. volume business ASP (164)

_____ 10. wizard (165)

a. text that appears at the bottom of every page

b. provides prepackaged applications, such as accounting, to businesses

c. intersection of a row and column in a spreadsheet

d. automated assistant that helps users complete a task

e. provides a means for sharing, distributing, and searching through documents

f. collection of drawings, diagrams, maps, and photographs that can be inserted

g. popular file format used by document management software to save converted documents

h. graphical image activated to cause a specific action to take place

i. rectangular area of the screen that displays data and information

j. screen view similar to how 35mm slides look on a light table

k. small symbol on the screen that moves as you move the mouse

l. small image that represents a program, document, or some other object

Short Answer

Write a brief answer to each of the following questions.

1. When using spreadsheet software, what is charting? _____ How are line charts, column charts, and pie charts different? _____

2. What are the features of personal information manager software? _____ Where might you find personal information manager software? _____

3. What are the benefits of document management software? _____ Why do businesses use document management software? _____

4. What are disadvantages of installed software? _____ How can you access a Web application? _____

5. In most programs, how do you start the online Help feature? _____ How is a wizard different from a template? _____

Beyond the Book

Read the following book elements, learn more about each using the Web, and then write a brief report.

1. Ethics & Issues — How Should Schools Deal with Internet Plagiarism? (141), Altering Digital Photographs — Art or Fraud? (153), Should Companies Monitor Employees' E-Mail? (161), or Copying Software — A Computer Crime! (167)

2. Career Corner — Help Desk Specialist (167)

3. Companies on the Cutting Edge — Adobe Systems or Microsoft (169)

4. FAQs (137, 142, 145, 148, 154, 157, 158, 162)

5. High-Tech Talk — Computer Viruses: Delivery, Infection, and Avoidance (168)

6. Looking Ahead — User Interfaces of the Future (137) or Driving Down the Web Highway (163)

7. Making Use of the Web — Finance (155)

8. Picture Yourself Using Software (132)

9. Technology Trailblazers — Dan Bricklin or Masayoshi Son (169)

10. Web Links (140, 144, 146, 150, 157, 158, 159, 160, 162, 166)

Learn It Online

Use the Learn It Online exercises to reinforce your understanding of the chapter concepts. To access the Learn It Online exercises, visit scsite.com/dc2007/ch3/learn.

1 At the Movies — Detect Spyware on Your Computer

To view the Detect Spyware on Your Computer movie, click the number 1 button. Locate your video and click the corresponding High-Speed or Dial-Up link, depending on your Internet connection. Watch the movie and then complete the exercise by answering the question that follows. Many of the programs installed on your computer also installed spyware along with the program you loaded. Several different types of spyware exist, two of which are keystroke recorders and advertising spyware. Spyware either collects information and sends it over the Internet to whoever installed it or stores it for later retrieval. Why might you want to detect and delete a keystroke recorder from your computer?

2 At the Movies — History of Adobe

To view the History of Adobe movie, click the number 2 button. Locate your video and click the corresponding High-Speed or Dial-Up link, depending on your Internet connection. Watch the movie and then complete the exercise by answering the question that follows. At the dawn of the computer age, computers were used mostly by scientists, and printers were large, cumbersome machines. The advent of desktop publishing gave average people access to the power of computing. Users finally were able to publish documents and images easily, and the computer became a tool for creative expression for everyone. Compare how you complete your homework assignments now to how homework was

done in the 1950s. How has desktop publishing changed the way students research and write reports?

3 Student Edition Labs — Word Processing

Click the number 3 button. A new browser window will open, displaying the Student Edition Labs. Follow the on-screen instructions, and complete the Word Processing Lab. When finished, click the Exit button. If required, submit your results to your instructor.

4 Student Edition Labs — Spreadsheets

Click the number 4 button. A new browser window will open, displaying the Student Edition Labs. Follow the on-screen instructions, and complete the Spreadsheets Lab. When finished, click the Exit button. If required, submit your results to your instructor.

5 Student Edition Labs — Databases

Click the number 5 button. A new browser window will open, displaying the Student Edition Labs. Follow the on-screen instructions, and complete the Databases Lab. When finished, click the Exit button. If required, submit your results to your instructor.

6 Student Edition Labs — Presentation Software

Click the number 6 button. A new browser window will open, displaying the Student Edition Labs. Follow the on-screen instructions, and complete the Presentation Software Lab. When finished, click the Exit button. If required, submit your results to your instructor.

7 Practice Test

Click the number 7 button. Answer each question. When completed, enter your name and click the Grade Test button to submit the

Learn It Online

quiz for grading. Make a note of any missed questions. If required, submit your score to your instructor.

8 Who Wants To Be a Computer Genius²?

Click the number 8 button to find out if you are a computer genius. Directions about how to play the game will be displayed. When you are ready to play, click the Play button. Submit your score to your instructor.

9 Wheel of Terms

Click the number 9 button to reinforce important terms you learned in this chapter by playing the Shelly Cashman Series version of this popular game. Directions about how to play the game will be displayed. When you are ready to play, click the Play button. Submit your score to your instructor.

10 DC Track and Field

Click the number 10 button to use what you have learned in this chapter to compete against other students in three track and field events. Directions about how to play the game will be displayed. When you are ready to play, click the start first event button. If required, submit your score to your instructor.

11 You're Hired!

Click the number 11 button to use what you have learned in this chapter to embark on the path to a career in computers. Directions about how to play the game will be displayed. When you are ready to play, click the begin game button. If required, submit your score to your instructor.

12 Crossword Puzzle Challenge

Click the number 12 button. Complete the puzzle to reinforce skills you learned in this chapter. Directions about how to play the game will be displayed. When you are ready to play, click the Play button. Submit the completed puzzle to your instructor.

13 Lab Exercises

Click the number 13 button. When the Lab Exercises menu appears, click the exercise assigned by your instructor. A new browser window will open. Follow the on-screen instructions to complete the exercise. When finished, click the Exit button. If required, submit your results to your instructor.

14 In the News

It is a computer user's worst fear — he or she opens an unfamiliar e-mail message or uses a disk of unknown origin and a computer virus is released that damages and/or deletes files. Fortunately, specialized software prevents such things from happening to your computer. Click the number 14 button and read a news article about antivirus programs. Which program does the article recommend? What does it do? Who will benefit from using this software? Why? Where can the software be obtained? Would you be interested in this software? Why or why not?

15 Chapter Discussion Forum

Select an objective from this chapter on page 133 about which you would like more information. Click the number 15 button and post a short message listing a meaningful message title accompanied by one or more questions concerning the selected objective. In two days, return to the threaded discussion by clicking the number 15 button. Submit to your instructor your original message and at least one response to your message.

16 Google Home Page

Click the number 16 button to learn how to make the Google home page your default home page. Explore the different sections of the Google home page (Images, Groups, News, Froogle, Local, and more). On the News page, use the Customize this page feature to rearrange the page and to add other sections. Print the Google News page and then step through the exercise. If required, submit your results to your instructor.

Learn How To

Use the Learn How To activities to learn fundamental skills when using a computer and accompanying technology. Complete the exercises and submit them to your instructor. To see a video of a Learn How To activity, visit scsite.com/dc2007/ch3/howto.

LEARN HOW TO 1: Save a File in Application Software

When you use application software, usually you either will create a new file or modify an existing file. If you turn off your computer or lose electrical power while working on the file, the file will not be retained. In order to retain the file, you must save it.

    To save a new file, you must complete several tasks:
1. Initiate an action indicating you want to save the file, such as clicking the Save button.
2. Designate where the file should be stored. This includes identifying both the device (such as drive C) and the folder (such as My Documents).
3. Specify the name of the file.
4. Click the Save button to save the file.

    Tasks 2 through 4 normally can be completed using a dialog box such as shown in Figure 3-46.
    If you close a program prior to saving a new or modified file, the program will display a dialog box asking if you want to save the file. If you click the Yes button, a modified file will be saved using the same file name in the same location. Saving a new file requires that you complete tasks 2 through 4.

Exercise
1. Start the WordPad program from the Accessories submenu on the All Programs submenu.
2. Type `Saving a file is the best insurance against losing work.`
3. Click the Save button on the WordPad toolbar. What dialog box is displayed? Where will the file be saved? What is the default file name? If you wanted to save the file on the desktop, what would you do? Click the Cancel button in the dialog box. Submit your answers to your instructor.
4. Click the Close button in the WordPad window. What happened? Click the Yes button in the WordPad dialog box. What happened? Place either a floppy disk in drive A or a USB drive in a USB port. Select either the floppy disk or the USB drive as the location for saving the file. Name the file, Chapter 3 How To 1. Save the file. What happened? Submit your answers to your instructor.

FIGURE 3-46

LEARN HOW TO 2: Install and Uninstall Application Software

When you purchase application software, you must install the software on the computer where you want to run it. The exact installation process varies with each program, but generally you must complete the following steps:
1. Insert the CD-ROM containing the application software into a drive.
2. The opening window will appear. If the CD-ROM contains more than one program, choose the program you want to install. Click the Continue or Next button.
3. Some file extractions will occur and then an Install Wizard will begin. You normally must accomplish the following steps by completing the directions within the wizard:
   a. Accept the terms of the license agreement.
   b. Identify where on your computer the software will be stored. The software usually selects a default location on drive C, and you normally will accept the default location.

Learn How To

c. Select any default options for the software.

d. Click a button to install the software.

4. A Welcome/Help screen often will be displayed. Click a button to finish the installation process.

At some point, you may want to remove software. Most software includes uninstall programming that will remove the program and all its software components. To uninstall a program, complete the following steps:

1. Click the Start button on the Windows taskbar.
2. Click Control Panel on the Start menu.
3. Click or double-click Add or Remove Programs. *The Add or Remove Programs window will open (Figure 3-47).*
4. Select the program you wish to remove. *In Figure 3-47, Macromedia Dreamweaver MX is selected as the program to remove.*
5. Click the Change/Remove button.
6. A dialog box will be displayed informing you that the software is being prepared for uninstall. You then will be informed that the process you are following will remove the program. You will be asked if you want to continue. To uninstall the program, click the Yes button.

The program will be removed from the computer.

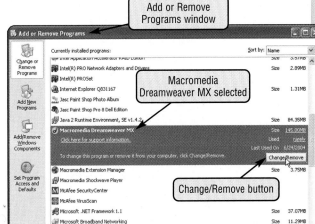

FIGURE 3-47

Exercise

1. Optional: Insert the CD-ROM containing the software you want to install into a drive and follow the instructions for installing the software. **Warning: If you are using a computer other than your own, particularly in a school laboratory, do not perform this exercise unless you have specific permission from your instructor.**
2. Optional: Follow the steps above to uninstall software you want to remove. Be aware that if you uninstall software, the software will not be available for use until you reinstall it. **Warning: If you are using a computer other than your own, particularly in a school laboratory, do not perform this exercise unless you have specific permission from your instructor.**

LEARN HOW TO 3: Check Application Software Version

Most application software will be modified from time to time by its developer. Each time the software is changed, it acquires a new version number and sometimes an entirely new name. To determine what version of software you have, perform the following steps:

1. Start the application program.
2. Click Help on the menu bar and then click About on the Help menu (the program name often follows the word, About). *The program displays the About window (Figure 3-48).*
3. To close the About window, click the OK button.

Depending on the software, in the About window you also might be able to determine further information.

FIGURE 3-48

Exercise

1. Start your Web browser and display the About window for the browser. What is the name of the browser? What version of the browser are you using? What is the product ID? What does the copyright notice say? Submit your answers to your instructor.
2. Start any other application software. Display the About window. What is the name of the program? What is the version number? What information do you find that you did not see in Exercise 1? Which window do you find more useful? Why? Submit your answers to your instructor.

Web Research

Use the Internet-based Web Research exercises to broaden your understanding of the concepts presented in this chapter. Visit scsite.com/dc2007/ch3/research to obtain more information pertaining to each exercise. To discuss any of the Web Research exercises in this chapter with other students, post your thoughts or questions at scsite.com/dc2007/ch3/forum.

① Scavenger Hunt   Use one of the search engines listed in Figure 2-10 in Chapter 2 on page 78 or your own favorite search engine to find the answers to the questions below. Copy and paste the Web address from the Web page where you found the answer. Some questions may have more than one answer. If required, submit your answers to your instructor. (1) What is the name of the latest Boeing flight deck added to Microsoft's Flight Simulator? (2) What video game did Atari begin selling at Sears under the Telegames label in 1975? (3) What inventor designed one of the first mechanical calculating devices, called the Codex? (4) What Web site features software that creates a game requiring a player to put numbers in nine rows of nine boxes?

② Search Sleuth   A virus is a potentially damaging computer program that can harm files and the operating system. The National Institute of Standards and Technology Computer Security Resource Center (csrc.nist.gov/virus/) is one of the more comprehensive Web sites discussing viruses. Visit this Web site and then use your word processing program to answer the following questions. Then, if required, submit your answers to your instructor. (1) The Virus Information page provides general information about viruses and links to various resources that provide more specific details. What two steps does the National Institute recommend to detect and prevent viruses from spreading? (2) Click the Symantec link in the Virus Resources & Other Areas of Interest section. What viruses are the latest threats, and when were they discovered? (3) Click Search at the top of the page and then type "Sasser worm" as the keyword in the Search text box. How many articles discuss the Sasser worm on the Symantec Web site? What three functions does the Sasser Removal Tool perform? (4) Click one of the Latest News links and review the material. Review the information you read and then write a 50-word summary.

③ Journaling   Respond to your readings in this chapter by writing at least one page about your reactions, evaluations, and reflections about the first time you used home, personal, and educational software. For example, have you prepared your income taxes using tax preparation programs? Have you enhanced or modified digital photos with paint/image editing software? What video games have you played on a home computer? You also can write about the new terms you learned by reading this chapter. If required, submit your journal to your instructor.

④ Expanding Your Understanding   Microsoft seeks to help customers use its products by maintaining the Microsoft Help and Support Web site (support.microsoft.com). This Web site has a link to the Knowledge Base, which contains more than 250,000 articles written by Microsoft employees who support the company's products. Also included are software downloads and updates, public newsgroups, methods of getting online or telephone assistance, and the Security Support Center. View this site and then search the Knowledge Base for information on Microsoft Word. Also view the common issues, updates, security issues, and visitors' top links listed on the Web site. Write a report summarizing your findings. If required, submit your report to your instructor.

⑤ Ethics in Action   A hacker is someone who tries to access a computer or network illegally. Although the activity sometimes is a harmless prank, it sometimes causes extensive damage. Some hackers say their activities give them a sense of excitement and test their skills. Others say their activities are a form of civil disobedience that allows them to challenge authority and force companies to make their products more secure. View online sites such as Hackers: Outlaws & Angels (tlc.discovery.com/convergence/hackers/hackers.html) that provide information about whether hackers provide some benefit to the Internet society. Write a report summarizing your findings and include a table of links to Web sites that provide additional details. If required, submit your report to your instructor.

Case Studies

Use the Case Studies to apply the concepts presented in the chapter to real-world situations. Visit scsite.com/dc2007/ch3/cases to obtain more information pertaining to each exercise. To discuss the Case Studies in this chapter with other students, visit scsite.com/dc2007/ch3/forum and post your thoughts or questions.

CASE STUDY 1 – Class Discussion   The owner of Mel's Hair Salon for Men and Women has decided to obtain a personal desktop computer for use in his business. In addition to using the computer for writing letters, developing advertising pieces, performing basic accounting, and maintaining lists of customers, the owner would like his employees to use a **digital camera** to take pictures of customers after they have had their hair done and create a file of printed full-color pictures of customers for marketing purposes. The owner has asked you to recommend the type of camera, software, and computer he should buy. Prepare a brief report detailing your findings and recommendations. Be prepared to discuss your recommendations in class.

CASE STUDY 2 – Class Discussion   Your manager at Dave's Office Supply Outlet intends to choose a spreadsheet program that the entire company will use. He prefers to learn about software using trade books — written texts that explain the features of a program and how to use it — rather than using online Help or tutorials. He has asked you to evaluate the **spreadsheet** trade books available in bookstores on the Web. Visit a bookstore Web site and other Web sites that sell books to survey the spreadsheet trade books available for Microsoft Excel, Lotus, Quattro Pro, and StarOffice Calc. Which spreadsheet program has the most books available? How difficult would it be to learn each program using the trade books at hand? Which trade book do you think is the best? Why? If you were going to purchase software solely on the basis of the related trade books, which program would you buy? Why? Be prepared to discuss your recommendations in class.

CASE STUDY 3 – Research   After attending a seminar on Web applications, the chief financial officer of Eastern Steel, Inc. has asked you to investigate the feasibility of using the Web to collect data from company offices and customers throughout the world. Recall that a **Web application** is application software that exists on a Web site. Users access the Web application through their browser. Use the Web and/or print media to create a brief report describing at least two Web applications and how Eastern Steel could use similar applications effectively. Include in your report a description of each application, a short overview of any online Help, and the Web address for each application. Write a brief report and share your findings with your class.

CASE STUDY 4 – Research   Frank's Custom Design frequently enhances its work with scanned photographs or graphics obtained with **illustration software**. The owner recently read that the Internet is providing a new resource for desktop publishers. Companies such as Corbis, Picture Network International, Muse, and Liaison International are offering archives of artwork and photographs. You have been asked to investigate the feasibility of using this new resource. Information about all four companies can be found on the World Wide Web. Pick two companies that provide digital images and find out more about their product. Prepare a brief report that answers the following questions. What kinds of illustrations are available? How are pictures on a specific subject located? How are the illustrations provided? What fees are involved? Would the cost be different for a high school student creating one paper than for an organization newsletter with a statewide distribution? Which company do you prefer? Why?

CASE STUDY 5 – Team Challenge   The new superintendent of Lisle Elementary School District 205 has recommended that **educational software** play a major role in the learning process at every grade level. In her presentation to the school board, she claimed that educational software is available for a wide variety of skills and subjects. She also indicated that educational software lets students learn at their own pace, shows infinite patience, and usually offers an entertaining approach. The president of the school board is not so sure. Unlike human instructors, educational software often does not recognize unique problems, fails to address individual goals, and provides limited feedback. Form a three-member team and investigate the use of educational software. Have each member of your team visit a software vendor's Web site, or an educational cooperative's Web site and list the advantages and disadvantages of using educational software. Select a program on the Web or from your school's education department library and use it. Note the subject being taught, the audience to which the software is directed, the approach used, and any special features. Then, meet with your team, discuss your findings, prepare a team report or PowerPoint presentation, and share it with your class.

CHAPTER FOUR

The Components of the System Unit

Picture Yourself Buying a Computer

Your neighbor, who is a computer guru and always has the latest computers and devices, just called to see if you want to buy one of his *old* computers. What he considers old actually still is state of the art. He says it would include the system unit, monitor, speakers, keyboard, and mouse.

He starts rattling off all the features while you frantically make quick notes. The system unit has a 3.2 GHz Pentium D processor with dual-core technology and 1 MB of L2 cache. It has 512 MB of dual channel SDRAM expandable to 4 GB, a 533 MHz bus, and integrated modem and networking capabilities. The back of the system unit has ports for a keyboard, a mouse, a monitor, speakers, a network, and a modem. It also has a serial port, a parallel port, seven USB ports (two in front and five in back), and a FireWire port. It is not Bluetooth-enabled, but you can buy a wireless port adapter if you need that capability. He says he will set up the computer for you, clean it for you once a year, and be available for personal support anytime. "Five hundred bucks," he says, "and it's yours." Sold!

After hanging up the telephone, you glance at all your notes. You know he gave you a great deal, but you have no idea what all these terms and numbers mean. To find out, you plan to read Chapter 4 to learn about processor chips, RAM, cache, adapter cards, and ports, and discover the many other components of the system unit.

After completing this chapter, you will be able to:

1. Differentiate among various styles of system units

2. Identify chips, adapter cards, and other components of a motherboard

3. Describe the components of a processor and how they complete a machine cycle

4. Identify characteristics of various personal computer processors on the market today

5. Define a bit and describe how a series of bits represents data

6. Explain how programs transfer in and out of memory

7. Differentiate among the various types of memory

8. Describe the types of expansion slots and adapter cards

9. Explain the differences among a serial port, a parallel port, a USB port, a FireWire port, and other ports

10. Describe how buses contribute to a computer's processing speed

11. Identify components in mobile computers and mobile devices

12. Understand how to clean a system unit

CONTENTS

THE SYSTEM UNIT

Whether you are a home user or a business user, you most likely will make the decision to purchase a new computer or upgrade an existing computer within the next several years. Thus, you should understand the purpose of each component in a computer. As Chapter 1 discussed, a computer includes devices used for input, processing, output, storage, and communications. Many of these components are part of the system unit.

The **system unit** is a case that contains electronic components of the computer used to process data. System units are available in a variety of shapes and sizes. The case of the system unit, sometimes called the *chassis*, is made of metal or plastic and protects the internal electronic components from damage. All computers have a system unit (Figure 4-1).

On desktop personal computers, the electronic components and most storage devices are part of the system unit. Other devices, such as the keyboard, mouse, microphone, monitor, printer, scanner, PC video camera, and speakers, normally occupy space outside the system unit. The trend is toward a smaller form factor, or size and shape, of the desktop personal computer system unit.

FIGURE 4-1   All sizes of computers have a system unit.

On notebook computers, the keyboard and pointing device often occupy the area on the top of the system unit, and the display attaches to the system unit by hinges. The location of the system unit on a Tablet PC varies, depending on the design of the Tablet PC. Some models build the system unit behind the display (as shown in Figure 4-1), while others position the system unit below the keyboard (shown later in the chapter). The system unit on a PDA and smart phone usually consumes the entire device. On these mobile devices, the display often is built into the system unit.

With game consoles, the input and output devices, such as controllers and a television, reside outside the system unit. On handheld game consoles and digital audio players, by contrast, the packaging around the system unit houses the input devices and display.

At some point, you might have to open the system unit on a desktop personal computer to replace or install a new electronic component. For this reason, you should be familiar with the electronic components of a system unit. Figure 4-2 identifies some of these components, which include the processor, memory, adapter cards, ports, drive bays, and the power supply.

The processor interprets and carries out the basic instructions that operate a computer. Memory typically holds data waiting to be processed and instructions waiting to be executed. The electronic components and circuitry of the system unit, such as the processor and memory, usually are part of or are connected to a circuit board called the motherboard. Many current motherboards also integrate modem and networking capabilities.

FIGURE 4-2 The system unit on a typical personal computer consists of numerous electronic components, some of which are shown in this figure. The sound card and video card are two types of adapter cards.

Adapter cards are circuit boards that provide connections and functions not built into the motherboard. Two adapter cards found in some desktop personal computers today are a sound card and a video card. Devices outside the system unit often attach to ports on the system unit by a connector on a cable. These devices may include a keyboard, mouse, microphone, monitor, printer, scanner, card reader/writer, digital camera, PC video camera, and speakers. A drive bay holds one or more disk drives. The power supply converts electricity from a power cord plugged in a wall outlet into a form that can be used by the computer.

The Motherboard

The **motherboard**, sometimes called a *system board*, is the main circuit board of the system unit. Many electronic components attach to the motherboard; others are built into it. Figure 4-3 shows a photograph of a current desktop personal computer motherboard and identifies components that attach to it, including adapter cards, a processor chip, and a memory module. Memory chips are installed on memory cards (modules) that fit in a slot on the motherboard.

A computer **chip** is a small piece of semiconducting material, usually silicon, on which integrated circuits are etched. An *integrated circuit* contains many microscopic pathways capable of carrying electrical current. Each integrated circuit can contain millions of elements such as resistors, capacitors, and transistors. A *transistor*, for example, can act as an electronic switch that opens or closes the circuit for electrical charges. Most chips are no bigger than one-half-inch square. Manufacturers package chips so the chips can be attached to a circuit board, such as a motherboard or an adapter card.

FIGURE 4-3   Many electronic components attach to the motherboard in a desktop personal computer, including a processor chip, memory module, and adapter cards.

PROCESSOR

The **processor**, also called the **central processing unit** (**CPU**), interprets and carries out the basic instructions that operate a computer. The processor significantly impacts overall computing power and manages most of a computer's operations. On larger computers, such as mainframes and supercomputers, the various functions performed by the processor extend over many separate chips and often multiple circuit boards. On a personal computer, all functions of the processor usually are on a single chip. Some computer and chip manufacturers use the term *microprocessor* to refer to a personal computer processor chip.

Processors contain a control unit and an arithmetic logic unit (ALU). These two components work together to perform processing operations. Figure 4-4 illustrates how other devices connected to the computer communicate with the processor to carry out a task.

The Control Unit

The **control unit** is the component of the processor that directs and coordinates most of the operations in the computer. The control unit has a role much like a traffic cop: it interprets each instruction issued by a program and then initiates the appropriate action to carry out the instruction. Read Ethics & Issues 4-1 for a related discussion.

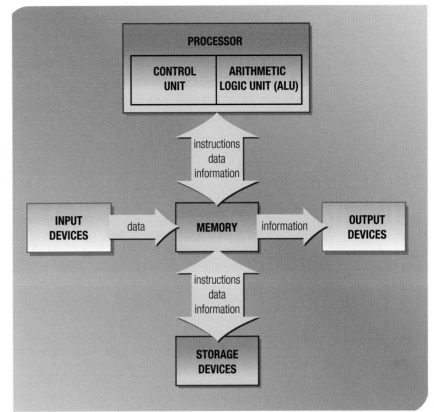

FIGURE 4-4   Most devices connected to the computer communicate with the processor to carry out a task. When a user starts a program, for example, its instructions transfer from a storage device to memory. Data needed by programs enters memory from either an input device or a storage device. The control unit interprets and executes instructions in memory, and the ALU performs calculations on the data in memory. Resulting information is stored in memory, from which it can be sent to an output device or a storage device for future access, as needed.

ETHICS & ISSUES 4-1

Can Computers Think?

Ever since a computer defeated world chess champion Gary Kasparov in a chess match, people have wondered, can computers think? As computer processors and software become more powerful, the question is more hotly debated. People who believe computers can think argue that, if a person had a conversation with a computer and was convinced the computer was really human, then the computer is intelligent. This criteria is known as the Turing Test, named after British mathematician Alan Turing who proposed the test in 1950. If a computer can pass a modern version of the Turing Test, it is considered to be intelligent, and it may win the prestigious $100,000 Loebner Prize. Opponents counter this argument by saying that, if a question written in a foreign language was submitted to a person who can read and write the language and a person who cannot read or write the language but has a list of questions and appropriate answers, it might be impossible to tell the response of one person from the other. But, the person who cannot read or write the language really does not understand it, any more than a computer really can think. Besides, computers lack an essential component of human thinking — common sense. Computers can consider millions of chess moves a second, but humans have the common sense to recognize that some moves are not worthy of consideration. Can computers think? Why or why not? If computers cannot think now, might they be able to think in the future? Why?

The Arithmetic Logic Unit

The **arithmetic logic unit** (*ALU*), another component of the processor, performs arithmetic, comparison, and other operations.

Arithmetic operations include basic calculations such as addition, subtraction, multiplication, and division. *Comparison operations* involve comparing one data item with another to determine whether the first item is greater than, equal to, or less than the other item. Depending on the result of the comparison, different actions may occur. For example, to determine if an employee should receive overtime pay, software instructs the ALU to compare the number of hours an employee worked during the week with the regular time hours allowed (e.g., 40 hours). If the hours worked are greater than 40, software instructs the ALU to perform calculations that compute the overtime wage.

Machine Cycle

For every instruction, a processor repeats a set of four basic operations, which comprise a *machine cycle* (Figure 4-5): (1) fetching, (2) decoding, (3) executing, and, if necessary, (4) storing. *Fetching* is the process of obtaining a program instruction or data item from memory. The term *decoding* refers to the process of translating the instruction into signals the computer can execute. *Executing* is the process of carrying out the commands. *Storing*, in this context, means writing the result to memory (not to a storage medium).

In some computers, the processor fetches, decodes, executes, and stores only one instruction at a time. In these computers, the processor waits until an instruction completes all four stages of the machine cycle (fetch, decode, execute, and store) before beginning work on the next instruction.

FIGURE 4-5   THE STEPS IN A MACHINE CYCLE

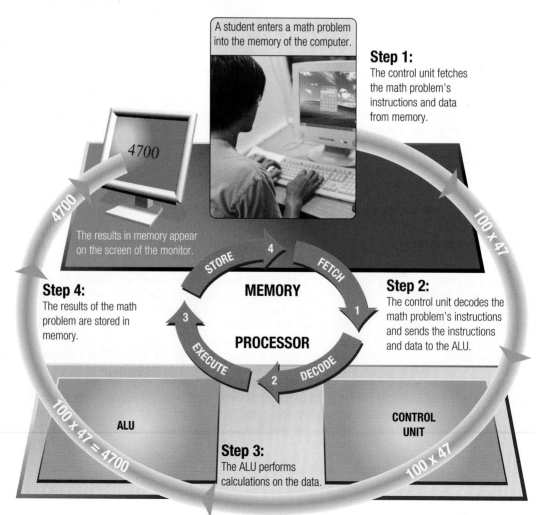

A student enters a math problem into the memory of the computer.

Step 1:
The control unit fetches the math problem's instructions and data from memory.

4700

The results in memory appear on the screen of the monitor.

STORE   4   FETCH

MEMORY

3   1

PROCESSOR

EXECUTE   2   DECODE

Step 4:
The results of the math problem are stored in memory.

Step 2:
The control unit decodes the math problem's instructions and sends the instructions and data to the ALU.

100 X 47

100 X 47 = 4700

ALU

CONTROL UNIT

100 X 47

Step 3:
The ALU performs calculations on the data.

Most of today's personal computers support a concept called pipelining. With *pipelining*, the processor begins fetching a second instruction before it completes the machine cycle for the first instruction. Processors that use pipelining are faster because they do not have to wait for one instruction to complete the machine cycle before fetching the next. Think of a pipeline as an assembly line. By the time the first instruction is in the last stage of the machine cycle, three other instructions could have been fetched and started through the machine cycle (Figure 4-6).

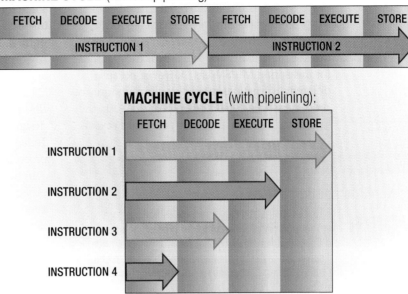

MACHINE CYCLE (without pipelining):

| FETCH | DECODE | EXECUTE | STORE | FETCH | DECODE | EXECUTE | STORE |

INSTRUCTION 1 · INSTRUCTION 2

MACHINE CYCLE (with pipelining):

| FETCH | DECODE | EXECUTE | STORE |

INSTRUCTION 1
INSTRUCTION 2
INSTRUCTION 3
INSTRUCTION 4

FIGURE 4-6 Most modern personal computers support pipelining. With pipelining, the processor fetches a second instruction before the first instruction is completed. The result is faster processing.

Registers

A processor contains small, high-speed storage locations, called *registers*, that temporarily hold data and instructions. Registers are part of the processor, not part of memory or a permanent storage device. Processors have many different types of registers, each with a specific storage function. Register functions include storing the location from where an instruction was fetched, storing an instruction while the control unit decodes it, storing data while the ALU computes it, and storing the results of a calculation.

The System Clock

The processor relies on a small quartz crystal circuit called the **system clock** to control the timing of all computer operations. Just as your heart beats at a regular rate to keep your body functioning, the system clock generates regular electronic pulses, or ticks, that set the operating pace of components of the system unit.

Each tick equates to a *clock cycle*. In the past, processors used one or more clock cycles to execute each instruction. Processors today often are *superscalar*, which means they can execute more than one instruction per clock cycle.

The pace of the system clock, called the **clock speed**, is measured by the number of ticks per second. Current personal computer processors have clock speeds in the gigahertz range. Giga

is a prefix that stands for billion, and a *hertz* is one cycle per second. Thus, one **gigahertz (GHz)** equals one billion ticks of the system clock per second. A computer that operates at 3.8 GHz has 3.8 billion (giga) clock cycles in one second (hertz).

The faster the clock speed, the more instructions the processor can execute per second. The speed of the system clock has no effect on devices such as a printer or disk drive. The speed of the system clock is just one factor that influences a computer's performance. Other factors, such as the type of processor chip, amount of cache, memory access time, bus width, and bus clock speed, are discussed later in this chapter.

FAQ 4-1

Does the system clock also keep track of the current date and time?

No, a separate battery-backed chip, called the *real-time clock*, keeps track of the date and time in a computer. The battery continues to run the real-time clock even when the computer is off. For more information, visit scsite.com/dc2007/ch4/faq and then click Computer Clock.

Some computer professionals measure a processor's speed according to the number of *MIPS* (*millions of instructions per second*) it can process. Current desktop personal computers can process more than 7,000 MIPS. No real standard for measuring MIPS exists, however, because different instructions require varying amounts of processing time. Read Looking Ahead 4-1 for a look at the next generation of processing speeds.

LOOKING AHEAD 4-1

Countries Seek Computing Speed Supremacy

The United States and Japan have been battling for years over the top spot in supercomputer processing speed, and China is entering this global race for national pride.

The world's fastest computers currently are located in the United States. IBM's Blue Gene/L, built for the U.S. Department of Energy's National Nuclear Security Agency, runs at more than 138 teraflops, or trillion, calculations per second, according to the Top500 Project, a group that monitors supercomputers throughout the world.

The Japanese government has set a goal of developing a supercomputer by 2011 that can perform more than a quadrillion calculations per second.

These fast computers are used in medical research, advanced climate forecasting, and other areas. They cost more than $1 billion to develop. For more information, visit scsite.com/dc2007/ch4/looking and then click Fastest Computer.

Comparison of Personal Computer Processors

The leading processor chip manufacturers for personal computers are Intel, AMD (Advanced Micro Devices), Transmeta, IBM, and Motorola. These manufacturers often identify their processor chips by a model name or model number. Figure 4-7 categorizes the historical development of the personal computer processor and documents the increases in clock speed and number of transistors in chips since 1982. The greater the number of transistors, the more complex and powerful the chip.

With its earlier processors, Intel used a model number to identify the various chips. After learning that processor model numbers could not be trademarked and protected from use by competitors, Intel began identifying its processors with names — thus emerged the series of processors known as the Pentium. Most high-performance desktop PCs use some type of **Pentium** processor. Many notebook computers and Tablet PCs use a **Pentium M** processor. Less expensive, basic PCs use a brand of Intel processor called the **Celeron**. The **Xeon** and **Itanium** processors, are ideal for workstations and low-end servers.

Today, AMD is the leading manufacturer of *Intel-compatible processors*, which have an internal design similar to Intel processors, perform the same functions, and can be as powerful, but often are less expensive. Transmeta, also a manufacturer of Intel-compatible processors, specializes in processors for mobile computers and devices. Intel and Intel-compatible processors are used in PCs.

Until recently, Apple computers used only an *IBM processor* or a *Motorola processor*, which had a design different from the Intel-style processor. Today's Apple computers, however, use Intel processors.

In the past, chip manufacturers listed a processor's clock speed in marketing literature and advertisements. As previously mentioned, though, clock speed is only one factor that impacts processing speed in today's computers. To help consumers evaluate various processors, manufacturers such as Intel and AMD now use a numbering scheme that more accurately reflects the processing speed of their chips.

Processor chips include technologies to improve processing performance. Some of Intel's processor chips contain *Hyper-Threading* (*HT*) *Technology*, which improves processing power and time by allowing the processor chip to mimic the power of two processors. For even higher levels of performance with lower levels of power consumption and heat emitted in the system unit, several processor chip manufacturers now offer dual-core and multicore processors. A *dual-core processor* is a chip that has two separate processors. Similarly, a *multicore processor* is a chip with two or more separate processors. Most processors have built-in instructions to improve the performance of multimedia and 3-D graphics. Processors for notebook computers include technology to integrate wireless capabilities and optimize and extend battery life. For example, Intel's *Centrino* mobile technology integrates wireless capabilities in notebook computers and Tablet PCs. PDAs and other smaller mobile devices often use a processor, such as AMD's Alchemy processor, that consumes less power yet offers high performance.

Another type of processor, called *system on a chip*, integrates the functions of a processor, memory, and a video card on a single chip. Lower-priced personal computers, Tablet PCs, networking devices, and consumer electronics such as audio players and game consoles sometimes have a system-on-a-chip processor. The goal of system-on-a-chip manufacturers is to create processors that have faster clock speeds, consume less power, are small, and are cost effective.

COMPARISON OF PERSONAL COMPUTER PROCESSORS

	NAME	DATE INTRODUCED/ UPDATED	MANUFACTURER	CLOCK SPEED*	NUMBER OF TRANSISTORS
SERVER PROCESSORS	Xeon MP	2002/2005	Intel	1.4–3.66 GHz	108–169 million
	Itanium 2	2003/2004	Intel	1.3–1.6 GHz	220–410 million
	Xeon	2001/2003	Intel	1.4–3.6 GHz	42–108 million
	Itanium	2001	Intel	733–800 MHz	25.4–60 million
	Pentium III Xeon	1999/2000	Intel	500–900 MHz	9.5–28 million
	Pentium II Xeon	1998/1999	Intel	400–450 MHz	7.5–27 million
	Opteron	2003	AMD	1.4–2.4 GHz	100 million
	Athlon MP	2002	AMD	1.53–2.25 GHz	54.3 million
DESKTOP PERSONAL COMPUTER PROCESSORS	Pentium Extreme Edition (dual-core)	2005	Intel	3.2 GHz	178 million
	Pentium D (dual-core)	2005	Intel	2.8–3.2 GHz	230 million
	Pentium 4 with HT Technology	2002/2005	Intel	2.4–3.8 GHz	55–178 million
	Pentium 4	2000/2005	Intel	1.3–3.8 GHz	42–125 million
	Pentium III	1999/2003	Intel	450 MHz–1.4 GHz	9.5–44 million
	Celeron D	2004/2005	Intel	2.4–3.2 GHz	26.2–125 million
	Celeron	1998/2003	Intel	266 MHz–2.8 GHz	7.5–55 million
	Pentium II	1997/1998	Intel	233–450 MHz	7.5 million
	Pentium Pro	1995/1999	Intel	150–200 MHz	5.5 million
	Pentium	1993/1997	Intel	75–233 MHz	3.3–4.5 million
	80486DX	1989/1994	Intel	25–100 MHz	1.6 million
	80386	1985/1990	Intel	16–33 MHz	275,000
	80286	1982	Intel	6–12 MHz	134,000
	Athlon 64 X2 (dual-core)	2005	AMD	2.0–2.8 GHz	233 million
	Athlon 64 FX	2005	AMD	2.6–2.8 GHz	114 million
	Sempron	2004	AMD	1.5–2 GHz	68.5 million
	Athlon 64	2003/2004	AMD	2–2.4 GHz	105.9–114 million
	Athlon	1999/2002	AMD	500 MHz–1.4 GHz	22–38 million
	Duron	1999/2001	AMD	600 MHz–1.3 GHz	25 million
	AMD–K6	1997/1999	AMD	300–450 MHz	8.8–21.3 million
	PowerPC (G1 to G5)	1994/2005	Motorola/IBM	60 MHz–2.7 GHz	2.8–58 million
	68040	1989	Motorola	25–40 MHz	1.2 million
	68030	1987	Motorola	16–50 MHz	270,000
	68020	1984	Motorola	16–33 MHz	190,000
MOBILE PROCESSORS	Celeron M	2004	Intel	900 MHz–1.6 GHz	55 million
	Pentium M	2003/2004	Intel	1–2.26 GHz	77–140 million
	Mobile Celeron	1999/2003	Intel	266 MHz–2.8 GHz	18.9 million
	Mobile Pentium	1997/2002	Intel	200 MHz–3.46 GHz	55 million
	Turion 64	2005	AMD	1.6–2.4 GHz	114 million
	Mobile Sempron	2004	AMD	1.6–1.8 GHz	37.5 million
	Mobile Athlon	2001/2002	AMD	1.4–2.2 GHz	37.5–105.9 million
	Mobile Duron	2000/2001	AMD	1.3 GHz	25 million
	Efficeon	2003	Transmeta	1–1.7 GHz	79 million
	Crusoe	2000	Transmeta	500 MHz–1 GHz	6.7 million

* Clock speed is not the only factor that determines processor performance.

FIGURE 4-7 A comparison of some processors.

Buying a Personal Computer

If you are ready to buy a new computer, the processor you select should depend on how you plan to use the computer. If you purchase an IBM-compatible PC or Apple computer, you will choose an Intel processor or an Intel-compatible processor (Figure 4-8).

Most users will realize greater processing performance with a dual-core/multicore processor. Each processor on a dual-core/multicore chip generally runs at a slower clock speed than a single-core processor, but dual-core/multicore chips typically reduce the power consumption and heat output, while increasing overall performance. For example, a dual-core processor can deliver one and one-half times more processing speed than a single-core processor.

If you plan to purchase an entertainment desktop computer, you will want it to use Intel's *Viiv technology*, which is designed to enhance digital entertainment through a home computer.

Instead of buying an entirely new computer, you might be able to upgrade your processor to increase the computer's performance. Be certain the processor you buy is compatible with your computer's motherboard; otherwise, you will have to replace the motherboard, too. Replacing a processor is a fairly simple process, whereas replacing a motherboard is much more complicated.

For detailed computer purchasing guidelines, read the Buyer's Guide 2007 feature that follows Chapter 8. Read Ethics & Issues 4-2 for a related discussion.

WEB LINK 4-2

Dual-Core Processors

For more information, visit scsite.com/dc2007/ch4/weblink and then click Dual-Core Processors.

GUIDELINES FOR SELECTING AN INTEL OR INTEL-COMPATIBLE PROCESSOR

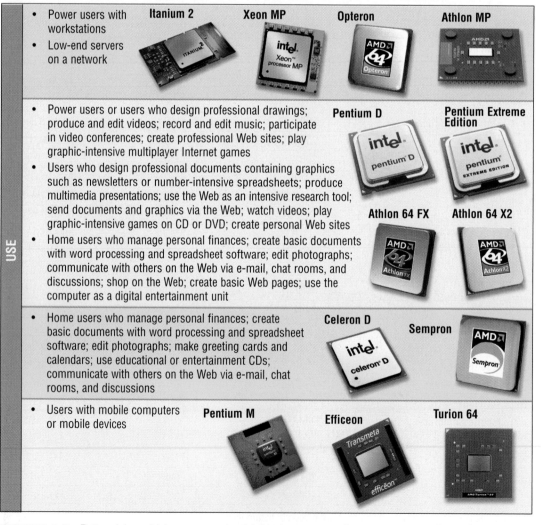

USE

- Power users with workstations
- Low-end servers on a network

Itanium 2   Xeon MP   Opteron   Athlon MP

- Power users or users who design professional drawings; produce and edit videos; record and edit music; participate in video conferences; create professional Web sites; play graphic-intensive multiplayer Internet games
- Users who design professional documents containing graphics such as newsletters or number-intensive spreadsheets; produce multimedia presentations; use the Web as an intensive research tool; send documents and graphics via the Web; watch videos; play graphic-intensive games on CD or DVD; create personal Web sites
- Home users who manage personal finances; create basic documents with word processing and spreadsheet software; edit photographs; communicate with others on the Web via e-mail, chat rooms, and discussions; shop on the Web; create basic Web pages; use the computer as a digital entertainment unit

Pentium D   Pentium Extreme Edition   Athlon 64 FX   Athlon 64 X2

- Home users who manage personal finances; create basic documents with word processing and spreadsheet software; edit photographs; make greeting cards and calendars; use educational or entertainment CDs; communicate with others on the Web via e-mail, chat rooms, and discussions

Celeron D   Sempron

- Users with mobile computers or mobile devices

Pentium M   Efficeon   Turion 64

FIGURE 4-8 Determining which processor to obtain when you purchase a computer depends on computer usage.

FAQ 4-2

What is Moore's Law?

Moore's Law is a prediction made by one of the founders of Intel, Gordon Moore, that the number of transistors and resistors placed on computer chips would double every year, with a proportional increase in computing power and decrease in cost. The chart below shows the growth of Intel processors. For more information, read the Technology Trailblazer article on page 219 and visit scsite.com/dc2007/ch4/faq and then click Moore's Law.

Intel Processor Chip Complexity

ETHICS & ISSUES 4-2

Discarded Computer Parts: Whose Problem Is It?

Experts estimate that about 1 billion computers will be discarded by 2010. The discarded items often are known as *e-waste*. As technology advances and prices fall, many people think of computers as disposable items. Computers contain several toxic elements, including lead, mercury, and barium. Computers thrown into landfills or burned in incinerators can pollute the ground and the air. A vast amount of e-waste ends up polluting third world countries. One solution is to recycle old computers. Some lawmakers prefer a more aggressive approach, such as setting up a recycling program that would be paid for by adding a $10 fee to a computer's purchase price, or forcing computer makers to be responsible for collecting and recycling their products. Manufacturers already have taken steps, but some claim that consumers should bear the responsibility of disposing of their old computer parts. Several have reduced the amount of toxic material in their products, and manufacturers have set up their own recycling programs, for which users pay a fee. One manufacturer admits, however, that only seven percent of the computers it has sold have been recycled. What can be done to ensure that computers are disposed of safely? Should government, manufacturers, or users be responsible for safe disposal? Why? How can computer users be motivated to recycle obsolete equipment?

Heat Sinks, Heat Pipes, and Liquid Cooling

Processor chips generate quite a bit of heat, which could cause the chip to burn up. Although the computer's main fan generates airflow, today's processors require additional cooling. A *heat sink* is a small ceramic or metal component with fins on its surface that absorbs and disperses heat produced by electrical components such as a processor (Figure 4-9). Some heat sinks are packaged as part of a processor chip. Others are installed on the top or the side of the chip. Because a heat sink consumes extra space, a smaller device called a *heat pipe* cools processors in notebook computers.

Some computers use liquid cooling technology to reduce the temperature of a processor. *Liquid cooling technology* uses a continuous flow of fluid(s), such as water and glycol, in a process that transfers the heated fluid away from the processor to a radiator-type grill, which cools the liquid, and then returns the cooled fluid to the processor.

FIGURE 4-9   A heat sink, which is attached to the top of a processor, prevents the chip from overheating. The heat sink fan, which attaches to the top of the heat sink, helps distribute air dissipated by the heat sink.

Parallel Processing

Parallel processing is a method that uses multiple processors simultaneously to execute a single program or task (Figure 4-10). Parallel processing divides a single problem into portions so that multiple processors work on their assigned portion of the problem at the same time. Parallel processing requires special software that recognizes how to divide the problem and then bring the results back together again.

Some personal computers implement parallel processing with dual-core processors or multicore processors. Others have two or more separate processor chips, respectively called dual processor or multiprocessor computers.

Supercomputers use parallel processing for applications such as weather forecasting. Some applications draw on the idle time of home users' personal computers to achieve parallel processing.

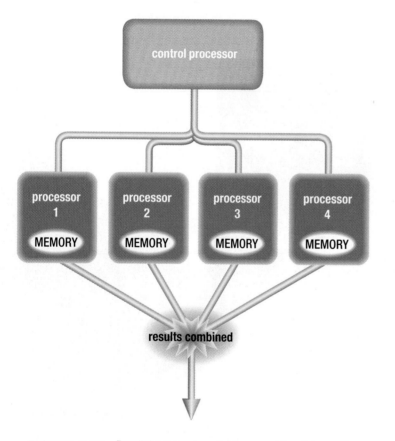

FIGURE 4-10 Parallel processing divides a problem into portions so that multiple processors work on their assigned portion of a problem at the same time. In this illustration, one processor, called the control processor, is managing the operations of four other processors.

Test your knowledge of pages 184 through 194 in Quiz Yourself 4-1.

QUIZ YOURSELF 4-1

Instructions: Find the true statement below. Then, rewrite the remaining false statements so they are true.

1. A computer chip is a small piece of semiconducting material, usually silicon, on which integrated circuits are etched.

2. Four basic operations in a machine cycle are: (1) comparing, (2) decoding, (3) executing, and, if necessary, (4) pipelining.

3. Processors contain a motherboard and an arithmetic logic unit (ALU).

4. The central processing unit, sometimes called a system board, is the main circuit board of the system unit.

5. The leading processor chip manufacturers for personal computers are Microsoft, AMD, IBM, Motorola, and Transmeta.

6. The pace of the system clock, called the clock speed, is measured by the number of ticks per minute.

7. The system unit is a case that contains mechanical components of the computer used to process data.

Quiz Yourself Online: To further check your knowledge of system unit styles, motherboards, processor components and machine cycles, and characteristics of personal computer processors, visit scsite.com/dc2007/ch4/quiz and then click Objectives 1 – 4.

DATA REPRESENTATION

To understand fully the way a computer processes data, you should know how a computer represents data. People communicate through speech by combining words into sentences. Human speech is **analog** because it uses continuous (wave form) signals that vary in strength and quality. Most computers are **digital**. They recognize only two discrete states: on and off. This is because computers are electronic devices powered by electricity, which also has only two states: on and off.

The two digits, 0 and 1, easily can represent these two states (Figure 4-11). The digit 0 represents the electronic state of off (absence of an electronic charge). The digit 1 represents the electronic state of on (presence of an electronic charge).

When people count, they use the digits in the decimal system (0 through 9). The computer, by contrast, uses a binary system because it recognizes only two states. The **binary system** is a number system that has just two unique digits, 0 and 1, called bits. A **bit** (short for *binary digit*) is the smallest unit of data the computer can process. By itself, a bit is not very informative.

When 8 bits are grouped together as a unit, they form a **byte**. A byte provides enough different combinations of 0s and 1s to represent 256 individual characters. These characters include numbers, uppercase and lowercase letters of the alphabet, punctuation marks, and others, such as the letters of the Greek alphabet.

The combinations of 0s and 1s that represent characters are defined by patterns called a coding scheme. In one coding scheme, the number 4 is represented as 00110100, the number 6 as 00110110, and the capital letter E as 01000101 (Figure 4-12). Two popular coding schemes are ASCII and EBCDIC (Figure 4-13). The *American Standard Code for Information Interchange* (*ASCII* pronounced ASK-ee) scheme is the most widely used coding system to represent data. Most personal computers and servers use the ASCII coding scheme. The *Extended Binary Coded Decimal Interchange Code* (*EBCDIC* pronounced EB-see-dik) scheme is used primarily on mainframe computers and high-end servers.

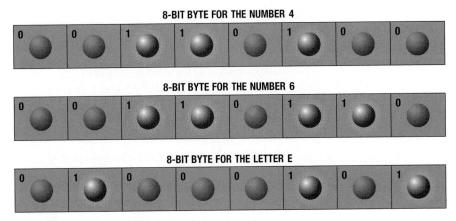

FIGURE 4-12   Eight bits grouped together as a unit are called a byte. A byte represents a single character in the computer.

The ASCII and EBCDIC coding schemes are sufficient for English and Western European languages but are not large enough for Asian and other languages that use different alphabets. *Unicode* is a 16-bit coding scheme that has the capacity of representing more than 65,000 characters and symbols. The Unicode coding scheme is capable of representing almost all the world's current written languages, as well as classic and historical languages. To allow for expansion, Unicode reserves 30,000 codes for future use and 6,000 codes for private use. Unicode is implemented in several operating systems, including Windows XP, Mac OS X, and Linux.

FIGURE 4-11   A computer circuit represents the 0 or the 1 electronically by the presence or absence of an electronic charge.

ASCII	SYMBOL	EBCDIC
00110000	0	11110000
00110001	1	11110001
00110010	2	11110010
00110011	3	11110011
00110100	4	11110100
00110101	5	11110101
00110110	6	11110110
00110111	7	11110111
00111000	8	11111000
00111001	9	11111001
01000001	A	11000001
01000010	B	11000010
01000011	C	11000011
01000100	D	11000100
01000101	E	11000101
01000110	F	11000110
01000111	G	11000111
01001000	H	11001000
01001001	I	11001001
01001010	J	11010001
01001011	K	11010010
01001100	L	11010011
01001101	M	11010100

ASCII	SYMBOL	EBCDIC
01001110	N	11010101
01001111	O	11010110
01010000	P	11010111
01010001	Q	11011000
01010010	R	11011001
01010011	S	11100010
01010100	T	11100011
01010101	U	11100100
01010110	V	11100101
01010111	W	11100110
01011000	X	11100111
01011001	Y	11101000
01011010	Z	11101001
00100001	!	01011010
00100010	"	01111111
00100011	#	01111011
00100100	$	01011011
00100101	%	01101100
00100110	&	01010000
00101000	(	01001101
00101001	)	01011101
00101010	*	01011100
00101011	+	01001110

FIGURE 4-13   Two popular coding schemes are ASCII and EBCDIC.

Unicode-enabled programming languages and software products include Java, XML, Microsoft Office, and Oracle.

Appendix A at the back of this book discusses the ASCII, EBCDIC, and Unicode schemes in more depth, along with the parity bit and number systems.

Coding schemes such as ASCII make it possible for humans to interact with a digital computer that processes only bits. When you press a key on a keyboard, a chip in the keyboard converts the key's electronic signal into a special code that is sent to the system unit. Then, the system unit converts the code into a binary form the computer can process and stores it in memory. Every character is converted to its

corresponding byte. The computer then processes the data as bytes, which actually is a series of on/off electrical states. When processing is finished, software converts the byte into a human-recognizable number, letter of the alphabet, or special character that is displayed on a screen or is printed (Figure 4-14). All of these conversions take place so quickly that you do not realize they are occurring.

Standards, such as those defined by ASCII, EBCDIC, and Unicode, also make it possible for components in computers to communicate with each other successfully. By following these and other standards, manufacturers can produce a component and be assured that it will operate correctly in a computer.

FIGURE 4-14 HOW A LETTER IS CONVERTED TO BINARY FORM AND BACK

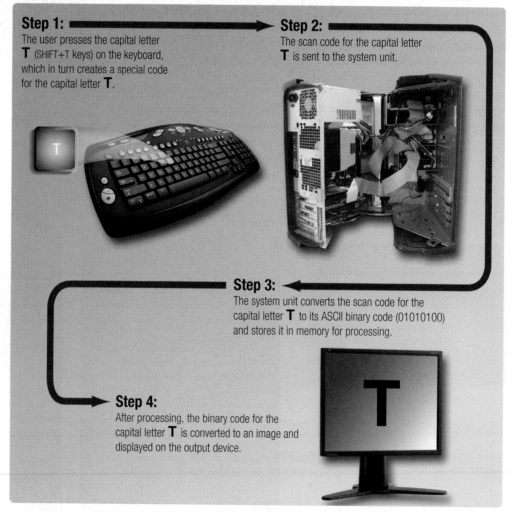

Step 1:
The user presses the capital letter **T** (SHIFT+T keys) on the keyboard, which in turn creates a special code for the capital letter **T**.

Step 2:
The scan code for the capital letter **T** is sent to the system unit.

Step 3:
The system unit converts the scan code for the capital letter **T** to its ASCII binary code (01010100) and stores it in memory for processing.

Step 4:
After processing, the binary code for the capital letter **T** is converted to an image and displayed on the output device.

MEMORY

Memory consists of electronic components that store instructions waiting to be executed by the processor, data needed by those instructions, and the results of processed data (information). Memory usually consists of one or more chips on the motherboard or some other circuit board in the computer.

Memory stores three basic categories of items: (1) the operating system and other system software that control or maintain the computer and its devices; (2) application programs that carry out a specific task such as word processing; and (3) the data being processed by the application programs and resulting information. This role of memory to store both data and programs is known as the *stored program concept*.

Bytes and Addressable Memory

A byte (character) is the basic storage unit in memory. When application program instructions and data are transferred to memory from storage devices, the instructions and data exist as bytes. Each byte resides temporarily in a location in memory that has an *address*. An address simply is a unique number that identifies the location of a byte in memory. The illustration in Figure 4-15 shows how seats in a concert hall are similar to addresses in memory: (1) a seat, which is identified by a unique seat number, holds one person at a time, and a

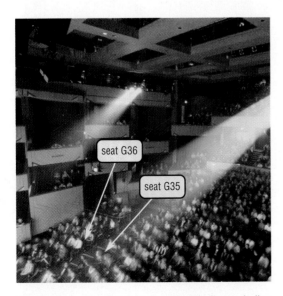

seat G36

seat G35

FIGURE 4-15 Seats in a concert hall are similar to addresses in memory: a seat holds one person at a time, and a location in memory holds a single byte; and both a seat and a byte can be empty.

location in memory, which is identified by a unique address, holds a single byte; and (2) both a seat, identified by a seat number, and a byte, identified by an address, can be empty. To access data or instructions in memory, the computer references the addresses that contain bytes of data.

Memory Sizes

Manufacturers state the size of memory chips and storage devices in terms of the number of bytes the chip or device has available for storage (Figure 4-16). Recall that storage devices hold data, instructions, and information for future use, while most memory holds these items temporarily. A **kilobyte** (**KB** or **K**) is equal to exactly 1,024 bytes. To simplify memory and storage definitions, computer users often round a kilobyte down to 1,000 bytes. For example, if a memory chip can store 100 KB, it can hold approximately 100,000 bytes (characters). A **megabyte** (**MB**) is equal to approximately 1 million bytes. A **gigabyte** (**GB**) equals approximately 1 billion bytes. A **terabyte** (**TB**) is equal to approximately 1 trillion bytes.

MEMORY AND STORAGE SIZES

Term	Abbreviation	Approximate Number of Bytes	Exact Amount of Bytes	Approximate Number of Pages of Text
Kilobyte	KB or K	1 thousand	1,024	1/2
Megabyte	MB	1 million	1,048,576	500
Gigabyte	GB	1 billion	1,073,741,824	500,000
Terabyte	TB	1 trillion	1,099,511,627,776	500,000,000

FIGURE 4-16 Terms commonly used to define memory and storage sizes.

Types of Memory

The system unit contains two types of memory: volatile and nonvolatile. When the computer's power is turned off, *volatile memory* loses its contents. *Nonvolatile memory*, by contrast, does not lose its contents when power is removed from the computer. Thus, volatile memory is temporary and nonvolatile memory is permanent. RAM is the most common type of volatile memory. Examples of nonvolatile memory include ROM, flash memory, and CMOS. The following pages discuss these types of memory.

RAM

Users typically are referring to RAM when discussing computer memory. **RAM** (*random access memory*), also called *main memory*, consists of memory chips that can be read from and written to by the processor and other devices. When you turn on power to a computer, certain operating system files (such as the files that determine how the Windows XP desktop appears) load into RAM from a storage device such as a hard disk. These files remain in RAM as long as the computer has continuous power. As additional programs and data are requested, they also load into RAM from storage.

The processor interprets and executes a program's instructions while the program is in RAM. During this time, the contents of RAM may change (Figure 4-17). RAM can accommodate multiple programs simultaneously.

Most RAM is volatile, which means it loses its contents when the power is removed from the computer. For this reason, you must save any data, instructions, and information you

FIGURE 4-17 HOW PROGRAM INSTRUCTIONS TRANSFER IN AND OUT OF RAM

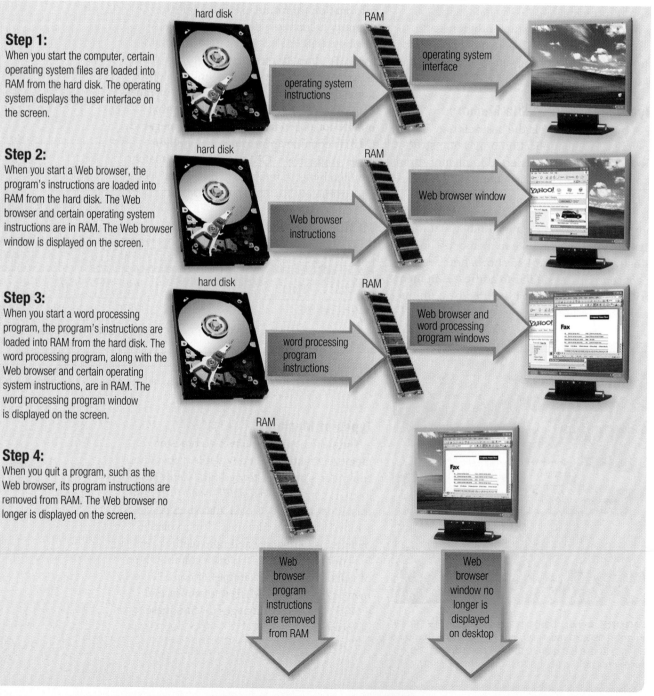

Step 1:
When you start the computer, certain operating system files are loaded into RAM from the hard disk. The operating system displays the user interface on the screen.

hard disk → operating system instructions → RAM → operating system interface

Step 2:
When you start a Web browser, the program's instructions are loaded into RAM from the hard disk. The Web browser and certain operating system instructions are in RAM. The Web browser window is displayed on the screen.

hard disk → Web browser instructions → RAM → Web browser window

Step 3:
When you start a word processing program, the program's instructions are loaded into RAM from the hard disk. The word processing program, along with the Web browser and certain operating system instructions, are in RAM. The word processing program window is displayed on the screen.

hard disk → word processing program instructions → RAM → Web browser and word processing program windows

Step 4:
When you quit a program, such as the Web browser, its program instructions are removed from RAM. The Web browser no longer is displayed on the screen.

RAM

Web browser program instructions are removed from RAM

Web browser window no longer is displayed on desktop

may need in the future. Saving is the process of copying data, instructions, and information from RAM to a storage device such as a hard disk.

Three basic types of RAM chips exist: dynamic RAM, static RAM, and magnetoresistive RAM.

- *Dynamic RAM* (*DRAM* pronounced DEE-ram) chips must be re-energized constantly or they lose their contents. Many variations of DRAM chips exist, most of which are faster than the basic DRAM. *Synchronous DRAM* (*SDRAM*) chips are much faster than DRAM chips because they are synchronized to the system clock. *Double Data Rate SDRAM* (*DDR SDRAM*) chips are even faster than SDRAM chips because they transfer data twice for each clock cycle, instead of just once, and DDR 2 is even faster than DDR. Dual channel SDRAM is faster than single channel SDRAM because it delivers twice the amount of data to the processor. *Rambus DRAM* (*RDRAM*) is yet another type of DRAM that is much faster than SDRAM because it uses pipelining techniques. Most personal computers today use some form of SDRAM chips or RDRAM chips.

- *Static RAM* (*SRAM* pronounced ESS-ram) chips are faster and more reliable than any variation of DRAM chips. These chips do not have to be re-energized as often as DRAM chips, thus, the term static. SRAM chips, however, are much more expensive than DRAM chips. Special applications such as cache use SRAM chips. A later section in this chapter discusses cache.

- A newer type of RAM, called *magnetoresistive RAM* (*MRAM* pronounced EM-ram), stores data using magnetic charges instead of electrical charges. Manufacturers claim that MRAM has greater storage capacity, consumes less power, and has faster access times than electronic RAM. Also, MRAM retains its contents after power is removed from the computer, which could prevent loss of data for users. As the cost of MRAM declines, experts predict MRAM could replace both DRAM and SRAM.

RAM chips usually reside on a **memory module**, which is a small circuit board. **Memory slots** on the motherboard hold memory modules (Figure 4-18). Three types of memory modules are SIMMs, DIMMs, and

RIMMs. A *SIMM* (*single inline memory module*) has pins on opposite sides of the circuit board that connect together to form a single set of contacts. With a *DIMM* (*dual inline memory module*), by contrast, the pins on opposite sides of the circuit board do not connect and thus form two sets of contacts. SIMMs and DIMMs typically hold SDRAM chips. A *RIMM* (*Rambus inline memory module*) houses RDRAM chips. For a more technical discussion about RAM, read the High-Tech Talk article on page 218 at the end of this chapter.

FIGURE 4-18 This photo shows a memory module being inserted in a motherboard.

WEB LINK 4-3

RAM

For more information, visit scsite.com/dc2007/ch4/weblink and then click RAM.

RAM CONFIGURATIONS The amount of RAM necessary in a computer often depends on the types of software you plan to use. A computer executes programs that are in RAM. Think of RAM as the workspace on the top of your desk. Just as the top of your desk needs a certain amount of space to hold papers, a computer needs a certain amount of memory to store programs, data, and information. The more RAM a computer has, the faster the computer will respond.

A software package typically indicates the minimum amount of RAM it requires. If you want the application to perform optimally, usually you need more than the minimum specifications on the software package. Some programs, such as operating systems, also have specified maximums.

Generally, home users running Windows XP and using basic application software such as word processing should have at least 256 MB of RAM. Most business users who work with accounting, financial, or spreadsheet programs, voice recognition, and programs requiring multimedia capabilities should have a minimum of 512 MB of RAM. Users creating professional Web sites or using graphics-intensive applications will want at least 2 GB of RAM.

Figure 4-19a lists guidelines for the amount of RAM for various types of users. Figure 4-19b shows advertisements that match to each user requirement. Advertisements normally list the type of processor, the clock speed of the processor, and the amount of RAM in the computer. The amount of RAM in computers purchased today ranges from 256 MB to 16 GB. In an advertisement, manufacturers specify the maximum amount of RAM a computer can hold, for example, 512 GB expandable to 2 GB. Read Ethics & Issues 4-3 for a related discussion.

FAQ 4-3

Can I add more RAM to my computer?

Check your computer documentation to see how much RAM you can add. RAM modules are relatively inexpensive and usually include easy-to-follow installation instructions. Be sure to purchase RAM compatible with your brand and model of computer. For more information, visit scsite.com/dc2007/ch4/faq and then click Upgrading RAM.

ETHICS & ISSUES 4-3

How Much Should You Pay for a Computer?

Today, you can buy a personal computer for less than $500 that can do more than one sold at nearly twice its cost three years ago. Some manufacturers even are offering basic computers for less than $300. Part of the plunge in prices is lower-cost components, but another factor is a growing demand for cheaper machines. Many of the new buyers are from families earning less than $40,000, far below the $50,000 average that once characterized typical computer buyers. These consumers are looking for inexpensive computers that are adequate for the most popular tasks. Spending more money on a computer means faster processors, more memory, 3-D graphics cards, higher-quality sound cards, more hard disk space, and other extras that some consider to be unnecessary, frivolous expenses. As one industry analyst asks, "Why buy a Porsche when you are going to drive only 55 miles per hour?" But others point out that perhaps you should spend more money and buy for the future in anticipation of more robust software and peripherals that can take advantage of more computing power. How might a greater availability of lower costing personal computers change the way people, schools, and businesses buy and use them? With respect to computers, does a higher price always mean greater usefulness? Why or why not? Who might be satisfied with less than the latest and greatest computer technology? Why?

FIGURE 4-19a (RAM guidelines)

RAM	256 MB to 1 GB	512 MB to 2 GB	2 GB and up
Use	Home and business users managing personal finances; using standard application software such as word processing; using educational or entertainment CD-ROMs; communicating with others on the Web	Users requiring more advanced multimedia capabilities; running number-intensive accounting, financial, or spreadsheet programs; using voice recognition; working with videos, music, and digital imaging; creating Web sites; participating in video conferences; playing Internet games	Power users creating professional Web sites; running sophisticated CAD, 3-D design, or other graphics-intensive software

FIGURE 4-19b (computers for sale)

Model	A200	P320	A280	P320	X225	A240
Processor	2.00 GHz Sempron processor	3.20 GHz Celeron D processor	2.80 GHz Athlon 64 X2 processor	3.2 GHz Pentium D processor	2.25 GHz Athlon MP processor	2.40 GHz Opteron processor
Memory	256 MB SDRAM	512 MB SDRAM	512 MB SDRAM	1 GB SDRAM	2 GB RDRAM	4 GB SDRAM

FIGURE 4-19 Determining how much RAM you need depends on the applications you intend to run on your computer. Advertisements for computers normally list the type of processor, the speed of the processor, and the amount of RAM installed.

Cache

Most of today's computers improve processing times with **cache** (pronounced cash). Two types of cache are memory cache and disk cache. This chapter discusses memory cache. Chapter 7 discusses disk cache.

Memory cache helps speed the processes of the computer because it stores frequently used instructions and data. Most personal computers today have two types of memory cache: L1 cache and L2 cache. Some also have L3 cache.

- *L1 cache* is built directly in the processor chip. L1 cache usually has a very small capacity, ranging from 8 KB to 128 KB. The more common sizes for personal computers are 32 KB or 64 KB.
- *L2 cache* is slightly slower than L1 cache but has a much larger capacity, ranging from 64 KB to 16 MB. When discussing cache, most users are referring to L2 cache. Current processors include *advanced transfer cache (ATC)*, a type of L2 cache built directly on the processor chip. Processors that use ATC perform at much faster rates than those that do not use it.

  Personal computers today typically have from 512 KB to 2 MB of advanced transfer cache. Servers and workstations have from 2 MB to 6 MB of advanced transfer cache.

- *L3 cache* is a cache on the motherboard that is separate from the processor chip. L3 cache exists only on computers that use L2 advanced transfer cache. Personal computers often have up to 2 MB of L3 cache; servers and workstations have from 2 MB to 9 MB of L3 cache.

Cache speeds up processing time because it stores frequently used instructions and data. When the processor needs an instruction or data, it searches memory in this order: L1 cache, then L2 cache, then L3 cache (if it exists), then RAM — with a greater delay in processing for each level of memory it must search (Figure 4-20). If the instruction or data is not found in memory, then it must search a slower speed storage medium such as a hard disk, CD, or DVD.

ROM

Read-only memory (**ROM** pronounced rahm) refers to memory chips storing permanent data and instructions. The data on most ROM chips cannot be modified — hence, the name read-only. ROM is nonvolatile, which means its contents are not lost when power is removed from the computer. In addition to computers, many devices contain ROM chips. For example, ROM chips in printers contain data for fonts.

WEB LINK 4-4

Cache
For more information, visit scsite.com/ dc2007/ch4/weblink and then click Cache.

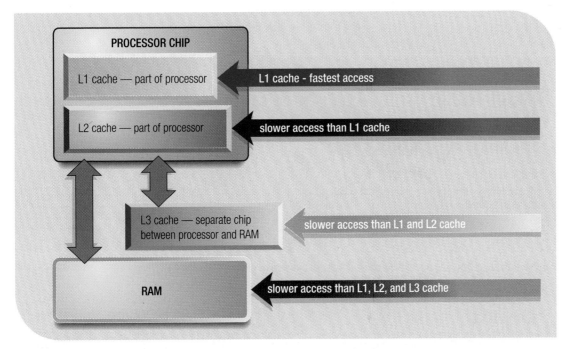

FIGURE 4-20 Cache helps speed processing times when the processor requests data, instructions, or information.

Manufacturers of ROM chips often record data, instructions, or information on the chips when they manufacture the chips. These ROM chips, called **firmware**, contain permanently written data, instructions, or information.

A *PROM (programmable read-only memory) chip* is a blank ROM chip on which a programmer can write permanently. Programmers use *microcode* instructions to program a PROM chip. Once a programmer writes the microcode on the PROM chip, it functions like a regular ROM chip and cannot be erased or changed.

A variation of the PROM chip, called an *EEPROM (electrically erasable programmable read-only memory) chip*, allows a programmer to erase the microcode with an electric signal.

Flash Memory

Flash memory is a type of nonvolatile memory that can be erased electronically and rewritten, similar to EEPROM. Most computers use flash memory to hold their startup instructions because it allows the computer easily to update its contents. For example, when the computer changes from standard time to daylight savings time, the contents of a flash memory chip (and the real-time clock chip) change to reflect the new time.

Flash memory chips also store data and programs on many mobile computers and devices, such as PDAs, smart phones, printers, digital cameras, automotive devices, audio players, digital voice recorders, and pagers. When you enter names and addresses in a PDA or smart phone, a flash memory chip stores the data. Some MP3 players store music on flash memory chips (Figure 4-21); others store music on tiny hard disks or flash memory cards. A later section in this chapter discusses flash memory cards, which contain flash memory on a removable device instead of a chip.

FAQ 4-4

How much music can I store on an MP3 player?

MP3 players that store music on flash memory chips can hold up to 700 songs. MP3 players with tiny hard disks have a much greater storage capacity — from 1,000 to 15,000 songs. For more information, visit scsite.com/dc2007/ch4/faq and then click MP3 Players.

FIGURE 4-21   HOW AN MP3 MUSIC PLAYER MIGHT STORE MUSIC IN FLASH MEMORY

Step 1:
Purchase and download MP3 music tracks from a Web site. With one end of a special cable connected to the system unit, connect the other end to the USB port in the MP3 player.

Step 2:
Instruct the computer to copy the MP3 music tracks to a flash memory chip in the MP3 player.

Step 3:
Plug the headphones in the MP3 player, push a button on the MP3 player, and listen to the music through the headphones.

USB port

flash memory chips

from the computer

MP3 player

headphones cable

CMOS

Some RAM chips, flash memory chips, and other types of memory chips use **complementary metal-oxide semiconductor** (**CMOS** pronounced SEE-moss) technology because it provides high speeds and consumes little power. CMOS technology uses battery power to retain information even when the power to the computer is off. Battery-backed CMOS memory chips, for example, can keep the calendar, date, and time current even when the computer is off. The flash memory chips that store a computer's startup information often use CMOS technology.

FAQ 4-5

What should I do if my computer's date and time are wrong?

First, try resetting the date and time. To do this in Windows XP, double-click the time at the right edge of the taskbar. If the computer continues to lose time or display an incorrect date, you may need to replace the CMOS battery on the motherboard that powers the system clock. For more information, visit scsite.com/dc2007/ch4/faq and then click CMOS Battery.

Memory Access Times

Access time is the amount of time it takes the processor to read data, instructions, and information from memory. A computer's access time directly affects how fast the computer processes data. Accessing data in memory can be more than 200,000 times faster than accessing data on a hard disk because of the mechanical motion of the hard disk.

Today's manufacturers use a variety of terminology to state access times (Figure 4-22). Some use fractions of a second, which for memory occurs in nanoseconds. A **nanosecond** (abbreviated *ns*) is one billionth of a second. A nanosecond is extremely fast (Figure 4-23). In fact, electricity travels about one foot in a nanosecond.

Other manufacturers state access times in MHz; for example, 533 MHz DDR SDRAM. If a manufacturer states access time in megahertz, you can convert it to nanoseconds by dividing 1 billion ns by the megahertz number. For example, 533 MHz equals approximately 1.9 ns (1,000,000,000/533,000,000).

The access time (speed) of memory contributes to the overall performance of the computer. Standard SDRAM chips can have access times up to 133 MHz (about 7.5 ns), and access times of the DDR SDRAM chips reach 677 MHz (about 1.5 ns). The higher the megahertz, the faster the access time; conversely, the lower the nanoseconds, the faster the access time. The faster RDRAM chips can have access times up to 1600 MHz (about 0.625 ns). ROM access times range from 25 to 250 ns.

While access times of memory greatly affect overall computer performance, manufacturers and retailers usually list a computer's memory in terms of its size, not its access time. Thus, an advertisement might describe a computer as having 512 MB of SDRAM upgradeable to 4 GB.

ACCESS TIME TERMINOLOGY

Term	Abbreviation	Speed
Millisecond	ms	One-thousandth of a second
Microsecond	µs	One-millionth of a second
Nanosecond	ns	One-billionth of a second
Picosecond	ps	One-trillionth of a second

FIGURE 4-22 Access times are measured in fractions of a second. This table lists the terms used to define access times.

10 million operations = 1 blink

FIGURE 4-23 It takes about one-tenth of a second to blink your eye, which is the equivalent of 100 million nanoseconds. In the time it takes to blink your eye, a computer can perform some operations 10 million times.

Test your knowledge of pages 194 through 203 in Quiz Yourself 4-2.

QUIZ YOURSELF 4-2

Instructions: Find the true statement below. Then, rewrite the remaining false statements so they are true.

1. A computer's memory access time directly affects how fast the computer processes data.

2. A gigabyte (GB) equals approximately 1 trillion bytes.

3. Memory cache helps speed the processes of the computer because it stores seldom used instructions and data.

4. Most computers are analog, which means they recognize only two discrete states: on and off.

5. Most RAM retains its contents when the power is removed from the computer.

6. Read-only memory (ROM) refers to memory chips storing temporary data and instructions.

Quiz Yourself Online: To further check your knowledge of bits, bytes, data representation, and types of memory, visit scsite.com/dc2007/ch4/quiz and then click Objectives 5 – 7.

EXPANSION SLOTS AND ADAPTER CARDS

WEB LINK 4-6

Sound Cards

For more information, visit scsite.com/dc2007/ch4/weblink and then click Sound Cards.

An **expansion slot** is a socket on the motherboard that can hold an adapter card. An **adapter card**, sometimes called an *expansion card*, is a circuit board that enhances functions of a component of the system unit and/or provides connections to peripherals. A **peripheral** is a device that connects to the system unit and is controlled by the processor in the computer. Examples of peripherals are modems, disk drives, printers, scanners, and keyboards.

Figure 4-24 lists currently used types of adapter cards. Sometimes, all functionality is built in the adapter card. With others, a cable connects the adapter card to a device, such as a digital video camera, outside the system unit. Figure 4-25 shows an adapter card being inserted in an expansion slot on a personal computer motherboard.

Some motherboards include all necessary capabilities and do not require adapter cards. Other motherboards may require adapter cards to provide capabilities such as sound and video. A **sound card** enhances the sound-generating capabilities of a personal computer by allowing sound to be input through a microphone and output through external speakers or headphones. A **video card**, also called a *graphics card*, converts computer output into a video signal that travels through a cable to the monitor, which displays an image on the screen.

TYPES OF ADAPTER CARDS

Adapter Card	Purpose
Disk controller	Connects disk drives
FireWire	Connects to FireWire devices
Graphics accelerator	Increases the speed at which graphics are displayed
MIDI	Connects musical instruments
Modem	Connects other computers through telephone or cable television lines
Network	Connects other computers and peripherals
PC-to-TV converter	Connects a television
Sound	Connects speakers or a microphone
TV tuner	Allows viewing of television channels on the monitor
USB 2.0	Connects to USB 2.0 devices
Video	Connects a monitor
Video capture	Connects a camcorder

FIGURE 4-24 Currently used adapter cards and their functions.

FIGURE 4-25 An adapter card being inserted in an expansion slot on the motherboard of a personal computer.

In the past, installing a card was not easy and required you to set switches and other elements on the motherboard. Many of today's computers support **Plug and Play**, which means the computer automatically can configure adapter cards and other peripherals as you install them. Having Plug and Play support means you can plug in a device, turn on the computer, and then immediately begin using the device.

PC Cards, Flash Memory Cards, and USB Flash Drives

Notebook and other mobile computers have at least one **PC Card slot**, which is a special type of expansion slot that holds a PC Card. A **PC Card** is a thin, credit card-sized device that adds memory, storage, sound, fax/modem, network, and other capabilities to mobile computers (Figure 4-26). Because of their small size and versatility, some consumer electronics products such as digital cameras use PC Cards.

All PC Cards conform to standards developed by the *Personal Computer Memory Card International Association* (these cards originally were called *PCMCIA cards*). These standards help to ensure the interchangeability of PC Cards among mobile computers. Although some PC cards contain tiny hard disks, many PC Cards are a type of flash memory card.

A **flash memory card** is a removable flash memory device that allows users to transfer data and information conveniently from mobile devices to their desktop computers (Figure 4-27). Many mobile and consumer devices, such as PDAs, smart phones, digital cameras, and digital audio players, use these memory cards. Some printers and computers have built-in card readers/writers or slots that read flash memory cards. In addition, you can purchase an external card reader/writer that attaches to any computer. Flash memory cards are available in a variety of shapes and sizes. The type of flash memory card you have will determine the type of card reader/writer you need. Storage capacities of flash memory cards range from 64 MB to 5 GB.

Another widely used type of removable flash memory is the USB flash drive (Figure 4-27). A *USB flash drive* is a flash memory storage device that plugs in a USB port on a computer or portable device. (The next section discusses USB ports.) Storage capacities of USB flash drives range from 64 MB to 5 GB.

Unlike adapter cards that require you to open the system unit and install the card on the motherboard, you can change a removable flash memory device without having to open the system unit or restart the computer. This feature, called *hot plugging*, allows you to insert and remove the removable flash memory and other devices while the computer is running.

FIGURE 4-26 A PC card slides in a PC Card slot on a notebook computer.

FIGURE 4-27 Removable flash memory devices are available in a range of sizes.

PORTS AND CONNECTORS

A **port** is the point at which a peripheral attaches to or communicates with a system unit so the peripheral can send data to or receive information from the computer. An external device, such as a keyboard, monitor, printer, mouse, and microphone, often attaches by a cable to a port on the system unit. Instead of port, the term **jack** sometimes is used to identify audio and video ports. The back of the system unit contains many ports; newer personal computers also have ports on the front of the system unit (Figure 4-28).

Ports have different types of connectors. A **connector** joins a cable to a peripheral. One end of a cable attaches to the connector on the system unit, and the other end of the cable attaches to a connector on the peripheral. Most connectors are available in one of two genders: male or female. *Male connectors* have one or more exposed pins, like the end of an electrical cord you plug in the wall. *Female connectors* have matching holes to accept the pins on a male connector, like an electrical wall outlet.

Sometimes, attaching a new peripheral to the computer is not possible because the connector on the system unit is the same gender as the connector on the cable. In this case, purchasing a gender changer solves this problem. A *gender changer* is a device that enables you to join two connectors that are both female or both male.

Manufacturers often identify the cables by their connector types to assist you with purchasing a cable to connect a computer to a peripheral. Figure 4-29 shows the different types of connectors on a system unit. Some system units include these connectors when you buy the computer. You add other connectors by inserting adapter cards on the motherboard. Certain adapter cards have ports that allow you to attach a peripheral to the adapter card.

Desktop personal computers may have a serial port, a parallel port, several USB ports, and a FireWire port. The next section discusses these and other ports.

FIGURE 4-28   The back of a system unit has many ports. Most computers have ports on the front of the system unit, also.

CONNECTOR TYPES

Connector Type	Picture	Connector Type	Picture
Audio in		Mouse	
Cable TV		Network	
Composite video in		Printer	
FireWire		Serial	
FM reception		Speaker	
Headphones		S-video in	
Keyboard		S-video out	
Microphone		Telephone line in	
Monitor		USB	

FIGURE 4-29 Examples of different types of connectors on a system unit.

Serial Ports

A **serial port** is a type of interface that connects a device to the system unit by transmitting data one bit at a time (Figure 4-30). Serial ports usually connect devices that do not require fast data transmission rates, such as a mouse, keyboard, or modem. The *COM port* (short for communications port) on the system unit is one type of serial port.

Some modems that connect the system unit to a telephone line use a serial port because the telephone line expects the data in a specific frequency. Serial ports conform to either the RS-232 or RS-422 standard, which specifies the number of pins used on the port's connector.

serial transmission of data

byte representation for number 1 (00110001)

byte representation for number 3 (00110011)

byte representation for number 5 (00110101)

connector

port

FIGURE 4-30
A serial port transmits data one bit at a time. One wire sends data, another receives data, and the remaining wires are used for other communications operations.

Parallel Ports

Unlike a serial port, a **parallel port** is an interface that connects devices by transferring more than one bit at a time (Figure 4-31). Originally, parallel ports were developed as an alternative to the slower speed serial ports.

Some printers can connect to the system unit using a parallel port. This parallel port can transfer eight bits of data (one byte) simultaneously through eight separate lines in a single cable.

byte representation for number 1 ⟶ 00110001
byte representation for number 3 ⟶ 00110011
byte representation for number 5 ⟶ 00110101

connector

port

FIGURE 4-31   A parallel port is capable of transmitting more than one bit at a time. The port shown in this figure has eight wires that transmit data; the remaining wires are used for other communications operations.

USB Ports

A **USB port**, short for *universal serial bus port*, can connect up to 127 different peripherals together with a single connector. Devices that connect to a USB port include the following: mouse, printer, digital camera, scanner, speakers, MP3 music player, CD, DVD, and removable hard disk. Personal computers typically have six to eight USB ports either on the front or back of the system unit (Figure 4-28 on page 206). The latest version of USB, called *USB 2.0*, is a more advanced and faster USB, with speeds 40 times higher than that of its predecessor.

To attach multiple peripherals using a single USB port, you can daisy chain the devices together outside the system unit. *Daisy chain* means the first USB device connects to the USB port on the computer, the second USB device connects to the first USB device, the third USB device connects to the second USB device, and so on. An alternative to daisy chaining is to use a USB hub. A **USB hub** is a device that plugs in a USB port on the system unit and contains multiple USB ports in which you plug cables from USB devices.

USB also supports hot plugging and Plug and Play, which means you can attach peripherals while the computer is running. With serial and parallel port connections, by contrast, you often must restart the computer after attaching the peripheral.

Some newer peripherals may attach only to a USB port. Others attach to either a serial or parallel port, as well as a USB port.

FAQ 4-6

Can older USB devices plug in a USB 2.0 port?

Yes. USB 2.0 is *backward compatible*, which means that it supports older USB devices as well as new USB 2.0 devices. Keep in mind, though, that older USB devices do not run any faster in a USB 2.0 port. For more information, visit scsite.com/dc2007/ch4/faq and then click USB 2.0.

FireWire Ports

Previously called an *IEEE 1394 port*, a **FireWire port** is similar to a USB port in that it can connect multiple types of devices that require faster data transmission speeds, such as digital video cameras, digital VCRs, color printers, scanners, digital cameras, and DVD drives, to a single connector. A FireWire port allows you to connect up to 63 devices together. You can use a FireWire hub to attach multiple devices to a single FireWire port. A **FireWire hub** is a device that plugs in a FireWire port on the system unit and contains multiple FireWire ports in which you plug cables from FireWire devices. The FireWire port supports Plug and Play.

Some newer peripherals may attach only to a FireWire port. Having standard ports and connectors, such as FireWire and USB, greatly simplify the process of attaching devices to a personal computer. For newer computers that do not have a serial or parallel port, users plug the device in a USB or FireWire port — as specified by the device's manufacturer. In general, FireWire has replaced audio, parallel, and SCSI ports, which are discussed in the next section. USB ports have replaced mouse, keyboard, serial, audio, parallel, and SCSI ports. Figure 4-32 shows how FireWire and USB ports are replacing other ports completely.

Special-Purpose Ports

Four special-purpose ports are MIDI, SCSI, IrDA, and Bluetooth. These ports are not included in typical computers. For a computer to have these ports, you must customize the computer purchase order. The following sections discuss MIDI, SCSI, IrDA, and Bluetooth ports.

MIDI PORT A special type of serial port that connects the system unit to a musical instrument, such as an electronic keyboard, is called a **MIDI port**. Short for *Musical Instrument Digital Interface*, MIDI (pronounced MID-dee) is the electronic music industry's standard that defines how devices, such as sound cards and synthesizers, represent sounds electronically. A *synthesizer*, which can be a peripheral or a chip, creates sound from digital instructions.

A system unit with a MIDI port has the capability of recording sounds that have been created by a synthesizer and then processing the sounds (the data) to create new sounds. Nearly every sound card supports the MIDI standard, so you can play and manipulate on one computer sounds that originally were created on another computer.

TRADITIONAL PORTS

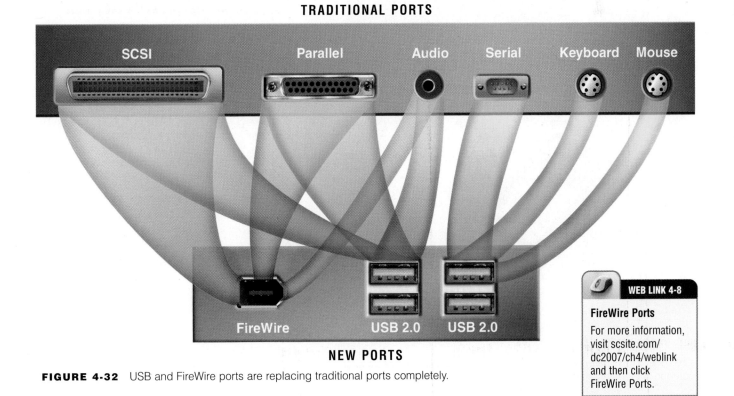

NEW PORTS

FIGURE 4-32 USB and FireWire ports are replacing traditional ports completely.

SCSI PORT   A special high-speed parallel port, called a **SCSI port**, allows you to attach SCSI (pronounced skuzzy) peripherals such as disk drives and printers. Depending on the type of *SCSI*, which stands for *small computer system interface*, you can daisy chain up to either 7 or 15 devices together. Some computers include a SCSI port. Others have a slot that supports a SCSI card.

IrDA PORT   Some devices can transmit data via infrared light waves. For these wireless devices to transmit signals to a computer, both the computer and the device must have an **IrDA port** (Figure 4-33). These ports conform to standards developed by the *IrDA* (*Infrared Data Association*).

To ensure nothing obstructs the path of the infrared light wave, you must align the IrDA port on the device with the IrDA port on the computer, similarly to the way you operate a television remote control. Devices that use IrDA ports include a PDA, smart phone, keyboard, mouse, printer, and pager. Several of these devices use a high-speed IrDA port, sometimes called a *fast infrared port*.

BLUETOOTH PORT   An alternative to IrDA, **Bluetooth** technology uses radio waves to transmit data between two devices (Figure 4-34). Unlike IrDA, the Bluetooth devices do not have to be aligned with each other. Many computers, peripherals, PDAs, smart phones, cars, and other consumer electronics are Bluetooth-enabled, which means they contain a small chip that allows them to communicate with other Bluetooth-enabled computers and devices. The latest version of Bluetooth, called Bluetooth 2.0, supports higher connection speeds and is backward compatible with its predecessors.

If you have a computer that is not Bluetooth enabled, you can purchase a Bluetooth wireless port adapter that will convert an existing USB port or serial port into a Bluetooth port. Also available are Bluetooth PC Cards for notebook computers and Bluetooth cards for PDAs and smart phones.

FAQ 4-7

How popular is Bluetooth?

Experts predict Bluetooth chip sales will grow to 720 million units by 2008 with revenues of $1.7 billion, as shown in the chart below. For more information, visit scsite.com/dc2007/ch4/faq and then click Bluetooth Growth.

Bluetooth Chip Sales History and Forecast

(bar chart: years 2001–2008 vertical axis; Millions of Units horizontal axis, 0 to 800)

Source: In-Stat/MDR

▸ TravelMate Series

acer

IrDA ports

notebook computer

smart phone

FIGURE 4-33   Many devices communicate wirelessly with desktop or notebook computers through IrDA ports.

FIGURE 4-34 This smart phone wirelessly communicates with a Bluetooth-enabled notebook computer.

BUSES

As explained earlier in this chapter, a computer processes and stores data as a series of electronic bits. These bits transfer internally within the circuitry of the computer along electrical channels. Each channel, called a **bus**, allows the various devices both inside and attached to the system unit to communicate with each other. Just as vehicles travel on a highway to move from one destination to another, bits travel on a bus (Figure 4-35).

Buses transfer bits from input devices to memory, from memory to the processor, from the processor to memory, and from memory to output or storage devices. Buses consist of two parts: a data bus and an address bus. The *data bus* transfers actual data and the *address bus* transfers information about where the data should reside in memory.

The size of a bus, called the *bus width*, determines the number of bits that the computer can transmit at one time. For example, a 32-bit bus can transmit 32 bits (4 bytes) at a time. On a 64-bit bus, bits transmit from one location to another 64 bits (8 bytes) at a time. The larger the number of bits handled by the bus, the faster the computer transfers data. Using the highway analogy again, assume that one lane

on a highway can carry one bit. A 32-bit bus is like a 32-lane highway. A 64-bit bus is like a 64-lane highway.

If a number in memory occupies 8 bytes, or 64 bits, the computer must transmit it in two separate steps when using a 32-bit bus: once for the first 32 bits and once for the second 32 bits. Using a 64-bit bus, the computer can transmit the number in a single step, transferring all 64 bits at once. The wider the bus, the fewer number of transfer steps required and the faster the transfer of data. Most personal computers today use a 64-bit bus.

In conjunction with the bus width, many computer professionals refer to a computer's word size. **Word size** is the number of bits the processor can interpret and execute at a given time. That is, a 64-bit processor can manipulate 64 bits at a time. Computers with a larger word size can process more data in the same amount of time than computers with a smaller word size. In most computers, the word size is the same as the bus width.

FIGURE 4-35 Just as vehicles travel on a highway, bits travel on a bus. Buses transfer bits from input devices to memory, from memory to the processor, from the processor to memory, and from memory to output or storage devices.

Every bus also has a clock speed. Just like the processor, manufacturers state the clock speed for a bus in hertz. Recall that one megahertz (MHz) is equal to one million ticks per second. Most of today's processors have a bus clock speed of 400, 533, or 800 MHz. The higher the bus clock speed, the faster the transmission of data, which results in applications running faster.

A computer has two basic types of buses: a system bus and an expansion bus. A *system bus* is part of the motherboard and connects the processor to main memory. An *expansion bus* allows the processor to communicate with peripherals. When computer professionals use the term bus by itself, they usually are referring to the system bus.

Expansion Bus

Some peripherals outside the system unit connect to a port on an adapter card, which is inserted in an expansion slot on the motherboard. This expansion slot connects to the expansion bus, which allows the processor to communicate with the peripheral attached to the adapter card. Data transmitted to memory or the processor travels from the expansion slot via the expansion bus and the system bus.

The types of expansion buses on a motherboard determine the types of cards you can add to the computer. Thus, you should understand these expansion buses commonly found in today's personal computers: PCI bus, AGP bus, USB, FireWire bus, and PC Card bus.

- The *PCI bus* (*Peripheral Component Interconnect bus*) is a high-speed expansion bus that connects higher speed devices. Types of cards you can insert in a PCI bus expansion slot include video cards, sound cards, SCSI cards, and high-speed network cards.
- The *Accelerated Graphics Port* (*AGP*) is a bus designed by Intel to improve the speed with which 3-D graphics and video transmit. With an AGP video card in an AGP bus slot, the AGP bus provides a faster, dedicated interface between the video card and memory. Newer processors support AGP technology.
- The *USB* (*universal serial bus*) and *FireWire bus* are buses that eliminate the need to install cards in expansion slots. In a computer with a USB, for example, USB devices connect to each other outside the system unit, and then a single cable attaches to the USB port. The USB port then connects to the USB, which connects to the PCI bus on the motherboard. The FireWire bus works in a similar fashion. With these buses, expansion slots are available for devices not compatible with USB or FireWire.
- The expansion bus for a PC Card is the *PC Card bus*. With a PC Card inserted in a PC Card slot, data travels on the PC Card bus to the PCI bus.

BAYS

After you purchase a computer, you may want to install an additional storage device, such as a disk drive, in the system unit. A **bay** is an opening inside the system unit in which you can install additional equipment. A bay is different from a slot, which is used for the installation of adapter cards. Rectangular openings, called **drive bays**, typically hold disk drives.

Two types of drive bays exist: external and internal. An *external drive bay* allows a user to access the drive from outside the system unit (Figure 4-36). CD drives, DVD drives, Zip drives, floppy disk drives, and tape drives are examples of devices installed in external drive bays. An *internal drive bay* is concealed entirely within the system unit. Hard disk drives are installed in internal bays.

WEB LINK 4-9

Buses

For more information, visit scsite.com/dc2007/ch4/weblink and then click Buses.

CD drive

DVD drive

floppy disk drive

FIGURE 4-36   External drive bays usually are located beside or on top of one another.

POWER SUPPLY

Many personal computers plug in standard wall outlets, which supply an alternating current (AC) of 115 to 120 volts. This type of power is unsuitable for use with a computer, which requires a direct current (DC) ranging from 5 to 12 volts. The **power supply** is the component of the system unit that converts the wall outlet AC power into DC power. Different motherboards and computers require different wattages on the power supply. If a power supply is not providing the necessary power, the computer will not function properly.

Built into the power supply is a fan that keeps the power supply and other components of the system unit cool. This fan dissipates heat generated by the processor and other components of the system unit. Many newer computers have additional fans near certain components in the system unit such as the processor, hard disk, and ports.

Some external peripherals such as an external modem, speakers, or a tape drive have an **AC adapter**, which is an external power supply. One end of the AC adapter plugs in the wall outlet and the other end attaches to the peripheral. The AC adapter converts the AC power into DC power that the peripheral requires.

FAQ 4-8

How many fans are in a system unit?

Most system units have at least three fans: one in the power supply, one on the case, and one on the processor heat sink. Some computers allow you to turn off noisy fans until they are needed. You also can purchase utility programs that slow or stop the fan until the temperature reaches a certain level. For more information, visit scsite.com/dc2007/ch4/faq and then click Computer Fan.

MOBILE COMPUTERS AND DEVICES

As businesses and schools expand to serve people across the country and around the world, increasingly more people need to use a computer while traveling to and from a main office or school to conduct business, communicate, or do homework. As Chapter 1 discussed, users with such mobile computing needs — known as mobile users — often have a mobile computer, such as a notebook computer or Tablet PC, or a mobile device such as a smart phone or PDA (Figure 4-37).

FIGURE 4-37 Users with mobile computing needs often have a notebook computer, PDA, and/or smart phone.

Weighing on average between 2.5 and 9 pounds, notebook computers can run either using batteries or using a standard power supply. Smaller PDAs and smart phones run strictly on batteries. Like their desktop counterparts, mobile computers and devices have a motherboard that contains electronic components that process data. Read Ethics & Issues 4-4 for a related discussion.

A notebook computer usually is more expensive than a desktop computer with the same capabilities because it is more costly to miniaturize the components. Notebook computers may have video, serial, parallel, modem,

network, FireWire, USB, headphones, and microphone ports (Figure 4-38).

Two basic designs of Tablet PC are available: slate and convertible. With the slate Tablet PC (shown in Figure 4-1 on page 184), all the hardware is behind the display — much like a PDA. Users can attach a removable keyboard to the slate Tablet PC. The display on the convertible Tablet PC, which is attached to a keyboard, can be rotated 180 degrees and folded down over the keyboard. Thus, the convertible Tablet PC can be repositioned to look like either a notebook computer or a slate Tablet PC. Tablet PCs usually include several slots and ports (Figure 4-39).

FIGURE 4-38 Ports on a typical notebook computer.

FIGURE 4-39 Ports and slots on a Tablet PC.

PDAs and smart phones are quite affordable, usually priced at a few hundred dollars or less. These mobile devices often have an IrDA port or are Bluetooth enabled so users can communicate wirelessly with other computers or devices such as a printer. Read Looking Ahead 4-2 for a look at the next generation of mobile computer.

LOOKING AHEAD 4-2

DNA Computer Works to Fight Cancer

One of the newest computers is so tiny that one trillion of them can fit inside a drop of water. The hardware of this biological invention is composed of enzymes that manipulate DNA, and the software is composed of actual DNA.

The concept for this computer had been proposed in 1936, but the actual computer was developed at the Weizmann Institute in Israel in 2001. Today, researchers at the Weizmann Institute are developing applications that process biological information. Their most current success is being able to program the computer to diagnose and treat cancer.

The researchers are hopeful they will be able to have the medical computer function inside a human cell. For more information, visit scsite.com/dc2007/ch4/looking and then click DNA Computer.

PUTTING IT ALL TOGETHER

When you purchase a computer, it is important to understand how the components of the system unit work. Many components of the system unit influence the speed and power of a computer. These include the type of processor, the clock speed of the processor, the amount of RAM, bus width, and the clock speed of the bus. The configuration you require depends on your intended use.

The table in Figure 4-40 lists the suggested minimum processor and RAM requirements based on the needs of various types of computer users.

SUGGESTED MINIMUM CONFIGURATIONS BY USER

User	Processor and RAM
HOME	Intel Celeron D or AMD Sempron or Intel Pentium 4 or AMD Athlon 64 Minimum RAM: 256 MB
SMALL OFFICE/ HOME OFFICE	Intel Pentium D or AMD Athlon 64 FX Minimum RAM: 512 MB
MOBILE	Intel Celeron M or Intel Pentium M or AMD Turion 64 Minimum RAM: 512 MB
POWER	Intel Itanium 2 or AMD Opteron or Intel Pentium Extreme Edition or Intel Xeon MP or AMD Athlon MP or AMD Athlon 64 X2 Minimum RAM: 2 GB
LARGE BUSINESS	Intel Pentium D or AMD Athlon 64 FX Minimum RAM: 1 GB

FIGURE 4-40 Suggested processor and RAM configurations by user.

KEEPING YOUR COMPUTER CLEAN

Over time, the system unit collects dust — even in a clean environment. Built up dust can block airflow in the computer, which can cause it to overheat, corrode, or even stop working. By cleaning your computer once or twice a year, you can help extend its life. This preventive maintenance task requires a few basic products (Figure 4-41):

- can of compressed air — removes dust and lint from difficult-to-reach areas
- lint-free antistatic wipes and swabs
- bottle of rubbing alcohol
- small computer vacuum (or small attachments on your house vacuum)
- antistatic wristband — to avoid damaging internal components with static electricity
- small screwdriver (may be required to open the case or remove adapter cards)

Before cleaning the computer, turn it off, unplug it from the electrical outlet, and unplug all cables from the ports. Blow away any dust from all openings on the computer case, such as drives, slots, and ports. Vacuum the power supply fan on the back of the computer case to remove any dust that has accumulated on it. Next, release short blasts of compressed air on the power supply fan. Then, use an antistatic wipe to clean the exterior of the case.

If you need assistance opening the computer case, refer to the instructions that came with the computer. Once the case is open, put the antistatic wristband on your wrist and attach its clip to the case of the computer. Use the antistatic wipes to clean dust and grime inside the walls of the computer case. Vacuum as much dust as possible from the interior of the case, including the wires, chips, adapter cards, and fan blades. Next, release short blasts of compressed air in areas the vacuum cannot reach. If the motherboard and adapter cards still look dirty, gently clean them with lint-free wipes or swabs lightly dampened with alcohol.

When finished, be sure all adapter cards are tightly in their expansion slots. Then close the case, plug in all cables, and attach the power cord. Write down the date you cleaned the computer so you have a record for your next cleaning.

If you do not feel comfortable cleaning the system unit yourself, have a local computer company clean it for you.

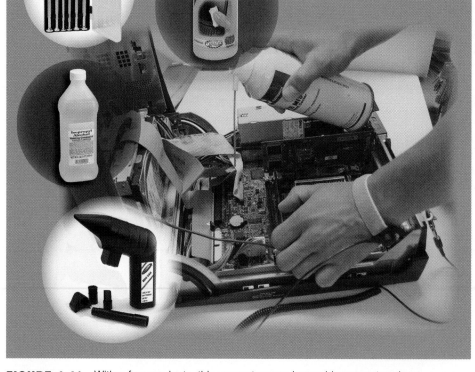

FIGURE 4-41   With a few products, this computer user keeps his computer clean.

FAQ 4-9

How do I clean components in the system unit?

Never pour or spray any form of liquid on the motherboard — or on any hardware. Always apply the liquid to a cloth or swab, and then use the cloth or swab to clean the hardware. If you can squeeze liquid out of the cloth or swab, then it is too moist. For more information, visit scsite.com/dc2007/ch4/faq and then click PC Hygiene.

Test your knowledge of pages 204 through 216 in Quiz Yourself 4-3.

QUIZ YOURSELF 4-3

Instructions: Find the true statement below. Then, rewrite the remaining false statements so they are true.

1. A bus is the point at which a peripheral attaches to or communicates with a system unit so the peripheral can send data to or receive information from the computer.

2. An AC adapter is a socket on the motherboard that can hold an adapter card.

3. Built into the power supply is a heater that keeps components of the system unit warm.

4. Serial ports can connect up to 127 different peripherals together with a single connector.

5. The higher the bus clock speed, the slower the transmission of data.

6. When cleaning the inside of the system unit, wear an antistatic wristband to avoid damaging internal components with static electricity.

Quiz Yourself Online: To further check your knowledge of expansion slots, adapter cards, ports, buses, components of mobile computers and devices, and cleaning a computer, visit scsite.com/dc2007/ch4/quiz and then click Objectives 8 – 12.

CHAPTER SUMMARY

Chapter 4 presented the components of the system unit; described how memory stores data, instructions, and information; and discussed the sequence of operations that occur when a computer executes an instruction. The chapter included a comparison of various personal computer processors on the market today. It also discussed how to clean a system unit.

CAREER CORNER

Computer Engineer

A *computer engineer* designs and develops the electronic components found in computers and peripheral devices. They also can work as researchers, theorists, and inventors. Companies may hire computer engineers for permanent positions or as consultants, with jobs that extend from a few months to a few years, depending on the project. Engineers in research and development often work on projects that will not be released to the general public for two years.

Responsibilities vary from company to company. All computer engineering work, however, demands problem-solving skills and the ability to create and use new technologies. The ability to handle multiple tasks and concentrate on detail is a key component. Assignments often are taken on as part of a team. Therefore, computer engineers must be able to communicate clearly with both computer personnel and computer users, who may have little technical knowledge.

Before taking in-depth computer engineering design and development classes, students usually take mathematics, physics, and basic engineering. Computer engineering degrees include B.S., M.S., and Ph.D. Because computer engineers employed in private industry often advance into managerial positions, many computer engineering graduates obtain a master's degree in business administration (M.B.A.). Most computer engineers earn between $63,500 and $106,500 annually, depending on their experience and employer, but salaries can exceed $125,000. For more information, visit scsite.com/dc2007/ch4/careers and then click Computer Engineer.

High-Tech Talk

RANDOM ACCESS MEMORY (RAM): THE GENIUS OF MEMORY

Inside your computer, RAM takes the form of separate microchip modules that plug in slots on the computer's motherboard. These slots connect through a line (bus) or set of electrical paths to the computer's processor. Before you turn on a computer, its RAM is a blank slate. As you start and use your computer, the operating system files, applications, and any data currently being used by the processor are written to and stored in RAM so the processor can access them quickly.

How is this data written to and stored in RAM? In the most common form of RAM, dynamic random access memory (DRAM), *transistors* (in this case, acting as switches) and a *capacitor* (as a data storage element) create a *memory cell*, which represents a single bit of data.

Memory cells are etched onto a silicon wafer in a series of columns (bitlines) and rows (wordlines), known as an *array*. The intersection of a column and row constitutes the *address* of the memory cell (Figure 4-42). Each memory cell has a unique address that can be found by counting across columns and then counting down by row. The address of a character consists of a series of memory cell addresses put together.

To write data to RAM, the processor sends the memory controller the address of a memory cell in which to store data. The *memory controller* organizes the request and sends the column and row address in an electrical charge along the appropriate address lines, which are very thin electrical lines etched into the RAM chip. This causes the transistors along those address lines to close.

These transistors act as a switch to control the flow of electrical current in an either closed or open circuit. While the transistors are closed, the software sends bursts of electricity along selected data lines. When the electrical charge traveling down the data line reaches an address line where a transistor is closed, the charge flows through the closed transistor and charges the capacitor.

A capacitor works as electronic storage that holds an electrical charge. Each charged capacitor along the address line represents a 1 bit. An uncharged capacitor represents a 0 bit. The combination of 1s and 0s from eight data lines forms a single byte of data.

The capacitors used in dynamic RAM, however, lose their electrical charge. The processor or memory controller continuously has to recharge all of the capacitors holding a charge (a 1 bit) before the capacitor discharges. During this *refresh operation*, which happens automatically thousands of times per second, the memory controller reads

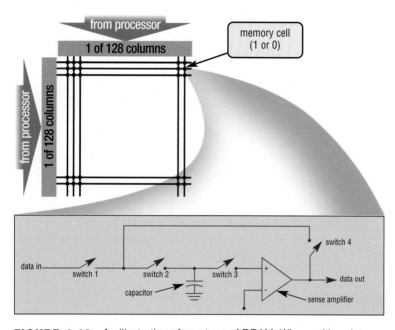

FIGURE 4-42 An illustration of one type of DRAM. When writing data, switches 1 and 2 in the circuit are closed and switches 3 and 4 are open. When reading data, switches 2, 3, and 4 in the circuit are closed and switch 1 is open. Most DRAM chips actually have arrays of memory cells (upper-left corner of figure) that are 16 rows deep.

memory and then immediately rewrites it. This refresh operation is what gives dynamic RAM its name. Dynamic RAM has to be refreshed continually, or it loses the charges that represent bits of data. A specialized circuit called a counter tracks the refresh sequence to ensure that all of the rows are refreshed.

The process of reading data from RAM uses a similar, but reverse, series of steps. When the processor gets the next instruction it is to perform, the instruction may contain the address of a memory cell from which to read data. This address is sent to the memory controller. To locate the memory cell, the memory controller sends the column and row address in an electrical charge down the appropriate address lines.

This electrical charge causes the transistors along the address line to close. At every point along the address line where a capacitor is holding a charge, the capacitor discharges through the circuit created by the closed transistors, sending electrical charges along the data lines.

A specialized circuit called a *sense amplifier* determines and amplifies the level of charge in the capacitor. A capacitor charge over a certain voltage level represents the binary value 1; a capacitor charge below that level represents a 0. The sensed and amplified value is sent back down the address line to the processor.

As long as a computer is running, data continuously is being written to and read from RAM. As soon as you shut down a computer, RAM loses its data. The next time you turn on a computer, operating system files and other data are again loaded into RAM and the read/write process starts all over. For more information, visit scsite.com/dc2007/ch4/tech and then click Memory.

Companies on the Cutting Edge

AMD
PC PROCESSOR SUPPLIER

Customer needs influence the integrated circuits *Advanced Micro Devices* (*AMD*) develops for the computing, communications, and consumer electronics industries. AMD calls this philosophy "customer-centric innovation."

As a global supplier of PC processors, AMD engineers its technologies at its Submicron Development Center (SDC) in Sunnyvale, California. The technologies are put into production at manufacturing facilities in the United States, Europe, Asia, and Japan.

Among the company's more successful line of processors is the AMD 64 family, which is composed of the AMD Athlon 64 processor for desktop and personal computers, the AMD Opteron processor for servers and workstations, and the AMD Turion mobile technology for notebook computers. The company is partnering with portable multimedia manufacturers, including TiVo, to use its Alchemy processor in providing high-performance video entertainment products. For more information, visit scsite.com/dc2007/ch4/companies and then click AMD.

INTEL
CHIP MAKER DOMINATES THE COMPUTER MARKET

When Gordon Moore and Robert Noyce started *Intel* in 1968, their goal was to replace magnetic core memory with semiconductor memory. Noyce and Moore, together with Andy Grove, refined the process of placing thousands of tiny electronic devices on a silicon chip. In 1971, the company introduced the Intel 4004, the first single-chip microprocessor.

When IBM chose the Intel 8008 chip for its new personal computer in 1980, Intel chips became standard for all IBM-compatible personal computers. Today, Intel's microprocessors are the building blocks in countless personal computers, servers, networks, and communications devices. In 2006, Intel introduced its Viiv technology, which is designed to enhance the entertainment experience in the digital home. For more information, visit scsite.com/dc2007/ch4/companies and then click Intel.

Technology Trailblazers

JACK KILBY
INTEGRATED CIRCUIT INVENTOR

Jack Kilby was awarded more than 60 patents during his lifetime, but one has changed the world. His integrated circuit, or microchip, invention made microprocessors possible.

Kilby started his work with miniature electrical components at Centralab, where he developed transistors for hearing aids. He then took a research position with Texas Instruments and developed a working model of the first integrated circuit, which was patented in 1959. Kilby applied this invention to various industrial, military, and commercial applications, including the first pocket calculator, called the Pocketronic.

Kilby is considered one of the more influential people in the world who has had the greatest impact on business computing in the past 50 years. He was awarded the Nobel Prize in physics in 2000 for his part in the invention of the integrated circuit, a product he believed will continue to change the world. For more information, visit scsite.com/dc2007/ch4/people and then click Jack Kilby.

GORDON MOORE
INTEL COFOUNDER

More than 40 years ago, *Gordon Moore* predicted that the number of transistors and resistors placed on computer chips would double every year, with a proportional increase in computing power and decrease in cost. This bold forecast, now known as Moore's Law, proved amazingly accurate for 10 years. Then, Moore revised the estimate to doubling every two years.

Convinced of the future of silicon chips, Moore cofounded Intel in 1968. Moore's lifelong interest in technology was kindled at an early age when he experimented with a neighbor's chemistry set. Even then, he displayed the passion for practical outcomes that has typified his work as a scientist and engineer.

Moore says that the semiconductor industry's progress will far surpass that of nearly all other industries. For more information, visit scsite.com/dc2007/ch4/people and then click Gordon Moore.

Discovering Computers
A Gateway to Information *2007*

4   The Components of the System Unit

Chapter Review

The Chapter Review section summarizes the concepts presented in this chapter. To listen to the audio version of this Chapter Review, visit scsite.com/dc2007/ch4/review. To obtain help from other students regarding any subject in this chapter, visit scsite.com/dc2007/ch4/forum and post your thoughts or questions.

① How Are Various Styles of System Units Different?   The **system unit** is a case that contains electronic components of the computer used to process data. On desktop personal computers, most storage devices also are part of the system unit. On notebook computers, the keyboard and pointing device often occupy the area on top of the system unit, and the display attaches to the system unit by hinges. On mobile devices, the display often is built into the system unit. With game consoles, the input and output devices, such as controllers and a television, reside outside the system unit. On handheld game consoles and digital music players, by contrast, the packaging around the system unit also houses the input devices and display.

② What Are Chips, Adapter Cards, and Other Components of the Motherboard?   The **motherboard** is the main circuit board of the system unit. The motherboard contains many electronic components including a processor chip, memory chips, expansion slots, and adapter cards. A **chip** is a small piece of semiconducting material, usually silicon, on which integrated circuits are etched. Expansion slots hold adapter cards that provide connections and functions not built into the motherboard.

③ What Are the Components of a Processor, and How Do They Complete a Machine Cycle?   The **processor** interprets and carries out the basic instructions that operate a computer. Processors contain a **control unit** that directs and coordinates most of the operations in the computer and an **arithmetic logic unit** (*ALU*) that performs arithmetic, comparison, and other operations. The *machine cycle* is a set of four basic operations — *fetching, decoding, executing,* and *storing* — that the processor repeats for every instruction. The control unit fetches program instructions and data from memory and decodes the instructions into commands the computer can execute.

④ What Are the Characteristics of Various Personal Computer Processors?   Intel produces the **Pentium** processor for high-performance PCs, the **Celeron** processor for basic PCs, and the **Xeon** and **Itanium** processors for workstations and low-end servers. AMD manufactures *Intel-compatible processors*, which have an internal design similar to Intel processors. A *dual-core processor* is a chip that has two separate processors. A *multicore processor* is a chip with two or more separate processors. Some devices have a *system on a chip* processor that integrates the functions of a processor, memory, and a video card on a single chip.

> *connect!*
> Visit scsite.com/dc2007/ch4/quiz or click the Quiz Yourself button. Click Objectives 1 – 4.

⑤ What Is a Bit, and How Does a Series of Bits Represent Data?   Most computers are **digital** and recognize only two discrete states: off and on. To represent these states, computers use the **binary system**, which is a number system that has just two unique digits — 0 (for off) and 1 (for on) — called bits. A **bit** is the smallest unit of data a computer can process. Grouped together as a unit, 8 bits form a **byte**, which provides enough different combinations of 0s and 1s to represent 256 individual characters. The combinations are defined by patterns, called coding schemes, such as *ASCII, EBCDIC,* and *Unicode*.

⑥ How Do Programs Transfer In and Out of Memory?   When an application program starts, the program's instructions load into memory from the hard disk. The program and operating system instructions are in memory, and the program's window is displayed on the screen. When you quit the program, the program instructions are removed from memory, and the program no longer is displayed on the screen.

Chapter Review

(7) What Are the Various Types of Memory?   The system unit contains volatile and nonvolatile memory. *Volatile memory* loses its contents when the computer's power is turned off. *Nonvolatile memory* does not lose its contents when the computer's power is turned off. RAM is the most common type of volatile memory. ROM, flash memory, and CMOS are examples of nonvolatile memory. **RAM** consists of memory chips that can be read from and written to by the processor and other devices. **ROM** refers to memory chips storing permanent data and instructions that usually cannot be modified. **Flash memory** can be erased electronically and rewritten. **CMOS** technology uses battery power to retain information even when the power to the computer is turned off.

connect
Visit scsite.com/dc2007/ch4/quiz or click the Quiz Yourself button. Click Objectives 5 – 7.

(8) What Are the Types of Expansion Slots and Adapter Cards?   An **expansion slot** is a socket on the motherboard that can hold an adapter card. An **adapter card** is a circuit board that enhances functions of a component of the system unit and/or provides a connection to a **peripheral** such as a modem, disk drive, printer, scanner, or keyboard. Several types of adapter cards exist. A **sound card** enhances the sound-generating capabilities of a personal computer. A **video card** converts computer output into a video signal that displays an image on the screen. Many computers today support **Plug and Play**, which enables the computer to configure adapter cards and peripherals automatically.

(9) How Are a Serial Port, a Parallel Port, a USB Port, a FireWire port, and Other Ports Different?   A **port** is the point at which a peripheral attaches to or communicates with a system unit so it can send data to or receive information from the computer. A **serial port**, which transmits data one bit at a time, usually connects devices that do not require fast data transmission, such as a mouse, keyboard, or modem. A **parallel port**, which transfers more than one bit at a time, sometimes connects a printer to the system unit. A **USB port** can connect up to 127 different peripherals together with a single connector. A **FireWire port** can connect multiple types of devices that require faster data transmission speeds. Four special-purpose ports are MIDI, SCSI, IrDA, and Bluetooth. A **MIDI port** connects the system unit to a musical instrument. A **SCSI port** attaches the system unit to SCSI peripherals, such as disk drives. An **IrDA port** and **Bluetooth** technology allow wireless devices to transmit signals to a computer via infrared light waves or radio waves.

(10) How Do Buses Contribute to a Computer's Processing Speed?   A **bus** is an electrical channel along which bits transfer within the circuitry of a computer, allowing devices both inside and attached to the system unit to communicate. The size of a bus, called the *bus width*, determines the number of bits that the computer can transmit at one time. The larger the bus width, the faster the computer transfers data.

(11) What Are the Components in Mobile Computers and Mobile Devices?   In addition to the motherboard, processor, memory, sound card, PC Card slot, and **drive bay**, a mobile computer's system unit also houses devices such as the keyboard, pointing device, speakers, and display. The system unit for a typical notebook computer often has video, serial, parallel, modem, network, FireWire, USB, headphone, and microphone ports. Tablet PCs usually include several slots and ports. PDAs often have an IrDA port or are Bluetooth enabled so users can communicate wirelessly.

(12) How Do You Clean a System Unit?   Before cleaning a system unit, turn off the computer and unplug it from the wall. Use a small vacuum and a can of compressed air to remove external dust. After opening the case, wear an antistatic wristband and vacuum the interior. Wipe away dust and grime using lint-free antistatic wipes and rubbing alcohol.

connect
Visit scsite.com/dc2007/ch4/quiz or click the Quiz Yourself button. Click Objectives 8 – 12.

Key Terms

You should know the Primary Terms and be familiar with the Secondary Terms. Use the list below to help focus your study. To further enhance your understanding of the Key Terms in this chapter, visit scsite.com/dc2007/ch4/terms. See an example of and a definition for each term, and access current and additional information about the term from the Web.

Primary Terms

(shown in bold-black characters in the chapter)

AC adapter (213)
access time (203)
adapter card (204)
analog (194)
arithmetic logic unit (188)
bay (212)
binary system (195)
bit (195)
Bluetooth (210)
bus (211)
byte (195)
cache (201)
Celeron (190)
central processing unit (CPU) (187)
chip (186)
clock speed (189)
complementary metal-oxide semiconductor (CMOS) (203)
connector (206)
control unit (187)
digital (194)
drive bays (212)
expansion slot (204)
FireWire hub (209)
FireWire port (209)
firmware (202)
flash memory (202)
flash memory card (205)
gigabyte (GB) (197)
gigahertz (GHz) (189)
IrDA port (210)
Itanium (190)

jack (206)
kilobyte (KB or K) (197)
megabyte (MB) (197)
memory (197)
memory cache (201)
memory module (199)
memory slots (199)
MIDI port (209)
motherboard (186)
nanosecond (203)
parallel port (208)
PC Card (205)
PC Card slot (205)
Pentium (190)
Pentium M (190)
peripheral (204)
Plug and Play (205)
port (206)
power supply (213)
processor (187)
RAM (198)
read-only memory (ROM) (201)
SCSI port (210)
serial port (207)
sound card (204)
system clock (189)
system unit (184)
terabyte (TB) (197)
USB hub (208)
USB port (208)
video card (204)
word size (211)
Xeon (190)

Secondary Terms

(shown in italic characters in the chapter)

Accelerated Graphics Port (AGP) (212)
address (197)
address bus (211)
advanced transfer cache (ATC) (201)
ALU (188)
American Standard Code for Information Interchange (ASCII) (195)
arithmetic operations (188)
binary digit (195)
bus width (211)
Centrino (190)
chassis (184)
clock cycle (189)
COM port (207)
comparison operations (188)
daisy chain (208)
data bus (211)
decoding (188)
DIMM (dual inline memory module) (199)
Double Data Rate SDRAM (DDR SDRAM) (199)
dual-core processor (190)
dynamic RAM (DRAM) (199)
EEPROM (electrically erasable programmable read-only memory) chip (202)
executing (188)
expansion bus (212)
expansion card (204)
Extended Binary Coded Decimal Interchange Code (EBCDIC) (195)
external drive bay (212)
fast infrared port (210)
female connectors (206)
fetching (188)
FireWire bus (212)
gender changer (206)
graphics card (204)
heat pipe (193)
heat sink (193)
hertz (189)
hot plugging (205)
Hyper-Threading (HT) Technology (190)
IBM processor (190)
IEEE 1394 port (209)
integrated circuit (186)
Intel-compatible processors (190)
internal drive bay (212)
IrDA (Infrared Data Association) (210)

L1 cache (201)
L2 cache (201)
L3 cache (201)
liquid cooling technology (193)
machine cycle (188)
magnetoresistive RAM (MRAM) (199)
main memory (198)
male connectors (206)
microcode (202)
microprocessor (187)
MIPS (millions of instructions per second) (190)
Motorola processor (190)
multicore processor (190)
Musical Instrument Digital Interface (209)
nonvolatile memory (197)
ns (203)
parallel processing (194)
PC Card bus (212)
PCI bus (Peripheral Component Interconnect bus) (212)
Personal Computer Memory Card International Association (PCMCIA) cards (205)
pipelining (189)
PROM (programmable read-only memory) chip (202)
Rambus DRAM (RDRAM) (199)
random access memory (198)
registers (189)
RIMM (Rambus inline memory module) (199)
SCSI (small computer system interface) (210)
SIMM (single inline memory module) (199)
static RAM (SRAM) (199)
stored program concept (197)
storing (188)
superscalar (189)
synchronous DRAM (SDRAM) (199)
synthesizer (209)
system board (186)
system bus (212)
system on a chip (190)
transistor (186)
Unicode (195)
universal serial bus port (208)
USB 2.0 (208)
USB flash drive (205)
Viiv technology (192)
volatile memory (197)

Checkpoint

Use the Checkpoint exercises to check your knowledge level of the chapter. The Beyond the Book exercises will help broaden your understanding of the concepts presented in this chapter. To complete the Checkpoint exercises interactively, visit scsite.com/dc2007/ch4/check.

 Label the Figure

Identify these components.

a. memory module

b. motherboard

c. adapter cards

d. expansion slots

e. processor chip in a processor slot

 True/False

Mark T for True and F for False. (See page numbers in parentheses.)

_____ 1. With game consoles, the input and output devices, such as controllers and a television, reside outside the system unit. (185)

_____ 2. The processor interprets and carries out the basic instructions that operate a computer. (187)

_____ 3. The speed of the system clock is the only factor that influences a computer's performance. (189)

_____ 4. A Pentium M processor typically is used for workstations and low-end servers. (192)

_____ 5. Replacing a motherboard is a fairly simple process, whereas replacing a processor is much more complicated. (192)

_____ 6. A heat sink is a small ceramic or metal component with fins on its surface that absorbs and disperses heat produced by electrical components. (193)

_____ 7. A byte is the smallest unit of data the computer can process. (195)

_____ 8. Coding schemes make it possible for humans to interact with a digital computer that processes only bits. (195)

_____ 9. Two types of cache are memory cache and disk cache. (201)

_____ 10. Read-only memory refers to memory chips storing permanent data and instructions. (201)

_____ 11. Serial ports usually connect devices that require fast data transmission rates. (207)

_____ 12. A USB port can connect up to eight different peripherals together with a single connector. (208)

Checkpoint

 Multiple Choice   Select the best answer. (See page numbers in parentheses.)

1. On _____, the display often is built into the system unit. (185)
   a. mobile devices
   b. notebook computers
   c. desktop personal computers
   d. all of the above

2. The processor also is called the _____. (187)
   a. central processing unit (CPU)
   b. adapter card
   c. motherboard
   d. chip

3. The _____ is the component of the processor that directs and coordinates most of the operations in the computer. (187)
   a. control unit
   b. arithmetic logic unit
   c. register
   d. machine cycle

4. _____ is the process of obtaining a program instruction or data item from memory. (188)
   a. Storing   b. Decoding
   c. Executing   d. Fetching

5. A processor contains small, high-speed storage locations, called _____, that temporarily hold data and instructions. (189)
   a. flash drives   b. registers
   c. jacks   d. heat sinks

6. Processors that can execute more than one instruction per clock cycle are said to be _____. (189)
   a. superscalar
   b. dual-core processors
   c. system on a chip
   d. flash drives

7. Dual-core/multicore processors _____. (192)
   a. reduce the power consumption
   b. reduce heat output
   c. increase overall performance
   d. all of the above

8. _____ is a 16-bit coding scheme that is capable of representing more than 65,000 characters and symbols, enough for almost all the world's current written languages. (195)
   a. ASCII   b. Unicode
   c. Microcode   d. EBCDIC

9. A(n) _____ is a unique number that identifies the location of a byte in memory. (197)
   a. register
   b. kilobyte
   c. address
   d. bit

10. A _____ is a type of memory module with pins on opposite sides of the circuit board that do not connect, and thus form two sets of contacts. (199)
    a. RIMM (Rambus inline memory module)
    b. DIMM (dual inline memory module)
    c. ROMM (Rambus online memory module)
    d. SIMM (single inline memory module)

11. Many of today's computers support _____, which means the computer automatically can configure adapter cards and other peripherals as you install them. (205)
    a. Pack and Go
    b. Plug and Play
    c. Pick and Choose
    d. Park and Ride

12. A _____ port is an interface that connects devices by transferring more than one bit at a time. (208)
    a. serial
    b. parallel
    c. USB
    d. mouse

13. Word size is the _____. (211)
    a. pace of the system clock
    b. size of the bus
    c. amount of time it takes the processor to read instructions from memory
    d. number of bits the processor can interpret and execute at a given time.

14. _____ usually are installed in internal bays. (212)
    a. Floppy disk drives
    b. Hard disk drives
    c. Zip drives
    d. CD drives

Checkpoint

Matching

Match the terms with their definitions. (See page numbers in parentheses.)

_____ 1. motherboard (186)
_____ 2. processor (187)
_____ 3. ALU (188)
_____ 4. register (189)
_____ 5. memory (197)
_____ 6. firmware (202)
_____ 7. flash memory (202)
_____ 8. expansion slot (204)
_____ 9. PC Card (205)
_____ 10. Bluetooth (210)

a. socket on the motherboard that can hold an adapter card
b. small, high-speed storage locations that temporarily hold data and instructions
c. electronic components that store instructions, data, and results of processed data
d. performs arithmetic, comparison, and other operations
e. ROM chips that contain permanently written data, instructions, or information
f. amount of time it takes the processor to read data, instructions, and information from memory
g. thin, credit card-sized device that adds memory, storage, sound, fax/modem, network, and other capabilities to mobile computers
h. nonvolatile memory that can be erased electronically and rewritten
i. technology that uses radio waves to transmit data between two devices
j. number of bits the processor can interpret and execute at a given time
k. main circuit board of the system unit
l. interprets and carries out the basic instructions that operate a computer

Short Answer

Write a brief answer to each of the following questions.

1. What is the motherboard? _____ What is a computer chip? _____
2. What are the four basic operations in a machine cycle? _____ What is pipelining, and how does it affect processing speed? _____
3. What is the system clock? _____ How does clock speed affect a computer's speed? _____
4. What is a system on a chip? _____ What types of devices typically have them? _____
5. What is a bus? _____ How does bus width affect a computer's data transfer speed? _____

Beyond the Book

Read the following book elements, learn more about each using the Web, and then write a brief report.

1. Ethics & Issues — Can Computers Think? (187), Discarded Computer Parts: Whose Problem Is It? (193), How Much Should You Pay for a Computer? (200), or Should Smart Shoes Be Banned from Competitive Events? (214)
2. Career Corner — Computer Engineer (217)
3. Companies on the Cutting Edge — AMD or Intel (219)
4. FAQs (189, 193, 200, 202, 203, 208, 210, 213, 216)
5. High-Tech Talk — Random Access

Memory (RAM): The Genius of Memory (218)
6. Looking Ahead — Countries Seek Computing Speed Supremacy (190) or DNA Computer Works to Fight Cancer (215)
7. Making Use of the Web — Resources (120)
8. Picture Yourself Buying a Computer (182)
9. Technology Trailblazers — Jack Kilby or Gordon Moore (219)
10. Web Links (186, 192, 199, 201, 202, 204, 205, 209, 212)

Learn It Online

Use the Learn It Online exercises to reinforce your understanding of the chapter concepts. To access the Learn It Online exercises, visit scsite.com/dc2007/ch4/learn.

① At the Movies — Computing Clusters

To view the Computing Clusters movie, click the number 1 button. Locate your video and click the corresponding High-Speed or Dial-Up link, depending on your Internet connection. Watch the movie and then complete the exercise by answering the questions below. Many graphics and animation programs have heavy data loads. When using a processing cluster, these difficult, memory-intensive tasks can be divided over several different computers linked through a network. Using multiple computers to perform a big job means it gets done faster. What types of tasks are best accomplished by a cluster? How would you handle a large, time-consuming project?

② At the Movies — USB Basics

To view the USB Basics movie, click the number 2 button. Locate your video and click the corresponding High-Speed or Dial-Up link, depending on your Internet connection. Watch the movie and then complete the exercise by answering the questions below. A universal serial bus (USB) is a peripheral bus standard developed by Intel which allows you to connect external equipment such as digital cameras and MP3 players to your computer. The USB enables the external equipment to communicate with your computer and share information and power. How can you tell if your USB port is working? What are some ways you can troubleshoot your USB ports?

③ Student Edition Labs — Understanding the Motherboard

Click the number 3 button. A new browser window will open, displaying the Student Edition Labs. Follow the on-screen instructions, and complete the Understanding the Motherboard Lab. When finished, click the Exit button. If required, submit your results to your instructor.

④ Student Edition Labs — Binary Numbers

Click the number 4 button. A new browser window will open, displaying the Student Edition Labs. Follow the on-screen instructions, and complete the Binary Numbers Lab. When finished, click the Exit button. If required, submit your results to your instructor.

⑤ Practice Test

Click the number 5 button. Answer each question. When completed, enter your name and click the Grade Test button to submit the quiz for grading. Make a note of any missed questions. If required, submit your score to your instructor.

⑥ Who Wants To Be a Computer Genius²?

Click the number 6 button to find out if you are a computer genius. Directions about how to play the game will be displayed. When you are ready to play, click the Play button. Submit your score to your instructor.

⑦ Wheel of Terms

Click the number 7 button to reinforce important terms you learned in this chapter by playing the Shelly Cashman Series version of this popular game. Directions about how to play the game will be displayed. When you are ready to play, click the Play button. Submit your score to your instructor.

Learn It Online

8 DC Track and Field

Click the number 8 button to use what you have learned in this chapter to compete against other students in three track and field events. Directions about how to play the game will be displayed. When you are ready to play, click the start first event button. If required, submit your score to your instructor.

9 You're Hired!

Click the number 9 button to use what you have learned in this chapter to embark on the path to a career in computers. Directions about how to play the game will be displayed. When you are ready to play, click the begin game button. If required, submit your score to your instructor.

10 Crossword Puzzle Challenge

Click the number 10 button. Complete the puzzle to reinforce skills you learned in this chapter. Directions about how to play the game will be displayed. When you are ready to play, click the Play button. Submit the completed puzzle to your instructor.

11 Lab Exercises

Click the number 11 button. When the Lab Exercises menu appears, click the exercise assigned by your instructor. A new browser window will open. Follow the on-screen instructions to complete the exercise. When finished, click the Exit button. If required, submit your results to your instructor.

12 In the News

In February 2006, the forerunner of the modern computer had its 60th anniversary. By today's standards for electronic computers, the ENIAC (Electronic Numerical Integrator And Computer) was a grotesque monster. With 30 separate units, plus a power supply and forced-air cooling, it weighed more than 30 tons. Its 19,000 vacuum tubes, 1,500 relays, and hundreds of thousands of resistors, capacitors, and inductors consumed almost 200 kilowatts of electrical power. The ENIAC performed fewer than 1,000 calculations per minute;

today, personal computers can process more than 300 million instructions per second. The rapid development of computing power and capabilities is astonishing, and the rate of that development is accelerating. Click the number 12 button and read a news article about the introduction of a new or improved computer component. What is the component? Who is introducing it? Will the component change the way people use computers? If so, how?

13 Chapter Discussion Forum

Select an objective from this chapter on page 183 about which you would like more information. Click the number 13 button, and post a short message listing a meaningful message title accompanied by one or more questions concerning the selected objective. In two days, return to the threaded discussion by clicking the number 13 button. Submit to your instructor your original message and at least one response to your message.

14 Configuring and Pricing Computers

Click the number 14 button to learn how to configure and price a custom computer. Research at least two manufacturers' Web sites, and get a quote from each site you visit. Make sure you include any software you may require. Also, add any upgrade items that you would like to have on your system including peripheral items (printer, scanner, etc.). Print the quotes from each site and submit the results to your instructor.

Learn How To

Use the Learn How To activities to learn fundamental skills when using a computer and accompanying technology. Complete the exercises and submit them to your instructor. Visit scsite.com/dc2007/ch4/howto to obtain more information pertaining to each activity.

LEARN HOW TO 1: Purchase and Install Memory in a Computer

One of the less expensive and more effective ways to speed up a computer, make it capable of processing more programs at the same time, and enable it to handle graphics, gaming, and other high-level programs is to increase the amount of memory. The process of increasing memory is accomplished in two phases — purchasing the memory and installing the memory. To purchase memory for a computer, complete the following steps:

1. Determine the amount of memory currently in the computer. For a method to do this, see Learn How To number 3 in Chapter 1.
2. Determine the maximum amount of memory your computer can contain. This value can change for different computers, based primarily on the number of slots on the motherboard available for memory and the size of the memory modules you can place in each slot. On most computers, different size memory modules can be inserted in slots. A computer, therefore, might allow a 128 MB, 256 MB, or 512 MB memory module to be inserted in each slot. To determine the maximum memory for a computer, in many cases you can multiply the number of memory slots on the computer by the maximum size memory module that can be inserted in each slot.

   For example, if a computer contains four memory slots and is able to accept memory modules of 128 MB, 256 MB, or 512 MB in each of its memory slots, the maximum amount of memory the computer can contain is 2 GB (4 x 512 MB).

   You can find the number of slots and the allowable sizes of each memory module by contacting the computer manufacturer, looking in the computer's documentation, or contacting sellers of memory such as Kingston (www.kingston.com) or Crucial (www.crucial.com) on the Web. These sellers have documentation for most computers, and even programs you can download to run on your computer that will specify how much memory your computer currently has and how much you can add.
3. Determine how much memory you want to add, which will be somewhere between the current memory and the maximum memory allowed on the computer.
4. Determine the current configuration of memory on the computer. For example, if a computer with four memory slots contains 512 MB of memory, it could be using one memory module of 512 MB in a single slot and the other three slots would be empty; two memory modules of 256 MB each in two slots with two slots empty; one memory module of 256 MB and two memory modules of 128 MB each in three slots with one slot empty; or four memory modules of 128 MB each in four slots with no slots empty. You may be required to look inside the system unit to make this determination. The current memory configuration on a computer will determine what new memory modules you should buy to increase the memory to the amount determined in Step 3.

   You also should be aware that a few computers require memory to be installed in matching pairs. This means a computer with four slots could obtain 512 MB of memory with two memory modules of 256 MB in two slots, or four memory modules of 128 MB in four slots.
5. Determine the number of available memory slots on your computer and the number and size memory modules you must buy to fulfill your requirement. Several scenarios can occur (in the following examples, assume you can install memory one module at a time).
   a. Scenario 1: The computer has one or more open slots. In this case, you might be able to purchase a memory module that matches the amount of memory increase you desire. For example, if you want to increase memory by 256 MB, you should purchase a 256 MB memory module for insertion in the open slot. Generally, you should buy the maximum size module you can for an open slot. So, if you find two empty slots and wish to increase memory by 256 MB, it is smarter to buy one 256 MB module and leave one empty slot rather than buy two 128 MB memory modules and use both slots. This allows you to increase memory again without removing currently used modules.

Learn How To

b. Scenario 2: The computer has no open slots. For example, a computer containing 512 MB of memory could have four slots each containing 128 MB memory modules. If you want to increase the memory on the computer to 1 GB, you will have to remove some of the 128 MB memory modules and replace them with the new memory modules you purchase. In this example, you want to increase the memory by 512 MB. You would have several options: (1) You could replace all four 128 MB memory modules with 256 MB memory modules; (2) You could replace all four 128 MB memory modules with two 512 MB memory modules; (3) You could replace one 128 MB memory module with a 512 MB memory module, and replace a second 128 MB module with a 256 MB memory module. Each of these options results in a total memory of 1 GB. The best option will depend on the price of memory and whether you anticipate increasing the memory size at a later time. The least expensive option probably would be number 3.

c. Scenario 3: Many combinations can occur. You may have to perform calculations to decide the combination of modules that will work for the number of slots on the computer and the desired additional memory.

6. Determine the type of memory to buy for the computer. Computer memory has many types and configurations, and it is critical that you buy the kind of memory for which the computer was designed. It is preferable to buy the same type of memory that currently is found in the computer. That is, if the memory is DDR SDRAM with a certain clock speed, then that is the type of additional memory you should place in the computer. The documentation for the computer should specify the memory type. In addition, the Web sites cited on the previous page, and others as well, will present a list of memory modules that will work with your computer. Enough emphasis cannot be placed on the fact that the memory you buy must be compatible with the type of memory usable on your computer. Because there are so many types and configurations, you must be especially diligent to ensure you purchase the proper memory for your computer.

7. Once you have determined the type and size of memory to purchase, buy it from a reputable dealer. Buying poor or mismatched memory is a major reason for a computer's erratic performance and is a difficult problem to troubleshoot.

After purchasing the memory, you must install it on your computer. Complete the following steps to install memory:

1. Unplug the computer, and remove all electrical cords and device cables from the ports on the computer. Open the case of the system unit. You may want to consult the computer's documentation to determine the exact procedure.

2. Ground yourself so you do not generate static electricity that can cause memory or other components within the system unit to be damaged. To do this, wear an antistatic wristband you can purchase inexpensively in a computer or electronics store; or, before you touch any component within the system unit, touch an unpainted metal surface. If you are not wearing an antistatic wristband, periodically touch an unpainted metal surface to dissipate any static electricity.

3. Within the system unit, find the memory slots on the motherboard. The easiest way to do this is look for memory modules that are similar to those you purchased. The memory slots often are located near the processor. If you cannot find the slots, consult the documentation. A diagram often is available to help you spot the memory slots.

4. Insert the memory module in the next empty slot. Orient the memory module in the slot to match the modules currently installed. A notch or notches on the memory module will ensure you do not install the module backwards. If your memory module is a DIMM, insert the module straight down into grooves on the clips and then apply gentle pressure. If your memory is SIMM, insert the module at a 45 degree angle and then rotate it to a vertical position until the module snaps into place.

5. If you must remove one or more memory modules before inserting the new memory, carefully release the clips before lifting the memory module out of the memory slot.

6. Plug in the machine and replace all the device cables without replacing the cover.

7. Start the computer. In most cases, the new memory will be recognized and the computer will run normally. If an error message appears, determine the cause of the error.

8. Replace the computer cover.

Exercise

1. Assume you have a computer that contains 256 MB of memory. It contains four memory slots. Each slot can contain 128 MB or 256 MB memory modules. Two of the slots contain 128 MB memory modules. What memory chip(s) would you buy to increase the memory on the computer to 512 MB? What is the maximum memory on the computer? Submit your answers to your instructor.

2. Assume you have a computer that contains 1 GB of memory. It contains four memory slots. Each slot can contain 128 MB, 256 MB, 512 MB, or 1 GB memory modules. Currently, each slot contains a 256 MB memory module. What combinations of memory modules will satisfy your memory upgrade to 2 GB? Visit a Web site to determine which of these combinations is the least expensive. Submit your answers and recommendations to your instructor.

Web Research

Use the Internet-based Web Research exercises to broaden your understanding of the concepts presented in this chapter. Visit scsite.com/dc2007/ch4/research to obtain more information pertaining to each exercise. To discuss any of the Web Research exercises in this chapter with other students, post your thoughts or questions at scsite.com/dc2007/ch4/forum.

① Scavenger Hunt   Use one of the <u>search engines</u> listed in Figure 2-8 in Chapter 2 on page 78 or your own favorite search engine to find the answers to the questions below. Copy and paste the Web address from the Web page where you found the answer. Some questions may have more than one answer. If required, submit your answers to your instructor. (1) Which Microsoft Windows operating systems support USB? (2) The USB port supports hot plugging or hot swapping. What is "hot plugging"? (3) What is the name of the suit that people wear when they work in chip manufacturing clean rooms? (4) What is CAS Latency? (5) What are rune stones and their connection to Danish King Harald Blatand (Bluetooth)? (6) What is the name of the type of memory that retains its contents until it is exposed to ultraviolet light?

② Search Sleuth   <u>Ask Jeeves</u> (ask.com) is one of the faster growing research Web sites. The search engine uses natural language, which allows researchers to type millions of questions each day using words a human would use rather than words a computer understands. Visit this Web site and then use your word processing program to answer the following questions. Then, if required, submit your answers to your instructor. (1) Click the P.G. Wodehouse link at the bottom of the home page. Who are P.G. Wodehouse and Bertie Wooster? (2) Click your browser's Back button or press the BACKSPACE key to return to the Ask Jeeves home page. Click the Search text box and then type What were the top selling DVDs this week? as the keywords in the Search text box. (3) Scroll through the links Ask Jeeves returns and then click one that provides the information requested. What three DVDs generated the best sales this past week? (4) Click your browser's Back button or press the BACKSPACE key to return to the Ask Jeeves home page. Click the Bloglines link at the bottom of the page. (5) Click the Today's hot topics link and review the material. Summarize the information you read and then write a 50-word summary.

③ Journaling   Respond to your readings in this chapter by writing at least one page containing your reactions, evaluations, and reflections about <u>cleaning your computer</u>. For example, have you tried cleaning a computer with the basic products recommended in this chapter? When? Where is the cleanest environment in your home to use the computer? If you do not feel comfortable cleaning the system unit yourself, where would you take it for this preventive maintenance? You also can write about the new terms you learned by reading this chapter. If required, submit your journal to your instructor.

④ Expanding Your Understanding   A <u>brick-and-click</u> business allows customers to conduct transactions at a physical location as well as online. Many banks and retailers, such as Citibank and Best Buy, are brick-and-click businesses. Choose a brick-and-click business and then visit the physical location and its Web site. Compare the type, availability, and cost of products or services. Write a report summarizing your findings, focusing on the advantages and disadvantages of conducting business at a physical location and online. If required, submit your report to your instructor.

⑤ Ethics in Action   More than 50 law enforcement agencies use handheld wireless devices to access commercial databases. For example, Massachusetts state police stationed at Logan International Airport use the <u>LocatePLUS Holdings Corporation</u>'s database, which has information on 98 percent of Americans. The data is composed of motor vehicle records, credit bureau reports, property tax payments, and telephone directories. Police say accessing this information helps them perform their jobs more efficiently. Privacy experts, in contrast, say that information collected for one purpose should not be available in other contexts. View online sites that provide information about commercial databases for sale. Write a report summarizing your findings, and include a table of links to Web sites that provide additional details. If required, submit your report to your instructor.

Case Studies

Use the Case Studies to apply the concepts presented in the chapter to real-world situations. Visit scsite.com/dc2007/ch4/cases to obtain more information pertaining to each exercise. To discuss the Case Studies in this chapter with other students, visit scsite.com/dc2007/ch4/forum and post your thoughts or questions.

CASE STUDY 1 — Class Discussion   You are the purchasing manager at TechnoInk, a company that specializes in designing and producing logos for local high school and college sports teams. The company has 35 nonnetworked computers that are used throughout the company for common business applications. The computers are four years old, and you would like to replace them. The director of information technology agrees, but he has reservations. He has asked you to complete a study on the cost of new computers, comparing the major features found on <u>system units</u> at three different price levels: less than $1,000; $1,000 to $1,750; and greater than $1,750. Prepare a brief summary report on the major features of system units at the various price levels. Include recommendations on which system units would meet the company's needs most economically. Be prepared to discuss your recommendations in class.

CASE STUDY 2 — Class Discussion   Universal Computing, Inc. has decided to upgrade several hundred PCs used in their offices nationwide. The Information Technology Department has recommended that the company again purchase PCs for approximately $1,500 each. The system units would include Pentium 4 processors with speeds of 3.80 GHz with 1 GB of RAM. From her days in college, the CFO has preferred Apple computers and currently uses an <u>Apple iMac</u> at home. She has hired you as a consultant to determine if the company would be better off purchasing iMacs in the same price range and with similar capabilities. Use the Web and/or print media to select a comparable iMac. Which one starts faster? Which one opens files faster? Which one loads Web pages faster? Is the iMac in the same price range as the PC? List any other advantages and disadvantages of each. Prepare a brief summary report and be prepared to discuss your findings in class.

CASE STUDY 3 — Research   Your family has decided to purchase a computer for use at home. Because you are enrolled in a computer course, you have been asked to make recommendations. Your instructor has pushed the premise "software drives hardware." List the application programs you and your family members plan to use. Visit the Web sites of the manufacturers of each application program, and note the capabilities required of the system unit (type of processor, amount of <u>RAM</u>, and so on). On the basis of your findings, what are the minimum system requirements you and your family would require in a personal computer? What system requirements would be sufficient to provide a "cushion" so that you could be sure the system also could run other, or new, application packages? Write a brief report and share your findings with your class.

CASE STUDY 4 — Research   Many system unit manufacturers provide a toll-free telephone number that customers can call with technical problems or questions. If the <u>service technician</u> determines a difficulty is a hardware problem that the customer can fix, the technician might ask the customer to open the system unit and make some adjustments. For this reason, every computer user can benefit by being familiar with the inside of the system unit. If you own a personal computer or have access to a personal computer, unplug the power supply and take the cover off the system unit. Be careful not to touch any of the system unit components. Make a sketch of the system unit and try to identify each part. By referring to the computer's *User Guide*, list some of the computer's specifications (clock speed, memory size, and so on). Compare your sketch and list with a classmate who has done this exercise with a different computer. How are the computers similar? How are they different?

CASE STUDY 5 — Team Challenge   The chief financial officer of SkateJam, Inc. has asked her Information Technology Department to look into replacing the company's desktop computers with <u>notebook computers</u>. The director of information technology has hired your team as consultants to examine the advantages and disadvantages of notebook computers. Form a three-member team and assign each team member one of the following companies — Dell, HP, and Apple. Have each member of your team use the Web and/or print media to find a notebook computer and a desktop computer with comparable middle-of-the-road system units sold by the company assigned to them. What is the price of each computer? How are the processors and RAM similar? How are they different? Meet with the members of your team to discuss results of your investigations. Is the notebook computer the better buy? If so, why? Write a summary report or use PowerPoint to create a group presentation and share your findings with the class.

CHAPTER FIVE

Input

Picture Yourself Going Digital

Your daughter claims you have been stuck in the last decade — still connected by cords, still writing appointments in a daily planner, still using the house telephone as your main method of communication, and still visiting photo labs to process 35 mm film. To get up to speed with digital technology, you have been using gift cards that you have received for birthdays and other occasions to purchase new devices for your computer.

First, you bought a wireless keyboard and mouse, which the sales clerk explained communicates via radio waves. More importantly to you, these two devices give you the freedom to work without the clutter of cords. You now can position the keyboard and mouse anywhere on your desk and not worry about whether the cord is long enough.

You then bought a smart phone that has PDA capabilities. First, you learned how to enter contact information and appointments and how to use the digital pen. Next, you learned how to send picture messages and post them to a Web site. You plan to send or post regular photo updates to keep friends and family up-to-date of all your activities.

Most recently, you purchased a digital camera. You have become quite adept at transferring the digital images to your computer, editing them with your photo editing software, printing the images in a variety of sizes, and, of course, e-mailing the pictures.

To learn more about keyboards, mouse devices, input for PDAs and smart phones, and digital cameras, read Chapter 5 and discover features of many other types of input devices.

After completing this chapter, you will be able to:

1. Define input
2. List the characteristics of a keyboard
3. Describe different mouse types and how they work
4. Summarize how various pointing devices work
5. Explain how voice recognition works
6. Describe various input devices for PDAs, smart phones, and Tablet PCs
7. Explain how a digital camera works
8. Describe the uses of PC video cameras, Web cams, and video conferencing
9. Discuss various scanners and reading devices and how they work
10. Explain the types of terminals
11. Summarize the various biometric devices
12. Identify alternative input devices for physically challenged users

CONTENTS

WHAT IS INPUT?

Input is any data and instructions entered into the memory of a computer. As shown in Figure 5-1, people have a variety of options for entering data or instructions into a computer.

As discussed in Chapter 1, *data* is a collection of unprocessed text, numbers, images, audio, and video. Once data is in memory, the computer interprets and executes instructions to process the data into information. Instructions entered into the computer can be in the form of programs, commands, and user responses.

- A *program* is a series of instructions that tells a computer what to do and how to do it. When a programmer writes a program, he or she enters the program into the computer by using a keyboard, mouse, or other input device. The programmer then stores the program in a file that a user can execute (run). When a user runs a program, the computer loads the program from a storage

keyboard

mouse

wheel

joystick

game controller

touch screen

control pad

biometric input

data collection device

MICR

magnetic stripe card reader

RFID reader

input

FIGURE 5-1 Users can enter data and instructions into a computer in a variety of ways.

medium into memory. Thus, a program is entered into a computer's memory.

- Programs respond to commands that a user issues. A *command* is an instruction that causes a program to perform a specific action. Users issue commands by typing or pressing keys on the keyboard, clicking a mouse button, speaking into a microphone, or touching an area on a screen.
- A *user response* is an instruction a user issues by replying to a question displayed by a program. A response to the question instructs the program to perform certain actions. Assume the program asks the question, Is the time card correct? If you answer Yes, the program processes the time card. If you answer No, the program gives you the opportunity to modify the time card entries.

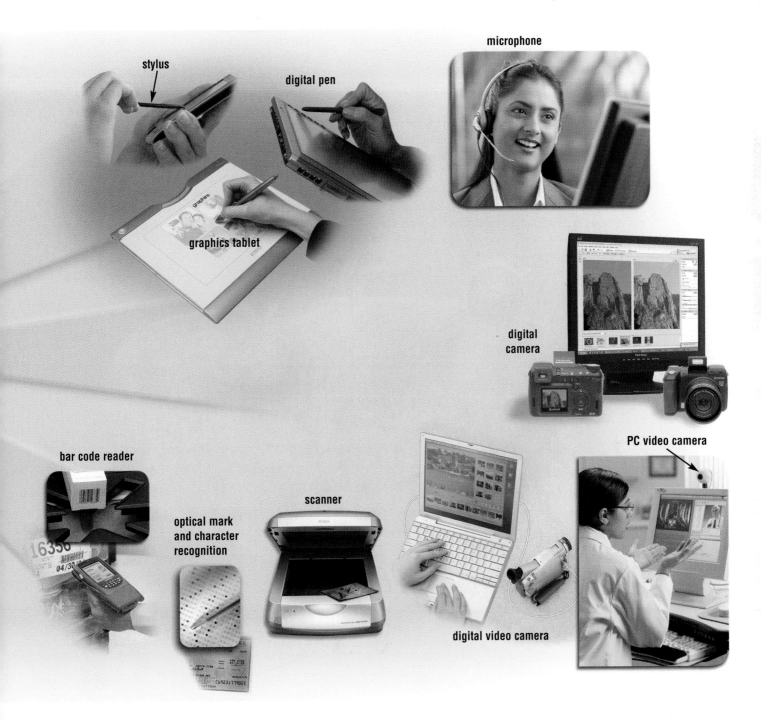

stylus

digital pen

microphone

graphics tablet

digital camera

PC video camera

bar code reader

optical mark and character recognition

scanner

digital video camera

WHAT ARE INPUT DEVICES?

An **input device** is any hardware component that allows users to enter data and instructions (programs, commands, and user responses) into a computer. Depending on the application and your particular requirements, the input device selected may vary. The following pages discuss a variety of input devices.

Storage devices, such as disk drives, serve as both input and output devices. Chapter 7 discusses storage devices.

THE KEYBOARD

Many people use a keyboard as one of their input devices. A **keyboard** is an input device that contains keys users press to enter data and instructions into a computer (Figure 5-2).

Desktop computer keyboards typically have from 101 to 105 keys. Keyboards for smaller computers such as notebook computers contain fewer keys. All computer keyboards have a typing area that includes the letters of the alphabet, numbers, punctuation marks, and other basic keys. Many desktop computer keyboards also have a numeric keypad on the right side of the keyboard. A keyboard also contains other keys that allow users to enter data and instructions into the computer. Read Ethics & Issues 5-1 for a related discussion.

Most of today's desktop computer keyboards are enhanced keyboards. An *enhanced keyboard* has twelve function keys along the top; it also has two CTRL keys, two ALT keys, and a set of arrow and additional keys between the typing area and the numeric keypad (Figure 5-2). *Function keys,* which are labeled with the letter F followed by a number, are special keys programmed to issue commands to a computer. The command associated with a function key may vary, depending on the program with which you are interacting. For example, the F3 key may issue one command to an operating system and an entirely different command to a word processing program. To issue commands, users often can press a function key in combination with other special keys (SHIFT, CTRL, ALT, and others).

FIGURE 5-2 On a desktop computer keyboard, you type using keys in the typing area and on the numeric keypad.

Keyboard Monitoring — Privacy Risk?

Are you curious about your spouse's long e-mail messages to a mutual friend? Are you concerned about your teenager's conversations in Internet chat rooms? Keyboard monitoring software can dispel your doubts. When installed on a computer, *keyboard monitoring software* records every keystroke in a hidden file, which later can be accessed by supplying the correct password. With keyboard monitoring software, you can see everything that was typed on the computer keyboard, including documents, e-mail, and other messages. Some programs also store a record of software used, Web sites visited, user logons, and periodic screen shots. The software can run completely undetected. With keyboard monitoring software, you can discover that your spouse is e-mailing gardening tips or recognize that your teenager has made a potentially dangerous contact in a chat room. Recently, courts ruled that law-enforcement agencies secretly can install keyboard monitoring software on suspects' computers if a proper search warrant is obtained. Many maintain, however, that keyboard monitoring software is an invasion of privacy, and some states have outlawed the secret installation of such software. Should keyboard monitoring software ever be used? If so, when? Some marketers of keyboard monitoring software recommend computer users be informed that the software is installed. Is this a good idea? Why or why not?

Nearly all keyboards have toggle keys. A *toggle key* is a key that switches between two states each time a user presses the key. When you press the NUM LOCK key, for example, it locks the numeric keypad so you can use the keypad to type numbers. When you press the NUM LOCK key again, the numeric keypad unlocks so the same keys can serve to move the insertion point. Many keyboards have status lights that light up when you activate a toggle key.

Keyboards also often have a WINDOWS key(s) and an APPLICATION key. When pressed, the WINDOWS key displays the Start menu, and the APPLICATION key displays an item's shortcut menu.

Keyboards also contain keys that allow you to position the insertion point, also known as a *cursor* in some programs. The **insertion point** is a symbol on the screen, usually a blinking vertical bar, that indicates where the next character you type will be displayed (Figure 5-3). Users can move the insertion point left, right, up, or down by pressing the arrow keys and other keys on the keyboard.

Newer keyboards include media control buttons that allow you to access the computer's CD/DVD drive and adjust speaker volume, and Internet control buttons that allow you to open an e-mail program, start a Web browser, and search the Internet. Some keyboards also have USB ports so a user can plug a USB device directly in the keyboard instead of in the system unit. Some keyboards include a fingerprint scanner, which is discussed later in this chapter.

A *gaming keyboard* is a keyboard designed specifically for users that enjoy playing games on the computer. Gaming keyboards typically include programmable keys so gamers can customize the keyboard to the game being played.

The keys on gaming keyboards light up so they are visible in all lighting conditions. Some even have small displays that show important game statistics, such as time or targets remaining.

What is the rationale for the arrangement of keys in the typing area?

The keys originally were arranged to reduce the frequency of key jams on old mechanical typewriters. Called a *QWERTY keyboard*, the first letters on the top alphabetic line spell QWERTY. A *Dvorak keyboard*, by contrast, places frequently typed letters in the middle of the typing area. Despite the Dvorak keyboard's logical design, most people and computers use a QWERTY keyboard. For more information, visit scsite.com/dc2007/ch5/faq and then click Keyboards.

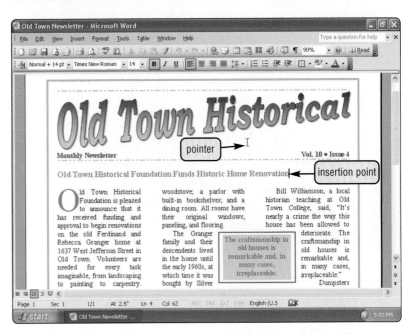

FIGURE 5-3 In most programs, such as Word, the insertion point is a blinking vertical bar. You use the keyboard or other input device to move the insertion point. The pointer, another symbol that is displayed on the screen, is controlled using a pointing device such as a mouse.

Keyboard Connections

Desktop computer keyboards often attach via a cable to a serial port, a keyboard port, or a USB port on the system unit. Some keyboards, however, do not use wires at all. A *wireless keyboard*, or *cordless keyboard*, is a battery-powered device that transmits data using wireless technology, such as radio waves or infrared light waves. Wireless keyboards often communicate with a receiver attached to a port on the system unit. The port type varies depending on the type of wireless technology. For example, a Bluetooth-enabled keyboard communicates via radio waves with a Bluetooth receiver that typically plugs in a USB port (Figure 5-4).

On notebook computers and some handheld computers, PDAs, and smart phones, the keyboard is built in the top of the system unit. To fit in these mobile computers and devices, the keyboards usually are smaller and have fewer keys. A typical notebook computer keyboard usually has only about 85 keys. To provide all of the functionality of a desktop computer keyboard, manufacturers design many of the keys to serve two or three purposes.

Keyboard Ergonomics

Regardless of size, many keyboards have a rectangular shape with the keys aligned in straight, horizontal rows. Users who spend a lot of time typing on these keyboards sometimes experience repetitive strain injuries (RSI) of their wrists and hands. For this reason, some manufacturers offer ergonomic keyboards. An *ergonomic keyboard* has a design that reduces the chance of wrist and hand injuries. Even keyboards that are not ergonomically designed attempt to offer a user more comfort by including a wrist rest or palm rest (Figure 5-2 on page 236).

The goal of **ergonomics** is to incorporate comfort, efficiency, and safety in the design of the workplace. Employees can be injured or develop disorders of the muscles, nerves, tendons, ligaments, and joints from working in an area that is not ergonomically designed.

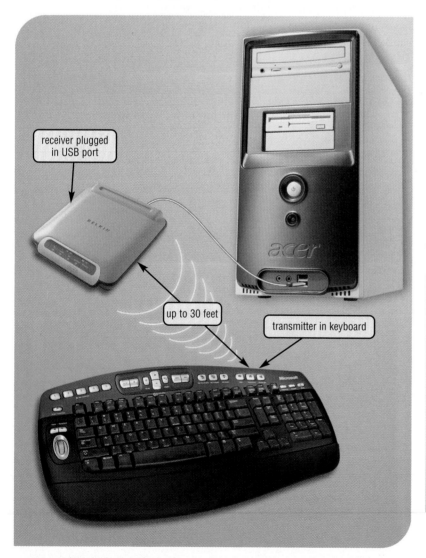

receiver plugged in USB port

up to 30 feet

transmitter in keyboard

FIGURE 5-4   Some personal computers have built-in Bluetooth technology. On computers that are not Bluetooth-enabled, you plug a Bluetooth receiver in a USB port on the system unit. A transmitter inside the keyboard communicates with the receiver, which should be within 30 feet from each other.

FAQ 5-2

What can I do to reduce chances of experiencing repetitive strain injuries?

Do not rest your wrist on the edge of a desk; use a wrist rest. Keep your forearm and wrist level so your wrist does not bend. Do hand exercises every 15 minutes. Keep your shoulders, arms, hands, and wrists relaxed while you work. Maintain good posture. Keep feet flat on the floor, with one foot slightly in front of the other. For more information, visit scsite.com/dc2007/ch5/faq and then click Repetitive Strain Injuries.

POINTING DEVICES

A **pointing device** is an input device that allows a user to control a pointer on the screen. In a graphical user interface, a **pointer** is a small symbol on the screen (Figure 5-3 on page 237) whose location and shape change as a user moves a pointing device. A pointing device can be used to move the insertion point; select text, graphics, and other objects; and click buttons, icons, links, and menu commands. The following sections discuss the mouse and other pointing devices.

MOUSE

A **mouse** is a pointing device that fits under the palm of your hand comfortably. The mouse is the most widely used pointing device on desktop computers.

With a mouse, users control the movement of the pointer, often called a *mouse pointer* in this case. As you move a mouse, the pointer on the screen also moves. Generally, you use the mouse to move the pointer on the screen to an object such as a button, a menu, an icon, a link, or text. Then, you press a mouse button to perform a certain action associated with that object. The top and sides of a mouse have one to four buttons; some also have a small wheel. The bottom of a mouse is flat and contains a mechanism that detects movement of the mouse.

Mouse Types

A *mechanical mouse* has a rubber or metal ball on its underside (Figure 5-5). When the ball rolls in a certain direction, electronic circuits in the mouse translate the movement of the mouse into signals the computer can process. You should place a mechanical mouse on a mouse pad. A **mouse pad** is a rectangular rubber or foam pad that provides better traction than the top of a desk. The mouse pad also protects the ball in the mouse from a build-up of dust and dirt, which could cause it to malfunction.

An optical mouse, by contrast, has no moving mechanical parts inside. Instead, an *optical mouse* uses devices that emit and sense light to detect the mouse's movement. Some use optical sensors, others use a laser (Figure 5-6). You can place an optical mouse on nearly all types of surfaces, eliminating the need for a mouse pad.

An optical mouse is more precise than a mechanical mouse and does not require cleaning as does a mechanical mouse, but it also is more expensive.

A mouse connects to a computer in several ways. Many types connect with a cable that attaches to a serial port, mouse port, or USB port on the system unit. A *wireless mouse*, or *cordless mouse*, is a battery-powered device that transmits data using wireless technology, such as radio waves or infrared light waves. The technology used for a wireless mouse is similar to that of a wireless keyboard discussed earlier. Some users prefer a wireless mouse because it frees up desk space and eliminates the clutter of a cord.

FIGURE 5-5 A mechanical mouse contains a small ball.

FIGURE 5-6a (optical mouse that uses optical sensor)

FIGURE 5-6b (optical mouse that uses laser)

FIGURE 5-6 An optical mouse uses an optical sensor or a laser. Many also include buttons you push with your thumb that enable forward and backward navigation through Web pages.

Using a Mouse

Windows users work with a mouse that has at least two buttons. For a right-handed user, the left button usually is the primary mouse button, and the right mouse button is the secondary mouse button. Left-handed people, however, can reverse the function of these buttons.

Operations you can perform with the mouse include point, click, right-click, double-click, triple-click, drag, right-drag, rotate wheel, press wheel button, and tilt wheel. The table in Figure 5-7 explains how to perform these mouse operations. Some programs also use keys in combination with the mouse to perform certain actions. The function of the mouse buttons and the wheel varies depending on the program. Read Ethics & Issues 5-2 for a related discussion.

Some programs support *mouse gestures*, where the user performs certain operations by holding a mouse button while moving the mouse in a particular pattern. For example, moving the mouse down and to the left may close all open windows. Mouse gestures minimize the amount of time users spend navigating through menus or toolbars because users can perform these tasks by simply moving (gesturing) the mouse.

FAQ 5-3

How do I use a wheel on a mouse?

Roll it forward or backward to scroll up or down. Tilt it to the right or left to scroll horizontally. Hold down the CTRL key while rolling the wheel to make the text on the screen bigger or smaller. These scrolling and zooming functions work with most software and also on the Web. For more information, visit scsite.com/dc2007/ch5/faq and then click Using a Mouse.

MOUSE OPERATIONS

Operation	Mouse Action	Example
Point	Move the mouse across a flat surface until the pointer on the desktop is positioned on the item of choice.	Position the pointer on the screen.
Click	Press and release the primary mouse button, which usually is the left mouse button.	Select or deselect items on the screen or start a program or program feature.
Right-click	Press and release the secondary mouse button, which usually is the right mouse button.	Display a shortcut menu.
Double-click	Quickly press and release the left mouse button twice without moving the mouse.	Start a program or program feature.
Triple-click	Quickly press and release the left mouse button three times without moving the mouse.	Select a paragraph.
Drag	Point to an item, hold down the left mouse button, move the item to the desired location on the screen, and then release the left mouse button.	Move an object from one location to another or draw pictures.
Right-drag	Point to an item, hold down the right mouse button, move the item to the desired location on the screen, and then release the right mouse button.	Display a shortcut menu after moving an object from one location to another.
Rotate wheel	Roll the wheel forward or backward.	Scroll vertically.
Press wheel button	Press the wheel button while moving the mouse on the desktop.	Scroll continuously.
Tilt wheel	Press the wheel toward the right or left.	Scroll horizontally.

FIGURE 5-7 The more common mouse operations.

OTHER POINTING DEVICES

The mouse is the most widely used pointing device today. Some users, however, work with other pointing devices. These include the trackball, touchpad, pointing stick, joystick, wheel, audio player control pad, gamepad, light pen, touch screen, stylus, and pens. The following sections discuss each of these pointing devices.

Trackball

Similar to a mechanical mouse that has a ball on the bottom, a **trackball** is a stationary pointing device with a ball on its top or side (Figure 5-8). The ball in most trackballs is about the size of a Ping-Pong ball.

To move the pointer using a trackball, you rotate the ball with your thumb, fingers, or the palm of your hand. In addition to the ball, a trackball usually has one or more buttons that work just like mouse buttons.

A trackball requires frequent cleaning because it picks up oils from fingers and dust from the environment. For users who have limited desk space, however, a trackball is a good alternative to a mouse because the device is stationary.

Touchpad

A **touchpad** is a small, flat, rectangular pointing device that is sensitive to pressure and motion (Figure 5-9). To move the pointer using a touchpad, slide your fingertip across the surface of the pad. Some touchpads have one or more buttons around the edge of the pad that work like mouse buttons. On most touchpads, you also can tap the pad's surface to imitate mouse operations such as clicking. Touchpads are found most often on notebook computers.

WEB LINK 5-2

Touchpad
For more information, visit scsite.com/dc2007/ch5/weblink and then click Touchpad.

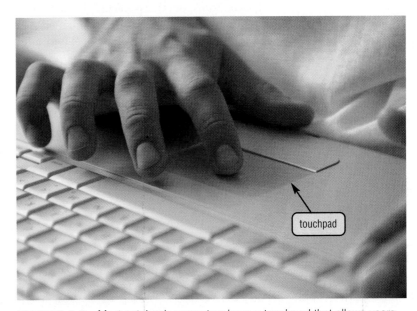

touchpad

FIGURE 5-8 A trackball is like an upside-down mouse.

FIGURE 5-9 Most notebook computers have a touchpad that allows users to control the movement of the pointer.

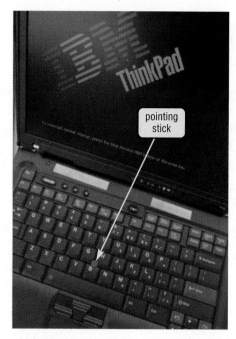

FIGURE 5-10
Some notebook computers include a pointing stick to allow a user to control the movement of the pointer.

WEB LINK 5-3

iPod Click Wheel

For more information, visit scsite.com/dc2007/ch5/weblink and then click iPod Click Wheel.

Pointing Stick

A **pointing stick** is a pressure-sensitive pointing device shaped like a pencil eraser that is positioned between keys on a keyboard (Figure 5-10). To move the pointer using a pointing stick, you push the pointing stick with a finger. The pointer on the screen moves in the direction you push the pointing stick. By pressing buttons below the keyboard, users can click and perform other mouse-type operations with a pointing stick.

A pointing stick does not require any additional desk space. IBM developed the pointing stick for its notebook computers.

Joystick and Wheel

Users running game software or flight and driving simulation software often use a joystick or wheel as a pointing device (Figure 5-11). A **joystick** is a vertical lever mounted on a base. You move the lever in different directions to control the actions of the simulated vehicle or player. The lever usually includes buttons called triggers that you press to activate certain events. Some joysticks also have additional buttons you set to perform other actions.

A **wheel** is a steering-wheel-type input device. Users turn the wheel to simulate driving a car, truck, or other vehicle. Most wheels also include foot pedals for acceleration and braking actions. A joystick and wheel typically attach via a cable to a USB port.

Audio Player Control Pad

The *control pad* on an audio player is a pointing device that enables users to scroll through and play music, adjust volume, and customize settings. Control pads typically contain buttons or wheels that are operated with a thumb or finger. For example, users rotate the iPod's *Click Wheel* to browse through its song lists and press the Click Wheel's buttons to play or pause a song, display a menu, and other actions (Figure 5-12).

FIGURE 5-12 You rotate the wheel or press buttons on the iPod's Click Wheel to select and play songs.

Gamepad

A **gamepad**, sometimes called a game controller, is a pointing device that controls the movement and actions of players or objects in video games or computer games. On the gamepad, users press buttons or move sticks in various directions to activate events. Gamepads communicate with a game console or a personal computer via wired or wireless technology.

Light Pen

A **light pen** is a handheld input device that can detect the presence of light. To select objects on the screen, a user presses the light pen against the surface of the screen or points the light pen at the screen and then presses a button on the pen. Light pens also are ideal for areas where employees' hands might contain food, dirt, grease, or other chemicals that could damage the computer.

FIGURE 5-11 Joysticks and wheels help a user control the actions of players and vehicles in game and simulation software.

Touch Screen

A **touch screen** is a touch-sensitive display device. Users can interact with these devices by touching areas of the screen. Because touch screens require a lot of arm movements, you do not enter large amounts of data using a touch screen. Instead, you touch words, pictures, numbers, letters, or locations identified on the screen.

Kiosks, which are freestanding computers, often have touch screens (Figure 5-13). Travelers use kiosks in airports to print tickets ordered online and in hotels for easy check in and check out. To allow easy access of your bank account from a car, many ATM machines have touch screens. Many handheld game consoles also have touch screens.

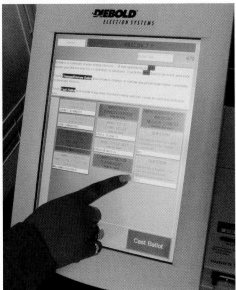

FIGURE 5-13 A voter uses a kiosk touch screen to cast ballots in an election.

Pen Input

Mobile users often enter data and instructions with a pen-type device. With **pen input**, users write, draw, and tap on a flat surface to enter input. The surface may be a monitor, a screen, a special type of paper, or a graphics tablet. Two devices used for pen input are the stylus and digital pen. A **stylus** is a small metal or plastic device that looks like a tiny ink pen but uses pressure instead of

ink (Figure 5-14). A **digital pen**, which is slightly larger than a stylus, is available in two forms: some are pressure-sensitive; others have built-in digital cameras.

Some mobile computers and nearly all mobile devices have touch screens. Instead of using a finger to enter data and instructions, most of these devices include a pressure-sensitive digital pen or stylus. You write, draw, or make selections on the computer screen by touching the screen with the pen or stylus. For example, Tablet PCs use a pressure-sensitive digital pen (Figure 5-15) and PDAs use a stylus. Pressure-sensitive digital pens, often simply called pens, typically provide more functionality than a stylus, featuring electronic erasers and programmable buttons.

Computers and mobile devices often use *handwriting recognition software* that translates the handwritten letters and symbols into characters that the computer or device can process.

FIGURE 5-14 PDAs and smart phones use a stylus.

WEB LINK 5-4

Touch Screen
For more information, visit scsite.com/ dc2007/ch5/weblink and then click Touch Screen.

FIGURE 5-15 Tablet PCs use a pressure-sensitive digital pen.

If you want to use pen input on a computer that does not have a touch screen, you can attach a graphics tablet to the computer. A **graphics tablet** is a flat, rectangular, electronic, plastic board. Architects, mapmakers, designers, artists, and home users create drawings and sketches by using a pressure-sensitive pen or a cursor on a graphics tablet (Figure 5-16). A *cursor* looks similar to a mouse, except it has a window with cross hairs, so the user can see through to the tablet. Each location on the graphics tablet corresponds to a specific location on the screen. When drawing on the tablet with a pen or cursor, the tablet detects and converts the movements into digital signals that are sent in the computer. Large-scale applications sometimes refer to the graphics tablet as a *digitizer*.

Digital pens that have built-in digital cameras work differently from pressure-sensitive digital pens. These pens look much like a ballpoint pen and typically do not contain any additional buttons. In addition to the tiny digital camera, these pens contain a processor, memory, and an ink cartridge. As you write or draw on special digital paper with the pen, it captures every handwritten mark by taking more than 100 pictures per second and then stores the images in the pen's memory. You transfer the images from the pen to a computer (Figure 5-17) or mobile device, such as a smart phone. Some pens have a cradle for transferring images; others communicate wirelessly using Bluetooth.

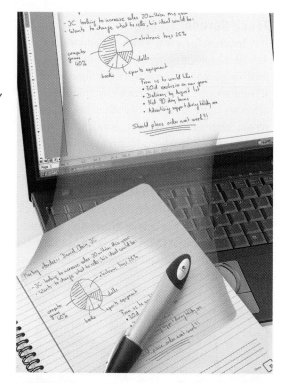

FIGURE 5-17 Some digital pens have built-in digital cameras that store handwritten marks and allow you to transfer your handwriting to a computer.

Test your knowledge of pages 234 through 244 in Quiz Yourself 5-1.

QUIZ YOURSELF 5-1

Instructions: Find the true statement below. Then, rewrite the remaining false statements so they are true.

1. A keyboard is an output device that contains keys users press to enter data in a computer.

2. A light pen is a flat, rectangular, electronic, plastic board.

3. A trackball is a small, flat, rectangular pointing device commonly found on notebook computers.

4. Input is any data or instructions entered into the memory of a computer.

5. Operations you can perform with a wheel include point, click, right-click, double-click, triple-click, drag, right-drag, rotate wheel, press wheel button, and tilt wheel.

6. PDAs use a pressure-sensitive digital pen, and Tablet PCs use a stylus.

Quiz Yourself Online: To further check your knowledge of input techniques, the keyboard, the mouse, and other pointing devices, visit scsite.com/dc2007/ch5/quiz and then click Objectives 1 – 4.

FIGURE 5-16a   (artist using a pen)

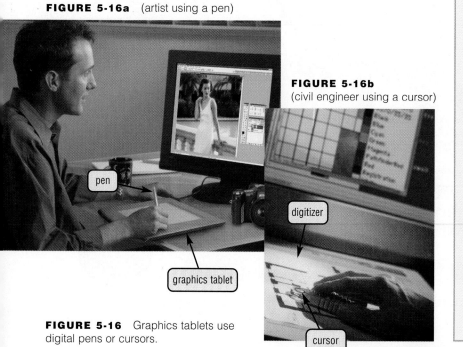

FIGURE 5-16b
(civil engineer using a cursor)

pen

graphics tablet

digitizer

cursor

FIGURE 5-16 Graphics tablets use digital pens or cursors.

VOICE INPUT

As an alternative to using a keyboard to enter data and instructions, some users talk to their computers and watch the spoken words appear on the screen as they talk. **Voice input** is the process of entering input by speaking into a microphone. The microphone may be a stand-alone peripheral that sits on top of a desk, or built in the computer or device, or in headphones or earphones. Some external microphones have a cable that attaches to a port on the sound card on the computer. Others communicate using wireless technology such as Bluetooth.

Voice recognition, also called *speech recognition*, is the computer's capability of distinguishing spoken words. Popular voice recognition programs include IBM ViaVoice and Dragon NaturallySpeaking. Many programs, such as Microsoft Office, support voice recognition. Figure 5-18 illustrates how Word recognizes dictated words and voice commands.

FIGURE 5-18 HOW TO DICTATE WORDS AND COMMANDS

Step 1:
Say, "dictation" to instruct the program you will be dictating and then say, "boat for sale."

Step 2:
Say, "voice command" to instruct the program you will be issuing commands and then say, "center."

Step 3:
Say, "select line." Say, "all caps" and then say, "font."

Step 4:
Say, "Stencil" and then say, "font size."

Step 5:
Say, "forty eight" and then say, "font color."

Step 6:
Say, "red" and then say, "end."

Voice recognition programs recognize a vocabulary of preprogrammed words. The vocabulary of voice recognition programs can range from two words to millions of words. The automated telephone system at your bank may ask you to answer questions by speaking the words Yes or No into the telephone. A voice recognition program on your computer, by contrast, may recognize up to two million words.

Most voice recognition programs are a combination of speaker dependent and speaker independent. With *speaker-dependent software*, the computer makes a profile of your voice, which means you have to train the computer to recognize your voice. To train the computer, you must speak words and phrases into the computer repeatedly. *Speaker-independent software* has a built-in set of word patterns so you do not have to train a computer to recognize your voice. Many products today include a built-in set of words that grows as the software learns your words.

Some voice recognition software requires *discrete speech*, which means you have to speak slowly and separate each word with a short pause. Most of today's products, however, allow you to speak in a flowing conversational tone, called *continuous speech*.

Keep in mind that the best voice recognition programs are 90 to 95 percent accurate, which means the software may interpret as many as one in ten words incorrectly.

FAQ 5-4

Which type of microphone is best?

For voice recognition software, headphones that have a microphone provide the highest quality because they typically do not pick up background noises. For group discussions, however, where multiple people will use the same microphone at the same time, you need a stand-alone or built-in microphone. For more information, visit scsite.com/dc2007/ch5/faq and then click Microphones.

WEB LINK 5-6

Voice Input

For more information, visit scsite.com/dc2007/ch5/weblink and then click Voice Input.

Audio Input

Voice input is part of a larger category of input called audio input. **Audio input** is the process of entering any sound into the computer such as speech, music, and sound effects. To enter high-quality sound into a personal computer, the computer must have a sound card. Users enter sound into a computer via devices such as microphones, tape players, CD/DVD players, or radios, each of which plugs in a port on the sound card.

Some users also enter music and other sound effects into a computer using external MIDI devices such as an electronic piano keyboard (Figure 5-19). As discussed in the previous chapter, in addition to being a port, *MIDI* (*musical instrument digital interface*) is the electronic music industry's standard that defines how digital musical devices represent sounds electronically. These devices connect to the sound card on a computer. Software that conforms to the MIDI standard allows users to compose and edit music and many other sounds. For example, you can change the speed, add notes, or rearrange the score to produce an entirely new sound.

FIGURE 5-19   An electronic piano keyboard is an external MIDI device that allows users to record music, which can be stored in the computer.

INPUT FOR PDAs, SMART PHONES, AND TABLET PCs

Mobile devices, such as the PDA and smart phone, and mobile computers, such as the Tablet PC, offer convenience for the mobile user. A variety of alternatives for entering data and instructions is available for these devices and computers.

PDAs

A user enters data and instructions into a PDA in many ways (Figure 5-20). PDAs ship with a basic stylus, which is the primary input device. Users often purchase a more elaborate stylus that has a ballpoint pen at one end and a stylus at the other. With the stylus, you enter data in two ways: using an on-screen keyboard or using handwriting recognition software that

digital camera

pen/stylus

scanner

on-screen keyboard

transfer data and instructions from desktop computer

cradle

FIGURE 5-20 Users enter data and instructions into a PDA using a variety of techniques.

is built in the PDA. For example, drawing a straight vertical line in a downward motion displays the number 1 on the PDA.

For users who prefer typing to handwriting, some PDAs have a built-in mini keyboard. Other users type on a desktop computer or notebook computer keyboard and transfer the data to the PDA. Some users prefer to enter data into a PDA using a portable keyboard. A *portable keyboard* is a full-sized keyboard you conveniently use with a PDA or other mobile device. Some portable keyboards physically attach to and remove from a PDA; others are wireless. Figure 5-21 shows a pocket-sized portable wireless keyboard that unfolds into a full-sized keyboard.

As an alternative to typing, some PDAs allow users to speak data and instructions into the device. Some PDAs also have cameras built in so you can take photographs and view them on a PDA. On other models, you simply attach a digital camera directly to the PDA. You also can use a PDA to scan small documents, such as business cards and product labels, by attaching a scanner to the PDA. For more information about PDAs, read the Personal Mobile Devices feature that follows this chapter.

Smart Phones

Voice is one method of input for smart phones. Instead of voice, many people use text messaging, instant messaging, and picture messaging to communicate with others.

TEXT MESSAGING Instead of calling someone's smart phone or cellular telephone, users can enter and send typed messages using *text messaging*. To send a text message, you type a short message, typically less than 160 characters, to another smart phone by pressing buttons on the telephone's keypad. As with chat rooms and instant messaging, text messaging uses abbreviations and emoticons to minimize the amount of typing required. For example, instead of typing the text, I am surprised, a user can type the emoticon, :-O.

INSTANT MESSAGING Recall that instant messaging (IM) is a real-time communications service that allows you to exchange messages with other online users. Some wireless Internet service providers (WISPs) partner with IM services so you can use your smart phone to communicate with computer users of the same IM service. For example, with Cingular Wireless service, users can send and receive instant messages with AOL Instant Messenger and Yahoo! Messenger.

FIGURE 5-21 This convenient portable wireless keyboard unfolds into a full-sized keyboard, to which you can attach a PDA.

PICTURE MESSAGING

With *picture messaging,* users can send graphics, pictures, video clips, and sound files, as well as short text messages to another smart phone with a compatible picture messaging service. Many smart phones today have a built-in camera so users easily can take pictures and videos and even incorporate short voice recordings in their picture messages (Figure 5-22). After taking the pictures, users can send them to another smart phone, e-mail them to any e-mail address, or post them on a Web site.

As an alternative to text messaging, some users write a message with a digital pen, transfer the message from the pen to the smart phone, and then use picture messaging to send the handwritten message. Read Ethics & Issues 5-3 for a related discussion.

Most smart phones include PDA capabilities. Thus, input devices used with PDAs typically also are available for smart phones.

Tablet PCs

The primary input device for a Tablet PC is a pressure-sensitive digital pen, which allows users to write on the device's screen. A Tablet PC's handwriting recognition software works similarly to that of a PDA. The computer converts the handwriting into characters it can process.

Both the slate and convertible designs of a Tablet PC provide a means for keyboard input for those users who prefer typing to handwriting. You can attach a removable keyboard to the slate Tablet PC. The convertible Tablet PC has an attached keyboard that can be rotated 180 degrees so the computer resembles a notebook computer.

To access peripherals at their home or office, users can slide their Tablet PC in a docking

FIGURE 5-22   Many smart phones include a digital camera so users can send pictures and videos to others.

ETHICS & ISSUES 5-3

Should Talking on a Cellular Phone While Driving Be Illegal?

Cellular phone sales are soaring. In addition to talking on the phone, many drivers are using their phones to send and receive text messages, instant messages, picture messages, and e-mail, and to access and view Web pages. For drivers, however, cellular phones may be a liability. Estimates vary widely, but studies link between 800 and 8,000 fatalities on U.S. highways to phone use. Because of their additional capabilities, some experts believe cellular phones pose an even greater risk. Many countries have placed bans or restrictions on the use of phones while driving. In the United States, several states have considered or enacted similar legislation. New York, for example, permits vehicle operators to use only hands-free phones. Yet, some studies report that just talking on a phone can cause enough driver inattention to trigger an accident. Supporters of a cellular phone ban cite a British study that found drivers talking on phones had reaction times 50 percent slower than when not talking on a phone, and 30 percent slower than drivers who were intoxicated. Opponents of a ban note, however, that other driver activities, like tuning a radio or having a conversation, can be equally distracting and that phones are a factor in fewer than 1 percent of crashes. Furthermore, drivers may have good reasons to use phones while driving, and laws may not take this into account. Should the use of phones be banned while driving? Why? What other measures, if any, could be taken to prevent drivers from endangering themselves and others while using phones?

station. A *docking station*, which is an external device that attaches to a mobile computer or device, contains a power connection and provides connections to peripherals. In the docking station, Tablet PC users can work with a full-sized keyboard, mouse, CD/DVD drives, and other desktop peripherals (Figure 5-23). The design of docking stations varies, depending on the type of mobile computer or the device to which they are attached.

FAQ 5-5

Can a mobile computer or device get a virus?

Yes. Mobile computers and devices can get a virus from a downloaded Web page. A virus can transfer from a desktop computer to a mobile device when users connect the two to synchronize data. Viruses also can transmit via wireless data transfer when two wireless devices communicate with one another, such as when receiving a text or picture message. For more information, visit scsite.com/dc2007/ch5/faq and then click Viruses and Mobile Devices.

FIGURE 5-23 To use a slate Tablet PC while working at a desk, insert the Tablet PC in a docking station. Devices such as a keyboard and CD drive can be plugged in the docking station.

DIGITAL CAMERAS

A **digital camera** allows users to take pictures and store the photographed images digitally, instead of on traditional film (Figure 5-24). While many digital cameras look like a traditional camera, some models attach to PDAs or are built in PDAs and smart phones. Mobile users such as real estate agents, insurance agents, general contractors, and photojournalists use digital cameras so they immediately can view photographed images on the camera. Home and business users have digital cameras to save the expense of film developing, duplication, and postage.

Some digital cameras use internal flash memory to store images. Others store images on mobile storage media, such as a flash memory card, memory stick, and mini-disc. Chapter 7 discusses these and other storage media in depth. Generally, higher-capacity storage devices can hold more pictures.

Digital cameras typically allow users to review, and sometimes edit, images while they are in the camera. Some digital cameras can connect to or communicate wirelessly with a printer or television, allowing users to print or view images directly from the camera.

FIGURE 5-24 With a digital camera, users can view photographed images immediately through a small screen on the camera to see if the picture is worth keeping.

Often users prefer to *download*, or transfer a copy of, the images from the digital camera to the computer's hard disk. With some digital cameras, images download through a cable that connects between the digital camera (or the camera's docking station) and a USB port or a FireWire port on the system unit. For cameras that store images on miniature mobile storage media, simply insert the media in a reading/writing device that communicates wirelessly or attaches to a port on the system unit. Copying images from the miniature media to the computer's hard disk is just like copying files from any other disk drive. Some cameras store images on a mini CD/DVD. In this case, insert the disc in the computer's disc drive and then copy the pictures to the computer's hard disk (or you can view the contents of the disc by inserting it in a CD or DVD player).

When you copy images to the hard disk in a computer, the images are available for editing with photo editing software, printing, faxing, sending via e-mail, including in another document, or posting to a Web site or photo community for everyone to see. Many users add pictures to greeting cards, a computerized photo album, a family newsletter, certificates, and awards.

The three basic types of digital cameras are studio cameras, field cameras, and point-and-shoot cameras. The most expensive and highest quality of the three is a *studio camera*, which is a stationary camera used for professional studio work. Often used by photojournalists, a *field camera* is a portable camera that has many lenses and other attachments. As with the studio camera, a field camera can be quite expensive. A *point-and-shoot camera* is much more affordable and lightweight and provides acceptable quality photographic images for the home or small business user. Figure 5-25 illustrates how one make of point-and-shoot digital camera works.

A point-and-shoot camera often features flash, zoom, automatic focus, and special effects. Some allow users to record short audio narrations for photographed images. Others even record short video clips in addition to still images. Point-and-shoot digital cameras often have a built-in TV out port, allowing users to

FIGURE 5-25 HOW A DIGITAL CAMERA MIGHT WORK

Step 1: Point to the image to photograph and take the picture. Light passes into the lens of the camera.

Step 2: The image is focused on a chip called a *charge-coupled device* (*CCD*).

Step 3: The CCD generates an analog signal that represents the image.

Step 4: The analog signal is converted to a digital signal by an analog-to-digital converter (ADC).

Step 5: A processor in the camera adjusts the quality of the image and usually stores the digital image on miniature mobile storage media inserted in the camera.

display photographed images or play recorded video clips directly on a television.

For additional information about digital cameras, read the Digital Imaging and Video Technology feature that follows Chapter 6.

Digital Camera Quality

One factor that affects the quality of a digital camera is its resolution. **Resolution** is the number of horizontal and vertical pixels in a display device. A *pixel* (short for picture element) is the smallest element in an electronic image (Figure 5-26). The greater the number of pixels the camera uses to capture an image, the better the quality of the image. Thus, the higher the resolution, the better the image quality, but the more expensive the camera.

Digital camera resolutions range from approximately 1 million to more than 8 million pixels (*MP*). A camera with a 5.1-megapixel (5,100,000 pixels) resolution will provide a better quality than one with a 3.2-megapixel resolution. As a general rule, a 1-megapixel camera is fine for pictures sent via e-mail or posted on the Web. For good quality printed photographs, users should have a 2-megapixel camera for 4 × 6 inch photographs, a 3-megapixel camera for 8 × 10 photographs, and 5-megapixel or greater camera for larger size prints.

Manufacturers often use pixels per inch to represent a digital camera's resolution. *Pixels per inch* (*ppi*) is the number of pixels in one inch of screen display. For example, a 2304 ×

1728 (pronounced 2304 by 1728) ppi camera has 2,304 pixels per vertical inch and 1,728 pixels per horizontal inch. Multiplying these two numbers together gives an approximate total number of megapixels. For example, 2304 times 1728 equals approximately 4 million, or 4 megapixels. If just one number is stated, such as 1600 ppi, then both the vertical and horizontal numbers are the same.

Many digital cameras provide a means to adjust the ppi to the desired resolution. With a lower ppi, you can capture and store more images in the camera. For example, a camera set at 800 × 600 ppi might capture and store 61 images, if it has sufficient storage capacity. The number of images may reduce to 24 on the same camera set at 1600 × 1200 ppi, because each image consumes more storage space.

The actual photographed resolution is known as the *optical resolution*. Some manufacturers state *enhanced resolution*, instead of, or in addition to, optical resolution. Optical resolution is different from enhanced resolution. The enhanced resolution usually is higher because it uses a special formula to add pixels between those generated by the optical resolution. Be aware that some manufacturers compute a digital camera's megapixels from the enhanced resolution, instead of optical resolution.

Another measure of a digital camera's quality is the number of bits it stores in a pixel. Each pixel consists of one or more bits of data. The more bits used to represent a pixel, the more colors and shades of gray that can be represented. One bit per pixel is enough for simple one-color images. For multiple colors and shades of gray, each pixel requires more than one bit of data. A point-and-shoot camera should be at least 24 bit.

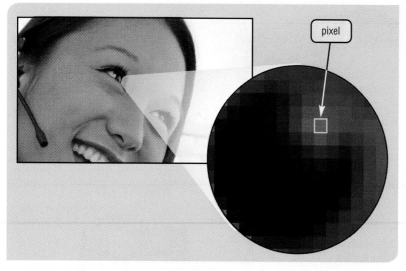

FIGURE 5-26 A pixel is a single point in an electronic image.

FAQ 5-7

What is dpi?

Some advertisements incorrectly use dpi to mean the same as ppi. The acronym *dpi*, which stands for *dots per inch*, is a measure of a print resolution. For screen resolution, the proper measurement term is ppi (pixels per inch). For more information, visit scsite.com/dc2007/ch5/faq and then click Resolution.

VIDEO INPUT

Video input is the process of capturing full-motion images and storing them on a computer's storage medium such as a hard disk or DVD.

Some video devices record video using analog signals. Computers, by contrast, use digital signals. To enter video from an analog device into a personal computer, the analog signal must be converted to a digital signal. To do this, plug a video camera, VCR, or other analog video device in a video capture port on the system unit. One type of adapter card that has a video capture port is a *video capture card*, which converts an analog video signal into a digital signal that a computer can process. Most new computers are not equipped with a video capture card because not all users have the need for this type of adapter card.

A **digital video (DV) camera**, by contrast, records video as digital signals instead of analog signals. Many DV cameras can capture still frames, as well as motion. To transfer recorded images to a hard disk or CD or DVD, users connect DV cameras directly to a USB port or a FireWire port on the system unit. Thus, the computer does not need a video capture card. Simply connect the video device to the computer and begin transferring images. After saving the video on a storage medium, such as a hard disk or DVD, you can play it or edit it using video editing software on a computer (Figure 5-27).

PC Video Cameras

A **PC video camera**, or **PC camera**, is a type of digital video camera that enables a home or small business user to capture video and still images, send e-mail messages with video attachments, add live images to instant messages, broadcast live images over the Internet, and make video telephone calls. During a *video telephone call*, both parties see each other as they communicate over the Internet (Figure 5-28). The cost of PC video cameras usually is less than $100.

Attached to the computer's USB port or FireWire port, a PC video camera usually sits on top of the monitor. For more flexibility, some PC video cameras are portable. That is, you can detach them from the base and use them as a stand-alone digital camera.

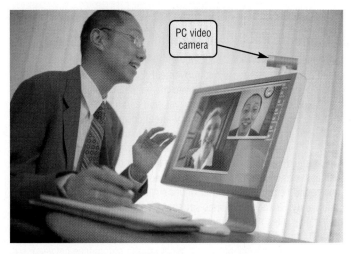

FIGURE 5-28 Using a PC video camera, home users can see each other as they communicate over the Internet.

video camera

video is displayed on computer screen

FIGURE 5-27 Home users can transfer videos to their computers and then use video editing software to edit the video.

Web Cams

A **Web cam** is any video camera that displays its output on a Web page. A Web cam attracts Web site visitors by showing images that change regularly. Home or small business users might use Web cams to show a work in progress, weather and traffic information, employees at work, photographs of a vacation, and countless other images. Read Ethics & Issues 5-4 for a related discussion.

Some Web sites have live Web cams that display still pictures and update the displayed image at a specified time or time intervals, such as 15 seconds. Another type of Web cam, called a *streaming cam*, has the illusion of moving images because it sends a continual stream of still images.

ETHICS & ISSUES 5-4

Should Cameras Be Able to Monitor Your Every Move?

In the world of George Orwell's classic novel *1984*, "Telescreens" constantly monitor each citizen's every word and movement. Since its publication more than 50 years ago, most people have viewed the novel as a warning against a future that should be avoided. Today, however, you can find cameras in every corner of public life. Whether it is on a busy street corner, on a casino floor, in a subway station, in the neighborhood grocery store, in an elevator, or even in the workplace, the watchful eye continues to become more and more ubiquitous. In Chicago, cameras monitor high-crime areas and even listen for gunshots. Businesses and governments claim that advances in the technology and the low cost as compared to other options allow them to provide greater security and safety. Privacy advocates say that the cameras violate the Constitution's guarantee against unreasonable searches. Many cases of abuse of video monitoring have been noted, such as stores secretly listening in on spouses discussing a potential purchase. What are the differences between George Orwell's Telescreens and the current state of video monitoring? What are the similarities? Would you feel more secure or more paranoid living in a continuously monitored society? Why? What are the benefits of video monitoring? Should you have nothing to fear from security cameras if you have done nothing wrong?

Video Conferencing

A **video conference** is a meeting between two or more geographically separated people who use a network or the Internet to transmit audio and video data (Figure 5-29). To participate in a video conference, you need video conferencing software along with a microphone, speakers, and a video camera attached to a computer.

As you speak, members of the meeting hear your voice on their speakers. Any image in front of the video camera, such as a person's face, appears in a window on each participant's screen. A *whiteboard* is another window on the screen that displays notes and drawings simultaneously on all participants' screens. This window provides multiple users with an area on which they can write or draw.

As the costs of video conferencing hardware and software decrease, increasingly more business meetings, corporate training, and educational classes will be conducted as video conferences.

FAQ 5-8

How popular is video conferencing?

A recent survey found that 40 percent of computer users participate in video conferences with desktop equipment. Annual expenditures exceed $7.7 billion on voice and video conferencing equipment. For more information, visit scsite.com/dc2007/ch5/faq and then click Video Conferencing.

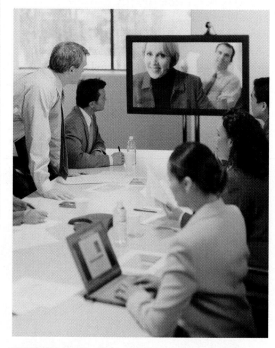

FIGURE 5-29 To save on travel expenses, many large businesses are turning to video conferencing.

Test your knowledge of pages 245 through 254 in Quiz Yourself 5-2.

SCANNERS AND READING DEVICES

Some input devices save users time by eliminating manual data entry. With these devices, users do not type, speak, or write into the computer. Instead, these devices capture data from a *source document*, which is the original form of the data. Examples of source documents include time cards, order forms, invoices, paychecks, advertisements, brochures, photographs, inventory tags, or any other document that contains data to be processed.

Devices that can capture data directly from a source document include optical scanners, optical readers, bar code readers, RFID readers, magnetic stripe card readers, and magnetic-ink character recognition readers. The following pages discuss each of these devices.

Optical Scanners

An *optical scanner*, usually called a **scanner**, is a light-sensing input device that reads printed text and graphics and then translates the results into a form the computer can process. Four types of scanners are flatbed, pen, sheet-fed, and drum (Figure 5-30).

TYPES OF SCANNERS

Scanner	Method of Scanning and Use	Scannable Items
Flatbed	• Similar to a copy machine • Scanning mechanism passes under the item to be scanned, which is placed on a glass surface	• Single-sheet documents • Bound material • Photographs • Some models include trays for slides, transparencies, and negatives
Pen or Handheld	• Move pen over text to be scanned, then transfer data to computer • Ideal for mobile users, students, and researchers • Some connect to a PDA or smart phone	• Any printed text
Sheet-fed	• Item to be scanned is pulled into a stationary scanning mechanism • Smaller than a flatbed scanner • A model designed specifically for photographs is called a *photo scanner*	• Single-sheet documents • Photographs • Slides (with an adapter) • Negatives
Drum	• Item to be scanned rotates around stationary scanning mechanism • Very expensive • Used in large businesses	• Single-sheet documents • Photographs • Slides • Negatives

FIGURE 5-30 This table describes the various types of scanners.

A **flatbed scanner** works in a manner similar to a copy machine except it creates a file of the document in memory instead of a paper copy (Figure 5-31). Once you scan a document or picture, you can display the scanned object on the screen, store it on a storage medium, print it, fax it, attach it to an e-mail message, include it in another document, or post it to a Web site or photo community for everyone to see.

As with a digital camera, the quality of a scanner is measured by the number of bits it stores in a pixel and the number of pixels per inch, or resolution. The higher each number, the better the quality, but the more expensive the scanner. Most of today's affordable color desktop scanners for the home or small business range from 30 to 48 bits and have an optical resolution ranging from 600 to 9600 ppi. Commercial scanners designed for power users range from 9600 to 14,000 ppi.

Many scanners include *OCR (optical character recognition) software*, which can read and convert text documents into electronic files. OCR software is useful if you need to modify a document but do not have the original word processing file. For example, if you scan a business report with a flatbed scanner and do not use OCR software, you cannot edit the report because the scanner saves the report as an image. This is because the scanner does not differentiate between text and graphics. OCR software, however, would convert the scanned image into a text file that you could edit, for example, with a word processing program. Current OCR software has a high success rate and usually can identify more than 99 percent of scanned material.

Businesses often use scanners for *image processing*, which consists of capturing, storing, analyzing, displaying, printing, and manipulating images. Image processing allows users to convert paper documents such as reports, memos, and procedure manuals into electronic images. Users distribute and publish these electronic documents on networks and the Internet.

Business users typically store and index electronic documents with an image processing system. An *image processing system* is similar to an electronic filing cabinet that provides access to exact reproductions of the original documents. Local governments, for example, use image processing systems to store property deeds and titles to provide the public and professionals, such as lawyers and loan officers, quick access to electronic documents.

FAQ 5-9

How can I improve the quality of scanned documents?

Place a blank sheet of paper behind translucent papers, newspapers, and other see-through types of paper. If the original image is crooked, draw a line on the back at the bottom of the image. Use that mark to align the original on the scanner. Use photo editing software to fix imperfections in images. For more information, visit scsite.com/dc2007/ch5/faq and then click Scanning.

FIGURE 5-31   HOW A FLATBED SCANNER WORKS

Step 1:
Place the document to be scanned face down on the glass window. Using buttons on the scanner or the scanner program, start the scanning process.

Step 2:
The scanner converts the document content to digital information, which is transmitted through the cable to the memory of the computer.

Step 3: Once in the memory of the computer, users can display the image, print it, e-mail it, include it in a document, or place it on a Web page.

Optical Readers

An *optical reader* is a device that uses a light source to read characters, marks, and codes and then converts them into digital data that a computer can process. Two technologies used by optical readers are optical character recognition and optical mark recognition.

OPTICAL CHARACTER RECOGNITION Optical **character recognition (OCR)** is a technology that involves reading typewritten, computer-printed, or hand-printed characters from ordinary documents and translating the images into a form that the computer can process. Most **OCR devices** include a small optical scanner for reading characters and sophisticated software to analyze what is read.

OCR devices range from large machines that can read thousands of documents per minute to handheld wands that read one document at a time. OCR devices read printed characters in an OCR font. A widely used OCR font is called OCR-A (Figure 5-32). During the scan of a document, an OCR device determines the shapes of characters by detecting patterns of light and dark. OCR software then compares these shapes with predefined shapes stored in memory and converts the shapes into characters the computer can process.

```
ABCDEFGHIJKLM
NOPQRSTUVWXYZ
1234567890
-=■;',./
```

FIGURE 5-32 A portion of the characters in the OCR-A font. Notice how characters such as the number 0 and the letter O are shaped differently so the reading device easily can distinguish between them.

Many companies use OCR characters on turnaround documents. A **turnaround document** is a document that you return (turn around) to the company that creates and sends it. For example, when consumers receive a bill, they often tear off a portion of the bill and send it back to the company with their payment (Figure 5-33). The portion of the bill they return usually has their payment amount, account number, and other information printed in OCR characters.

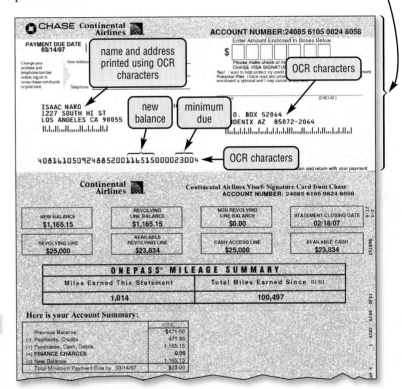

FIGURE 5-33 OCR characters frequently are used with turnaround documents. With this bill, you tear off the top portion and return it with a payment.

OPTICAL MARK RECOGNITION Optical **mark recognition (OMR)** is a technology that reads hand-drawn marks such as small circles or rectangles. A person places these marks on a form, such as a test, survey, or questionnaire answer sheet. With a test, the OMR device first scans the answer key sheet to record correct answers based on patterns of light. The OMR device then scans the remaining documents and matches their patterns of light against the answer key sheet.

Bar Code Readers

A **bar code reader**, also called a **bar code scanner**, is an optical reader that uses laser beams to read bar codes by using light patterns that pass through the bar code lines (Figure 5-34). A **bar code** is an identification code that consists of a set of vertical lines and spaces of different widths. The bar code represents data that identifies the manufacturer and the item.

Manufacturers print a bar code either on a product's package or on a label that is affixed to a product. A variety of products such as groceries, books, clothing, vehicles, mail, and packages have bar codes. Each industry uses its own type of bar code. The United States Postal Service (USPS) uses a POSTNET bar code. Retail and grocery stores use the *UPC* (*Universal Product Code*) bar code (Figure 5-35). Read Ethics & Issues 5-5 for a related discussion.

WEB LINK 5-8

Bar Code Readers

For more information, visit scsite.com/dc2007/ch5/weblink and then click Bar Code Readers.

FIGURE 5-34 A bar code reader uses laser beams to read bar codes on products such as groceries and books.

ETHICS & ISSUES 5-5

Scanner Errors at the Checkout Counter?

Have you ever taken an item to a store's checkout and discovered that the price displayed when the item's bar code was scanned was different from the price shown on a shelf tag, sign, or advertisement? If you have, you are not alone. A government survey found that eight percent of the time, an item's scanned price is different from the price presented elsewhere. When an item is scanned at a store's checkout counter, a computer finds the item's price in the store's database. Store owners claim that discrepancies between the scanned price and a listed price are the result of human error — either failure to update the store's price database or incorrect shelf tags, signs, or advertisements. Yet, some consumer advocates claim that the discrepancy sometimes is intentional. They accuse stores of *scanner fraud*, insisting that some stores advertise one price and then charge another, hoping buyers will not recognize the difference. Most states have laws that protect consumers against scanner fraud. Some laws even require stores to pay consumers an immediate reward, sometimes $5 or more, if the consumer finds a scanner error. Who do you think is responsible for differences between scanned prices and posted costs? Why? Should stores be responsible for pricing errors? Why or why not?

check character verifies accuracy of scanned UPC symbol

number system character identifies type of product

manufacturer identification number (Shaw's in this case)

item number (1 gallon of skim milk)

FIGURE 5-35 This UPC identifies a carton of skim milk.

RFID Readers

RFID (*radio frequency identification*) is a technology that uses radio signals to communicate with a tag placed in or attached to an object, an animal, or a person. RFID tags, which contain a memory chip and an antenna, are available in many shapes and sizes and sometimes are embedded in glass, labels, or cards. Some RFID tags are as small as a grain of sand; others are the size of a luggage tag. An **RFID reader** reads information on the tag via radio waves. RFID readers can be handheld devices or mounted in a stationary object such as a doorway.

Many retailers see RFID as an alternative to bar code identification because it does not require direct contact or line-of-site transmission. Each product in a store would contain a tag that identifies the product (Figure 5-36). As consumers remove products from the store shelves and walk through a checkout area, an RFID reader reads the tag(s) and communicates with a computer that calculates the amount due, eliminating the need for checking out each item.

Other uses of RFID include tracking times of runners in a marathon; tracking location of soldiers, employee wardrobes, and airline baggage; checking lift tickets of skiers; gauging pressure and temperature of tires on a vehicle; checking out library books; and tracking payment as vehicles pass through booths on tollway systems. Read Ethics & Issues 5-6 for a related discussion. Read Looking Ahead 5-1 for a look at the next generation of RFID.

FIGURE 5-36 RFID readers read information stored on an RFID tag and then communicate this information to computers, which instantaneously compute payments and update inventory records. In this example, the RFID tag is embedded in a label attached to the garment.

RFID tag embedded in label attached to garment

memory chip

ETHICS & ISSUES 5-6

Ready for RFID?

Move over bar codes, make way for RFID. RFID (radio frequency identification) uses a tiny computer chip that can be mounted on a tag attached to a product or sewn into an article of clothing. For merchants, RFID can help to locate items in a warehouse and identify items that need to be replenished. For consumers, RFID can supply detailed product information, reduce costs associated with inventory management, and someday let buyers bypass check-out lines and take purchases directly from the store, with the item's cost charged to their card. Even casinos are beginning to use RFID in betting chips to stop counterfeiting and track patrons' habits. Privacy advocates worry, however, that RFID could obliterate a buyer's anonymity. They fear that with an RFID reader, any individual or organization could track a purchaser's movements and make that information available to marketers or government agencies. To protect privacy, privacy advocates insist that merchants should be forced to disable RFID transmitters as soon as buyers leave a store. Would you be comfortable purchasing a product that includes RFID? Why or why not? Should buyers be allowed to request that RFID transmitters be disabled after they make a purchase, or should merchants be required to render transmitters inoperative when the product leaves the store? Why?

LOOKING AHEAD 5-1

RFID Sensors Simplify, Monitor Tasks

Burnt microwave meals may become a thing of the past with the development of RFID technology. Just wave the packaging in front of a food-enabled scanner and let the microwave determine how long to cook the food at a particular temperature.

Many uses for RFID sensors are planned. They could determine when a soccer ball crosses a goal line or a marathon runner crosses the finish line, signal when a child passes a doorway in his pajamas or an inmate enters restricted areas, and track packages by sensing and transmitting product locations. On the battlefield, they could sense vehicle and missile movement. In hospitals, patient wristbands could monitor when a particular drug and dosage is administered. For more information, visit scsite.com/dc2007/ch5/looking and then click RFID Uses.

Magnetic Stripe Card Readers

A **magnetic stripe card reader**, often called a *magstripe reader*, reads the magnetic stripe on the back of credit cards, entertainment cards, bank cards, and other similar cards. The stripe, which is divided in three horizontal tracks, contains information identifying you and the card issuer (Figure 5-37). Some information stored in the stripe includes your name, account number, the card's expiration date, and a country code.

When a consumer swipes a credit card through the magstripe reader, it reads the information stored on the magnetic stripe on the card. If the magstripe reader rejects your card, it is possible that the magnetic stripe on the card is scratched, dirty, or erased. Exposure to a magnet or magnetic field can erase the contents of a card's magnetic stripe.

In many cases, a magstripe reader is part of a point-of-sale terminal. The function of point-of-sale terminals is discussed later in this chapter.

FIGURE 5-37 A magnetic stripe card reader reads information encoded on the stripe on the back of your credit card.

MICR Readers

MICR (*magnetic-ink character recognition*) devices read text printed with magnetized ink. An **MICR reader** converts MICR characters into a form the computer can process. The banking industry almost exclusively uses MICR for check processing. Each check in your checkbook has precoded MICR characters beginning at the lower-left edge (Figure 5-38). The MICR characters represent the bank number, the customer account number, and the check number. These numbers may appear in a different order than the ones shown in the sample in Figure 5-38.

When a bank receives a check for payment, it uses an MICR inscriber to print the amount of the check in MICR characters in the lower-right corner. The check then is sorted or routed to the customer's bank, along with thousands of others. Each check is inserted in an MICR reader, which sends the check information — including the amount of the check — to a computer for processing. When you balance your checkbook, verify that the amount printed in the lower-right corner is the same as the amount written on the check; otherwise, your statement will not balance.

The banking industry has established an international standard not only for bank numbers, but also for the font of the MICR characters. This standardization makes it possible for people to write checks in other countries.

bank routing number   account number   check number   check amount

FIGURE 5-38 The MICR characters preprinted on the check represent the bank routing number, the customer account number, and the check number. The amount of the check in the lower-right corner is added after the check is cashed.

Data Collection Devices

Instead of reading or scanning data from a source document, a *data collection device* obtains data directly at the location where the transaction or event takes place. For example, employees use bar code readers, PDAs, handheld computers, or other mobile devices to collect data wirelessly (Figure 5-39). These types of data collection devices are used in restaurants, factories, warehouses, the outdoors, or other locations where heat, humidity, and cleanliness are not easy to control.

Data collection devices and many mobile computers and devices have the capability of wirelessly transmitting data over a network or the Internet. Increasingly more users today send data wirelessly to central office computers using these devices.

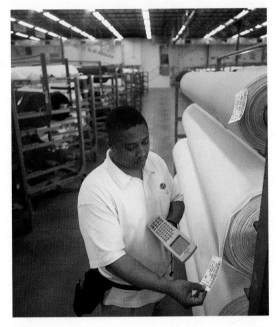

FIGURE 5-39 A warehouse employee uses this rugged handheld computer, which includes a bar code reader, that wirelessly transmits information about the scanned item to the company's inventory system.

TERMINALS

A *terminal* consists of a keyboard, a monitor, a video card, and memory. Often, these components are housed in a single unit.

Terminals fall into three basic categories: dumb terminals, smart terminals, and special-purpose terminals. A *dumb terminal* has no processing power; thus, it cannot function as an independent device. Users enter data and instructions in a dumb terminal and then transmit the data to a host computer over a network. The host computer processes the input and then, if necessary, sends information (output) back to the dumb terminal. The host computer usually is a server or mainframe. A *smart terminal* has a processor, giving it the capability of performing some functions independent of the host computer. In recent years, personal computers have replaced most smart terminals.

Special-purpose terminals perform specific tasks and contain features uniquely designed for use in a particular industry. Two widely used special-purpose terminals are point-of-sale (POS) terminals and automated teller machines.

Point-of-Sale Terminals

The location in a retail or grocery store where a consumer pays for goods or services is the *point of sale* (POS). Most retail stores use a **POS terminal** to record purchases, process credit or debit cards, and update inventory.

In a grocery store, the POS terminal is a combination of an electronic cash register, bar code reader, and printer. When the checkout clerk scans the bar code on the food product, the computer uses the manufacturer and item numbers to look up the price of the item and the complete product name in a database. Then, the price of the item in the database shows on the display device, the name of the item and its price print on a receipt, and the item being sold is recorded so the inventory can be updated. Thus, the output from a POS terminal serves as input to other computers to maintain sales records, update inventory, verify credit, and perform other activities associated with the sales transactions that are critical to running the business. Some POS terminals are Web-enabled, which allows updates to inventory at geographically separate locations.

Many POS terminals handle credit card or debit card payments and thus also include a magstripe reader. After swiping your card through the reader, the POS terminal connects to a system that authenticates the purchase. Once the transaction is approved, the terminal prints a receipt for the customer.

A self-service POS terminal allows consumers to perform all checkout-related activities (Figure 5-40). That is, they scan the items, bag the items, and pay for the items themselves. Consumers with small orders find the self-service POS terminals convenient because these terminals often eliminate the hassle of waiting in long lines.

which verifies that you are the holder of the bankcard. When your transaction is complete, the ATM prints a receipt for your records.

magstripe reader

FIGURE 5-41   An ATM is a self-service banking terminal that allows customers to access their bank accounts.

touch screen with graphical user interface

magstripe reader scans credit or debit card

bar code reader reads UPC labels

FIGURE 5-40   Many grocery stores offer self-serve checkouts, where the consumers themselves use the POS terminals to scan purchases, scan their store saver card and coupons, and then pay for the goods.

Automated Teller Machines

An **automated teller machine (ATM)** is a self-service banking machine that connects to a host computer through a network (Figure 5-41). Banks place ATMs in convenient locations, including grocery stores, convenience stores, retail outlets, shopping malls, and gas stations, so customers conveniently can access their bank accounts.

Using an ATM, people withdraw cash, deposit money, transfer funds, or inquire about an account balance. Some ATMs have a touch screen; others have special buttons or keypads for entering input. To access a bank account, you insert a plastic bankcard in the ATM's magstripe reader. The ATM asks you to enter a password, called a *personal identification number (PIN)*,

BIOMETRIC INPUT

Biometrics is the technology of authenticating a person's identity by verifying a personal characteristic. Biometric devices grant users access to programs, systems, or rooms by analyzing some biometric identifier. A *biometric identifier* is a physiological (related to physical or chemical activities in the body) or behavioral characteristic. Examples include fingerprints, hand geometry, facial features, voice, signatures, and eye patterns.

A *biometric device* translates a personal characteristic (the input) into a digital code that is compared with a digital code stored in the computer. If the digital code in the computer does not match the personal characteristic's code, the computer denies access to the individual.

The most widely used biometric device today is a fingerprint scanner. A **fingerprint scanner** captures curves and indentations of a fingerprint. With the cost of fingerprint scanners less than $100, home and small business users install fingerprint scanners to authenticate users before they can access a personal computer. External fingerprint scanners usually plug into a parallel or USB port. To save on desk space, some newer keyboards and notebook computers have a fingerprint scanner built into them, which allows users to log on to Web sites via their fingerprint instead of entering a user name and password (Figure 5-42). For a technical discussion about fingerprint scanners, read the High-Tech Talk article on page 268.

A *face recognition system* captures a live face image and compares it with a stored image to determine if the person is a legitimate user. Some buildings use face recognition systems to secure access to rooms. Law enforcement, surveillance systems, and airports use face recognition to protect the public. Some notebook computers use this security technique to safeguard a computer. The computer will not start unless the user is legitimate. These programs are becoming more sophisticated and can recognize people with or without glasses, makeup, or jewelry, and with new hairstyles.

Biometric devices measure the shape and size of a person's hand using a *hand geometry system* (Figure 5-43). Because their cost is more than $1,000, larger companies use these systems as time and attendance devices or as security devices. Colleges use hand geometry systems to verify students' identities. Day-care centers and hospital nurseries use them to verify parents who pick up their children.

A *voice verification system* compares a person's live speech with their stored voice pattern. Larger organizations sometimes use voice verification systems as time and attendance devices. Many companies also use this technology for access to sensitive files and networks. Some financial services use voice verification systems to secure telephone banking transactions. These systems use speaker-dependent voice recognition software. That is, users train the computer to recognize their inflection patterns.

A *signature verification system* recognizes the shape of your handwritten signature, as well as measures the pressure exerted and the motion used to write the signature. Signature verification systems use a specialized pen and tablet.

FIGURE 5-42 Keyboard with built-in fingerprint scanner.

FIGURE 5-43 A hand geometry system verifies this student's identity before he is allowed access to the school recreation center.

High security areas use iris recognition systems. The camera in an *iris recognition system* uses iris recognition technology to read patterns in the iris of the eye (Figure 5-44). These patterns are as unique as a fingerprint. Iris recognition systems are quite expensive and are used by government security organizations, the military, and financial institutions that deal with highly sensitive data. Some organizations use *retinal scanners*, which work similarly but instead scan patterns of blood vessels in the back of the retina.

WEB LINK 5-9

Biometric Input

For more information, visit scsite.com/dc2007/ch5/weblink and then click Biometric Input.

Sometimes, fingerprint, iris, retina, and other biometric data are stored on a smart card. A **smart card**, which is comparable in size to a credit card or ATM card, stores the personal data on a thin microprocessor embedded in the card (Figure 5-45). Smart cards add an extra layer of protection. For example, when a user places a smart card through a smart card reader, the computer compares a fingerprint stored on the card with the one read by the fingerprint scanner. Some credit cards are smart cards; that is, the microprocessor contains the card holder's information instead of a magnetic stripe.

FAQ 5-10

How popular is biometric technology?

One study estimates that revenues from biometric solutions has and will continue to grow by about 35 percent annually for the next several years, as shown in the chart below. For more information, visit scsite.com/dc2007/ch5/faq and then click Biometrics.

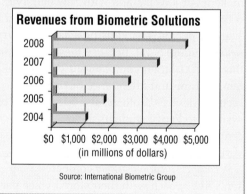

Revenues from Biometric Solutions

2008
2007
2006
2005
2004

$0 $1,000 $2,000 $3,000 $4,000 $5,000
(in millions of dollars)

Source: International Biometric Group

FIGURE 5-44 An iris recognition system.

smart card reader

microprocessor on smart card

FIGURE 5-45 A smart card reader reads data stored on a smart card's microprocessor.

PUTTING IT ALL TOGETHER

When you purchase a computer, you should have an understanding of the input devices included with the computer, as well as those you may need that are not included. Many factors influence the type of input devices you may use: the type of input desired, the hardware and software in use, and the desired cost. The type of input devices you require depends on your intended use. Figure 5-46 outlines several suggested input devices for specific computer users.

SUGGESTED INPUT DEVICES BY USER

User	Input Device
HOME	• Enhanced keyboard or ergonomic keyboard • Mouse • Stylus for PDA or smart phone • Joystick or wheel • 30-bit 600 x 1200 ppi color scanner • 3-megapixel digital camera • Headphones that include a microphone • PC video camera
SMALL OFFICE/ HOME OFFICE	• Enhanced keyboard or ergonomic keyboard • Mouse • Stylus and portable keyboard for PDA or smart phone, or digital pen for Tablet PC • 36-bit 600 x 1200 ppi color scanner • 3-megapixel digital camera • Headphones that include a microphone • PC video camera
MOBILE	• Wireless mouse for notebook computer • Touchpad or pointing stick on notebook computer • Stylus and portable keyboard for PDA or smart phone, or digital pen for Tablet PC • 3- or 4-megapixel digital camera • Headphones that include a microphone • Fingerprint scanner for notebook computer
POWER	• Enhanced keyboard or ergonomic keyboard • Mouse • Stylus and portable keyboard for PDA or smart phone • Pen for graphics tablet • 48-bit 1200 x 1200 ppi color scanner • 6- to 8-megapixel digital camera • Headphones that include a microphone • PC video camera
LARGE BUSINESS	• Enhanced keyboard or ergonomic keyboard • Mouse • Stylus and portable keyboard for PDA or smart phone, or digital pen for Tablet PC • Touch screen • Light pen • 42-bit 1200 x 1200 ppi color scanner • OCR/OMR readers, bar code readers, MICR reader, or data collection devices • Microphone • Video camera for video conferences • Fingerprint scanner or other biometric device

FIGURE 5-46   This table recommends suggested input devices.

INPUT DEVICES FOR PHYSICALLY CHALLENGED USERS

The ever-increasing presence of computers in everyone's lives has generated an awareness of the need to address computing requirements for those who have or may develop physical limitations. The **Americans with Disabilities Act (ADA)** requires any company with 15 or more employees to make reasonable attempts to accommodate the needs of physically challenged workers.

Besides voice recognition, which is ideal for blind or visually impaired users, several other input devices are available. A *keyguard* is a metal or plastic plate placed over the keyboard that allows users to rest their hands on the keyboard without accidentally pressing any keys (Figure 5-47). A keyguard also guides a finger or pointing device so a user presses only one key at a time.

Keyboards with larger keys also are available. Still another option is the *on-screen keyboard*, in which a graphic of a standard keyboard is displayed on the user's screen (Figure 5-48).

Various pointing devices are available for users with motor disabilities. Small trackballs that the user controls with a thumb or one finger can be attached to a table, mounted to a wheelchair, or held in the user's hand. Another option for people with limited hand movement is a *head-mounted pointer* to control the pointer or insertion point (Figure 5-49). To simulate the functions of a mouse button, a user works with switches that control the pointer. The switch might be a hand pad, a foot pedal, a receptor that detects facial motions, or a pneumatic instrument controlled by puffs of air.

Two exciting developments in this area are gesture recognition and computerized implant devices. Both in the prototype stage, they attempt to provide users with a natural computer interface.

With *gesture recognition*, the computer will detect human motions. Computers with gesture recognition capability have the potential to recognize sign language, read lips, track facial movements, or follow eye gazes. For paralyzed or speech impaired individuals, a doctor will implant a computerized device into the brain. This device will contain a transmitter. As the user thinks thoughts, the transmitter will send signals to the computer.

FIGURE 5-47 A keyguard.

FIGURE 5-48 As you click letters on the on-screen keyboard, they appear in the document at the location of the insertion point.

FIGURE 5-49 A camera/receiver mounted on the monitor tracks the position of the head-mounted pointer, which is reflective material that this user is wearing on the brim of her hat. As the user moves her head, the pointer on the screen also moves.

Test your knowledge of pages 255 through 266 in Quiz Yourself 5-3.

QUIZ YOURSELF 5-3

Instructions: Find the true statement below. Then, rewrite the remaining false statements so they are true.

1. A fingerprint scanner captures curves and indentations of a signature.
2. After swiping a credit card through an MICR reader, a POS terminal connects to a system that authenticates the purchase.
3. ATMs ask you to enter a password, called a biometric identifier, which verifies that you are the holder of the bankcard.
4. Four types of source documents are flatbed, pen, sheet-fed, and drum.
5. Retail and grocery stores use the POSTNET bar code.
6. RFID is a technology that uses laser signals to communicate with a tag placed in an object, an animal, or a person.
7. The Americans with Disabilities Act (ADA) requires any company with 15 or more employees to make reasonable attempts to accommodate the needs of physically challenged workers.

Quiz Yourself Online: To further check your knowledge of scanners and reading devices, terminals, biometric devices, and input for physically challenged users, visit scsite.com/dc2007/ch5/quiz and then click Objectives 9 – 12.

CHAPTER SUMMARY

Input is any data and instructions you enter into the memory of a computer. This chapter described the various techniques of entering input and several commonly used input devices (read Looking Ahead 5-2 for a look at the next generation of input devices). Topics presented included the keyboard, mouse, and other pointing devices; voice input; input for PDAs, smart phones, and Tablet PCs; digital cameras; video input; scanners and reading devices; terminals; biometric input; and input devices for physically challenged users.

LOOKING AHEAD 5-2

Wearable Computers Make Performance Statement

Frodo, the hero in the *Lord of the Rings* trilogy, wears a durable, inconspicuous tunic that saves his life. You, too, may one day wear a garment with biosensors that may save your life by detecting health problems and summoning emergency help.

While this clothing is practical, other researchers are creating the newest fashions and accessories outfitted with computers. For example, reporters may one day wear trench coats equipped with 10 cameras to give a 360-degree panoramic view of the scene. Children wearing the Dog@watch jacket and watch might transmit their location via a GPS unit and wireless computer. Buttons on your jacket also may serve as cameras, sunglasses may have a built-in audio player, and your shirt might display text messages from a friend. For more information, visit scsite.com/dc2007/ch5/looking and then click Wearable Computers.

CAREER CORNER

Data Entry Clerk

Data entry clerks have an essential role in today's information-producing industry. A *data entry clerk* enters data into documents, databases, and other applications using computer keyboards and visual display devices. Duties can include manipulating, editing, and maintaining data to ensure that it is accurate and up-to-date, and researching information.

Some data entry clerks telecommute. Although they generally use keyboards, they also work with other input from scanners or electronically transmitted files. Because of the nature of their job, data entry clerks often sit for hours typing in front of monitors. They can be susceptible to repetitive stress injuries and neck, back, and eye strain. To prevent these injuries, many offices use ergonomically designed input devices and incorporate regularly scheduled exercise breaks.

Data entry clerks usually are high school graduates with keyboarding skills. Some employers require an associate's degree or at least two years of post-high-school education plus two years of office experience. Data entry training, basic language skills, and familiarity with word processing, spreadsheet, and database programs are important. Data entry often serves as a stepping-stone to other administrative positions. The average annual salary for data entry clerks is around $24,000. Salaries start at about $21,500 and, with experience, can exceed $33,000. For more information, visit scsite.com/dc2007/ch5/careers and then click Data Entry Clerk.

High-Tech Talk

BIOMETRICS: PERSONALIZED SECURITY

Biometric authentication is based on the measurement of an individual's unique physiological and behavioral characteristics. The most common measurements, described earlier in this chapter, such as fingerprints, hand geometry, facial features, and eye patterns are physiological biometrics. Some of the more novel measurements, such as body odor, brain wave patterns, DNA, ear shape, sweat pores, and vein patterns also fall into the category of physiological biometrics. Voice scan and signature scan are examples of behavioral biometrics.

Any biometric technology process involves two basic steps — enrollment and matching. To illustrate these steps, this High-Tech Talk uses the most common biometric technology, finger-scan technology.

ENROLLMENT Enrollment is the process in which a user presents the fingerprint data to be stored in a template for future use, as shown in the top of Figure 5-50. This initial template is called the *enrollment template*. Creating the enrollment template involves four basic steps: (1) acquire fingerprint, (2) extract fingerprint feature, (3) create enrollment template, and (4) store enrollment template. The enrollment template usually is created only after the user has submitted several samples of the same fingerprint. Most fingerprint images will have false details, usually caused by cuts, scars, or even dirt, which must be filtered out.

The first step, acquire fingerprint, presents a major challenge to finger-scan technology. The quality of a fingerprint may vary substantially from person to person and even finger to finger. The two main methods of acquiring images are optical and silicon. With optical technology, a camera is used to register the fingerprint image against a plastic or glass platen (scanner). Silicon technology uses a silicon chip as a platen, which usually produces a higher quality fingerprint image than optical devices.

The second step, extract fingerprint feature, involves thinning the ridges of the raw image to a minuscule size and then converting the characteristics to binary format. Fingerprints are comprised of ridges and valleys that have unique patterns, such as arches, loops, and swirls. Irregularities and discontinuities in these ridges and valleys are known as *minutiae*. Minutiae are the distinctive characteristics upon which most finger-scan technology is based. The fingerprint-feature extraction process used is highly sophisticated, patented, and a closely-held vendor secret.

In the third step, the binary format is used to create the enrollment template. The fourth and final step involves storing the template on a storage device, such as a hard disk or smart card for future use when the same person attempts to be authenticated.

MATCHING Matching is the process of comparing a match template to an enrollment template. A *match template* is created when the user attempts to gain access through a fingerprint scanner. Most computer and network systems are set up so that the person also must claim an identity, such as a user name, along with the fingerprint. In this case, the match template is compared directly to the enrollment template for that user name. Other systems, such as those used for criminal investigations, will search the entire enrollment template database for a match.

The match template is created in the same fashion as the enrollment template described earlier. Rather than storing the match template on disk, however, it is compared to the user's stored enrollment template, as shown in the bottom of Figure 5-50. The result of the matching process is a score. The score is compared against a threshold. The threshold is a predefined number that can be adjusted depending on the desired level of security.

The scoring process leads to the decision process. The decision process will produce one of three actions: (1) the threshold has been exceeded, thereby resulting in a match; (2) the threshold has not been met, thereby resulting in a nonmatch; or (3) the data may have been insufficient, resulting in the system requesting a new sample from the user to begin a new comparison.

Finger-scan technology is likely to continue to grow as the centerpiece of the biometric industry. For more information, visit scsite.com/dc2007/ch5/tech and then click Biometrics.

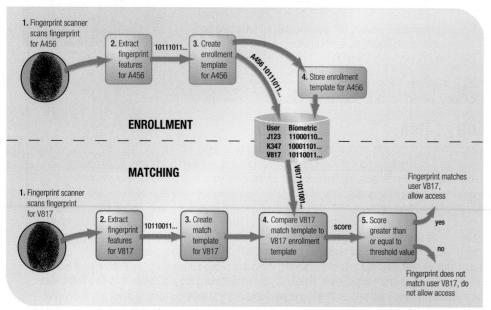

FIGURE 5-50 The two steps in biometric technology.

Companies on the Cutting Edge

LOGITECH
PERSONAL INTERFACE PRODUCTS LEADER

The average Internet user has more than 40 inches of cords on his desktop, according to a *Logitech* survey. This company is working to reduce desktop clutter with a variety of cordless peripherals, including mouse devices, keyboards, mobile headphones and earphones, and game controllers.

A market leader, Logitech has sold more than 50 million wireless devices. It also designs, manufactures, and markets corded devices. The company's retail sales account for more than 85 percent of its revenue.

Two engineering students from Stanford University, Italian-born Pierluigi Zappacosta and Swiss-born Daniel Borel, launched Logitech in 1981. Today, the corporation is the world's largest manufacturer of the mouse, having sold more than 500 million since the company's founding. For more information, visit scsite.com/dc2007/ch5/companies and then click Logitech.

Palm
HANDHELD COMPUTING DEVICES MANUFACTURER

The PalmPilot holds the distinction of being the most rapidly adopted new computing product ever manufactured. More than two million units of this PDA were sold since Palm Computing introduced the product in 1996.

Palm Computing was founded in 1992 and became a subsidiary of 3Com Corp. in 1997. In 2000, the Palm subsidiary became an independent, publicly traded company. In 2003, shareholders voted to spin off PalmSource, Inc., maker of the Palm operating system, as an independent company called palmOne, Inc., and acquire Handspring, Inc. In 2005, the company changed its name to *Palm*, Inc., after it acquired full rights to the brand name, Palm.

The Palm product family includes the Zire and Tungsten handheld devices, LifeDrive storage devices, and the Treo smart phones. For more information, visit scsite.com/dc2007/ch5/companies and then click Palm.

Technology Trailblazers

CHARLES WALTON
RFID DEVELOPER

The next time you use a key card to unlock a door, you can thank *Charles Walton* for simplifying your life. He holds the first patent in RFID technology, issued in 1973, which he called "an automatic identification system."

He believed his invention would interest General Motors executives, but they thought his automatic door lock reader was too futuristic. He then went to lock manufacturer Schlage, where management licensed his technology. Walton also created an automatic toll collection system more than 20 years ago. He has been awarded more than 50 patents, 10 of which are for his RFID-related products.

Today, Walton continues to invent RFID and other technologies in his Los Gatos, California laboratory. For more information, visit scsite.com/dc2007/ch5/people and then click Charles Walton.

DOUGLAS ENGELBART
CREATOR OF THE MOUSE

The phrase "point and click" might not be part of every computer user's vocabulary if *Douglas Engelbart* had not pursued his engineering dreams. In 1964, he developed the first prototype computer mouse with the goal of making it easier to move a cursor around a computer screen.

Ten years later, engineers at Xerox refined Engelbart's prototype and showed the redesigned product to Apple's Steve Jobs, who applied the concept to his graphical Macintosh computer. The mouse was mass produced in the mid-1980s, and today it is the most widely used pointing device.

Engelbart currently serves as director of the Bootstrap Institute, a company he founded with his daughter to form strategic alliances and consequently improve corporations' performances. For more information, visit scsite.com/dc2007/ch5/people and then click Douglas Engelbart.

Quizzes and Learning Games

Computer Genius
Crossword Puzzle
DC Track and Field
Practice Test
Quiz Yourself
Wheel of Terms
You're Hired!

Exercises

Case Studies
Chapter Review
Checkpoint
Key Terms
Learn How To
Learn It Online
Web Research

Beyond the Book

Career Corner
Companies
FAQs
High-Tech Talk
Looking Ahead
Making Use of the Web
Trailblazers
Web Links

Features

Chapter Forum
Install Computer
Lab Exercises
Maintain Computer
Tech News
Timeline 2007

Chapter Review

The Chapter Review section summarizes the concepts presented in this chapter. To listen to the audio version of this Chapter Review, visit scsite.com/dc2007/ch5/review. To obtain help from other students regarding any subject in this chapter, visit scsite.com/dc2007/ch5/forum and post your thoughts or questions.

(1) What Is Input? **Input** is any *data* or instructions entered into the memory of a computer. An **input device** is any hardware component that allows users to enter data and instructions.

(2) What Are the Characteristics of a Keyboard? A **keyboard** is an input device that contains keys users press to enter data into a computer. Computer keyboards have a typing area that includes letters of the alphabet, numbers, punctuation marks, and other basic keys. Most keyboards also have *function keys* programmed to issue commands; keys used to move the **insertion point**, usually a blinking vertical bar, on the screen; and *toggle keys* that switch between two states when pressed. A *gaming keyboard* is a keyboard designed specifically for users that enjoy playing games on the computer.

(3) What Are Different Mouse Types, and How Do They Work? A **pointing device** is an input device that allows users to control a small graphical symbol, called a **pointer**, on the computer screen. A **mouse** is a pointing device that fits under the palm of your hand. As you move a mouse, the pointer on the screen also moves. A *mechanical mouse* translates the movement of a ball on its underside into signals the computer can process. An *optical mouse* uses devices that emit and sense light to detect the mouse's movement. A *cordless mouse* transmits data using wireless technology.

(4) How Do Pointing Devices Work? A **trackball** is a stationary pointing device with a ball that you rotate to move the pointer. A **touchpad** is a flat, pressure-sensitive device that you slide your finger across to move the pointer. A **pointing stick** is a device positioned on the keyboard that you push to move the pointer. A **joystick** is a vertical lever that you move to control a simulated vehicle or player. A **wheel** is a steering-wheel-type device that you turn to simulate driving a vehicle. The *control pad* on an audio player is a pointing device that enables users to scroll through and play music, adjust volume, and customize settings. A **gamepad**, sometimes called a game controller, is a pointing device that controls the movement and actions of players or objects in video games or computer games. A **light pen** is a light-sensitive device that you press against or point at the screen to select objects. A **touch screen** is a touch-sensitive display device that you interact with by touching areas of the screen. A **stylus** and a **digital pen** use pressure to write or draw.

Visit scsite.com/dc2007/ch5/quiz or click the Quiz Yourself button. Click Objectives 1 – 4.

(5) How Does Voice Recognition Work? **Voice recognition** is the computer's capability of distinguishing spoken words. Voice recognition programs recognize a vocabulary of preprogrammed words. Most voice recognition programs are a combination of *speaker-dependent software*, which makes a profile of your voice, and *speaker-independent software*, which has a built-in set of word patterns.

(6) What Are Input Devices for PDAs, Smart Phones, and Tablet PCs? A primary input device for a PDA is a basic stylus. Some PDAs have a built-in keyboard or support voice input. You can attach a full-sized *portable keyboard* to a PDA. Voice is one input method for smart phones. Users can send typed messages using *text messaging*. Some smart phones can use IM to communicate over the Internet, and many have a camera so that users can use *picture messaging*. The primary input device for a Tablet PC is a digital pen, with which users can write on the device's screen. If you slide a Tablet PC into a *docking station*, you can use a full-sized keyboard, mouse, and other peripherals.

Chapter Review

(7) How Does a Digital Camera Work?   A **digital camera** allows users to take pictures and store the photographed images digitally. When you take a picture, light passes into the camera lens, which focuses the image on a *charge-coupled device (CCD)*. The CCD generates an analog signal that represents the image. An analog-to-digital converter (ADC) converts the analog signal to a digital signal. A processor in the camera stores the digital image on the camera's storage media. The image is downloaded to a computer's hard disk via cable or copied from the camera's storage media.

(8) How Are PC Video Cameras, Web Cams, and Video Conferencing Used?   A **PC video camera** is a digital video camera that enables users to capture video and still images and then send or broadcast the images over the Internet. A **Web cam** is any video camera that displays its output on a Web page. A **video conference** is a meeting between geographically separated people who use a network or the Internet to transmit audio and video data.

connect
Visit scsite.com/dc2007/ch5/quiz or click the Quiz Yourself button. Click Objectives 5 – 8.

(9) What Are Various Types of Scanners and Reading Devices, and How Do They Work?
A **scanner** is a light-sensing input device that reads printed text and graphics and translates the results into a form the computer can process. A **flatbed scanner** works in a manner similar to a copy machine except it creates a file of the document. An *optical reader* uses a light source to read characters, marks, and codes and converts them into digital data. **Optical character recognition (OCR)** reads characters from ordinary documents. **Optical mark recognition (OMR)** reads hand-drawn marks such as small circles. A **bar code reader** is an optical reader that uses laser beams to read a **bar code**, or identification code. **RFID** (*radio frequency identification*) uses radio signals to communicate with an embedded tag. **MICR** (*magnetic-ink character recognition*) reads text printed with magnetized ink.

(10) What Are Types of Terminals?   A *terminal* consists of a keyboard, a monitor, a video card, and memory. A *dumb terminal* has no processing power and relies on a host computer for processing. A *smart terminal* has a processor and can perform some functions independent of the host computer. POS terminals and ATMs are special-purpose terminals. A **POS (point-of-sale) terminal** records purchases, processes credit or debit cards, and updates inventory. An **automated teller machine (ATM)** is a self-service banking machine that connects to a host computer. To access a bank account, you insert a bankcard into the ATM's card reader and enter a *personal identification number (PIN)*.

(11) What Are Various Biometric Devices?   A *biometric device* translates a personal characteristic into digital code that is compared with a digital code stored in the computer to identify an individual. A **fingerprint scanner** captures curves and indentations of a fingerprint. A *face recognition system* captures a live face image. A *hand geometry system* measures the shape and size of a hand. A *voice verification system* compares live speech with a stored voice pattern. A *signature verification system* recognizes the shape of a signature. An *iris recognition system* reads patterns in the iris of the eye. *Retinal scanners* scan patterns of blood vessels in the back of the retina.

(12) What Are Alternative Input Devices for Physically Challenged Users?   Voice recognition is ideal for visually impaired users. A *keyguard* is a plate placed over the keyboard that allows users with limited hand mobility to rest their hands and press only one key at a time. Keyboards with larger keys or an *on-screen keyboard* displayed on a user's screen also are available. A small trackball or a *head-mounted pointer* helps users with limited hand movement to control the pointer. Two developments in the prototype stage are *gesture recognition* and computerized implant devices.

connect
Visit scsite.com/dc2007/ch5/quiz or click the Quiz Yourself button. Click Objectives 9 – 12.

Key Terms

You should know the Primary Terms and be familiar with the Secondary Terms. Use the list below to help focus your study. To further enhance your understanding of the Key Terms in this chapter, visit scsite.com/dc2007/ch5/terms. See an example of and a definition for each term, and access current and additional information about the term from the Web.

Primary Terms

(shown in bold-black characters in the chapter)

Americans with Disabilities Act (ADA) (266)
audio input (246)
automated teller machine (ATM) (262)
bar code (258)
bar code reader (258)
bar code scanner (258)
digital camera (250)
digital pen (243)
digital video (DV) camera (253)
ergonomics (238)
fingerprint scanner (262)
flatbed scanner (256)
gamepad (242)
graphics tablet (244)
input (234)
input device (236)
insertion point (237)
joystick (242)
keyboard (236)
light pen (242)
magnetic stripe card reader (260)
MICR (260)
MICR reader (260)
mouse (239)
mouse pad (239)
OCR devices (257)
optical character recognition (OCR) (257)
optical mark recognition (OMR) (257)
PC camera (253)
PC video camera (253)
pen input (243)
pointer (239)
pointing device (239)
pointing stick (242)
POS terminal (261)
resolution (252)
RFID (259)
RFID reader (259)
scanner (255)
smart card (264)
stylus (243)
touch screen (243)
touchpad (241)
trackball (241)
turnaround document (257)
video conference (254)
video input (253)
voice input (245)
voice recognition (245)
Web cam (254)
wheel (242)

Secondary Terms

(shown in italic characters in the chapter)

biometric device (262)
biometric identifier (262)
biometrics (262)
charge-coupled device (CCD) (251)
Click Wheel (242)
command (235)
continuous speech (246)
control pad (242)
cordless keyboard (238)
cordless mouse (239)
cursor (application program) (237)
cursor (graphics tablet) (244)
data (234)
data collection device (261)
digitizer (244)
discrete speech (246)
docking station (250)
download (251)
dumb terminal (261)
enhanced keyboard (236)
enhanced resolution (252)
ergonomic keyboard (238)
face recognition system (263)
field camera (251)
function keys (236)
gaming keyboard (237)
gesture recognition (266)
hand geometry system (263)
handwriting recognition software (243)
head-mounted pointer (266)
image processing (256)
image processing system (256)
iris recognition system (264)
keyguard (266)
magnetic-ink character recognition (260)
magstripe reader (260)
mechanical mouse (239)
MIDI (musical instrument digital interface) (246)
mouse gestures (240)
mouse pointer (239)
MP (252)
OCR (optical character recognition) software (256)
on-screen keyboard (266)
optical mouse (239)
optical reader (257)
optical resolution (252)
optical scanner (255)
personal identification number (PIN) (262)
picture messaging (249)
pixel (252)
pixels per inch (ppi) (252)
point-and-shoot camera (251)
point of sale (POS) (261)
portable keyboard (248)
program (234)
radio frequency identification (259)
retinal scanners (264)
signature verification system (263)
smart terminal (261)
source document (255)
speaker-dependent software (246)
speaker-independent software (246)
speech recognition (245)
streaming cam (254)
studio camera (251)
terminal (261)
text messaging (248)
toggle key (237)
UPC (Universal Product Code) (258)
user response (235)
video capture card (253)
video telephone call (253)
voice verification system (263)
whiteboard (254)
wireless keyboard (238)
wireless mouse (239)

Learn It Online

⑧ DC Track and Field

Click the number 8 button to use what you have learned in this chapter to compete against other students in three track and field events. Directions about how to play the game will be displayed. When you are ready to play, click the start first event button. If required, submit your score to your instructor.

⑨ You're Hired!

Click the number 9 button to use what you have learned in this chapter to embark on the path to a career in computers. Directions about how to play the game will be displayed. When you are ready to play, click the begin game button. If required, submit your score to your instructor.

⑩ Crossword Puzzle Challenge

Click the number 10 button. Complete the puzzle to reinforce skills you learned in this chapter. Directions about how to play the game will be displayed. When you are ready to play, click the Submit button. Submit the completed puzzle to your instructor.

⑪ Lab Exercises

Click the number 11 button. When the Lab Exercises menu appears, click the exercise assigned by your instructor. A new browser window will open. Follow the on-screen instructions to complete the exercise. When finished, click the Exit button. If required, submit your results to your instructor.

⑫ In the News

Many people spend a great deal of time jotting notes on scratch pads, napkins, or self-stick notes. This may be fine for the occasional thought; however, in a situation where you would rather concentrate on the substance of the ideas being expressed, you may need a more sophisticated method for taking notes. Tape recorders have long been the mainstay for recording lectures, interviews, or one's thoughts, but they are restricted by the fact that the tapes last only so long before they

have to be flipped over or switched altogether. One new development is the voice pen, which is a flash-memory-based recording device. It records digitally, which offers higher quality over standard tapes, easy indexing, and instant erasure. It is approximately the size of a small cellular telephone or remote control unit and can record up to 500 minutes on long play settings. Click the number 12 button and read a news article about a new or improved input device, an input device being used in a new way, or an input device being made more available. What is the device? Who is promoting it? How will it be used? Will the input device change the number, or effectiveness, of potential users? If so, why?

⑬ Chapter Discussion Forum

Select an objective from this chapter on page 233 about which you would like more information. Click the number 13 button and post a short message listing a meaningful message title accompanied by one or more questions concerning the selected objective. In two days, return to the threaded discussion by clicking the number 13 button. Submit to your instructor your original message and at least one response to your message.

⑭ eHow.com

Click the number 14 button to learn how to use eHow.com to locate information on a project you want to learn how to complete. Read other users contributions' and then perform the project. Write a brief report about your experience and then post your report to the topic you chose so that others can learn from your experience. Print your report and submit to your instructor.

Learn How To

Use the Learn How To activities to learn fundamental skills when using a computer and accompanying technology. Complete the exercises and submit them to your instructor. To see a video of a Learn How To activity, visit scsite.com/dc2007/ch5/howto.

LEARN HOW TO 1: Install and Use a PC Video Camera

A PC video camera, sometimes called a Web cam, is a digital video camera that allows you to capture video and still images. The videos can be used in live instant messages or for live images over the Internet. Recordings of the videos can be included on Web pages or in e-mail messages as attachments. In addition, some cameras include software that enables you to establish a visual security environment where the camera can be used to detect and record movement in its general vicinity.

Using a PC video camera requires two phases: 1) purchasing and installing the PC video camera, and 2) using the video camera to transmit live video or to record video or digital images.

To purchase and install a PC video camera, complete the following steps:

1. Determine how you want to use the video camera in order to decide the quality of camera you require and the camera software you need. PC video cameras range in price from about $25 to more than $125, and vary in picture quality, features, and accompanying software. If you are not sure of all features and prices, search the Web to determine the best camera for your use.
2. After making your purchase, you will find that most cameras are accompanied by a CD-ROM containing the software that enables the camera to communicate and work with the computer. Often, the instructions with the device will specify that you should place the CD-ROM in a CD or DVD drive and follow the on-screen instructions to install the software on the computer.
3. After the software is installed, you likely will be told to connect the camera to the computer. You do so by connecting the USB cable first to the camera and then to a USB port on your computer. When the camera is connected, you will be able to start the camera software from either the All Programs submenu or the Windows taskbar.

Once you have started the camera software, you will be able to use the camera for any of the tasks you require. Each camera and its accompanying software will allow you to create a video, use instant messaging to send live video to your IM contacts, and other uses as well. In addition, you often will be able to control the quality of your video output by modifying brightness, contrast, and clarity. With many cameras, you will be able to zoom in and out, and, from your keyboard, enter commands to move the camera lens left, right, up, and down.

On some cameras, you even can use a feature called face tracking, where the camera will remain focused on your face even when you move. This feature allows you to be more natural and not be concerned with always making sure you are placed exactly right for the camera.

As you can see, once you have purchased and installed a PC video camera, you will open an entirely new world of communication right from your computer.

Exercise

1. Assume you have decided to purchase a PC video camera to use for instant messaging. Search the Web to find the highest rated cameras available for purchase that can be used for your purposes. What is the most expensive camera you found? The least expensive? What features distinguish the two? Based on your use of the camera for instant messaging, what camera would you choose to buy? Why? Submit your answers to your instructor.
2. Optional: Purchase a PC video camera or borrow one from a friend. Install the camera software on a computer. Warning: If you are using a computer that is not your own, complete this exercise only with the owner's permission. Connect the camera to the computer. Practice with the camera and the accompanying software. What features does the software provide? Which feature do you find the most compelling? What features could you do without? Record a video of yourself answering these questions. Submit the video to your instructor.

Learn How To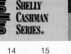

LEARN HOW TO 2: Use the On-Screen Keyboard for Physically Challenged Users

Everyone who uses a computer must enter data and instructions into the computer. For people with limited hand and arm mobility, this can prove a daunting task. Windows XP and a variety of other applications provide a number of aids that can be useful. One of these is the on-screen keyboard.

The on-screen keyboard allows a user to view the keyboard on the screen and select characters to enter by using several different methods. To display and use the on-screen keyboard, complete the following steps:

1. Click the Start button on the Windows taskbar, point to All Programs on the Start menu, point to Accessories on the All Programs submenu, point to Accessibility on the Accessories submenu, and then click On-Screen Keyboard on the Accessibility submenu. *The On-Screen Keyboard window opens. In addition, an On-Screen Keyboard dialog box might appear that indicates the on-screen keyboard provides a minimum level of functionality and that a more robust product might be needed for daily use.* If this dialog box is displayed, click the OK button to close it.
2. In the On-Screen Keyboard window, click Settings on the menu bar. Ensure a checkmark is next to Always on Top.
3. If necessary, click Settings on the menu bar again. Click Typing Mode on the Settings menu. *The Typing Mode dialog box is displayed (Figure 5-51).*
4. Ensure the Click to select button is selected and then click the OK button in the Typing Mode dialog box.
5. Start your Web browser and click the Address bar.
6. Using the on-screen keyboard, enter the characters www.cnn.com and then click the ent key.
7. When the cnn.com Web page appears, click the Enter Symbol box in the Business at CNNMoney section of the page. Using the on-screen keyboard, enter ibm and then click the ent key.
8. After finding the stock price for IBM, close the browser window.
9. Start the WordPad program (see Learn How To number 1 on page 48).
10. In the On-Screen Keyboard window, click Settings on the menu bar and then click Typing Mode on the Settings menu.
11. Ensure the Hover to select button is selected in the Typing Mode dialog box. Click the Minimum time to hover box arrow and select 1.00 seconds in the list. Click the OK button.
12. Click in the WordPad window to position the insertion point.
13. You can cause a character to be entered in the WordPad window by placing the mouse pointer over the desired key (hovering) for one second. Type the following using the on-screen keyboard: Accessibility tools are vital for computer users.
14. Close the WordPad window and then close the On-Screen Keyboard window.

Typing Mode dialog box

Click to select option button

Hover to select option button

Joystick or key to select option button

OK button

FIGURE 5-51

You have seen how one of the Accessibility tools within Windows XP functions. You are encouraged to explore all of the tools and discover how these tools can be useful to those people for whom they were designed.

Exercise

1. Start WordPad and then display the on-screen keyboard. In the On-Screen Keyboard window, click Settings on the menu bar and then click Typing Mode. In the Typing Mode dialog box, select Joystick or key to select. Click the Advanced button. Ensure the Keyboard key box contains a checkmark and then click Space in the list. Click the OK buttons to close the dialog boxes. Then, on the Keyboard menu, select Block Layout. Click in the WordPad window and then press the SPACEBAR. What happened? Keep pressing the SPACEBAR until you cause a character to be entered in the WordPad window. Use the bksp key on the on-screen keyboard to backspace and erase the character, and then use the on-screen keyboard to type On-Screen Keyboard usage in the WordPad window. When you are done, close the WordPad window and the On-Screen Keyboard window. Which means of using the on-screen keyboard (click a key, hover, or the SPACEBAR) did you find easiest to use? Why? Why would a physically challenged person prefer one method over another? Prepare your answers using the on-screen keyboard and then submit your answers to your instructor.

Web Research

Use the Internet-based Web Research exercises to broaden your understanding of the concepts presented in this chapter. Visit scsite.com/dc2007/ch5/research to obtain more information pertaining to each exercise. To discuss any of the Web Research exercises in this chapter with other students, post your thoughts or questions at scsite.com/dc2007/ch5/forum.

(1) Scavenger Hunt   Use one of the <u>search engines</u> listed in Figure 2-10 in Chapter 2 on page 78 or your own favorite search engine to find the answers to the questions below. Copy and paste the Web address from the Web page where you found the answer. Some questions may have more than one answer. If required, submit your answers to your instructor. (1) The primary inventor of the first commercial typewriter wanted to persuade people to buy and use the device, so he ordered the keys to allow users to type as quickly as possible. Who was the QWERTY keyboard's primary inventor? (2) What are reasonable accommodations that employers must make to comply with the Americans with Disabilities Act? (3) Who holds patents awarded in the 1950s for automatic video scanning and inspection methods, which led to bar code technology?

(2) Search Sleuth   <u>MetaCrawler</u> (metacrawler.com) is a different type of search Web site because it returns combined results from leading search engines. Visit this Web site and then use your word processing program to answer the following questions. Then, if required, submit your answers to your instructor. (1) Click the Tools & Tips link at the top of the page. Browse and then explore some of the tools, such as Search Tips and FAQs. (2) Scroll down and then read some of the information contained in the Popular Searches section. What are some of the popular MetaCrawler search terms? (3) Click your browser's Back button or press the BACKSPACE key twice to return to the MetaCrawler home page. What are the six most popular searches today? Click a link for one of these popular searches and scroll through the results MetaCrawler returns. (4) Click your browser's Back button or press the BACKSPACE key to return to the MetaCrawler home page. Click the Search text box and then type `What are the top selling digital cameras?` as the keywords in the Search text box. (5) Scroll through the links MetaCrawler returns and then click one that provides the information requested. What are three popular digital cameras? Read the information and then write a 50-word summary.

(3) Journaling   Respond to your readings in this chapter by writing at least one page about your reactions, evaluations, and reflections about using <u>input devices</u>. For example, do you recall the first time you used a mouse? What experiences have you had with voice recognition? Do you own a PDA or Tablet PC, digital camera, or smart phone? Have you ever participated in a video conference? How do you reduce the chances of experiencing repetitive strain injuries? You also can write about the new terms you learned by reading this chapter. If required, submit your journal to your instructor.

(4) Expanding Your Understanding   Journalists, attorneys, law enforcement officials, and students consider tape recorders and notepads essential components of their daily activities. An alternate means of capturing information is a <u>voice pen</u>, which is a flash-memory-based recording device approximately the size of a small smart phone. Visit a local electronics store or view electronics Web sites to learn more about voice pens. Compare their features, cost, recording time, and warranty. Write a report summarizing your findings, focusing on comparing and contrasting the voice pens. If required, submit your report to your instructor.

(5) Ethics in Action   Some reports suggest that a global surveillance system is monitoring e-mail messages, telephone calls, and faxes. This organization known as <u>Echelon</u> attempts to intercept more than three billion satellite, microwave, cellular, and fiber-optic messages per day, according to the reports. The National Security Agency is forbidden to monitor U.S. citizens, but privacy experts contend that at least 90 percent of U.S. communication is gathered and reviewed. View online sites that provide information about Echelon, including Echelon Watch (www.echelonwatch.org). Write a report summarizing your findings, and include a table of links to Web sites that provide additional details. If required, submit your report to your instructor.

Case Studies

Use the Case Studies to apply the concepts presented in the chapter to real-world situations. Visit scsite.com/dc2007/ch5/cases to obtain more information pertaining to each exercise. To discuss the Case Studies in this chapter with other students, visit scsite.com/dc2007/ch5/forum and post your thoughts or questions.

CASE STUDY 1 — Class Discussion   You work in the Efficiency Analysis department of one of the largest retail companies in the world, with multiple stores in every state and many other countries. For the past 25 years, the company has used optical scanners at checkout counters that read the UPC bar code on products to determine from a database the price to charge customers. The company is considering replacing the optical scanners with <u>radio frequency identification</u>, or RFID. The reader receives the code identifying the product via a chip with an antenna that is part of the box or label on the outside of the product. Your manager has asked you to draft a memo outlining the impact such a change would have on the company, its suppliers, and its customers. Be prepared to discuss your findings in class.

CASE STUDY 2 — Class Discussion   You have been asked to serve on your company's Voice Recognition Committee. The committee has been charged with investigating the feasibility of using voice recognition as a primary method for entering data and instructions into the company's computers. The chairperson of the committee has asked for your opinion on the use of <u>voice recognition</u>. When would voice recognition be an advantage over the keyboard and mouse? Might it ever be a disadvantage? Why? Prepare a brief report and be prepared to discuss your recommendations in class.

CASE STUDY 3 — Research   While attending college part-time for the past two years, you have worked as a data entry clerk for Salmon Mirror. Recently, you began to feel an unusual pain in your right wrist. Your doctor diagnosed the problem as <u>carpal tunnel syndrome</u>, which is the most well-known of a series of musculoskeletal disorders that fall under the umbrella of repetitive strain injuries (RSIs). Your doctor made several recommendations to relieve the pain, one of which was to find a new job. Before you begin job hunting, however, you want to learn more about this debilitating injury. Use the Web and/or print media to investigate carpal tunnel syndrome. Prepare a report and/or PowerPoint presentation on your findings. Include information about carpal tunnel syndrome warning signs, risk factors, suggestions about proper workstation ergonomics, and procedures for healing the injury. Share your report or presentation with your class.

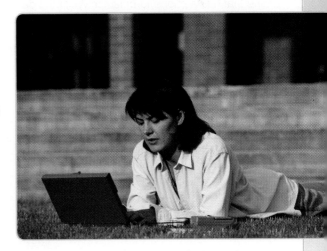

CASE STUDY 4 — Research   An electronics company where you are employed as an analyst spends hundreds of thousands of dollars each year on travel to the multiple locations where they operate around the country. In an effort to curb the ever-increasing costs of travel, the CFO has asked you to look into the feasibility of adopting <u>video conferencing</u> at all of its major locations. Use the Web and/or print media to determine the advantages and disadvantages of video conferencing. Can the technology replace all or most face-to-face meetings? What are the costs of common video conferencing systems and the recurring costs their use incurs? Compare those costs to the cost of travel for a team of three people making six trips per year between New York and Los Angeles, including hotel, airline, and food expenses. Write a brief report or use PowerPoint to create a presentation and share your findings with your class.

CASE STUDY 5 — Team Challenge   The Transportation Security Administration (TSA) is looking into ways to expedite the airport screening experience of frequent flyers without compromising security. The TSA has hired your team as consultants to investigate <u>biometric technology</u>. In particular, they want your team to review three biometric devices for screening frequent flyers — fingerprint scanner, face recognition system, and iris recognition system. Form a three-member team and have each team member choose a different biometric device. Using the Web and/or print media, have each team member determine the advantages and disadvantages of their chosen biometric device. Include in each report how frequent flyer applicants would apply, accuracy rates of the device, and whether the device would indeed enhance security or open a loophole for terrorists. As a team, merge your findings into a team report and/or PowerPoint presentation and share your recommendations with your class.

Special Feature

Personal Mobile Devices

Mobile devices that usually can fit in your pocket, such as PDAs, smart phones, and smart pagers, are referred to as personal mobile devices (Figure 1). Page 22 in Chapter 1 discusses PDAs and smart phones. A **PDA** provides personal organizer functions, such as calendar, appointment book, address book, calculator, and notepad. A **smart phone** is an Internet-enabled telephone that usually provides PDA functionality. A **smart pager** is a wireless mobile device that provides data services, such as e-mail alerts, news alerts, and Internet access. Smart pagers usually provide PDA functionality, such as an address book and calendar. Additionally, some smart pagers include telephone capabilities.

Because the various types of personal mobile devices often offer similar capabilities, they typically are categorized by their form factor. A device's **form factor** refers to its size, shape, and configuration. For example, Figure 1 shows a smart phone that has a PDA form factor and a smart phone that has a phone form factor. While the device with the phone form factor may include PDA functionality, its main purpose is to be used as a phone. Its smaller size may make using it as a PDA more cumbersome than the smart phone with a PDA form factor. The PDA form factor, while larger, provides a better interface for accessing the PDA functionality.

Most personal mobile devices allow you to enhance their functionality through the use of accessories — such as headsets, cameras, and memory cards — and software. Not long ago, PDA (personal digital assistant) software consisted of a few programs, such as a to-do list and an address book. PDAs previously contained embedded software, meaning that a user could not change the software or add programs to the PDA. Today's PDAs, smart phones, and smart pagers allow for as much choice and versatility in their software as a typical personal computer. Most personal mobile devices come equipped with a rich set of programs. In some cases, a user may want to use enhanced versions of the included software, such as an enhanced calculator program, or install additional software, such as a game. Many personal mobile devices allow the user to play music, such as MP3 files.

This special feature provides an overview of accessories and software available for personal mobile devices. The final section of the feature lists the criteria you should consider when deciding which personal mobile device is right for you.

smart pager

PDA

smart phone with
phone form factor

smart phone with
PDA form factor

FIGURE 1   Your choice of a personal mobile device depends on the features you require, the desired form factor, the available accessories, and the available software for the device.

PERSONAL MOBILE DEVICE OPERATING SYSTEMS

As with personal computers, personal mobile devices run an operating system. A personal mobile device runs software made only for the operating system of the device. Personal mobile devices can be categorized by the operating system that each runs. Figure 2 lists the common personal mobile device operating systems, the manufacturer, and a brief description of the operating system.

PERSONAL MOBILE DEVICE OPERATING SYSTEMS

Operating System	Manufacturer	Device Types	Description
Palm OS (versions 5 and later)	PalmSource	PDA Smart phone	The latest version of the operating system for Palm OS-based PDAs supports faster processors, multimedia, and more memory.
Palm OS (earlier versions)	PalmSource	PDA Smart phone	Several PDA manufacturers continue to use earlier versions of the Palm OS operating system because of the simplicity and lower power requirements, resulting in longer usage between recharges.
Windows Mobile for Pocket PC	Microsoft	PDA	The Windows Mobile operating system tightly integrates with Microsoft's Windows operating systems and includes scaled-down versions of many of Microsoft's popular programs, including Word, Outlook, Excel, and MSN Messenger.
Windows Mobile for Pocket PC Phone Edition	Microsoft	Smart phone with PDA form factor	The Pocket PC Phone Edition includes enhancements for the Windows Mobile operating system geared for phone use, such as enhancing the contact manager with the ability to dial a telephone number. This edition includes all of the Windows Mobile PDA functionality.
Windows Mobile for Smartphone	Microsoft	Smart phone with phone form factor	The Smartphone edition of the Windows Mobile operating system is designed for smaller screens and devices with less functionality than a typical PDA.
Blackberry	Research in Motion (RIM)	Smart pager Smart phone with PDA form factor	The Blackberry operating system runs on devices supplied by RIM. The devices include enhanced messaging and e-mail features when compared to smart phones.
Symbian OS	Symbian	Smart phone	Symbian OS is a popular PDA operating system commonly used on cellular telephones. Symbian OS is more popular in Europe and with business users.
Embedded Linux	Open source	PDA Smart phone	Some PDAs use a scaled-down version of the free Linux operating system.

FIGURE 2 Personal mobile device capabilities depend on the operating system that they run.

ACCESSORIES FOR PERSONAL MOBILE DEVICE SOFTWARE

Most personal mobile devices have the capability to take advantage of add-on accessories. For example, using an external keyboard with a device greatly enhances the ability to enter data or notes quickly. Figure 3 lists the more common accessories available for a personal mobile device.

ACCESSORIES FOR PERSONAL MOBILE DEVICES

Accessory	Description
Keyboard	External keyboards provide much faster input when taking notes as opposed to using a small, built-in keyboard on a device. Keyboards may be wireless or attached to the device using a special cable.
Memory card	Memory cards provide additional storage space for a device. Some memory cards may include hardware enhancements such as wireless capability, a camera, or Bluetooth capability. Some cards come with preinstalled software or a vast amount of data, such as a dictionary, on them.
Car kit	Car kits allow you to integrate a device with your car by providing mounting and/or hands-free operation of a device.
Chargers	Special chargers allow you to recharge a device's battery almost anywhere, such as an airplane, hotel, or foreign country. Some chargers provide emergency battery backup in case the device's batteries start running low when no electrical outlet is nearby.
Camera	Add-on cameras provide picture and video taking capability to devices with no such built-in functionality.
Case	Most mobile devices can be placed in a case or holster for protection while the device is not in use. Some devices include built-in flip screens to protect the device. You may want a case that fits comfortably in your pocket, or one that includes a belt clip. A good case protects the device when it is dropped from a height of 3 or 4 feet.
Headset/earphones	Headsets allow you to wear a combined earpiece and microphone while keeping the device in your hand, pocket, or next to you. Some headsets use Bluetooth to communicate wirelessly with the device. Earphones are used when you want to listen to sound on your device, such as when listening to music or an e-book, or when watching a video.
GPS receiver	A GPS receiver contains an antenna, radio receiver, and processor and receives signals from GPS satellites to determine a location and/or speed. GPS receivers turn a personal mobile device into a complete GPS unit. The receivers typically include software that you must install on the device.

FIGURE 3 Some accessories for personal mobile devices are common to most devices, while others are specialized.

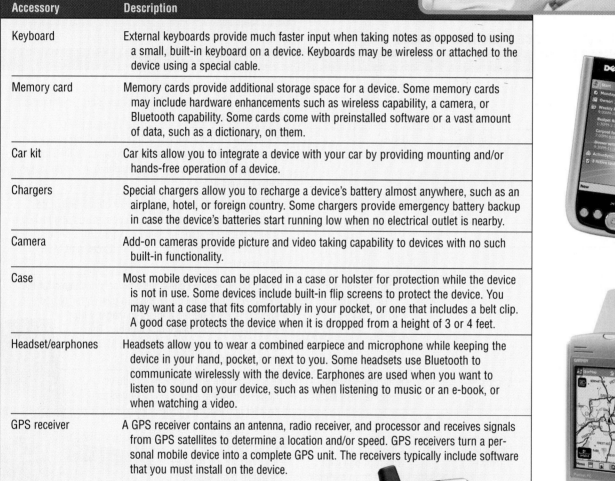

BUILT-IN PERSONAL MOBILE DEVICE SOFTWARE

Most personal mobile devices include several programs that provide basic functionality, such as an **address book** and **date book**. Figure 4 lists the types of software that usually are preinstalled on a personal mobile device.

BUILT-IN PERSONAL MOBILE DEVICE SOFTWARE

Application	Description
Address book and contacts	Maintains a list of acquaintances, including names, addresses, telephone numbers, e-mail addresses, and notes.
To-do list	Maintains a list of tasks. Tasks can be categorized and assigned a priority.
Calculator	Offers functionality of standard desktop calculators.
Datebook and calendar	Maintains appointments and important dates, such as birthdays and holidays. A user also sets audio or visual alarms to trigger when an appointment time arrives.
Memos and notepad	Keeps track of notes.
Launcher	The interface that allows a user to execute, or launch, programs, shown on the PDA screen in the figure below.
Dialer	Smart phones typically include dialer software that assists you in using the telephone capabilities of a device. Some dialer software is integrated into the operating system so that you use dialing capabilities in other applications. For example, you can select a telephone number in the word processing program and request that the number be dialed.

FIGURE 4 Personal mobile devices typically contain this preinstalled software.

SYNCHRONIZATION SOFTWARE

Most personal mobile devices allow a user to share data and information between his or her personal computer and the device. The software that enables the sharing is called **synchronization software**. A personal mobile device may synchronize, or sync (pronounced sink), with a personal computer or a server on a network. Corporations often standardize their synchronization software so that employees share data across the corporate network, and so the data is backed up properly on a server. Figure 5 lists popular synchronization software for personal mobile devices.

SYNCHRONIZATION SOFTWARE FOR PERSONAL MOBILE DEVICES

Application	Description	Samples
Built-in	Most devices include software that the user loads on a personal computer that allows the computer to communicate with the device and share data and information.	• The Palm OS includes HotSync software • Pocket PC PDAs include ActiveSync software • Blackberry devices use the Blackberry Desktop Software
Synching many sources	Some device users have data and information stored in many places. For example, users may want to have their address books on the Web, on their personal computers, on their cellular phones, and on their PDAs. Special synchronization software allows users to keep all of the address books up-to-date.	• Intellisync Handheld Edition • PocketMirror • XTNDConnect Server
SyncML	**SyncML** is a standard that is being adopted by many companies that create personal mobile devices. SyncML allows for common information stored on a device to be shared among many devices, such as cellular telephones, other personal mobile devices, and personal computers.	• IBM WebSphere Everyplace Access • Intellisync Handheld Edition • fusionOne MightyPhone • Symbian based devices use SyncML
iSync	Apple's iSync software allows a user to keep a calendar and contact information synchronized up to the minute between a smart phone, an Apple iPod, a Palm OS device, or multiple Macs.	• Apple iSync

FIGURE 5   Personal mobile devices use synchronization software to share data and information with a personal computer or server.

BUSINESS SOFTWARE

Most programs used on a personal mobile device have some counterpart program on a desktop computer. For example, both a personal computer and a PDA or smart phone may include a word processing program. Many business programs have counterparts on personal mobile devices. The personal mobile device versions of these programs generally have fewer features and options. For example, a word processing program on a PDA may not have a spelling checker, and a spreadsheet program may not include all of the built-in calculations of its desktop computer counterpart. A smart phone with a phone form factor may allow you only to view documents, rather than edit documents. Figure 6 lists business software for personal mobile devices.

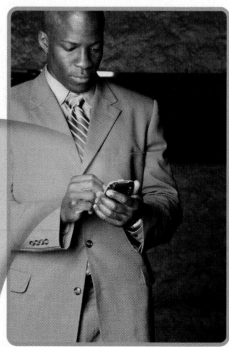

BUSINESS SOFTWARE FOR PERSONAL MOBILE DEVICES

Application	Description	Samples
Word processing	Allows for simple creation, editing, and viewing of documents.	• Documents To Go • WordSmith • PocketWord
Spreadsheet	Allows a user to create, edit, and view worksheets on a personal mobile device.	• PocketExcel • TinySheet • Quickoffice • SmartSheet
Readers	Allows read-only (view only) access to word processing documents, spreadsheets, or databases that a user downloads to a personal mobile device from a personal computer. Readers are useful for taking large documents on the road to read them without the ability to modify them. Some readers allow the user to view all of these types of documents, while others are targeted to specific desktop program counterparts, such as presentation viewers or word processing document viewers.	• Pocket SlideShow • TealDoc • iSilo • Microsoft Reader for Pocket PC
Database and list management	Allows creation, editing, and viewing of databases or lists. List management is a popular use of personal mobile devices. Some examples of lists that are handy to store on a device include shopping lists, to-do lists, exercise logs, and automobile maintenance logs.	• HanDBase • thinkDB • SmartList To Go • JFile • ListPro • Mobile Data Viewer
Financial	Financial software includes programs to manage a bank account, track expenses during a trip, manage a budget, or track an investment portfolio. Many personal computer financial programs include personal mobile device companion software that keeps the information on a device synchronized with the financial information on a personal computer or the Web.	• Microsoft Money for Windows Mobile-based Pocket PC • Pocket Quicken • BankBook • Ultrasoft Money • Handy Expense

FIGURE 6   Business software provides scaled-down versions of common desktop programs.

SOFTWARE FOR WIRELESS DEVICES

Most of the software used to interact with the Internet using a personal computer has a counterpart on wireless mobile devices. Some devices come equipped with e-mail software or a Web browser. Often, special servers allow the device to communicate securely with corporate databases or Web sites. For personal mobile devices that do not include wireless Internet connectivity, a special modem connects the device to the Internet. Often, a device without built-in wireless capability can be connected to a mobile phone that can connect the device to the Internet. Web content and e-mail also synchronize to the device from a personal computer, and the information may be browsed offline while using the device. Figure 7 provides a list of popular communications software for personal mobile devices.

COMMUNICATIONS SOFTWARE FOR PERSONAL MOBILE DEVICES

Application	Description	Samples
E-mail	Used for composing and reading e-mail. Many personal mobile devices include a pre-installed e-mail program.	• Pocket Outlook • riteMail • Mail+ • SnapperMail
Web browsers	Allows Web browsing. Some browsers use an **intermediate server** to make the pages smaller by stripping out images or making images smaller. Others attempt to display the full Web page on the personal mobile device. Many personal mobile devices include a preinstalled Web browser.	• Pocket Internet Explorer • ThunderHawk • AvantGo • Opera browser
Clipping	**Web clippings** are programs that gather and display only the critical elements, or clips, of a Web page.	• Travelocity.com • The Weather Channel • Moviefone.com
Instant messaging	Instant messaging programs usually allow the user to use the same instant messaging ID as that used on a personal computer.	• MSN Messenger • AIM for Palm OS • Agile Messenger

FIGURE 7 Communications software allows a mobile device to access the Internet and other data sources while the user is away from the classroom or office.

CORPORATE/GOVERNMENT SOFTWARE

Large organizations, such as corporations and government agencies, take advantage of personal mobile devices' capability of keeping current information in the hands of their personnel. The organization's central employee telephone book is kept up-to-date and synchronized to each employee's device on a regular basis. Executives synchronize key corporate information. Traveling sales personnel and field technicians synchronize appointments, e-mail, notes about contact with customers, product lists, and sales information. Corporate/government software for personal mobile devices is listed in Figure 8.

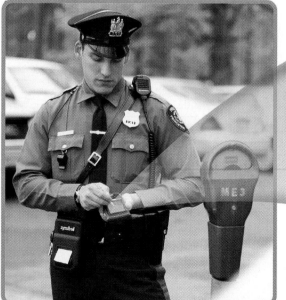

CORPORATE/GOVERNMENT SOFTWARE FOR PERSONAL MOBILE DEVICES

Application	Description	Samples
Executive	Executives keep up-to-date corporate information on their personal mobile devices. Executives may keep current sales information, financial information, and inventory information available to make informed decisions.	• mySAP.com • Siebel 7 Mobile Solutions
Sales	Sales people working out of the office are perhaps the largest group of personal mobile device users. The devices are useful for keeping product information handy, keeping scheduled appointments, and maintaining customer information.	• Siebel 7 Mobile Sales • Salesforce.com • ActionNames
Field technicians and mobile workers	Field technicians visit customer locations to troubleshoot problems. Personal mobile devices help technicians keep track of customer information, maintain up-to-date information on replacement parts, and log troubleshooting information.	• UPS and FedEx use specialized devices and software for their drivers to track package pickups and drop offs.
Military and law enforcement	The military and law enforcement agencies deploy personal mobile devices to manage the special needs of the military and law enforcement.	• Most software of this nature is custom made for the needs of particular agencies. Such programs help track cases or serve as legal references.
Connecting and synchronizing with corporate data sources	Several solutions exist for synchronizing corporate data with personal mobile devices. Special software keeps track of user permissions and makes certain that the right people get the data they require on a day-to-day basis.	• Intellisync Data Sync • MessageWireless
Large organization management issues	In organizations with thousands of personal mobile device users, the support of those devices becomes tedious, especially when users install unsupported software on the devices that may interfere with the corporate software and data for which the device was intended. Server software may detect these conflicts when the user synchronizes with the corporate server and deletes or reports the offending software.	• Much of the software of this nature is custom built for each enterprise, as needs and infrastructure of each organization are different.

FIGURE 8   Large organizations utilize special software to keep their employees synchronized.

MEDICAL SOFTWARE

One of the largest communities to adopt personal mobile device software in significant numbers is the medical community. Physicians and other medical workers routinely use specialized software to track patient charts, check information on drugs, and browse electronic versions of large reference books. The end result is a savings in time and money, and an increase in the level of care for the patient. Figure 9 lists some popular medical software for personal mobile devices.

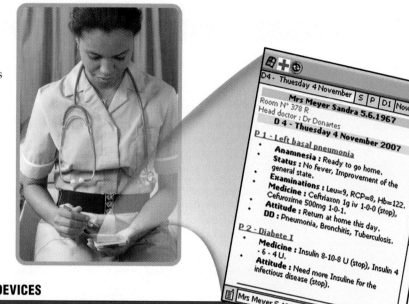

MEDICAL SOFTWARE FOR PERSONAL MOBILE DEVICES

Application	Description	Samples
Patient and case management	Patient and case management programs allow medical workers to enter information as they interact with the patient. This eliminates transcription errors or the need for the worker to find a workstation to do his or her work.	• MedLogs • PatientKeeper Personal • Handy Patients • MD Coder PocketPC Edition
Drug information and drug interactions	Allows for fast access to critical drug information, such as dosages and drug interactions.	• Epocrates Rx • eDrugsDatabase • Dr Drugs
Reference books	Medical workers often rely on a large collection of references to do their jobs. Electronic versions of many popular references, such as the *Physicians' Desk Reference*, are available in electronic format and are kept up-to-date easily through regular downloads.	• PDRDrugs • eDrugs Database • DiagnosisPro for Pocket PC • MedRules
Prescriptions	With electronic prescribing, physicians write prescriptions electronically. Physicians print legible prescriptions and hand the prescriptions to the patient. If the personal mobile device is connected to the Internet or hospital network, the physician checks the patient's medication or medical history.	• iScribe • PocketRx • Medicalis
Medical calculations	Medical workers often make quick calculations for medication dosages or patient status. Programs assist many of these calculations and target the worker's specialty.	• MedMath • MedCalc • Medical MathPad

FIGURE 9 The medical community quickly has become one of the larger users of specialized PDA software.

SCIENTIFIC SOFTWARE

The mobility of personal mobile devices makes them valuable tools for scientific use. Researchers use these devices to gather and record data in the field and later download the data to a personal computer or server. Scientists also use specialized software targeted to their specific field, such as astronomy or meteorology, as a replacement for bulky reference manuals or observation notes (Figure 10).

SCIENTIFIC SOFTWARE FOR PERSONAL MOBILE DEVICES

Application	Description	Samples
Data gathering	Scientists can enter observations quickly into a personal mobile device. These programs often are used in the field for gathering research statistics.	• iCollect
Calculations and conversions	Users can perform specialized calculations or data conversions. Many fields of science, such as astronomy, require special calculations that are useful to have available on a personal mobile device.	• ME Tools • CoolCalc for the Pocket PC • Convert It! • APCalc Converter
Reference	Scientists can look up information quickly, rather than using cumbersome manuals or textbooks.	• ChemRef Basic • Packed Periodic Table • Gene • ABC's of Science
Astronomy	Observers can follow the stars. With the large number of amateur astronomers in the world, programs specific to astronomy are some of the more popular scientific titles.	• Pocket Universe • Planetarium • Astronomist • Pocket Stars
Weather	Meteorologists' specific needs are addressed because these programs allow quick calculations or data gathering in a changing environment. Some programs are linked to add-on hardware that measure temperature, humidity, and other meteorological data.	• Weather Manager • WorldMate • Weather Calculator for Palm OS • Weather.com

FIGURE 10 Scientific programs help scientists manage complex information.

TRAVEL SOFTWARE

The portable nature of personal mobile devices makes them ideal for the business or leisure traveler. Even a night on the town can be enhanced by a list of popular hot spots. The user keeps his or her itinerary handy along with maps and directions while traveling to new places. A GPS-enabled mobile device tracks a user's route and keeps the user on course. Wireless connectivity allows the user to book flights and hotels from the back of a taxi cab. Figure 11 lists travel software for personal mobile devices.

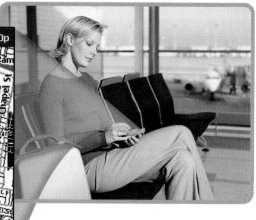

TRAVEL SOFTWARE FOR PERSONAL MOBILE DEVICES

Application	Description	Samples
Itinerary consolidation	Manages travel itineraries, including flights, hotels, and car rentals. The software may keep track of travel preferences and make suggestions about travel and accommodations when planning a new trip.	• Traveler (Pocket PC edition) • Time Traveler • WorldMate
Mapping	Mapping software may download maps from the Web or a personal computer. Or, the software may include maps. The software may suggest travel routes from point to point, or simply serve as a reference.	• Vindigo for Palm OS or Pocket PC • Pocket Streets • HandMap
City guides	City guides are one of the more popular personal mobile device programs. The user installs city guides for specific cities or an entire country. Guides include restaurant listings and ratings, hotels, directions, popular attractions, and local customs.	• Intelliguide Professional • Vindigo for Palm OS or Pocket PC • WorldMate • Frommer's Port@ble Guide • iFodor's
Hotel and flight	Users can view current hotel and flight information while planning a trip. Some of these programs require the device to connect to the Internet. Others occasionally allow downloading the information to a device from a personal computer. Some programs link to booking systems on the Internet, so the user makes reservations directly from a personal mobile device.	• OAG Club • SkyGuide
GPS	Usually requires additional GPS hardware connected to the device. Some software includes mapping data or only displays and saves GPS information, such as location and speed.	• GPS Port@ble Navigator — Travelers Edition • GPS Wireless Navigation System • GPS Atlas

FIGURE 11 Travel software acts as a personal concierge for the business or leisure traveler.

EDUCATIONAL SOFTWARE

With so much to organize, students and instructors greatly benefit from mobile software geared for educational uses (Figure 12). Students load textbook chapters or entire textbooks onto expansion cards and use special software to read the books and highlight key material. Instructors distribute electronic versions of the class syllabus, automatically updating each student's calendar on the students' devices. Some schools even acquire PDAs for the entire student body and require their use in the classroom.

EDUCATIONAL SOFTWARE FOR PERSONAL MOBILE DEVICES

Application	Description	Samples
E-books and references	E-books are electronic versions of books. E-books are specially formatted files that may be viewed using Reader software, as noted in Figure 6 on page 287. Many e-books are available at no cost, and many authors and publishing companies make e-books available to those who have purchased a hard copy of a particular book.	• TomeRaider • PocketLingo Pro • Formulas for Palm OS • Speed Reader Plus • The collected works of William Shakespeare for Microsoft Reader • eWord for Blackberry • Mobipocket Reader Pro for Symbian OS
Class schedules and course management	Helps instructors and students manage their respective schedules. The information may include syllabus details distributed in electronic format by an instructor. The software also may link to a central data repository of a school. The software helps track grading, assignments, to-do lists, instructor office hours, and notes.	• 4.0Student by Handmark course management • Pocket ClassPro for Pocket PC • MyClasses
Roster	Manages grading, rosters, attendance, and contact information for students.	• Teachers PET • Head Start • Teach File
Review	Includes programs for quizzing students and reviewing coursework. Students often train the application to help them review troublesome material.	• Herbert's Math Time • Mental Arithmetic • Quizzler

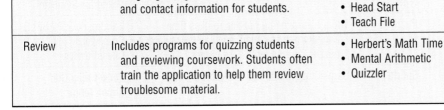

FIGURE 12 Educational software benefits both students and instructors.

MULTIMEDIA SOFTWARE

Most personal mobile devices include the capability of viewing images, and some are powerful enough to view short video clips. Some devices also double as audio players, allowing the user to take his or her favorite music anywhere. Devices that are more recent contain, or allow the user to attach, a camera or recording device to capture video or audio and then download the captured media to a personal computer. Some image viewers allow the user to use a personal mobile device as an electronic picture frame while the device rests in its cradle on the user's desk. Popular multimedia software for personal mobile devices is listed in Figure 13.

MULTIMEDIA SOFTWARE FOR PERSONAL MOBILE DEVICES

Application	Description	Samples
Picture viewer	Allows a user to view images uploaded to a personal mobile device using software on a personal computer or camera. Some viewers have a slide show mode that rotates through a list of images automatically.	• SplashPhoto • PocketPhoto • Palbum Picture Viewer • Resco Photo Viewer for Smartphone • Pictures
Video player	Allows the user to watch video clips on a personal mobile device.	• Windows Media Player Mobile • PocketTV for Pocket PC • ActiveSky Media Player
Audio player	Permits a user to listen to his or her favorite music or record and playback voice recordings for meetings or personal audio notes. Some devices are equipped with additional hardware such as microphones, headphones, or audio controls to enhance the audio experience.	• AudioPlus • Windows Media Player Mobile • Today Player

FIGURE 13   Multimedia software gives personal mobile device users the ability to view images, watch video, and listen to audio.

ENTERTAINMENT SOFTWARE

While on the train ride to work or waiting at the airport, a personal mobile device user can enjoy his or her favorite games. The infrared port or wireless connectivity of a device allows a user to play some games against other players. Most devices include buttons to control games. Figure 14 lists popular entertainment software for personal mobile devices.

ENTERTAINMENT SOFTWARE FOR PERSONAL MOBILE DEVICES

Application	Description	Samples
Strategy	Includes classic board games such as chess, backgammon, and Monopoly.	• PocketChess • ChessGenius • Handmark Monopoly • SimCity
Card	Includes casino games, solitaire games, and other card games.	• AcidSolitaire • BlackJack++ • Pocket Cribbage
Action	Games that require quick reflexes, including many arcade-style games.	• Tomb Raider • Bejeweled • Breakfast • Vexed for Symbian
Puzzle	Thought-provoking puzzles to pass time and sharpen the mind, such as crossword puzzles, mazes, and word games.	• Handmark SCRABBLE • Crossword • ChessPuzzles
Sports	Games that mimic real-life sports.	• Pocket Mini Golf • Smart Tennis • Bowling Master

FIGURE 14   Entertainment software allows a user to relax with a personal mobile device and enjoy his or her favorite games.

OBTAINING AND INSTALLING PERSONAL MOBILE DEVICE SOFTWARE

Software often is available at computer or electronics stores. A significant number of programs are available as shareware, freeware, or trial editions at various Web sites. Most of the software listed in the previous figures is accessible on the Web sites listed in Figure 15. Because software for personal mobile devices usually is smaller than the personal computer counterparts, downloading the software from the Web to your personal computer and then uploading it to your device often is the best alternative when you want to try something new. Software downloaded from the Web to a personal computer requires that the software be installed using the device's synchronization software. Additionally, some personal computer application software includes accompanying mobile device software that corresponds with the personal computer software. Wireless devices, such as smart phones and smart pagers, may allow you to download new software over the wireless connection.

Software for personal mobile devices sold in a retail location often is supplied on a CD-ROM. The CD-ROM first installs the software on a personal computer. The device's synchronization software then is used to load the software onto the device while the device is connected to the personal computer. Depending on the type of software installed, this process may be automatic. Some software is packaged as an add-on card that the user inserts into the device's expansion slot. Some Web sites allow the user to browse a software catalog from a wireless device's Web browser and download the software directly to the device. When synchronizing a personal mobile device on a corporate network, some companies automatically install software to the employees' devices with no interaction required from the employee.

WHERE TO OBTAIN PERSONAL MOBILE DEVICE SOFTWARE

Application	Description	Samples
Web sites	Software publishers make their products available at their Web sites. Several Web sites also exist specifically to distribute mobile device software. Tens of thousands of titles are available, and most can be downloaded on a trial basis.	palmgear.com handandgo.com pdamd.com tucows.com
Retail	Many popular software titles can be purchased at electronic and computer stores. The most popular titles at these locations include productivity and entertainment software.	bestbuy.com compusa.com
Develop in-house	Many corporations develop their own personal mobile device software to use internally to meet specific needs. These programs usually tap into existing corporate databases of product and customer information. The companies that produce mobile device operating systems often make the development tools for such software available at no cost or a minimal cost.	palmsource.com microsoft.com/windows/mobile/ developers blackberry.net/developers symbian.com/developer
For an updated list of where to obtain PDA software, visit scsite.com/dc2007/ch5/pda.		

FIGURE 15 Personal mobile device software is available from a number of sources.

HOW TO PURCHASE A PERSONAL MOBILE DEVICE

Whether you choose a PDA, smart phone, or smart pager depends on where, when, and how you will use the device. If you need to stay organized when you are on the go, then a PDA may be the right choice. PDAs typically are categorized by the operating system they run (Figure 2 on page 283). If you need to stay organized and in touch when on the go, then a smart phone or smart pager may be the right choice. Like PDAs, smart phones and smart pagers are categorized by the operating system they run. The six primary operating systems for these devices are the Palm OS, Windows Mobile for Pocket PC, Windows Mobile for Smartphone, Symbian OS, Blackberry, and Embedded Linux.

This section lists guidelines you should consider when purchasing a PDA, smart phone, or smart pager. You also should visit the Web sites listed in Figure 16 to gather more information about the type of personal mobile device that best suits your computing needs.

 1 DETERMINE THE PROGRAMS YOU PLAN TO RUN ON YOUR DEVICE.

All PDAs and most smart phones and smart pagers can handle basic organizer-type software such as a calendar, address book, and notepad. The availability of other software depends on the operating system you choose. The depth and breadth of software for the Palm OS is significant, with more than 20,000 basic programs and over 600 wireless programs. Devices that run Windows-based operating systems, such as Windows Mobile or Windows Smartphone, may have fewer programs available, but the operating system and application software are similar to those with which you are familiar, such as Word and Excel. Some Symbian-based smart phones also include the capability to read and/or edit Microsoft Office documents. Consider if you want extras on the device, such as the capability of playing MP3 music files.

2 CONSIDER HOW MUCH YOU WANT TO PAY.

The price of a personal mobile device can range from $100 to $800, depending on its capabilities. Some Palm OS devices are at the lower end of the cost spectrum, and Windows-based devices often are at the higher end. A PDA will be less expensive than a smart phone with a similar configuration. For the latest prices, capabilities, and accessories, visit the Web sites listed in Figure 16.

3 DETERMINE WHETHER YOU NEED WIRELESS ACCESS TO THE INTERNET AND E-MAIL OR MOBILE TELEPHONE CAPABILITIES WITH YOUR DEVICE.

Smart pagers give you access to e-mail and other data and Internet services. Smart phones typically include these features, but also include the capability to make and receive phone calls on cellular networks. Some PDAs and smart phones include wireless networking capability to allow you to connect to the Internet wirelessly. These wireless features and services allow personal mobile device users to access real-time information from anywhere to help make decisions while on the go.

 4 FOR WIRELESS DEVICES, DETERMINE HOW AND WHERE YOU WILL USE THE SERVICE.

When purchasing a wireless device, you must subscribe to a wireless service. Determine if the wireless network (carrier) you choose has service in the area where you plan to use the device. Some networks have high-speed data networks only in certain areas, such as large cities or business districts. Also, a few carriers allow you to use your device in other countries.

When purchasing a smart phone, determine if you plan to use the device more as a phone, PDA, or wireless data device. Some smart phones, such as those based on the Pocket PC Phone edition or the Palm OS, are geared more for use as a PDA and have a PDA form factor. Other smart phones, such as those based on Microsoft Smartphone or Symbian operating systems, mainly are phone devices that include robust PDA functionality. Research in Motion Blackberry-based smart phones include robust data features that are oriented to accessing e-mail and wireless data services.

 5 MAKE SURE YOUR DEVICE HAS ENOUGH MEMORY.

Memory (RAM) is not a major issue with low-end devices with monochrome displays and basic organizer functions. Memory is a major issue, however, for high-end devices that have color displays and wireless features. Without enough memory, the performance level of your device will drop dramatically. If you plan to purchase a high-end device running the Palm OS operating system, the device should have at least 32 MB of RAM. If you plan to purchase a high-end device running the Windows Mobile operating system, the PDA should have at least 64 MB of RAM.

6 PRACTICE WITH THE TOUCH SCREEN, HANDWRITING RECOGNITION, AND BUILT-IN KEYBOARD BEFORE DECIDING ON A MODEL.

To enter data into a PDA or smart phone, you use a pen-like stylus to handwrite on the screen or a keyboard. The keyboard either slides out or is mounted on the front of the device. With handwriting recognition, the device translates the handwriting into a computerized font. You also can use the stylus as a pointing device to select items on the screen and enter data by tapping on an on-screen keyboard. By practicing data entry before buying a device, you can learn if one device may be easier for you to use than another. You also can buy third-party software to improve a device's handwriting recognition.

7 DECIDE WHETHER YOU WANT A COLOR DISPLAY.

Pocket PC devices usually come with a color display that supports as many as 65,536 colors. Palm OS devices also have a color display, but the less expensive models display in 4 to 16 shades of gray. Smart phones and smart pagers also have the option for color displays. Having a color display does result in greater on-screen detail, but it also requires more memory and uses more power. Resolution also influences the quality of the display.

8 COMPARE BATTERY LIFE.

Any mobile device is good only if it has the power required to run. For example, Palm OS devices with monochrome screens typically have a much longer battery life than Pocket PC devices with color screens. The use of wireless networking will shorten battery time considerably. To help alleviate this problem, most devices have incorporated rechargeable batteries that can be recharged by placing the device in a cradle or connecting it to a charger.

9 SERIOUSLY CONSIDER THE IMPORTANCE OF ERGONOMICS.

Will you put the device in your pocket, a carrying case, or wear it on your belt? How does it feel in your hand? Will you use it indoors or outdoors? Many screens are unreadable outdoors. Do you need extra ruggedness, such as would be required in construction, in a plant, or in a warehouse? A smart phone with a PDA form factor may be larger than a typical PDA. A smart phone with a phone form factor may be smaller, but have fewer capabilities.

10 CHECK OUT THE ACCESSORIES.

Determine which accessories you want for your personal mobile device. Accessories include carrying cases, portable mini- and full-sized keyboards, removable storage, modems, synchronization cradles and cables, car chargers, wireless communications, global positioning system modules, digital camera modules, expansion cards, dashboard mounts, replacement styli, hands-free headsets, and more.

11 DECIDE WHETHER YOU WANT ADDITIONAL FUNCTIONALITY.

In general, off-the-shelf Microsoft operating system-based devices have broader functionality than devices with other operating systems. For example, voice-recording capability, e-book players, MP3 players, and video players are standard on most Pocket PC devices. If you are leaning towards a Palm OS device and want these additional functions, you may need to purchase additional software or expansion modules to add them later. Determine whether your employer permits devices with cameras on the premises, and if not, do not consider devices with cameras.

12 DETERMINE WHETHER SYNCHRONIZATION OF DATA WITH OTHER DEVICES OR PERSONAL COMPUTERS IS IMPORTANT.

Most devices come with a cradle that connects to the USB or serial port on your computer so you can synchronize data on your device with your desktop or notebook computer. Increasingly more devices are Bluetooth and/or wireless networking enabled, which gives them the capability of synchronizing wirelessly. Many devices today also have an infrared port that allows you to synchronize data with any device that has a similar infrared port, including desktop and notebook computers or other personal mobile devices.

Web Site	Web Address
Hewlett-Packard	hp.com
CNET Shopper	shopper.cnet.com
Palm	palm.com
Microsoft	windowsmobile.com pocketpc.com microsoft.com/smartphone
PDA Buyers Guide	pdabuyersguide.com
Research in Motion	rim.com
Danger	danger.com
Symbian	symbian.com
Wireless Developer Network	wirelessdevnet.com
Sharp	www.myzaurus.com

For an updated list of reviews and information about personal mobile devices and their Web addresses, visit scsite.com/dc2007/ch5/pda.

FIGURE 16 Web site reviews and information about personal mobile devices.

CHAPTER SIX

Output

Picture Yourself Saving Money Using a Computer

While eating lunch with some friends, your conversation centers around rising prices and the cost of hotels, postage stamps, greeting cards, gasoline, and services such as banking and film developing. After the discussion, each of you decides to take measures to reduce some of these costs by using your computers.

Instead of paying for personal checks and postage, you decide to use online banking to pay your bills and balance your statements while viewing them on a computer monitor. For those items that still must be mailed through the postal service, you will print the postage stamps on your printer. You also will print addresses directly on the envelopes or print mailing labels. You soon discover that not only do you save on costs but also the amount of time it takes to complete these activities. No more time spent driving to the post office!

With greeting card software, you will design your own greeting cards on the computer screen, personalizing them with pictures and special notes, and then print them in color on card paper. You also will make personalized T-shirts as gifts by printing pictures on T-shirt transfer paper and then ironing the transfer on a plain T-shirt.

The next time photo paper is on sale, you plan to stock up. With the photo paper in the printer, you will print copies of your digital pictures in a variety of sizes — wallet, 4 × 6, 5 × 7, and 8 × 10.

Read Chapter 6 to learn about various types of monitors, printers, and paper and to discover many other forms of output.

OBJECTIVES

After completing this chapter, you will be able to:

1. Describe the four categories of output

2. Summarize the characteristics of LCD monitors, LCD screens, and plasma monitors

3. Describe the characteristics of a CRT monitor and factors that affect its quality

4. Explain the relationship between graphics chips and monitors

5. Describe various ways to print

6. Differentiate between a nonimpact printer and an impact printer

7. Summarize the characteristics of ink-jet printers, photo printers, laser printers, thermal printers, mobile printers, label and postage printers, and plotters and large-format printers

8. Describe the uses of speakers, headphones, and earphones

9. Identify the output characteristics of fax machines and fax modems, multifunction peripherals, data projectors, joysticks, wheels, and gamepads

10. Identify output options for physically challenged users

CONTENTS

WHAT IS OUTPUT?

Output is data that has been processed into a useful form. That is, computers process data (input) into information (output). A computer generates several types of output, depending on the hardware and software being used and the requirements of the user.

Users view output on a screen, print it, or hear it through speakers, headphones, or earphones. Monitors, notebook computers, Tablet PCs, PDAs, and smart phones have screens that allow users to view documents, Web sites, e-mail messages, and other types of output. Some printers produce black-and-white documents, and others produce brilliant colors, enabling users to print color documents, photographs, and transparencies. Through the computer's speakers, headphones, or earphones, users listen to sounds, music, and voice messages.

While working with a computer, a user encounters four basic categories of output: text, graphics, audio, and video (Figure 6-1). Very often, a single form of output, such as a Web page, includes more than one of these categories.

- Text — Examples of text-based output are memos, letters, announcements, press releases, reports, advertisements, newsletters, envelopes, mailing labels, and e-mail messages. On the Web, users view and print many other types of text-based output. These include newspapers, magazines, books, play or television show transcripts, stock quotes, famous speeches, and historical lectures.

- Graphics — Output often includes graphics to enhance its visual appeal and convey information. Business letters have logos. Reports include charts. Newsletters use drawings, clip art, and photographs. Users print high-quality photographs taken with a

FIGURE 6-1 Four categories of output are text, graphics, audio, and video.

digital camera, eliminating the need for film or film developers. Many Web sites use animated graphics, such as blinking icons, scrolling messages, or simulations.

- Audio — Users insert their favorite music CD in a CD or DVD drive and listen to the music while working on the computer. Software such as games, encyclopedias, and simulations often have musical accompaniments for entertainment and audio clips, such as narrations and speeches, to enhance understanding. On the Web, users tune into radio and television stations and listen to audio clips or live broadcasts of interviews, talk shows, sporting events, news, music, and concerts. They also use the Internet to conduct real-time conversations with friends, coworkers, or family members, just as if they were speaking on the telephone.
- Video — As with audio, software and Web sites often include video clips to enhance

understanding. Users watch a live or prerecorded news report, view a movie, see a doctor perform a life-saving surgery, observe a hurricane in action, or enjoy a live performance of their favorite musician or musical group on the computer.

Attaching a video camera to the computer allows users to watch home movies on the computer. They also can attach a television's antenna or cable to the computer and watch a television program on the computer screen.

An **output device** is any type of hardware component that conveys information to one or more people. Commonly used output devices include display devices; printers; speakers, headphones, and earphones; fax machines and fax modems; multifunction peripherals; data projectors; and force-feedback joysticks, wheels, and gamepads. This chapter discusses each of these output devices.

DISPLAY DEVICES

A **display device**, or simply *display*, is an output device that visually conveys text, graphics, and video information. Information on a display device, sometimes called *soft copy*, exists electronically and appears for a temporary period.

Display devices consist of a screen and the components that produce the information on the screen. Desktop computers typically use a monitor as their display device. A **monitor** is a display device that is packaged as a separate peripheral. Most monitors have a tilt-and-swivel base that allows users to adjust the angle of the screen to minimize neck strain and reduce glare from overhead lighting. Monitor controls permit users to adjust the brightness, contrast, positioning, height, and width of images.

Most mobile computers and devices integrate the display and other components into the same physical case. For example, the display on a notebook computer attaches with hinges. Some PDA and smart phone displays also attach with a hinge to the device; with others, the display is built into the PDA or smart phone case.

Most display devices show text, graphics, and video information in color. Some, however, are monochrome. *Monochrome* means the information appears in one color (such as white, amber, green, black, blue, or gray) on a different color background (such as black or grayish-white). Some PDAs and other mobile devices use monochrome displays because they require less battery power.

Two types of display devices are flat-panel displays and CRT monitors. The following sections discuss each of these display devices.

FAQ 6-1

What can I do to ease eyestrain while using my computer?

Blink your eyes every five seconds. Adjust the room lighting. Use larger fonts or zoom a display. Take an eye break every 30 minutes: look into the distance and focus on an object for 20 to 30 seconds, roll your eyes in a complete circle, and then close your eyes for at least 30 seconds. If you wear glasses, ask your doctor about computer glasses. For more information, visit scsite.com/dc2007/ch6/faq and then click Eye Strain.

FLAT-PANEL DISPLAYS

A *flat-panel display* is a lightweight display device with a shallow depth and flat screen that typically uses LCD (liquid crystal display) or gas plasma technology. Types of flat-panel displays include LCD monitors, LCD screens, and plasma monitors.

LCD Monitors and Screens

An **LCD monitor**, also called a *flat panel monitor*, is a desktop monitor that uses a liquid crystal display to produce images (Figure 6-2). These monitors produce sharp, flicker-free images.

LCD monitors have a small *footprint*; that is, they do not take up much desk space. For additional space savings, some LCD monitors are wall mountable. LCD monitors are available in a variety of sizes, with the more common being 15, 17, 18, 19, 20, 21, and 23 inches — some are 30 or 40 inches. You measure a monitor the same way you measure a television, that is, diagonally from one corner to the other.

Determining what size monitor to purchase depends on your intended use. A large monitor allows you to view more information on the screen at once, but usually is more expensive. You may want to invest in a 19-inch monitor if you use multiple applications at one time or do a lot of research on the Web. Users working with intense graphics applications, such as desktop publishing and engineering, typically have larger monitors.

FIGURE 6-2   An LCD monitor is thin and lightweight.

For an even wider screen area, some users position two or more monitors side by side or stacked (Figure 6-3). For example, one monitor can show the left side of a document, game, graphic design, or other item, with the other monitor showing the right side. This arrangement also is convenient if you want to run multiple applications simultaneously. Users of side-by-side or stacked monitors include music editors, video editors, network administrators, gamers, researchers, Web developers, graphic designers, and engineers.

Mobile computers, such as notebook computers and Tablet PCs, and mobile devices, such as PDAs and smart phones, often have built-in LCD screens (Figure 6-4). Notebook computer screens are available in a variety of sizes, with the more common being 14.1, 15.4, and 17 inches. Tablet PC screens range from 8.4 inches to 14.1 inches. PDA screens average 3.5 inches. On smart phones, screen sizes range from 2.5 to 3.5 inches.

FIGURE 6-3 Users sometimes have multiple monitors stacked or side by side to increase their viewing area.

FAQ 6-2

Can I read a book on a PDA or smart phone screen?

Yes, you can download an electronic book, called an *e-book*, to a mobile device or computer. To read an e-book, your mobile device or computer requires a reader program such as *Microsoft Reader* or *Adobe Reader*. Both of these programs can be downloaded free on the Web. For more information, visit scsite.com/dc2007/ch6/faq and then click E-Books.

notebook computer

Tablet PC

PDA

smart phone

FIGURE 6-4 Notebook computers and Tablet PCs have color LCD screens. Many PDAs and smart phones also have color displays.

LCD Technology

A **liquid crystal display** (**LCD**) uses a liquid compound to present information on a display device. Computer LCDs typically contain fluorescent tubes that emit light waves toward the liquid-crystal cells, which are sandwiched between two sheets of material. When an electrical charge passes through the cells, the cells twist. This twisting causes some light waves to be blocked and allows others to pass through, creating images on the display.

LCD monitors and LCD screens produce color using either passive-matrix or active-matrix technology. An *active-matrix display*, also known as a *TFT* (*thin-film transistor*) *display*, uses a separate transistor to apply charges to each liquid crystal cell and thus displays high-quality color that is viewable from all angles. A newer type of TFT technology, called *organic LED* (*OLED*), uses organic molecules that produce an even brighter, easier-to-read display than standard TFT displays. OLEDs are less expensive to produce, consume less power, and can be fabricated on flexible surfaces. Read Looking Ahead 6-1 for a look at the next generation of OLEDs.

A *passive-matrix display* uses fewer transistors, requires less power, and is less expensive than an active-matrix display. The color on a passive-matrix display often is not as bright as an active-matrix display. Users view images on a passive-matrix display best when working directly in front of it.

LOOKING AHEAD 6-1

Rollable Displays Lock and Roll

Your newspaper arrives each morning at your front door rolled up and secured with a rubber band or in a plastic bag. Your computer monitor soon may arrive rolled up so you can transport it easily in your book bag or luggage.

Flexible screens are being developed to curve against your car's dashboard and bend around corners. In 2005, Philips Polymer Vision introduced the Readius prototype, a pocket-sized electronic document reader that unrolls a 5-inch-long display. The paper-like mobile reader can display text, graphics, and maps. When users are finished viewing the screen, they simply retract the display back into the device, which measures less than 4 inches high.

Rollable screens should prove useful as electronics shrink in size, for they will permit large displays in small, pocket-size mobile devices. For more information, visit scsite.com/dc2007/ch6/looking and then click Rollable Displays.

LCD Quality

The quality of an LCD monitor or LCD screen depends primarily on its resolution, response time, brightness, pixel pitch, and contrast ratio.

- **Resolution** is the number of horizontal and vertical pixels in a display device. For example, a monitor that has a 1600 × 1200 resolution displays up to 1600 pixels per horizontal row and 1200 pixels per vertical row, for a total of 1,920,000 pixels to create a screen image. Recall that a *pixel* (short for picture element) is a single point in an electronic image. A higher resolution uses a greater number of pixels and thus provides a smoother, sharper, and clearer image. As you increase the resolution, however, some items on the screen appear smaller, such as menu bars, toolbars, and rulers (Figure 6-5).

  With LCD monitors and screens, resolution generally is proportional to the size of the device. For example, a 17-inch LCD monitor typically has a resolution of 1280 × 1024, while a 20-inch LCD monitor has a resolution of 1600 × 1200. LCDs are geared for a specific resolution, called the *native resolution*. When set at other resolutions, the quality may not be as good as the native resolution.

- *Response time* of an LCD monitor or screen is the time in milliseconds (ms) that it takes to turn a pixel on or off. LCD monitors' and screens' response times range from 8 to 25 ms. The lower the number, the faster the response time.

- Brightness of an LCD monitor or LCD screen is measured in nits. A *nit* is a unit of visible light intensity equal to one candela (formerly called candlepower) per square meter. The *candela* is the standard unit of luminous intensity. LCD monitors and screens today range from 200 to 350 nits. The higher the nits, the brighter the images.

- *Pixel pitch*, sometimes called *dot pitch*, is the distance in millimeters between pixels on a display device. Text created with a smaller dot pitch is easier to read. Advertisements normally specify a monitor's pixel pitch or dot pitch. Average pixel pitch on LCD monitors and screens should be .28 mm or lower. The lower the number, the sharper the image.

- *Contrast ratio* describes the difference in light intensity between the brightest white and darkest black that can be displayed on an LCD monitor. Contrast ratios today range from 400:1 to 800:1. Higher contrast ratios represent colors better.

FIGURE 6-5a (screen resolution at 800 × 600)

FIGURE 6-5b (screen resolution at 1600 × 1200)

FIGURE 6-5 A higher screen resolution displays smaller images on the screen. This comparison illustrates that all elements on the screen become smaller when the resolution is increased from 800 × 600 to 1600 × 1200. The higher resolution also displays more text on the screen.

Graphics Chips, Ports, and LCD Monitors

A cable on a monitor plugs in a port on the system unit, which enables communications from a graphics chip. This chip, called the *graphics processing unit*, controls the manipulation and display of graphics on a display device. The graphics processing unit either is integrated on the motherboard or resides on a video card in a slot in the motherboard. Video cards usually contain a fan or heat sink to keep this and other chips from overheating.

LCD monitors use a digital signal to produce a picture. To display the highest quality images, an LCD monitor should plug in a *DVI (Digital Video Interface) port*, which enables digital signals to transmit directly to the LCD monitor. Current models of system units either have an integrated DVI chip or contain a video card that has a DVI port. They usually also have a standard monitor port and an *S-video port*, allowing users to connect external devices such as a television, DVD player, or video recorder, to the computer (Figure 6-6).

Over the years, several video standards have been developed to define the resolution, number of colors, and other display properties.

Current video standards include *SVGA* (Super Video Graphics Array), which has a resolution of 800 × 600; *XGA* (eXtended Graphics Array), a resolution of 1024 × 768; *SXGA* (Super XGA), a resolution of 1280 × 1024; and *UGA* (Ultra XGA), a resolution of 1600 × 1200. Many display devices have resolutions beyond UGA, such as 2048 × 1536. Some display devices support all of these standards; others support only a subset of them. For a display device to show images as defined by a video standard, both the display device and graphics processing unit must support the same video standard.

standard monitor port

S-video port

DVI port

FIGURE 6-6 Ports on current video cards.

The number of colors a graphics processing unit displays is determined by bit depth. The *bit depth*, also called *color depth*, is the number of bits used to store information about each pixel. For example, a video card with a 24-bit depth uses 24 bits to store information about each pixel. Thus, this video card can display 2^{24} or 16.7 million colors. The greater the number of bits, the better the resulting image. Today's video cards typically have a 24-bit depth or a 32-bit depth.

A video card or motherboard, in the case of integrated video, must have enough video memory to generate the resolution and number of colors you want to display. This memory, which often is 128 MB or 256 MB on current video cards, stores information about each pixel.

FAQ 6-3

How much do video cards cost?

Although video cards for the home user cost less than $100, professional artists and designers use video cards that can cost up to $1,500. These cards have more than 384 MB of memory and support resolutions of 2048 × 1536. For more information, visit scsite.com/dc2007/ch6/faq and then click Video Cards.

WEB LINK 6-2

Plasma Technology
For more information, visit scsite.com/dc2007/ch6/weblink and then click Plasma Technology.

Plasma Monitors

Large business or power users sometimes have plasma monitors, which often measure more than 60 inches wide (Figure 6-7). A **plasma monitor** is a display device that uses gas plasma technology, which sandwiches a layer of gas between two glass plates.

When voltage is applied, the gas releases ultraviolet (UV) light. This UV light causes the pixels on the screen to glow and form an image.

Plasma monitors offer larger screen sizes and higher display quality than LCD monitors but are more expensive. These monitors also can hang directly on a wall.

FAQ 6-4

What is the largest monitor to date?

The Sydney Olympics had a monitor wall that contained more than 400 screens, measuring about 150 feet wide and 7½ feet tall. For more information, visit scsite.com/dc2007/ch6/faq and then click Monitor Wall.

Televisions

Home users sometimes use their television as a display device. Connecting a computer to an analog television requires a converter that translates the digital signal from the computer into an analog signal that the television can display. The best analog televisions have a resolution of only 520 × 400 pixels. Thus, users are turning to *digital television* (*DTV*) for crisper, higher-quality output on their LCD or plasma televisions.

Digital television signals provide two major advantages over analog signals. First, digital signals produce a higher-quality picture. Second, many programs can be broadcast on a single digital channel, whereas only one program can be broadcast on an analog channel. Today, all broadcast stations must transmit digital signals, as mandated by the FCC.

HDTV (*high-definition television*) is the most advanced form of digital television, working with digital broadcast signals, transmitting digital sound, supporting wide screens, and providing resolutions up to 1920 × 1080 pixels. With HDTV, the broadcast signals are digitized when they are sent via over-the-air (OTA) broadcasts from

FIGURE 6-7 Large plasma monitors can measure more than 60 inches wide.

local television networks, satellite, or cable. To receive the HDTV signals via OTA broadcasts, you need a VHF/UHF antenna; via satellite, you need an HDTV-compatible satellite receiver/tuner; and via cable, you need an HDTV-compatible cable box.

With game consoles, such as Microsoft's Xbox 360 and Sony's PlayStation 3, the output device often is a television (Figure 6-8). Users plug one end of a cable in the game console and the other end in the video port on the television. Although some game consoles include a small LCD screen (usually 5 inches or smaller), home users often prefer the larger television displays for game playing, watching movies, and browsing the Internet on a television connected to a game console.

FAQ 6-5

Who plays video games?

Studies have shown that people between 18 and 34 years of age spend the most time playing video games. This age group spends more money on video games than in movie theaters. For more information, visit scsite.com/dc2007/ch6/faq and then click Video Gaming.

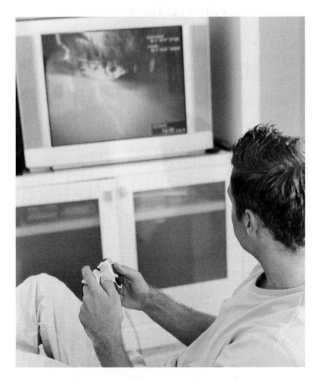

FIGURE 6-8 Video game players often use a television as their game console's output device.

CRT MONITORS

A **CRT monitor** is a desktop monitor that contains a cathode-ray tube (Figure 6-9). A *cathode-ray tube* (*CRT*) is a large, sealed glass tube. The front of the tube is the screen. Tiny dots of phosphor material coat the screen on a CRT. Each dot consists of a red, a green, and a blue phosphor. The three dots combine to make up each pixel. Inside the CRT, an electron beam moves back and forth across the back of the screen. This causes the dots on the front of the screen to glow, which produces an image on the screen.

CRT monitors have a much larger footprint than do LCD monitors; that is, they take up more desk space. CRT monitors for desktop computers are available in various sizes, with the more common being 15, 17, 19, 21, and 22 inches. In addition to monitor size, advertisements also list a CRT monitor's viewable size. The *viewable size* is the diagonal measurement of the actual viewing area provided by the screen in the CRT monitor. A 21-inch monitor, for example, may have a viewable size of 20 inches.

In the past, CRT monitor screens were curved slightly. Today's models have flat screens. A flat screen reduces glare, reflection, and distortion of images. With a flat screen, users do not notice as much eyestrain and fatigue.

A CRT monitor costs less than an LCD monitor, but it also generates more heat and uses more power than an LCD monitor. To help reduce the amount of electricity used by monitors and other computer components, the United States Department of Energy (DOE) and the United States Environmental Protection Agency (EPA) developed the **ENERGY STAR program**. This program encourages manufacturers to create energy-efficient devices that require little power when they are not in use. Monitors and devices that meet ENERGY STAR guidelines display an ENERGY STAR label.

FIGURE 6-9 The core of a CRT monitor is a cathode-ray tube.

CRT monitors produce a small amount of electromagnetic radiation. *Electromagnetic radiation* (*EMR*) is a magnetic field that travels at the speed of light. Excessive amounts of EMR can pose a health risk. To be safe, all high-quality CRT monitors comply with MPR II standards. *MPR II* is a set of standards that defines acceptable levels of EMR for a monitor. To protect yourself even further, sit at arm's length from the CRT monitor because EMR travels only a short distance. In addition, EMR is greatest on the sides and back of the CRT monitor.

FAQ 6-6

Is a flat display the same as a flat-panel display?

No. A *flat display* refers to a CRT monitor that has a flat screen. A flat-panel display, by contrast, has a shallow depth and uses LCD, gas plasma, or some technology other than CRT. For more information, visit scsite.com/dc2007/ch6/faq and then click Flat-Panel Displays.

Quality of a CRT Monitor

The quality of a CRT monitor depends largely on its resolution, dot pitch, and refresh rate.

- Most CRT monitors support a variety of screen resolutions. Standard CRT monitors today usually display up to a maximum of 1800 × 1440 pixels, with 1280 × 1024 often the norm. High-end CRT monitors (for the power user) can display 2048 × 1536 pixels or more. The display resolution you choose is a matter of preference. Larger monitors typically look best at a higher resolution, and smaller monitors look best at a lower resolution.
- As with LCD monitors, text created with a smaller dot pitch, or pixel pitch, is easier to read. To minimize eye fatigue, use a CRT monitor with a dot pitch of .27 millimeters or lower.
- Electron beams inside a CRT monitor "draw" an image on the entire screen many times per second so the phosphor dots, and therefore the image, do not fade. The number of times the image is drawn per second is called the *refresh rate*, or *scan rate*. A CRT monitor's refresh rate, which is expressed in hertz (Hz), should be fast enough to maintain a constant, flicker-free image. A slower refresh rate causes the image to fade and then flicker as it is redrawn. This flicker can lead to eye fatigue and cause headaches for some users.

A high-quality CRT monitor will provide a vertical refresh rate of at least 68 Hz. This means the image on the screen redraws itself vertically 68 times in a second.

Graphics Chips and CRT Monitors

Many CRT monitors use an analog signal to produce an image. As with an LCD monitor, a cable on the CRT monitor plugs in a port on the system unit, which enables communications from a graphics chip. If the graphics chip resides on a video card, for example, the video card converts digital output from the computer into an analog video signal and sends the signal through the cable to the monitor, which displays output on the screen (Figure 6-10).

As with LCD monitors, the greater the video card's bit depth, the better the resulting image. Both the video card and the monitor must support the video standard to generate the desired resolution and number of colors, and the video card must have enough memory to generate the resolution and number of colors you want to display. Some users place additional video cards in their system unit, allowing multiple monitors to display output from a single computer simultaneously.

FAQ 6-7

What type of video content do users view on display devices?

Music videos and newscasts are the most widely viewed video content on display devices, as shown in the chart below. For more information, visit scsite.com/dc2007/ch6/faq and then click Video Output Content.

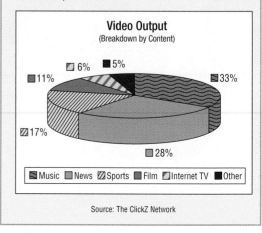

Video Output
(Breakdown by Content)

- 6%
- 5%
- 11%
- 33%
- 17%
- 28%

■ Music ■ News ▨ Sports ■ Film ▨ Internet TV ■ Other

Source: The ClickZ Network

FIGURE 6-10 HOW VIDEO TRAVELS FROM THE PROCESSOR TO A CRT MONITOR VIA A VIDEO CARD

Step 1:
The processor sends digital video data to the video card.

00100110110101101

processor

video card

Step 2:
The video card's digital-to-analog converter (DAC) converts the digital video data to an analog signal.

Step 3:
The analog signal is sent through a cable to the CRT monitor.

Step 4:
The CRT monitor separates the analog signal into red, green, and blue signals.

Step 5:
Electron guns fire the three color signals to the front of the CRT.

Step 6:
An image is displayed on the screen when the electrons hit phosphor dots on the back of the screen.

Test your knowledge of pages 300 through 309 in Quiz Yourself 6-1.

QUIZ YOURSELF 6-1

Instructions: Find the true statement below. Then, rewrite the remaining false statements so they are true.

1. A lower resolution uses a greater number of pixels and thus provides a smoother image.

2. An output device is any type of software component that conveys information to one or more people.

3. Documents often include text to enhance their visual appeal and convey information.

4. LCD monitors have a larger footprint than CRT monitors.

5. Types of CRTs include LCD monitors, LCD screens, and plasma monitors.

6. You measure a monitor diagonally from one corner to the other.

Quiz Yourself Online: To further check your knowledge of output, flat-panel displays, and CRT monitors, visit scsite.com/dc2007/ch6/quiz and then click Objectives 1 – 4.

PRINTERS

A **printer** is an output device that produces text and graphics on a physical medium such as paper or transparency film. Printed information, called *hard copy*, exists physically and is a more permanent form of output than that presented on a display device (soft copy).

A hard copy, also called a *printout*, is either in portrait or landscape orientation (Figure 6-11). A printout in *portrait orientation* is taller than it is wide, with information printed across the shorter width of the paper. A printout in *landscape orientation* is wider than it is tall, with

information printed across the widest part of the paper. Letters, reports, and books typically use portrait orientation. Spreadsheets, slide shows, and graphics often use landscape orientation.

Home computer users might print less than a hundred pages a week. Small business computer users might print several hundred pages a day. Users of mainframe computers, such as large utility companies that send printed statements to hundreds of thousands of customers each month, require printers that are capable of printing thousands of pages per hour.

To meet this range of printing needs, many different printers exist with varying speeds, capabilities, and printing methods. Figure 6-12 presents a list of questions to help you decide on the printer best suited to your needs.

The following pages discuss various ways of producing printed output, as well as many different types of printers.

FIGURE 6-11a   (portrait orientation)

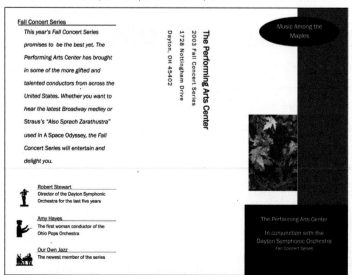

FIGURE 6-11b   (landscape orientation)

FIGURE 6-11   Portrait orientation is taller than it is wide. Landscape orientation is wider than it is tall.

1. What is my budget?
2. How fast must my printer print?
3. Do I need a color printer?
4. What is the cost per page for printing?
5. Do I need multiple copies of documents?
6. Will I print graphics?
7. Do I want to print photographs?
8. Do I want to print directly from a memory card or other type of miniature storage media?
9. What types of paper does the printer use?
10. What sizes of paper does the printer accept?
11. Do I want to print on both sides of the paper?
12. How much paper can the printer tray hold?
13. Will the printer work with my computer and software?
14. How much do supplies such as ink and paper cost?
15. Can the printer print on envelopes and transparencies?
16. How many envelopes can the printer print at a time?
17. How much do I print now, and how much will I be printing in a year or two?
18. Will the printer be connected to a network?
19. Do I want wireless printing capability?

FIGURE 6-12   Questions to ask when purchasing a printer.

Producing Printed Output

Until a few years ago, printing a document required connecting a computer to a printer with a cable via the USB or parallel port on the computer. Although many users today continue to print using this method, a variety of printing options are available, as shown in Figure 6-13.

Today, wireless printing technology makes the task of printing from a notebook computer, Tablet PC, PDA, smart phone, or digital camera much easier. As discussed in Chapter 4, two wireless technologies for printing are Bluetooth and infrared. With *Bluetooth printing*, a computer or other device transmits output to a printer via radio waves. The computer or other device and the printer do not have to be aligned with each

other; rather, they need to be within an approximate 30-foot range. With *infrared printing*, a printer communicates with a computer or other device using infrared light waves. To print from a smart phone, for example, a user lines up the IrDA port on the smart phone with the IrDA port on the printer.

Users can print images taken with a digital camera without downloading the images to the computer using a variety of techniques. Some cameras connect directly to a printer via a cable. Others store images on media cards that can be removed and inserted in the printer. Some printers have a docking station, into which the user inserts the camera to print pictures stored in the camera.

WEB LINK 6-3

Printing Digital Camera Images

For more information, visit scsite.com/ dc2007/ch6/weblink and then click Printing Digital Camera Images.

FIGURE 6-13 Users print documents and pictures using a variety of printing methods.

Finally, many home and business users print to a central printer on a network. Their computer may communicate with the network printer via cables or wirelessly.

Nonimpact Printers

A **nonimpact printer** forms characters and graphics on a piece of paper without actually striking the paper. Some spray ink, while others use heat or pressure to create images.

Commonly used nonimpact printers are ink-jet printers, photo printers, laser printers, thermal printers, mobile printers, label and postage printers, plotters, and large-format printers.

Ink-Jet Printers

An **ink-jet printer** is a type of nonimpact printer that forms characters and graphics by spraying tiny drops of liquid ink onto a piece of paper. Ink-jet printers have become a popular type of color printer for use in the home. A reasonable quality ink-jet printer costs less than $100.

Ink-jet printers produce text and graphics in both black-and-white and color on a variety of paper types (Figure 6-14). These printers normally use individual sheets of paper stored in one or two removable or stationary trays. Ink-jet printers accept papers in many sizes, ranging from 3 × 5 inches to 8½ × 14 inches. Available paper types include plain paper, ink-jet paper, photo paper, glossy paper, and banner paper. Most ink-jet

FIGURE 6-14 Ink-jet printers are a popular type of color printer used in the home.

printers can print photographic-quality images on any of these types of paper.

Ink-jet printers also print on other materials such as envelopes, labels, index cards, greeting card paper (card stock), transparencies, and iron-on T-shirt transfers. Many ink-jet printers include software for creating greeting cards, banners, business cards, letterheads, and transparencies.

As with many other input and output devices, one factor that determines the quality of an ink-jet printer is its resolution. Printer resolution is measured by the number of *dots per inch* (*dpi*) a printer can print. With an ink-jet printer, a dot is a drop of ink. A higher dpi means the drops of ink are smaller. Most ink-jet printers can print from 600 to 4800 dpi.

As shown in Figure 6-15, the higher the dpi, the better the print quality. The difference in quality becomes noticeable when the size of the printed image increases. That is, a wallet-sized image printed at 600 dpi may look similar in quality to one printed at 1200 dpi. When you increase the size of the image, to 8 × 10 for example, the printout of the 600 dpi resolution

may look grainier than the one printed using a 1200 dpi resolution.

The speed of an ink-jet printer is measured by the number of pages per minute (ppm) it can print. Most ink-jet printers print from 3 to 26 ppm. Graphics and colors print at a slower rate. For example, an ink-jet printer may print 20 ppm for black text and only 15 ppm for color and/or graphics.

The print head mechanism in an ink-jet printer contains ink-filled print cartridges. Each cartridge has fifty to several hundred small ink holes, or nozzles. The steps in Figure 6-16 illustrate how a drop of ink appears on a page. The ink propels through any combination of the nozzles to form a character or image on the paper.

FIGURE 6-15 You will notice a higher quality output with printers that can print at a higher dpi.

FIGURE 6-16 HOW AN INK-JET PRINTER WORKS

Step 1:
A small resistor heats the ink, causing the ink to boil and form a vapor bubble.

Step 2:
The vapor bubble forces the ink through the nozzle.

Step 3:
Ink drops onto the paper.

Step 4:
As the vapor bubble collapses, fresh ink is drawn into the firing chamber.

When the print cartridge runs out of ink, you simply replace the cartridge. Most ink-jet printers have at least two print cartridges: one containing black ink and the other(s) containing colors. Cartridges with black ink cost $15 to $30 each. Color ink cartridge prices range from $20 to $35 each. The number of pages a single cartridge can print varies by manufacturer and the type of documents you print. For example, black ink cartridges typically print from 200 to 800 pages, and color ink cartridges from 125 to 450 pages. Read Ethics & Issues 6-1 for a related discussion.

ETHICS & ISSUES 6-1

Is It Ethical to Refill an Ink-Jet Cartridge?

In 1903, King Camp Gillette introduced an innovative product — a safety razor with disposable blades. Gillette accompanied his product with an even more innovative idea — sell the razor, which was purchased once, at or below cost, and rely on sales of the razor blades, which were purchased repeatedly, for profit. The idea made Gillette a millionaire. Manufacturers of ink-jet printers use a similar approach. The printers are inexpensive, often less than $100. The ink cartridges the printers use, however, can cost from $30 to $50 each time they are replaced. To avoid the high cost of cartridges, some people get cartridges refilled cheaply by a third party vendor. At least one printer company legally prohibits the practice, and violators may be breaking patent and contract law if they refill a cartridge. Additionally, some printer manufacturers have inserted special chips that keep a cartridge from being refilled and, some claim, shut down a cartridge before it really is out of ink. Opponents of these practices say that the printer companies are gouging customers and that no legitimate reason exists why someone should not be able to refill an ink-jet cartridge in the same way a soap dispenser can be refilled. Should manufacturers be allowed to prevent people from refilling ink cartridges? Why? Would you use an ink refill kit? Why or why not?

Photo Printers

A **photo printer** is a color printer that produces photo-lab-quality pictures (Figure 6-17). Some photo printers print just one or two sizes of images, for example, 3 × 5 inches and 4 × 6 inches. Others print up to letter size, legal size, or even larger. Some even print panoramic photographs. Generally, the more sizes the printer prints, the more expensive the printer.

Many photo printers use ink-jet technology. With models that can print letter-sized documents, users connect the photo printer to their computer and use it for all their printing needs. For a few hundred dollars, this type of photo printer is ideal for the home or small business user. Other photo printer technologies are discussed later in the chapter. Read Ethics & Issues 6-2 for a related discussion.

prints only 4 × 6 size

prints 4 × 6, 5 × 7, 8 × 10, 8½ × 11, and panoramic sizes

prints 4 × 6, 5 × 7, 8 × 10, 8½ × 11, 11 × 14, 13 × 19, and panoramic sizes

FIGURE 6-17 Photo printers print in a range of sizes.

Who Is Responsible for Stopping Counterfeiting?

Some college students found a solution to their money problems: they made their own. With a scanner, personal computer, and color printer, they produced bogus bills and passed more than $1,000 in counterfeit currency before they were caught. As printer and scanner quality continues to improve, it is estimated that more than $1 million in fraudulent funds is produced every week. Police have arrested counterfeiters ranging from high school students to senior citizens. As one federal agent points out, counterfeiting has gone from a high-skill, low-tech job to a high-tech, low-skill job. While counterfeiters used to specialize in higher-domination bills ($20, $50, and $100), today phony $10, $5, and even $1 bills are circulated. Spotting fake money is not that difficult, but most people never look that closely. Manufacturers of printers have introduced technology to produce lines or streaks when a printed image contains too much bank-note green color. Producers of scanners often include technology that prevents the scanner from scanning currency. Should the manufacturers of high-quality printers and scanners take responsibility for this problem? Why or why not? It is illegal to pass counterfeit currency knowingly. Should it be illegal to offer templates knowingly online that could be used to produce counterfeit documents? Can you offer any other possible solutions?

Many photo printers have a built-in card slot so the printer can print digital photographs directly from a media card. Simply remove the media card from the digital camera and insert it in the printer's card slot. Then, push buttons on the printer to select the desired photo, specify the number of copies, and indicate the size of the printed image. Some photo printers have built-in LCD color screens, allowing users to view and enhance the pictures before printing them.

Laser Printers

A **laser printer** is a high-speed, high-quality nonimpact printer (Figure 6-18). Laser printers are available in both black-and-white and color models. A laser printer for personal computers ordinarily uses individual 8½ × 11-inch sheets of paper stored in one or more removable trays that slide in the printer case. Some laser printers have built-in trays that accommodate different sizes of paper, while others require separate trays for letter- and legal-sized paper. Most laser printers have a manual feed slot where you can insert individual sheets and envelopes. You also can print transparencies on a laser printer.

Laser printers print text and graphics in high-quality resolutions, usually 1200 dpi for black-and-white printers and up to 2400 dpi for color printers. While laser printers usually cost more than ink-jet printers, they also are much faster. A laser printer for the home and small office user typically prints black-and-white text at speeds of 15 to 50 ppm. Color laser printers print 4 to 27 ppm. Laser printers for large business users print more than 150 ppm.

What type of paper is available for a photo printer?

Many photo papers are available in various surface finishes, brightness, and weights. Surface finishes include high gloss, soft gloss, satin, or matte. The higher the brightness rating, the more brilliant the whiteness. The greater the paper weight, which is measured in pounds, the thicker the paper. In the United States, the weight of paper is stated in pounds per 500 sheets of 17 × 22-inch paper, each sheet of which equals four letter-sized sheets. For more information, visit scsite.com/dc2007/ch6/faq and then click Photo Paper.

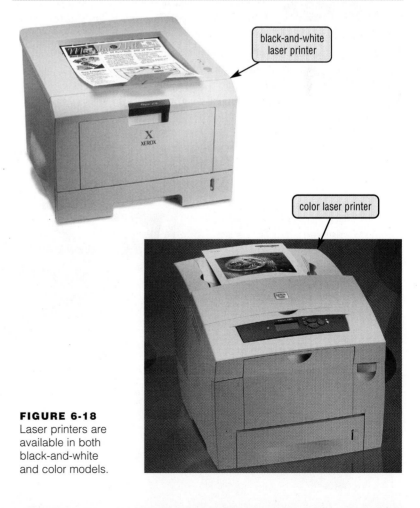

black-and-white laser printer

color laser printer

FIGURE 6-18
Laser printers are available in both black-and-white and color models.

Depending on the quality, speed, and type of laser printer, the cost ranges from a few hundred to a few thousand dollars for the home and small office user, and several hundred thousand dollars for the large business user. Color laser printers are slightly higher priced than otherwise equivalent black-and-white laser printers.

When printing a document, laser printers process and store the entire page before they actually print it. For this reason, laser printers sometimes are called page printers. Storing a page before printing requires that the laser printer has a certain amount of memory in the device.

Depending on the amount of graphics you intend to print, a laser printer for the home or small business user can have up to 544 MB of memory and a 20 GB hard disk. To print a full-page 1200-dpi picture, for instance, you might need 32 MB of memory in the printer. If the printer does not have enough memory to print the picture, either it will print as much of the picture as its memory will allow, or it will display an error message and not print any of the picture.

Laser printers use software that enables them to interpret a *page description language* (*PDL*), which tells the printer how to lay out the contents of a printed page. When you purchase a laser printer, it comes with at least one of two common page description languages: PCL or PostScript. Developed by Hewlett-Packard, a leading printer manufacturer, *PCL* (*Printer Control Language*) is a standard printer language

that supports the fonts and layout used in standard office documents. Professionals in the desktop publishing and graphic art fields commonly use *PostScript* because it is designed for complex documents with intense graphics and colors.

Operating in a manner similar to a copy machine, a laser printer creates images using a laser beam and powdered ink, called *toner*. The laser beam produces an image on a special drum inside the printer. The light of the laser alters the electrical charge on the drum wherever it hits. When this occurs, the toner sticks to the drum and then transfers to the paper through a combination of pressure and heat (Figure 6-19).

When the toner runs out, you replace the toner cartridge. Toner cartridge prices range from $50 to $100 for about 5,000 printed pages.

FAQ 6-10

How do I dispose of toner cartridges?

Do not throw them in the garbage. The housing contains iron, metal, and aluminum that is not biodegradable. The ink toner inside the cartridges contains toxic chemicals that pollute water and soil if discarded in dumps. Instead, recycle empty toner cartridges. Contact your printer manufacturer to see if it has a recycling program. For more information, visit scsite.com/dc2007/ch6/faq and then click Recycling Toner Cartridges.

FIGURE 6-19   HOW A BLACK-AND-WHITE LASER PRINTER WORKS

Step 1:
After the user sends an instruction to print a document, the drum rotates as gears and rollers feed a sheet of paper into the printer.

Step 2:
A rotating mirror deflects a low-powered laser beam across the surface of a drum.

Step 3:
The laser beam creates a charge that causes toner to stick to the drum.

Step 4:
As the drum continues to rotate and press against the paper, the toner transfers from the drum to the paper.

Step 5:
A set of rollers uses heat and pressure to fuse the toner permanently to the paper.

Thermal Printers

A **thermal printer** generates images by pushing electrically heated pins against heat-sensitive paper. Basic thermal printers are inexpensive, but the print quality is low and the images tend to fade over time. Self-service gas pumps often print gas receipts using a built-in lower-quality thermal printer.

Two special types of thermal printers have high print quality. A *thermal wax-transfer printer* generates rich, nonsmearing images by using heat to melt colored wax onto heat-sensitive paper. Thermal wax-transfer printers are more expensive than ink-jet printers, but less expensive than many color laser printers.

A *dye-sublimation printer*, sometimes called a *digital photo printer*, uses heat to transfer colored dye to specially coated paper. Most dye-sublimation printers create images that are of photographic quality (Figure 6-20). Professional applications requiring high image quality, such as photography studios, medical labs, and security identification systems, use dye-sublimation printers. These high-end printers cost thousands of dollars and print images in a wide range of sizes. Most dye-sublimation printers for the home or small business user, by contrast, typically print images in only one or two sizes and are much slower than their professional counterparts. These lower-end dye-sublimation printers are comparable in cost to a photo printer based on ink-jet technology. Some are small enough for the mobile user to carry the printer in a briefcase.

Mobile Printers

A **mobile printer** is a small, lightweight, battery-powered printer that allows a mobile user to print from a notebook computer, Tablet PC, PDA, or smart phone while traveling (Figure 6-21). Barely wider than the paper on which they print, mobile printers fit easily in a briefcase alongside a notebook computer.

Mobile printers mainly use ink-jet, thermal, thermal wax-transfer, or dye-sublimation technology. Many of these printers connect to a parallel port or USB port. Others have a built-in wireless port through which they communicate with the computer wirelessly.

FIGURE 6-20a (dye-sublimation printer for the professional)

FIGURE 6-20b (dye-sublimation printer for the home or small office user)

FIGURE 6-20 The printers shown in this figure use dye-sublimation technology to create photographic-quality output.

FIGURE 6-21 A mobile printer is a compact printer that allows the mobile user to print from a notebook computer or mobile device.

Label and Postage Printers

A **label printer** is a small printer that prints on an adhesive-type material (Figure 6-22) that can be placed on a variety of items such as envelopes, packages, CDs, DVDs, audio-cassettes, photographs, file folders, and toys. Most label printers also print bar codes. Label printers typically use thermal technology.

A *postage printer* is a special type of label printer that has a built-in digital scale and prints postage stamps. Postage printers allow users to buy and print digital postage, called *Internet postage*, right from their computer. That is, you purchase an amount of postage from an authorized postal service Web site. As you need a stamp, you print it on the postage printer. Each time a postage stamp prints, your postage account is updated.

FIGURE 6-22
A label printer.

Plotters and Large-Format Printers

Plotters are sophisticated printers used to produce high-quality drawings such as blue-prints, maps, and circuit diagrams. These printers are used in specialized fields such as engineering and drafting and usually are very costly. Current plotters use a row of charged wires (called styli) to draw an electrostatic pattern on specially coated paper and then fuse toner to the pattern. The printed image consists of a series of very small dots, which provides high-quality output.

Using ink-jet printer technology, but on a much larger scale, a **large-format printer** creates photo-realistic-quality color prints. Graphic artists use these high-cost, high-performance printers for signs, posters, and other professional quality displays (Figure 6-23).

Plotters and large-format printers can accommodate paper with widths up to 60 inches because blueprints, maps, signs, posters and other such drawings and displays can be quite large. Some plotters and large-format printers use individual sheets of paper, while others take large rolls.

Impact Printers

An **impact printer** forms characters and graphics on a piece of paper by striking a mechanism against an inked ribbon that physically contacts the paper. Impact printers characteristically are noisy because of this striking activity. These printers commonly produce *near letter quality* (*NLQ*) output, which is print quality slightly less clear than what is acceptable for business letters. Companies may use impact printers for routine jobs such as printing mailing labels, envelopes, and invoices. Impact printers also are ideal for printing multipart forms because they easily print through many layers of paper. Factories and retail counters use impact printers because these printers withstand dusty environments, vibrations, and extreme temperatures.

Two commonly used types of impact printers are dot-matrix printers and line printers.

FIGURE 6-23 Graphic artists use large-format printers to print signs, posters, and other professional quality displays.

DOT-MATRIX PRINTERS A **dot-matrix printer** is an impact printer that produces printed images when tiny wire pins on a print head mechanism strike an inked ribbon (Figure 6-24). When the ribbon presses against the paper, it creates dots that form characters and graphics.

Most dot-matrix printers use *continuous-form paper*, in which thousands of sheets of paper are connected together end to end. The pages have holes along the sides to help feed the paper through the printer.

The print head mechanism on a dot-matrix printer contains 9 to 24 pins, depending on the manufacturer and the printer model. A higher number of pins means the printer prints more dots per character, which results in higher print quality.

The speed of a dot-matrix printer is measured by the number of characters per second (cps) it can print. The speed of most dot-matrix printers ranges from 300 to 1100 characters per second (cps), depending on the desired print quality.

LINE PRINTERS A **line printer** is a high-speed impact printer that prints an entire line at a time (Figure 6-25). The speed of a line printer is measured by the number of lines per minute (lpm) it can print. Some line printers print as many as 3,000 lpm. Mainframes, servers, or networked applications, such as manufacturing, distribution, or shipping, often use line printers. These printers typically use 11 x 17-inch continuous-form paper.

Two popular types of line printers used for high-volume output are band and shuttle-matrix. A *band printer* prints fully formed characters when hammers strike a horizontal, rotating band that contains shapes of numbers, letters of the alphabet, and other characters. A *shuttle-matrix printer* functions more like a dot-matrix printer. The difference is the shuttle-matrix printer moves a series of print hammers back and forth horizontally at incredibly high speeds, as compared with standard line printers. Unlike a band printer, a shuttle-matrix printer prints characters in various fonts and font sizes.

FIGURE 6-25 A line printer is a high-speed printer often connected to a mainframe, server, or network.

continuous-form paper

FIGURE 6-24 A dot-matrix printer produces printed images when tiny pins strike an inked ribbon.

Test your knowledge of pages 310 through 319 in Quiz Yourself 6-2.

QUIZ YOURSELF 6-2

Instructions: Find the true statement below. Then, rewrite the remaining false statements so they are true.

1. A laser printer generates images by pushing electrically heated pins against heat-sensitive paper.
2. A photo printer creates images using a laser beam and powdered ink, called toner.
3. An ink-jet printer is a type of impact printer that forms characters and graphics by spraying tiny drops of liquid nitrogen onto a piece of paper.
4. Printed information is called soft copy.
5. Two commonly used types of impact printers are ink-jet printers and line printers.
6. With Bluetooth printing, a computer or other device transmits output to a printer via radio waves.

Quiz Yourself Online: To further check your knowledge of ways to print and various type of printers, visit scsite.com/dc2007/ch6/quiz and then click Objectives 5 – 7.

SPEAKERS, HEADPHONES, AND EARPHONES

An **audio output device** is a component of a computer that produces music, speech, or other sounds, such as beeps. Three commonly used audio output devices are speakers, headphones, and earphones.

Most personal computers have a small internal speaker that usually emits only low-quality sound. Thus, many personal computer users add surround sound **speakers** to their computers to generate a higher-quality sound for playing games, interacting with multimedia presentations, listening to music CDs, and viewing DVDs (Figure 6-26).

Most surround sound computer speaker systems include one or two center speakers and two or more *satellite speakers* that are positioned so sound emits from all directions. Speakers typically have tone and volume controls, allowing users to adjust settings. To boost the low bass sounds, surround sound speaker systems also include a *subwoofer*.

Surround sound systems are available in a variety of configurations. For example, a 2.1 speaker system contains two speakers and a subwoofer. A 5.1 speaker system has four satellite speakers, a center speaker, and a subwoofer. A 6.1 speaker system has four satellite speakers, a front center speaker, a rear center speaker, and a subwoofer.

In many cases, users connect the speakers and subwoofer to ports on the sound card. With wireless speakers, however, a transmitter connects to the sound card, which wirelessly communicates with the speakers. To take full advantage of high-end surround sound speaker systems, be sure the sound card in the computer is compatible with the speaker system. For a more technical discussion about how sound cards produce sound, read the High-Tech Talk article on page 328.

FIGURE 6-26 Most personal computer users add high-quality surround sound speaker systems to their computers.

When using speakers, anyone in listening distance can hear the output. In a computer laboratory or other crowded environment, speakers might not be practical. Instead, users can plug headphones or earphones in a port on the sound card, in a speaker, or on the front of the system unit. With headphones or earphones, only the individual wearing the headphones or earphones hears the sound from the computer. The difference is that **headphones** cover or are placed outside of the ear (Figure 6-27), whereas **earphones**, or *earbuds*, rest inside the ear canal (shown in Figure 6-1 on page 300).

Electronically produced voice output is growing in popularity. **Voice output** occurs when you hear a person's voice or when the computer talks to you through the speakers on the computer. In some software applications, the computer can speak the contents of a document through voice output. On the Web, you can listen to (or download and then listen to) interviews, talk shows, sporting events, news, recorded music, and live concerts from many radio and television stations. Some Web sites dedicate themselves to providing voice output, where you can hear songs, quotes, historical lectures, speeches, and books (Figure 6-28). Read Ethics & Issues 6-3 for a related discussion.

WEB LINK 6-7

Earphones
For more information, visit scsite.com/dc2007/ch6/weblink and then click Earphones.

FIGURE 6-27 In a crowded environment where speakers are not practical, users wear headphones or earphones to hear audio output.

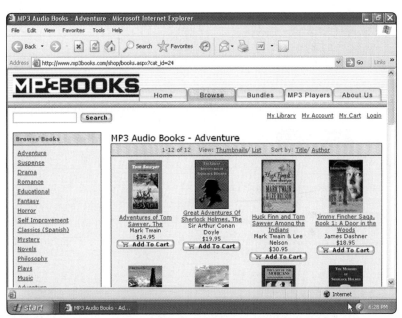

FIGURE 6-28 Through this Web site, users can purchase and then download a book in digital audio format and then listen to the book's contents via their computer's speakers or an audio player such as an iPod.

ETHICS & ISSUES 6-3

Is the Use of Digital Audio Books and E-Books Fair to All Students?

Digital audio books and e-books for notebook computers, PDAs, and even MP3 players are beginning to replace and supplement textbooks at some schools. Recently, a high school became the first to eliminate all textbooks and provide notebook computers to all 340 of its students. Internet access is required for the students to complete their school work. The computers include all course assignments and e-book versions of textbooks. Digital audio books, which are played on MP3 players such as an iPod, can include entire textbooks or supplementary course information, such as lecture notes or textbook chapter summaries. Proponents of the new wave of electronic textbooks claim that they are less expensive than traditional textbooks, alleviate back and posture problems associated with hefty textbooks, and provide more material to students in a smaller package. Opponents argue that requiring students to have access to certain technology, such as the Internet or an MP3 player, is unfair to those without the means or desire to take advantage of the technology. Also, if the school makes the electronic textbooks optional, those who can afford to take advantage of the technology may have an unfair advantage over those who can not. Would you use a digital audio book or an e-book? Why or why not? Are schools being fair to all students when the school requires access to certain technology, such as the Internet, a notebook computer, or an MP3 player? Why or why not? How can schools adopt even more technology and remain fair to all students?

Very often, voice output works with voice input. For example, when you call an airline to check the status of gates, terminals, and arrival times, your voice interacts with a computer-generated voice output. Another example is *Internet telephony*, which allows users to speak to other users over the Internet using their desktop computer, mobile computer, or mobile device.

Sophisticated programs enable the computer to converse with you. Talk into the microphone and say, "I'd like today's weather report." The computer replies, "For which city?" You reply, "Chicago." The computer says, "Sunny and 80 degrees."

OTHER OUTPUT DEVICES

In addition to display devices, printers, and speakers, many other output devices are available for specific uses and applications. These devices include fax machines and fax modems, multifunction peripherals, data projectors, and force-feedback joysticks, wheels, and gamepads.

Fax Machines and Fax Modems

A **fax machine** is a device that codes and encodes documents so they can be transmitted over telephone lines. The documents can contain text, drawings, or photographs, or can be handwritten. The term *fax* refers to a document that you send or receive via a fax machine.

A stand-alone fax machine scans an original document, converts the image into digitized data, and transmits the digitized image (Figure 6-29). A fax machine at the receiving end reads the incoming data, converts the digitized data back into an image, and prints or stores a copy of the original image.

Many computers include fax capability by using a fax modem. A *fax modem* is a modem that also allows you to send (and sometimes receive) electronic documents as faxes (Figure 6-30). A fax modem transmits computer-prepared documents, such as a word processing letter, or documents that have been digitized with a scanner or digital camera. A fax modem transmits these faxes to a fax machine or to another fax modem.

WEB LINK 6-8

Fax Modems

For more information, visit scsite.com/dc2007/ch6/weblink and then click Fax Modems.

FIGURE 6-29   A stand-alone fax machine.

PC Card fax modem

internal fax modem card in system unit

fax machine

FIGURE 6-30   A fax modem allows users to send (and sometimes receive) electronic documents as faxes to a fax machine or another computer.

When a computer (instead of a fax machine) receives a fax, users can view the fax on the screen, saving the time and expense of printing it. If necessary, you also can print the fax. The quality of a viewed or printed fax is less than that of a word processing document because the fax actually is an image. Optical character recognition (OCR) software, which was discussed in Chapter 5, enables you to convert the image to text and then edit it.

A fax modem can be an external device that plugs in a port on the system unit, an internal adapter card inserted in an expansion slot on the motherboard, a chip integrated on the motherboard, or a PC Card that inserts in a PC Card slot.

Multifunction Peripherals

A **multifunction peripheral** is a single device that looks like a copy machine but provides the functionality of a printer, scanner, copy machine, and perhaps a fax machine (Figure 6-31). The features of these devices, which sometimes are called *all-in-one devices*, vary. For example, some use color ink-jet printer technology, while others include a black-and-white laser printer.

Small offices and home office (SOHO) users have multifunction peripherals because these devices require less space than having a separate printer, scanner, copy machine, and fax machine. Another advantage of these devices is they are significantly less expensive than if you purchase each device separately. If the device breaks down, however, you lose all four functions, which is the primary disadvantage.

Data Projectors

A **data projector** is a device that takes the text and images displaying on a computer screen and projects them on a larger screen so an audience can see the image clearly (Figure 6-32). For example, many classrooms use data projectors so all students easily can see an instructor's presentation on the screen.

Some data projectors are large devices that attach to a ceiling or wall in an auditorium. Others are small portable devices. Two types of smaller, lower-cost units are LCD projectors and DLP projectors.

WEB LINK 6-9

Multifunction Peripherals

For more information, visit scsite.com/dc2007/ch6/weblink and then click Multifunction Peripherals.

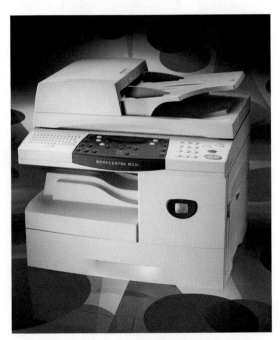

FIGURE 6-31 This multifunction peripheral is a color printer, scanner, copy machine, and fax machine all-in-one device.

computer

data projector

FIGURE 6-32 A data projector projects an image from a computer screen on a larger screen so an audience easily can see the image.

An *LCD projector*, which uses liquid crystal display technology, attaches directly to a computer, and uses its own light source to display the information shown on the computer screen. Because LCD projectors tend to produce lower-quality images, users often prefer DLP projectors for their sharper, brighter images.

A *digital light processing* (*DLP*) *projector* uses tiny mirrors to reflect light, which produces crisp, bright, colorful images that remain in focus and can be seen clearly even in a well-lit room. Some newer televisions use DLP instead of LCD or plasma technology. Read Looking Ahead 6-2 for a look at the next generation of digital cinema projectors.

Force-Feedback Joysticks, Wheels, and Gamepads

As discussed in Chapter 5, joysticks, wheels, and gamepads are input devices used to control movement and actions of a player or object in computer games, simulations, and video games. Today's joysticks, wheels, and gamepads also include *force feedback*, which is a technology that sends resistance to the device in response to actions of the user (Figure 6-33). For example, as you use the simulation software to drive from a smooth road onto a gravel alley, the steering wheel trembles or vibrates, making the driving experience as realistic as possible. In addition to games, these devices are used in practical training applications such as in the military and aviation.

LOOKING AHEAD 6-2

Digital Cinema Just the Right Picture

Computers have influenced the motion picture business by modifying how movies are produced, distributed, and exhibited. Major movie studios are part of the *Digital Cinema Initiative* (DCI), and they plan to release all of their theatrical feature films worldwide in digital format. The new technology's superior sound and visual clarity have been heralded as the greatest innovations since talkies replaced silent movies 80 years ago.

The seven larger Hollywood movie studios have developed final system requirements and specifications that enable manufacturers to develop standardized digital theater equipment. These uniform standards were created along with a compression scheme, which allows the studios to distribute the movies without having to make thousands of prints, thus saving millions of dollars annually.

With the equipment and compression standards in place, manufacturers now can intensify their efforts to develop digital cinema projectors. For more information, visit scsite.com/dc2007/ch6/looking and then click Digital Cinema.

FIGURE 6-33 Gaming devices often provide force feedback, giving the user a realistic experience.

PUTTING IT ALL TOGETHER

Many factors influence the type of output devices you should use: the type of output desired, the hardware and software in use, and the anticipated cost. Figure 6-34 outlines several suggested monitors, printers, and other output devices for various types of computer users.

SUGGESTED OUTPUT DEVICES BY USER

User	Monitor	Printer	Other
HOME	• 17- or 19-inch LCD monitor	• Ink-jet color printer; or • Photo printer	• Speakers • Headphones or earphones • Force-feedback joystick, wheel, and/or gamepad
SMALL OFFICE/ HOME OFFICE	• 19- or 21-inch LCD monitor • Color LCD screen on Tablet PC, PDA, or smart phone	• Multifunction peripheral; or • Ink-jet color printer; or • Laser printer (black-and-white or color) • Label printer • Postage printer	• Fax machine • Speakers
MOBILE	• 15.7-inch LCD screen on notebook computer • Color LCD screen on Tablet PC, PDA, or smart phone	• Mobile color printer • Ink-jet color printer; or • Laser printer for in-office use (black-and-white or color) • Photo printer	• Fax modem • Headphones or earphones • DLP data projector
POWER	• 23-inch LCD monitor	• Laser printer (black-and-white or color) • Plotter or large-format printer; or • Photo printer; or • Dye-sublimation printer	• Fax machine or fax modem • Speakers • Headphones or earphones
LARGE BUSINESS	• 19- or 21-inch LCD monitor • Color LCD screen on Tablet PC, PDA, or smart phone	• High-speed laser printer • Laser printer, color • Line printer (for large reports from a mainframe) • Label printer	• Fax machine or fax modem • Speakers • Headphones or earphones • DLP data projector

FIGURE 6-34   This table recommends suggested output devices for various types of users.

OUTPUT DEVICES FOR PHYSICALLY CHALLENGED USERS

As Chapter 5 discussed, the growing presence of computers has generated an awareness of the need to address computing requirements for those with physical limitations. Read Ethics & Issues 6-4 for a related discussion.

For users with mobility, hearing, or vision disabilities, many different types of output devices are available. Hearing-impaired users, for example, can instruct programs to display words instead of sounds. With the Windows XP operating system, users also can set options to make programs easier to use. The Magnifier command, for example, enlarges text and other items in a window on the screen (Figure 6-35).

Visually impaired users can change Windows XP settings, such as increasing the size or changing the color of the text to make the words easier to read. Instead of using a monitor, blind users can work with voice output. That is, the computer reads the information that is displayed on the screen. Another alternative is a *Braille printer*, which prints information on paper in Braille (Figure 6-36).

FIGURE 6-36
A Braille printer.

location of line that contains mouse pointer is magnified at top of screen

FIGURE 6-35 The Magnifier command in Windows XP enlarges text and other on-screen items for visually impaired users.

ETHICS & ISSUES 6-4

Should Web Sites Be Held Accountable for Accessibility Levels for Physically Challenged People?

The World Wide Web Consortium (W3C) has published accessibility guidelines for Web sites. The guidelines specify measures that Web site designers can take to increase accessibility for physically challenged users. Among its guidelines, the W3C urges Web site designers to provide equivalent text for audio or visual content, include features that allow elements to be activated and understood using a variety of input and output devices, and make the user interface follow principles of accessible design. A recent report found that most Web sites do not meet all of the W3C guidelines. This failure is disappointing, because many physically challenged users could benefit from the Web's capability to bring products and services into the home. Ironically, a survey discovered that more than 50 percent of the Web sites run by disability organizations also fail to meet the W3C guidelines. Critics contend that these Web sites neglect the needs of their users and fail to lead by example. Web site apologists contend, however, that many sponsoring organizations lack the funding necessary to comply with the guidelines. Should the government require that all Web sites meet the W3C accessibility guidelines? Why or why not? Do Web sites run by disability organizations have a moral obligation to meet the guidelines? Why? What can be done to encourage people and organizations to make their Web sites more accessible?

Test your knowledge of pages 320 through 327 in Quiz Yourself 6-3.

QUIZ YOURSELF 6-3

Instructions: Find the true statement below. Then, rewrite the remaining false statements so they are true.

1. A digital light processing (DLP) projector uses tiny lightbulbs to reflect light.
2. A stand-alone fax machine scans an original document, converts the image into digitized data, and transmits the digitized image.
3. Many personal computer users add surround sound printer systems to their computers to generate a higher-quality sound.
4. Multifunction peripherals require more space than having a separate printer, scanner, copy machine, and fax machine.
5. Some joysticks, wheels, and gamepads include real-time action, which is a technology that sends resistance to the device in response to actions of the user.

Quiz Yourself Online: To further check your knowledge of speakers, headphones, and earphones; other output devices; and output for physically challenged users, visit scsite.com/dc2007/ch6/quiz and then click Objectives 8 – 10.

CHAPTER SUMMARY

Computers process and organize data (input) into information (output). This chapter described the various methods of output and several commonly used output devices. Output devices presented were flat-panel displays; CRT monitors; printers; speakers, headphones, and earphones; fax machines and fax modems; multifunction peripherals; data projectors; and force-feedback joysticks, wheels, and gamepads.

Graphic Designer/Illustrator

Graphic designers and *graphic illustrators* are artists, but many do not create original works. Instead, they portray visually the ideas of their clients. Illustrators create pictures for books and other publications and sometimes for commercial products, such as greeting cards. They work in fields such as fashion, technology, medicine, animation, or even cartoons. Illustrators often prepare their images on a computer. Designers combine practical skills with artistic talent to convert abstract concepts into designs for products and advertisements. Many use computer-aided design (CAD) tools to create, visualize, and modify designs. Designer careers usually are specialized in particular areas, such as:

- Graphic designers — book covers, stationery, and CD covers
- Commercial and industrial designers — products and equipment
- Costume and theater designers — costumes and settings for theater and television
- Interior designers — layout, decor, and furnishings of homes and buildings
- Merchandise displayers — commercial displays
- Fashion designers — clothing, shoes, and other fashion accessories

Certificate, two-year, four-year, and masters-level educational programs are available within design areas. About 30 percent of graphic illustrators/designers choose to freelance, while others work with advertising agencies, publishing companies, design studios, or specialized departments within large companies. Salaries range from $30,000 to $80,000-plus, based on experience and educational background. For more information, visit scsite.com/dc2007/ch6/careers and then click Graphic Designer/Illustrator.

High-Tech Talk

SOUND CARDS: BRINGING YOUR COMPUTER TO LIFE

Speakers, headphones, earphones, and other audio output devices rely on sound cards or integrated sound card functionality to produce sounds such as music, voice, beeps, and chimes. Sound cards contain the chips and circuitry to record and play back a wide range of sounds using analog-to-digital conversion and digital-to-analog conversion, as described in the Chapter 1 High-Tech Talk on page 38.

To record a sound, the sound card must be connected to an input device, such as a microphone or audio CD player. The input device sends the sound to the sound card as an analog signal. The analog signal flows to the sound card's analog-to-digital-converter (ADC). The ADC converts the signal into digital (binary) data of 1s and 0s by sampling the signal at set intervals.

The analog sound is a continuous waveform, with a range of frequencies and volumes. To represent the waveform in a recording, the computer would have to store the waveform's value at every instant in time. Because this is not possible, the sound is recorded using a sampling process. *Sampling* involves breaking up the waveform into set intervals and representing all values during that interval with a single value.

Several factors in the sampling process — sampling rate, audio resolution, and mono or stereo recording — affect the quality of the recorded sound during playback.

- *Sampling rate*, also called sampling frequency, refers to the number of times per second the sound is recorded. The more frequently a sound is recorded, the smaller the intervals and the better the quality. The sampling frequency used for audio CDs, for example, is 44,100 times per second, which is expressed in hertz (Hz) as 44,100 Hz. Cassette-tape-quality multimedia files use a sampling rate of 22,050 Hz; and basic Windows sounds use a sampling rate of 11,025 Hz.

- *Audio resolution* — defined as a bit rate such as 8-bit, 16-bit, or 24-bit — refers to the number of bytes used to represent the sound at any one interval. A sound card using 8-bit resolution, for example, represents a sound with any 1 of 256 values (2^8). A 16-bit sound card uses any 1 of 65,536 values (2^{16}) for each interval. Using a higher resolution provides a finer measurement scale, which results in a more accurate representation of the value of each sample and better sound quality. With 8-bit resolution, the sound quality is like that of an AM radio; 16-bit resolution gives CD-quality sound, and a 24-bit resolution is used for high-quality digital audio editing.

- Mono or stereo recording refers to the number of channels used during recording. *Mono* means that the same sound emits from both the left and right speaker during playback; *stereo* means that two separate channels exist in the recording: one each for the left and right speakers. Most sound cards support stereo recording for better playback.

After the ADC converts the analog sound through sampling, the digital data flows to the digital signal processor (DSP) on the sound card. The DSP then requests instructions from the sound card's memory chip on how to process the digital data. Typically, the DSP then compresses the digital data to save space. Finally, the DSP sends the compressed data to the computer's main processor, which stores the data in .WAV, .MP3, or other audio file format.

To play a recorded sound, such as a WAV, an MP3, or a CD track, the main processor retrieves the sound file from a hard disk, CD, or other storage device (Figure 6-37). The processor then sends the digital data to the DSP, which decompresses the data and looks to the memory chip to determine how to recreate the sound.

The DSP then sends the digital signals to the sound card's digital-to-analog converter (DAC), which converts the sound in digital format back to an analog electrical voltage. An output device, such as a speaker, uses an amplifier to strengthen the electrical voltage. This causes the speaker's cone to vibrate, recreating the sound.

All of this happens in an instant. The next time your computer beeps or chirps, consider the complex process required to make that simple sound. Then, insert your favorite CD and hear your computer come to life with the sweet music provided courtesy of the sound card. For more information, visit scsite.com/dc2007/ch6/tech and then click Sound Cards.

CD

sound

main processor

intel pentium D

sound in digital format

sound card

DSP

DAC/ADC

digital signals

analog electrical voltage

sound to speaker

amplifier

speakers

FIGURE 6-37
The path of sound from media to speakers.

Companies on the Cutting Edge

HEWLETT-PACKARD
TECHNOLOGY FOR BUSINESS AND LIFE

If you have printed a document recently, chances are the printer manufacturer was *Hewlett-Packard (HP)*. Market analysts estimate that 60 percent of printers sold today bear the HP logo, and HP says it ships one million printers each week.

HP is noted for a range of high-quality printers, disk storage systems, UNIX and Windows servers, and notebook, desktop, and handheld computers. In 2005, HP acquired Snapfish, an online photo service, and also unveiled the world's fastest home photo printing devices.

William Hewlett and David Packard started the company in a one-car garage in 1939 with the goal of manufacturing test and measurement equipment. HP has been developing personal information devices, including calculators and computers, for more than 30 years. For more information, visit scsite.com/dc2007/ch6/companies and then click Hewlett-Packard.

VIEWSONIC
VISUAL TECHNOLOGY LEADER

We live in a "display-centric world" according to industry leaders at *ViewSonic*. Our computer displays, whether viewed on a PDA, a desktop monitor, or a flat-panel screen, influence how we access and control the informative and entertaining output.

ViewSonic's products focus on visual technology, including CRT and LCD monitors, data projectors, plasma screens, and high-definition television. The company also designs mobile products, such as Tablet PCs and wireless monitors.

President and CEO James Chu founded ViewSonic in 1987 with the goal of increasing workers' productivity while creating an ergonomically comfortable work-space. He developed the company's logo consisting of three colorful Gouldian finches to represent outstanding quality and value, radiant color, and crisp resolution. For more information, visit scsite.com/dc2007/ch6/companies and then click ViewSonic.

Technology Trailblazers

STEVE JOBS
APPLE COMPUTER AND PIXAR COFOUNDER

Steve Jobs has an uncompromising drive for perfection. He helped build the first desktop personal computer, cofounded Apple Computer Corporation, marketed a revolutionary operating system, and became a millionaire all before his 35th birthday.

Under his direction, Apple took advantage of advances in both memory and battery technology to develop the iPod, the world's most popular digital audio player. He also is known as being a brilliant motivator and having the ability to bring out the best performance from his employees.

Under Jobs's supervision, Pixar's award-winning animation studios have created some of the most beloved animated films, such as *Toy Story*, *Toy Story 2*, *A Bug's Life*, *Monsters, Inc.*, and *Finding Nemo*. For more information, visit scsite.com/dc2007/ch6/people and then click Steve Jobs.

DONNA DUBINSKY
Palm Cofounder

PDAs are ubiquitous, partly due to the efforts of *Donna Dubinsky*. In the mid-1990s, she sensed that people wanted to own an electronic version of their paper appointment books. She and Jeff Hawkins introduced the original Palm Pilot prototype made of mahogany and cardboard at Palm Computing in 1996. Sales of more than two million units made the Palm Pilot the most rapidly adopted new computing product ever manufactured.

Dubinsky and Hawkins left Palm in 1998 to cofound Handspring, where they introduced several successful products, including the Treo smart phone. In 2003, Handspring merged with the Palm hardware group to create palmOne, now called Palm.

Dubinsky currently serves as CEO and chairman of Numenta, Inc., which develops computer memory. For more information, visit scsite.com/dc2007/ch6/people and then click Donna Dubinsky.

Chapter Review

The Chapter Review section summarizes the concepts presented in this chapter. To listen to the audio version of this Chapter Review, visit scsite.com/dc2007/ch6/review. To obtain help from other students regarding any subject in this chapter, visit scsite.com/dc2007/ch6/forum and post your thoughts or questions.

(1) What Are the Four Categories of Output? **Output** is data that has been processed into a useful form. Four categories of output are text, graphics, audio, and video. An **output device** is any hardware component that conveys information to one or more people.

(2) What Are LCD Monitors, LCD Screens, and Plasma Monitors? LCD monitors, LCD screens, and plasma monitors are types of flat-panel displays. A *flat-panel display* is a display with a shallow depth that typically uses LCD or gas plasma technology. An **LCD** monitor is a desktop monitor that uses a liquid crystal display to produce images. A **liquid crystal display** (**LCD**) uses a liquid compound to present information on a display. A **plasma monitor** is a display device that uses gas plasma technology, which substitutes a layer of gas for the liquid crystal material in an LCD monitor. Although some game consoles include a small LCD screen (usually 5 inches or smaller), home users often prefer the larger television displays for game playing, watching movies, and browsing the Internet on a television connected to a game console.

(3) What Is a CRT Monitor, and What Factors Affect Its Quality? A **CRT monitor** is a desktop monitor that contains a *cathode-ray tube (CRT)*. The screen on the front of the CRT is coated with tiny dots of red, green, and blue phosphor that combine to make up each *pixel*, which is a single element in an electronic image. As an electron beam inside the CRT moves back and forth across the back of the screen, the dots glow, which produces an image. The quality of a CRT monitor depends largely on its resolution, dot pitch, and refresh rate. **Resolution** is the number of horizontal and vertical pixels in a display device. *Dot pitch*, sometimes called *pixel pitch*, is the distance in millimeters between pixels on a display device. *Refresh rate* is the speed that a monitor redraws the images on the screen.

(4) How Are Graphics Chips and CRT Monitors Related? Many CRT monitors use an analog signal to produce an image. A cable on the CRT monitor plugs in a port on the system unit, which enables communications from a graphics chip. If the graphics chip is on a video card, the card converts digital output from the computer into an analog video signal and sends the signal through a cable to the CRT monitor, which displays output on the screen.

> *connect*   Visit scsite.com/dc2007/ch6/quiz or click the Quiz Yourself button. Click Objectives 1 – 4.

(5) What Are the Various Ways to Print? Users can print by connecting a computer to a printer with a cable that plugs in a port on the computer. *Bluetooth printing* uses radio waves to transmit output to a printer. With *infrared* printing, a computer or other device communicates with the printer via infrared light waves. Some digital cameras connect directly to a printer via a cable; others store images on media cards that can be removed and inserted in the printer. Networked computers can communicate with the network printer via cables or wirelessly.

(6) How Is a Nonimpact Printer Different from an Impact Printer? A **printer** is an output device that produces text and graphics on a physical medium, such as paper or transparency film. A **nonimpact printer** forms characters and graphics on a piece of paper without actually striking the paper. Commonly used nonimpact printers are ink-jet printers, photo printers, laser printers, thermal printers, mobile printers, label and postage printers, plotters, and large-format printers. An **impact printer** forms characters and graphics on a piece of paper by striking a mechanism against an inked ribbon that physically contacts the paper. Two commonly used types of impact printers are a **dot-matrix printer** and a **line printer**.

Chapter Review

⑦ What Are Ink-Jet Printers, Photo Printers, Laser Printers, Thermal Printers, Mobile Printers, Label and Postage Printers, and Plotters and Large-Format Printers?   An ink-jet **printer** is a type of nonimpact printer that forms characters and graphics by spraying tiny drops of liquid ink onto a piece of paper. A **photo printer** is a color printer that produces photo-lab-quality pictures. A **laser printer** is a high-speed, high-quality nonimpact printer that operates in a manner similar to a copy machine, creating images using a laser beam and powdered ink, called *toner*. A **thermal printer** generates images by pushing electronically heated pins against heat-sensitive paper. A **mobile printer** is a small, lightweight, battery-powered printer that allows a mobile user to print from a notebook computer. A **label printer** is a small printer that prints on an adhesive-type material that can be placed on a variety of items. A *postage printer* is a special type of label printer that has a built-in scale and prints postage stamps. **Plotters** are sophisti-cated printers used to produce high-quality drawings. A **large-format printer** uses ink-jet technology on a large scale to create photo-realistic-quality color prints.

> *connect*
> Visit scsite.com/dc2007/ch6/quiz or click the Quiz Yourself button. Click Objectives 5 – 7.

⑧ How Are Speakers, Headphones, and Earphones Used?   Speakers, headphones, and earphones are three commonly used audio output devices. An **audio output device** is a component of a computer that produces sound. Many personal computer users add stereo **speakers** to their computers to generate a higher-quality sound. With headphones or earphones, only the individual wearing the headphones or earphones hears the sound from the computer. The difference is that **headphones** cover or are placed outside of the ear, whereas **earphones**, or *earbuds*, rest inside the ear canal.

⑨ What Are Fax Machines and Fax Modems, Multifunction Peripherals, Data Projectors, Joysticks, Wheels, and Gamepads?   A **fax machine** is a device that codes and encodes documents so they can be transmitted over telephone lines. A document sent or received via a fax machine is a *fax*. Many computers include fax capability using a *fax modem,* which is a modem that allows you to send (and sometimes receive) electronic documents as faxes. A **multifunction peripheral** is a single device that looks like a copy machine but provides the func-tionality of a printer, scanner, copy machine, and per-haps a fax machine. A **data projector** is a device that takes the text and images displaying on a computer screen and projects them onto a larger screen so an audience of people can see the image clearly. Joysticks, wheels, and gamepads are input devices used to control actions of a player or vehicle. Today's joy-sticks, wheels, and gamepads also include *force feedback*, which is a technology that sends resistance to the device in response to actions of the user.

⑩ What Output Options Are Available for Physically Challenged Users?
Hearing-impaired users can instruct programs to display words instead of sound. With Windows XP, visually impaired users can enlarge items on the screen and change other settings, such as increasing the size or changing the color of text to make words easier to read. Blind users can work with voice output instead of a monitor. Another alternative is a *Braille printer*, which prints information in Braille on paper.

> *connect*
> Visit scsite.com/dc2007/ch6/quiz or click the Quiz Yourself button. Click Objectives 8 – 10.

Key Terms

You should know the Primary Terms and be familiar with the Secondary Terms. Use the list below to help focus your study. To further enhance your understanding of the Key Terms in this chapter, visit scsite.com/dc2007/ch6/terms. See an example of and a definition for each term, and access current and additional information about the term from the Web.

Primary Terms

(shown in bold-black characters in the chapter)

audio output device (320)
CRT monitor (307)
data projector (323)
display device (302)
dot-matrix printer (319)
earphones (321)
ENERGY STAR program (307)
fax machine (322)
HDTV (306)
headphones (321)
impact printer (318)
ink-jet printer (312)
label printer (318)
large-format printer (318)
laser printer (315)
LCD monitor (302)
line printer (319)
liquid crystal display (LCD) (304)
mobile printer (317)
monitor (302)
multifunction peripheral (323)
nonimpact printer (312)
output (300)
output device (301)
photo printer (314)
plasma monitor (306)
plotters (318)
printer (310)
resolution (304)
speakers (320)
thermal printer (317)
voice output (321)

Secondary Terms

(shown in italic characters in the chapter)

active-matrix display (304)
all-in-one devices (323)
band printer (319)
bit depth (306)
Bluetooth printing (311)
Braille printer (326)
candela (304)
cathode-ray tube (CRT)
 (307)
color depth (306)
continuous-form paper
 (319)
contrast ratio (304)
digital light processing
 (DLP) projector (324)
digital photo printer (317)
digital television (DTV)
 (306)
display (302)
dot pitch (304)
dots per inch (dpi) (313)
DVI (Digital Video
 Interface) port (305)
dye-sublimation printer
 (317)
earbuds (321)
electromagnetic radiation
 (EMR) (308)
fax (322)
fax modem (322)
flat-panel monitor (302)
flat-panel display (302)
footprint (302)
force feedback (324)
graphics processing unit
 (305)
hard copy (310)
high-definition television
 (306)
infrared printing (311)
Internet postage (318)

Internet telephony (322)
landscape orientation (310)
LCD projector (324)
monochrome (302)
MPR II (308)
native resolution (304)
near letter quality (NLQ)
 (318)
nit (304)
organic LED (OLED) (304)
page description language
 (PDL) (316)
passive-matrix display
 (304)
PCL (Printer Control
 Language) (316)
pixel (304)
pixel pitch (304)
portrait orientation (310)
postage printer (318)
PostScript (316)
printout (310)
refresh rate (308)
response time (304)
satellite speakers (320)
scan rate (308)
shuttle-matrix printer (319)
soft copy (302)
subwoofer (320)
S-video port (305)
SVGA (305)
SXGA (305)
TFT (thin-film transistor)
 display (304)
thermal wax-transfer
 printer (317)
toner (316)
UGA (305)
viewable size (307)
XGA (305)

Checkpoint

Use the Checkpoint exercises to check your knowledge level of the chapter. The Beyond the Book exercises will help broaden your understanding of the concepts presented in this chapter. To complete the Checkpoint exercises interactively, visit scsite.com/dc2007/ch6/check.

Label the Figure

Identify the ports on this video card.

a. S-video port
b. DVI port
c. standard monitor port

1. ___
2. ___
3. ___

True/False

Mark T for True and F for False. (See page numbers in parentheses.)

_____ 1. A computer generates several types of output, depending on the hardware and software being used and the requirements of the user. (300)

_____ 2. Information on a display device sometimes is called soft copy. (302)

_____ 3. Most mobile computers and devices do not integrate the display and other components into the same physical case. (302)

_____ 4. Some PDAs and other mobile devices use monochrome displays because they require less battery power. (302)

_____ 5. A pixel is a unit of visible light intensity equal to one candela per square meter. (304)

_____ 6. LCD monitors use an analog signal to produce a picture. (305)

_____ 7. With game consoles, the output device often is a television. (307)

_____ 8. A printout in portrait orientation is taller than it is wide. (310)

_____ 9. With Bluetooth printing, a computer or other device transmits output to a printer via infrared light waves. (311)

_____ 10. Many photo printers use ink-jet technology. (314)

_____ 11. A laser printer is a high-speed, low-quality nonimpact printer. (315)

_____ 12. A multifunction peripheral is a single device that looks like a copy machine but provides the functionality of a printer, scanner, copy machine, and perhaps a fax machine. (323)

Checkpoint

 Multiple Choice   Select the best answer. (See page numbers in parentheses.)

1. Examples of text-based documents are _____. (300)
   a. drawings, clip art, and photographs
   b. home movies and live performances
   c. music, narrations, and speeches
   d. letters, reports, and mailing labels

2. A passive-matrix display _____ an active-matrix display. (304)
   a. uses more transistors than
   b. requires more power than
   c. often is not as bright as
   d. is more expensive than

3. _____ uses organic molecules that produce an even brighter, easier-to-read display than standard TFT displays. (304)
   a. HDTV   b. OLED
   c. LCD   d. LED

4. _____ describes the difference in light intensity between the brightest white and darkest black that can be displayed on an LCD monitor. (304)
   a. Contrast ratio
   b. Brightness
   c. Dot pitch
   d. Bit depth

5. For a display device to show images as defined by a video standard, both the display device and the graphics processing unit must _____. (305)
   a. be the same size
   b. contain a heat sink or fan
   c. use an analog signal
   d. support the same video standard

6. Plasma monitors offer larger screens _____. (306)
   a. but lower display quality than LCD monitors and are less expensive
   b. but lower display quality than LCD monitors and are more expensive
   c. and higher display quality than LCD monitors but are less expensive
   d. and higher display quality than LCD monitors but are more expensive

7. The viewable size of a monitor is the _____ measurement of the actual viewing area provided by the screen in the monitor. (307)
   a. horizontal
   b. vertical
   c. three-dimensional
   d. diagonal

8. Printer resolution is measured by the number of _____ a printer can print. (313)
   a. pages per minute (ppm)
   b. dots per inch (dpi)
   c. lines per minute (lpm)
   d. pixels per inch (ppi)

9. Laser printers usually cost _____. (315)
   a. more than ink-jet printers and are faster
   b. less than ink-jet printers and are faster
   c. more than ink-jet printers and are slower
   d. less than ink-jet printers and are slower

10. The speed of a(n) _____ is measured by the number of characters per second (cps) it can print. (319)
    a. dot-matrix printer
    b. laser printer
    c. ink-jet printer
    d. thermal printer

11. _____ occurs when you hear a person's voice or when the computer talks to you through the speakers on the computer. (321)
    a. Voice input
    b. Force feedback
    c. Voice output
    d. Internet telephony

12. A(n) _____ is a device that takes the text and images displaying on a computer screen and projects them on a larger screen so an audience can see the image clearly. (323)
    a. DLP projector
    b. LCD projector
    c. data projector
    d. all of the above

13. The disadvantage of multifunction peripherals is that _____. (323)
    a. they require more space than having separate devices
    b. if the multifunction peripheral breaks down, all functions are lost
    c. they are significantly more expensive than purchasing each device separately
    d. all of the above

14. The _____ command in Windows XP enlarges text and other on-screen items for visually impaired users. (326)
    a. Magnifier
    b. On-Screen Keyboard
    c. Narrator
    d. Utility Manager

Checkpoint

Matching

Match the terms with their definitions. (See page numbers in parentheses.)

_____ 1. soft copy (302)

_____ 2. LCD monitor (302)

_____ 3. pixel pitch (304)

_____ 4. nit (304)

_____ 5. bit depth (306)

_____ 6. electromagnetic radiation (EMR) (308)

_____ 7. hard copy (310)

_____ 8. nonimpact printer (312)

_____ 9. LCD projector (324)

_____ 10. DLP projector (324)

a. information on a display device that exists electronically and appears for a temporary period

b. printed information that exists physically and is a more permanent form of output

c. distance in millimeters between pixels on a display device

d. unit of visible light intensity equal to one candela per square meter

e. changes the brightness and contrast of pixels surrounding each letter

f. the number of bits used to store information about each pixel

g. attaches directly to a computer and uses its own light source to display information

h. a desktop monitor that uses a liquid crystal display to produce images

i. magnetic field that travels at the speed of light

j. forms characters and graphics on a piece of paper without actually striking the paper

k. uses many shades of gray from white to black to enhance the quality of graphics

l. uses tiny mirrors to reflect light, which produces crisp, bright, colorful images

Short Answer

Write a brief answer to each of the following questions.

1. What determines the quality of an LCD monitor or LCD screen? _____ What are the differences between active-matrix and passive-matrix displays? _____

2. What factors determine a CRT monitor's quality? _____ What is the ENERGY STAR program? _____

3. How is portrait orientation different from landscape orientation? _____ What is continuous-form paper? _____

4. What are two types of wireless printing technology? _____ How do they differ in how they communicate with a computer or other device? _____

5. What are two common types of impact printers? _____ What are the differences between the two types? _____

Beyond the Book

Read the following book elements, learn more about each using the Web, and then write a brief report.

1. Ethics & Issues — Is It Ethical to Refill an Ink-Jet Cartridge? (314), Who Is Responsible for Stopping Counterfeiting? (315), Is the Use of Digital Audio Books and E-Books Fair to All Students? (321), or Should Web Sites Be Held Accountable for Accessibility Levels for Physically Challenged People? (327)

2. Career Corner — Graphic Designer/Illustrator (327)

3. Companies on the Cutting Edge — Hewlett-Packard (329) or ViewSonic (329)

4. FAQs (302, 303, 306, 307, 308, 312, 315, 316)

5. High-Tech Talk — Sound Cards: Bringing Your Computer to Life (328)

6. Looking Ahead — Rollable Displays Lock and Roll (304), or Digital Cinema Just the Right Picture (324)

7. Making Use of the Web — Government (122)

8. Picture Yourself Saving Money Using a Computer (298)

9. Technology Trailblazers — Steve Jobs and Donna Dubinsky (329)

10. Web Links (304, 306, 311, 314, 316, 321, 322, 323, 324)

Learn It Online

Use the Learn It Online exercises to reinforce your understanding of the chapter concepts. To access the Learn It Online exercises, visit scsite.com/dc2007/ch6/learn.

① At the Movies — Plasma vs. LCD

To view the Plasma vs. LCD movie, click the number 1 button. Locate your video and click the corresponding High-Speed or Dial-Up link, depending on your Internet connection. Watch the movie and then complete the exercise by answering the questions that follow. Basic differences exist between plasma and LCD-display TVs, and those differences may affect your choice as a consumer. By understanding those differences, you will be able to choose the display options that best suit your needs. Compare and contrast the two technologies using simple criteria such as cost and size. What are the pros and cons of each display technology? How does a plasma TV display its picture? What are the disadvantages of plasma?

② At the Movies — Essential Dorm Room Gadgets

To view the Essential Dorm Room Gadgets movie, click the number 2 button. Locate your video and click the corresponding High-Speed or Dial-Up link, depending on your Internet connection. Watch the movie and then complete the exercise by answering the questions that follow. As a rule, most college students have little, if any, disposable income. Some great and affordable gadgets are available, however, that can make a dorm room more functional for study and more fun for play. How would a network interface improve a dorm room?

③ Student Edition Labs — Peripheral Devices

Click the number 3 button. A new browser window will open, displaying the Student Edition Labs. Follow the on-screen instructions to complete the Peripheral Devices Lab. When finished, click the Exit button. If required, submit your results to your instructor.

④ Student Edition Labs — Working with Graphics

Click the number 4 button. A new browser window will open, displaying the Student Edition Labs. Follow the on-screen instructions to complete the Working with Graphics Lab. When finished, click the Exit button. If required, submit your results to your instructor.

⑤ Practice Test

Click the number 5 button. Answer each question. When completed, enter your name and click the Grade Test button to submit the quiz for grading. Make a note of any missed questions. If required, submit your results to your instructor.

⑥ Who Wants To Be a Computer Genius²?

Click the number 6 button to find out if you are a computer genius. Directions about how to play the game will be displayed. When you are ready to play, click the Play button. Submit your score to your instructor.

⑦ Wheel of Terms

Click the number 7 button to reinforce important terms you learned in this chapter by playing the Shelly Cashman Series version of this popular game. Directions about how to play the game will be displayed. When you are ready to play, click the Play button. Submit your score to your instructor.

Learn It Online

⑧ DC Track and Field

Click the number 8 button to use what you have learned in this chapter to compete against other students in three track and field events. Directions about how to play the game will be displayed. When you are ready to play, click the start first event button. If required, submit your score to your instructor.

⑨ You're Hired!

Click the number 9 button to use what you have learned in this chapter to embark on the path to a career in computers. Directions about how to play the game will be displayed. When you are ready to play, click the begin game button. If required, submit your score to your instructor.

⑩ Crossword Puzzle Challenge

Click the number 10 button. Complete the puzzle to reinforce skills you learned in this chapter. Directions about how to play the game will be displayed. When you are ready to play, click the Submit button. Submit the completed puzzle to your instructor.

⑪ Lab Exercises

Click the number 11 button. When the Lab Exercises menu appears, click the exercise assigned by your instructor. A new browser window will open. Follow the on-screen instructions to complete the exercise. When finished, click the Exit button. If required, submit your results to your instructor.

⑫ Choosing a Printer

The printer is a key component of any new personal computer that you purchase. Whether you are printing black-and-white reports or producing photo-lab-quality pictures, determining which printer is best for your individual needs requires some research. Printers are available in a range of speeds and capabilities. Click the number 12 button for a tutorial about how to select the printer that is best for your particular requirements.

⑬ In the News

Display device technology continues to advance. Not long ago, computer users would have considered connecting their $1,000 computers to a color television instead of paying outrageous prices for a color monitor. Today, you can purchase a 20-inch monitor that is faster and sharper than that color television for less than $300. Yet, as prices fall, consumers surely will purchase the display devices for HDTV and crystal-clear Internet access. Click the number 13 button and then read a news article about a new or improved output device. What is the device? Who manufactures it? How is the output device better than, or different from, earlier devices? Who do you think is most likely to use the device? Why?

⑭ Chapter Discussion Forum

Select an objective from this chapter on page 299 about which you would like more information. Click the number 14 button and post a short message listing a meaningful message title accompanied by one or more questions concerning the selected objective. In two days, return to the threaded discussion by clicking the number 14 button. Submit to your instructor your original message and at least one response to your message.

⑮ Howstuffworks.com

Click the number 15 button to learn how to use Howstuffworks.com to discover how a laser printer works in comparison to an ink-jet printer. Follow the instructions to get to the computer peripherals page. Read the articles about how both types of printers work. Write a report listing the major differences between the printers. Which type of printer would you recommend to your fellow students? Why? Print your report and submit it to your instructor.

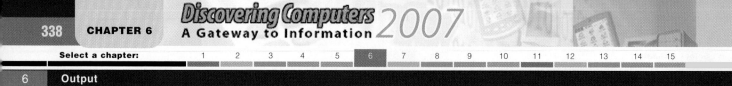
Learn How To

Use the Learn How To activities to learn fundamental skills when using a computer and accompanying technology. Complete the exercises and submit them to your instructor. To see a video of a Learn How To activity, visit scsite.com/dc2007/ch6/howto.

LEARN HOW TO 1: Adjust the Sound on a Computer

Every computer today contains a sound card and associated hardware and software that allow you to play and record sound. You can adjust the sound by completing the following steps:

1. Click the Start button on the Windows taskbar and then click Control Panel on the Start menu.
2. When the Control Panel window opens, click Sounds, Speech, and Audio Devices and then click Adjust the system volume; or double-click Sounds and Audio Devices. *The Sounds and Audio Devices Properties dialog box is displayed (Figure 6-38).*
3. To adjust the volume for all devices connected to the sound card, drag the Device volume slider left or right to decrease or increase the volume.
4. If you want to mute the sound on the computer, click the Mute check box so it contains a checkmark, and then click the OK button or the Apply button.
5. If you want to place the volume icon on the Windows taskbar, click the Place volume icon in the taskbar check box so it contains a checkmark, and then click the OK button or the Apply button. You can click the icon on the taskbar to set the volume level or mute the sound.
6. To make sound and other adjustments for each device on the computer, click the Advanced button in the Device volume area. *The Play Control or Recording Control window opens, depending on prior choices for this window (Figure 6-39).*
7. If the Recording Control window is opened, click Options on the window menu bar, click Properties on the Options menu, click the Playback option button, and then click the OK button.
8. In the Play Control window, Play Control volume is the same as the volume adjusted in the Sounds and Audio Devices Properties dialog box. The other columns in the Play Control window refer to devices found on the computer. To select the columns that are displayed, click Options on the menu bar and then click Properties. With Playback selected, place checkmarks in the check boxes for those devices you want to be displayed in the Control window.
9. To adjust volumes, drag the Volume sliders up or down for each device. To adjust the speaker balance, drag the Balance sliders.

Sounds and Audio Devices Properties dialog box

type of sound card

Device volume slider

Advanced button

Mute check box

Place volume icon in the taskbar check box

Apply button

OK button

FIGURE 6-38

Play Control window

Balance sliders

Options menu

Play Control Volume slider

Advanced button

Volume sliders

FIGURE 6-39

Learn How To

10. If the Advanced button is not displayed in the Play Control window, click Options on the menu bar and then click Advanced Controls on the Options menu. Click the Advanced button. You can control the Bass and Treble settings by using the sliders in the Tone Controls area of the Advanced Controls for Play Control dialog box.

Exercise

1. Open the Control Panel window and then display the Sounds and Audio Devices Properties dialog box. What kind of sound card is on the computer? Click the Place volume icon in the taskbar check box and then click the Apply button. What change did you notice on the Windows taskbar? Do the same thing again. What change occurred on the Windows taskbar? Click the Advanced button in the Device volume area. Ensure the Play Control window is open. What devices are chosen for control in the Play Control window? How would you change what devices are chosen? Submit your answers to your instructor.

LEARN HOW TO 2: Control Printing on Your Computer

When you print using a computer, you control printing at two different points: first, before the printing actually begins, and second, after the document has been sent to the printer and either is physically printing or is waiting to be printed. To set the parameters for printing and then print the document, complete the following steps:

1. Click File on the menu bar of the program that will be used for printing and then click Print on the File menu. *The Print dialog box is displayed (Figure 6-40). The Print dialog box will vary somewhat depending on the program used.*

2. In the Print dialog box, make the selections for what printer will be used, what pages will be printed, the number of copies to be printed, and any other choices available. For further options, click the Properties button (or, sometimes, the Preferences button) or click the Options button.

3. Click the OK button or the Print button. The document being printed is sent to a print queue, which is an area on disk storage from which documents actually are printed.

When you click the Print button to send the document to the print queue, a printer icon [] may appear on the Windows taskbar. To see the print queue and control the actual printing of documents on the printer, complete the following steps:

FIGURE 6-40

1. If the printer icon appears on the Windows taskbar, double-click it; otherwise, click the Start button on the Windows taskbar, click Printers and Faxes on the Start menu, and then double-click the printer icon with the checkmark. The checkmark indicates the default printer. *A window opens with the name of the printer on the title bar. All the documents either printing or waiting to be printed are listed in the window. The Status column indicates whether the document is printing or waiting. In addition, the owner of the file, number of pages, size, date and time submitted, and printer port are listed.*

2. If you click Printer on the menu bar in the printer window, you can set printing preferences from the Printer menu. In addition, you can pause all printing and cancel all printing jobs from the Printer menu.

3. If you select a document in the document list and then click Document on the menu bar, you can cancel the selected document for printing, or you can pause the printing for the selected document. To continue printing for the selected document, click Document on the menu bar and then click Resume on the Document menu.

Exercise

1. Start WordPad from the Accessories submenu. Type The Print dialog box is displayed by clicking Print on the File menu.

2. Display the Print dialog box and then click the Preferences button. What choices do you have in the Layout sheet? Close the Printing Preferences dialog box. How do you select the number of copies you want to print? How would you print pages 25–35 of a document? Submit your answers to your instructor.

Web Research

Use the Internet-based Web Research exercises to broaden your understanding of the concepts presented in this chapter. Visit scsite.com/dc2007/ch6/research to obtain more information pertaining to each exercise. To discuss any of the Web Research exercises in this chapter with other students, post your thoughts or questions at scsite.com/dc2007/ch6/forum.

(1) **Scavenger Hunt** Use one of the <u>search engines</u> listed in Figure 2-10 in Chapter 2 on page 78 or your own favorite search engine to find the answers to the questions below. Copy and paste the Web address from the Web page where you found the answer. Some questions may have more than one answer. If required, submit your answers to your instructor. (1) What company introduced the first laser printer? When? (2) What was the selling price of the first DeskJet ink-jet printer Hewlett-Packard released in 1988? (3) Who developed the liquid crystal display? (4) What is the model number of the IBM printer that could play musical notes? (5) What is an ambient light sensor on a monitor?

(2) **Search Sleuth** Some search engines use computers to index the World Wide Web automatically, so they generally find more Web sites that human indexers can catalog. One of the most aggressive automatic, or robot, search engines is <u>AltaVista</u> (altavista.com), which attempts to catalog the entire World Wide Web. AltaVista and many other search engines have a wildcard matching feature. Assume that you want to search for all information pertaining to flat-panel displays, including LCD monitors and screens, and plasma monitors. In this instance, you could use the wildcard symbol (*) to indicate missing letters. Your search query would be *flat-panel display, where the * substitutes for any variation of the words, flat-panel display. Visit this Web site and then use your word processing program to answer the following questions. Then, if required, submit your answers to your instructor. (1) Click the Help link and then click the Search link. Scroll down and then read about the different types of searches AltaVista emphasizes in its Basic Help page. What are these searches? (2) Click your browser's Back button or press the BACKSPACE key twice to return to the AltaVista home page. (3) Use the wildcard option and type *flat-panel display. (4) Scroll through the results until you reach the AltaVista News section. Read at least two of the news stories and then write a 50-word summary.

(3) **Journaling** Respond to your readings in this chapter by writing at least one page about your reactions, evaluations, and reflections about using <u>output devices</u>. For example, have you printed photos taken with a digital camera? What type of photo paper did you use? Do you purchase recyclable printer supplies, such as toner or ink-jet cartridges? Where would you dispose of old monitors and printers and used toner? How do you attempt to reduce eyestrain while using a computer? You also can write about the new terms you learned by reading this chapter. If required, submit your journal to your instructor.

(4) **Expanding Your Understanding** If you are using a Tablet PC and your coworker is using a PDA, it is cumbersome to transfer files from one device to the other. Engineers are developing <u>digital pens</u> that might ease the file exchange process. Using this special pen, one user can select a file on his computer and then place the pen on the other user's computer to transfer the file. Other digital pens allow users to write or draw and then retrieve all the handwritten information on a computer. Visit a local electronics store or Web site to learn more about digital pens. Compare their features, cost, file transfer process, and warranty. Write a report summarizing your findings, focusing on comparing and contrasting the digital pens. If required, submit your report to your instructor.

(5) **Ethics in Action** <u>Internet addiction disorder</u> (IAD) may be affecting some Internet users. People claim to be addicted when they spend up to 10 hours a day online, they occasionally binge for extended Internet sessions, and they suffer withdrawal symptoms when they have not been online for some time. "Netomania" is not a recognized disorder, however, and some researchers believe the Internet problem is just a symptom of other psychiatric disorders, such as manic-depression. View online sites that provide information about IAD, including the Center for Online and Internet Addiction (netaddiction.com). Write a report summarizing your findings and include a table of links to Web sites that provide additional details. If required, submit your report to your instructor.

Case Studies

Use the Case Studies to apply the concepts presented in the chapter to real-world situations. Visit scsite.com/dc2007/ch6/cases to obtain more information pertaining to each exercise. To discuss the Case Studies in this chapter with other students, visit scsite.com/dc2007/ch6/forum and post your thoughts or questions.

Case Study 1 – Class Discussion   You are a manager of a 30-member income tax accounting group. Your company provides desktop computers for each of the accountants. The current computers have 17-inch CRT monitors. The accountants have been complaining that the monitors are too small. Use the Web and/or print media to investigate the costs associated with upgrading the current monitors to 19-inch or 20-inch <u>flat-panel display devices</u>. What are the advantages and disadvantages of flat-panel display devices? What is the best screen size? Why? When you have finished reviewing flat-panel display device characteristics, write a brief report to your supervisor summarizing your recommendations. Include a list of the five factors you think are the most important to consider when purchasing a flat-panel display device. Be prepared to discuss your recommendations in class.

Case Study 2 — Class Discussion   The price of <u>color laser printers</u> has dropped considerably over the past few years to a point where the price between a color laser printer and black-and-white laser printer is not as significant as it once was. The company at which you are employed as a buyer, has decided to upgrade the black-and-white laser printers used by its administrative staff throughout the company to color laser printers. Your manager has asked you to send him a brief report that lists the advantages and disadvantages of black-and-white laser printers versus color laser printers. Include both initial and recurring cost estimates for both black-and-white and color printers. Be prepared to discuss your recommendations in class.

Case Study 3 — Research   Printing requirements vary greatly among users. The local insurance agency where you are employed part time is shopping for a <u>printer</u>. The owner is aware that you are taking a computer class and has asked you to assist her in making a decision on what printer to buy. Figure 6-12 on page 310 lists several questions that should be considered when choosing a printer. Use what you learned in class to answer the questions posed in Figure 6-12. Answer each question according to what you believe to be your employer's needs. Then, use the Web and/or print media to find at least two printers that fit the requirements. List the name of each printer and note their advantages and disadvantages. Which of the two printers would you buy? Why? Prepare a report and/or PowerPoint presentation and share your findings with your class.

Case Study 4 — Research   While printers produce an image on a page from top to bottom, <u>plotters</u> can draw on any part of a page at random, and then move on to any other part. This capability, coupled with their capacity to use large sheets of paper, makes plotters particularly valuable to people who produce maps or blueprints. A local engineering firm that has used hand drawings for the past 50 years has hired you to assist them in purchasing three 42-inch plotters with a maximum print length of 300 feet and at least 1200 × 600 dpi. What is the advantage or disadvantage of using a plotter compared to simply creating a drawing by hand? Use the Web and/or print media to research both the initial and recurring costs of plotters that meet the stated requirements from three different manufacturers. Include in your research how long each plotter takes to produce an image and other noteworthy information. Prepare a report and/or PowerPoint presentation summarizing your findings.

Case Study 5 — Team Challenge   Three accountants at the company you work for want to go off on their own and set up a small accounting office with approximately 20 to 25 employees. They have hired your group as consultants to help with the setup. The goal is to determine the type of output devices you think they will need within the office. Consider the types and number of printers, types and number of display devices, <u>audio devices</u>, microphones, LCD projectors, considerations for the physically challenged, and whether fax machines, fax modems, and/or multifunction peripherals are needed. Form a three-member team and assign each team member one or more categories of output devices. Have the team members use the Web and/or print media to research their assignments. Combine your findings in a table listing the advantages and disadvantages of the various devices, your team's recommendations, and a short explanation of why the team selected each device. Share your findings with your class.

Digital Imaging and Video Technology

Everywhere you look, people are capturing moments they want to remember. They take pictures or make movies of their vacations, birthday parties, activities, accomplishments, sporting events, weddings, and more. Because of the popularity of digital cameras and digital video cameras, increasingly more people desire to capture their memories digitally, instead of on film. With digital technology, photographers have the ability to modify and share the digital images and videos they create. When you use special hardware and/or software, you can copy, manipulate, print, and distribute digital images and videos using your personal computer and the Internet. Amateurs can create professional quality results by using more sophisticated hardware and software.

digital camera (input)

digital video camera (input)

FireWire or USB 2.0

television (output)

FIGURE 1 The top portion of the figure shows a typical home digital imaging setup, and the lower portion of the figure shows a typical home setup for editing personal video.

Digital photography and recordings deliver significant benefits over film-based photography and movie making. With digital cameras, no developing is needed. Instead, the images reside on storage media such as a hard disk, DVD, or flash memory card. Unlike film, storage media can be reused, which reduces costs, saves time, and provides immediate results. Digital technology allows greater control over the creative process, both while taking pictures and video and in the editing process. You can check results immediately after capturing a picture or video to determine whether it meets your expectations. If you are dissatisfied with a picture or video, you can erase it and recapture it, again and again.

As shown in the top portion of Figure 1, a digital camera functions as an input device when it transmits pictures through a cable to a personal computer via a USB port or FireWire port. Using a digital camera in this way allows you to edit the pictures, save them on storage media, and print them on a photographic-quality printer via a parallel port or USB port.

The lower portion of Figure 1 illustrates how you might use a digital video camera with a personal computer. The process typically is the same for most digital video cameras. You capture the images or video with the video camera. Next, you connect the video camera to your personal computer using a FireWire or USB 2.0 port, or you place the storage media used on the camera in the computer. The video then is copied or downloaded to the computer's hard disk. Then, you can edit the video using video editing software. If desired, you can preview the video during the editing process on a television. Finally, you save the finished result to the desired media, such as a VHS tape or DVD+RW or, perhaps, e-mail the edited video. In this example, a VCR and a DVD player also can be used to input video from a VHS tape or a DVD.

USB

USB

photographic-quality printer
(output)

personal computer

S-video-in

DVD recorder
(input, output, storage)

S-video

S-video-out

VCR (input, output, storage)

DIGITAL IMAGING TECHNOLOGY

Digital imaging technology involves capturing and manipulating still photographic images in an electronic format. The following sections outline the steps involved in the process of using digital imaging technology.

1 Select a Digital Camera

A **digital camera** is a type of camera that stores photographed images electronically instead of on traditional film. Digital cameras are divided into three categories (Figure 2) based mainly on image resolution, features, and of course, price. The image resolution is measured in pixels (short for picture element). The image quality increases with the number of pixels. The image resolution usually is measured in **megapixels** (million of pixels), often abbreviated as **MP**. Features of digital cameras include red-eye reduction, zoom, autofocus, flash, self-timer, and manual mode for fine-tuning settings. Figure 3 summarizes the three categories of digital cameras.

(a) point-and-shoot

(b) field

(c) studio

FIGURE 2 The point-and-shoot digital camera (a) requires no adjustments before shooting. The field digital camera (b) offers improved quality and features that allow you to make manual adjustments before shooting and use a variety of lenses. The studio digital camera (c) offers better color and resolution and greater control over exposure and lenses.

TYPES OF DIGITAL CAMERAS

Type	Resolution Range	Features	Price
Point-and-shoot	Less than 5 MP	Fully automatic; fits in your pocket; easy to use; ideal for average consumer usage.	Less than $500
Field cameras	Greater than 6 MP	Used by photojournalists; portable but flexible; provides ability to change lenses and use other attachments; great deal of control over exposure and other photo settings.	$600 to $2,000
Studio cameras	Greater than 6 MP	Stationary camera used for professional studio work; flexible; widest range of lenses and settings.	$1,500 and up

FIGURE 3 Digital cameras often are categorized by image resolution, features, and price.

2 Take Pictures

Digital cameras provide you with several options that are set before a picture is taken. Three of the more important options are the resolution, compression, and image file format in which the camera should save the picture. While a camera may allow for a very high resolution for a large print, you may choose to take a picture at a lower resolution if the image does not require great detail or must be a small size. For example, you may want to use the image on a Web page where smaller image file sizes are beneficial.

Compression results in smaller image file sizes. Figure 4 illustrates the image file sizes for varying resolutions and compressions under standard photographic conditions using a 4-megapixel digital camera. Figure 4 also shows the average picture size for a given resolution. The camera may take more time to save an image at lower compression, resulting in a longer delay before the camera is ready to take another picture. A higher compression, however, may result in some loss of image quality. If a camera has a 16 MB flash memory card, you can determine the number of pictures the card can hold by dividing 16 MB by the file size. Flash memory cards are available in sizes from 16 MB to 8 GB.

Most digital cameras also allow you to choose an image file format. Two popular file formats are TIFF and JPEG. The **TIFF** file format saves the image uncompressed. All of the image detail is captured and stored, but the file sizes can be large. The **JPEG** file format is compressed. The resolution of the image may be the same as a TIFF file, but some detail may be lost in the image.

Finally, before you take the photograph, you should choose the type of media on which to store the resulting image file. Some cameras allow for a choice of media to which you can store the image, such as a CompactFlash card or Memory Stick, while others allow for only one type of storage media. One major advantage of a digital camera is that you easily can erase pictures from its media, freeing up space for new pictures.

IMAGE FILE SIZE WITH A FOUR MEGAPIXEL DIGITAL CAMERA

Resolution in Pixels	COMPRESSION			Picture Size in Inches
	Low	Medium	High	
	Resulting Image File Size			
2272 × 1704	2 MB	1.1 MB	556 KB	11 x 17
1600 × 1200	1 MB	558 KB	278 KB	8 x 10
1024 × 768	570 KB	320 KB	170 KB	4 x 6
640 × 480	249 KB	150 KB	84 KB	3 x 5

FIGURE 4 Image file sizes for varying resolutions and compressions under standard photographic conditions using a 4-megapixel digital camera.

③ Transfer and Manage Image Files

The method of transferring images from the camera to the personal computer differs greatly depending on the capabilities of both. Digital cameras use a variety of storage media (Figure 5). If your camera uses a flash memory card such as CompactFlash, Memory Stick, SmartMedia, or Secure Digital (SD), you can remove the media from the camera and place it in a slot on the personal computer or in a device, such as a card reader, connected to the personal computer. Your camera or card reader also may connect to the personal computer using a USB, USB 2.0, or FireWire (Figure 6) port. When you insert the memory card or connect the camera, software on the personal computer guides you through the process of transferring the images to the hard disk. Some operating systems and software recognize a memory card or camera as though it is another hard disk on the computer. This feature allows you to access the files, navigate them, and then copy, delete, or rename the files while the media still is in the camera.

After you transfer the files to the hard disk on your personal computer, you should organize the files by sorting them or renaming them so that information, such as the subject, date, time, and purpose, is saved along with the image. Finally, before altering the images digitally or using the images for other purposes, you should back up the images to another location, such as a CD or DVD, so the original image is recoverable.

SD Card

CompactFlash

Memory Stick

FIGURE 5 SD Cards, CompactFlash, and Memory Sticks are popular storage devices for digital cameras.

FIGURE 6 Using a USB or FireWire connection, you can add a card reader to your personal computer.

④ Edit Images

Image editing software allows you to edit digital images. The following list summarizes the more common image enhancements or alterations:

- Adjust the contrast and brightness; correct lighting problems; or help give the photograph a particular feeling, such as warm or stark.
- Remove red-eye.
- Crop an image to remove unnecessary elements and resize it.
- Rotate the image to change its orientation.
- Add elements to the image, such as descriptive text, a date, a logo, or decorative items; create collages or add missing elements.
- Replace individual colors with a new color.
- Add special effects, such as texture or motion blurring to enhance the image.

Figure 7 shows some of the effects available in Jasc's Paint Shop Pro on the Artistic Effects submenu.

FIGURE 7 The capability of applying effects separates digital photography from film photography.

⑤ Print Images

Once an image is digitally altered, it is ready to be printed. You can print images on a personal color printer or send them to a professional service that specializes in digital photo printing.

When printing the images yourself, make sure that the resolution used to create the image was high enough for the size of the print you want to create. For example, if the camera used a resolution of 640 × 480 pixels, then the ideal print size is a wallet size. If you print such an image at a size of 8 x 10 inches, then the image will appear **pixilated**, or blurry. Use high-quality photo paper for the best results. A photo printer gives the best results when printing digital photography.

Many services print digital images, either over the Internet or through traditional photo developing locations and kiosks (Figure 8), such as those found in drug stores or shopping marts. Some services allow you to e-mail or upload the files to the service, specify the size, quality, and quantity of print; and then receive the finished prints via the postal service. Other services allow you to drop off flash memory cards, CD-ROMs, or floppy disks at a photo shop and later pick up the prints, just as you do with traditional photo developing shops.

FIGURE 8
A Pixel Magic Imaging Photo Ditto kiosk allows you to print digital images in high resolution on photo paper.

6 Distribute Images Electronically

Rather than printing images, you often need to use the images electronically. Depending on the electronic use of the image, the image may require additional processing. If you use the images on a Web site or want to e-mail a photo, you probably want to send a lower-resolution image. Image editing software allows you to lower the resolution of the image, resulting in a smaller file size. You also should use standard file formats when distributing an electronic photo. The JPEG format is viewable using most personal computers or Web browsers. Some online services allow you to upload and share your photos free of charge and will automatically change your photos to a lower resolution and JPEG format.

You can store very high resolution photos on a DVD or a CD. **DVD and CD mastering software** (Figure 9) allows you to create slide show presentations on a recordable DVD or CD that can play in many home DVD players or personal computer DVD drives.

Finally, you should back up and store images that you distribute electronically with the same care as you store your traditional film negatives.

FIGURE 9 Nero PhotoShow Elite and similar software applications allow you to create your own photo slide show on DVD or CD.

DIGITAL VIDEO TECHNOLOGY

Digital video technology allows you to input, edit, manage, publish, and share your videos using a personal computer. With digital video technology, you can transform home videos into Hollywood-style movies by enhancing the videos with scrolling titles and transitions, cutting out or adding scenes, and adding background music and voice-over narration. The following sections outline the steps involved in the process of using digital video technology.

1 Select a Video Camera

Video cameras record in either analog or digital format. **Analog formats** include 8mm, Hi8, VHS, VHS-C, and Super VHS-C. The last three formats use the types of tapes similar to those used in a standard VCR. **Digital formats** include Mini-DV, MICROMV, Digital8, and DVD. Digital video cameras fall into three general categories: high-end consumer, consumer, and webcasting and monitoring (Figure 10). Consumer digital video cameras are by far the most popular type among consumers. Digital video cameras provide more features than analog video cameras, such as a higher level of zoom, better sound, or greater control over color and lighting.

(a) high-end consumer

(b) consumer

(c) webcasting and monitoring

FIGURE 10 The high-end consumer digital video camera (a) can produce professional-grade results. The consumer digital video camera (b) produces amateur-grade results. The webcasting and monitoring digital video camera (c) is appropriate for webcasting and security monitoring.

2 Record a Video

Most video cameras provide you with a choice of recording programs, which sometimes are called automatic settings. Each recording program includes a different combination of camera settings, so you can adjust the exposure and other functions to match the recording environment. Usually, several different programs are available, such as point-and-shoot, point-and-shoot with manual adjustment, sports, portrait, spotlit scenes, and low light. You also have the ability to select special digital effects, such as fade, wipe, and black and white. If you are shooting outside on a windy day, then you can enable the wind screen to prevent wind noise. If you are shooting home videos, then the point-and-shoot recording program is sufficient.

3 Transfer and Manage Videos

After recording the video, the next step is to transfer the video to your personal computer. Most video cameras connect directly to a USB 2.0 or FireWire port on your personal computer (Figure 11). Transferring video with a digital camera is easy, because the video already is in a digital format that the computer can understand.

An analog camcorder or VCR requires additional hardware to convert the analog signals to a digital format before the video can be manipulated on a personal computer. The additional hardware includes a special video capture card using a standard RCA video cable or an S-video cable (Figure 12). *S-video* cables provide sharper

images and greater overall quality. When you use video capture hardware with an analog video, be sure to close all open programs on your computer because capturing video requires a great deal of processing power.

FIGURE 11 A digital video camera is connected to the personal computer via a FireWire or USB 2.0 port. No additional hardware is needed.

FIGURE 12 An analog camcorder or VCR is connected to the personal computer via an S-video port on a video capture card.

When transferring video, plan to use approximately 15 to 30 gigabytes of hard disk storage space per hour of digital video. A typical video project requires about four times the amount of raw footage as the final product. Therefore, at the high end, a video that lasts an hour may require up to 120 gigabytes of storage for the raw footage, editing process, and final video. This storage requirement can vary depending on the software you use to copy the video from the video camera to the hard disk and the format you select to save the video. For example, Microsoft claims that the latest version of its Windows Movie Maker can save 15 hours of video in 10 gigabytes when creating video for playback on a computer, but saves only 1 hour of video in 10 gigabytes when creating video for playback on a DVD or VCR.

The video transfer requires application software on the personal computer (Figure 13). Windows XP includes the Windows Movie Maker software that allows you to transfer the video from your video camera. Depending on the length of video and the type of connection used, the video may take a long time to download. Make certain that no other programs are running on your personal computer while transferring the video.

When transferring video, the software may allow you to choose a file format and a codec to store the video. A video **file format** holds the video information in a manner specified by a vendor, such as Apple or Microsoft. Three of the more popular file formats are listed in Figure 14.

File formats support codecs to encode the audio and video into the file formats. A particular file format may be able to store audio and video in a number of different codecs. A **codec** specifies how the audio and video is compressed and stored within the file. Figure 15 shows some options available for specifying a file format and codec in a video capture application. The dialog box in Figure 15 allows the user to determine whether the video is smoother in playback or if the video is more crisp, meaning that it includes more detail. The file format and codec you choose often is based on what you plan to do with the movie. For example, if you plan to stream video over the Web using Real's Helix software, the best choice for the file format is the RealMedia format, which uses the RealVideo codec.

After transferring the video to a personal computer, and before manipulating the video, you should store the video files in appropriate folders, named correctly, and backed up. Most video transfer application software helps manage these tasks.

POPULAR VIDEO FILE FORMATS

File Format	File Extensions
Apple QuickTime	.MOV or .QT
Microsoft Windows Media Video	.WMV or .ASF
Real RealMedia	.RM or .RAM

FIGURE 14 Apple, Microsoft, and Real offer the more popular video file formats.

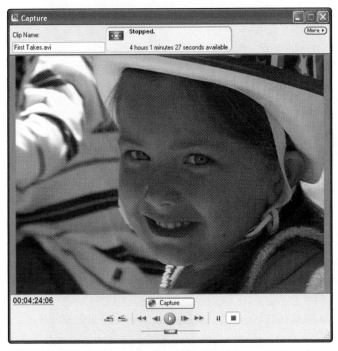

FIGURE 13 Some video editing software allows you to transfer your video from any video source to a hard disk. This dialog box allows the user to set various video parameters for capturing video from a camera or other device.

FIGURE 15 Video editing software applications allow you to specify a combination of file format and codec when saving a video.

4 Edit a Video

Once the video is stored on your hard disk, the next step is to edit, or manipulate, the video. If you used a video capture card to transfer analog video to your computer (Figure 12 on page 348), the files may require extra initial processing. When you use a video capture card, some of the video frames may be lost in the transfer process. Some video editing programs allow you to fix this problem with **frame rate correction** tools.

The first step in the editing process is to split the video into smaller pieces, or *scenes*, that you can manipulate more easily. This process is called *splitting*. Most video software automatically splits the video into scenes, thus sparing you the task. After splitting, you should cut out unwanted scenes or portions of scenes. This process is called *pruning*.

After you create the scenes you want to use in your final production, you edit each individual scene. You can *crop*, or change the size of, scenes. That is, you may want to cut out the top or a side of a scene that is irrelevant. You also can resize the scene. For example, you may be creating a video that will be displayed in a Web browser.

Making a smaller video, such as 320 × 200 pixels instead of 640 × 480 pixels, results in a smaller file that transmits faster over the Internet.

If video has been recorded over a long period, using different cameras or under different lighting conditions, the video may need color correction. *Color correction tools* (Figure 16) analyze your video and match brightness, colors, and other attributes of video clips to ensure a smooth look to the video.

You can add logos, special effects, or titles to scenes. You can place a company logo or personal logo in a video to identify yourself or the company producing the video. Logos often are added on the lower-right corner of a video and remain for the duration of the video. Special effects include warping, changing from color to black and white, morphing, or zoom motion. *Morphing* is a special effect in which one video image is transformed into another image over the course of several frames of video, creating the illusion of metamorphosis. You usually add titles at the beginning and end of a video to give the video context. A training video may have titles throughout the video to label a particular scene, or each scene may begin with a title.

FIGURE 16 Color correction tools in video editing software allow a great deal of control over the mood of your video creation.

The next step in editing a video is to add audio effects, including voice-over narration and background music. Many video editing programs allow you to add additional tracks, or *layers*, of sound to a video in addition to the sound that was recorded on the video camera. You also can add special audio effects.

The final step in editing a video is to combine the scenes into a complete video (Figure 17). This process involves ordering scenes and adding transition effects between scenes (Figure 18). Video editing software allows you to combine scenes and separate each scene with a transition. *Transitions* include fading, wiping, blurry, bursts, ruptures, erosions, and more.

FIGURE 17 In Windows Movie Maker 2, scenes, shown on the top, are combined into a sequence on the bottom of the screen.

FIGURE 18 Smooth and dynamic transitions eliminate the hard cuts between scenes typically found in raw footage.

⑤ Distribute the Video

After editing the video, the final step is to distribute it or save it on an appropriate medium. You can save video in a variety of formats. Using special hardware, you can save the video on standard video tape. *A digital-to-analog converter* is necessary to allow your personal computer to transmit video to a VCR. A digital-to-analog converter may be an external device that connects to both the computer and input device, or may be a video capture card inside the computer.

Video also can be stored in digital formats in any of several DVD formats, on CD-R, or on video CD (VCD). *DVD* or *CD creation software*, which often is packaged with video editing software, allows you to create, or *master*, DVDs and CDs. You can add interactivity to your DVDs. For example, you can allow viewers to jump to certain scenes using a menu (Figure 19). A *video CD* (*VCD*) is a CD format that stores video on a CD-R that can be played in many DVD players.

You also can save your video creation in electronic format for distribution over the Web or via e-mail. Your video editing software must support the file format and codec you want to use. For example, RealNetworks's Helix media delivery system allows you to save media files in the RealVideo file formats.

Professionals use hardware and software that allow them to create a film version of digital video that can be played in movie theaters. This technology is becoming increasingly popular and has been used in such movies as the recent *Lord of the Rings* movies. Some Hollywood directors believe that eventually, all movies will be recorded and edited digitally.

After creating your final video for distribution or your personal video collection, you should backup the final video file. You can save your scenes for inclusion in other video creations or create new masters using different effects, transitions, and ordering of scenes.

FIGURE 19 DVD mastering software allows you to create interactive menus on your DVD.

CHAPTER SEVEN

Storage

Picture Yourself Working with Mobile Storage Media

At the end of the job interview, the supervisor asks, "When can you start?" You are thrilled to get this job with the local newspaper. The flexible hours are a perfect arrangement with your school schedule. As an added bonus, the job will give you experience toward your major — computer technology.

You will be working with the photojournalists in the office — more precisely, with their mobile media. The photojournalists take many pictures while on various assignments. All of them use digital cameras. Your job is to print pictures taken by the photojournalists. Because the photo-journalists each use different makes and models of cameras, the digital pictures are stored on a variety of mobile media. Some of the cameras use flash memory cards such as CompactFlash cards, xD Picture cards, and Memory Sticks. One photojournalist transfers his pictures to a USB flash drive, from which you print the images. Some copy their pictures on a CD, and another gives you a Zip disk containing all her pictures.

After you receive the media, you insert it in the appropriate card reader, card slot, drive, or port. You then begin the process of storing the images on a hard disk and finally printing the images. The office has a very liberal personal use policy that allows you to print your own digital pictures during off-the-clock time — as long as you supply the paper. When you are away from the office, however, you print personal pictures using an in-store kiosk.

To learn about these various types of mobile media, read Chapter 7 and discover many other types of storage devices.

After completing this chapter, you will be able to:

1. Differentiate between storage devices and storage media

2. Describe the characteristics of magnetic disks

3. Describe the characteristics of a hard disk

4. Differentiate between floppy disks and Zip disks

5. Describe the characteristics of optical discs

6. Differentiate among CD-ROMs, recordable CDs, rewritable CDs, DVD-ROMs, recordable DVDs, and rewritable DVDs

7. Identify the uses of tape

8. Discuss PC Cards and the various types of miniature mobile storage media

9. Identify uses of microfilm and microfiche

CONTENTS

STORAGE

Storage holds data, instructions, and information for future use. Every computer uses storage to hold system software and application software. To start up, a computer locates an operating system (system software) in storage and loads it into memory. When a user issues a command to start application software, such as a word processing program or a Web browser, the operating system locates the program in storage and loads it into memory.

In addition to programs, users store a variety of data and information on mainframe computers, servers, desktop computers, notebook computers, Tablet PCs, handheld computers,

PDAs, and smart phones. For example, all types of users store digital photographs; appointments, schedules, and contact/address information; and correspondence, such as letters and e-mail messages. Other items stored by specific types of users include the following:

- The home user might also store budgets, bank statements, a household inventory, records of stock purchases, tax data, homework assignments, recipes, music, and videos.
- The small office/home office user also often stores faxes, business reports, financial records, tax data, travel records, customer orders, payroll records, inventory records, and Web pages.

FIGURE 7-1 A variety of storage media.

- The mobile user usually also stores faxes, presentations, travel records, homework assignments, and quotations.
- The power user also stores diagrams, drawings, blueprints, designs, marketing literature, corporate newsletters, product catalogs, videos, audio recordings, multimedia presentations, and Web pages.
- The large business user also accesses many stored items such as tax data, inventory records, presentations, contracts, marketing literature, and Web pages. The large business user accesses hundreds or thousands of employee, customer, and vendor records, including data and information about orders, invoices, payments, and payroll.

Storage requirements among these users vary greatly. Home users, small office/home office users, and mobile users typically have much smaller storage requirements than the large business user or power user. For example, a home user may need 160 billion bytes of storage, while large businesses may require 50 trillion bytes of storage.

A **storage medium** (media is the plural), also called *secondary storage*, is the physical material on which a computer keeps data, instructions, and information. Examples of storage media are hard disks, floppy disks, Zip disks, CDs and DVDs, tape, PC Cards, flash memory cards, USB flash drives, and microfilm (Figure 7-1). Memory, by contrast, typically consists of one or more chips on the motherboard or some other circuit board in the computer.

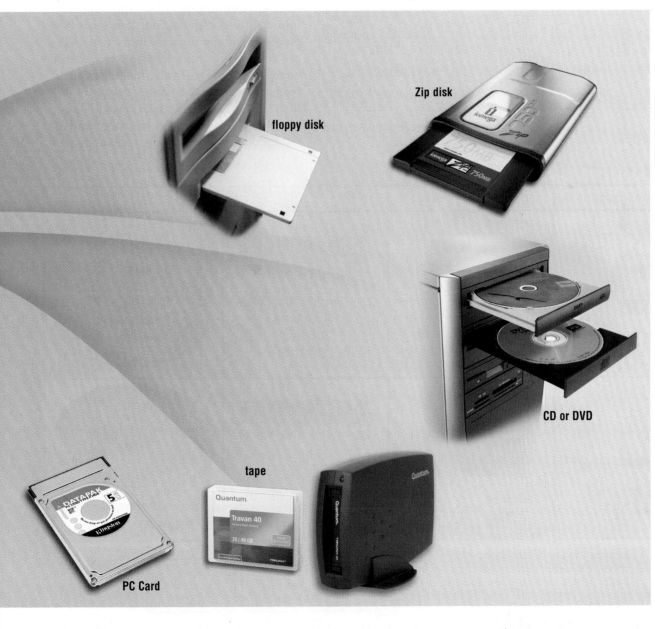

floppy disk

Zip disk

CD or DVD

tape

PC Card

Capacity is the number of bytes (characters) a storage medium can hold. Figure 7-2 identifies the terms manufacturers use to define the capacity of storage media. For example, a reasonably priced USB flash drive can store up to 256 MB of data (approximately 256 million bytes) and a typical hard disk has 160 GB (approximately 160 billion bytes) of storage capacity.

Items on a storage medium remain intact even when power is removed from the computer. Thus, a storage medium is nonvolatile. Most memory, by contrast, holds data and instructions temporarily and thus is volatile. Figure 7-3 illustrates the concept of volatility. For an analogy, think of a filing cabinet that holds file folders as a storage medium, and the top of your desk as memory. When you want to work with a file, you remove it from the filing cabinet (storage medium) and place it on your desk (memory). When you are finished with the file, you remove it from your desk (memory) and return it to the filing cabinet (storage medium).

A **storage device** is the computer hardware that records and/or retrieves items to and from storage media. **Writing** is the process of transferring data, instructions, and information from memory to a storage medium. **Reading** is the process of transferring these items from a storage medium into memory. When storage devices write data on storage media, they are creating output. Similarly, when storage devices read from storage media, they function as a source of input. Nevertheless, they are categorized as storage devices, not as input or output devices.

STORAGE TERMS

Storage Term	Approximate Number of Bytes	Exact Number of Bytes
Kilobyte (KB)	1 thousand	2^{10} or 1,024
Megabyte (MB)	1 million	2^{20} or 1,048,576
Gigabyte (GB)	1 billion	2^{30} or 1,073,741,824
Terabyte (TB)	1 trillion	2^{40} or 1,099,511,627,776
Petabyte (PB)	1 quadrillion	2^{50} or 1,125,899,906,842,624
Exabyte (EB)	1 quintillion	2^{60} or 1,152,921,504,606,846,976
Zettabyte (ZB)	1 sextillion	2^{70} or 1,180,591,620,717,411,303,424
Yottabyte (YB)	1 septillion	2^{80} or 1,208,925,819,614,629,174,706,176

FIGURE 7-2   The capacity of a storage medium is measured by the number of bytes it can hold.

AN ILLUSTRATION OF VOLATILITY

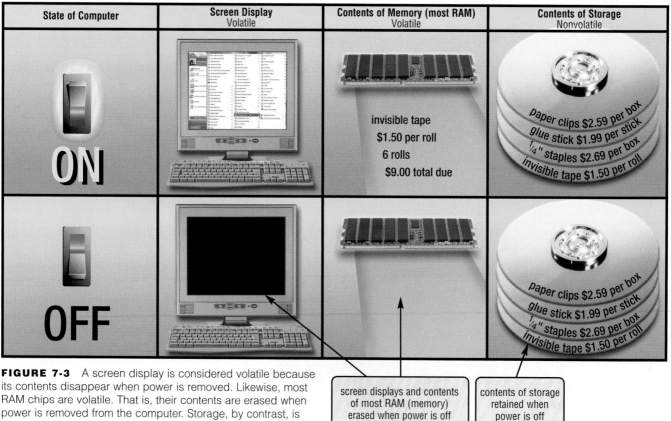

State of Computer	Screen Display Volatile	Contents of Memory (most RAM) Volatile	Contents of Storage Nonvolatile
ON		invisible tape $1.50 per roll 6 rolls $9.00 total due	paper clips $2.59 per box glue stick $1.99 per stick 1/4" staples $2.69 per box invisible tape $1.50 per roll
OFF			paper clips $2.59 per box glue stick $1.99 per stick 1/4" staples $2.69 per box invisible tape $1.50 per roll

screen displays and contents of most RAM (memory) erased when power is off

contents of storage retained when power is off

FIGURE 7-3   A screen display is considered volatile because its contents disappear when power is removed. Likewise, most RAM chips are volatile. That is, their contents are erased when power is removed from the computer. Storage, by contrast, is nonvolatile. Its contents remain when power is off.

The speed of storage devices and memory is defined by access time. **Access time** measures (1) the amount of time it takes a storage device to locate an item on a storage medium or (2) the time required to deliver an item from memory to the processor. The access time of storage devices is slow, compared with the access time of memory. Memory (chips) accesses items in billionths of a second (nanoseconds). Storage devices, by contrast, access items in thousandths of a second (milliseconds).

Instead of, or in addition to access time, some manufacturers state a storage device's transfer rate because it affects access time. *Transfer rate* is the speed with which data, instructions, and information transfer to and from a device. Transfer rates for disks are stated in *KBps* (kilobytes per second) and *MBps* (megabytes per second).

Numerous types of storage media and storage devices exist to meet a variety of users' needs. Figure 7-4 shows how different types of storage media and memory compare in terms of transfer rates and uses. This chapter discusses these and other storage media.

MAGNETIC DISKS

Magnetic disks use magnetic particles to store items such as data, instructions, and information on a disk's surface. Depending on how the magnetic particles are aligned, they represent either a 0 bit or a 1 bit. Recall from Chapter 4 that a bit (binary digit) is the smallest unit of data a computer can process. Thus, the alignment of the magnetic particles represents the data.

Before any data can be read from or written on a magnetic disk, the disk must be formatted. **Formatting** is the process of dividing the disk into tracks and sectors (Figure 7-5), so the operating system can store and locate data and information on the disk. A *track* is a narrow recording band that forms a full circle on the surface of the disk. The disk's storage locations consist of pie-shaped sections, which break the tracks into small arcs called *sectors*. On a magnetic disk, a sector typically stores up to 512 bytes of data.

For reading and writing purposes, sectors are grouped into clusters. A *cluster* is the smallest unit of disk space that stores data and information. Each cluster, also called an *allocation unit*, consists of two to eight sectors (the number varies depending on the operating system). Even if a file consists of only a few bytes, it uses an entire cluster. Each cluster holds data from only one file. One file, however, can span many clusters.

faster transfer rates	Stores...
Memory	Memory (most RAM)	Items waiting to be interpreted and executed by the processor
Storage	Hard Disk	Operating system, application software, user data and information, including pictures, music, and videos
	Flash Memory Cards and USB Flash Drives	Digital pictures or files to be transported
	CDs and DVDs	Software, backups, movies, music
	Tape	Backups
	Floppy Disk	Small files to be transported
slower transfer rates		

FIGURE 7-4 A comparison of different types of storage media and memory in terms of relative speed and uses. Memory is faster than storage but is expensive and not practical for all storage requirements. Storage is less expensive but is slower than memory.

FIGURE 7-5 Tracks form circles on the surface of a magnetic disk. The disk's storage locations are divided into pie-shaped sections, which break the tracks into small arcs called sectors.

Sometimes, a sector has a flaw and cannot store data. When you format a disk, the operating system marks these bad sectors as unusable. For a technical discussion about formatting, read the High-Tech Talk article on page 382.

Three types of magnetic disks are hard disks, floppy disks, and Zip disks. Some of these disks are portable; others are not. With respect to a storage medium, the term *portable* means you can remove the medium from one computer and carry it to another computer.

Hard Disks

A **hard disk**, also called a *hard disk drive*, is a storage device that contains one or more inflexible, circular platters that magnetically store data, instructions, and information. Home users store documents, spreadsheets, presentations, databases, e-mail messages, Web pages, digital photographs, music, videos, and software on hard disks. Businesses use hard disks to store correspondence, reports, financial records, e-mail messages, customer orders and invoices, payroll records, inventory records, presentations, contracts, marketing literature, schedules, and Web sites.

The system unit on most desktop and notebook computers contains at least one hard disk.

The entire device is enclosed in an airtight, sealed case to protect it from contamination. A hard disk that is mounted inside the system unit sometimes is called a *fixed disk* because it is not portable (Figure 7-6). Portable hard disks are discussed later in this chapter.

Current personal computer hard disks have storage capacities from 80 to 500 GB and more. Traditionally, hard disks stored data using *longitudinal recording*, which aligned the magnetic particles horizontally around the surface of the disk. With *perpendicular recording*, by contrast, hard disks align the magnetic particles vertically, or perpendicular to the disk's surface, making much greater storage capacities possible. Experts estimate that hard disks using perpendicular recording will provide storage capacities about 10 times greater than disks that use longitudinal recording. Read Looking Ahead 7-1 for a look at the next generation of hard disk storage capacities. Hard disks are read/write storage media. That is, you can read from and write on a hard disk any number of times. If the computer contains only one hard disk, the operating system designates it as drive C. Additional hard disks are assigned the next available drive letter.

WEB LINK 7-1

Perpendicular Recording

For more information, visit scsite.com/dc2007/ch7/weblink and then click Perpendicular Recording.

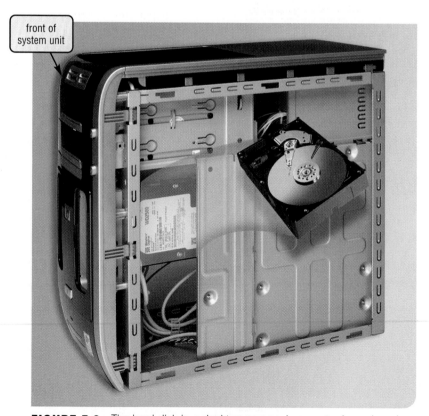

front of system unit

FIGURE 7-6   The hard disk in a desktop personal computer is enclosed inside an airtight, sealed case inside the system unit.

Have personal computer hard disk capacities grown much since their inception?

Yes, hard disk capacities have grown phenomenally over the past several years, as shown in the chart to the right. This trend is expected to continue at a rate of 60 percent annually. For more information, visit scsite.com/dc2007/ch7/faq and then click Hard Disk Capacities.

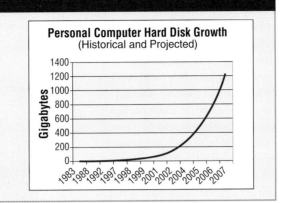

Personal Computer Hard Disk Growth
(Historical and Projected)

Heat Increases Disk Capacity

Things are heating up in the data storage industry. Engineers at IBM Research are testing the use of heat to record data inexpensively on magnetic media, such as hard disks.

Within the next ten years, the researchers predict that this new technique will allow storage of more than one terabit per square inch, which is the equivalent of 25 DVDs on an area the size of a postage stamp. With this capacity, a hard disk that can store seven terabits will be commonplace.

IBM calls this new storage system *Millipede*. It uses heated tips mounted on the ends of cantilevers, in a fashion similar to the way the stylus on an old phonograph sat on the grooves of vinyl records. For more information, visit scsite.com/dc2007/ch7/looking and then click Heated Storage.

CHARACTERISTICS OF A HARD DISK Characteristics of a hard disk include its capacity, platters, read/write heads, cylinders, sectors and tracks, revolutions per minute, transfer rate, and access time. Figure 7-7 shows characteristics of a sample 120 GB hard disk. The following paragraphs discuss each of these characteristics.

The capacity of a hard disk is determined from the number of platters it contains, together with composition of the magnetic coating on the platters. A *platter* is made of aluminum, glass, or ceramic and is coated with an alloy material that allows items to be recorded magnetically on its surface. The coating usually is three millionths of an inch thick.

SAMPLE HARD DISK CHARACTERISTICS

Advertised capacity	120 GB
Platters	3
Read/write heads	6
Cylinders	16,383
Bytes per sector	512
Sectors per track	63
Sectors per drive	234,441,648
Revolutions per minute	7,200
Transfer rate	133 MB per second
Access time	8.9 ms

FIGURE 7-7 Characteristics of a sample 120 GB hard disk. The actual disk's capacity sometimes is different from the advertised capacity because of bad sectors on the disk.

On desktop computers, platters most often have a *form factor*, or size, of approximately 3.5 inches in diameter; on notebook computers and mobile devices, the form factor is 2.5 inches or less. A typical hard disk has multiple platters stacked on top of one another. Each platter has two read/write heads, one for each side. The hard disk has arms that move the read/write heads to the proper location on the platter (Figure 7-8). A *read/write head* is the mechanism that reads items and writes items in the drive as it barely touches the disk's recording surface.

The location of the read/write heads often is referred to by its cylinder. A *cylinder* is the vertical section of a track that passes through all platters (Figure 7-9). A single movement of the read/write head arms accesses all the platters in a cylinder. If a hard disk has two platters

top view of a platter

track

sector

read/write head

side view of a platter

sides

cylinder

FIGURE 7-9 A cylinder is the vertical section of track through all platters on a hard disk.

FIGURE 7-8 HOW A HARD DISK WORKS

Step 2:
A small motor spins the platters while the computer is running.

Step 3:
When software requests a disk access, the read/write heads determine the current or new location of the data.

Step 1:
The circuit board controls the movement of the head actuator and a small motor.

Step 4:
The head actuator positions the read/write head arms over the correct location on the platters to read or write data.

(four sides), each with 1,000 tracks, then it will have 1,000 cylinders with each cylinder consisting of 4 tracks (2 tracks for each platter).

While the computer is running, the platters in the hard disk rotate at a high rate of speed. This spinning, which usually is 5,400 to 15,000 *revolutions per minute* (*rpm*), allows nearly instant access to all tracks and sectors on the platters. The platters typically continue to spin until power is removed from the computer. (On many computers, the hard disk stops spinning after a specified time to save power.) The spinning motion creates a cushion of air between the platter and its read/write head. This cushion ensures that the read/write head floats above the platter instead of making direct contact with the platter surface. The distance between the read/write head and the platter is about two millionths of one inch.

As shown in Figure 7-10, this close clearance leaves no room for any type of contamination. Dirt, hair, dust, smoke, and other particles could cause the hard disk to have a head crash. A *head crash* occurs when a read/write head touches the surface of a platter, usually resulting in a loss of

FIGURE 7-10   The clearance between a disk read/write head and the platter is about two millionths of an inch. A smoke particle, dust particle, human hair, or other contaminant could render the drive unusable.

data or sometimes loss of the entire drive. Although current internal hard disks are built to withstand shocks and are sealed tightly to keep out contaminants, head crashes do occasionally still occur. Thus, it is crucial that you back up your hard disk regularly. A **backup** is a duplicate of a file, program, or disk that you can use in case the original is lost, damaged, or destroyed. Chapter 8 discusses backup techniques.

Depending on the type of hard disk, transfer rates range from 15 MBps to 320 MBps. Access time for today's hard disks ranges from approximately 3 to 12 ms (milliseconds).

Hard disks improve their access time by using disk caching. *Disk cache* (pronounced cash), sometimes called a buffer, consists of a memory chip(s) on a hard disk that stores frequently accessed items such as data, instructions, and information (Figure 7-11). Disk cache and memory cache work in a similar fashion. When a processor requests data, instructions, or information from the hard disk, the hard disk first checks its disk cache — before moving any mechanical parts to access the platters. If the requested item is in disk cache, the hard disk sends it to the processor. If the hard disk does not find the requested item in the disk cache, then the processor must wait for the hard disk to locate and transfer the item from the disk to the processor. Hard disks today contain between 2 MB and 16 MB of disk cache. The greater the disk cache, the faster the hard disk.

Step 1:
A special-purpose chip on the hard disk, called a controller, receives a request for data, instructions, or information from the processor.

Step 2a:
The controller first checks disk cache for the requested item.

Step 2b:
If the controller does not find the requested item in disk cache, it locates the requested item on the hard disk's platters.

Step 3:
The controller transfers the requested item to the processor.

processor

disk cache

controller

FIGURE 7-11   HOW DISK CACHE WORKS

FAQ 7-2

How do manufacturers specify hard disk reliability?

Hardware manufacturers often specify a device's service life (expected useful life) and *MTBF* (mean time between failures), which is the total number of hours all devices were observed operating divided by the total number of failures that occurred. Although MTBF can be as high as 1.4 million hours for hard disks, many people rely on the service life estimate instead. For more information, visit scsite.com/dc2007/ch7/faq and then click MTBF.

FIGURE 7-12 This hard disk has a form factor of 0.85 inch and storage capacities up to 8 GB.

MINIATURE HARD DISKS Many mobile devices and consumer electronics include miniature hard disks, which provide users with greater storage capacities than flash memory. These tiny hard disks, some of which have form factors of less than one inch (Figure 7-12), are found in devices such as audio players, digital cameras, smart phones, and PDAs. Miniature hard disks have storage capacities that range from 2 GB to 120 GB. Miniature hard disks with greater storage capacities typically use perpendicular recording.

PORTABLE HARD DISKS Portable hard disks either are external or removable and have storage capacities up to 500 GB or higher.

An **external hard disk**, shown in the left picture in Figure 7-13, is a separate free-standing hard disk that connects with a cable to a USB port or FireWire port on the system unit. As with the internal hard disk, the entire hard disk is enclosed in an airtight, sealed case.

A **removable hard disk** is a hard disk that you insert and remove from either a dock or a drive. Sometimes the dock or drive is built in the system unit. Others are external devices that connect with a cable to a USB port or FireWire port on the system unit.

Removable hard disks that insert in a dock are self-contained units, similar to external hard disks. Removable hard disks that insert in a drive, shown in the right picture in Figure 7-13, read from and write on the removable hard disk.

External hard disks and removable hard disks offer the following advantages over internal hard disks (fixed disks):

- Transport a large number of files
- Back up important files or an entire internal hard disk (several external hard disk models allow you to back up simply by pushing a button on the disk)
- Easily store large audio and video files
- Secure your data; for example, at the end of a work session, remove the hard disk and lock it up, leaving no data in the computer
- Add storage space to a notebook computer or Tablet PC
- Add storage space to a desktop computer without having to open the system unit
- Share a drive with multiple computers

As the prices of portable hard disks drop, increasingly more users will purchase one to supplement a home or office internal hard disk. Keep in mind, though, that external or removable hard disks transfer data at slower rates than internal hard disks.

external hard disk

one type of removable hard disk

FIGURE 7-13 Examples of portable hard disks.

HARD DISK CONTROLLERS   A *disk controller* consists of a special-purpose chip and electronic circuits that control the transfer of data, instructions, and information from a disk to and from the system bus and other components in the computer. That is, it controls the interface between the hard disk and the system bus. A disk controller for a hard disk, called the hard disk controller, may be part of a hard disk or the motherboard, or it may be a separate adapter card inside the system unit.

In their personal computer advertisements, vendors usually state the type of hard disk interface supported by the hard disk controller. Thus, you should understand the types of available hard disk interfaces. In addition to USB and FireWire (external hard disk interfaces), three other types of hard disk interfaces for internal use in personal computers are SATA, EIDE, and SCSI.

- *SATA* (*Serial Advanced Technology Attachment*), the newest type of hard disk interface, uses serial signals to transfer data, instructions, and information. The primary advantage of SATA interfaces is their cables are thinner, longer, more flexible, and less susceptible to interference than cables used by hard disks that use parallel signals. SATA interfaces have data transfer rates of up to 300 MBps. In addition to hard disks, SATA interfaces support connections to CD and DVD drives.
- *EIDE* (*Enhanced Integrated Drive Electronics*) is a hard disk interface that uses parallel signals to transfer data, instructions, and information. EIDE interfaces can support up to four hard disks at 137 GB per disk. These interfaces have data transfer rates up to 100 MBps. EIDE interfaces also provide connections for CD and DVD drives and tape drives. Some manufacturers market their EIDE interfaces as Fast ATA or Ultra ATA.
- *SCSI* interfaces, which also use parallel signals, can support up to eight or fifteen peripheral devices. Supported devices include hard disks, CD and DVD drives, tape drives, printers, scanners, network cards, and much more. Recall from Chapter 4 that SCSI is an acronym for Small Computer System Interface. Some computers have a built-in SCSI interface, while others use an adapter card to add a SCSI interface. SCSI interfaces provide up to 320 MBps data transfer rates.

FAQ 7-3

What are the transfer rates of USB and FireWire?

USB 2.0, also called *Hi-Speed USB*, has transfer rates up to 480 *Mbps* (megabits per second). FireWire has transfer rates up to 800 Mbps. For more information, visit scsite.com/dc2007/ch7/faq and then click USB and FireWire.

MAINTAINING DATA STORED ON A HARD DISK Most manufacturers guarantee their hard disks to last approximately three to five years. Many last much longer with proper care. To prevent the loss of items stored on a hard disk, you regularly should perform preventive maintenance such as defragmenting or scanning the disk for errors. Chapter 8 discusses these and other utilities in depth.

ONLINE STORAGE   Some users choose online storage instead of storing data locally on a hard disk. **Online storage** is a service on the Web that provides hard disk storage to computer users, usually for a minimal monthly fee (Figure 7-14). Fee arrangements for use of these Internet hard disks vary. For example, one online storage service charges $10 per month for 5 GB of storage. Many offer free trial periods.

WEB LINK 7-4

Online Storage
For more information, visit scsite.com/dc2007/ch7/weblink and then click Online Storage.

FIGURE 7-14   An example of one Web site advertising its online storage service.

Users subscribe to an online storage service for a variety of reasons:

• To access files on the Internet hard disk from any computer or device that has Internet access

• To store large audio, video, and graphics files on an Internet hard disk instantaneously, instead of spending time downloading to a local hard disk

• To allow others to access files on their Internet hard disk so others can listen to an audio file, watch a video clip, or view a picture — instead of e-mailing the file to them

• To view time-critical data and images immediately while away from the main office or location; for example, doctors can view x-ray images from another hospital, home, or office, or while on vacation

• To store offsite backups of data (Chapter 8 presents this and other backup strategies)

Once users subscribe to the online storage service, they can save on the Internet hard disk in the same manner they save on their local hard disk or any other drive.

Floppy Disks

A **floppy disk**, also called a *diskette*, is a portable, inexpensive storage medium that consists of a thin, circular, flexible plastic Mylar film with a magnetic coating enclosed in a square-shaped plastic shell. Although the exterior of current floppy disks is not bendable, users refer to this storage medium as a floppy disk because of the flexible film inside the rigid plastic 3.5-inch outer cover.

A standard floppy disk can store up to 500 double-spaced pages of text, several digital photographs, or a small audio file. Floppy disks are not as widely used as they were 15 years ago because of their low storage capacity. They are used, however, for specific applications. For example, some users work with floppy disks to transport small files to and from nonnetworked personal computers, such as from school or work to home.

A **floppy disk drive** is a device that reads from and writes on a floppy disk. A user

inserts a floppy disk in and removes it from a floppy disk drive. In the past, desktop personal computers and notebook computers had a floppy disk drive installed inside the system unit (Figure 7-15a). Most computers today do not include a floppy disk drive as standard equipment. On these computers, you can use an *external floppy disk drive*, in which the drive is a separate device with a cable that plugs in a port on the system unit (Figure 7-15b). These external drives are attached to the computer

FIGURE 7-15a (floppy disk drive installed inside a desktop computer)

FIGURE 7-15b (external floppy disk drive attached to computer with a cable)

FIGURE 7-15 Two types of floppy disk drives.

only when the user needs to access items on a floppy disk.

If a personal computer has one floppy disk drive, it is named drive A. To read from or write on a floppy disk, a floppy disk drive must support that floppy disk's density. *Density* is the number of bits in an area on a storage medium. A disk with a higher density has more bits in an area and thus has a larger storage capacity. Most standard floppy disks today are high density (*HD*).

The average time it takes a current floppy disk drive to locate an item on a disk (access time) is 84 milliseconds, or approximately 1/12 of a second. The transfer rates range from 250 to 500 KBps.

You can read from and write on a floppy disk any number of times. To protect a floppy disk from accidentally being erased, the plastic outer shell on the disk contains a write-protect notch in its corner. A **write-protect notch** is a small opening that has a tab you slide to cover or expose the notch. If the write-protect notch is open, the drive cannot write on the floppy disk. If the write-protect notch is covered, or closed, the drive can write on the floppy disk. A floppy disk drive can read from a floppy disk whether the write-protect notch is open or closed. On the opposite corner, some floppy disks have a second opening without a small tab. This opening identifies the disk as a high-density floppy disk.

A floppy disk is a type of magnetic media that stores data in tracks and sectors. A typical floppy disk stores data on both sides of the disk, has 80 tracks on each side of the recording surface, and has 18 sectors per track. To compute a disk's storage capacity, you multiply the number of sides on the disk, the number of tracks on the disk, the number of sectors per track, and the number of bytes in a sector. For example, the following is the formula for a high-density 3.5-inch floppy disk: 2 (sides) $\times$ 80 (tracks) $\times$ 18 (sectors per track) $\times$ 512 (bytes per sector) = 1,474,560 bytes. Disks often store system files in some tracks, which means the available capacity on a disk may be less than the total possible capacity.

Zip Disks

A **Zip disk** is a type of portable magnetic media that can store from 100 MB to 750 MB of data. The larger capacities make it easy to transport many files or large items such as graphics, audio, or video files. Another use of Zip disks is to back up important data and information.

Zip disks are slightly larger than and about twice as thick as a 3.5-inch floppy disk. A **Zip drive** is a high-capacity disk drive developed by Iomega Corporation that reads from and writes on a Zip disk (Figure 7-16). These drives cannot read standard 3.5-inch floppy disks.

Many users prefer to purchase an external Zip drive, which connects to a USB port or FireWire port on the system unit. The external Zip drive is convenient for users with multiple computers, because it allows them to move the drive from computer to computer as needed. As an alternative, some users prefer to order a computer with a built-in Zip drive.

FIGURE 7-16 An external Zip drive and Zip disk.

Test your knowledge of pages 354 through 365 in Quiz Yourself 7-1.

QUIZ YOURSELF 7-1

Instructions: Find the true statement below. Then, rewrite the remaining false statements so they are true.

1. Miniature hard disks are a type of optical disc.
2. Hard disks contain one or more inflexible, circular platters that magnetically store data, instructions, and information.
3. SATA is a hard disk interface that uses parallel signals to transfer data, instructions, and information.
4. Storage media is the computer hardware that records and/or retrieves items to and from a storage device.
5. Three types of manual disks are hard disks, floppy disks, and Zip disks.
6. Users can move an internal Zip drive from computer to computer as needed by connecting the drive to a USB port or FireWire port on the system unit.

Quiz Yourself Online: To further check your knowledge of storage devices and storage media, hard disks, floppy disks, and Zip disks, visit scsite.com/dc2007/ch7/quiz and then click Objectives 1 – 4.

OPTICAL DISCS

An *optical disc* is a type of storage media that consists of a flat, round, portable disc made of metal, plastic, and lacquer that is written and read by a laser. (Recall from Chapter 1 that the term disk is used for magnetic media, and disc is used for optical media.) Optical discs used in personal computers are 4.75 inches in diameter and less than one-twentieth of an inch thick. Smaller computers and devices, however, use *mini discs* that have a diameter of 3 inches or less.

Optical discs primarily store software, data, digital photographs, movies, and music. Some optical disc formats are read only, meaning users cannot write (save) on the media. Others are read/write, which allows users to save on the disc just as they save on a hard disk.

Nearly every personal computer today has some type of optical disc drive installed in a drive bay. On these drives, you push a button to slide out a tray, insert the disc, and then push the same button to close the tray (Figure 7-17). Other convenient features on most of these drives include a volume control button and a headphone port (or jack) so you can use head-phones to listen to audio without disturbing others nearby.

With some discs, you can read and/or write on one side only. Manufacturers usually place a silk-screened label on the top layer of these single-sided discs. You insert a single-sided disc in the drive with the label side up. Other discs are double-sided. Simply remove the disc from the drive, flip it over, and reinsert it in the drive

Push the button to slide out the tray.

Insert the disc, label side up.

Push the same button to close the tray.

FIGURE 7-17 On optical disc drives, you push a button to slide out a tray, insert the disc, and then push the same button to close the tray.

to use the other side of the disc. Double-sided discs often have no label; instead each side of the disc is identified with small writing around the center of the disc.

The drive designation of an optical disc drive usually follows alphabetically after that of all the hard disks and portable disks. For example, if the computer has one internal hard disk (drive C) and an external hard disk (drive D), then the first optical disc drive is drive E. A second optical disc drive would be drive F.

Optical discs store items by using microscopic pits (indentations) and lands (flat areas) that are in the middle layer of the disc (Figure 7-18). A high-powered laser light creates the pits. A lower-powered laser light reads items from the disc by reflecting light through the bottom of the disc, which usually is either solid gold or silver in color. The reflected light is converted into a series of bits the computer can process. A land causes light to reflect, which is read as binary digit 1. Pits absorb the light; this absence of light is read as binary digit 0.

Optical discs commonly store items in a single track that spirals from the center of the disc to the edge of the disc. As with a hard disk, this single track is divided into evenly sized sectors on which items are stored (Figure 7-19).

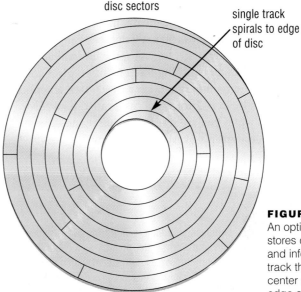

disc sectors

single track spirals to edge of disc

FIGURE 7-19
An optical disc typically stores data, instructions, and information in a single track that spirals from the center of the disc to the edge of a disc.

FIGURE 7-18   HOW A LASER READS DATA ON AN OPTICAL DISC

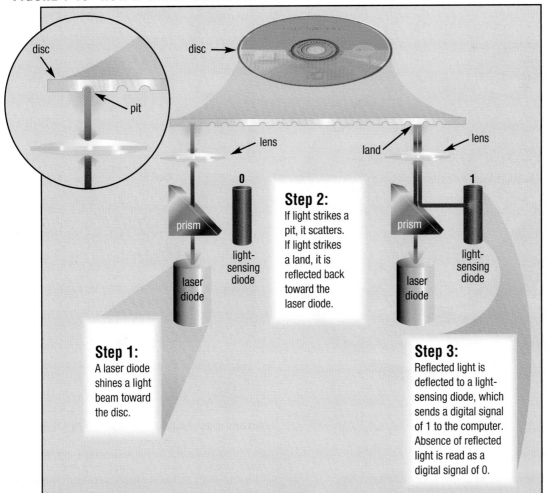

disc

disc

pit

lens

land

lens

0

1

prism

prism

light-sensing diode

light-sensing diode

laser diode

laser diode

Step 1:
A laser diode shines a light beam toward the disc.

Step 2:
If light strikes a pit, it scatters. If light strikes a land, it is reflected back toward the laser diode.

Step 3:
Reflected light is deflected to a light-sensing diode, which sends a digital signal of 1 to the computer. Absence of reflected light is read as a digital signal of 0.

Care of Optical Discs

Manufacturers claim that a properly cared for high-quality optical disc will last 5 years but could last up to 100 years. Figure 7-20 offers some guidelines for the proper care of optical discs. Never bend a disc; it may break. Do not expose discs to extreme temperatures or humidity. The ideal temperature range for disc storage is 50 to 70 degrees Fahrenheit. Stacking discs, touching the underside of discs, or exposing them to any type of contaminant may scratch a disc. Place an optical disc in its protective case, called a *jewel box*, when you are finished using it and store in an upright (vertical) position.

FAQ 7-4

Can I clean a disc?

Yes, you can remove dust, dirt, smudges, and fingerprints from the surface of an optical disc. Moisten a soft cloth with warm water or rubbing alcohol and then wipe the disc in straight lines from the center outward. You also can repair scratches on the surface with a specialized disc repair kit. For more information, visit scsite.com/dc2007/ch7/faq and then click Cleaning and Repairing Discs.

Types of Optical Discs

Many different formats of optical discs exist today. Two general categories are CDs and DVDs, with DVDs having a much greater storage capacity than CDs. Specific formats include CD-ROM, CD-R, CD-RW, DVD-ROM, DVD-R, DVD+R, DVD-RW, DVD+RW, and DVD+RAM. Figure 7-21 identifies each of these optical disc formats and specifies whether a user can read from the disc, write to the disc, and/or erase the disc. The following sections describe characteristics unique to each of these disc formats.

OPTICAL DISC FORMATS

Optical Disc	Read	Write	Erase
CD-ROM	Y	N	N
CD-R	Y	Y	N
CD-RW	Y	Y	Y
DVD-ROM	Y	N	N
DVD-R DVD+R	Y	Y	N
DVD-RW DVD+RW DVD+RAM	Y	Y	Y

FIGURE 7-21 Manufacturers sell CD-ROM and DVD-ROM media prerecorded (written) with audio, video, and software. Users cannot change the contents of these discs. Users, however, can purchase the other formats of CDs and DVDs as blank media and record (write) their own data, instructions, and information on these discs.

DO store the disc in a jewel box when not in use.

DO NOT eat, smoke, or drink near a disc.

DO NOT expose the disc to excessive heat or sunlight.

DO hold a disc by its edges.

DO NOT touch the underside of the disc.

DO NOT stack discs.

FIGURE 7-20 Some guidelines for the proper care of optical discs.

CD-ROMs

A **CD-ROM** (pronounced SEE-DEE-rom), or *compact disc read-only memory*, is a type of optical disc that users can read but not write (record) or erase — hence, the name read-only. Manufacturers write the contents of standard CD-ROMs. A standard CD-ROM is called a *single-session disc* because manufacturers write all items on the disc at one time. Software manufacturers often distribute their programs using CD-ROMs (Figure 7-22).

A typical CD-ROM holds from 650 MB to 1 GB of data, instructions, and information. To read a CD-ROM, insert the disc in a **CD-ROM drive** or a CD-ROM player. Because audio CDs and CD-ROMs use the same laser technology, you may be able to use a CD-ROM drive to listen to an audio CD while working on the computer. Some music companies, however, configure their CDs so the music will not play on a computer. They do this to protect themselves from customers illegally copying and sharing the music. Read Ethics & Issues 7-1 for a related discussion.

The speed of a CD-ROM drive determines how fast it installs programs and accesses the disc. Original CD-ROM drives were single-speed drives with transfer rates of 150 KBps (kilobytes per second). Manufacturers measure all optical disc drives relative to this original CD-ROM drive. They use an X to denote the original transfer rate of 150 KBps. For example, a 48X CD-ROM drive has a data transfer rate of 7,200 (48 × 150) KBps, or 7.2 MBps.

Current CD-ROM drives have transfer rates, or speeds, ranging from 48X to 75X or faster. The higher the number, the faster the CD-ROM drive. Faster CD-ROM drives are more expensive than slower drives.

WEB LINK 7-5

CD-ROMs

For more information, visit scsite.com/dc2007/ch7/weblink and then click CD-ROMs.

ETHICS & ISSUES 7-1

Does Music Sharing Harm CD Sales?

With over a billion songs illegally available on file sharing networks, such as eDonkey, the music industry claims that sharing music is harming CD sales, which results in less money in the artists' pockets. A recent study by researchers at Harvard University and the University of North Carolina showed that the availability and sharing of recent CD releases did not have an effect on the sales of the CDs. The researchers found that those who obtained the music from the Internet were often the least likely to purchase the CDs in the first place. While music publishing companies have seen a modest decline in sales since the advent of music sharing, they have released significantly fewer titles, and some claim that the quality of music has declined. Also, CD sales may have been exceptionally high in the 1990s as people replaced older media, such as cassette tapes and vinyl albums, with the newer CD format. While clearly in violation of the music publishers' copyright, does music sharing harm CD sales? Why? Is it possible that music sharing actually results in higher sales for record companies in some cases? Why or why not? Are the music industry's complaints justified or are they being greedy? Why?

FIGURE 7-22 Encyclopedias, games, simulations, and many other programs are distributed on CD-ROM.

PICTURE CDs   A Kodak **Picture CD** is a single-session CD-ROM that stores digital versions of a single roll of film using a jpg file format. Many film developers offer Picture CD service for consumers when they drop off film to be developed. That is, in addition to printed photographs and negatives, you also receive a Picture CD containing the film's pictures. The resolution of images stored on a Picture CD usually is 1024 × 1536 pixels. The additional cost for a Picture CD is about $10 per roll of film.

Most optical disc drives can read a Picture CD. Using photo editing software and photographs on the Picture CD, you can remove red eye, crop the photograph, enhance colors, trim away edges, adjust the lighting, and edit just about any aspect of a photograph. In addition, a Picture CD allows you to print copies of the photographs on glossy paper with an ink-jet printer. If you do not have a printer to print the images, many stores have kiosks at which you can print pictures from a Picture CD or other media (Figure 7-23).

FAQ 7-5

How do I share my digital pictures with others?

You can send them as e-mail attachments, copy them to online storage, or post them to a personal Web page or a photo community. At a *photo community*, users can create online photo albums and share their digital photographs on the Web. Some photo communities provide free, unlimited storage space; others charge a nominal fee. For more information, visit scsite.com/dc2007/ch7/faq and then click Photo Communities.

FIGURE 7-23   HOW A PICTURE CD WORKS

Step 1:
Drop off the film to be developed. Mark the Picture CD box on the film-processing envelope.

Step 2:
When you pick up prints and negatives, a Picture CD contains digital images of each photograph.

Step 3:
At home, print images from the Picture CD on your ink-jet or photo printer. At a store, print images from the Picture CD at a kiosk.

CD-Rs and CD-RWs

A **CD-R** (*compact disc-recordable*) is a multisession optical disc on which users can write, but not erase, their own items such as text, graphics, and audio. *Multisession* means you can write on part of the disc at one time and another part at a later time. Each part of a CD-R, however, can be written on only one time, and the disc's contents cannot be erased.

Writing on the CD-R requires a *CD recorder* or a **CD-R drive**. A CD-R drive usually can read both audio CDs and standard CD-ROMs. These drives read at speeds of 48X or more and write at speeds of 40X or more. Manufacturers often list the write speed first, for example, as 40/48.

A **CD-RW** (*compact disc-rewritable*) is an erasable multisession disc you can write on multiple times. CD-RW overcomes the major disadvantage of CD-R because it allows users to write and rewrite data, instructions, and information on the CD-RW disc multiple times — instead of just once. Reliability of the disc tends to drop, however, with each successive rewrite.

To write on a CD-RW disc, you must have CD-RW software and a **CD-RW drive**. These drives have write speeds of 52X or more, rewrite speeds of 24X or more, and read speeds of 52X or more. Manufacturers state the speeds in this order; that is, write speed, rewrite speed, and read speed is stated as 52/24/52. Most CD-RW drives can read audio CDs, CD-ROMs, CD-Rs, and CD-RWs.

Many personal computers today include a CD-RW drive as a standard feature so users can burn their own discs. The process of writing on an optical disc is called *burning*. Some operating systems, such as Windows XP, include the capability of burning discs.

Using a CD-RW disc, users easily back up large files from a hard disk. Another popular use of CD-RW and CD-R discs is to create audio CDs. For example, users can record their own music and save it on a CD, purchase and download MP3 songs from the Web, or rearrange tracks on a purchased music CD. The process of copying audio and/or video data from a purchased disc and saving it on digital media is called *ripping*. Read Ethics & Issues 7-2 for a related discussion.

WEB LINK 7-7

CD-Rs and CD-RWs
For more information, visit scsite.com/ dc2007/ch7/weblink and then click CD-Rs and CD-RWs.

FAQ 7-6

Is it legal to copy songs or movies to a disc or other media?

It is legal to copy songs or movies from a disc that you obtained legally, if you use the copied music or movie for your own personal use. If you share the copy with a friend, however, you are violating copyright law. It is legal to download copyrighted material if the copyright holder has granted permission to do so. In most cases, you pay a fee. For more information, visit scsite.com/dc2007/ ch7/faq and then click Copying Songs and Movies.

ETHICS & ISSUES 7-2

Is It Ethical to Use Pirated CDs or DVDs?

Recently, several highly anticipated, big-budget movies were being watched in homes around the world — before the movies even were released to theaters. CD-R and DVD-R technology makes copying music and movies easy and affordable. People use CD-R and DVD-R technology to copy CDs and DVDs they have purchased, borrowed, or downloaded from the Internet. At some campuses, students use college servers to create music Web sites, download copyrighted music, and then record and distribute unauthorized copies. The recording industry claims this practice is unfair to the industry and, in essence, steals from the recording artists. Others, however, insist that bootlegged music actually is a marketing vehicle, influencing listeners who pay to attend concerts eventually to purchase the CD. The music industry has gone as far as placing technology on CDs that makes them impossible or very difficult to copy. Opponents to this practice say that these measures infringe on the CD owner's right to fair use, such as making personal backup copies, which courts have upheld as exceptions to copyright laws. Is it ethical to download and copy portions of a music CD, or an entire music CD, from the Internet? Why? If you purchase a CD, is it ethical to make copies for yourself? For a friend? Why? Should recording or movie companies be able to use formatting techniques to keep people from copying CDs or DVDs? What practices should be allowed within the doctrine of fair use?

DVD-ROMs

A **DVD-ROM** (*digital versatile disc-read-only memory* or *digital video disc-read-only memory*) is an extremely high-capacity optical disc on which users can read but not write or erase. Manufacturers write the contents of DVD-ROMs and distribute them to consumers. DVD-ROMs store movies, music, music videos, huge databases, and complex software (Figure 7-24).

The storage capacity of a DVD-ROM is more than enough to hold a telephone book containing every resident in the United States. Not only is the storage capacity of a DVD-ROM greater than that of a CD, a DVD-ROM's quality also far surpasses that of CDs because images are stored at higher resolution.

To read a DVD-ROM, you must have a **DVD-ROM drive** or DVD player. Most DVD-ROM drives also can read audio CDs, CD-ROMs, CD-Rs, and CD-RWs. DVD-ROM drives can read DVDs at speeds of 16X or more and CDs at speeds of 52X or more.

Although the size and shape of a CD-ROM and DVD-ROM are similar, a DVD-ROM stores data, instructions, and information in a slightly different manner and thus achieves a higher storage capacity. Widely used DVD-ROMs are capable of storing 4.7 GB to 17 GB, depending on the storage techniques used (Figure 7-25). The first storage technique involves making the disc denser by packing the pits closer together. The second involves using two layers of pits. For this technique to work, the lower layer of pits is semi-transparent so the laser can read through it to the upper layer. This technique doubles the capacity of the disc. Finally, some DVD-ROMs are double-sided. Two newer, quite expensive competing DVD formats are Blu-ray and HD-DVD. A *Blu-ray disc* currently has storage capacities of 27 GB, with expectations of exceeding 100 GB in the future. The *HD-DVD disc*, which stands for high-density-DVD, has storage capacities up to 45 GB. Read Looking Ahead 7-2 for a look at the competing HD-DVD and Blu-ray technologies.

A mini-DVD that has grown in popularity is the UMD, which works specifically with the PlayStation Portable handheld game console. The *UMD* (Universal Media Disc), which has a diameter of about 2.4 inches, can store up to 1.8 GB of games, movies, or music (Figure 7-26).

FAQ 7-7

What is a DVD/CD-RW drive?

It is a combination drive that reads DVD and CD media; it also writes to CD-RW media. This drive allows you to watch a DVD or burn a CD. For more information, visit scsite.com/dc2007/ch7/faq and then click DVD/CD-RW Drives.

DVD-ROM STORAGE CAPACITIES

Sides	Layers	Storage Capacity
1	1	4.7 GB
1	2	8.5 GB
2	1	9.4 GB
2	2	17 GB

FIGURE 7-25 Storage capacities of DVD-ROMs.

FIGURE 7-24 A DVD-ROM is an extremely high-capacity optical disc.

FIGURE 7-26 This UMD contains the movie, *Spider-Man 2*.

LOOKING AHEAD 7-2

Next-Generation DVDs a Burning Question

Two incompatible recording formats are battling for supremacy in the next generation of high-definition video discs. Traditional DVD backers, including Time-Warner, Toshiba, Intel, Microsoft, and NEC, are supporting the HD-DVD format, while several consumer electronics and high-tech companies, such as Sony, Philips, and Matsushita, are favoring Blu-ray. The major movie studios have split their support between the two technologies.

Both formats offer superior picture quality, a feature that will become increasingly important as consumers purchase more high-definition television products. Compared to the HD-DVD discs, Blu-ray discs will cost more to manufacture, but they will hold more data. The format rivalry is affecting the multibillion dollar market for DVD players, personal computer drivers, and optical discs. For more information, visit scsite.com/dc2007/ch7/looking and then click DVD Formats.

Recordable and Rewritable DVDs

Many types of recordable and rewritable DVD formats are available. *DVD-R* and *DVD+R* are competing DVD-recordable formats, each with up to 4.7 GB storage capacity. Both allow users to write on the disc once and read (play) it many times. In concept, DVD-R and DVD+R are similar to CD-R.

Instead of recordable DVDs, however, most users work with rewritable DVDs because these discs can be written on multiple times and also erased. Three competing rewritable DVD formats exist, each with storage capacities up to 4.7 GB per side: **DVD-RW**, **DVD+RW**, and **DVD+RAM**. These rewritable DVDs are similar in concept to CD-RW. With DVD-RW and DVD+RW discs, a user can erase and write (record) more than 1,000 times. To write on these discs, you must have a DVD-RW drive, a DVD+RW drive, or a DVD recorder. DVD-RW and DVD+RW drives have rewrite speeds of 12X or more, and read speeds of 40X or more. The drives usually can read DVD-ROM, DVD-R, DVD+R, and all CD media, and they can write on DVD-RW or DVD+RW, DVD-R, CD-R, and CD-RW media.

DVD+RAM (DVD+random access memory) allows users to erase and record on a DVD+RAM disc more than 100,000 times. These discs can be read by DVD+RAM drives and some DVD-ROM drives and players.

As the cost of DVD technologies becomes more reasonable, many industry professionals expect that DVD eventually will replace all CD media.

FAQ 7-8

Do any digital video cameras record movies on DVD?

Yes. Video cameras that store at least 120 minutes of recording on mini-DVD-RW/CD-RW media are available. Once recorded, users can view the DVD media in a standard computer DVD drive or a DVD player. Many video cameras include the capability of editing the video right in the camera. For more information, visit scsite.com/dc2007/ch7/faq and then click DVD Video Recorders.

WEB LINK 7-8

DVDs

For more information, visit scsite.com/dc2007/ch7/weblink and then click DVDs.

Test your knowledge of pages 366 through 373 in Quiz Yourself 7-2.

QUIZ YOURSELF 7-2

Instructions: Find the true statement below. Then, rewrite the remaining false statements so they are true.

1. A CD-RW is a type of optical disc on which users can read but not write (record) or erase.

2. A DVD-RAM is a single-session disc that stores digital versions of a single roll of film using a jpg file format.

3. DVDs have the same storage capacities as CDs.

4. Optical discs are written and read by mirrors.

5. Single session means you can write on part of the disc at one time and another part at a later time.

6. Three competing rewritable DVD formats are DVD-RW, DVD+RW, and DVD+RAM.

Quiz Yourself Online: To further check your knowledge of optical discs and various optical disc formats, visit scsite.com/dc2007/ch7/quiz and then click Objectives 5 – 6.

TAPE

One of the first storage media used with mainframe computers was tape. **Tape** is a magnetically coated ribbon of plastic capable of storing large amounts of data and information at a low cost. Tape no longer is used as a primary method of storage. Instead, business and home users utilize tape most often for long-term storage and backup.

Comparable to a tape recorder, a **tape drive** reads and writes data and information on a tape. Although older computers used reel-to-reel tape drives, today's tape drives use tape cartridges. A *tape cartridge* is a small, rectangular, plastic housing for tape (Figure 7-27). Tape cartridges that contain quarter-inch-wide tape are slightly larger than audiocassette tapes. Business and home users sometimes back up personal computer hard disks to tape. Transfer rates of tape drives range from 1.25 MBps to 6 MBps.

Some personal computers have external tape units. Others have the tape drive built into the system unit. On larger computers, tape cartridges are mounted in a separate cabinet called a *tape library*.

Tape storage requires *sequential access*, which refers to reading or writing data consecutively. As with a music tape, you must forward or rewind the tape to a specific point to access a specific piece of data. For example, to access item W requires passing through points A through V sequentially.

Hard disks, CDs, and DVDs all use direct access. *Direct access*, also called *random access*, means that the device can locate a particular data item or file immediately, without having to move consecutively through items stored in front of the desired data item or file. When writing or reading specific data, direct access is much faster than sequential access.

FIGURE 7-27   A tape drive and a tape cartridge.

PC CARDS

As discussed in Chapter 4, a **PC Card** is a thin, credit-card-sized device that fits into a PC Card slot. Different types and sizes of PC Cards add storage, additional memory, fax/modem, networking, sound, and other capabilities to a desktop or notebook computer. PC Cards commonly are used in notebook computers (Figure 7-28).

Originally, PC Cards were called PCMCIA cards. Three kinds of PC Cards are available: Type I, Type II, and Type III (Figure 7-29). The only difference in size among the three types is their thickness. Some digital cameras use a Type II or Type III PC Card to store photographs. PC Cards that house a hard disk have storage capacities up to 5 GB. The advantage of a PC Card for storage is portability. You easily can transport large amounts of data, instructions, and information from one computer to another using a Type II or Type III PC Card.

FIGURE 7-28   A PC Card in a notebook computer.

PC CARDS

Category	Thickness	Use
Type I	3.3 mm	RAM, SRAM, flash memory
Type II	5.0 mm	Modem, LAN, SCSI, sound, TV tuner, hard disk, or other storage
Type III	10.5 mm	Rotating storage such as a hard disk

FIGURE 7-29   Various uses of PC Cards.

MINIATURE MOBILE STORAGE MEDIA

Miniature mobile storage media allow mobile users easily to transport digital images, music, or documents to and from computers and other devices (Figure 7-30). Many desktop computers, notebook computers, Tablet PCs, PDAs, smart phones, digital cameras, and audio players have built-in slots or ports to read from and write on miniature mobile storage media. For computers or devices without built-in slots, users insert the media in separate peripherals such as a card reader/writer, which typically plugs in a USB port, or a device such as a *digital photo viewer*, which connects to a television port for on-screen picture viewing. The following sections discuss the widely used miniature storage media: flash memory cards, USB flash drives, and smart cards.

FIGURE 7-30 Many types of computers and devices use miniature mobile storage media.

Flash Memory Cards

Previously, this chapter discussed miniature hard disks (magnetic media) and mini discs such as the UMD (optical media). Flash memory cards, by contrast, are a type of *solid-state media*, which means they consist entirely of electronic components and contain no moving parts. Common types of flash memory cards include *CompactFlash (CF), SmartMedia, Secure Digital (SD), xD Picture Card,* and *Memory Stick.* The table in Figure 7-31 compares storage capacities and uses of these media.

Depending on the device, manufacturers claim miniature mobile storage media can last from 10 to 100 years. Transfer rates range from about 1 MBps to 10 MBps or more, depending on the device. Flash memory cards are quite expensive compared to other storage media.

For example, the cost of a 4 GB CompactFlash card is the same as a 120 GB hard disk.

To view, edit, or print images and information stored on miniature mobile storage media, you transfer the contents to your desktop computer or other device such as a digital photo viewer. Some printers have slots to read PC Cards and flash memory cards. If your computer or printer does not have a built-in slot, you can purchase a *card reader/writer,* which is a device that reads and writes data, instructions, and information stored on PC Cards or flash memory cards. Card reader/writers usually connect to the USB port, FireWire port, or parallel port on the system unit. The type of card you have will determine the type of card reader/writer needed. Figure 7-32 shows how one type of flash memory card works with a card reader/writer.

VARIOUS FLASH MEMORY CARDS

Media Name	Storage Capacity	Use
CompactFlash	64 MB to 8 GB	Digital cameras, PDAs, smart phones, photo printers, audio players, notebook computers, desktop computers
SmartMedia	32 MB to 128 MB	Digital cameras, photo printers, audio players
Secure Digital	64 MB to 1 GB	Digital cameras, digital video cameras, PDAs, smart phones, photo printers, audio players
xD Picture Card	64 MB to 1 GB	Digital cameras, photo printers
Memory Stick	256 MB to 4 GB	Digital cameras, digital video cameras, PDAs, photo printers, smart phones, handheld game consoles, notebook computers

FIGURE 7-31 A variety of flash memory cards.

FIGURE 7-32   HOW ONE TYPE OF FLASH MEMORY CARD WORKS

Step 1:
When you insert a memory card in a card reader/writer or card slot, the memory card's metallic conductors make contact with connectors in the card reader/writer or card slot, allowing the transfer of pictures and other items between the card and the reading/writing device.

metallic conductors

write-protect switch

card reader/writer

memory card

Step 4:
Some memory cards contain write-protect switches, which prevent users from accidentally erasing pictures and other items stored on the flash memory chips.

controller chip

notch

Step 2:
A notch on the side of the memory card prevents the card from accidentally slipping out of the card reader/writer or card slot.

flash memory chips

registers

Step 3:
Flash memory chips store pictures and other types of data and information. When requested, the controller transfers items stored on the flash memory chips to the metallic conductors, using registers for temporary storage, as needed.

USB Flash Drives

A **USB flash drive**, sometimes called a *pen drive*, is a flash memory storage device that plugs in a USB port on a computer or mobile device (Figure 7-33). USB flash drives are convenient for mobile users because they are small and lightweight enough to be transported on a keychain or in a pocket. With a USB flash drive, users easily transfer documents, pictures, music, and videos from one computer to another. Current USB flash drives have data transfer rates of about 12 MBps and storage capacities up to 4 GB.

USB flash drives have become the mobile user's primary portable storage device, making the floppy disk nearly obsolete because they have much greater storage capacities and are much more convenient to carry.

FIGURE 7-33   A USB flash drive.

Smart Cards

A **smart card**, which is similar in size to a credit card or ATM card, stores data on a thin microprocessor embedded in the card. Smart cards contain a processor and have input, process, output, and storage capabilities. When you insert the smart card in a specialized card reader, the information on the smart card is read and, if necessary, updated (Figure 7-34).

Uses of smart cards include storing medical records, vaccination data, and other health-care and identification information; tracking information such as customer purchases or employee attendance; storing a prepaid amount of money; and authenticating users such as for Internet purchases. Read Ethics & Issues 7-3 for a related discussion.

FAQ 7-9

Are some credit cards smart cards?

Yes. More than 60 million people around the world have a smart Visa card, which contains a microchip filled with their personal information. Credit card smart cards offer the consumer the convenience of using the card to make purchases in stores and online. For more information, visit scsite.com/dc2007/ch7/faq and then click Credit Card Smart Cards.

ETHICS & ISSUES 7-3

Should the World Become a Cashless Society?

Do you toss your loose change in a jar with the hopes of making a special purchase with the savings someday? Futurists predict that this practice may one day go the way of making purchases with silver and gold. Some forecasters say that the world is moving toward a cashless society. One form of payment that could end the need for cash is the smart card, which can store a dollar amount on a thin microprocessor and update the amount whenever a transaction is made. Advocates claim that smart cards would eliminate muggings and robberies, make it difficult to purchase illegal goods, and reduce taxes by identifying tax cheats. Smart cards already are common in Europe, but many Americans cite privacy concerns as reasons to avoid them. Several high-profile security breaches at credit reporting and credit card companies have heightened these concerns. In a recent survey, most Americans said that they would not use a smart card even if privacy was guaranteed. A cash purchase usually is anonymous. Yet, a smart card purchase preserves a record of the transaction that could become available to other merchants, advertisers, government agencies, or hackers. Considering the advantages and disadvantages, should the world become a cashless society? Why or why not? Would you be comfortable using a smart card instead of cash for all transactions? Why?

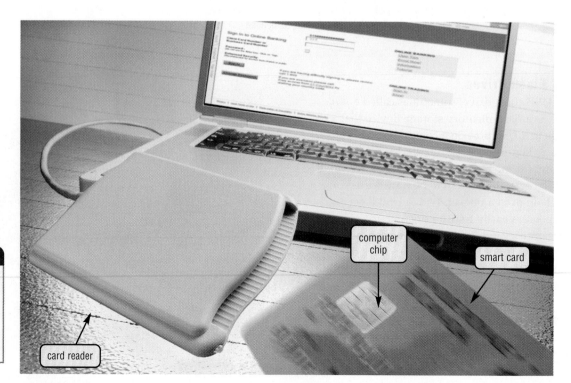

FIGURE 7-34 A smart card and smart card reader.

MICROFILM AND MICROFICHE

Microfilm and microfiche store microscopic images of documents on roll or sheet film. **Microfilm** is a 100- to 215-foot roll of film. **Microfiche** is a small sheet of film, usually about 4 × 6 inches. A *computer output microfilm recorder* is the device that records the images on the film. The stored images are so small that you can read them only with a microfilm or microfiche reader (Figure 7-35).

Applications of microfilm and microfiche are widespread. Libraries use these media to store back issues of newspapers, magazines, and genealogy records. Some large organizations use microfilm and microfiche to archive inactive files. Some banks use them to store transactions and canceled checks. The U.S. Army uses them to store personnel records.

The use of microfilm and microfiche provides a number of advantages. They greatly reduce the amount of paper firms must handle. They are inexpensive and have the longest life of any storage media (Figure 7-36).

ENTERPRISE STORAGE

A large business, commonly referred to as an enterprise, has hundreds or thousands of employees in offices across the country or around the world. Enterprises use computers and computer networks to manage and store huge volumes of data and information about customers, suppliers, and employees (Figure 7-37).

To meet their large-scale needs, enterprises use special hardware geared for heavy use, maximum availability, and maximum efficiency. One or more servers on the network have the sole purpose of providing storage to connected users. For high-speed storage access, entire networks are dedicated exclusively to connecting devices that provide storage to other servers. In an enterprise, some storage systems can provide more than 185 terabytes (trillion bytes) of storage capacity. CD-ROM servers and DVD-ROM servers hold hundreds of CD-ROMs or DVD-ROMs.

An enterprise's storage needs usually grow daily. Thus, the storage solutions an enterprise chooses must be able to store its data and information requirements today and tomorrow.

FIGURE 7-35   Images on microfilm can be read only with a microfilm reader.

MEDIA LIFE EXPECTANCIES* (when using high-quality media)

Media Type	Guaranteed Life Expectancy	Potential Life Expectancy
Magnetic disks	3 to 5 years	20 to 30 years
Optical discs	5 to 10 years	50 to 100 years
Microfilm	100 years	500 years

* according to manufacturers of the media

FIGURE 7-36   Microfilm is the medium with the longest life.

FIGURE 7-37   An enterprise uses computers and high-capacity storage devices.

PUTTING IT ALL TOGETHER

Many factors influence the type of storage devices you should use: the amount of data, instructions, and information to be stored; the hardware and software in use; and the desired cost. The table in Figure 7-38 outlines several suggested storage devices for various types of computer users.

CATEGORIES OF USERS

User	Typical Storage Devices
HOME	• 160 GB hard disk • Online storage • CD or DVD drive • Card reader/writer • USB flash drive
SMALL OFFICE/ HOME OFFICE	• 250 GB hard disk • Online storage • CD or DVD drive • External hard disk for backup • USB flash drive
MOBILE	• 100 GB hard disk • Online storage • CD or DVD drive • Card reader/writer • Portable hard disk for backup • USB flash drive and/or 5 GB PC Card hard disk
POWER	• CD or DVD drive • 500 GB hard disk • Online storage • Portable hard disk for backup • USB flash drive

LARGE BUSINESS	• Desktop Computer
	  - 250 GB hard disk
	  - CD or DVD drive
	  - Smart card reader
	  - Tape drive
	  - USB flash drive
	• Server or Mainframe
	  - Network storage server
	  - 40 TB hard disk system
	  - CD-ROM or DVD-ROM server
	  - Microfilm or microfiche

FIGURE 7-38 Recommended storage devices for various users.

Test your knowledge of pages 374 through 380 in Quiz Yourself 7-3.

QUIZ YOURSELF 7-3

Instructions: Find the true statement below. Then, rewrite the remaining false statements so they are true.

1. A smart card stores data on a thin magnetic stripe embedded in the card.
2. A USB flash drive is a flash memory storage device that plugs in a parallel port on a computer or mobile device.
3. Flash memory cards are a type of magnetic media, which means they consist entirely of electronic components and contain no moving parts.
4. Microfilm and microfiche have the shortest life of any storage media.
5. Tape storage requires direct access, which refers to reading or writing data consecutively.
6. The only difference in size among Type I, Type II, and Type III PC Cards is their thickness.

Quiz Yourself Online: To further check your knowledge of tape, PC Cards, miniature mobile storage media, and microfilm and microfiche, visit scsite.com/dc2007/ch7/quiz and then click Objectives 7 – 9.

CHAPTER SUMMARY

Storage holds data, instructions, and information, which includes pictures, music, and videos, for future use. Users depend on storage devices to provide access to their storage media for years and decades to come. Read Ethics & Issues 7-4 for a discussion about the future of storage.

This chapter identified and discussed various storage media and storage devices. Storage media covered included internal hard disks, portable hard disks, floppy disks, Zip disks, CD-ROMs, recordable CDs, rewritable CDs, DVD-ROMs, recordable DVDs, tape, PC Cards, flash memory cards, USB flash drives, smart cards, and microfilm and microfiche.

ETHICS & ISSUES 7-4

Who Should Be Looking at Your Medical Records?

A medical transcriber based in Pakistan and hired by a U.S. medical center threatened to post private medical records to the Internet if she was not paid more. With the widespread use of computers and an explosion in data storage capacity around the world, private information, such as medical records, requires increased diligence by companies, governments, and individuals to maintain this privacy. The government would like most Americans' health care records available in electronic format by 2014. Updates to the Health Insurance Portability and Accountability Act (HIPAA) effective in 2003 set rigorous standards for medical record privacy. The law, however, still leaves much of your medical information at risk. The law does not cover financial records, education records, or employment records — each of which may contain medical information about you. Your medical information also may be examined by insurance companies, government agencies, the Medical Information Bureau (MIB), employers, and the courts. You also inadvertently may pass on medical information to direct marketers when you participate in informal health screenings or surveys. Some people have found that discussing medical conditions via Internet chat rooms or newsgroups has resulted in unwanted attention, and they later regret the disclosures. Proponents of greater electronic access to medical records claim that more access means that physicians can be better prepared when they see patients, physicians will make fewer errors, and insurance companies can better root out fraud. Should more limits be placed on what other people can do with your medical information? Why or why not? What are the advantages of increased access to medical records? What are the disadvantages?

CAREER CORNER

Computer Technician

The demand for computer technicians is growing in every organization and industry. For many, this is the entry point for a career in the computer/information technology field. The responsibilities of a *computer technician*, also called a computer service technician, include a variety of duties. Most companies that employ someone with this title expect the technician to have basic across-the-board knowledge of concepts in the computer electronics field. Some of the tasks are hardware repair and installation; software installation, upgrade, and configuration; and troubleshooting client and/or server problems. Because the computer field is changing rapidly, technicians must work to remain abreast of current technology and become aware of future developments. Computer technicians generally work with a variety of users, which requires expert people skills, especially the ability to work with groups of nontechnical users.

Most entry-level computer technicians possess the *A+ certification*. This certification attests that a computer technician has demonstrated knowledge of core hardware and operating system technology including installation, configuration, diagnosing, preventive maintenance and basic networking that meets industry standards and has at least six months of experience in the field. The Electronics Technicians Association also provides a Computer Service Technician (CST) certification program.

Because this is an entry-level position, the pay scale is not as high as other more demanding and skilled positions. Individuals can expect an average annual starting salary of around $34,000 to $44,000. Companies pay more for computer technicians with experience and certification. For more information, visit scsite.com/dc2007/ch7/careers and then click Computer Technician.

High-Tech Talk

DISK FORMATTING AND FILE SYSTEMS

Formatting a disk can be compared to starting a library. Before any books can be put in place, you must install the bookshelves and a catalog system. Similarly, a disk must have a file system set up to make it ready to receive data. This is true of many different storage media — including floppy disks, hard disks, removable hard disks, and CDs and DVDs — all of which must be formatted, to allow a way to organize and find files saved on the disk.

This discussion focuses on the formatting process required to take a hard disk from its newly manufactured state to a fully functional storage medium. Three main steps are involved in the process of formatting a hard disk: (1) low-level (physical) formatting, (2) partitioning, and (3) high-level (logical) formatting.

A hard disk must be formatted physically before it can be formatted logically. The hard disk manufacturer usually performs a hard disk's physical formatting, or *low-level formatting*. A hard drive physically formats a hard disk by writing a pattern of 1s and 0s on the surface of the disk. The 1s and 0s act as small electronic markers, which divide the hard disk platter into its basic physical elements: tracks, sectors, and cylinders.

These elements define the way data is written on and read from the disk physically. As the read/write head moves over the spinning disks, it reads the electronic markers that define the tracks, sectors, and cylinders to determine where it is in relation to the data on the disk's surface.

Once a hard disk has been formatted physically, it can be partitioned. *Partitioning* is the process of dividing the hard disk into regions called partitions. Each partition occupies a group of adjacent cylinders. Partitioning allows you to organize a hard disk into segments and lets you run multiple operating systems on a single computer. You also can keep the entire hard disk as one partition. After a disk partition has been formatted, it is referred to as a *volume*.

After a hard disk has been formatted physically and partitioned, it must be formatted logically. Logical formatting, known as *high-level formatting*, places a file system on the disk. A *file system* allows an operating system to use the space available on a hard disk to store and retrieve files. The operating system uses the file system to store information about the disk's directory, or folder, structure.

The file system also defines the size of the clusters used to store data on the hard disk. A cluster, or *block*, is made up of two or more sectors on a single track on a hard disk. Even if a file has a size of 1 byte, a cluster as large as 64 KB might be used to store the file on large drives. The number of sectors and tracks and, therefore, the number of clusters that a drive can create on a disk's surface determine the capacity of the disk.

While creating the file system during logical formatting, the drive creates a special table in the disk's first sector, sector 0. This table stores entries that the operating system uses to locate files on a disk. Each entry in the table takes up a certain number of bits, which is why file systems often are referred to as 12-bit, 16-bit, or 32-bit. The content of each entry consists of a whole number, which identifies one or more clusters where the file is stored.

Depending on the operating system used to format the disk, the file system can be one of several types, as shown in the table in Figure 7-39. Whatever file system is used, the file system is the interface between the operating system and drives. For more information, visit scsite.com/dc2007/ch7/tech and then click Disk Formatting.

File System	Description	Key Features
FAT (also called FAT12 and FAT16)	The standard file system for DOS and Windows. Because of its widespread use, FAT also is accessible by most other operating systems.	• FAT12 is used for floppy disk drives and very small hard disks (up to 16 MB) • FAT16 is used for small to moderate-sized hard disk volumes (up to 2 GB)
VFAT (Virtual FAT)	A newer protected-mode version of the FAT file system, introduced with Windows 95.	• Supports long file names up to 255 characters • Faster than FAT because the computer can read files at least 32 bits at a time
FAT32	A 32-bit version of FAT, introduced with Windows 95.	• Same key features as VFAT • Used for medium-sized to very large hard disk volumes (up to 2 terabytes)
NTFS (NT File System)	The 32-bit file system currently used for Windows NT, Windows 2000, and Windows XP.	• 32- or 64-bit entries in file system table • Fully recoverable file system, designed to restore consistency after a system crash • Used for medium-sized to very large hard disk volumes (up to 16 billion GB)
WinFS (Windows Future Storage)	The file storage subsystem that can be used with Windows XP and Windows Vista.	• Uses database technology; allows users to query for data items • Instead of representing a file with a single name, will represent individual domain objects such as e-mail messages or address book entries

FIGURE 7-39 Comparison of various file systems.

Companies on the Cutting Edge

MAXTOR
INFORMATION STORAGE SUPPLIER

Consumers understand the need to back up their data, but fewer than 25 percent of computer users back up their data on a weekly basis. Hard-disk manufacturer *Maxtor* has been persuading people to save copies of their important documents so they will suffer less data loss in the event of a fire or natural disaster.

Maxtor is a leading manufacturer of hard disks and storage solutions for desktop computers, high-performance servers, and consumer electronics, including digital video recorders and game consoles. Its wholly owned subsidiary, MMC Technology, manufactures nearly 50 million disks each year.

Maxtor launched its Backup Awareness campaign in 2005 to educate consumers about the critical need to protect their data. For more information, visit scsite.com/dc2007/ch7/companies and then click Maxtor.

SANDISK CORPORATION
WORLD'S LARGEST FLASH MEMORY CARD SUPPLIER

The next time you buy milk at the grocery store or shampoo at the drug store, you might want to purchase a flash memory card for your digital camera, too. *SanDisk Corporation* products can be found in more than 100,000 retail stores across the United States, including Rite Aid and Kmart.

With retail sales of flash memory cards soaring, SanDisk executives believe consumers buy multiple flash memory cards to store their digital photographs in much the same manner as they formerly stored film negatives in shoe boxes. They also prefer to take a separate flash memory card to digital photo processing centers, which produce high-quality prints.

SanDisk is the only company with the rights to manufacture and sell every flash card format. For more information, visit scsite.com/dc2007/ch7/companies and then click SanDisk.

Technology Trailblazers

AL SHUGART
STORAGE EXPERT

Al Shugart enjoys fixing broken items and developing new technology. The day after receiving his bachelor's degree in 1951, he went to work at IBM to repair broken machines. IBM then promoted him to supervisor of the product development team that developed the first removable rigid read/write disk drive.

He left IBM in 1969 and went to work as vice president of product development for Memorex. In 1973, he started Shugart Associates, a pioneer in the manufacture of floppy disks. Six years later, he and some associates founded Seagate Technology, Inc., which is a leader in designing and manufacturing storage products.

Today he serves as president and CEO of Al Shugart International, a venture capital firm in California. For more information, visit scsite.com/dc2007/ch7/people and then click Al Shugart.

MARK DEAN
IBM INVENTOR

The next generation of IBM's hardware and software might be the work of *Mark Dean*. As vice president of IBM's Almaden Research Center lab in California, Dean is responsible for developing innovative products.

His designs are used in more than 40 million personal computers manufactured each year. He has more than 40 patents or patents pending, including four of the original seven for the architecture of the original personal computer.

Dean joined IBM in 1979 after graduating at the top of his class at the University of Tennessee. Dean earned his Ph.D. degree at Stanford, and he headed a team at IBM that invented the first CMOS microprocessor to operate at 1 gigahertz (1,000 MHz). For more information, visit scsite.com/dc2007/ch7/people and then click Mark Dean.

384 **CHAPTER 7**

Discovering Computers
A Gateway to Information *2007*

Select a chapter:
1 2 3 4 5 6 7 8 9 10 11 12 13 14 15

7   Storage

Chapter Review

The Chapter Review section summarizes the concepts presented in this chapter. To listen to the audio version of this Chapter Review, visit scsite.com/dc2007/ch7/review. To obtain help from other students regarding any subject in this chapter, visit scsite.com/dc2007/ch7/forum and post your thoughts or questions.

(1) **How Are Storage Devices Different from Storage Media?** A **storage medium** (media is the plural) is the physical material on which a computer keeps data, instructions, and information, which includes pictures, music, and videos. The number of bytes (characters) a storage medium can hold is its **capacity**. A **storage device** is the computer hardware that records and/or retrieves items to and from storage media. **Writing** is the process of transferring items from memory to a storage medium, and **reading** is the process of transferring these items from a storage medium into memory.

(2) **What Are the Characteristics of Magnetic Disks?** *Magnetic disks* use magnetic particles to store data, instructions, and information on a disk's surface. Before any data can be read from or written on a magnetic disk, the disk must be formatted. **Formatting** is the process of dividing the disk into *tracks* and *sectors*. Three types of magnetic disks are floppy disks, Zip disks, and hard disks.

(3) **What Are the Characteristics of a Hard Disk?** A **hard disk**, also called a *hard disk drive*, is a storage device that contains one or more inflexible, circular platters that store data, instructions, and information. A *platter* is made of aluminum, glass, or ceramic and is coated with a material that allows items to be recorded magnetically on its surface. Each platter has two read/write heads, one for each side. The location of a *read/write head* often is referred to by its *cylinder,* which is the vertical section of a track that passes through all platters. While the computer is running, the platters rotate at 5,400 to 15,000 *revolutions per minute* (rpm), which allows nearly instant access to all tracks and sectors on the platters. The spinning creates a cushion of air between the platters and the read/write heads. A *head crash* occurs when a read/write head touches the surface of a platter, usually resulting in a loss of data. A **backup** is a duplicate of a file, program, or disk that you can use in case the original is lost, damaged, or destroyed.

(4) **What Are the Differences between Floppy Disks and Zip Disks?** A **floppy disk** is a portable, inexpensive storage medium that consists of a thin, circular, flexible plastic Mylar film with a magnetic coating enclosed in a square-shaped plastic shell. A standard floppy disk can store up to 500 double-spaced pages of text, several digital photographs, or a small audio file. A **floppy disk drive** is a device that reads from and writes on a floppy disk. A **Zip disk** is a type of portable magnetic media that can store from 100 MB to 750 MB of data. The larger capacities make it easy to transport many files or large items. Another popular use of Zip disks is to back up important data and information.

Visit scsite.com/dc2007/ch7/quiz or click the Quiz Yourself button. Click Objectives 1 – 4.

(5) **What Are the Characteristics of Optical Discs?** An *optical disc* is a type of storage media that consists of a flat, round, portable disc made of metal, plastic, and lacquer that is written and read by a laser. Optical discs, which primarily store software, data, digital photographs, movies, and music, contain microscopic pits (indentations) and lands (flat areas) in their middle layer. Optical discs commonly store items in a single track that spirals from the center of the disc to its edge. Like a hard disk, the single track is divided into evenly sized sectors.

Chapter Review

Common optical discs used today are CD-ROM, CD-R, CD-RW, DVD-ROM, Blu-ray disc, HD-DVD disc, UMD, DVD-R, DVD+R, DVD-RW, DVD+RW, and DVD+RAM.

(6) How Are CD-ROMs, Recordable CDs, Rewritable CDs, DVD-ROMs, Recordable DVDs, and Rewritable DVDs Different?   A **CD-ROM**, or *compact disc read-only memory*, is a type of optical disc that uses laser technology to store items. A typical CD-ROM holds from 650 MB to 1 GB of data, instructions, and information. Users can read the contents of standard CD-ROMs but cannot erase or modify their contents. A **CD-R** (*compact disc-recordable*) is a *multisession* disc on which users can record their own items. Each part of a CD-R can be written on only one time, and the disc's contents cannot be erased. A **CD-RW** (*compact disc-rewritable*) is an erasable disc that can be written on multiple times. A **DVD-ROM** (*digital versatile disc-ROM* or *digital video disc-ROM*) is an extremely high capacity optical disk capable of storing from 4.7 GB to 17 GB. Not only is the storage capacity of a DVD-ROM greater than that of a CD-ROM, a DVD-ROM's quality also far surpasses that of a CD-ROM. **DVD-RW** and **DVD+RW** discs are a recordable version of DVD that allows users to erase and record more than 1,000 times. **DVD+RAM** allows users to erase and record on a DVD+RAM more than 100,000 times.

connect Visit scsite.com/dc2007/ch7/quiz or click the Quiz Yourself button. Click Objectives 5 – 6.

(7) How Is Tape Used?   **Tape** is a magnetically coated ribbon of plastic capable of storing large amounts of data and information at a low cost. A **tape drive** reads and writes data and information on tape. Businesses and home users sometimes back up personal computer hard disks on tape.

(8) What Are PC Cards and Other Types of Miniature Mobile Storage Media?   A **PC Card** is a thin, credit-card-sized device that fits into a PC Card slot to add storage or other capabilities to a desktop or notebook computer. Many desktop and notebook computers, Tablet PCs, PDAs, smart phones, digital cameras, and music players have built-in slots or ports for miniature mobile storage media. Common types of miniature mobile storage media include flash memory cards, USB flash drives, and smart cards. A **USB flash drive** is a flash memory storage device that plugs in a port on a computer or mobile device. Common flash memory cards include *CompactFlash* (*CF*), *SmartMedia*, *Secure Digital* (*SD*), *xD Picture Card*, and *Memory Stick*. A **smart card**, which is similar in size to a credit or ATM card, stores data on a thin microprocessor embedded in the card.

(9) How Are Microfilm and Microfiche Used?   **Microfilm** is a 100- to 215-foot roll of film. **Microfiche** is a small sheet of film, usually about 4 × 6 inches. Libraries use microfilm and microfiche to store back issues of newspapers, magazines, and records; some large organizations use them to archive inactive files; some banks use them to store transactions and canceled checks; and the U.S. Army uses them to store personnel records.

connect Visit scsite.com/dc2007/ch7/quiz or click the Quiz Yourself button. Click Objectives 7 – 9.

Key Terms

You should know the Primary Terms and be familiar with the Secondary Terms. Use the list below to help focus your study. To further enhance your understanding of the Key Terms in this chapter, visit scsite.com/dc2007/ch7/terms. See an example of and a definition for each term, and access current and additional information about the term from the Web.

Primary Terms

(shown in bold-black characters in the chapter)

access time (357)
backup (361)
capacity (356)
CD-R (371)
CD-R drive (371)
CD-ROM (369)
CD-ROM drive (369)
CD-RW (371)
CD-RW drive (371)
DVD+RAM (373)
DVD+RW (373)
DVD-ROM (372)
DVD-ROM drive (372)
DVD-RW (373)
external hard disk (362)
floppy disk (364)
floppy disk drive (364)
formatting (357)
hard disk (358)
microfiche (379)
microfilm (379)
online storage (363)
PC Card (374)
Picture CD (370)
reading (356)

removable hard disk (362)
smart card (378)
storage device (356)
storage medium (355)
tape (374)
tape drive (374)
USB flash drive (377)
write-protect notch (365)
writing (356)
Zip disk (365)
Zip drive (365)

Secondary Terms

(shown in italic characters in the chapter)

allocation unit (357)
Blu-ray disc (372)
burning (371)
card reader/writer (376)
CD recorder (371)
cluster (357)
compact disc read-only memory (369)
compact disc-recordable (371)
compact disc-rewritable (371)
CompactFlash (CF) (376)
computer output microfilm recorder (379)
cylinder (360)
density (365)
digital photo viewer (375)
digital versatile disc-read-only memory (372)
digital video disc-read-only memory (372)
direct access (374)
disk cache (361)
disk controller (363)
diskette (364)
DVD+R (373)
DVD-R (373)
EIDE (Enhanced Integrated Drive Electronics) (363)
external floppy disk drive (364)

fixed disk (358)
form factor (360)
hard disk drive (358)
head crash (360)
HD (365)
HD-DVD disc (372)
jewel box (368)
KBps (357)
longitudinal recording (358)
magnetic disks (357)
MBps (357)
Memory Stick (376)
mini discs (366)
multisession (371)
optical disc (366)
pen drive (377)
perpendicular recording (358)
platter (359)
portable (358)
random access (374)
read/write head (360)
revolutions per minute (rpm) (360)
ripping (371)
SATA (Serial Advanced Technology Attachment) (363)
SCSI (363)
secondary storage (355)
sectors (357)
Secure Digital (SD) (376)
sequential access (374)
single-session disc (369)
SmartMedia (376)
solid-state media (376)
storage (354)
tape cartridge (374)
tape library (374)
track (357)
transfer rate (357)
UMD (372)
xD Picture Card (376)

Checkpoint

Use the Checkpoint exercises to check your knowledge level of the chapter. The Beyond the Book exercises will help broaden your understanding of the concepts presented in this chapter. To complete the Checkpoint exercises interactively, visit scsite.com/dc2007/ch7/check.

Label the Figure

Identify the storage media.

a. CD or DVD
b. USB flash drive
c. tape
d. miniature hard disk
e. external hard disk
f. flash memory card
g. Zip disk
h. internal hard disk

1. ___
2. ___
3. ___
4. ___
5. ___
6. ___
7. ___

True/False

Mark T for True and F for False. (See page numbers in parentheses.)

_____ 1. Every computer uses storage to hold software, specifically, system software and application software. (354)

_____ 2. A storage medium is the physical material on which a computer keeps data, instructions, and information. (355)

_____ 3. Reading is the process of transferring data, instructions, and information from memory to a storage medium. (356)

_____ 4. Formatting is the process of dividing the disk into tracks and sectors. (357)

_____ 5. A cluster can hold data from many files. (357)

_____ 6. A typical hard disk contains multiple platters. (360)

_____ 7. A removable hard disk is a separate, free-standing hard disk that connects with a cable to a port on the system unit. (362)

_____ 8. SCSI interfaces can support up to eight or fifteen peripheral devices. (363)

_____ 9. All optical discs are double-sided. (366)

_____ 10. A UMD can store up to 2.8 GB of games, movies, or music. (372)

_____ 11. When writing or reading specific data, direct access is much slower than sequential access. (374)

_____ 12. Smart cards contain a processor and have input, process, output, and storage capabilities. (378)

Checkpoint

 Multiple Choice   Select the best answer. (See page numbers in parentheses.)

1. Examples of storage media include all of the following, except _____. (355)
   a. CDs and DVDs
   b. floppy disks and hard disks
   c. monitors and printers
   d. tape and PC Cards

2. _____ is the speed with which data, instructions, and information transfer to and from a device. (357)
   a. Formatting
   b. Access time
   c. Transfer rate
   d. Reading

3. On desktop computers, platters most often have a form factor, or size, of approximately _____ in diameter. (360)
   a. 3.5 inches
   b. 2.5 inches
   c. 88 mm
   d. 1.6 inches

4. Portable hard disks offer all of the following advantages over internal hard disks, except _____. (362)
   a. they can transport a large number of files
   b. they can add storage space to a notebook computer
   c. they can be shared with multiple computers
   d. they can transfer data at much faster rates

5. Users store data and information on online storage to _____. (364)
   a. save time by storing large files instantaneously
   b. allow others to access files
   c. store offsite backups of data
   d. all of the above

6. _____ is the number of bits in an area on a storage medium. (365)
   a. Capacity
   b. Density
   c. KBps
   d. Allocation unit

7. A Zip disk can store from _____ of data. (365)
   a. 10 MB to 75 MB
   b. 100 MB to 750 MB
   c. 10 GB to 75 GB
   d. 100 GB to 750 GB

8. A(n) _____ is a type of storage media that consists of a flat, round, portable disc made of metal, plastic, and lacquer that is written and read by a laser. (366)
   a. floppy disk
   b. hard disk
   c. optical disc
   d. pen drive

9. All of the following are guidelines for the proper care of optical discs except _____. (368)
   a. do not expose the disc to extreme temperatures
   b. do not stack discs
   c. do not hold a disc by its edges
   d. do not eat, smoke, or drink near a disc

10. The process of copying audio and/or video data from a purchased disc and saving it on digital media is called _____. (371)
    a. formatting   b. ripping
    c. burning   d. reading

11. A storage technique that a DVD-ROM uses to achieve a higher storage capacity than a CD-ROM is _____. (372)
    a. making the disc denser by packing the pits closer together
    b. using two layers of pits
    c. using both sides of the disc
    d. all of the above

12. _____ storage requires sequential access. (374)
    a. Hard disk
    b. UMD
    c. Tape
    d. CD

13. Which of the following is not true of flash memory cards? (376)
    a. they are a type of solid-state media
    b. they are quite expensive compared to other storage media
    c. they can last 10 to 100 years
    d. they contain moving parts

14. Microfilm and microfiche _____. (379)
    a. greatly increase the amount of paper firms must handle
    b. are expensive
    c. have the longest life of any storage media
    d. all of the above

Checkpoint

Matching
Match the terms with their definitions. (See page numbers in parentheses.)

_____ 1. capacity (356)

_____ 2. cluster (357)

_____ 3. form factor (360)

_____ 4. cylinder (360)

_____ 5. disk cache (361)

_____ 6. disk controller (363)

_____ 7. Zip disk (365)

_____ 8. HD-DVD disc (372)

_____ 9. tape drive (374)

_____ 10. pen drive (377)

a. vertical section of a track that passes through all platters

b. the number of bytes (characters) a storage medium can hold

c. piece of metal on a floppy disk that slides to expose the surface of the disk

d. flash memory storage device that plugs in a USB port

e. smallest unit of disk space that stores data and information

f. memory chips that the processor uses to store frequently accessed items

g. reads and writes data and information on a tape

h. newer, expensive type of DVD with storage capacities up to 45 GB

i. size of hard disk platters on desktop computers

j. type of portable magnetic media that can store from 100 MB to 750 MB of data

k. special-purpose chip and electronic circuits that control the transfer of items to and from the system bus

Short Answer
Write a brief answer to each of the following questions.

1. What is access time? _____ What is the difference between a sector and a track? _____

2. Why is a hard disk inside the system unit sometimes called a fixed disk? _____ What are the different types of portable hard disks? _____

3. What is longitudinal recording? _____ What is the benefit of perpendicular recording over longitudinal recording? _____

4. How is a single-session disc different from a multisession disc? _____ How is a CD-R different from a CD-RW? _____

5. What are the common types of flash memory cards? _____ What is a card reader/writer and how might it attach to your computer? _____

Beyond the Book
Read the following book elements, learn more about each using the Web, and then write a brief report.

1. Ethics & Issues — Does Music Sharing Harm CD Sales? (369), Is It Ethical to Use Pirated CDs or DVDs? (371), Should the World Become a Cashless Society? (378), or Who Should Be Looking at Your Medical Records? (381)

2. Career Corner — Computer Technician (381)

3. Companies on the Cutting Edge — Maxtor or SanDisk Corporation (383)

4. FAQs (359, 361, 363, 368, 370, 371, 372, 373, 378)

5. High-Tech Talk — Disk Formatting and File Systems (382)

6. Looking Ahead — Heat Increases Disk Capacity (359) or Next-Generation DVDs a Burning Question (373)

7. Making Use of the Web — Shopping and Auctions (123)

8. Picture Yourself Working with Mobile Storage Media (352)

9. Technology Trailblazers — Al Shugart or Mark Dean (383)

10. Web Links (358, 362, 363, 369, 370, 371, 373, 377, 378)

Quizzes and Learning Games

Computer Genius
Crossword Puzzle
DC Track and Field
Practice Test
Quiz Yourself
Wheel of Terms
You're Hired!

Exercises

Case Studies
Chapter Review
Checkpoint
Key Terms
Learn How To
▶ Learn It Online
Web Research

Beyond the Book

Career Corner
Companies
FAQs
High-Tech Talk
Looking Ahead
Making Use of the Web
Trailblazers
Web Links

Features

Chapter Forum
Install Computer
Lab Exercises
Maintain Computer
Tech News
Timeline 2007

Learn It Online

Use the Learn It Online exercises to reinforce your understanding of the chapter concepts. To access the Learn It Online exercises, visit scsite.com/dc2007/ch7/learn.

① At the Movies — Repair Your CD Scratches

To view the Repair Your CD Scratches movie, click the number 1 button. Locate your video and click the corresponding High-Speed or Dial-Up link, depending on your Internet connection. Watch the movie and then complete the exercise by answering the questions that follow. Just because your favorite CD has a few scratches is no reason to discard it. A few options are available to help you keep those scratched CDs playing smoothly longer. How does resurfacing work to restore your scratched CDs? What common household product can be used to repair a CD?

② At the Movies — Online Data Storage Options

To view the Online Data Storage Options movie, click the number 2 button. Locate your video and click the corresponding High-Speed or Dial-Up link, depending on your Internet connection. Watch the movie and then complete the exercise by answering the question that follows. Online data storage broadens your options for file sharing and frees up space on your personal computer. If you store files online, anyone who knows the password can access them from anywhere in the world. Several free storage systems offer a moderate amount of space; however, if you need more you can sign up and pay for additional storage for as little as $15 a month. What are some of the most important reasons for backing up your files online?

③ Student Edition Labs — Maintaining a Hard Drive

Click the number 3 button. A new browser window will open, displaying the Student Edition Labs. Follow the on-screen instructions to complete the Maintaining a Hard Drive Lab. When finished, click the Exit button. If required, submit your results to your instructor.

④ Student Edition Labs — Managing Files and Folders

Click the number 4 button. A new browser window will open, displaying the Student Edition Labs. Follow the on-screen instructions to complete the Managing Files and Folders Lab. When finished, click the Exit button. If required, submit your results to your instructor.

⑤ Practice Test

Click the number 5 button. Answer each question. When completed, enter your name and click the Grade Test button to submit the quiz for grading. Make a note of any missed questions. If required, submit your results to your instructor.

⑥ Who Wants To Be a Computer Genius²?

Click the number 6 button to find out if you are a computer genius. Directions about how to play the game will be displayed. When you are ready to play, click the Play button. Submit your score to your instructor.

⑦ Wheel of Terms

Click the number 7 button to reinforce important terms you learned in this chapter by playing the Shelly Cashman Series version of this popular game. Directions about how to play the game will be displayed. When you are ready to play, click the Play button. Submit your score to your instructor.

Learn It Online

⑧ DC Track and Field

Click the number 8 button to use what you have learned in this chapter to compete against other students in three track and field events. Directions about how to play the game will be displayed. When you are ready to play, click the start first event button. If required, submit your score to your instructor.

⑨ You're Hired!

Click the number 9 button to use what you have learned in this chapter to embark on the path to a career in computers. Directions about how to play the game will be displayed. When you are ready to play, click the begin game button. If required, submit your score to your instructor.

⑩ Crossword Puzzle Challenge

Click the number 10 button. Complete the puzzle to reinforce skills you learned in this chapter. Directions about how to play the game will be displayed. When you are ready to play, click the Submit button. Submit the completed puzzle to your instructor.

⑪ Lab Exercises

Click the number 11 button. When the Lab Exercises menu appears, click the exercise assigned by your instructor. A new browser window will open. Follow the on-screen instructions to complete the exercise. When finished, click the Exit button. If required, submit your results to your instructor.

⑫ In the News

Hitachi sells a small disk drive, about the size of a quarter, which is capable of storing up to 4 GB of information, as much as 50 CDs. The drive is used in devices such as PDAs or digital cameras. What other storage devices are on the horizon? Click the number 12 button and read a news article about a new or improved storage device. What is the device? Who manufactures it? How is the storage device better than, or different from, earlier devices? How will the device be used? Why?

⑬ Chapter Discussion Forum

Select an objective from this chapter on page 353 about which you would like more information. Click the number 13 button and post a short message listing a meaningful message title accompanied by one or more questions concerning the selected objective. In two days, return to the threaded discussion by clicking the number 13 button. Submit to your instructor your original message and at least one response to your message.

⑭ Blogs

Click the number 14 button to learn how to use blogs to find information about a topic. Follow the instructions to use MSNBC.com's Blogs Etc. to find a blog about a popular topic, such as the hottest national news story or another topic of national interest. Write a report comparing opinions of two different people about the selected topic. Print your report and submit to your instructor.

Learn How To

Use the Learn How To activities to learn fundamental skills when using a computer and accompanying technology. Complete the exercises and submit them to your instructor. To see a video of a Learn How To activity, visit scsite.com/dc2007/ch7/howto.

LEARN HOW TO 1: Maintain a Hard Disk

A computer's hard disk is used for the majority of storage requirements. It is important, therefore, to ensure that each hard disk on a computer is operating at peak efficiency.

Three tasks that maximize disk operations are detecting and repairing disk errors by using the Check Disk utility program; removing unused or unnecessary files and folders by using the Disk Cleanup utility program; and, consolidating files and folders into contiguous storage areas using the Disk Defragmenter utility program.

A. Check Disk

To detect and repair disk errors using the Check Disk utility program, complete the following steps:

1. Click the Start button on the Windows taskbar and then click My Computer on the Start menu.
2. When the My Computer window opens, right-click the hard disk icon for drive C (or any other hard disk you want to select), and then click Properties on the shortcut menu.
3. In the Properties dialog box, if necessary click the Tools tab.
   The Tools sheet contains buttons to start the Check Disk program, the Defragment program, and the Backup program (Figure 7-40).
4. Click the Check Now button. *The Check Disk dialog box is displayed.*
5. To do a complete scan of the disk and correct any errors that are found, place a checkmark in the Scan for and attempt recovery for bad sectors check box, and then click the Start button. Four phases of checking the disk will occur. While the checking is in progress, the disk being checked cannot be used for any purpose whatsoever; furthermore, once it has started, the process cannot be stopped.
6. When the four phases are complete (this may take more than one-half hour, depending on the size of the hard disk and how many corrections must occur), a dialog box is displayed with the message, Disk Check Complete. Click the OK button in the dialog box.

FIGURE 7-40

B. Cleanup Disk

After checking the disk, your next step can be to clean up the disk by removing any programs and data that are not required for the computer. To do so, complete the following steps:

1. Click the General tab (Figure 7-40) in the disk drive Properties dialog box to display the General sheet.
2. Click the Disk Cleanup button in the General sheet.
3. The Disk Cleanup dialog box is displayed and contains a message that indicates the amount of space that can be freed up is being calculated.
4. After the calculation is complete, the Disk Cleanup dialog box specifies the amount of space that can be freed up and the files to delete, some of which are checked automatically (Figure 7-41). Select those items from which you wish to delete files.
5. Click the OK button in the Disk Cleanup dialog box.
6. A dialog box asks if you are sure you want to perform these actions. Click the Yes button. The Disk Cleanup dialog box illustrates the progress of the cleanup. When the cleanup is complete, the dialog box closes.

Learn How To

C. Defragment Disk

The next step in disk maintenance is to defragment all the files on the disk. When a file is stored on disk, the data in the file sometimes is stored contiguously, and other times is stored in a noncontiguous manner. When a file is stored in a noncontiguous manner, it can take significantly longer to find and retrieve data from the file. Therefore, one of the more useful utilities to speed up disk operations is the defragmentation program, which combines all files so that no files are stored in a noncontiguous manner. To use the defragmentation program, complete the following steps:

1. If necessary, click the Tools tab in the Properties dialog box for the hard disk to be defragmented.
2. Click the Defragment Now button in the Tools sheet. *The Disk Defragmenter window opens (Figure 7-42). This window displays the hard disks on the computer and shows the size and amount of free space for each disk. During defragmentation, the Estimated disk usage before defragmentation area and the Estimated disk usage after defragmentation area display the layout of the data on the disk. If you click the Analyze button, the disk will be analyzed for its data layout but defragmentation will not occur.*
3. Click the Defragment button. The defragmentation process begins. The amount of processing completed is shown on the status bar at the bottom of the window. The defragmentation process can consume more than one hour in some cases. You can pause or stop the operation at any time by clicking the Pause or Stop button in the Disk Defragmenter window.
4. When the process is complete, the Disk Defragmenter dialog box displays the message, Defragmentation is complete for (C:). Click the View Report button to see a complete report about the hard disk.
5. Click the Close button to close the Disk Defragmenter dialog box.

FIGURE 7-41

FIGURE 7-42

Exercise

Caution: The exercises for this chapter that require the actual disk maintenance are optional. If you are performing these exercises on a computer that is not your own, obtain explicit permission to complete these exercises. Keep in mind that these exercises can require significant computer time and the computer may be unusable during this time.

1. Display the Properties dialog box for a hard disk found on the computer. Display the Tools sheet. Click the Check Now button and then place a checkmark in the Scan for and attempt recovery for bad sectors check box. Click the Start button. How long did it take to complete the check of the hard disk? Were any errors discovered and corrected? Submit your answers to your instructor.
2. Display the Properties dialog box for a hard disk found on the computer. Display the General sheet. What is the capacity of the hard disk? How much space is used? How much free space is available? Click the Disk Cleanup button. How much space can be freed up if you use the Disk Cleanup program? Click the OK button to clean up the disk. How long did it take to perform the disk cleanup? Submit your answers to your instructor.
3. Display the Properties dialog box for a hard disk found on the computer. Display the Tools sheet. Click the Defragment Now button. In the Disk Defragmenter window, click the Analyze button. Does the hard disk need to be defragmented? Click the View Report button. How many files are stored on the disk? What is the average size of the files stored on the disk? If necessary, click the Defragment button in the Analysis Report window. How long did defragmentation require? Submit your answers to your instructor.

Web Research

Use the Internet-based Web Research exercises to broaden your understanding of the concepts presented in this chapter. Visit scsite.com/dc2007/ch7/research to obtain more information pertaining to each exercise. To discuss any of the Web Research exercises in this chapter with other students, post your thoughts or questions at scsite.com/dc2007/ch7/forum.

① Scavenger Hunt   Use one of the <u>search engines</u> listed in Figure 2-10 in Chapter 2 on page 78 or your own favorite search engine to find the answers to the questions that follow. Copy and paste the Web address from the Web page where you found the answer. Some questions may have more than one answer. If required, submit your answers to your instructor. (1) What are the three different laser powers used in a CD-rewritable recorder? How do two of the powers affect the recording layer? During writing, to what temperature does the laser beam selectively heat areas of the recording material? (2) What was the diameter of the first floppy disk? (3) What is the Red Book standard? (4) What is the function of a hard disk's actuator? (5) What is areal density? What unit of measurement is used to describe this density? (6) What is IBM's Millipede project?

② Search Sleuth   Many computer users search the World Wide Web by typing words in the search text box, and often they are overwhelmed when the search engine returns thousands of possible Web sites. You can narrow your search by typing quotation marks around phrases and by adding words that give details about the phrase. <u>Go.com</u> is a Web portal developed by the Walt Disney Internet Group. It features a search engine, the latest ABC news and ESPN sports stories, stock market quotes, weather forecasts, maps, and games. Visit this Web site and then use your word processing program to answer the following questions. Then, if required, submit your answers to your instructor. (1) What are five of the listings in the Top Ten Searches area? Click one of these search topics. What are the first three search results listed? (2) Click the Search for text box at the top of the page. Type "USB flash drive" in the box. How many pages of search results are returned that are not Sponsored links? What are Sponsored results? (3) Click the Search for text box after the words, "USB flash drive." Add +"2 GB" and +"data reliability" as the search terms. How many pages of search results are returned that are not Sponsored links? (4) Review your search results and then write a 50-word summary of your findings.

③ Journaling   Respond to your readings in this chapter by writing at least one page about your reactions, evaluations, and reflections about using <u>storage devices</u>. For example, have you used USB flash drives, smart cards, or Zip disks? How do you care for your mobile storage media? Do you own a credit card smart card? What is the storage capacity of your school, office, or home computer's hard disk? Have you copied a CD or DVD? You also can write about the new terms you learned by reading this chapter. If required, submit your journal to your instructor.

④ Expanding Your Understanding   Bill Gates, Microsoft's chief software architect, considers <u>holographic storage</u> an impressive new storage system. The holographic process can store more than 100 movie, photo, and music files on one disc holding one terabyte of data. View Web sites to learn more about holographic storage. What factors are driving the rush to develop this system? How are images stored? What companies are researching and developing this technology? Write a report summarizing your findings, focusing on the possible uses of this storage medium and current engineering efforts to commercialize the technology. If required, submit your report to your instructor.

⑤ Ethics in Action   The United States Federal Bureau of Investigation used a controversial program until January 2005 to monitor and store the e-mail and Internet activity of suspected criminals. Originally called Carnivore, the surveillance program was renamed <u>DCS1000</u>. The program was designed to track the activities of potential terrorists, spies, drug traffickers, and organized crime ring members. FBI agents needed to obtain a court order to monitor an individual, but privacy advocates claim the software tracked people not covered under the court order. View online sites that provide information about DCS1000 or Carnivore, including HowStuffWorks (computer.howstuffworks.com/carnivore.htm). Write a report summarizing your findings, and include a table of links to Web sites that provide additional details. If required, submit your report to your instructor.

Case Studies

Use the Case Studies to apply the concepts presented in the chapter to real-world situations. Visit scsite.com/dc2007/ch7/cases to obtain more information pertaining to each exercise. To discuss the Case Studies in this chapter with other students, visit scsite.com/dc2007/ch7/forum and post your thoughts or questions.

CASE STUDY 1 — Class Discussion   The owner of the motorcycle repair shop where you are employed as a part-time office manager is tired of continually upgrading the company's computer system. After attending a seminar on how small businesses can make use of the Internet, she asked you to look into the feasibility of using online storage (also called an Internet hard disk), rather than purchasing additional storage for the company's computer. Write a brief report outlining the advantages and disadvantages of using online storage. Compare Yahoo! Briefcase and Google's Gmail online storage offerings. Which company offers the best arrangement? Why? Be prepared to discuss your recommendations in class.

CASE STUDY 2 — Class Discussion   Paul's Trucking Company has hired you as an IT consultant. The company plans to purchase 15 computers for use in the accounting department. The first task assigned to you by the president of the company is to recommend the number and types of CD and DVD drives to include with the computers they plan to purchase. They want to use CDs and/or DVDs to share data and information between employees and to back up critical files. Create a brief memo that includes a table summarizing the advantages and disadvantages of using CD-ROM, recordable CD, rewritable CD, DVD-ROM, recordable DVD, and rewritable DVD. Include in the table both the approximate cost of the drive and the media. Be prepared to discuss your findings in class.

CASE STUDY 3 — Research   An old aphorism claims, "You never can have too much money." Many computer users support a similar maxim, "You never can have too much storage." Your manager at MJ National Bank where you are employed as an analyst, however, is tired of buying more hardware to meet the bank's storage needs. She wants you to investigate alternative ways to improve storage capacity. Use the Web and/or print media to find out more about hard disk partitions and data compression as a means of increasing storage capacity. How do partitions increase the capacity of hard disks? What kind of data compression is most suitable for communications devices? What are the most well known data compression algorithms? How can compression ratios of different algorithms be compared? What are some formats for data compression archives? Prepare a report and/or PowerPoint presentation and share your findings with your class.

CASE STUDY 4 — Research   A major national retail chain, where you are employed as a technology buyer, has grown enormously over the past few years. The growth has required the company to triple its storage capacity each year to keep pace with its expanding business. Your manager, who is up for promotion, wants to impress his boss by expanding the storage capacity by tenfold this year while staying under the budget earmarked for storage improvements. He has asked you to look into the latest cutting-edge storage technologies, such as holographic and heat-assisted storage. Use the Web and/or print media to develop a features/benefits breakdown that compares the latest storage technologies to the more traditional hard disk technology. What do the different technologies entail? Are they available today? If not, when? What are their costs? Prepare a report and/or PowerPoint presentation summarizing your findings.

CASE STUDY 5 — Team Challenge   Your team has been assigned to do IT research for a new local magazine-subscription telemarketing company that is about to open for business. The company's business plan calls for 150 telemarketers to make a minimum of 100 calls a day. If a telemarketer does not meet the minimum number of calls, then he or she is required to finish the calls from home. The company plans to buy used computers for each telemarketer to use at home. The company also has to decide on the type of storage device to provide the telemarketers so that when they have to make calls from home, they have a way to take the necessary data home with them. Senior management has narrowed down their choice to three storage devices — rewritable CDs, rewritable DVDs, or USB flash drives. Form a three-member team and have each team member choose a different storage device. Using the Web and/or print media, have each team member determine the advantages and disadvantages of their chosen device. Include such features as capacity, access time, durability of media, and cost. As a team, merge your findings into a team report and/or PowerPoint presentation and share your recommendations with your class.

CHAPTER EIGHT

Operating Systems and Utility Programs

Picture Yourself Getting a Virus through E-Mail

With a break between classes, you and some classmates sit outside and enjoy the nice weather. Everyone decides to exchange e-mail addresses and phone numbers, so you can communicate while away from school.

Later that night at home, you notice a classmate has sent you a picture via e-mail. As soon as you open the picture, your computer freezes. You click the mouse button. Nothing happens. You press a key on the keyboard. The computer beeps. You click the mouse again. Still no response. You restart the computer. The Windows XP desktop never appears.

At that moment, your smart phone rings. A panicked friend says his computer stopped working as soon as he opened that picture. Realizing the picture file probably had a virus, you call a technical support hotline. After explaining the situation, the support technician asks you several questions, and you answer: Did you have antivirus software installed on the computer? "No." Were the operating system's firewall settings enabled? "I don't know." Do you have a backup of the computer's hard disk? "No, I haven't learned how to burn CDs to make backups." Can you find the computer's recovery disc? "Yes, it's right here." The bad news is you lost *everything* on your computer and had to reinstall Windows XP — the good news is your computer is functional again. Now, you need to protect your computer from future infections.

Read Chapter 8 to learn about antivirus software, firewall settings, backups, and recovery discs, and discover features of most operating systems and utility programs.

SYSTEM SOFTWARE

When you purchase a personal computer, it usually has system software installed on its hard disk. **System software** consists of the programs that control or maintain the operations of the computer and its devices. System software serves as the interface between the user, the application software, and the computer's hardware.

Two types of system software are operating systems and utility programs. Several types of utility programs are provided with an operating system. Other utility programs are available stand-alone, that is, as programs separate from the operating system. This chapter discusses the operating system and its functions, as well as several types of utility programs for personal computers.

OPERATING SYSTEMS

An **operating system** (**OS**) is a set of programs containing instructions that coordinate all the activities among computer hardware resources. Most operating systems perform similar functions that include starting a computer, providing a user interface, managing programs, managing memory, scheduling jobs, configuring devices, establishing an Internet connection,

FIGURE 8-1 Most operating systems perform the functions illustrated in this figure.

monitoring performance, and providing file management utilities. Some operating systems also allow users to control a network and administer security (Figure 8-1).

In most cases, the operating system is installed and resides on the computer's hard disk. On handheld computers and many mobile devices such as PDAs and smart phones, however, the operating system may reside on a ROM chip.

Different sizes of computers typically use different operating systems. For example, a mainframe computer does not use the same operating system as a personal computer. Even the same types of computers, such as desktop

computers, may not use the same operating system. Furthermore, the application software designed for a specific operating system may not run when using another operating system. For example, PCs often use Windows XP, and iMacs use Mac OS X. When purchasing application software, you must ensure that it works with the operating system installed on your computer.

The operating system that a computer uses sometimes is called the *platform*. On purchased application software, the package identifies the required platform (operating system). A *cross-platform* program is one that runs the same on multiple operating systems.

provide a user interface

manage programs

manage memory

monitor performance

establish an Internet connection

schedule jobs and configure devices

OPERATING SYSTEM FUNCTIONS

Many different operating systems exist, designed for all types of computers. Regardless of the size of the computer, however, most operating systems provide similar functions. The following sections discuss functions common to most operating systems. The operating system handles many of these functions automatically, without requiring any instructions from a user.

Starting a Computer

The process of starting or restarting a computer is called **booting**. When turning on a computer that has been powered off completely, you are performing a **cold boot**. A **warm boot**, by contrast, is the process of using the operating system to restart a computer. A warm boot properly closes any open processes and programs. With Windows XP, you can perform a warm boot by clicking the Start button on the taskbar, clicking Turn Off Computer on the Start menu, and then clicking the Restart button in the Turn off computer dialog box (Figure 8-2). Some computers have a reset button that when pressed restarts a computer as if it had been powered off. A reset button does not properly close open processes.

When you install new software, often an on-screen prompt instructs you to restart the computer. In this case, a warm boot is appropriate. If your computer stops responding, try to restart it with a warm boot first. If it does not respond to the warm boot, then try pushing the reset button on the computer, if the computer has a reset button. As a last resort, restart the computer with a cold boot; that is, push the power button.

Each time you boot a computer, the kernel and other frequently used operating system instructions are loaded, or copied, from the hard disk (storage) into the computer's memory (RAM). The *kernel* is the core of an operating system that manages memory and devices, maintains the computer's clock, starts applications, and assigns the computer's resources, such as devices, programs, data, and information. The kernel is *memory resident*, which means it remains in memory while the computer is running. Other parts of the operating system are *nonresident*, that is, these instructions remain on the hard disk until they are needed.

When you boot a computer, a series of messages may be displayed on the screen. The actual information displayed varies depending on the make and type of the computer and the equipment installed. The boot process, however, is similar for large and small computers.

The steps in the following paragraphs explain what occurs during a cold boot on a personal computer using the Windows XP operating system. The steps in Figure 8-3 illustrate and correspond to the steps discussed in the following paragraphs.

Step 1: When you turn on the computer, the power supply sends an electrical signal to the components in the system unit.

Step 2: The charge of electricity causes the processor chip to reset itself and find the ROM chip(s) that contains the BIOS. The **BIOS** (pronounced BYE-ose), which stands for *basic input/output system*, is firmware that contains the computer's startup instructions.

Step 3: The BIOS executes a series of tests to make sure the computer hardware is connected properly and operating correctly. The tests, collectively called the *power-on self test* (*POST*), check the various system components including the buses, system clock, adapter cards, RAM chips, mouse, keyboard, and drives. As the POST executes, LEDs (tiny lights) flicker on devices such as the disk drives and keyboard. Beeps also may sound, and messages may be displayed on the screen.

Step 4: The POST results are compared with data in a CMOS chip. As discussed in Chapter 4, CMOS is a technology that uses battery power to retain information when the computer is off. The CMOS chip stores configuration information about the computer, such as the amount of memory; type of disk drives, keyboard, and monitor; the current date and time; and other startup information. It also detects any new devices

Turn off computer

Stand By   Turn Off   Restart

puts computer in low-power consumption state

performs a warm boot

Cancel

FIGURE 8-2 To reboot a running computer, click the Restart button in the Turn off computer dialog box.

connected to the computer. If any problems are identified, the computer may beep, display error messages, or cease operating — depending on the severity of the problem.

Step 5: If the POST completes successfully, the BIOS searches for specific operating system files called *system files*. The BIOS may look first to see if a USB flash drive plugged in a USB port, or a disc in a CD or DVD drive, or a disk in a floppy disk drive contains the system files. If these ports or drives do not contain media or if the system files are not

on media in the port or drive, the BIOS looks in drive C (the designation usually given to the first hard disk) for the system files.

Step 6: Once located, the system files load into memory (RAM) from storage (usually the hard disk) and execute. Next, the kernel of the operating system loads into memory. Then, the operating system in memory takes control of the computer.

Step 7: The operating system loads system configuration information. In Windows XP, the *registry* consists of several files

FIGURE 8-3 HOW A PC BOOTS UP

Step 1:
The power supply sends a signal to the components in the system unit.

Step 2:
The processor finds the ROM chip(s) that contains the BIOS (basic input/output system).

Step 3:
The BIOS performs the POST (power-on self test), which checks components, such as the mouse, keyboard, and adapter cards.

Step 4:
The results of the POST are compared with data in a CMOS chip.

Step 5:
The BIOS sometimes looks for the system files on a USB flash drive, on a CD or DVD drive, or in a floppy disk drive, and then drive C (hard disk).

Step 6:
The system files and the kernel of the operating system load into memory (RAM) from storage (hard disk).

Step 7:
The operating system loads configuration information, may request user information, and displays the desktop on the screen.

system unit

CD drive
DVD drive
floppy disk drive
Pentium 4 processor
(RAM) memory modules
CMOS
hard disk
sound card
video card
USB flash drive

that contain the system configuration information. Windows XP constantly accesses the registry during the computer's operation for information such as installed hardware and software devices and individual user preferences for mouse speed, passwords, and other information.

Necessary operating system files are loaded into memory. On some computers, the operating system verifies that the person attempting to use the computer is a legitimate user. Finally, the Windows XP desktop and icons are displayed on the screen. The operating system executes programs in the *Startup folder*, which contains a list of programs that open automatically when you boot the computer.

RECOVERY DISK   A **boot drive** is the drive from which your personal computer boots (starts). In most cases, drive C (the hard disk) is the boot drive. Sometimes a hard disk becomes damaged and the computer cannot boot from the hard disk. In this case, you can boot from a special disk, called a **recovery disk** or a **boot disk**, that contains a few system files that will start the computer. When you purchase a computer, it usually includes a recovery disk in the form of a CD. If you do not have a recovery disk, the operating system usually provides a means to create one. Many users today create a recovery disk on a USB flash drive.

FAQ 8-1

When I am finished using the computer, can I simply turn it off?

No! You must use the operating system's shut-down procedure so various processes are closed in sequence and items in memory released properly. Depending on the computer, several shut-down options exist. The Turn Off command removes power from the computer. Restart does a warm boot. *Hibernate* saves all documents in memory and then turns off the computer. *Stand By* places the entire computer in a low-power state but does not turn it off. With Hibernate and Stand By, the next time you resume work on the computer, the desktop is restored exactly to how you left it. For more information, visit scsite.com/dc2007/ch8/faq and then click Shut-Down Options.

Providing a User Interface

You interact with software through its user interface. That is, a **user interface** controls how you enter data and instructions and how information is displayed on the screen. Three types of user interfaces are command-line, menu-driven, and graphical. Operating systems often use a combination of these interfaces to define how a user interacts with a computer.

COMMAND-LINE INTERFACE   To configure devices, manage system resources, and troubleshoot network connections, network administrators and other advanced users work with a command-line interface. In a *command-line interface*, a user types commands or presses special keys on the keyboard (such as function keys or key combinations) to enter data and instructions (Figure 8-4a). Command-line interfaces often are difficult to use because they require exact spelling, grammar, and punctuation. Minor errors, such as a missing period, generate an error message. Command-line interfaces, however, give a user more control to manage detailed settings. For a technical discussion about a command-line interface, read the High-Tech Talk article on page 430.

When working with a command-line interface, the set of commands entered into the computer is called the *command language*. Programs that contain command language instructions are called *scripts*. Network administrators and Web page programmers often use scripts.

MENU-DRIVEN INTERFACE   A *menu-driven interface* provides menus as a means of entering commands (Figure 8-4b). Menu-driven interfaces are easier to learn than command-line interfaces because users do not have to learn the rules of entering commands.

GRAPHICAL USER INTERFACE   Most users today work with a graphical user interface. With a *graphical user interface* (GUI), you interact with menus and visual images such as buttons and other graphical objects to issue commands. Many current GUI operating systems incorporate features similar to those of a Web browser. The Windows XP screen shown in Figure 8-4c, for example, contains links and navigation buttons such as the Back button and the Forward button.

FIGURE 8-4a (command-line)

FIGURE 8-4b (menu-driven)

FIGURE 8-4c (graphical)

FIGURE 8-4 Examples of command-line, menu-driven, and graphical user interfaces.

Managing Programs

Some operating systems support a single user and only one running program at a time. Others support thousands of users running multiple programs. How an operating system handles programs directly affects your productivity.

A *single user/single tasking* operating system allows only one user to run one program at a time. For example, if you are working in a graphics program and want to check e-mail messages, you must quit the graphics program before you can run the e-mail program. Early systems were single user/single tasking. Most of today's operating systems are multitasking. PDAs, smart phones, and other small computing

devices, however, often use a single user/single tasking operating system.

A *single user/multitasking* operating system allows a single user to work on two or more programs that reside in memory at the same time. Using the example just cited, if you are working with a single user/multitasking operating system, you do not have to quit the graphics program to run the e-mail program. Both programs can run concurrently. Users today typically run multiple programs concurrently. It is common to have an e-mail program and Web browser open at all times, while working with application programs such as word processing or graphics.

When a computer is running multiple programs concurrently, one program is in the foreground and the others are in the background. The one in the *foreground* is the active program, that is, the one you currently are using. The other programs running but not in use are in the *background*. In Figure 8-5, the PowerPoint program, which is showing a slide show, is in the foreground, and three other programs are running in the background (HP Image Zone, Hallmark Card Studio, and iTunes). For example, iTunes can be playing music while you are modifying the slide show.

The foreground program typically displays on the desktop, and the background programs are partially or completely hidden behind the foreground program. You easily can switch between foreground and background programs. To make a program active (in the foreground) in Windows XP, click its program button on the taskbar. This causes the operating system to place all other programs in the background.

In addition to application programs, an operating system manages other processes. These processes include utilities or routines that provide support to other programs or

FIGURE 8-5 The foreground program, PowerPoint, is displayed on the desktop. The other programs (HP Image Zone, Hallmark Card Studio, and iTunes) are in the background.

hardware. Some are memory resident. Others run as they are required. Figure 8-6 shows a list of all processes running on a Windows XP computer. The list contains the applications programs running, as well as other programs and processes.

Some operating systems use preemptive multitasking to prevent any one process from monopolizing the computer's resources. With *preemptive multitasking*, the operating system interrupts a program that is executing and passes control to another program waiting to be executed. An advantage of preemptive multitasking is the operating system regains control if one program stops operating properly.

A *multiuser* operating system enables two or more users to run programs simultaneously. Networks, servers, mainframes, and super-computers allow hundreds to thousands of users to connect at the same time, and thus are multiuser.

A *multiprocessing* operating system supports two or more processors running programs at the same time. Multiprocessing involves the coordinated processing of programs by more than one processor. Multiprocessing increases a computer's processing speed.

A computer with separate processors also can serve as a fault-tolerant computer. A *fault-tolerant computer* continues to operate when one of its components fails, ensuring that no data is lost. Fault-tolerant computers have duplicate components such as processors, memory, and disk drives. If any one of these components fails, the computer switches to the duplicate component and continues to operate. Airline reservation systems, communications networks, automated teller machines, and other systems that must be operational at all times use fault-tolerant computers.

Managing Memory

The purpose of **memory management** is to optimize the use of random access memory (RAM). As discussed in Chapter 4, RAM consists of one or more chips on the motherboard that hold items such as data and instructions while the processor interprets and executes them. The operating system allocates, or assigns, data and instructions to an area of memory while they are being processed. Then, it carefully monitors the contents of memory. Finally, the operating system releases these items from being monitored in memory when the processor no longer requires them.

If you have multiple programs running simultaneously, it is possible to run out of RAM. For example, assume an operating system requires 128 MB of RAM, an antivirus program — 128 MB of RAM, a Web browser — 32 MB of RAM, a business software suite — 64 MB of RAM, and a photo editing program — 128 MB of RAM. With all these programs running simultaneously, the total RAM required would be 480 MB of RAM (128 + 128 + 32 + 64 + 128). If the computer has only 256 MB of RAM, the operating system may have to use virtual memory to solve the problem.

FIGURE 8-6 An operating system manages multiple programs and processes while you use the computer.

With **virtual memory**, the operating system allocates a portion of a storage medium, usually the hard disk, to function as additional RAM (Figure 8-7). As you interact with a program, part of it may be in physical RAM, while the rest of the program is on the hard disk as virtual memory. Because virtual memory is slower than RAM, users may notice the computer slowing down while it uses virtual memory.

The area of the hard disk used for virtual memory is called a *swap file* because it swaps (exchanges) data, information, and instructions between memory and storage. A *page* is the amount of data and program instructions that can swap at a given time. The technique of swapping items between memory and storage, called *paging*, is a time-consuming process for the computer.

When an operating system spends much of its time paging, instead of executing application software, it is said to be *thrashing*. If application software, such as a Web browser, has stopped responding and the hard disk's LED blinks repeatedly, the operating system probably is thrashing.

FAQ 8-2

How can I stop a computer from thrashing?

Try to quit the program that stopped responding. If the computer does not respond and continues to thrash, do a warm boot. When the computer reboots, check whether the available hard disk space is less than 200 MB. If it is, remove unnecessary files from the hard disk and if possible uninstall seldom used programs. Defragment the hard disk (discussed later in this chapter). If thrashing continues to occur, you may need to install more RAM in the computer. For more information, visit scsite.com/dc2007/ch8/faq and then click Optimizing Memory.

Scheduling Jobs

The operating system determines the order in which jobs are processed. A **job** is an operation the processor manages. Jobs include receiving data from an input device, processing instructions, sending information to an output device, and transferring items from storage to memory and from memory to storage.

FIGURE 8-7   HOW A COMPUTER MIGHT USE VIRTUAL MEMORY

page swapped out

RAM (physical memory)

disk (virtual memory)

swap file

Step 1:
The operating system transfers the least recently used data and program instructions from RAM to the hard disk because RAM is needed for other functions.

Step 2:
The operating system transfers data and program instructions from the hard disk to RAM when they are needed.

page swapped in

A mulituser operating system does not always process jobs on a first-come, first-served basis. Sometimes, one user may have a higher priority than other users. In this case, the operating system adjusts the schedule of jobs.

Sometimes, a device already may be busy processing one job when it receives a second job. This occurs because the processor operates at a much faster rate of speed than peripheral devices. For example, if the processor sends five print jobs to a printer, the printer can print only one document at a time.

While waiting for devices to become idle, the operating system places items in buffers. A **buffer** is a segment of memory or storage in which items are placed while waiting to be transferred from an input device or to an output device.

The operating system commonly uses buffers with print jobs. This process, called **spooling**, sends print jobs to a buffer instead of sending them immediately to the printer. The buffer holds the information waiting to print while the printer prints from the buffer at its own rate of speed. By spooling print jobs to a buffer, the processor can continue interpreting and executing instructions while the printer prints. This allows users to work on the computer for other tasks while a printer is printing. Multiple print jobs line up in a **queue** (pronounced Q)

in the buffer. A program, called a *print spooler*, intercepts print jobs from the operating system and places them in the queue (Figure 8-8).

Configuring Devices

A **driver**, short for *device driver*, is a small program that tells the operating system how to communicate with a specific device. Each device on a computer, such as the mouse, keyboard, monitor, printer, card reader/writer, and scanner, has its own specialized set of commands and thus requires its own specific driver. When you boot a computer, the operating system loads each device's driver. These devices will not function without their correct drivers.

If you attach a new device to a computer, such as a printer or scanner, its driver must be installed before you can use the device. Today, many devices and operating systems support Plug and Play. As discussed in Chapter 4, **Plug and Play** means the operating system automatically configures new devices as you install them. Specifically, it assists you in the device's installation by loading the necessary drivers automatically and checking for conflicts with other devices. With Plug and Play, a user plugs in a device, turns on the computer, and then uses the device without having to configure the system manually.

WEB LINK 8-2

Plug and Play

For more information, visit scsite.com/dc2007/ch8/weblink and then click Plug and Play.

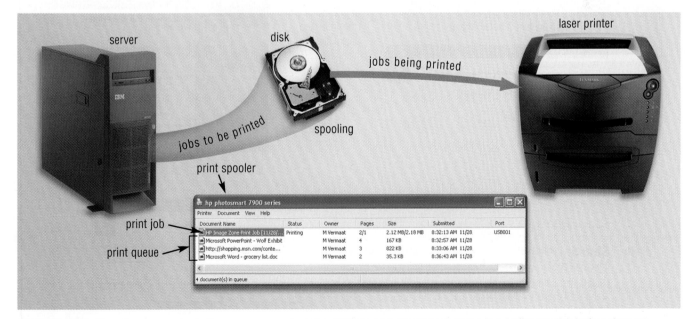

FIGURE 8-8   Spooling increases both processor and printer efficiency by placing print jobs in a buffer on disk before they are printed. This figure illustrates three jobs in the queue with one job printing.

For devices that are not Plug and Play, Windows XP provides a wizard to guide users through the installation steps. Figure 8-9 shows how to install a driver for a printer. You follow the same general steps to install drivers for any type of hardware. For many devices, the computer's operating system may include the necessary drivers. If it does not, you can install the drivers from the CD provided with the purchased device.

When you attach a Plug and Play device to a computer, the operating system determines an

FIGURE 8-9   HOW TO INSTALL DRIVERS FOR NEW HARDWARE IN WINDOWS XP

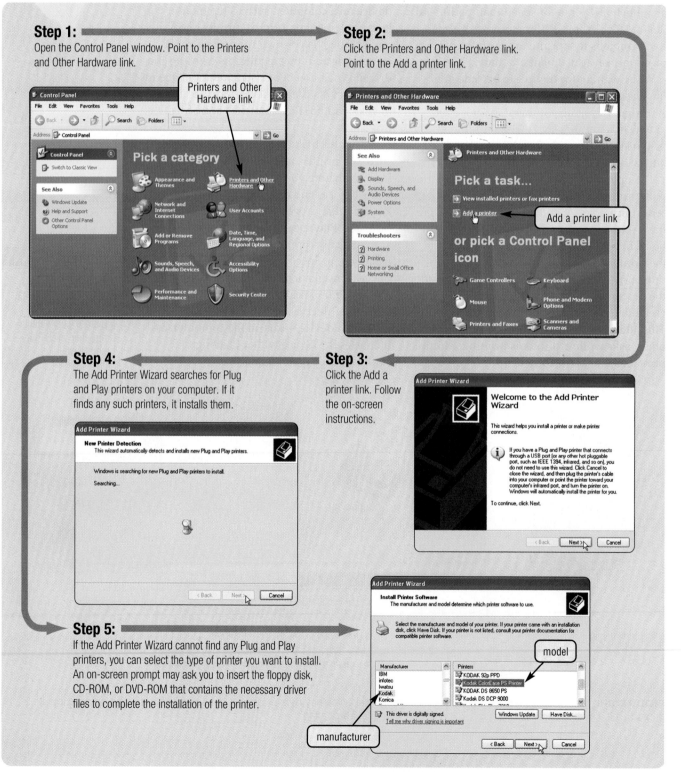

Step 1:
Open the Control Panel window. Point to the Printers and Other Hardware link.

Step 2:
Click the Printers and Other Hardware link. Point to the Add a printer link.

Step 4:
The Add Printer Wizard searches for Plug and Play printers on your computer. If it finds any such printers, it installs them.

Step 3:
Click the Add a printer link. Follow the on-screen instructions.

Step 5:
If the Add Printer Wizard cannot find any Plug and Play printers, you can select the type of printer you want to install. An on-screen prompt may ask you to insert the floppy disk, CD-ROM, or DVD-ROM that contains the necessary driver files to complete the installation of the printer.

appropriate IRQ to use. An *IRQ* (*interrupt request line*) is a communications line between a device and the processor.

FAQ 8-3

What if I do not have the driver for a device?

When reinstalling an operating system, you may have to supply a device's driver. If you do not have the original driver disc, visit the manufacturer's Web site. Most post drivers for download at no cost, or they may suggest a similar driver that will work. If you do not have Internet access, call the manufacturer and request a new disc via the postal service. For more information, visit scsite.com/dc2007/ch8/faq and then click Drivers.

Establishing an Internet Connection

Operating systems typically provide a means to establish Internet connections. For example, Windows XP includes a New Connection Wizard that guides users through the process of setting up a connection between a computer and an Internet service provider (Figure 8-10).

Some operating systems also include a Web browser and an e-mail program, enabling you to begin using the Web and communicate with others as soon as you set up the Internet connection. Some also include a built-in firewall to protect computers from unauthorized intrusions. Read Ethics & Issues 8-1 for a related discussion.

Monitoring Performance

Operating systems typically contain a performance monitor. A **performance monitor** is a program that assesses and reports information about various computer resources and devices (Figure 8-11). For example, users can monitor the processor, disks, memory, and network usage. A performance monitor also can check the number of reads and writes to a disk.

The information in performance reports helps users and administrators identify a problem with resources so they can try to resolve any problems. If a computer is running extremely slow, for example, the performance monitor may determine that the computer's memory is being used to its maximum. Thus, you might consider installing additional memory in the computer.

ETHICS & ISSUES 8-1

What Should Be in an Operating System?

Microsoft includes a Web browser, movie making software, a word processing program, plug-ins, a personal firewall, anti-spyware, and other programs, utilities, and features with its Windows operating system. Apple bundles QuickTime, CD burning software, and other programs, utilities, and features into Mac OS X. Manufacturers say that combining additional features and programs with their operating systems is a convenience for consumers and sometimes integral to the operating systems' performance. Microsoft's bundling of its Web browser with its Windows operating system was the proximate cause of an antitrust action against the software giant. Recently, the European Union ordered Microsoft to remove its media player from the Windows XP operating system as a result of antitrust action. Critics also insist that bundling applications with an operating system forces consumers to pay for programs that may be inferior to those available elsewhere. Is bundling applications with an operating system fair, or is it a monopolistic practice? Why? Who should decide what an operating system should include? Why? Should computer manufacturers be allowed to choose which bundled applications are installed on computers that they ship to customers? Why or why not?

FIGURE 8-10   To display the New Connection Wizard in Windows XP, click the Start button, point to All Programs, point to Accessories, point to Communications, and then click New Connection Wizard on the Communications submenu.

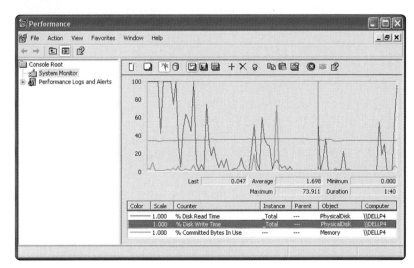

FIGURE 8-11   The System Monitor above is tracking disk read time, disk write time, and the amount of bytes in use.

Providing File Management and Other Utilities

Operating systems often provide users with the capability of managing files, viewing images, securing a computer from unauthorized access, uninstalling programs, scanning disks, defragmenting disks, diagnosing problems, backing up files and disks, and setting up screen savers. A later section in the chapter discusses these utilities in depth. Read Ethics & Issues 8-2 for a related discussion.

ETHICS & ISSUES 8-2

Who Is Responsible for Operating System Security?

A few years ago, the Sasser worm infected almost one million computers in the stretch of a weekend. Surprisingly, most computer users already had the necessary means to stop this worm before it even got started. The Windows XP operating system comes equipped with built-in firewall protection that could have stopped the worm, but, by default, the feature was turned off. Microsoft later released a service pack, or update, for the operating system in which the feature was turned on by default. Most operating system manufacturers allow users automatically to download and install up-to-date security patches. It is up to the users to make use of this service properly. Sometimes, as was the case with the Sasser worm, the updates come too late. Often, users are not technically savvy enough to keep up with the security updates or to configure a network connection with a firewall properly. Who should be responsible for operating system security? Why? Should operating system manufacturers be required to send security updates to computer users? Why or why not? Who should enforce such requirements, and what should the punishments be for not meeting the requirements? Should users be required to take responsibility for worms and viruses that they spread to others due to lax security? Why or why not?

Controlling a Network

Some operating systems are network operating systems. A **network operating system**, or *network OS*, is an operating system that organizes and coordinates how multiple users access and share resources on a network. Resources include hardware, software, data, and information. For example, a network OS allows multiple users to share a printer, Internet access, files, and programs.

Some operating systems have network features built into them. In other cases, the network OS is a set of programs separate from the operating system on the client computers that access the network. When not connected to the network, the client computers use their own operating system. When connected to the network, the network OS may assume some of the operating system functions.

The *network administrator*, the person overseeing network operations, uses the network OS to add and remove users, computers, and other devices to and from the network. The network administrator also uses the network operating system to install software and administer network security.

Administering Security

The network administrator uses the network OS to establish permissions to resources. These permissions define who can access certain resources and when they can access those resources.

For each user, the network administrator establishes a user account, which enables a user to access, or **log on** to, a computer or a network. Each user account typically consists of a user name and password (Figure 8-12). A **user name**, or **user ID**, is a unique combination of characters, such as letters of the alphabet or numbers, that identifies one specific user. Many users select a combination of their first and last names as their user name. A user named Henry Baker might choose H Baker as his user name.

A **password** is a private combination of characters associated with the user name that allows access to certain computer resources. Some operating systems allow the network administrator to assign passwords to files

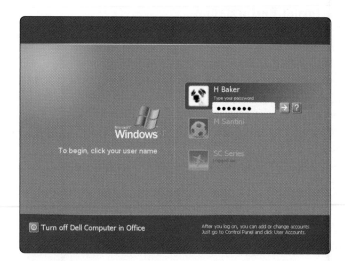

FIGURE 8-12   Most multiuser operating systems allow each user to log on, which is the process of entering a user name and a password into the computer.

and commands, restricting access to only authorized users.

To prevent unauthorized users from accessing computer resources, keep your password confidential. While entering your password, most computers hide the actual password characters by displaying some other characters, such as asterisks (*) or dots. After entering a user name and password, the operating system compares the user's entry with a list of authorized user names and passwords. If the entry matches the user name and password kept on file, the operating system grants the user access. If the entry does not match, the operating system denies access to the user.

The operating system records successful and unsuccessful logon attempts in a file. This allows the network administrator to review who is using or attempting to use the computer. Network administrators also use these files to monitor computer usage.

To protect sensitive data and information further as it travels over the network, a network operating system may encrypt it. *Encryption* is the process of encoding data and information into an unreadable form. Network administrators can set up a network to encrypt data as it travels over the network to prevent unauthorized users from reading the data. When an authorized user attempts to read the data, it automatically is decrypted, or converted back into a readable form.

Test your knowledge of pages 398 through 411 in Quiz Yourself 8-1.

OPERATING SYSTEM UTILITY PROGRAMS

A **utility program**, also called a **utility**, is a type of system software that allows a user to perform maintenance-type tasks, usually related to managing a computer, its devices, or its programs. Most operating systems include several built-in utility programs (Figure 8-13). Users often buy stand-alone utilities, however, because they offer improvements over those included with the operating system.

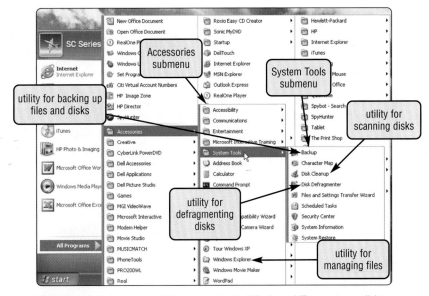

FIGURE 8-13 Many utilities available in Windows XP are accessible through the Accessories and System Tools submenus.

Utility programs included with most operating systems provide the following functions: managing files, viewing images, securing a computer from unauthorized access, uninstalling programs, scanning disks, defragmenting disks, diagnosing problems, backing up files and disks, and setting up screen savers. The following sections briefly discuss each of these utilities.

File Manager

A **file manager** is a utility that performs functions related to file and disk management. Windows XP includes a file manager called *Windows Explorer*. Some of the file and disk management functions that a file manager performs are formatting and copying disks; displaying a list of files on a storage medium (Figure 8-14); checking the amount of used or free space on a storage medium; organizing, copying, renaming, deleting, moving, and sorting files; and creating shortcuts. A **shortcut** is an icon on the desktop that provides a user with immediate access to a program or file.

Formatting is the process of preparing a disk for reading and writing. Most hard disk manufacturers preformat their disks. If you must format media, you can do so using the file manager. For a technical discussion about formatting, read the High-Tech Talk article on page 382 in Chapter 7.

Image Viewer

An **image viewer** is a utility that allows users to display, copy, and print the contents of a graphics file. With an image viewer, users can see images without having to open them in a paint or image editing program. Windows XP includes an image viewer called *Windows Picture and Fax Viewer* (Figure 8-15). To display a file in this image viewer, simply double-click the thumbnail of the image in the file manager. For example, double-clicking a thumbnail in Windows Explorer (Figure 8-14) displays the image in a Windows Picture and Fax Viewer window.

FIGURE 8-15   Windows Picture and Fax Viewer allows users to see the contents of a graphics file.

FIGURE 8-14   With Windows Explorer, which is the file manager included with Windows XP, users can display a list of graphics files on a disk. In this case, thumbnails of the files are displayed.

Personal Firewall

A **personal firewall** is a utility that detects and protects a personal computer from unauthorized intrusions. Personal firewalls constantly monitor all transmissions to and from a computer.

When connected to the Internet, your computer is vulnerable to attacks from a hacker. A *hacker* is someone who tries to access a computer or network illegally. Users with broadband Internet connections, such as through DSL and Internet cable television service, are even more susceptible than those with dial-up access because the Internet connection is always on.

The latest update to Windows XP automatically enables the built-in personal firewall upon installation. This firewall, called Windows Firewall, is easy to access and configure (Figure 8-16). If your operating system does not include a personal firewall or you want additional protection, you can purchase a stand-alone personal firewall utility or a hardware firewall, which is a device such as a router that has a built-in firewall.

Uninstaller

An **uninstaller** is a utility that removes a program, as well as any associated entries in the system files. In Windows XP, the uninstaller is available through the Add/Remove Programs command in the Control Panel.

When you install a program, the operating system records the information it uses to run the software in the system files. The uninstaller deletes files and folders from the hard disk, as well as removes program entries from the system files.

FAQ 8-5

Should I use the file manager to delete a program?

No! If you remove software from a computer by deleting the files and folders associated with the program without running the uninstaller, the system file entries are not updated. This may cause the operating system to display error messages when you start the computer. If the program has an uninstaller, always use it to remove software. For more information, visit scsite.com/dc2007/ch8/faq and then click Uninstalling Programs.

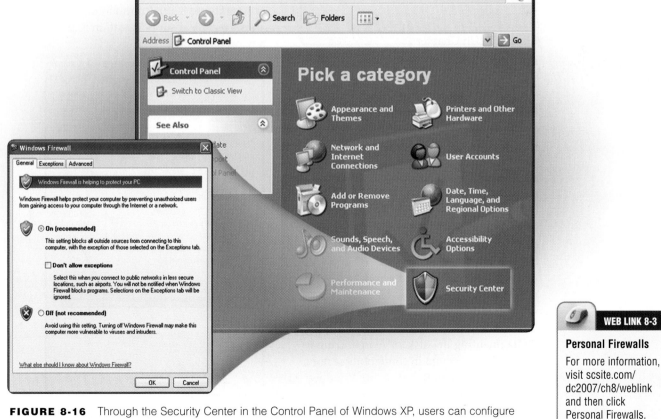

FIGURE 8-16   Through the Security Center in the Control Panel of Windows XP, users can configure Windows Firewall, which is a personal firewall utility built into the latest upgrade of Windows XP.

WEB LINK 8-3

Personal Firewalls

For more information, visit scsite.com/dc2007/ch8/weblink and then click Personal Firewalls.

Disk Scanner

A **disk scanner** is a utility that (1) detects and corrects both physical and logical problems on a hard disk and (2) searches for and removes unnecessary files. A physical disk problem is a problem with the media such as a scratch on the surface of the disk. A logical disk problem is a problem with the data, such as a corrupt file. Windows XP includes two disk scanner utilities. One detects problems and the other searches for and removes unnecessary files such as temporary files (Figure 8-17).

FIGURE 8-17 Disk Cleanup searches for and removes unnecessary files.

Disk Defragmenter

A **disk defragmenter** is a utility that reorganizes the files and unused space on a computer's hard disk so the operating system accesses data more quickly and programs run faster. When an operating system stores data on a disk, it places the data in the first available sector on the disk. It attempts to place data in sectors that are contiguous (next to each other), but this is not always possible. When the contents of a file are scattered across two or more noncontiguous sectors, the file is *fragmented*.

Fragmentation slows down disk access and thus the performance of the entire computer. **Defragmenting** the disk, or reorganizing it so the files are stored in contiguous sectors, solves this problem (Figure 8-18). Windows XP includes a disk defragmenter available on the System Tools submenu.

disk after defragmentation process

FIGURE 8-18 A fragmented disk has many files stored in noncontiguous sectors. Defragmenting reorganizes the files so they are located in contiguous sectors, which speeds access time.

Diagnostic Utility

A **diagnostic utility** compiles technical information about your computer's hardware and certain system software programs and then prepares a report outlining any identified problems. For example, Windows XP includes the diagnostic utility, *Dr. Watson*, which diagnoses problems as well as suggests courses of action (Figure 8-19). Information in the report assists technical support staff in remedying any problems.

FIGURE 8-19 Dr. Watson is a diagnostic utility included with Windows.

Backup Utility

A **backup utility** allows users to copy, or *back up*, selected files or an entire hard disk to another storage medium such as CD, DVD, external hard disk, tape, or USB flash drive. During the backup process, the backup utility monitors progress and alerts you if it needs additional discs or tapes. Many backup programs *compress*, or shrink the size of, files during the backup process. By compressing the files, the backup program requires less storage space for the backup files than for the original files.

Because they are compressed, you usually cannot use backup files in their backed up form. In the event you need to use a backup file, a **restore program** reverses the process and returns backed up files to their original form. Backup utilities include restore programs.

You should back up files and disks regularly in the event your originals are lost, damaged, or destroyed. Windows XP includes a backup utility (Figure 8-20). Instead of backing up to a local disk storage device, some users opt to use online storage to back up their files. As described in Chapter 7, online storage is a service on the Web that provides hard disk storage to computer users, usually for a minimal monthly fee.

FIGURE 8-20 A backup utility allows users to copy files or an entire hard disk to another storage medium.

Screen Saver

A **screen saver** is a utility that causes a display device's screen to show a moving image or blank screen if no keyboard or mouse activity occurs for a specified time (Figure 8-21). When you press a key on the keyboard or move the mouse, the screen saver disappears and the screen returns to the previous state.

FIGURE 8-21 A Windows XP screen saver.

Screen savers originally were developed to prevent a problem called *ghosting*, in which images could be permanently etched on a monitor's screen. Although ghosting is not as severe of a problem with today's displays, manufacturers continue to recommend that users install screen savers for this reason. Screen savers also are popular for security, business, and entertainment purposes. To secure a computer, users configure their screen saver to require a password to deactivate. In addition to those included with the operating system, many screen savers are available in stores and on the Web for free or a minimal fee.

TYPES OF OPERATING SYSTEMS

Many of the first operating systems were device dependent and proprietary. A *device-dependent* program is one that runs only on a specific type or make of computer. *Proprietary software* is privately owned and limited to a specific vendor or computer model. Some operating systems still are device dependent. The trend today, however, is toward *device-independent* operating systems that run on computers provided by a variety of manufacturers. The advantage of device-independent operating systems is you can retain existing application software and data files even if you change computer models or vendors.

WEB LINK 8-4

Screen Savers
For more information, visit scsite.com/ dc2007/ch8/weblink and then click Screen Savers.

When you purchase a new computer, it typically has an operating system preinstalled. As new versions of the operating system are released, users upgrade their existing computers to incorporate features of the new version. An upgrade usually costs less than purchasing the entire operating system.

Some software manufacturers, such as Microsoft and IBM, release free downloadable updates to their software, often called a *service pack*. Users also can order service packs on CD for a minimal shipping fee. Service packs provide enhancements to the original software and fix bugs (errors) in the software. Read Ethics & Issues 8-3 for a related discussion.

New versions of an operating system usually are downward compatible. That is, they recognize and work with application software written for an earlier version of the operating system (or platform). The application software, by contrast, is said to be upward compatible, meaning it will run on new versions of the operating system.

The three basic categories of operating systems that exist today are stand-alone, network, and embedded. The table in Figure 8-22 lists specific names of operating systems in each category. The following pages discuss the operating systems listed in the table.

CATEGORIES OF OPERATING SYSTEMS

Category	Operating System Name
Stand-alone	• DOS • Early Windows versions (Windows 3.x, Windows 95, Windows NT Workstation, Windows 98, Windows 2000 Professional, Windows Millennium Edition) • Windows XP • Windows Vista • Mac OS X • UNIX • Linux
Network	• NetWare • Early Windows Server versions (Windows NT Server, Windows 2000 Server) • Windows Server 2003 • UNIX • Linux • Solaris
Embedded	• Windows CE • Windows Mobile • Palm OS • Embedded Linux • Symbian OS

FIGURE 8-22 Examples of stand-alone, network, and embedded operating systems. Some stand-alone operating systems include the capability of configuring small home or office networks.

ETHICS & ISSUES 8-3

Should Software Manufacturers Be Liable for Defective Software?

Several years ago in Panama, 28 patients receiving radiation treatment were given massive overdoses of radiation due to a software bug. Over the next several years, at least 12 of these patients died due to radiation poisoning and others were considered to be at risk of developing further complications. In another mishap, bugs in a sports car's braking system caused a warning light to not illuminate when problems were detected with the brakes. It is estimated that defective software costs U.S. businesses more than $60 billion annually. In a software license, software manufacturers usually include a disclaimer that limits the manufacturer's liability in the event that software malfunctions. Due to the increase in viruses, worms, and well-publicized software failures, such as the one that caused the power blackout in much of the northeastern U.S. a few years ago, many people are calling for the government to force software manufacturers to assume more liability. Software manufacturers claim that more liability — and consequently more cost — will result in less software and fewer features. They further claim that hardware manufacturers instead should be held responsible. Should the government enact more rules regarding software quality and liability? Why or why not? Who should be held accountable, if anyone, when faulty software causes injury or financial loss? Why? Will the free market or costly lawsuits eventually force makers of bug-ridden software to go out of business?

STAND-ALONE OPERATING SYSTEMS

A **stand-alone operating system** is a complete operating system that works on a desktop computer, notebook computer, or mobile computing device. Some stand-alone operating systems are called *client operating systems* because they also work in conjunction with a network operating system. Client operating systems can operate with or without a network. Other stand-alone operating systems include networking capabilities, allowing the home and small business user to set up a small network.

Examples of stand-alone operating systems are DOS, Windows XP, Windows Vista, Mac OS X, UNIX, and Linux. The following paragraphs briefly discuss these operating systems.

DOS

The term **DOS** (*Disk Operating System*) refers to several single user operating systems developed in the early 1980s by Microsoft for personal computers. The two more widely used versions of DOS were PC-DOS and MS-DOS. The functionality of these two operating systems was essentially the same.

DOS used a command-line interface when Microsoft first developed it. Later versions included both command-line and menu-driven user interfaces. At its peak, DOS was a widely used operating system, with an estimated 70 million computers running it. DOS hardly is used today because it does not offer a graphical user interface and it cannot take full advantage of modern 32-bit personal computer processors.

Windows XP

In the mid-1980s, Microsoft developed its first version of Windows, which provided a graphical user interface (GUI). Since then, Microsoft continually has updated its Windows operating system, incorporating innovative features and functions with each subsequent version (Figure 8-23). **Windows XP** is a fast, reliable Windows operating system, providing quicker startup, better performance, increased security, and a simpler visual look than previous Windows versions. Using Windows XP, home and small office users easily can set up a network and secure it from hackers with Windows Firewall. Windows Messenger, included with Windows XP, enables users to send instant messages. Windows XP also includes Windows Media Player, which allows users to listen to Internet radio stations, play

HIGHLIGHTS OF STAND-ALONE WINDOWS VERSIONS

Windows Version	Year Released	Highlights
Windows 3.x	1990	• Provided a GUI • An operating environment only — worked in combination with DOS
Windows NT 3.1	1993	• Client OS that connected to a Windows NT Advanced Server • Interface similar to Windows 3.x
Windows 95	1995	• True multitasking operating system • Improved GUI • Included support for networking, Plug and Play technology, longer file names, and e-mail
Windows NT Workstation 4.0	1996	• Client OS that connected to a Windows NT Server • Interface similar to Windows 95 • Network integration
Windows 98	1998	• Upgrade to Windows 95 • More integrated with the Internet; included *Internet Explorer* (a Web browser) • Faster system startup and shutdown, better file management, support for multimedia technologies (e.g., DVDs), and USB connectivity
Windows Millennium Edition	2000	• Upgrade to Windows 98 • Designed for the home user who wanted music playing, video editing, and networking capabilities
Windows 2000 Professional	2000	• Upgrade to Windows NT Workstation 4.0 • Complete multitasking client OS designed for business personal computers • Certified device drivers, faster performance, adaptive Start menu, image viewer, enhanced for mobile users
Windows XP	2001	• Upgrade to Windows Millennium Edition called Windows XP Home Edition • Upgrade to Windows 2000 Professional called Windows XP Professional • Windows XP Tablet PC Edition designed for Tablet PC users • Windows XP Media Center Edition designed for PCs used for home entertainment • Windows XP Professional x64 Edition designed for workstations that use 64-bit processors • Improved interface and increased performance in all editions
Windows XP SP2 (Service Pack 2)	2004	• Enhancement to Windows XP that offers more built-in security technologies • Improved firewall utility • Automatic blocking of Internet pop-up advertisements
Windows Vista	2006	• Upgrade to Windows XP • Easier to navigate user interface • Enhanced administration of user accounts • Improved firewall • Simplified customization techniques • New Document Explorer and Virtual Folders improve searching and organizing capabilities • Improved performance and reliability

FIGURE 8-23   Microsoft has released many versions of Windows.

MP3 and other music formats, copy music and data to CDs, and watch DVD movies.

Windows XP is available in five editions: Home Edition, Professional (Figure 8-24), Media Center Edition, Tablet PC Edition, and Professional x64 Edition.

- With *Windows XP Home Edition*, users easily can organize and share digital pictures, download and listen to music, create and edit videos, network home computers, send and receive instant messages, and recover from problems with easy-to-use tools.
- *Windows XP Professional* includes all the capabilities of Windows XP Home Edition and also offers greater data security, remote access to a computer, simpler administration of groups of users, multiple language user interface, and support for a wireless network.

- *Windows XP Media Center Edition* includes all features of Windows XP Professional and is designed for Media Center PCs. A *Media Center PC* is a home entertainment personal computer that includes a mid- to high-end processor, large-capacity hard disk, CD and DVD drives, a remote control, and advanced graphics and audio capabilities. These computers often use a television as their display device. Users access digital entertainment such as television programs, movies, music, radio, and photographs via a remote control device (Figure 8-25).
- *Windows XP Tablet PC Edition* includes all features of Windows XP Professional and provides additional features designed to make users more productive while working on their Tablet PC. With Windows Tablet PC Edition, users can write on the screen or issue instructions to the Tablet PC using a digital pen.
- *Windows XP Professional x64 Edition* is designed for power users with workstations that use 64-bit processors. It manages multicore processors and can support up to 128 GB of RAM and 16 TB of virtual memory.

FAQ 8-6

How many people use Windows?

According to Microsoft, the number of Windows PCs will grow to more than one billion by 2010. Studies by industry analysts estimate that 96 percent of desktop computers worldwide currently use Windows. For more information, visit scsite.com/dc2007/ch8/faq and then click Windows Users.

FIGURE 8-24   Windows XP, with its simplified look, is a fast, reliable Windows operating system.

FIGURE 8-25   With Windows XP Media Center Edition, users access recorded videos, pictures, music, television programs, radio stations, or movies via a remote control device.

Windows Vista

Windows Vista, the successor to Windows XP, is Microsoft's fastest, most reliable and efficient operating system to date, offering quicker application start up, built-in diagnostics, automatic recovery, improved security, and enhanced searching and organizing capabilities (Figure 8-26). The table in Figure 8-27 highlights features of Windows Vista.

Windows Vista is available in several editions, which are grouped in two general categories: Home and Business. The Windows Vista Home category includes several editions, each designed for a different level of user. All home editions include a firewall, parental controls, search capability, a photo library, and movie maker. For more advanced home users, other editions also include features such as media center functionality, DVD authoring, HDTV support, wireless networking automatic configuration, and Tablet PC support. The Windows Vista Business category also includes several editions, designed for small businesses to large enterprises. To take advantage of all features and capabilities of Windows Vista, your computer should have 512 MB of RAM.

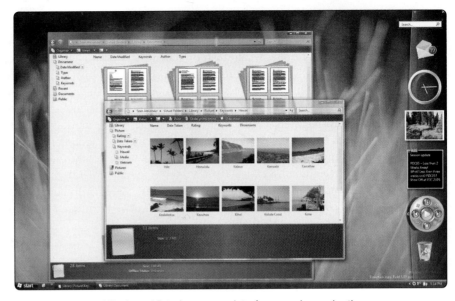

FIGURE 8-26 Windows Vista has a new interface, easier navigation and searching techniques, and improved security.

WINDOWS VISTA FEATURES

Reliability and Performance	• New Sleep state combines resume speed of Windows XP Standby mode and low power consumption of Hibernate mode • Automatically detects and fine tunes performance problems • Built-in hardware diagnostics detect and repair problems automatically • Automatically recovers from failures, including restoring an unbootable computer to a usable state
Security	• User Account Protection allows administrators to restrict permissions • Improved firewall • Protects users from dangerous Web sites
Information Management	• *Document Explorer* (replaces My Documents in Windows XP) helps users locate documents by showing thumbnails that preview documents' content and allowing users to adjust thumbnail size to view a document without opening it • *Virtual Folders* store search criteria as part of the folder that instantly runs each time the folder opens, enabling users easily to locate documents stored anywhere on the computer • Use Quick Search to locate files based on file name or any other property saved with the file • Easily share files with other users
Appearance and Navigation	• Easy-to-navigate interface with translucent windows to minimize distraction • Flip through thumbnails of open windows using the mouse or keyboard • Windows Sidebar connects to personalized mini-applications, called gadgets, such as weather, photos, or headline news • Improved wizards • Common dialog boxes shared by all applications
Communications and the Internet	• Enhanced Internet Explorer • Improved e-mail program with built-in spam filter • Consistent and secure wireless network connections

FIGURE 8-27 Some features of Windows Vista.

Mac OS X

Since it was released in 1984 with Macintosh computers, Apple's **Macintosh operating system** has set the standard for operating system ease of use and has been the model for most of the new GUIs developed for non-Macintosh systems. The latest version, **Mac OS X**, is a multitasking operating system available only for computers manufactured by Apple (Figure 8-28).

Mac OS X includes features from previous versions of the Macintosh operating system such as large photo-quality icons, built-in networking support, e-mail, online shopping, enhanced speech recognition, CD burning, and enhanced multimedia capabilities. In addition, Mac OS X includes these features:

- New desktop search technology
- Dashboard, a desktop area for mini-applications
- Built-in, fast Web browser
- Parental controls
- Accessibility interface reads e-mail messages
- 3-D personal video and audio conferencing
- Filter to eliminate junk e-mail messages
- Contact lists synchronized with PDA or Bluetooth-enabled smart phone
- Latest version of QuickTime to listen to music and view videos on the Internet
- Easy networking of computers and devices
- Windows network connection and shared Windows documents

WEB LINK 8-6

Mac OS X

For more information, visit scsite.com/dc2007/ch8/weblink and then click Mac OS X.

UNIX

UNIX (pronounced YOU-nix) is a multitasking operating system developed in the early 1970s by scientists at Bell Laboratories. Bell Labs (a subsidiary of AT&T) was prohibited from actively promoting UNIX in the commercial marketplace because of federal regulations. Bell Labs instead licensed UNIX for a low fee to numerous colleges and universities, where UNIX obtained a wide following. UNIX was implemented on many different types of computers. After deregulation of the telephone companies in the 1980s, UNIX was licensed to many hardware and software companies.

Several versions of this operating system exist, each slightly different. When programmers move application software from one UNIX version to another, they sometimes have to rewrite some of the programs. Although some versions of UNIX have a command-line interface, most versions of UNIX offer a graphical user interface (Figure 8-29).

Today, a version of UNIX is available for most computers of all sizes. Power users often work with UNIX because of its flexibility and power. Manufacturers such as Sun and IBM sell personal computers and workstations with a UNIX operating system.

WEB LINK 8-7

UNIX

For more information, visit scsite.com/dc2007/ch8/weblink and then click UNIX.

FIGURE 8-28 Mac OS X is the operating system used with Apple Macintosh computers.

FIGURE 8-29 Some versions of UNIX have a graphical user interface.

Linux

Linux is one of the faster growing operating systems. **Linux** (pronounced LINN-uks) is a popular, multitasking UNIX-type operating system. In addition to the basic operating system, Linux also includes many free programming languages and utility programs.

Linux is not proprietary software like the operating systems discussed thus far. Instead, Linux is *open source software*, which means its code is provided for use, modification, and redistribution. It has no restrictions from the copyright holder regarding modification of the software's internal instructions and redistribution of the software. Many programmers have donated time to modify and redistribute Linux to make it the best possible version of UNIX. Promoters of open source software state two main advantages: users who modify the software share their improvements with others, and customers can personalize the software to meet their needs. Read Ethics & Issues 8-4 for a related discussion.

Some versions of Linux are command-line. Others are GUI. The two most popular GUIs available for Linux are GNOME and KDE. Some companies such as Red Hat market software applications that run on their own version of Linux (Figure 8-30). Many application programs, utilities, and plug-ins have Linux versions, including OpenOffice.org, StarOffice, Mozilla, Netscape, Yahoo! Messenger, RealPlayer, QuickTime, and Acrobat Reader.

Users obtain Linux in a variety of ways. Some download it free from the Web. Others purchase it from vendors such as Red Hat or IBM, who bundle their own software with the operating system. Linux CD-ROMs are included in many Linux books and also are available for purchase from vendors. Some retailers such as Dell will preinstall Linux on a new computer's hard disk on request. Read Looking Ahead 8-1 for a look at the next generation of Linux.

ETHICS & ISSUES 8-4

Closed Source vs. Open Source Operating Systems

Linux is a fast-growing, innovative operating system. One of the features that make it different from other operating systems is that Linux is open source and its source code, along with any changes, remains public. Since its introduction in 1991, Linux has been altered, adapted, and improved by thousands of programmers. Unlike Linux, most operating systems are proprietary, and their program code often is a zealously guarded secret. At one large software developer, an employee reported that application programmers had little opportunity to contribute to operating system programs because they had no access to the operating system program source code. Supporters of open source maintain that source code should be open to the public so that it can be scrutinized, corrected, and enhanced. In light of concerns about security and fears of possible virus problems, however, some people are not sure open source software is a good idea. Besides, they argue, companies and programmers should be able to control, and profit from, the operating systems they create. On the other hand, open source software can be scrutinized for errors by a much larger group of people and changes can be made immediately. Are open source operating systems a good idea? Why or why not? How can the concerns about open source operating systems be addressed? What are the advantages and disadvantages of open versus closed source operating systems? Does the open source model lead to better software?

FIGURE 8-30 Red Hat provides a version of Linux called Red Hat Enterprise Linux.

LOOKING AHEAD 8-1

The Future of Linux

The Linux operating system has been altered and enhanced since Linus Torvalds wrote the initial source code in 1991. With hundreds of programmers donating their time to make Linux the best possible version of UNIX, the software literally has changed on a daily basis.

As these developers work to improve Linux, their efforts are helping to shape the software's future. Open source experts predict this operating system will command six percent of the computer market in a few years. They also believe the key to Linux's success is an initiative to get the product into schools as a viable alternative to Microsoft Windows. Expect to see Linux applications in the manufacturing, medicine, biometrics, and entertainment environments. For more information, visit scsite.com/dc2007/ch8/looking and then click Linux Future.

Test your knowledge of pages 411 through 421 in Quiz Yourself 8-2.

NETWORK OPERATING SYSTEMS

As discussed earlier in this chapter, a network operating system is an operating system that is designed specifically to support a network. A network operating system typically resides on a server. The client computers on the network rely on the server(s) for resources. Many of the client operating systems discussed in the previous section work in conjunction with a network operating system.

Some of the stand-alone operating systems discussed in the previous section include networking capability; however, network operating systems are designed specifically to support all sizes of networks, including medium to large-sized businesses and Web servers. Examples of network operating systems include NetWare, Windows Server 2003, UNIX, Linux, and Solaris.

NetWare

Novell's *NetWare* is a network operating system designed for client/server networks. NetWare has a server portion that resides on the network server and a client portion that resides on each client computer connected to the network. NetWare supports open source software and runs on all types of computers from mainframes to personal computers.

The server portion of NetWare allows users to share hardware devices attached to the server (such as a printer), as well as e-mail, databases, or any other files and software

stored on the server. The client portion of NetWare communicates with the server. Client computers also can have their own stand-alone operating system such as Windows XP, Mac OS X, or a Linux-based client.

Windows Server 2003

Windows Server 2003 is an upgrade to Windows 2000 Server, which was an upgrade to Windows NT Server. Windows Server 2003, which includes features of previous server versions, offers the following capabilities:
- Web site management and hosting
- Delivery and management of multimedia across intranets and the Internet
- Document storage in Web folders
- Central information repository about network users and resources with *Active Directory*
- Client support using Windows XP and earlier versions of Windows, Mac OS X, UNIX, and Linux

To meet the needs of all sizes of businesses, the **Windows Server 2003 family** includes five products:
- *Windows Small Business Server 2003* designed for businesses with fewer than 75 users and limited networking expertise
- *Windows Server 2003, Standard Edition* for the typical small- to medium-sized business network
- *Windows Server 2003, Enterprise Edition* for medium- to large-sized businesses, including those with e-commerce operations; available in 64-bit version

- *Windows Server 2003, Datacenter Edition* for businesses with huge volumes of transactions and large-scale databases; available in 64-bit version
- *Windows Server 2003, Web Edition* for Web server and Web hosting businesses

Windows Server 2003 is part of Windows Server System. In addition to Windows Server 2003, *Windows Server System* provides developers with dynamic development tools that allow businesses and customers to connect and communicate easily via the Internet. Through Windows Server System, programmers have the ability to use *Web services*, which are Web applications created with any programming language or any operating system to communicate and share data seamlessly.

UNIX

In addition to being a stand-alone operating system, UNIX also is a network operating system. That is, UNIX is capable of handling a high volume of transactions in a multiuser environment and working with multiple processors using multiprocessing. For this reason, some computer professionals call UNIX a *multipurpose operating system* because it is both a stand-alone and network operating system. Many Web servers use UNIX as their operating system.

Linux

Some network servers use Linux as their operating system. Thus, Linux also is a multipurpose operating system. With Linux, a network administrator can configure the network, administer security, run a Web server, and process e-mail. Clients on the network can run Linux, UNIX, or Windows. Versions of Linux include both the Netscape and Mozilla Web browsers.

Solaris

Solaris, a version of UNIX developed by Sun Microsystems, is a network operating system designed specifically for e-commerce applications. Solaris manages high-traffic accounts and incorporates security necessary for Web transactions. Client computers often use a desktop program, such as GNOME desktop, that communicates with the Solaris operating system.

EMBEDDED OPERATING SYSTEMS

The operating system on most PDAs and small devices, called an **embedded operating system**, resides on a ROM chip. Popular embedded operating systems today include Windows CE, Windows Mobile, Palm OS, Embedded Linux, and Symbian OS. The following sections discuss these operating systems.

Windows CE

Windows CE is a scaled-down Windows operating system designed for use on communications, entertainment, and computing devices with limited functionality. Examples of devices that use Windows CE include Voice over IP devices, industrial control devices, point-of-sale terminals, security robots, navigation systems, media players, ticket machines, and computerized sewing machines (Figure 8-31).

FIGURE 8-31 This sewing machine uses Windows CE to assist with stitching quilts, garments, crafts, decorations, and embroidery.

Windows CE is a GUI that supports color, sound, multitasking, multimedia, e-mail, Internet access, and Web browsing. A built-in file viewer allows users to view files created in popular applications such as Word, Excel, and PowerPoint.

Devices equipped with Windows CE can communicate wirelessly with computers and other devices using Bluetooth or other wireless technologies, as long as the device is equipped with the necessary communications hardware.

Windows Mobile

Windows Mobile, an operating system based on Windows CE, includes functionality, applications, and a user interface designed for specific types of devices. Windows Mobile-based devices include PDAs, called the **Pocket PC**, and smart phones (Figure 8-32). With the Windows Mobile operating system and a Pocket PC or smart phone, users have access to all the basic PIM (personal information manager) functions such as contact lists, schedules, tasks, calendars, and notes. Information on the PDA or smart phone easily synchronizes with a personal computer or prints on a printer using a cable or a wireless technology.

Windows Mobile, which has a Windows XP look, also provides numerous additional features that allow users to check e-mail, browse the Web, listen to music, take pictures or record video, watch a video, send and receive instant messages, record a voice message, manage finances, or read an e-book. Many applications such as Word, Excel, Outlook, and Internet

Explorer, have scaled-down versions that run with Windows Mobile. Some devices with Windows Mobile also support handwriting and voice input. With the Pocket PC Phone Edition devices, users can make telephone calls and send text messages using the PDA.

Palm OS

A competing operating system to Windows Mobile is *Palm OS*, which runs on PDAs and smart phones (Figure 8-33). With Palm OS devices, users manage schedules and contacts, telephone messages, project notes, reminders, task and address lists, and important dates and appointments. Information on the PDA or smart phone easily synchronizes with a personal computer or prints on a printer using a cable or a wireless technology. Palm users also can exchange information with other Palm users wirelessly through IrDA technology.

Palm OS includes handwriting recognition software, called Graffiti. Many Palm OS devices allow users to connect wirelessly to the Internet, browse the Web, send and receive e-mail messages and instant messages, listen to music, record voice messages, and view digital photos. The latest version of Palm OS includes improved security for data transmission, allows for biometric identification, and supports the use of smart cards.

FIGURE 8-32 Windows Mobile runs on Pocket PCs and many smart phones.

FIGURE 8-33 Palm OS runs on PDAs and smart phones.

Embedded Linux

Embedded Linux is a scaled-down Linux operating system designed for PDAs, smart phones, smart watches, set-top boxes, Internet telephones, and many other types of devices and computers requiring an embedded operating system (Figure 8-34). PDAs and smart phones with embedded Linux offer calendar and address book and other PIM functions, touch screens, and handwriting recognition. Many also allow you to connect to the Internet, take pictures, play videos, listen to music, and send e-mail and instant messages. Devices that use embedded Linux synchronize with desktop computers using a variety of technologies including Bluetooth.

FIGURE 8-34
A PDA that uses embedded Linux.

Symbian OS

Symbian OS is an open source multitasking operating system designed for smart phones (Figure 8-35). In addition to making telephone calls, users of Symbian OS can maintain contact lists; save appointments; browse the Web; and send and receive text and picture messages, e-mail messages, and faxes using a smart phone. Users enter data by pressing keys on the keypad or keyboard, touching the screen, writing on the screen with a stylus, or speaking into the smart phone. Symbian OS allows users to communicate wirelessly using a variety of technologies including Bluetooth and IrDA.

FIGURE 8-35 This smart phone uses the Symbian OS.

STAND-ALONE UTILITY PROGRAMS

Although operating systems typically include some built-in utilities, many stand-alone utility programs are available for purchase. For example, you can purchase personal firewall, backup utilities, and screen savers. These stand-alone utilities typically offer improvements over those features built into the operating system or provide features not included in an operating system.

Other functions provided by stand-alone utilities include protecting against viruses, removing spyware and adware, filtering Internet content, converting files, compressing files, burning CDs and DVDs, and maintaining a personal computer. The following sections discuss each of these utilities.

Antivirus Programs

The term, computer **virus**, describes a potentially damaging computer program that affects, or infects, a computer negatively by altering the way the computer works without the user's knowledge or permission. More specifically, a computer virus is a segment of program code from some outside source that implants itself in a computer. Once the virus is in a computer, it can spread throughout and may damage your files and operating system.

Currently, more than 81,000 known virus programs exist with an estimated 6 new virus programs discovered each day. Computer viruses do not generate by chance. The programmer of a virus, known as a *virus author*, intentionally writes a virus program. Some virus authors find writing viruses a challenge. Others write virus programs to cause destruction. Writing a virus program usually requires significant programming skills.

Some viruses are harmless pranks that simply freeze a computer temporarily or display sounds or messages. The Music Bug virus, for example, instructs the computer to play a few chords of music. Other viruses destroy or corrupt data stored on the hard disk of the infected computer. If you notice any unusual changes in your computer's performance, it may be infected with a virus. Figure 8-36 outlines some common symptoms of virus infection.

SIGNS OF VIRUS INFECTION

- An unusual message or image is displayed on the computer screen
- An unusual sound or music plays randomly
- The available memory is less than what should be available
- A program or file suddenly is missing
- An unknown program or file mysteriously appears
- The size of a file changes without explanation
- A file becomes corrupted
- A program or file does not work properly
- System properties change

FIGURE 8-36 Viruses attack computers in a variety of ways. This list indicates some of the more common signs of virus infection.

Viruses are just one type of malicious software. *Malware* (short for malicious software) is software that acts without a user's knowledge and deliberately alters the computer's operations. In addition to viruses, worms and Trojan horses are malware.

A **worm**, such as Sasser or Zotob, copies itself repeatedly, for example, in memory or over a network, using up system resources and possibly shutting the system down. A **Trojan horse** (named after the Greek myth) hides within or looks like a legitimate program such as a screen saver. A certain condition or action usually triggers the Trojan horse. Unlike a virus or worm, a Trojan horse does not replicate itself to other computers. For a more technical discussion about computer viruses, read the High-Tech Talk article in Chapter 3 on page 168.

To protect a computer from virus attacks, users should install an antivirus program and update it frequently. An **antivirus program** protects a computer against viruses by identifying and removing any computer viruses found in memory, on storage media, or on incoming files (Figure 8-37). Most antivirus programs also protect against worms and Trojan horses. When you purchase a new computer, it often includes antivirus software.

The two more popular antivirus programs are McAfee VirusScan and Norton AntiVirus. As an alternative to purchasing these products on CD, both McAfee and Norton offer Web-based antivirus programs. That is, during your paid subscription period, the program continuously protects the computer against viruses.

FIGURE 8-37 An antivirus program scans memory, disks, and incoming e-mail messages and attachments for viruses and attempts to remove any viruses it finds.

FAQ 8-8

What steps should I take to prevent virus infections on my computer?

Set up the antivirus software to scan on a regular basis. Update your virus definitions regularly. Never open an e-mail attachment unless you are expecting the attachment and it is from a trusted source. If you use Windows, install the latest updates. Set macro security in programs such as word processing and spreadsheet so you can enable or disable macros. Back up files regularly. For more information, visit scsite.com/dc2007/ch8/faq and then click Preventing Virus Infections.

Spyware Removers

Spyware is a program placed on a computer without the user's knowledge that secretly collects information about the user, often related to Web browsing habits. Spyware often enters a computer as a result of a user installing a new program. The spyware program communicates information it collects to some outside source while you are online.

Adware is a program that displays an online advertisement in a banner or pop-up window on Web pages, e-mail, or other Internet services. Sometimes, spyware is hidden in adware. A **spyware remover** is a program that detects and deletes spyware, adware, and other similar programs. Most spyware removers cost less than $50; some are available on the Web at no cost. Some operating systems include adware blockers.

Internet Filters

Filters are programs that remove or block certain items from being displayed. Three widely used Internet filters are anti-spam programs, Web filters, and pop-up blockers.

ANTI-SPAM PROGRAMS *Spam* is an unsolicited e-mail message or newsgroup posting sent to many recipients or newsgroups at once. Spam is Internet junk mail. The content of spam ranges from selling a product or service, to promoting a business opportunity, to advertising offensive material. An **anti-spam program** is a filtering program that attempts to remove spam before it reaches your inbox. If your e-mail program does not include an anti-spam program, many anti-spam programs are available at no cost on the Web. Internet access providers often filter spam as a service for their subscribers.

Should anti-spam programs be installed on home computers?

Yes. With more than 65 percent of all e-mail categorized as spam, home and business users could lose valuable time sifting through messages related to the variety of subjects shown in the chart below. For more information, visit scsite.com/dc2007/ch8/faq and then click Anti-Spam Programs.

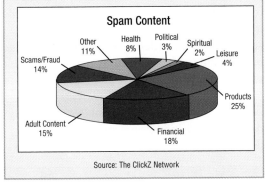

Spam Content

- Other 11%
- Health 8%
- Political 3%
- Spiritual 2%
- Leisure 4%
- Scams/Fraud 14%
- Products 25%
- Adult Content 15%
- Financial 18%

Source: The ClickZ Network

WEB FILTERS **Web filtering software** is a program that restricts access to certain material on the Web. Some restrict access to specific Web sites; others filter sites that use certain words or phrases. Many businesses use Web filtering software to limit employee's Web access. Some schools, libraries, and parents use this software to restrict access to minors.

POP-UP BLOCKERS A *pop-up ad* is an Internet advertisement that appears in a new window in the foreground of a Web page displayed in your browser. A **pop-up blocker** is a filtering program that stops pop-up ads from displaying on Web pages. If your operating system does not block pop-up ads, many pop-up blockers can be downloaded from the Web at no cost.

File Conversion

A *file conversion utility* transforms the contents of a file or data from one format to another. When a business develops a new information system, often the data in the current system is not in the correct format for the new system. Thus, part of the system development process is to convert data — instead of having users reenter all the existing data in the new system. On a smaller scale, when home users purchase new software, they may need to convert files so the files will be displayed properly in the new software.

File Compression

A **file compression utility** shrinks the size of a file(s). A compressed file takes up less storage space than the original file. Compressing files frees up room on the storage media and improves system performance. Attaching a compressed file to an e-mail message, for example, reduces the time needed for file transmission. Uploading and downloading compressed files to and from the Internet reduces the file transmission time.

Compressed files, sometimes called **zipped files**, usually have a .zip extension. When you receive or download a compressed file, you must uncompress it. To **uncompress**, or *unzip*, a file, you restore it to its original form. Some operating systems such as Windows XP include uncompress capabilities. To compress a file, however, you need a stand-alone file compression utility. Two popular stand-alone file compression utilities are PKZIP and WinZip (Figure 8-38).

zip extension

compressed files

percent compressed

FIGURE 8-38   WinZip is a popular file compression utility.

CD/DVD Burning

CD/DVD burning software writes text, graphics, audio, and video files on a recordable or rewritable CD or DVD. This software enables the home user easily to back up contents of their hard disk on a CD/DVD and make duplicates of uncopyrighted music or movies. CD/DVD burning software usually also includes photo editing, audio editing, and video editing capabilities (Figure 8-39).

When you buy a recordable or rewritable CD or DVD, it typically includes CD/DVD burning software. You also can buy CD/DVD burning software for a cost of less than $100.

Personal Computer Maintenance

Operating systems typically include a diagnostic utility that diagnoses computer problems but does not repair them. A **personal computer maintenance utility** identifies and fixes operating system problems, detects and repairs disk problems, and includes the capability of improving a computer's performance. Additionally, some personal computer maintenance utilities continuously monitor a computer while you use it to identify and repair problems before they occur. Norton SystemWorks is a popular personal computer maintenance utility designed for Windows operating systems (Figure 8-40).

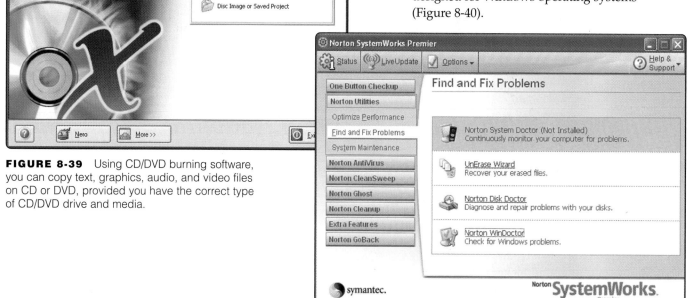

FIGURE 8-39 Using CD/DVD burning software, you can copy text, graphics, audio, and video files on CD or DVD, provided you have the correct type of CD/DVD drive and media.

FIGURE 8-40 A popular maintenance program for Windows users.

Test your knowledge of pages 422 through 428 in Quiz Yourself 8-3.

QUIZ YOURSELF 8-3

Instructions: Find the true statement below. Then, rewrite the remaining false statements so they are true.

1. A pop-up blocker shrinks the size of a file(s).

2. An anti-spam program protects a computer against viruses by identifying and removing any computer viruses found in memory, on storage media, or on incoming files.

3. Examples of network operating systems include NetWare, Windows Server 2003, UNIX, Linux, and Solaris.

4. Pocket PCs use Palm OS as their operating system.

5. Web filtering software writes text, graphics, audio, and video files to a recordable or rewritable CD or DVD.

Quiz Yourself Online: To further check your knowledge of network operating systems, embedded operating systems, and stand-alone utility programs, visit scsite.com/dc2007/ch8/quiz and then click Objectives 7 – 9.

CHAPTER SUMMARY

This chapter defined an operating system and then discussed the functions common to most operating systems. Next, it introduced several utility programs commonly found in operating systems. The chapter discussed a variety of stand-alone operating systems, network operating systems, and embedded operating systems (read Looking Ahead 8-2 for a look at the next generation of operating systems). Finally, the chapter described several stand-alone utility programs.

LOOKING AHEAD 8-2

Online Operating Systems Proposed

Microsoft Windows' dominance in the operating system world is being challenged by proposed Web operating systems. Experts predict that within a few years computer users will see Google, Yahoo!, and Mozilla release Internet-enabled products.

If these operating systems come to fruition, computer users will access content and manage data using a Web browser. They will be unaware of when their computer is retrieving information from the Web or from their local computer. Applications will be written for this Web browser and will not be dependent upon a specific machine or cellular phone.

Proposed applications include reading e-mail, blogs, and news offline, backing up files to an online service, and managing audio and video files. For more information, visit scsite.com/dc2007/ch8/looking and then click Operating Systems.

CAREER CORNER

Systems Programmer

System software is a key component in any computer. A *systems programmer* evaluates, installs, and maintains system software and provides technical support to the programming staff.

Systems programmers work with the programs that control computers, such as operating systems, network operating systems, and database systems. They identify current and future processing needs and then recommend the software and hardware necessary to meet those needs. In addition to selecting and installing system software, systems programmers must be able to adapt system software to the requirements of an organization, provide regular maintenance, measure system performance, determine the impact of new or updated software on the system, design and implement special software, and provide documentation. Because they are familiar with the entire system, systems programmers often help application programmers to diagnose technical problems.

Systems programmers must be acquainted thoroughly with a variety of operating systems. They must be able to think logically, pay attention to detail, work with abstract concepts, and devise solutions to complex problems. Systems programmers often work in teams and interact with programmers and nontechnical users, so communications skills are important.

Most systems programmers have a four-year B.S. degree in Computer Science or Information Technology. Depending on responsibilities and experience, salaries range from $55,000 to more than $110,000. For more information, visit scsite.com/dc2007/ch8/careers and then click Systems Programmer.

High-Tech Talk

WINDOWS XP: A USEFUL WAY TO COMPLETE A WIDE RANGE OF TASKS

When Microsoft developed the Windows XP operating system, it gave it a fresh, new graphical user interface. You still, however, can complete many important tasks using the command-line interface. Microsoft's first operating system, MS-DOS, was based entirely on a command-line interface. Today, Windows XP supports many of the original MS-DOS commands — and many new commands that help you complete tasks.

With Windows XP, you enter commands via a command shell. A *command shell* is a program with a nongraphical, command-line interface that provides an environment to run text-based application software and utility programs. The Windows XP command shell is called *Command Prompt*; the file name for the Command Prompt application is cmd.exe.

To open the Command Prompt window, click the Start button and point to All Programs, point to Accessories on the All Programs submenu, and then click Command Prompt on the Accessories submenu. Clicking Run on the Start menu and then typing cmd in the Run dialog box also opens the Command Prompt window. To execute a command, type one command per line and then press the ENTER key. Many commands allow you to enter one or more *options*, or *arguments*, which are additions to a command that change or refine the command in a specified manner. To close the Command Prompt window, type exit and then press the ENTER key or click the Close button in the Command Prompt window.

The Command Prompt window allows you to complete a wide range of tasks, including troubleshooting network connections. The *ping command*, for example, allows you to test TCP/IP connectivity for network and Internet connections (Figure 8-4a on page 403). When you enter the ping command with an IP address, your computer sends a special packet called ICMP Echo to that address. If everything is working, a reply comes back; if not, the ping times out. You also can use *TRACERT* (*traceroute*), a command-line utility that traces a data packet's path to its destination. When you enter tracert scsite.com, for example, the tracert utility traces the path from your computer to the Shelly Cashman Web server (Figure 8-41). The tracert command sends information to each device (called a hop) three times. The traceroute program sends the information three times to give you some idea of the variance in transit times. The time it takes for the device to respond each time is displayed. When you access a Web site, your request usually will pass through several routers before you connect to the destination server. For example, the tracert command for scsite.com passed through 15 other routers before connecting to the destination server (www.scsite.com).

You also can use the Windows XP Command Prompt to help manage your computer. When you enter the *systeminfo command*, Command Prompt queries your computer for basic system information, including operating system configuration and hardware properties, such as RAM and disk space. If you enter the *tasklist command*, the Command Prompt window returns a list of processes running on a computer, with each process identified by a process ID (PID). You can terminate any process by entering the *taskkill command* and the PID as the argument. Network administrators can use this command to fix problems on networked computers by closing applications.

The Windows XP Command Prompt also supports commands used to manage the files and file system on your hard disk. The *chkdsk command* checks for and corrects errors on the disk. You also can defragment your hard disk by entering the *defrag command*, with an argument specifying the drive to defragment (for example, defrag c:). When you are done working, you can use the *shutdown command* to shut down or restart your local or a remote computer.

In most cases, the command-line tools perform functions similar to the GUI application. The Disk Defragmenter utility and the defrag command, for example, provide similar functionality. In others, the command-line tools provide additional functionality. For instance, the *diskpart command* starts the command-line version of the DiskPart utility and gives you access to advanced features not available in the GUI version.

The commands discussed here are just some of the wide range of commands supported by Windows XP. For more information, visit scsite.com/dc2007/ch8/tech and then click Windows XP Command Prompt.

Windows XP Command Prompt window

tracert scsite.com command

time required for device to respond to request

names of routers along path

hops required to reach destination

destination address

FIGURE 8-41
An example of the tracert command.

Companies on the Cutting Edge

RED HAT
OPEN SOURCE SOFTWARE DISTRIBUTOR

When you were young, you were taught to share. University professors share their research with colleagues throughout the world; and *Red Hat* shares software code, or instructions, with computer users.

Red Hat is the largest supplier of open source software, which allows buyers to view, modify, and perhaps improve, the software. The company delivers the software improvements to customers through the Red Hat Network, the company's Internet service.

Bob Young and Marc Ewing founded Red Hat in 1994 and started distributing a version of the Red Hat Linux operating system complete with documentation and support. Today, Linux is Red Hat's most well-known product. Subscriptions to the company's premium Linux software have helped boost the company to profitability. The subscriptions include tested updates, security fixes, and technical information updated daily. For more information, visit scsite.com/dc2007/ch8/companies and then click Red Hat.

SYMBIAN
HANDHELD COMPUTING DEVICES MANUFACTURER

The next time you send a text message using your smart phone, you may be using an operating system developed by *Symbian*. This British company's operating system is the global industry standard and is licensed to 11 leading cellular telephone manufacturers, including Ericsson, Matsushita (Panasonic), Motorola, Nokia, and Psion, which account for more than 39 million cellular phones worldwide.

In 1994, former CEO Colly Myers began experimenting with his programming expertise with the goal of developing a full operating system for a handset rivaling that found on a mainframe computer. Four years later, he convinced Ericsson, Motorola, and Nokia to invest in his product.

The Symbian open standards allow manufacturers to customize services and user interfaces, including graphics, e-mail, and touch screens. For more information, visit scsite.com/dc2007/ch8/companies and then click Symbian.

Technology Trailblazers

ALAN KAY
COMPUTER PIONEER

Chances are that every time you use your computer you use one of *Alan Kay*'s ideas. More than 35 years ago — long before the personal computer became ubiquitous — he was developing a notebook computer complete with a flat screen, wireless network, and storage. More than 20 years ago, he engineered a graphical user interface, object-oriented languages, and personal computer networks.

Kay did much of his early work at the U.S. Defense Department's Advance Research Project Agency (DARPA) and Xerox's Palo Alto Research Center (PARC). Today he is a computer science professor at UCLA and president of the Viewpoints Research Institute, a nonprofit organization dedicated to helping children develop fluency in critical thinking, math, and science. For more information, visit scsite.com/dc2007/ch8/people and then click Alan Kay.

LINUS TORVALDS
LINUX CREATOR

When *Linus Torvalds* developed a new operating system in 1991, he announced his project in an Internet newsgroup, made the source code available, and asked for suggestions. Computer users responded by reviewing the system and offering enhancements. Three years later, Torvalds released a much-enhanced version of an open source operating system he called Linux.

Torvalds developed the innovative operating system when he was a 21-year-old computer science student in Finland. Today, Linux is estimated to be running on at least 10 percent of computers and is Microsoft's main competitor. Torvalds leads the development of Linux as a fellow at OSDL (Open Source Development Labs), a not-for-profit consortium of companies dedicated to developing and promoting the operating system. In 2005, Torvalds predicted Linux will be a prominent part of the desktop market within the next 10 years. For more information, visit scsite.com/dc2007/ch8/people and then click Linus Torvalds.

Chapter Review

The Chapter Review section summarizes the concepts presented in this chapter. To listen to the audio version of this Chapter Review, visit scsite.com/dc2007/ch8/review. To obtain help from other students regarding any subject in this chapter, visit scsite.com/dc2007/ch8/forum and post your thoughts or questions.

(1) What Are the Types of System Software?   **System software** consists of the programs that control or maintain the operations of a computer and its devices. Two types of system software are operating systems and utility programs. An **operating system (OS)** contains instructions that coordinate all the activities among computer hardware resources. A **utility program** performs maintenance-type tasks, usually related to managing a computer, its devices, or its programs.

(2) What Is the Startup Process on a Personal Computer?   **Booting** is the process of starting or restarting a computer. When a user turns on a computer, the power supply sends a signal to the system unit. The processor chip finds the ROM chip(s) that contains the **BIOS**, which is firmware with the computer's startup instructions. The BIOS performs the *power-on self test* (*POST*) to check system components and compares the results with data in a CMOS chip. If the POST completes successfully, the BIOS searches for the *system files* and the *kernel* of the operating system, which manages memory and devices, and loads them into memory from storage. Finally, the operating system loads configuration information, requests any necessary user information, and displays the desktop on the screen.

(3) What Are the Functions of an Operating System?   The operating system provides a user interface, manages programs, manages memory, schedules jobs, configures devices, establishes an Internet connection, and monitors performance. The **user interface** controls how data and instructions are entered and how information is displayed. Three types of user interfaces are a *command-line interface*, a *menu-driven interface*, and a *graphical user interface* (*GUI*). Managing programs refers to how many users, and how many programs, an operating system can support at one time. An operating system can be *single user/single tasking*, *single user/multitasking*, *multiuser*, or *multiprocessing*. **Memory management** optimizes the use of random access memory (RAM). If memory is insufficient, the operating system may use **virtual memory**, which allocates a portion of a storage medium to function as additional RAM. Scheduling jobs determines the order in which jobs are processed. A **job** is an operation the processor manages. Configuring devices involves loading each device's driver when a user boots the computer. A **driver** is a program that tells the operating system how to communicate with a specific device. Establishing an Internet connection sets up a connection between a computer and an Internet service provider. A **performance monitor** is an operating system program that assesses and reports information about computer resources and devices.

(4) How Can Operating Systems Help Administrators Control a Network and Manage Security?   A **network operating system**, or *network OS*, is an operating system that organizes and coordinates how multiple users access and share network resources. A *network administrator* uses the network OS to add and remove users, computers, and other devices to and from the network. A network administrator also uses the network OS to administer network security. For each user, the network administrator establishes a user account that enables the user to **log on**, or access, the network by supplying the correct **user name** and **password**.

Visit scsite.com/dc2007/ch8/quiz or click the Quiz Yourself button. Click Objectives 1 – 4.

(5) What Is the Purpose of the Utilities Included with Most Operating Systems?   Most operating systems include several built-in utility programs. A **file manager** performs functions related to file and disk management. An **image viewer** displays, copies, and prints the contents of a graphics file. A **personal firewall** detects and protects a computer from unauthorized intrusions. An **uninstaller** removes a program and any associated entries in the system files. A **disk scanner** detects and corrects problems on a disk and searches for and removes unnecessary files. A **disk defragmenter** reorganizes the files and unused space on a computer's hard disk. A

Chapter Review

diagnostic utility compiles and reports technical information about a computer's hardware and certain system software programs. A **backup utility** is used to copy, or *back up*, selected files or an entire hard disk. A **screen saver** displays a moving image or blank screen if no keyboard or mouse activity occurs for a specified time.

6 What Are Features of Several Stand-Alone Operating Systems? A **stand-alone operating system** is a complete operating system that works on a desktop computer, notebook computer, or mobile computing device. Stand-alone operating systems include DOS, Windows XP, Windows Vista, Mac OS X, UNIX, and Linux. **DOS** (*Disk Operating System*) refers to several single user, command-line operating systems developed for personal computers. **Windows XP** is a fast, reliable Windows operating system, providing better performance, increased security, and a simpler look. **Windows Vista**, successor to Windows XP, is Microsoft's fastest, most reliable and efficient operating system to date, offering quicker application start up, built-in diagnostics, automatic recovery, improved security, and enhanced searching and organizing capabilities. **Mac OS X** is a multitasking operating system available only for Apple computers. **UNIX** is a multitasking operating system developed at Bell Laboratories. **Linux** is a popular, multitasking UNIX-type operating system that is *open source software*, which means its code is available to the public.

Visit scsite.com/dc2007/ch8/quiz or click the Quiz Yourself button. Click Objectives 5 – 6.

7 What Are Various Network Operating Systems? Network operating systems include NetWare, Windows Server 2003, UNIX, Linux, and Solaris. Novell's *NetWare* is a network OS designed for client/server networks. **Windows Server 2003** is an upgrade to Windows 2000 Server and includes features of previous server versions. Linux, like UNIX, is a *multipurpose operating system* because it is both a stand-alone and network operating system. *Solaris*, a version of UNIX developed by Sun Microsystems, is a network OS designed for e-commerce applications.

8 What Devices Use Embedded Operating Systems? Most PDAs and small devices have an **embedded operating system** that resides on a ROM chip. Popular embedded operating systems include Windows CE, Windows Mobile, Palm OS, embedded Linux, and Symbian OS. **Windows CE** is a scaled-down Windows operating system designed for use on communications, entertainment, and computing devices with limited functionality. **Windows Mobile**, an operating system based on Windows CE, provides a user interface designed for a specific type of devices, such as PDAs, called the **Pocket PC**. *Palm OS* is an operating system used on PDAs and smart phones.

9 What Is the Purpose of Several Stand-Alone Utility Programs? Stand-alone utility programs offer improvements over features built into the operating system or provide features not included in the operating system. An **antivirus program** protects computers against a **virus**, or potentially damaging computer program, by identifying and removing any computer viruses. A **spyware remover** detects and deletes *spyware*, *adware*, and other similar programs. Internet filter programs can include an **anti-spam** program, **Web filtering software**, and a **pop-up blocker**. A **file compression utility** shrinks the size of a file so that it takes up less storage space. A *file conversion utility* transforms the contents of a file from one format to another. **CD/DVD burning software** writes to a recordable or rewritable CD or DVD. A **personal computer maintenance utility** identifies and repairs operating system problems or disk problems, and improves a computer's performance.

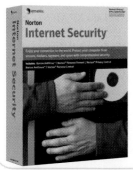

Visit scsite.com/dc2007/ch8/quiz or click the Quiz Yourself button. Click Objectives 7 – 9.

Key Terms

You should know the Primary Terms and be familiar with the Secondary Terms. Use the list below to help focus your study. To further enhance your understanding of the Key Terms in this chapter, visit scsite.com/dc2007/ch8/terms. See an example of and a definition for each term, and access current and additional information about the term from the Web.

Primary Terms

(shown in bold-black characters in the chapter)

anti-spam program (426)
antivirus program (426)
backup utility (415)
BIOS (400)
boot disk (402)
boot drive (402)
booting (400)
buffer (407)
CD/DVD burning software (428)
cold boot (400)
defragmenting (414)
diagnostic utility (414)
disk defragmenter (414)
disk scanner (414)
DOS (417)
driver (407)
embedded operating system (423)
file compression utility (427)
file manager (412)
formatting (412)
image viewer (412)
job (406)
Linux (421)
log on (410)
Mac OS X (420)
Macintosh operating system (420)
memory management (405)
network operating system (410)
operating system (OS) (398)
password (410)
performance monitor (409)

personal computer maintenance utility (428)
personal firewall (413)
Plug and Play (407)
Pocket PC (424)
pop-up blocker (427)
queue (407)
recovery disk (402)
restore program (415)
screen saver (415)
shortcut (412)
spooling (407)
spyware remover (426)
stand-alone operating system (416)
system software (398)
Trojan horse (426)
uncompress (427)
uninstaller (413)
UNIX (420)
user ID (410)
user interface (402)
user name (410)
utility (411)
utility program (411)
virtual memory (406)
virus (425)
warm boot (400)
Web filtering software (427)
Windows CE (423)
Windows Mobile (424)
Windows Server 2003 (422)
Windows Server 2003 family (422)
Windows Vista (419)
Windows XP (417)
worm (426)
zipped files (427)

Secondary Terms

(shown in italic characters in the chapter)

Active Directory (422)
adware (426)
back up (415)
background (404)
basic input/output system (400)
client operating systems (416)
command language (402)
command-line interface (402)
compress (415)
cross-platform (399)
device driver (407)
device-dependent (415)
device-independent (415)
Disk Operating System (417)
Document Explorer (419)
Dr. Watson (414)
embedded Linux (425)
encryption (411)
fault-tolerant computer (405)
file conversion utility (427)
foreground (404)
fragmented (414)
ghosting (415)
graphical user interface (GUI) (402)
hacker (413)
IRQ (interrupt request line) (409)
kernel (400)
malware (426)
Media Center PC (418)
memory resident (400)
menu-driven interface (402)
multiprocessing (405)
multipurpose operating system (423)
multiuser (405)
NetWare (422)
network administrator (410)
network OS (410)
nonresident (400)
open source software (421)
page (406)
paging (406)
Palm OS (424)
platform (399)
pop-up ad (427)
power-on self test (POST) (400)

preemptive multitasking (405)
print spooler (407)
proprietary software (415)
registry (401)
scripts (402)
service pack (416)
single user/multitasking (403)
single user/single tasking (403)
Solaris (423)
spam (426)
spyware (426)
Startup folder (402)
swap file (406)
Symbian OS (425)
system files (401)
thrashing (406)
unzip (427)
Virtual Folders (419)
virus author (425)
Web services (423)
Windows Explorer (412)
Windows Picture and Fax Viewer (412)
Windows Server 2003, Datacenter Edition (423)
Windows Server 2003, Enterprise Edition (422)
Windows Server 2003, Standard Edition (422)
Windows Server 2003, Web Edition (423)
Windows Server System (423)
Windows Small Business Server 2003 (422)
Windows XP Home Edition (418)
Windows XP Media Center Edition (418)
Windows XP Professional (418)
Windows XP Professional x64 Edition (418)
Windows XP Tablet PC Edition (418)

Checkpoint

Use the Checkpoint exercises to check your knowledge level of the chapter. The Beyond the Book exercises will help broaden your understanding of the concepts presented in this chapter. To complete the Checkpoint exercises interactively, visit scsite.com/dc2007/ch8/check.

Label the Figure

Identify the various elements of virtual memory.

a. Forward button

b. link

c. command prompt

d. command entered by user

e. background program

f. menu names

g. menu

True/False

Mark T for True and F for False. (See page numbers in parentheses.)

_____ 1. All sizes of computers typically use the same operating system. (399)

_____ 2. Booting is the process of starting or restarting a computer. (400)

_____ 3. A user interface controls how you enter data and instructions and how information is displayed on the screen. (402)

_____ 4. When a computer is running multiple programs concurrently, one program is in the background and the others are in the foreground. (404)

_____ 5. Encryption is the process of encoding data and information into an unreadable form. (411)

_____ 6. A disk scanner is a utility that reorganizes the files and unused space on a computer's hard disk so the operating system accesses data more quickly and programs run faster. (414)

_____ 7. Some stand-alone operating systems are called client operating systems because they also work in conjunction with a network operating system. (416)

_____ 8. Linux is open source software, which means its code cannot be modified or redistributed. (421)

_____ 9. Most antivirus programs do not protect against worms or Trojan horses. (426)

_____ 10. A pop-up blocker is a filtering program that stops pop-up ads from displaying on Web pages. (427)

Checkpoint

 Multiple Choice

Select the best answer. (See page numbers in parentheses.)

1. The _____ chip, which uses battery power, stores configuration information about the computer. (400)
   a. CMOS
   b. POST
   c. BIOS
   d. RAM

2. In Windows XP, the _____ consists of several files that contain the system configuration information. (401)
   a. shortcut
   b. page
   c. registry
   d. swap file

3. _____ often are difficult to use because they require exact spelling, grammar, and punctuation. (402)
   a. Graphical user interfaces
   b. Menu-driven interfaces
   c. Command-line interfaces
   d. All of the above

4. When an operating system spends much of its time paging, instead of executing application software, it is said to be _____. (406)
   a. booting
   b. thrashing
   c. spooling
   d. formatting

5. A _____ is a small program that tells the operating system how to communicate with a specific device. (407)
   a. buffer
   b. device
   c. performance monitor
   d. driver

6. Defragmenting reorganizes the files on a disk so they are located in _____ access time. (414)
   a. noncontiguous sectors, which slows
   b. noncontiguous sectors, which speeds
   c. contiguous sectors, which speeds
   d. contiguous sectors, which slows

7. Windows XP includes the _____, Dr. Watson, which detects problems as well as suggests courses of action. (414)
   a. file manager
   b. backup utility
   c. image viewer
   d. diagnostic utility

8. _____ is a complete operating system that works on a desktop computer, notebook computer, or mobile computing device. (416)
   a. A stand-alone operating system
   b. A network operating system
   c. A stand-alone utility program
   d. An embedded operating system

9. _____ used a command-line interface when Microsoft first developed it, although later versions included menu-driven user interfaces. (417)
   a. Windows XP
   b. DOS
   c. Mac OS X
   d. UNIX

10. _____ store(s) search criteria as part of the folder that instantly runs each time the folder opens, enabling users easily to locate documents stored anywhere on the computer. (419)
    a. Virtual Folders
    b. Document Explorer
    c. A buffer
    d. A screen saver

11. _____, developed by Sun Microsystems, manages high-traffic accounts and incorporates security necessary for Web transactions. (423)
    a. Solaris
    b. Linux
    c. Windows Server 2003
    d. Netware

12. _____ is an open source multitasking operating system designed for smart phones. (425)
    a. Solaris
    b. Linux
    c. Palm OS
    d. Symbian OS

13. A _____ is malware that does not replicate itself to other computers. (426)
    a. virus
    b. Trojan horse
    c. worm
    d. all of the above

14. _____ is a program that displays an online advertisement in a banner or pop-up window on Web pages, e-mail, or other Internet services. (426)
    a. Spyware
    b. A Trojan horse
    c. Adware
    d. A pop-up ad

Checkpoint

Matching

Match the terms with their definitions. (See page numbers in parentheses.)

_____ 1. recovery disk (402)
_____ 2. fault-tolerant computer (405)
_____ 3. page (406)
_____ 4. spooling (407)
_____ 5. IRQ (409)
_____ 6. user name (410)
_____ 7. image viewer (412)
_____ 8. restore program (415)
_____ 9. proprietary software (415)
_____ 10. virus (425)

a. communications line between a device and the processor
b. hides within or looks like a legitimate program such as a screen saver
c. continues to operate when one of its components fails
d. with virtual memory, the amount of data and program instructions that can be swapped at a given time
e. reverses the backup process and restores backed up files
f. unique combination of characters that identifies one specific user
g. potentially damaging computer program that affects, or infects, a computer negatively by altering the way the computer works without the user's knowledge or permission
h. disk that contains a few system files that will start the computer
i. privately owned and limited to a specific vendor or computer model
j. a utility that allows users to display, copy, and print the contents of a graphics file
k. process that sends print jobs to a buffer instead of sending them immediately to the printer
l. program that tells the operating system how to communicate with a device

Short Answer

Write a brief answer to each of the following questions.

1. How is a cold boot different from a warm boot? _____ How is a memory-resident part of an operating system different from a nonresident part of an operating system? _____

2. What is a user interface? _____ How are a command-line interface, a menu-driven interface, and a graphical user interface different? _____

3. What is the purpose of memory management? _____ What is the purpose of virtual memory, and where is virtual memory stored? _____

4. What is the difference between device-dependent and device-independent software? _____ What is proprietary software? _____

5. What is the difference between spyware and adware? _____ What are three widely used Internet filters? _____

Beyond the Book

Read the following book elements, learn more about each using the Web, and then write a brief report.

1. Ethics & Issues — What Should Be in an Operating System? (409), Who Is Responsible for Operating System Security? (410), Should Software Manufacturers Be Liable for Defective Software? (416), or Closed Source vs. Open Source Operating Systems (421)

2. Career Corner — Systems Programmer (429)

3. Companies on the Cutting Edge – Red Hat or Symbian (431)

4. FAQs (402, 406, 409, 411, 413, 418, 423, 426, 427)

5. High-Tech Talk — Windows XP: A Useful Way to Complete a Wide Range of Tasks (430)

6. Looking Ahead — The Future of Linux (421) or Online Operating Systems Proposed (429)

7. Making Use of the Web — Weather, Sports, and News (124)

8. Picture Yourself Getting a Virus through E-Mail (396)

9. Technology Trailblazers — Alan Kay or Linus Torvalds (431)

10. Web Links (401, 407, 413, 415, 419, 420, 423, 424, 427)

Learn It Online

Use the Learn It Online exercises to reinforce your understanding of the chapter concepts.
To access the Learn It Online exercises, visit scsite.com/dc2007/ch8/learn.

(1) At the Movies — Windows XP Media Center Edition

To view the Windows XP Media Center Edition movie, click the number 1 button. Locate your video and click the corresponding High-Speed or Dial-Up link, depending on your Internet connection. Watch the movie and then complete the exercise by answering the questions that follow. Windows XP Media Center Edition 2004 is software that easily can enable advanced multimedia interactivity on your computer. With one touch of the remote control, you can activate your music, photographs, videos, radio shows, or television programs. Why is the Windows XP Media Center prone to viruses? How can you make sure your computer is protected from viruses?

(2) At the Movies — Beam DVDs From Room to Room

To view the Beam DVDs From Room to Room movie, click the number 2 button. Locate your video and click the corresponding High-Speed or Dial-Up link, depending on your Internet connection. Watch the movie and then complete the exercise by answering the question that follows. With a moderately priced audio/video sender and receiver system you easily could hook up a small camera and monitor in any room in the house. What are the pros and cons of using video monitoring in your home?

(3) Student Edition Labs — Installing and Uninstalling Software

Click the number 3 button. A new browser window will open, displaying the Student Edition Labs. Follow the on-screen instructions to complete the Installing and Uninstalling Software Lab. When finished, click the Exit button. If required, submit your results to your instructor.

(4) Practice Test

Click the number 4 button. Answer each question. When completed, enter your name and click the Grade Test button to submit the quiz for grading. Make a note of any missed questions. If required, submit your results to your instructor.

(5) Who Wants To Be a Computer Genius²?

Click the number 5 button to find out if you are a computer genius. Directions about how to play the game will be displayed. When you are ready to play, click the Play button. Submit your score to your instructor.

(6) Wheel of Terms

Click the number 6 button to reinforce important terms you learned in this chapter by playing the Shelly Cashman Series version of this popular game. Directions about how to play the game will be displayed. When you are ready to play, click the Play button. Submit your score to your instructor.

(7) DC Track and Field

Click the number 7 button to use what you have learned in this chapter to compete against other students in three track and field events. Directions about how to play the game will be displayed. When you are ready to play, click the start first event button. If required, submit your score to your instructor.

Learn It Online

8 You're Hired!

Click the number 8 button to use what you have learned in this chapter to embark on the path to a career in computers. Directions about how to play the game will be displayed. When you are ready to play, click the begin game button. If required, submit your score to your instructor.

9 Crossword Puzzle Challenge

Click the number 9 button. Complete the puzzle to reinforce skills you learned in this chapter. Directions about how to play the game will be displayed. When you are ready to play, click the Submit button. Submit the completed puzzle to your instructor.

10 Lab Exercises

Click the number 10 button. When the Lab Exercises menu appears, click the exercise assigned by your instructor. A new browser window will open. Follow the on-screen instructions to complete the exercise. When finished, click the Exit button. If required, submit your results to your instructor.

11 In the News

When Windows XP was introduced in October 2001, hundreds queued up at computer outlets. It is unclear, however, whether the anticipation was caused by the new operating system or by the promotions many dealers offered. Click the number 11 button and read a news article about the impact, quality, or promotion of an operating system. What operating system was it? What was done to sell the operating system? Is the operating system recommended? Why or why not?

12 Chapter Discussion Forum

Select an objective from this chapter on page 397 about which you would like more information. Click the number 12 button and post a short message listing a meaningful message title accompanied by one or more questions concerning the selected objective. In two days, return to the threaded discussion by clicking the number 12 button. Submit to your instructor your original message and at least one response to your message.

13 Airline Schedules

Click the number 13 button to learn how to use the Internet to price, reserve, and track airline flights. Follow the instructions to use Southwest Airlines' Web site to price a flight from Chicago to Las Vegas. Using the Schedules link, check for available flights for the dates you select. Once you have selected a flight, use the Reservations link to price the flight. Print a copy of the pricing for your selected flight. Check the status of a current flight comparable to the flight you priced. Write a report comparing the different fares available and summarizing what information is available when you check the status of a flight. Include in your report what the circumstances would have to be for you to choose a more expensive flight. Print your report and submit it to your instructor.

Learn How To

Use the Learn How To activities to learn fundamental skills when using a computer and accompanying technology. Complete the exercises and submit them to your instructor. Visit scsite.com/dc2007/ch8/howto to obtain more information pertaining to each activity.

LEARN HOW TO 1: Install a Computer

Once you have purchased a computer, you must install it for use. Based on years of experience, a set of guidelines for installing and using your computer has been developed. To examine these guidelines, complete the following steps:
1. Start the browser on your computer.
2. Type the Web address scsite.com/dc2007 in the Address box and then press the ENTER key.
3. Click the Chapter 8 link in the top navigation bar.
4. Click Install Computer in the left sidebar below the heading, Beyond the Book.
5. Read the material presented about how to install a computer.

Exercise
1. Using your Web search skills, research the latest recommendations with respect to proper ergonomics for using a computer. What information did you find that you did not know before? What changes would you make to your current computer setup that might make you more productive? Submit your answers to your instructor.
2. Many people report illnesses or injuries from using computers. Perform research in a library or on the Web to discover the five most common ailments associated with using a computer. Determine the actions people can take to minimize or eliminate these ailments. Submit a report to your instructor describing your findings.
3. Your computer lab at school contains multiple computers for student use. Using the knowledge you have obtained from this Learn How To activity, evaluate the computer installation in your school lab. In a report to your instructor, specify those items you think can be improved in the lab.

LEARN HOW TO 2: Maintain a Computer

While computers are amazingly resilient and reliable, you still should perform certain activities to ensure they maintain peak performance. To learn about these activities, complete the following steps:
1. Start the browser on your computer.
2. Type the Web address scsite.com/dc2007 in the Address box and then press the ENTER key.
3. Click the Chapter 8 link in the top navigation bar.
4. Click Maintain Computer in the left sidebar below the heading, Beyond the Book.
5. Read the material presented about how to maintain a computer.

Exercise
1. On either your computer or the computer on which you are working, perform a hardware and software inventory of at least five hardware devices and five application programs on the computer. List the vendor, product, vendor Web address, vendor e-mail address, and vendor support telephone number. Submit your inventory to your instructor.
2. Record the serial number of the computer on which you are working. Then, record the serial number for seven different application programs on the computer. Submit this information to your instructor.

Learn How To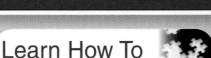

LEARN HOW TO 3: Keep Windows XP Up-to-Date

Keeping Windows XP up-to-date is a critical part of keeping your computer in good working order. The updates made available by Microsoft for no charge over the Internet will keep errors from occurring on your computer and will ensure that all security safeguards are in place. To update Windows, complete the following steps:

1. Click the Start button on the Windows taskbar, point to All Programs, and then click Windows Update on the All Programs submenu (Figure 8-42). *A browser window will open and display the Windows Update page.*
2. Click the Express Install (Recommended) link. Your computer will be examined and then a list of recommended updates for your computer will be shown.
3. If necessary, select those updates you wish to install and then click the Install button. Be aware that some updates might take 20 minutes or more to download and install, based primarily on your Internet access speed.
4. Often, after installation of updates, you must restart your computer to allow those updates to take effect. Be sure to save any open files before restarting your computer.

   You also can schedule automatic updates for your computer. To do so, complete the following steps:
1. Click the Start button on the Windows taskbar and then click Control Panel on the Start menu.
2. In the Control Panel window, ensure that Category view is displayed, and then click Performance and Maintenance.
3. In the Performance and Maintenance window, click System.
4. In the System Properties dialog box, click the Automatic Updates tab. *The Automatic Updates sheet is displayed in the System Properties dialog box (Figure 8-43).*
5. Select the option you want to use for Windows updates. Microsoft, together with all security and operating system experts, strongly recommends you select Automatic so updates will be installed on your computer automatically. Notice that if you select Automatic, you also should select a time when your computer will be on and be connected to the Internet. A secondary choice is to download the suggested updates and then choose when you want to install them.
6. When you have made your selection, click the OK button in the System Properties dialog box.

   Updating Windows on your computer is vital to maintain security and operational integrity.

FIGURE 8-42

FIGURE 8-43

Exercise

1. Open the Windows Update window in your browser. Make a list of the recommended updates to Windows XP on the computer you are using. Add to the list the Custom Install updates that are available. If you are using your own computer, install the updates of your choice on your computer. Submit the list of updates to your instructor.
2. Optional: If you are not using your own computer, do not complete this exercise. Display the Automatic Updates sheet in the System Properties dialog box. Select the level of automatic updates you want to use. Write a report justifying your choice of automatic updates and then submit the report to your instructor.

Web Research

Use the Internet-based Web Research exercises to broaden your understanding of the concepts presented in this chapter. Visit scsite.com/dc2007/ch8/research to obtain more information pertaining to each exercise. To discuss any of the Web Research exercises in this chapter with other students, post your thoughts or questions at scsite.com/dc2007/ch8/forum.

① Scavenger Hunt Use one of the <u>search engines</u> listed in Figure 2-10 in Chapter 2 on page 78 or your own favorite search engine to find the answers to the questions that follow. Copy and paste the Web address from the Web page where you found the answer. Some questions may have more than one answer. If required, submit your answers to your instructor. (1) What is the UNIX billennium? (2) The term, spool, is an acronym for what words? What company invented the term? (3) What did Gary Kildall develop in 1974 while working for Intel? (4) What is the basis of the lawsuit Caldera Inc. filed against Microsoft in 1996? (5) What is Larry the cow's relationship to Linux?

② Search Sleuth A search engine using a <u>concept-based search system</u> seeks Web sites containing a search term along with related concepts. For example, if you search for "operating systems," this type of search engine also returns links to books, professional organizations, and other operating system-related topics. Many researchers consider Excite (excite.com) the best concept-based search engine. Visit this Web site and then use your word processing program to answer the following questions. Then, if required, submit your answers to your instructor. (1) Click the Help link at the bottom of the page. What are some Search Tools & Tips listed in the Searches and Classified area? (2) Click the Back button, click the Search the Web text box, and then type Linux in the box. How many search results are returned that are not sponsored links? (3) Click the View Results by Search Engine option button near the top of the page. What are three search engines Excite used to return results? Which search engine returned the most links? (4) Click two of the links that discuss Linux news and information. Review these articles and then write a 50-word summary of your findings.

③ Journaling Respond to your readings in this chapter by writing at least one page about your reactions, evaluations, and reflections about using <u>stand-alone utility programs</u>. For example, does your computer have an antivirus program? If so, how often do you check for new virus definition updates? Has a virus ever infected one of your files or your computer? Do you have a backup of your hard disk? Do you have a recovery disk? Do you have a personal firewall? You also can write about the new terms you learned by reading this chapter. If required, submit your journal to your instructor.

④ Expanding Your Understanding Instant messaging (IM) is moving into the workplace. According to America Online, 59 percent of Internet users use IM, and 27 percent of these people use IM at work. Computer industry analysts predict this method of electronic communication will overtake e-mail during the next few years. With IM's popularity comes <u>spim</u>, a junk message. Yahoo! reports that 2 percent of the instant messages sent over its network are spim. View Web sites to learn more about IM's popularity and spim. What programs allow you to filter instant messages? Write a report summarizing your findings, focusing on the possible uses of this method of communication in the workplace. If required, submit your report to your instructor.

⑤ Ethics in Action Several automobile insurers, including Progressive Casualty Insurance Company, are promising drivers insurance premium discounts if they install a data recorder in their cars to track their driving and then exercise good driving behavior. Progressive customers voluntarily taking part in this <u>TripSense</u> program upload the data from their monitors monthly and hope to decrease their insurance bills by a maximum of 25 percent. Privacy experts predict more insurance companies will offer this monitoring system and that it eventually will become mandatory. These critics fear that negative data will be used against poor drivers and possibly be subpoenaed in litigation. View online sites that provide information about vehicle monitoring devices. Write a report summarizing your findings and include a table of links to Web sites that provide additional details. If required, submit your report to your instructor.

Case Studies

Use the Case Studies to apply the concepts presented in the chapter to real-world situations. Visit scsite.com/dc2007/ch8/cases to obtain more information pertaining to each exercise. To discuss the Case Studies in this chapter with other students, visit scsite.com/dc2007/ch8/forum and post your thoughts or questions.

CASE STUDY 1 — Class Discussion Many students at the local college have been using the college's computers to download music from the Internet. You have been asked to serve on a student committee to draft a policy addressing this questionable use of the college's computers. Is it the college's responsibility to block music downloads? Why or why not? How would the college prevent students from **downloading music**? What is the difference between taping a song heard on the radio and downloading music from the Internet? Should violators be expelled, fined, required to attend a seminar on the ethical use of computers, or given a verbal warning? What recommendations would you give to the committee regarding the downloading of music? Draft a memo addressed to all students regarding this matter. Be prepared to discuss your recommendations in class.

CASE STUDY 2 — Class Discussion It is legal to **copy songs from a CD**, provided it was purchased legally. A principal at a local high school, however, has learned that students have been copying popular tracks from purchased music CDs to other CDs using the school's computer and then selling the CDs for $1.00 each. As the dean of students, what action would you take against the students copying the CDs? What action would you take against students buying the illegal copies? Write a brief report, and be prepared to discuss your recommendations in class.

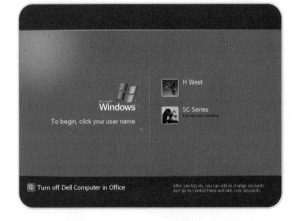

CASE STUDY 3 — Research Your uncle is buying a new computer both for personal use and to operate his consulting business, which he runs out of his home. He is undecided on the Windows operating system to purchase with his new computer. **Windows XP** Professional is intended for business and power users. Windows XP Home Edition is designed for home computing. He has asked you to help him decide if he should buy one or the other. Use the Web and/or print media to develop a report that lists the differences. Which Windows XP Professional features are not available in Windows XP Home Edition? Submit your report or use PowerPoint to create a presentation and share your findings with your class.

CASE STUDY 4 — Research Many programs are available for users of personal computers. The owner of the party supply store, Crazy Pete's Party Palace, where you work part time is interested in purchasing an **antivirus program**. Because you are taking a computer class, he has asked you to help him choose the best program. Choose at least two competing manufacturers of antivirus programs. Use the Web and/or print media and compare the programs. For each program, answer the following questions: What is the program's function? What are the system requirements? How easy is the program to use? Does it include a firewall? Does it protect against spam, spyware, and adware? How do you obtain updates to the program? How much does the program cost? In your opinion, is the program worth the price? Why or why not? Which one would you buy? Why? Write a brief report or use PowerPoint to create a presentation and share your findings with your class.

CASE STUDY 5 — Team Challenge Your team members are employed as analysts at Soap-n-Suds, an international manufacturer of laundry soaps. The company currently uses an early version of the Windows operating system on its 5,000 desktop computers. Next year, the company plans to upgrade the operating system and, if necessary, its desktop computers. The vice-president of information technology has asked your team to compare the latest desktop versions of the Windows operating system, the **Mac operating system**, and the Linux operating system. Assign each member of your team an operating system. Have each member use the Web and/or print media to develop a feature/benefit report. What is the initial cost of the operating system per computer? What are the memory and storage requirements? Will the operating system require the company to purchase new computers? Are training costs involved? Which one is best at avoiding viruses, spam, and spyware? Which operating system is easier to use? Why? Can Microsoft Office run under the operating system? As a team, merge your findings into a team report and/or PowerPoint presentation and share your findings with your class.

Special Feature

Buyer's Guide 2007:
How to Purchase a Personal Computer

At some point, perhaps while you are taking this course, you may decide to buy a personal computer. The decision is an important one and will require an investment of both time and money. Like many buyers, you may have little computer experience and find yourself unsure of how to proceed. You can get started by talking to your friends, coworkers, and instructors about their computers. What type of computers did they buy? Why? For what purposes do they use their computers? You also should answer the following four questions to help narrow your choices to a specific computer type, before reading this Buyer's Guide.

(a) desktop computer

(b) mobile computer (notebook computer or Tablet PC)

(c) personal mobile device (smart phone or PDA)

Should I buy a desktop or mobile computer or personal mobile device?

For what purposes will I use the computer?

Should I buy a Mac or PC?

Should the computer I buy be compatible with the computers at school or work?

1 **Do you want a desktop computer, mobile computer, or personal mobile device?** A desktop computer (Figure 1a) is designed as a stationary device that sits on or below a desk or table in a location such as a home, office, or dormitory room. A desktop computer must be plugged into an electrical outlet to operate. A mobile computer, such as a notebook computer or Tablet PC (Figure 1b), is smaller than a desktop computer, more portable, and has a battery that allows you to operate it for a period without an electrical outlet. A personal mobile device (Figure 1c) runs on a battery for a longer period of time than a notebook computer or Tablet PC and can fit in your pocket.

Desktop computers are a good option if you work mostly in one place and have plenty of space in your work area. Desktop computers generally give you more performance for your money.

Increasingly, more desktop computer users are buying mobile computers to take advantage of their portability to work in the library, at school, while traveling, and at home. The past disadvantages of mobile computers, such as lower processor speeds, poor-quality monitors, weight, short battery life, and significantly higher prices, have all but disappeared when compared with desktop computers.

FIGURE 1

If you are thinking of using a mobile computer to take notes in class or in business meetings, then consider a Tablet PC with handwriting and drawing capabilities. Typically, note-taking involves writing text notes and drawing charts, schematics, and other illustrations. By allowing you to write and draw directly on the screen with a digital pen, a Tablet PC eliminates the distracting sound of the notebook keyboard tapping and allows you to capture drawings. Some notebook computers can convert to Tablet PCs.

A personal mobile device, such as a smart phone or a PDA, is ideal if you require a pocket-sized computing device as you move from place to place. Personal mobile devices provide personal organizer functions, such as a calendar, appointment book, address book, and many other applications. The small size of the processor, screen, and keyboard, however, limit a personal mobile device's capabilities when compared with a desktop or notebook computer or a Tablet PC. For this reason, most people who purchase personal mobile devices also have a desktop or notebook computer to handle heavy-duty applications.

Drawbacks of mobile computers and personal mobile devices are that they tend to have a shorter useful lifetime than desktop computers and lack the high-end capabilities. Their portability makes them susceptible to vibrations, heat or cold, and accidental drops, which can cause components such as hard disks or display devices to fail. Also, because of their size and portability, they are easy to lose and are the prime targets of thieves.

2 **For what purposes will you use the computer?**
Having a general idea of the purposes for which you want to use your computer will help you decide on the type of computer to buy. At this point in your research, it is not necessary to know the exact application software titles or version numbers you might want to use. Knowing that you plan to use the computer primarily to create word processing, spreadsheet, database, and presentation documents, however, will point you in the direction of a desktop or notebook computer. If you want the portability of a smart phone or PDA, but you need more computing power, then a Tablet PC may be the best alternative. You also must consider that some application software runs only on a Mac, while others run only on a PC with the Windows operating system. Still other software may run only on a PC running the UNIX or Linux operating system.

3 **Should the computer be compatible with the computers at school or work?** If you plan to bring work home, telecommute, or take distance education courses, then you should purchase a computer that is compatible with those at school or work.

Compatibility is primarily a software issue. If your computer runs the same operating system version, such as Microsoft Windows XP, and the same application software, such as Microsoft Office, then your computer will be able to read documents created at school or work and vice versa. Incompatible hardware can become an issue if you plan to connect directly to a school or office network using a cable or wireless technology. You usually can obtain the minimum system requirements from the Information Technology department at your school or workplace.

4 **Should the computer be a Mac or PC?** If you ask a friend, coworker, or instructor, which is better — a Mac or a PC — you may be surprised by the strong opinion expressed in the response. No other topic in the computer industry causes more heated debate. The Mac has strengths, especially in the areas of graphics, movies, photos, and music. The PC, however, has become the industry standard with 95 percent of the market share. Figure 2 compares features of the Mac and PC in several different areas. Overall, the Mac and PC have more similarities than differences, and you should consider cost, compatibility, and other factors when choosing whether to purchase a Mac or PC.

Area	Comparison
Cost and availability	A Mac is priced slightly higher than a PC. Mac peripherals also are more expensive. The PC offers more available models from a wide range of vendors. You can custom build, upgrade, and expand a PC for less money than a Mac.
Exterior design	The Mac has a more distinct and stylish appearance than most PCs.
Free software	Although free software for the Mac is available on the Internet, significantly more free software applications are available for the PC.
Market share	The PC dominates the personal computer market. While the Mac sells well in education, publishing, Web design, graphics, and music, the PC is the overwhelming favorite of businesses.
Operating system	Users claim that Mac OS X provides a better all-around user experience than Microsoft Windows XP. Both the Mac and PC supports other operating systems, such as Linux and UNIX.
Program control	Both have simple and intuitive graphical user interfaces. The Mac relies more on the mouse and less on keyboard shortcuts than the PC. The mouse on the Mac has one button, whereas the mouse on a PC has a minimum of two buttons.
Software availability	The basic application software most users require, such as Microsoft Office, is available for both the Mac and PC. More specialized software, however, often is available only for PCs. Many programs are released for PCs long before they are released for Macs.
Speed	Historically, the PC has provided faster processors than the Mac. Apple, however, has begun to ship some models of the Mac with PC-like Intel processors.
Viruses	Dramatically fewer viruses attack Macs. Mac viruses also generally are less infectious than PC viruses.

FIGURE 2 Comparison of Mac and PC features.

After evaluating the answers to these four questions, you should have a general idea of how you plan to use your computer and the type of computer you want to buy. Once you have decided on the type of computer you want, you can follow the guidelines presented in this Buyer's Guide to help you purchase a specific computer, along with software, peripherals, and other accessories.

Many of the desktop computer guidelines presented also apply to the purchase of a notebook computer, Tablet PC, and personal mobile device. Later in this Buyer's Guide, sections on purchasing a notebook computer or Tablet PC address additional considerations specific to those computer types.

This Buyer's Guide concentrates on recommendations for purchasing a desktop computer or mobile computer. For recommendations on purchasing a personal mobile device, see page 296 in the Personal Mobile Devices feature that follows Chapter 5.

Type of Computer	Web Site	Web Address
PC	CNET Shopper	shopper.cnet.com
	PC World Magazine	pcworld.com
	BYTE Magazine	byte.com
	PC Magazine	zdnet.com/reviews
	Yahoo! Computers	computers.yahoo.com
	MSN Shopping	shopping.msn.com
	Dave's Guide to Buying a Home Computer	css.msu.edu/PC-Guide
Mac	Macworld Magazine	macworld.com
	Apple	apple.com
	Switch to Mac Campaign	apple.com/switch

For an updated list of hardware and software reviews and their Web site addresses, visit scsite.com/dc2007/ch8/buyers.

FIGURE 3 Hardware and software reviews.

HOW TO PURCHASE A DESKTOP COMPUTER

Once you have decided that a desktop computer is most suited to your computing needs, the next step is to determine specific software, hardware, peripheral devices, and services to purchase, as well as where to buy the computer.

① Determine the specific software you want to use on your computer. Before deciding to purchase software, be sure it contains the features necessary for the tasks you want to perform. Rely on the computer users in whom you have confidence to help you decide on the software to use. The minimum requirements of the software you select may determine the operating system (Microsoft Windows XP, Linux, UNIX, Mac OS X) you need. If you have decided to use a particular operating system that does not support software you want to use, you may be able to purchase similar software from other manufacturers.

Many Web sites and trade magazines, such as those listed in Figure 3, provide reviews of software products. These Web sites frequently have articles that rate computers and software on cost, performance, and support.

Your hardware requirements depend on the minimum requirements of the software you will run on your computer. Some software requires more memory and disk space than others, as well as additional input, output, and storage devices. For example, suppose you want to run software that can copy one CD's or DVD's contents directly to another CD or DVD, without first copying the data to your hard disk. To support that, you should consider a desktop computer or a high-end notebook computer, because the computer will need two CD or DVD drives: one that reads from a CD or DVD, and one that reads from and writes on a CD or DVD. If you plan to run software that allows your computer to work as an entertainment system, then you will need a CD or DVD drive, quality speakers, and an upgraded sound card.

② Look for bundled software. When you purchase a computer, it may come bundled with software. Some sellers even let you choose which software you want. Remember, however, that bundled software has value only if you would have purchased the software even if it had not come with the computer. At the very least, you probably will want word processing software and a browser to access the Internet. If you need additional applications, such as a spreadsheet, a database, or presentation graphics, consider purchasing Microsoft Works, Microsoft Office, OpenOffice.org, or Sun StarOffice, which include several programs at a reduced price.

③ Avoid buying the least powerful computer available. Once you know the application software you want to use, you then can consider the following important criteria about the computer's components: (1) processor speed, (2) size and types of memory (RAM) and storage, (3) types of input/output devices, (4) types of ports and adapter cards, and (5) types of communications devices. The information in Figures 4 and 5 can help you determine what system components are best for you. Figure 4 outlines considerations for specific hardware components. Figure 5 (on page 449) provides a Base Components worksheet that lists PC recommendations for each category of user discussed in this book: Home User,

Small Office/Home Office User, Mobile User, Power User, and Large Business User. In the worksheet, the Home User category is divided into two groups: Application Home User and Game Home User. The Mobile User recommendations list criteria for a notebook computer, but do not include the PDA or Tablet PC options.

Computer technology changes rapidly, meaning a computer that seems powerful enough today may not serve your computing needs in a few years. In fact, studies show that many users regret not buying a more powerful computer. To avoid this, plan to buy a computer that will last you for two to three years. You can help delay obsolescence by purchasing the fastest processor, the most memory, and the largest hard disk you can afford. If you must buy a less powerful computer, be sure you can upgrade it with additional memory, components, and peripheral devices as your computer requirements grow.

CD/DVD Drives: Most computers come with a CD-RW drive. A CD-RW drive allows you to create your own custom data CDs for data backup or data transfer purposes. It also will allow you to store and share video files, digital photos, and other large files with other people who have access to a CD-ROM drive. An even better alternative is to upgrade to a DVD±RW combination drive. It allows you to read DVDs and CDs and to write data on (burn) a DVD or CD. A DVD has a capacity of at least 4.7 GB versus the 650 MB capacity of a CD.

Card Reader/Writer: A card reader/writer is useful for transferring data directly to and from a removable flash memory card, such as the ones used in your camera or audio player. Make sure the card reader/writer can read from and write on the flash memory cards that you use.

Digital Camera: Consider an inexpensive point-and-shoot digital camera. They are small enough to carry around, usually operate automatically in terms of lighting and focus, and contain storage cards for storing photographs. A 3- to 4-megapixel camera with a 64 MB, 128 MB, or 256 MB storage card is fine for creating images for use on the Web or to send via e-mail.

Digital Video Capture Device: A digital video capture device allows you to connect your computer to a camcorder or VCR and record, edit, manage, and then write video back on a VCR tape, a CD, or a DVD. The digital video capture device can be an external device or an adapter card. To create quality video (true 30 frames per second, full-sized TV), the digital video capture device should have a USB 2.0 or FireWire port. You will find that a standard USB port is too slow to maintain video quality. You also will need sufficient storage: an hour of data on a VCR tape takes up about 5 GB of disk storage.

Floppy Disk Drive: The floppy disk drive is useful for backing up and transferring small files, collectively less than 1.44 MB. Users prefer the faster and higher capacity USB flash drives and CD/DVD drives for backup and file transfer purposes. Consider a floppy disk drive only if your work environment requires it.

Hard Disk: It is recommended that you buy a computer with 60 to 80 GB if your primary interests are browsing the Web and using e-mail and Office suite-type applications; 80 to 100 GB if you also want to edit digital photographs; 100 to 120 GB if you plan to edit digital video or manipulate large audio files even occasionally; and 120 to 300 GB if you will edit digital video, movies, or photography often; store audio files and music; or consider yourself to be a power user.

Joystick/Wheel: If you use your computer to play games, then you will want to purchase a joystick or a wheel. These devices, especially the more expensive ones, provide for realistic game play with force feedback, programmable buttons, and specialized levers and wheels.

Keyboard: The keyboard is one of the more important devices used to communicate with the computer. For this reason, make sure the keyboard you purchase has 101 to 105 keys, is comfortable and easy to use, and has a USB connection. A wireless keyboard should be considered, especially if you have a small desk area.

Microphone: If you plan to record audio or use speech recognition to enter text and commands, then purchase a close-talk headset with gain adjustment support.

Modem: Most computers come with a modem so that you can use your telephone line to dial out and access the Internet. Some modems also have fax capabilities. Your modem should be rated at 56 Kbps.

Monitor: The monitor is where you will view documents, read e-mail messages, and view pictures. A minimum of a 17" screen is recommended, but if you are planning to use your computer for graphic design or game playing, then you may want to purchase a 19" or 21" monitor. The LCD flat panel monitor should be considered, especially if space is an issue.

FIGURE 4   Hardware guidelines.

(continued on next page)

(continued from previous page)

Mouse: As you work with your computer, you use the mouse constantly. For this reason, spend a few extra dollars, if necessary, and purchase a mouse with an optical sensor and USB connection. The optical sensor replaces the need for a mouse ball, which means you do not need a mouse pad. For a PC, make sure your mouse has a wheel, which acts as a third button in addition to the top two buttons on the left and right. An ergonomic design is also important because your hand is on the mouse most of the time when you are using your computer. A wireless mouse should be considered to eliminate the cord and allow you to work at short distances from your computer.

Network Card: Most computers come with a network card. A network card allows you to connect to a network or use broadband (cable or DSL) to connect to the Internet.

Port Hub Expander: If you plan to connect several peripheral devices to your computer at the same time, then you need to be concerned with the number of ports available on your computer. If your computer does not have enough ports, then you should purchase a port hub expander. A port hub expander plugs into a single FireWire port or USB port and gives several additional ports.

Printer: Your two basic printer choices are ink-jet and laser. Color ink-jet printers cost on average between $50 and $300. Laser printers cost from $200 to $2,000. In general, the cheaper the printer, the lower the resolution and speed, and the more often you are required to change the ink cartridge or toner. Laser printers print faster and with a higher quality than an ink-jet, and their toner on average costs less. If you want color, then go with a high-end ink-jet printer to ensure quality of print. Duty cycle (the number of pages you expect to print each month) also should be a determining factor. If your duty cycle is on the low end — hundreds of pages per month — then stay with a high-end ink-jet printer, rather than purchasing a laser printer. If you plan to print photographs taken with a digital camera, then you should purchase a photo printer. A photo printer is a dye-sublimation printer or an ink-jet printer with higher resolution and features that allow you to print quality photographs.

Processor: For a PC, a 2.8 GHz Intel or AMD processor is more than enough processor power for application home and small office/home office users. Game home, large business, and power users should upgrade to faster processors.

RAM: RAM plays a vital role in the speed of your computer. Make sure the computer you purchase has at least 512 MB of RAM. If you have extra money to invest in your computer, then consider increasing the RAM to 1 GB or more. The extra money for RAM will be well spent.

Scanner: The most popular scanner purchased with a computer today is the flatbed scanner. When evaluating a flatbed scanner, check the color depth and resolution. Do not buy anything less than a color depth of 48 bits and a resolution of 1200 x 2400 dpi. The higher the color depth, the more accurate the color. A higher resolution picks up the more subtle gradations of color.

Sound Card: Computers come with a standard sound card that supports the Sound Blaster and General MIDI standards and should be capable of recording and playing digital audio. If you plan to turn your computer into an entertainment system or are a game home user, then you will want to spend the extra money and upgrade from the standard sound card.

Speakers: Once you have a good sound card, quality speakers and a separate subwoofer that amplifies the bass frequencies of the speakers can turn your computer into a premium stereo system.

PC Video Camera: A PC video camera is a small camera used to capture and display live video (in some cases with sound), primarily on a Web page. You also can capture, edit, and share video and still photos. The camera sits on your monitor or desk. Recommended minimum specifications include 640 x 480 resolution, a video with a rate of 30 frames per second, and a USB 2.0 or FireWire port.

USB Flash Drive: If you work on different computers and need access to the same data and information, then this portable miniature mobile storage device is ideal. USB flash drive capacity varies from 16 MB to 4 GB.

Video Graphics Card: Most standard video cards satisfy the monitor display needs of application home and small office users. If you are a game home user or a graphic designer, you will want to upgrade to a higher quality video card. The higher refresh rates will further enhance the display of games, graphics, and movies.

Wireless LAN Access Point: A Wireless LAN Access Point allows you to network several computers, so they can share files and access the Internet through a single cable modem or DSL connection. Each device that you connect requires a wireless card. A Wireless LAN Access Point can offer a range of operations up to several hundred feet, so be sure the device has a high-powered antenna.

BASE COMPONENTS

	Application Home User	Game Home User	Small Office/Home Office User	Mobile User	Large Business User	Power User
HARDWARE						
Processor	Pentium 4 at 2.8 GHz	Pentium 4 at 3.0 GHz	Pentium 4 at 3.0 GHz	Pentium 4M at 2.4 GHz	Pentium 4 at 3.4 GHz	Multiple Itanium at 1.6 GHz
RAM	512 MB	1 GB	512 MB	512 MB	2 GB	2 GB
Cache	256 KB L2	512 KB L2	512 KB L2	512 KB L2	512 KB L2	2 MB L3
Hard Disk	80 GB	120 GB	120 GB	60 GB	160 GB	300 GB
Monitor/LCD Flat Panel	17" or 19"	21"	19" or 21"	15.7" Wide Display	19" or 21"	23"
Video Graphics Card	256 MB	512 MB	256 MB	32 MB	128 MB	256 MB
CD/DVD Bay 1	CD-RW	CD-RW	CD-RW	CD-RW/DVD	CD-RW	CR-RW/DVD
CD/DVD Bay 2	DVD+RW	DVD+RW	DVD+RW	DVD+RW	DVD+RW	DVD+RW
Printer	Color Ink-Jet	Color Ink-Jet	18 ppm Laser	Portable Ink-Jet	50 ppm Laser	10 ppm Laser
PC Video Camera	Yes	Yes	Yes	Yes	Yes	Yes
Fax/Modem	Yes	Yes	Yes	Yes	Yes	Yes
Microphone	Close-Talk Headset With Gain Adjustment	Close-Talk Headset With Gain Adjustment	Close-Talk Headset With Gain Adjustment	Close-Talk Headset With Gain Adjustment	Close-Talk Headset With Gain Adjustment	Close-Talk Headset With Gain Adjustment
Speakers	Stereo	Full-Dolby Surround	Stereo	Stereo	Stereo	Full-Dolby Surround
Pointing Device	IntelliMouse or Optical Mouse	Laser Mouse and Joystick	IntelliMouse or Optical Mouse	Touchpad or Pointing Stick and Laser Mouse	IntelliMouse or Optical Mouse	IntelliMouse or Laser Mouse and Joystick
Keyboard	Yes	Yes	Yes	Built-In	Yes	Yes
Backup Disk/Tape Drive	250 MB Zip®	External or Removable Hard Disk	External or Removable Hard Disk	External or Removable Hard Disk	Tape Drive	External or Removable Hard Disk
USB Flash Drive	128 MB	256 MB	256 MB	256 MB	4 GB	2 GB
Sound Card	Sound Blaster Compatible	Sound Blaster Audigy 2	Sound Blaster Compatible	Built-In	Sound Blaster Compatible	Sound Blaster Audigy 2
Network Card	Yes	Yes	Yes	Yes	Yes	Yes
TV-Out Connector	Yes	Yes	Yes	Yes	Yes	Yes
USB Port	6	8	6	2	8	8
FireWire Port	2	2	2	1	2	2
SOFTWARE						
Operating System	Windows XP Home Edition with Service Pack 2	Windows XP Home Edition with Service Pack 2	Windows XP Professional with Service Pack 2	Windows XP Professional with Service Pack 2	Windows XP Professional with Service Pack 2	Windows XP Professional with Service Pack 2
Application Suite	Office 2003 Standard Edition	Office 2003 Standard Edition	Office 2003 Small Business Edition	Office 2003 Small Business Edition	Office 2003 Professional	Office 2003 Professional
Antivirus	Yes, 12-Mo. Subscription	Yes, 12-Mo. Subscription	Yes, 12-Mo. Subscription	Yes, 12-Mo. Subscription	Yes, 12-Mo. Subscription	Yes, 12-Mo. Subscription
Internet Access	Cable, DSL, or Dial-up	Cable or DSL	Cable, DSL, or Dial-up	Wireless or Dial-up	LAN/WAN (T1/T3)	Cable or DSL
OTHER						
Surge Protector	Yes	Yes	Yes	Portable	Yes	Yes
Warranty	3-Year Limited, 1-Year Next Business Day On-Site Service	3-Year Limited, 1-Year Next Business Day On-Site Service	3-year On-Site Service	3-Year Limited, 1-Year Next Business Day On-Site Service	3-year On-Site Service	3-year On-Site Service
Other		Wheel	Postage Printer	Docking Station Carrying Case Fingerprint Scanner Portable Data Projector		Graphics Tablet Plotter or Large-Format Printer

Optional Components for all Categories	
802.11g Wireless Card	Graphics Tablet
Bluetooth™ Enabled	iPod Audio Player
Biometric Input Device	IrDA Port
Card Reader/Writer	Mouse Pad/Wrist Rest
Digital Camera	Multifunction Peripheral
Digital Video Capture	Photo Printer
Digital Video Camera	Port Hub Expander
Dual-Monitor Support with Second Monitor	Portable Data Projector
Ergonomic Keyboard	Scanner
External Hard Disk	TV/FM Tuner
Floppy Disk Drive	Uninterruptible Power Supply

FIGURE 5 Base desktop and mobile computer components and optional components. A copy of the Base Components worksheet is part of the Data Files for Students. To obtain a copy of the Data Files for Students, see the inside back cover of this book for instructions.

Consider upgrades to the mouse, keyboard, monitor, printer, microphone, and speakers. You use these peripheral devices to interact with your computer, so you should make sure they are up to your standards. Review the peripheral devices listed in Figure 4 on pages 447 and 448 and then visit both local computer dealers and large retail stores to test the computers on display. Ask the salesperson what input and output devices would be best for you and whether you should upgrade beyond what comes standard. Consider purchasing a wireless keyboard and wireless mouse to eliminate bothersome wires on your desktop. A few extra dollars spent on these components when you initially purchase a computer can extend its usefulness by years.

Determine whether you want to use telephone lines or broadband (cable or DSL) to access the Internet. If your computer has a modem, then you can access the Internet using a standard telephone line. Ordinarily, you call a local or toll-free 800 number to connect to an ISP (see Guideline 6 on the next page). Using a dial-up Internet connection is relatively inexpensive but slow.

DSL and cable connections provide much faster Internet connections, which are ideal if you want faster file download speeds for software, digital photos, and music. As you would expect, they also are more expensive. DSL, which is available through local telephone companies, also may require that you subscribe to an ISP. Cable is available through your local cable television provider and some online service providers (OSPs). If you get cable, then you would not use a separate Internet service provider or online service provider.

6 **If you are using a dial-up or wireless connection to connect to the Internet, then select an ISP or OSP.** You can access the Internet via telephone lines in one of two ways: an ISP or an OSP. Both provide Internet access for a monthly fee that ranges from $6 to $25. Local ISPs offer Internet access to users in a limited geographic region, through local telephone numbers. National ISPs provide access for users nationwide (including mobile users), through local and toll-free telephone numbers and cable. Because of their size, national ISPs generally offer more services and have a larger technical support staff than local ISPs. OSPs furnish Internet access as well as members-only features for users nationwide. Figure 6 lists several national ISPs and OSPs. Before you choose an ISP or OSP, compare such features as the number of access hours, monthly fees, available services (e-mail, Web page hosting, chat), and reliability.

Company	Service	Web Address
America Online	OSP	aol.com
AT&T Worldnet	ISP	www.att.net
Comcast	OSP	comcast.net
CompuServe	OSP	compuserve.com
EarthLink	ISP	earthlink.net
Juno	OSP	juno.com
NetZero	OSP	netzero.com
MSN	OSP	msn.com
SBC Yahoo!	ISP/OSP	myhome.prodigy.net

For an updated list of national ISPs and OSPs and their Web site addresses, visit scsite.com/dc2007/ch8/buyers.

FIGURE 6   National ISPs and OSPs.

7 **Use a worksheet to compare computers, services, and other considerations.** You can use a separate sheet of paper to take notes on each vendor's computer and then summarize the information on a worksheet, such as the one shown in Figure 7. You can use Figure 7 to compare prices for either a PC or a Mac. Most companies advertise a price for a base computer that includes components housed in the system unit (processor, RAM, sound card, video card), disk drives (floppy disk, hard disk, CD-ROM, CD-RW, DVD-ROM, and DVD±RW), a keyboard, mouse, monitor, printer, speakers, and modem. Be aware, however, that some advertisements list prices for computers with only some of these components. Monitors and printers, for example, often are not included in a base computer's price. Depending on how you plan to use the computer, you may want to invest in additional or more powerful components. When you are comparing the prices of computers, make sure you are comparing identical or similar configurations.

PC or MAC Cost Comparison Worksheet

Dealers list prices for computers with most of these components (instead of listing individual component costs). Some dealers do not supply a monitor. Some dealers offer significant discounts, but you must subscribe to an Internet service for a specified period to receive the discounted price. To compare computers, enter overall system price at top and enter a 0 (zero) for components included in the system cost. For any additional components not covered in the system price, enter the cost in the appropriate cells.

Items to Purchase	Desired System (PC)	Desired System (Mac)	Local Dealer #1	Local Dealer #2	Online Dealer #1	Online Dealer #2	Comments
OVERALL SYSTEM							
Overall System Price	< $1,500	< $1500					
HARDWARE							
Processor	Pentium® 4 at 2.8 GHz	Power PC G5 at 1.6 GHz					
RAM	1 GB	1 GB					
Cache	256 KB L2	256 KB L2					
Hard Disk	120 GB	120 GB					
Monitor/LCD Flat Panel	17 Inch	17 Inch					
Video Graphics Card	128 MB	128 MB					
Floppy Disk Drive	3.5 Inch	NA					
USB Flash Drive	128 MB	128 MB					
CD/DVD Bay 1	CD-RW	DVD±RW					
CD/DVD Bay 2	DVD±RW	NA					
Speakers	Stereo	Stereo					
Sound Card	Sound Blaster Compatible	Sound Blaster Compatible					
USB Ports	6	6					
FireWire Port	2	2					
Network Card	Yes	Yes					
Fax/Modem	56 Kbps	56 Kbps					
Keyboard	Standard	Apple Pro Keyboard					
Pointing Device	IntelliMouse	Intellimouse or Apple Pro Mouse					
Microphone	Close-Talk Headset with Gain Adjustment	Close-Talk Headset with Gain Adjustment					
Printer	Color Ink-Jet	Color Ink-Jet					
SOFTWARE							
Operating System	Windows XP Media Center Edition	Mac OS X					
Application Software	Office 2003 Small Business Edition	Office 2004 for Mac					
Antivirus	Yes - 12 Mo. Subscription	Yes - 12 Mo. Subscription					
OTHER							
Card Reader							
Digital Camera	4-Megapixel	4-Megapixel					
Floppy Disk Drive	3.5 Inch	NA					
Internet Connection	1-Year Subscription	1-Year Subscription					
Joystick	Yes	Yes					
PC Video Camera	With Microphone	With Microphone					
Port Hub Expander							
Scanner							
Surge Protector							
Warranty	3-Year On-Site Service	3-Year On-Site Service					
Wireless Card	Internal	Internal					
Wireless LAN Access Point	LinkSys	Apple AirPort					
Total Cost			$	$	$	$	

FIGURE 7   A worksheet is an effective tool for summarizing and comparing components and prices of different computer vendors. A copy of the Computer Cost Comparison Worksheet is part of the Data Files for Students. To obtain a copy of the Data Files for Students, see the inside back cover of this book for instructions.

8 **If you are buying a new computer, you have several purchasing options: buying from your school bookstore, a local computer dealer, a local large retail store, or ordering by mail via telephone or the Web.**   Each purchasing option has certain advantages. Many college bookstores, for example, sign exclusive pricing agreements with computer manufacturers and, thus, can offer student discounts. Local dealers and local large retail stores, however, more easily can provide hands-on support. Mail-order companies that sell computers by telephone or online via the Web (Figure 8) often provide the lowest prices, but extend less personal service. Some major mail-order companies, however, have started to provide next-business-day, on-site services. A credit card usually is required to buy from a mail-order company. Figure 9 lists some of the more popular mail-order companies and their Web site addresses.

9 **If you are buying a used computer, stay with name brands such as Dell, Gateway, Hewlett-Packard, and Apple.**   Although brand-name equipment can cost more, most brand-name computers have longer, more comprehensive warranties, are better supported, and have more authorized centers for repair services. As with new computers, you can purchase a used computer from local computer dealers, local large retail stores, or mail

order via the telephone or the Web. Classified ads and used computer sellers offer additional outlets for purchasing used computers. Figure 10 lists several major used computer brokers and their Web site addresses.

10 **If you have a computer and are upgrading to a new one, then consider selling or trading in the old one.**   If you are a replacement buyer, your older computer still may have value. If you cannot sell the computer through the classified ads, via a Web site, or to a friend, then ask if the computer dealer will buy your old computer. An increasing number of companies are taking trade-ins, but do not expect too much money for your old computer. Other companies offer free disposal of your old PC.

11 **Be aware of hidden costs.**   Before purchasing, be sure to consider any additional costs associated with buying a computer, such as an additional telephone line, a cable or DSL modem, an uninterruptible power supply (UPS), computer furniture, a USB flash drive, paper, and computer training classes you may want to take. Depending on where you buy your computer, the seller may be willing to include some or all of these in the computer purchase price.

Type of Computer	Company	Web Address
PC	CNET Shopper	shopper.cnet.com
	Hewlett-Packard	hp.com
	CompUSA	compusa.com
	TigerDirect	tigerdirect.com
	Dell	dell.com
	Gateway	gateway.com
Macintosh	Apple Computer	store.apple.com
	ClubMac	clubmac.com
	MacConnection	macconnection.com
	PC & MacExchange	macx.com

For an updated list of new mail-order computer companies and their Web site addresses, visit scsite.com/dc2007/ch8/buyers.

FIGURE 9   Computer mail-order companies.

Company	Web Address
Amazon.com	amazon.com
TECHAGAIN	techagain.com
American Computer Exchange	americancomputerex.com
U.S. Computer Exchange	usce.org
eBay	ebay.com

For an updated list of used computer mail-order companies and their Web site addresses, visit scsite.com/dc2007/ch8/buyers.

FIGURE 10   Used computer mail-order companies.

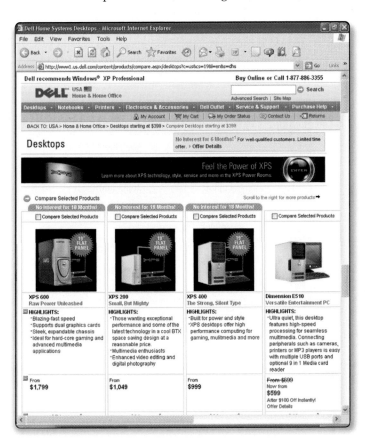

FIGURE 8   Mail-order companies, such as Dell, sell computers online.

Consider more than just price. The lowest-cost computer may not be the best long-term buy. Consider such intangibles as the vendor's time in business, the vendor's regard for quality, and the vendor's reputation for support. If you need to upgrade your computer often, you may want to consider a leasing arrangement, in which you pay monthly lease fees, but can upgrade or add on to your computer as your equipment needs change. No matter what type of buyer you are, insist on a 30-day, no-questions-asked return policy on your computer.

 Avoid restocking fees. Some companies charge a restocking fee of 10 to 20 percent as part of their money-back return policy. In some cases, no restocking fee for hardware is applied, but it is applied for software. Ask about the existence and terms of any restocking policies before you buy.

 Use a credit card to purchase your new computer. Many credit cards offer purchase protection and extended warranty benefits that cover you in case of loss of or damage to purchased goods. Paying by credit card also gives you time to install and use the computer before you have to pay for it. Finally, if you are dissatisfied with the computer and are unable to reach an agreement with the seller, paying by credit card gives you certain rights regarding withholding payment until the dispute is resolved. Check your credit card terms for specific details.

Consider purchasing an extended warranty or service plan. If you use your computer for business or require fast resolution to major computer problems, consider purchasing an extended warranty or a service plan through a local dealer or third-party company. Most extended warranties cover the repair and replacement of computer components beyond the standard warranty. Most service plans ensure that your technical support calls receive priority response from technicians. You also can purchase an on-site service plan that states that a technician will come to your home, work, or school within 24 hours. If your computer includes a warranty and service agreement for a year or less, think about extending the service for two or three years when you buy the computer.

HOW TO PURCHASE A NOTEBOOK COMPUTER

f you need computing capability when you travel or to use in lecture or meetings, you may find a notebook computer to be an appropriate choice. The guidelines mentioned in the previous section also apply to the purchase of a notebook computer. The following are additional considerations unique to notebook computers.

 Purchase a notebook computer with a sufficiently large active-matrix screen. Active-matrix screens display high-quality color that is viewable from all angles. Less expensive, passive-matrix screens sometimes are difficult to see in low-light conditions and cannot be viewed from an angle. Notebook computers typically come with a 12.1-inch, 13.3-inch, 14.1-inch, 15.4-inch, or 17-inch display. For most users, a 14.1-inch display is satisfactory. If you intend to use your notebook computer as a desktop computer replacement, however, you may opt for a 15.7-inch or 17-inch display. Notebook computers with these larger displays weigh seven to ten pounds, however, so if you travel a lot and portability is essential, you might want a lighter computer with a smaller display. The lightest notebook computers, which weigh less than 3 pounds, are equipped with a 12.1-inch display. Regardless of size, the resolution of the display should be at least 1024 x 768 pixels. To compare the monitor size on various notebook computers, visit the company Web sites in Figure 11.

Type of Notebook	Company	Web Address
PC	Acer	global.acer.com
	Dell	dell.com
	Fujitsu	fujitsu.com
	Gateway	gateway.com
	Hewlett-Packard	hp.com
	Lenovo	lenovo.com/us/en/
	NEC	nec.com
	Sony	sony.com
	Toshiba	toshiba.com
Mac	Apple	apple.com

For an updated list of companies and their Web site addresses, visit scsite.com/dc2007/ch8/buyers.

FIGURE 11 Companies that sell notebook computers.

CENTURY COMPUTERS
Performance Guarantee
(See reverse for terms & conditions of this contract)

Invoice #: 1984409   Effective Date: 10/12/07
Invoice Date: 10/12/07   Expiration Date: 10/12/10

Customer Name: Leon, Richard   System & Serial Numbers
Date: 10/12/07   IMB computer
Address: 1123 Roxbury   S/N: US759290C
       Sycamore, IL 60178
Day phone: (815) 555-0303
Evening Phone: (728) 555-0203

John Smith   *10/12/07*
Print Name of Century's Authorized Signature   Date

Experiment with different keyboards and pointing devices. Notebook computer keyboards are far less standardized than those for desktop computers. Some notebook computers, for example, have wide wrist rests, while others have none. Notebook computers also use a range of pointing devices, including pointing sticks, touchpads, and trackballs. Before you purchase a notebook computer, try various types of keyboard and pointing devices to determine which is easiest for you to use. Regardless of the pointing device you select, you also may want to purchase a regular mouse to use when you are working at a desk or other large surface.

Make sure the notebook computer you purchase has a CD and/or DVD drive. Most notebook computers come with a CD and/or a DVD drive. Although DVD drives are slightly more expensive, they allow you to play CDs and DVD movies using your notebook computer and a headset.

If necessary, upgrade the processor, memory, and disk storage at the time of purchase. As with a desktop computer, upgrading your notebook computer's memory and disk storage usually is less expensive at the time of initial purchase. Some disk storage is custom designed for notebook computer manufacturers, meaning an upgrade might not be available in the future. If you are purchasing a lightweight notebook computer, then it should include at least a 2.4 GHz processor, 512 MB RAM, and 80 GB of storage.

The availability of built-in ports and a port extender on a notebook computer is important. A notebook computer does not have a lot of room to add adapter cards. If you know the purpose for which you plan to use your notebook computer, then you can determine the ports you will need. Most notebooks come with common ports, such as a mouse port, IrDA port, serial port, parallel port, video port, a FireWire port, and multiple USB ports. If you plan to connect your notebook computer to a TV, however, then you will need a PCtoTV port. If you want to connect to networks at school or in various offices via a network cable, make sure the notebook computer you purchase has a network port. If your notebook computer does not come with a network port, then you will have to purchase an external network card that slides into an expansion slot in your notebook computer, as well as a network cable. While newer iPod audio players connect to a USB port, older ones require a FireWire port.

 If you plan to use your notebook computer for note-taking at school or in meetings, consider a notebook computer that converts to a Tablet PC. Some computer manufacturers have developed convertible notebook computers that allow the screen to rotate 180 degrees on a central hinge and then fold down to cover the keyboard and become a Tablet PC (Figure 12). You then can use a stylus to enter text or drawings into the computer by writing on the screen.

FIGURE 12
The HP Compaq tc4200 Tablet PC converts to a notebook computer.

Purchase a notebook computer with a built-in wireless network connection. A wireless network connection can be useful when you travel or as part of a home network. Increasingly more airports, hotels, and cafes have wireless networks that allow you to connect to the Internet. Many users today are setting up wireless home networks. With a wireless home network, the desktop computer functions as the server, and your notebook computer can access the desktop computer from any location in the house to share files and hardware, such as a printer, and browse the Web. If your notebook computer does not come with a built-in wireless network connection, you can purchase an external one that slides into your notebook computer. Most home wireless networks allow connections from distances of 150 to 800 feet.

If you are going to use your notebook computer for long periods without access to an electrical outlet, purchase a second battery. The trend among notebook computer users today is power and size over battery life, and notebook computer manufacturers have picked up on this. Many notebook computer users today are willing to give up longer battery life for a larger screen, faster processor, and more storage. In addition, some manufacturers typically sell the notebook with the lowest capacity battery. For this reason, you need to be careful in choosing a notebook computer if you plan to use it without access to electrical outlets for long periods, such as an airplane flight. You also might want to purchase a second battery as a backup. If you anticipate running your notebook computer on batteries frequently, choose a computer that uses lithium-ion batteries, which last longer than nickel cadmium or nickel hydride batteries.

9 **Purchase a well-padded and well-designed carrying case.** An amply padded carrying case will protect your notebook computer from the bumps it will receive while traveling. A well-designed carrying case will have room for accessories such as spare floppy disks, CDs and DVDs, a user manual, pens, and paperwork (Figure 13).

FIGURE 13 A well-designed notebook computer carrying case.

10 **If you travel overseas, obtain a set of electrical and telephone adapters.** Different countries use different outlets for electrical and telephone connections. Several manufacturers sell sets of adapters that will work in most countries.

11 **If you plan to connect your notebook computer to a video projector, make sure the notebook computer is compatible with the video projector.** You should check, for example, to be sure that your notebook computer will allow you to display an image on the computer screen and projection device at the same time (Figure 14). Also, ensure that your notebook computer has the ports required to connect to the video projector.

12 **For improved security, consider a fingerprint scanner.** More than a quarter of a million notebook computers are stolen or lost each year. If you have critical information stored on your notebook computer, then consider purchasing one with a fingerprint scanner (Figure 15) to protect the data if your computer is stolen or lost. Fingerprint security offers a level of protection that extends well beyond the standard password protection.

FIGURE 15 Fingerprint scanner technology offers greater security than passwords.

FIGURE 14 A notebook computer connected to a video projector projects the image displayed on the screen.

HOW TO PURCHASE A TABLET PC

The Tablet PC (Figure 16) combines the mobility features of a traditional notebook computer with the simplicity of pencil and paper, because you can create and save Office-type documents by writing and drawing directly on the screen with a digital pen. Tablet PCs use the Windows XP Tablet PC Edition operating system, which expands on Windows XP Professional by including digital pen and speech capabilities. A notebook computer and a Tablet PC have many similarities. For this reason, if you are considering purchasing a Tablet PC, review the guidelines for purchasing a notebook computer, as well as the guidelines below.

FIGURE 16 The lightweight Tablet PC, with its handwriting capabilities, is the latest addition to the family of mobile computers.

 Make sure the Tablet PC fits your mobile computing needs. The Tablet PC is not for every mobile user. If you find yourself in need of a computer in class or you are spending more time in meetings than in your office, then the Tablet PC may be the answer. Before you invest money in a Tablet PC, however, determine the programs you plan to use on it. You should not buy a Tablet PC simply because it is a new and interesting type of computer. For additional information on the Tablet PC, visit the Web sites listed in Figure 17. You may have to use the search capabilities on the home page of the companies listed to locate information about the Tablet PC.

Company	Web Address
Fujitsu	fujitsu.com
Hewlett-Packard	hp.com
Microsoft	microsoft.com/windowsxp/tabletpc
ViewSonic	viewsonic.com
For an updated list of companies and their Web site addresses, visit scsite.com/dc2007/ch8/buyers.	

FIGURE 17 Companies involved with Tablet PCs and their Web sites.

 Decide whether you want a convertible or pure Tablet PC. Convertible Tablet PCs have an attached keyboard and look like a notebook computer. You rotate the screen and lay it flat against the computer for note-taking. The pure Tablet PCs are slim and lightweight, weighing less than four pounds. They have the capability of easily docking at a desktop to gain access to a large monitor, keyboard, and mouse. If you spend a lot of time attending lectures or meetings, then the pure Tablet PC is ideal. Acceptable specifications for a Tablet PC are shown in Figure 18.

TABLET PC SPECIFICATIONS

Dimensions	12" × 9" × 1.2"
Weight	Less than 4 Pounds
Processor	Pentium M processor at 1 GHz
RAM	1 GB
Hard Disk	40 GB
Display	12.1" TFT
Digitizer	Electromagnetic Digitizer
Battery	4-Cell (3-Hour)
USB	2
FireWire	1
Docking Station	Grab and Go with CD-ROM, Keyboard, and Mouse
Bluetooth Port	Yes
Wireless	802.11a/b/g Card
Network Card	10/100 Ethernet
Modem	56 Kbps
Speakers	Internal
Microphone	Internal
Operating System	Windows XP Tablet PC Edition
Application Software	Office Small Business Edition
Antivirus Software	Yes – 12 Month Subscription
Warranty	1-Year Limited Warranty Parts and Labor

FIGURE 18 Tablet PC specifications.

 Be sure the weight and dimensions are conducive to portability. The weight and dimensions of the Tablet PC are important because you carry it around like a notepad. The Tablet PC you buy should weigh four pounds or less. Its dimensions should be approximately 12 inches by 9 inches by 1.2 inches.

Port availability, battery life, and durability are even more important with a Tablet PC than they are with a notebook computer.
Make sure the Tablet PC you purchase has the ports required for the applications you plan to run. As with any mobile computer, battery life is important especially if you plan to use your Tablet PC for long periods without access to an electrical outlet. A Tablet PC must be durable because if you use it the way it was designed to be used, then you will be handling it much like you handle a pad of paper.

 Experiment with different models of the Tablet PC to find the digital pen that works best for you. The key to making use of the Tablet PC is to be comfortable with its handwriting capabilities and on-screen keyboard. Not only is the digital pen used to write on the screen (Figure 19), you also use it to make gestures to complete tasks, in a manner similar to the way you use a mouse. Figure 20 compares the standard point-and-click of a mouse with the gestures made with a digital pen. Other gestures with the digital pen replicate some of the commonly used keys on a keyboard.

FIGURE 19 A Tablet PC lets you handwrite notes and draw on the screen using a digital pen.

Mouse	Digital Pen
Point	Point
Click	Tap
Double-click	Double-tap
Right-click	Tap and hold
Click and drag	Drag

FIGURE 20 Standard point-and-click of a mouse compared with the gestures made with a digital pen.

 Check out the comfort level of handwriting in different positions. You should be able to handwrite on a Tablet PC with your hand resting on the screen. You also should be able to handwrite holding the Tablet PC in one hand, as well as with it sitting in your lap.

 Make sure the LCD display device has a resolution high enough to take advantage of Microsoft's ClearType technologies.
Tablet PCs use a digitizer under a standard 10.4-inch motion-sensitive LCD display to make the digital ink on the screen look like real ink on paper. To ensure you get the maximum benefits from the new ClearType technology, make sure the LCD display has a resolution of 800 × 600 in landscape mode and a 600 × 800 in portrait mode.

 Test the built-in Tablet PC microphone and speakers. With many application software packages recognizing human speech, such as Microsoft Office, it is important that the Tablet PC's built-in microphone operates at an acceptable level. If the microphone is not to your liking, you may want to purchase a close-talk headset with your Tablet PC. Increasingly more users are sending information as audio files, rather than relying solely on text. For this reason, you also should check the speakers on the Tablet PC to make sure they meet your standards.

Consider a Tablet PC with a built-in PC video camera. A PC video camera adds streaming video and still photography capabilities to your Tablet PC, while still allowing you to take notes in lectures or meetings.

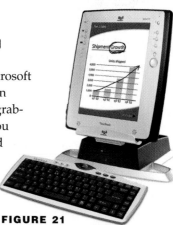 **Review the docking capabilities of the Tablet PC.** The Microsoft Windows XP Tablet PC Edition operating system supports a grab-and-go form of docking, so you can pick up and take a docked Tablet PC with you, just as you would pick up a notepad on your way to a meeting (Figure 21).

FIGURE 21
A Tablet PC docked to create a desktop computer with the Tablet PC as the monitor.

Wireless access to the Internet and your e-mail is essential with a Tablet PC. Make sure the Tablet PC has wireless networking, so you can access the Internet and your e-mail anytime and anywhere. Your Tablet PC also should include standard network connections, such as dial-up and Ethernet connections.

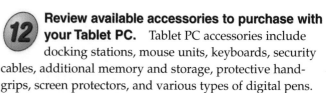 **Review available accessories to purchase with your Tablet PC.** Tablet PC accessories include docking stations, mouse units, keyboards, security cables, additional memory and storage, protective handgrips, screen protectors, and various types of digital pens.

APPENDIX A

Coding Schemes and Number Systems

CODING SCHEMES

As discussed in Chapter 4, a computer uses a coding scheme to represent characters. This section of the appendix presents the ASCII, EBCDIC, and Unicode coding schemes and discusses parity.

ASCII and EBCDIC

Two popular coding schemes that represent characters in a computer are ASCII and EBCDIC. The **American Standard Code for Information Interchange**, or ASCII (pronounced ASK-ee), coding scheme is the most widely used coding scheme to represent data. Many personal computers and midrange servers use ASCII. The **Extended Binary Coded Decimal Interchange Code**, or EBCDIC (pronounced EB-see-dik), coding scheme is used primarily on mainframe computers and high-end servers. As shown in Figure A-1, the combination of bits (0s and 1s) is unique for each character in the ASCII and EBCDIC coding schemes.

When a computer uses the ASCII or EBCDIC coding scheme, it stores each represented character in one byte of memory. Other binary formats exist, however, that the computer sometimes uses to represent numeric data. For example, a computer may store, or pack, two numeric characters in one byte of memory. The computer uses these binary formats to increase storage and processing efficiency.

Unicode

The 256 characters and symbols that are represented by ASCII and EBCDIC codes are sufficient for English and western European languages but are not large enough for Asian and other languages that use different alphabets. Further compounding the problem is that many of these languages use symbols, called **ideograms**, to represent multiple words and ideas. One solution to this situation is Unicode. **Unicode** is a 16-bit coding scheme that has the capacity of representing all the world's current languages, as well as classic and historical languages, in more than 65,000 characters and symbols.

ASCII	SYMBOL	EBCDIC
00110000	0	11110000
00110001	1	11110001
00110010	2	11110010
00110011	3	11110011
00110100	4	11110100
00110101	5	11110101
00110110	6	11110110
00110111	7	11110111
00111000	8	11111000
00111001	9	11111001
01000001	A	11000001
01000010	B	11000010
01000011	C	11000011
01000100	D	11000100
01000101	E	11000101
01000110	F	11000110
01000111	G	11000111
01001000	H	11001000
01001001	I	11001001
01001010	J	11010001
01001011	K	11010010
01001100	L	11010011
01001101	M	11010100
01001110	N	11010101
01001111	O	11010110
01010000	P	11010111
01010001	Q	11011000
01010010	R	11011001
01010011	S	11100010
01010100	T	11100011
01010101	U	11100100
01010110	V	11100101
01010111	W	11100110
01011000	X	11100111
01011001	Y	11101000
01011010	Z	11101001
00100001	!	01011010
00100010	"	01111111
00100011	#	01111011
00100100	$	01011011
00100101	%	01101100
00100110	&	01010000
00101000	(	01001101
00101001	)	01011101
00101010	*	01011100
00101011	+	01001110

FIGURE A-1

A Unicode code for a symbol, as shown in Figure A-2, is obtained by appending the symbol's corresponding digit in the left-most column to the end of the symbol's corresponding three-digit code in the column heading. For

	003	004	005	006	007
0	0 0030	@ 0040	P 0050	` 0060	p 0070
1	1 0031	A 0041	Q 0051	a 0061	q 0071
2	2 0032	B 0042	R 0052	b 0062	r 0072
3	3 0033	C 0043	S 0053	c 0063	s 0073
4	4 0034	D 0044	T 0054	d 0064	t 0074
5	5 0035	E 0045	U 0055	e 0065	u 0075
6	6 0036	F 0046	V 0056	f 0066	v 0076
7	7 0037	G 0047	W 0057	g 0067	w 0077
8	8 0038	H 0048	X 0058	h 0068	x 0078
9	9 0039	I 0049	Y 0059	i 0069	y 0079
A	: 003A	J 004A	Z 005A	j 006A	z 007A
B	; 003B	K 004B	[005B	k 006B	{ 007B
C	< 003C	L 004C	\ 005C	l 006C	| 007C
D	= 003D	M 004D	] 005D	m 006D	} 007D
E	> 003E	N 004E	^ 005E	n 006E	~ 007E
F	? 003F	O 004F	_ 005F	o 006F	DEL 007F

FIGURE A-2

example, the Unicode for the capital letter C is 0043. In Unicode, 30,000 codes are reserved for future use, such as ancient languages, and 6,000 codes are reserved for private use. Existing ASCII coded data is fully compatible with Unicode because the first 256 codes are the same. Unicode is implemented in several operating systems, including Windows XP, Mac OS X, and Linux. Unicode-enabled programming languages and software include Java, XML, Microsoft Office, and Oracle. Some experts believe that Unicode eventually will replace all other coding schemes.

Parity

Regardless of the coding scheme used to represent characters in memory, it is important that the computer store characters accurately. For each byte of memory, most computers have at least one extra bit, called a **parity bit**, that the computer uses for error checking. A parity bit can detect if one of the bits in a byte has been changed inadvertently. While such errors are extremely rare (most computers never have a parity error during their lifetime), they can occur because of voltage fluctuations, static electricity, or a memory failure.

Computers are either odd- or even-parity machines. In computers with odd-parity, the total number of on bits in the byte (including the parity bit) must be an odd number (Figure A-3). In computers with even parity, the total number of on bits must be an even number. The computer checks parity each time it uses a memory location. When the computer moves data from one location to another in memory, it compares the parity bits of both the sending and receiving locations to see if they are the same. If the computer detects a difference or if the wrong number of bits is on (e.g., an odd number in a computer with even parity), an error message is displayed. Many computers use multiple parity bits that enable them to detect and correct a single-bit error and detect multiple-bit errors.

FIGURE A-3

NUMBER SYSTEMS

This section of the appendix describes the number systems used with computers. Technical computer personnel require a thorough knowledge of this subject, but most users need only a general understanding of number systems and how they relate to computers.

The binary (base 2) number system is used to represent the electronic status of the bits in memory. It also is used for other purposes such as addressing the memory locations. Another number system commonly used with computers is **hexadecimal** (base 16). The computer uses the hexadecimal number system to communicate with a programmer when a problem with a program exists, because it would be difficult for the programmer to understand the 0s and 1s of binary code. Figure A-4 shows how the decimal values 0 through 15 are represented in binary and hexadecimal number systems.

DECIMAL	BINARY	HEXADECIMAL
0	0000	0
1	0001	1
2	0010	2
3	0011	3
4	0100	4
5	0101	5
6	0110	6
7	0111	7
8	1000	8
9	1001	9
10	1010	A
11	1011	B
12	1100	C
13	1101	D
14	1110	E
15	1111	F

FIGURE A-4

The mathematical principles that apply to the binary and hexadecimal number systems are the same as those that apply to the decimal number system. To help you better understand these principles, this section starts with the familiar decimal system, then progresses to the binary and hexadecimal number systems.

The Decimal Number System

The decimal number system is a base 10 number system (deci means ten). The base of a number system indicates how many symbols it uses. The decimal number system uses 10 symbols: 0 through 9. Each of the symbols in the number system has a value associated with it. For example, 3 represents a quantity of three and 5 represents a quantity of five.

The decimal number system also is a positional number system. This means that in a number such as 143, each position in the number has a value associated with it. When you look at the decimal number 143, the 3 is in the ones, or units, position and represents three ones (3×1); the 4 is in the tens position and represents four tens (4×10); and the 1 is in the hundreds position and represents one hundred (1×100). The number 143 is the sum of the values in each position of the number ($100 + 40 + 3 = 143$). The chart in Figure A-5 shows how you can calculate the positional values (hundreds, tens, and units) for a number system. Starting on the right and working to the left, the base of the number system, in this case 10, is raised to consecutive powers ($10^0, 10^1, 10^2$). These calculations are a mathematical way of determining the place values in a number system.

When you use number systems other than decimal, the same principles apply. The base of the number system indicates the number of symbols that it uses, and each position in a number system has a value associated with it. By raising the base of the number system to consecutive powers beginning with zero, you can calculate the positional value.

power of 10	10^2	10^1	10^0	1	4	3	=
				(1×10^2) +	(4×10^1) +	(3×10^0)	=
positional value	100	10	1	(1×100) +	(4×10) +	(3×1)	=
number	1	4	3	100 +	40 +	3	= 143

FIGURE A-5

The Binary Number System

As previously discussed, binary is a base 2 number system (bi means two), and the symbols it uses are 0 and 1. Just as each position in a decimal number has a place value associated with it, so does each position in a binary number. In binary, the place values, moving from right to left, are successive powers of two (2^0, 2^1, 2^2, 2^3 or 1, 2, 4, 8). To construct a binary number, place ones in the positions where the corresponding values add up to the quantity you want to represent and place zeros in the other positions. For example, in a four-digit binary number, the binary place values are (from right to left) 1, 2, 4, and 8. The binary number 1001 has ones in the positions for the values 1 and 8 and zeros in the positions for 2 and 4. Therefore, as shown in Figure A-6, the quantity represented by binary 1001 is 9 (8 + 0 + 0 + 1).

The Hexadecimal Number System

The hexadecimal number system uses 16 symbols to represent values (hex means six). These include the symbols 0 through 9 and A through F (Figure A-4 on the previous page). The mathematical principles previously discussed also apply to hexadecimal (Figure A-7).

The primary reasons the hexadecimal number system is used with computers are (1) it can represent binary values in a more compact and readable form, and (2) the conversion between the binary and the hexadecimal number systems is very efficient.

An eight-digit binary number (a byte) can be represented by a two-digit hexadecimal number. For example, in the ASCII code, the character M is represented as 01001101. This value can be represented in the hexadecimal number system as 4D. One way to convert this binary number (4D) to a hexadecimal number is to divide the binary number (from right to left) into groups of four digits, calculate the value of each group, and then change any two-digit values (10 through 15) to the symbols A through F that are used in the hexadecimal number system (Figure A-8).

power of 2	2^3	2^2	2^1	2^0
positional value	8	4	2	1
binary	1	0	0	1

	1	0	0	1	=
	(1×2^3) +	(0×2^2) +	(0×2^1) +	(1×2^0) =	
	(1×8) +	(0×4) +	(0×2) +	(1×1) =	
	8 +	0 +	0 +	1 =	9

FIGURE A-6

power of 16	16^1	16^0
positional value	16	1
hexadecimal	A	5

	A	5	=
	(10×16^1) +	(5×16^0)	=
	(10×16) +	(5×1)	=
	160 +	5	= 165

FIGURE A-7

positional value	8421	8421
binary	0100	1101
decimal	4	13
hexadecimal	4	D

FIGURE A-8

APPENDIX B

Quiz Yourself Answers

Following are possible answers to the Quiz Yourself boxes throughout the book.

Quiz Yourself 1-1

1. A computer is ~~a motorized~~an electronic device that processes ~~output~~input into ~~input~~output.
2. A storage device records (~~reads~~writes) and/or retrieves (~~writes~~reads) items to and from storage media.
3. An ~~output~~input device is any hardware component that allows you to enter data and instructions into a computer.
4. True Statement
5. Computers have the ~~dis~~advantages of fast speeds, ~~high~~low failure rates, producing consistent results, storing ~~small~~enormous amounts of data, and communicating with others.
6. Three commonly used ~~input~~output devices are a printer, a monitor, and speakers.

Quiz Yourself 1-2

1. A ~~resource~~network is a collection of computers and devices connected together via communications devices and transmission media.
2. True Statement
3. Popular ~~system~~application software includes Web browsers, word processing software, spreadsheet software, database software, and presentation graphics software.
4. The ~~Internet~~Web is one of the more popular services on the ~~Web~~Internet.
5. Two types of ~~application~~system software are the operating system and utility programs.

Quiz Yourself 1-3

1. A ~~desktop computer~~notebook computer (or laptop computer) is a portable, personal computer designed to fit on your lap.
2. True Statement
3. Each ~~large business~~home user spends time on the computer for different reasons that include budgeting and personal financial management, Web access, communications, and entertainment.
4. A ~~home~~power user requires the capabilities of a workstation or other powerful computer.
5. ~~Mainframes~~Supercomputers are the fastest, most powerful computers — and the most expensive.
6. The elements of an information system are hardware, ~~e-mail~~software, data, people, and ~~the Internet~~procedures.
7. With ~~embedded computers~~online banking, users access account balances, pay bills, and copy monthly

transactions from the bank's computer right into their personal computers.

Quiz Yourself 2-1

1. True Statement
2. ~~A WISP~~An IP address (or Internet Protocol address) is a number that uniquely identifies each computer or device connected to the Internet.
3. ~~An IP address~~A domain name, such as www.google.com, is the text version of ~~a domain name~~an IP address.
4. Dial-up access takes place when the modem in your computer uses ~~the cable television network~~a standard telephone line to connect to the Internet.
5. The World Wide Web Consortium (W3C) oversees research and ~~owns~~sets standards and guidelines for many areas of the Internet.

Quiz Yourself 2-2

1. True Statement
2. A ~~Web browser~~subject directory classifies Web pages in an organized set of categories, such as sports or shopping, and related subcategories.
3. Audio and video files are ~~downloaded~~compressed to reduce their file sizes.
4. Popular ~~portals~~players include iTunes, RealPlayer, and Windows Media Player.
5. The more widely used ~~search engines~~Web browsers for personal computers are Internet Explorer, Netscape, Firefox, Mozilla, Opera, and Safari.
6. To develop a Web page, you do not have to be a computer programmer.
7. To improve your Web searches, use ~~general~~specific nouns and put the ~~least~~most important terms first in the search text.

Quiz Yourself 2-3

1. True Statement
2. An e-mail address is a combination of a user name and ~~an e-mail program~~a domain name that identifies a user so he or she can receive Internet e-mail.
3. ~~Business~~Consumer-to-consumer e-commerce occurs when one consumer sells directly to another, such as in an online auction.
4. FTP is an Internet standard that permits file ~~reading~~uploading and ~~writing~~downloading with other computers on the Internet.
5. ~~Spam~~Internet telephony uses the Internet (instead of the public switched telephone network) to connect a calling party to one or more called parties.
6. Netiquette is the code of ~~un~~acceptable behaviors while on the Internet.
7. On a newsgroup, a ~~subscription~~thread (or threaded discussion) consists of the original article and all subsequent related replies.

Quiz Yourself 3-1

1. True Statement
2. ~~Public domain~~Packaged software is mass produced, copyrighted retail software that meets the needs of a wide variety of users, not just a single user or company.
3. To use ~~system~~application software, your computer must be running ~~application~~system software.
4. When an application is started, the program's instructions load from ~~memory~~a storage medium into ~~a storage medium~~memory.

Quiz Yourself 3-2

1. ~~Audio~~Video editing software typically includes ~~video~~audio editing capabilities.
2. ~~Enterprise computing~~Image editing software provides the capabilities of paint software and also includes the ability to modify existing images.
3. Millions of people use ~~spreadsheet~~word processing software every day to develop documents such as letters, memos, reports, fax cover sheets, mailing labels, newsletters, and Web pages.
4. Professional ~~accounting~~DTP (or desktop publishing) software is ideal for the production of high-quality color documents such as textbooks, corporate newsletters, marketing literature, product catalogs, and annual reports.
5. ~~Spreadsheet~~Presentation graphics software is application software that allows users to create visual aids for presentations to communicate ideas, messages, and other information to a group.
6. Two of the more widely used ~~CAD programs~~software suites are Microsoft Office and Sun StarOffice.
7. True Statement

Quiz Yourself 3-3

1. An ~~anti-spam~~antivirus program protects a computer against viruses by identifying and removing any computer viruses found in memory, on storage media, or in incoming files.
2. ~~Computer~~Web-based training is a type of ~~Web~~computer-based training that uses Internet technology and consists of application software on the Web.
3. True Statement
4. ~~Legal~~Personal finance software is a simplified accounting program that helps home users and small office/home office users balance their checkbooks, pay bills, track investments, and evaluate financial plans.
5. ~~Personal DTP~~Photo editing software is a popular type of image editing software that allows users to edit digital photographs.

Quiz Yourself 4-1

1. True Statement
2. Four basic operations in a machine cycle are: (1) ~~comparing~~fetching, (2) decoding, (3) executing, and, if necessary, (4) ~~pipelining~~storing.
3. Processors contain a ~~motherboard~~control unit and an arithmetic logic unit (ALU).
4. The ~~central processing unit~~motherboard, sometimes called a system board, is the main circuit board of the system unit.
5. The leading processor chip manufacturers for personal computers are ~~Microsoft~~Intel, AMD, IBM, Motorola, and Transmeta.
6. The pace of the system clock, called the clock speed, is measured by the number of ticks per ~~minute~~second.
7. The system unit is a case that contains ~~mechanical~~electronic components of the computer used to process data.

Quiz Yourself 4-2

1. True Statement
2. A gigabyte (GB) equals approximately 1 ~~trillion~~billion bytes.
3. Memory cache helps speed the processes of the computer because it stores ~~seldom~~frequently used instructions and data.
4. Most computers are ~~analog~~digital, which means they recognize only two discrete states: on and off.
5. Most RAM ~~retains~~loses its contents when the power is removed from the computer.
6. Read-only memory (ROM) refers to memory chips storing ~~temporary~~permanent data and instructions.

Quiz Yourself 4-3

1. A ~~bus~~port is the point at which a peripheral attaches to or communicates with a system unit so the peripheral can send data to or receive information from the computer.
2. An ~~AC adapter~~expansion slot is a socket on the motherboard that can hold an adapter card.
3. Built into the power supply is a ~~heater~~fan that keeps components of the system unit ~~warm~~cool.
4. ~~Serial~~USB ports can connect up to 127 different peripherals together with a single connector type.
5. The higher the bus clock speed, the ~~slower~~faster the transmission of data.
6. True Statement

Quiz Yourself 5-1

1. A keyboard is an ~~output~~input device that contains keys users press to enter data in a computer.
2. A ~~light pen~~graphics tablet is a flat, rectangular, electronic plastic board.

3. A ~~trackball~~ touch pad is a small, flat, rectangular pointing device commonly found on notebook computers.
4. True Statement
5. Operations you can perform with a ~~wheel~~ mouse include point, click, right-click, double-click, triple-click, drag, right-drag, rotate wheel, press wheel button, and tilt wheel.
6. ~~PDAs~~ Tablet PCs use a pressure-sensitive digital pen, and ~~Tablet PCs~~ PDAs use a stylus.

Quiz Yourself 5-2

1. True Statement
2. DV cameras record video as ~~analog~~ digital signals.
3. ~~Instant messaging~~ Voice recognition (or speech recognition) is the computer's capability of distinguishing spoken words.
4. Many smart phones today have a built-in camera so users easily can send ~~text~~ picture messages.
5. The ~~lower~~ higher the resolution of a digital camera, the better the image quality, but the more expensive the camera.

Quiz Yourself 5-3

1. A fingerprint scanner captures curves and indentations of a ~~signature~~ fingerprint.
2. After swiping a credit card through ~~an MICR~~ a magstripe (or magnetic stripe card) reader, a POS terminal connects to a system that authenticates the purchase.
3. ATMs ask you to enter a password, called a ~~biometric identifier~~ PIN (or personal identification number), which verifies that you are the holder of the bankcard.
4. Four types of ~~source documents~~ scanners are flatbed, pen, sheet-fed, and drum.
5. Retail and grocery stores use the ~~POSTNET~~ UPC (Universal Product Code) bar code.
6. RFID is a technology that uses ~~laser~~ radio signals to communicate with a tag placed in an object, an animal, or a person.
7. True Statement

Quiz Yourself 6-1

1. A ~~lower~~ higher resolution uses a greater number of pixels and thus provides a smoother image.
2. An output device is any type of ~~software~~ hardware component that conveys information to one or more people.
3. Documents often include ~~text~~ graphics to enhance their visual appeal and convey information.
4. ~~LCD~~ CRT monitors have a larger footprint than ~~CRT~~ LCD monitors.
5. Types of ~~CRTs~~ flat-panel displays include LCD monitors, LCD screens, and plasma monitors.
6. True Statement

Quiz Yourself 6-2

1. A ~~laser~~ thermal printer generates images by pushing electrically heated pins against heat-sensitive paper.
2. A ~~photo~~ laser printer creates images using a laser beam and powdered ink, called toner.
3. An ink-jet printer is a type of impact printer that forms characters and graphics by spraying tiny drops of liquid ~~nitrogen~~ ink onto a piece of paper.
4. Printed information is called ~~soft~~ hard copy.
5. Two commonly used types of impact printers are ~~ink-jet~~ dot-matrix printers and line printers.
6. True Statement

Quiz Yourself 6-3

1. A digital light processing (DLP) projector uses tiny ~~lightbulbs~~ mirrors to reflect light.
2. True Statement
3. Many personal computer users add surround sound ~~printer systems~~ speakers to their computers to generate a higher-quality sound.
4. Multifunction peripherals require ~~more~~ less space than having a separate printer, scanner, copy machine, and fax machine.
5. Some joysticks, wheels, and gamepads include ~~real-time action~~ force feedback, which is a technology that sends resistance to the device in response to actions of the user.

Quiz Yourself 7-1

1. Miniature hard disks are a type of ~~optical disc~~ magnetic disk.
2. True Statement
3. SATA is a hard disk interface that uses ~~parallel~~ serial signals to transfer data, instructions, and information.
4. ~~Storage media~~ A storage device is the computer hardware that records and/or retrieves items to and from a ~~storage device~~ storage media.
5. Three types of ~~manual~~ magnetic disks are hard disks, floppy disks, and Zip disks.
6. Users can move an ~~internal~~ external Zip drive from computer to computer as needed by connecting the drive to a USB port or FireWire port on the system unit.

Quiz Yourself 7-2

1. A ~~CD-RW~~ CD-ROM is a type of optical disc on which users can read but not write (record) or erase.
2. A ~~DVD-RAM~~ Picture CD is a single-session disc that stores digital versions of a single roll of film using a jpg file format.
3. DVDs have the ~~same~~ much greater storage capacities ~~as~~ than CDs.
4. Optical discs are written and read by ~~mirrors~~ a laser.

5. ~~Single session~~Multisession means you can write on part of the disc at one time and another part at a later time.
6. True Statement

Quiz Yourself 7-3

1. A smart card stores data on a thin ~~magnetic stripe~~microprocessor embedded in the card.
2. A USB flash drive is a flash memory storage device that plugs in a ~~parallel~~USB port on a computer or mobile device.
3. Flash memory cards are a type of ~~magnetic~~solid-state media, which means they consist entirely of electronic components and contain no moving parts.
4. Microfilm and microfiche have the ~~shortest~~longest life of any storage media.
5. Tape storage requires ~~direct~~sequential access, which refers to reading or writing data consecutively.
6. True Statement

Quiz Yourself 8-1

1. A ~~buffer~~driver is a small program that tells the operating system how to communicate with a specific device.
2. A ~~cold~~warm boot is the process of using the operating system to restart a computer.
3. A password is a ~~public~~private combination of characters associated with the user name that allows access to certain computer resources.
4. Firmware that contains the computer's startup instructions is called the ~~kernel~~BIOS.
5. The program you currently are using is in the ~~background~~foreground, and the other programs running but not in use are in the ~~foreground~~background.
6. Two types of system software are operating systems and ~~application~~utility programs.
7. True Statement

Quiz Yourself 8-2

1. A ~~file manager~~firewall is a utility that detects and protects a personal computer from unauthorized intrusions.
2. ~~Fragmenting~~Defragmenting a disk is the process of reorganizing it so the files are stored in contiguous sectors.
3. ~~Linux~~Windows XP is available in five editions: Home Edition, Professional, Media Center Edition, Tablet PC Edition, and Professional x64 Edition.
4. True Statement
5. ~~Windows XP~~Linux is a UNIX-type operating system that is open source software.
6. You should ~~uninstall~~back up files and disks regularly in the event your originals are lost, damaged, or destroyed.

Quiz Yourself 8-3

1. A ~~pop-up blocker~~file compression utility shrinks the size of a file(s).
2. An ~~anti-spam~~antivirus program protects a computer against viruses by identifying and removing any computer viruses found in memory, on storage media, or on incoming files.
3. True Statement
4. Pocket PCs use ~~Palm OS~~Windows Mobile as their operating system.
5. ~~Web filtering~~CD/DVD burning software writes text, graphics, audio, and video files to a recordable or rewritable CD or DVD.

APPENDIX C

Computer Acronyms

Acronym	Description	Page
AA	Audible Audio	87
AAC	Advanced Audio Coding	87
AC	alternating current	213
ADA	Americans with Disabilities Act	266
ADC	analog-to-digital converter	38
AGP	Accelerated Graphics Port	212
AIFF	Audio Interchange File Format	87
ALU	arithmetic logic unit	188
AMD	Advanced Micro Devices	219
AOL	America Online	72, 82
ARPA	Advanced Research Projects Agency	69
ARPANET	Advanced Research Projects Agency network	69
ASCII	American Standard Code for Information Interchange	195
ASF	Advanced Streaming (or Systems) Format	87
ASP	application service provider	164
ATC	advanced transfer cache	201
ATM	automated teller machine	262
B2B	business-to-business	92
B2C	business-to-consumer	92
BIOS	basic input/output system	400
Bit	binary digit	195
BMP	bit map	85
BTW	by the way	100
C2C	consumer-to-consumer	92
CAD	computer-aided design	151, 327
CAI	computer-aided instruction	160
CAM	computer-aided manufacturing	36
CBT	computer-based training	160
CCD	charge-coupled device	251
CD	compact disc	8, 9, 17, 27, 89, 357
CD-R	compact disc-recordable	371
CD-ROM	compact disc read-only memory	369-70
CD-RW	compact disc-rewritable	371
CF	CompactFlash	376
CMOS	complementary metal-oxide semiconductor	203
COBOL	COmmon Business-Oriented Language	53
COM port	communications port	207
CPU	central processing unit	8, 187
CRT	cathode-ray tube	307
CST	Computer Service Technician	381
DAC	digital-to-analog converter	38
DDR SDRAM	double data rate synchronous dynamic random access memory	199
DHCP	Dynamic Host Configuration Protocol	102
DIMM	dual inline memory module	199
DL	distance learning	166
DLP projector	digital light processing projector	324
DNS	domain name system	74
DOS	Disk Operating System	417
Dpi	dots per inch	252, 313
DRAM	dynamic random access memory	199

Acronym	Description	Page
DSL	Digital Subscriber Line	70, 449
DSP	digital signal processor	38
DTP	desktop publishing	152
DTV	digital television	306
DV camera	digital video camera	253
DVD	digital versatile disc or digital video disc	8, 17, 59, 89, 357
DVD+R	digital versatile disc or digital video disc recordable	373
DVD-R	digital versatile disc or digital video disc recordable	373
DVD+RAM	digital versatile disc or digital video disc + random access memory	373
DVD-ROM	digital versatile disc or digital video disc read-only memory	9, 372
DVD+RW	digital versatile disc or digital video disc + rewritable	373
DVD-RW	digital versatile disc or digital video disc + rewritable	373
DVI	Digital Video Interface	305
EB	exabyte	356
EBCDIC	Extended Binary Coded Decimal Interchange Code	195
E-book	electronic book	61, 303
E-commerce	electronic commerce	28, 30, 60, 61, 91-92
EEPROM	electrically erasable programmable read-only memory	202
E-file	electronic filing	157
EIDE	Enhanced Integrated Drive Electronics	363
E-mail	electronic mail	12, 31, 69, 92-95, 101, 161
EMR	electromagnetic radiation	308
ENIAC	Electronic Numerical Integrator and Computer	52
FAQ	frequently asked questions	6, 100
Fax	facsimile	322-23
Fortran	FORmula TRANslator	53
FTP	File Transfer Protocol	68, 96, 134, 161
FWIW	for what it's worth	100
FYI	for your information	100
GB	gigabyte	197, 356
GHz	gigahertz	189
GIF	Graphics Interchange Format	85
GIGO	garbage in, garbage out	10
GPU	graphics processing unit	305
GUI	graphical user interface	15, 137, 402, 420, 421
HD	high density	364
HD-DVD	high-density-DVD	372
HDTV	high-definition television	306-7
HIPAA	Health Insurance Portability and Accountability Act	381
HP	Hewlett-Packard	329
http	Hypertext Transfer Protocol	76
Hz	hertz	189
IBM	International Business Machines	53, 54, 55, 138

Appendix C *Computer Acronyms*

Acronym	Description	Page
IC	integrated circuit	186
ICANN	Internet Corporation for Assigned Names and Numbers	74
IM	instant messaging	98
IMHO	in my humble opinion	100
Interactive TV	interactive television	307
IP address	Internet Protocol address	73, 102
IPng	Internet Protocol Next Generation	102
IPv6	Internet Protocol version 6	102
IrDA	Infrared Data Association	210
IRQ	interrupt request	409
IS	information system	25
ISP	Internet service provider	72
IT	information technology	25
JPEG	Joint Photographic Experts Group	85, 345
K	kilobyte	197
KB	kilobyte	197
KBps	kilobytes per second	357, 369
L1 cache	Level 1 cache	201
L2 cache	Level 2 cache	201
L3 cache	Level 3 cache	201
LAN	local area network	55
LCD	liquid crystal display	304
Mac OS	Macintosh Operating System	19
Mac OS X	Macintosh Operating System X	39, 135, 195, 420
MB	megabyte	197, 356
MBps	megabytes per second	357, 365
Mbps	megabits per second	365
M-commerce	mobile commerce	91
MHz	megahertz	203
MIB	Medical Information Bureau	381
MICR	magnetic-ink character recognition	260
MIDI	Musical Instrument Digital Interface	209, 246
MIPS	millions of instructions per second	190
Modem	modulate/demodulate	9
MP	million pixels	252
MP3	Moving Pictures Experts Group Audio Layer 3 (MPEG-3)	86, 87, 89, 202
MPEG	Moving Pictures Experts Group	88
MRAM	magnetoresistive random access memory	199
µs	microsecond	203
ms	millisecond	203
MS-DOS	Microsoft Disk Operating System	417, 430
MSN	Microsoft Network, The	72, 82
MT/ST	Magnetic Tape/Selectric Typewriter	54
MTBF	mean time between failures	361
Netiquette	Internet etiquette	100
NLQ	near letter quality	318
ns	nanosecond	203
NSF	National Science Foundation	70
OCR	optical character recognition	257
OLE	object linking and embedding	57
OLED	organic light emitting diode	304
OMR	optical mark recognition	257
OS	operating system	15-16, 398-425
OSP	online service provider	72
PB	petabyte	356

Acronym	Description	Page
PC	personal computer	19-20, 445
PC-DOS	personal computer Disk Operating System	417
PCI bus	Peripheral Component Interconnect bus	212
PCL	Printer Control Language	316
PCMCIA	Personal Computer Memory Card International Association	205
PC-to-TV port	personal computer-to-television port	453
PDA	personal digital assistant	22, 31, 265, 282, 325
PDF	Portable Document Format	150
PDL	page description language	316
PIM	personal information manager	148
PIN	personal identification number	262
Pixel	picture element	252, 304
PNG format	Portable Network Graphics format	85
POP	point of presence	72
POP	Post Office Protocol	95
POP3	Post Office Protocol 3	95
POS	point of sale	261
POST	power-on self test	400
ppi	pixels (picture elements) per inch	252
PROM chip	programmable read-only memory chip	202
ps	picosecond	203
QT	QuickTime	87
RA	RealAudio	87
RAM	random access memory	197, 198-200
RDRAM	Rambus dynamic random access memory	199
RFID	radio frequency identification	259
RIAA	Recording Industry Association of America	63
RIMM	Rambus inline memory module	199
ROM	read-only memory	201-2
Rpm	revolutions per minute	360
RSS 2.0	Really Simple Syndication	84
SATA	Serial Advanced Technology Attachment	362-63
SCSI	small computer system interface	210
SD	Secure Digital	376
SDRAM	synchronous dynamic random access memory	199, 203
SIMM	single inline memory module	199
SMTP	simple mail transfer protocol	94
SOHO	small office/home office	28
SRAM	static random access memory	199
SVGA	super video graphics array	305
SXGA	Super Extended Graphics Array	305
TB	terabyte	197, 356
TFT display	thin-film transistor display	304
TIFF	Tagged Image File Format	85, 345
TRACERT	traceroute	430
TTFN	ta ta for now	100
TYVM	thank you very much	100
UGA	Ultra Extended Graphics Array	305
Ultra XGA	Ultra Extended Graphics Array	305
UMD	Universal Media Disc	372
UNIVAC I	UNIVersal Automatic Computer	52
uPC	ultra personal computer	21
UPC	Universal Product Code	258
UPS	uninterruptible power supply	451
URL	Uniform Resource Locator	76

Acronym	Description	Page
USB	universal serial bus	207, 212
User ID	user identification	410
VCD	video CD	351
Voice over IP	voice over Internet Protocol	99
VR	virtual reality	88
W3C	World Wide Web Consortium	70, 327
WAV	Windows waveform	87
WBT	Web-based training	166

Acronym	Description	Page
WinFS	Windows Future Storage	382
WISP	wireless Internet service provider	72
WMA	Windows Media Audio	87, 89, 202
WWW	World Wide Web	75, 103
WYSIWYG	what you see is what you get	137
XGA	Extended Graphics Array	305
YB	yottabyte	356
ZB	zettabyte	356

Jobs
outsourcing, 10
Joystick: Pointing device used for games or flight and driving simulations that is a vertical lever mounted on a base. **242**
force feedback and, 324
purchasing desktop computer and, 447
JPEG: Format that compresses graphics to reduce their file size. **85, 345**
Picture CD using, 370

K, 197. *See also* **Kilobyte**
Kay, Alan, 431
Kazaa, 369
KB, 197. *See also* **Kilobyte**
KBps: Kilobytes per second. **357,** 369
Kbps. *See* Kilo (thousand) bits per second
Kemeny, John, 54
Kernel: The core of an operating system that manages memory and devices, maintains the computer's clock, starts applications, and assigns the computer's resources. **400,** 401
Keyboard: Input device that contains keys users press to enter data and instructions into a computer. 7, **236–38**
BIOS testing, 400
connections, 238
ergonomics, 238
fingerprint scanner on, 263
health issues, 238
keyguard for, 266
on-screen, 247, 266
personal mobile device and, 284
portable, 248
purchasing desktop computer and, 447, 449
purchasing notebook computer and, 453
terminal, 261
Keyboard monitoring software, 237

Keyguard: Metal or plastic plate placed over the keyboard that allows users to rest their hands on the keyboard without accidentally pressing any keys. **266**
Keywords: Words or phrases entered in a search engine's text box to find information on a Web page. 80–81
Kilby, Jack, 53, 219
Kilobyte (KB or K): Exactly 1,024 bytes. **197.** *See also* **K; KB**
Kiosk: Freestanding computer, usually with a touch screen, used by some businesses in public locations. **30,** 242
Kodak, Picture CD and, 370

L1 cache: A type of memory cache that is built directly into the processor chip, with a capacity of 8 KB to 16 KB. **201**
L2 cache: A type of memory cache that is slightly slower than L1 cache, but has a much larger capacity, ranging from 64 KB to 16 MB. **201**
L3 cache: Cache on the motherboard that is separate from the processor. **201**
Label: Text entered in a worksheet cell that identifies the worksheet data and helps organize the worksheet. **143**
Label printer: Small printer that prints on adhesive-type material that can be placed on items such as envelopes, packages, CDs, DVDs, audio cassettes, photographs, file folders, and toys. **318**
LAN, 55. *See also* **Local area network**

Landscape orientation: A printout that is wider than it is tall with information printed across the widest part of the paper. **310**
Landscaping software. *See* **Home design/ landscaping software**
Laptop computer, 20. *See also* **Notebook computer**
Large business user: Computer user working for a business that has hundreds or thousands of employees in offices across a region, the country, or the world. 26, **30,** 31
input devices, 265
operating systems for, 422
output devices, 310, 315, 325
printers, 310, 315
processor selection and, 215
storage and, 355, 380
Large-format printer: Printer that creates photo-realistic quality color prints, used mainly by graphic artists. **318**
Laser printer: Type of high-speed, high-quality nonimpact printer that creates images using a laser beam and powdered ink called toner. **315–16**
Layers, 351
LCD, 304. *See also* **Liquid crystal display**
LCD monitor: Desktop monitor that uses a liquid crystal display instead of a cathode-ray tube to produce images on a screen, resulting in a sharp, flicker-free display. **302–7,** 325
quality of, 304
on mobile computers and devices, 303
See also **Flat-panel monitor**

LCD projector: Projector that uses liquid crystal display technology that attaches directly to a computer and uses its own light source to display the information shown on the computer screen. **324**
Learning
computer-based training and, 160
computers used in, 32
distance, 166
educational software for, 160
online, 82
Left-handed mouse users, 240
Legal issues
copyright. *See* **Copyright**
Legal software: Application software that assists in the preparation of legal documents and provides legal information to individuals, families, and small businesses. **157**
Light pen: Handheld input device that can detect the presence of light. **242**
Line chart: Chart that shows a trend during a period of time, as indicated by a rising or falling line. **144**
Line printer: Type of high-speed impact printer that prints an entire line at a time. **319**
Link: Built-in connection to another related Web page or part of a Web page. Short for hyperlink. **77**
animation, 86
search engine and, 79, 80
Linux: Popular, multitasking UNIX-type operating system. 58, 60, 64, 195, **421,** 423, 431
future of, 421

Personal finance software: Simplified accounting program that helps home users or small office/home office users manage finances. **156**

Personal firewall: Utility program that detects and protects a personal computer and its data from unauthorized intrusions. **162, 413**

Personal identification number (PIN), ATM: Password that can be used with a bankcard at an ATM, which verifies the user is the holder of the bankcard. **262.** *See also* **PIN**

Personal information manager (PIM): Application software that includes features to help users organize personal information. **148.** *See also* **PIM**

Personal mobile devices, 282–97
accessories for, 284
installing software on, 295
operating systems and, 283
purchasing, 296–97
software for, 285–94

Personal paint/image editing software: Application software that provides an easy-to-use interface, usually with more simplified capabilities that allows users to draw pictures, shapes, and other images. **158**

Personal photo editing software: Type of image editing software that allows users to edit digital photographs and create electronic photo albums. **159, 251, 370**

Personal use, software for, 155–60

Personal Web site, 84

Petabyte (PB), 356

Phishing: Scam in which a perpetrator sends an official looking e-mail that attempts to obtain your personal and financial information. 65

Photo printer: Type of nonimpact color printer that produces photo-lab-quality pictures. **314**–15
paper for, 315
storage media for, 376

Photo sharing community: Web site that allows users to create an online photo album and store their electronic photographs. **14,** 159, 251, 256, **370**

Photographs, 85
altering, 153
clip art, 139
editing, 153, 159
online print service for, 159
personal DTP software, 158
Picture CDs and, 370

Physically challenged users
input devices for, 266
output devices for, 326–27

Picosecond (ps), 203

Picture CD: Single-session CD-ROM that stores digital versions of a single roll of film using a jpg file format. **370**

Picture messaging: Service that allows users to send graphics, pictures, video clips, and sound files, as well as short text messages to another smart phone, PDA, or computer. 249. *See also* **MMS (multimedia message service)**

Pictures
scanning, 256

Pie chart: Chart that is displayed in the shape of a round pie cut into slices to show the relationship of parts to a whole. **144**

PIM. *See also* **Personal information manager**

PIN, 262, 567. *See also* **Personal identification number (PIN)**

Ping command, 430

Pipelining: Concept in which the processor begins fetching a second instruction before it completes the machine cycle for the first instruction. **189**

Pixar, 329

Pixel: The smallest element in an electronic image. Short for picture element. **252, 304**
CRT monitor, 307, 308
digital camera and, 252
distance between, 308
scanners and, 256

Pixel pitch: The distance in millimeters between pixels on a display device. **304,** 308. *See also* **Dot pitch**

Pixels per inch (ppi): Number of pixels in one inch of screen display. **252.** *See also* **Ppi**

Pixilated, 346

PKZIP, 427

Plagiarism, Internet, 141

Plasma monitor: Display device that uses gas plasma technology, which sandwiches a layer of gas between two glass plates. **306**

Platform: Set of programs containing instructions that coordinate all the activities among computer hardware resources. **399**

Platter: Component of a hard disk that is made of aluminum, glass, or ceramic and is coated with an alloy material that allows items to be recorded magnetically on its surface. **359**–60

Player: Software used by a person to listen to an audio file on a computer. **86**

Plotters: Sophisticated printers that produce high-quality drawings such as blueprints, maps, and circuit diagrams using a row of charged wires (called styli) to draw an electrostatic pattern on specially coated paper and then fuse toner to the pattern. **318**

Plug and Play: Technology that gives a computer the capability to configure adapter cards and other peripherals automatically as a user installs them. **205,** 208, **407**–8

Plug-in: Program that extends the capability of a browser; often used to enhance multimedia. **89**

PNG format: Graphics format that improves upon the GIF format. **85**

Pocket PC: Type of PDA. **424**

Podcast: Recorded audio, usually an MP3 file, stored on a Web site that can be downloaded to a computer or a portable digital audio player such as an iPod. **14, 86**

Point: Measure of font size, equal to about 1/72 of an inch in height. **141**

Point of presence (POP): Access point on the Internet to which a user connects when using dial-up access. **72.** *See also* **POP**

Point of sale (POS): Location in a retail or grocery store where a consumer pays for goods or services. **261.** *See also* **POS**

PHOTO CREDITS

Chapter 1: Picture Yourself, © Digital Vision/Getty Images; Picture Yourself, Courtesy of Sandisk Corporation; Picture Yourself, © Masterfile/Masterfile www.masterfile.com; Picture Yourself, ©Tony Freeman/Photo Edit — All rights reserved.; Picture Yourself, © Digital Vision/Getty images; Picture Yourself, ©Davis Barber/Photo Edit — All rights reserved; Picture Yourself, © Burazin/Getty Images; Picture Yourself, Courtesy of 3Com Corporation; Picture Yourself, Courtesy of Bluetooth SIG; Figure 1-1a, © Rubberball; Figure 1-1b, © Mark Scott/Getty Images; Figure 1-1b2, Courtesy of Sony Ericsson Mobile Communications AB. All Rights Reserved.; Figure 1-1c, © Thierry Dosogne/Getty Images; Figure 1-1d1, © Patrick Olear/Photo Edit — All rights reserved.; Figure 1-1d2, Courtesy of xThink, Inc.; Figure 1-1e1, © Jennifer Burrell/Masterfile; Figure 1-1e2, © Kim Kulish/Corbis; Figure 1-1f, © David Young-Wolff/Photo Edit — All rights reserved.; Figure 1-3a, Courtesy of Acer America Corp.; Figure 1-3b, Courtesy of Logitech, Inc.; Figure 1-3c, Courtesy of Logitech, Inc.; Figure 1-3d1, Courtesy of Western Digital Corporation. WD RAPTOR® and WD CAVIAR®; are registered trademarks, and the HARD DRIVE BY WD™ logo is a trademark of WD in the U.S. and other countries.; Figure 1-3d2, Courtesy of Umax Systems GmbH; Figure 1-3e, Courtesy of Sandisk Corporation; Figure 1-3f, Courtesy of Sandisk Corporation; Figure 1-3g, Courtesy of Linksys, a Division of Cisco Systems Inc.; Figure 1-3h, Courtesy of Umax Systems GmbH; Figure 1-3i, Courtesy of Epson America, Inc.; Figure 1-4, Courtesy of Seagate Technology; Figure 1-5, ©Rachel Epstein/Photo Edit; Looking Ahead 1-1, © P/WIDE WORLD PHOTOS; Figure 1-6a,b,c, Courtesy of Sony Electronics Inc.; Figure 6-1a3, Courtesy of TallyGenicom; Figure 1-7a, Courtesy of Acer America Corp.; Figure 1-7b, Courtesy of Sony Electronics Inc.; Figure 1-7c, © Gateway Inc.; Figure 1-7d, Courtesy of Acer America Corp.; Figure 1-7e, Courtesy of Nokia; Figure 1-7f, Courtesy of Sony Electronics Inc.; Figure 1-11, © Mark Richards/Photo Edit — All rights reserved.; Figure 1-12, Courtesy of Acer America Corp.; Figure 1-15, Courtesy of Lenovo; Figure 1-16a, Courtesy of Apple Computer, Inc.; Figure 1-16b, Courtesy of Apple Computer, Inc.; Figure 1-17, Courtesy of Sony Electronics Inc.; Figure 1-18, Courtesy of Motion Computing, Inc.; Figure 1-19, Courtesy of San Francisco-based OQO Inc. www.oqo.com; Figure 1-20a, Photo by Business Wire via Getty Images; Figure 1-20b, Courtesy of Belkin Corporation; Figure 1-21a, Courtesy of Nokia; Figure 1-21b, Courtesy of Nokia; Figure 1-21c, Courtesy of Nokia; Figure 1-21d, Courtesy of Nokia; Figure 1-21e, Courtesy of Nokia; Figure 1-22a, Photo by Microsoft via Getty Images; Figure 1-22b, © PRNewsFoto/Nintendo of America; Figure 1-23, Courtesy of Sun Microsystems, Inc.; Figure 1-24, Courtesy of IBM Corporation; Figure 1-25, COPicture YourselfRIGHT: JAMSTEC/ESC; Figure 1-26a, Toyota photo; Figure 1-26b, © Patti McConville/Imagestate; Figure 1-26c, Toyota photo; Figure 1-26d, Toyota photo; Figure 1-26e, © DiMaggio/Kalish/CORBIS; Figure 1-26f, Toyota photo; Figure 1-27, Step 3, Courtesy of Fujitsu Siemens Computers; Figure 1-27, Step 4, Courtesy of IBM Corporation; Figure 1-28a, Courtesy of Intuit Inc.; Figure 1-28, © Comstock Images; Figure 1-29, Courtesy of Sony Electronics Inc.; Figure 1-30, © Paul Barton/CORBIS; Figure 1-31a, © C. Görling/zefa/Corbis; Figure 1-31b, © Masterfile/Masterfile www.masterfile.com; Figure 1-31c, Courtesy of Sony Ericsson Mobile Communications AB. All Rights Reserved; Figure 1-31d, © Patrick Olear/Photo Edit — All rights reserved.; Figure 1-32, © Mark Harmel/Alamy; Figure 1-33, © Dynamic Graphics Group/IT Stock Free/Alamy; Figure 1-34, Courtesy of IBM Corporation; Figure 1-35a, © Comstock Images; Figure 1-35b, © Paul Barton/CORBIS; Figure 1-35c, © C. Görling/zefa/Corbis; Figure 1-35d, © Mark Harmel/Alamy; Figure 1-35e, © Dynamic Graphics Group/IT Stock Free/Alamy; Looking Ahead 1-2, Courtesy of Sony Electronics Inc.; Figure 1-36, © David Roth/Getty Images; Figure 1-38, Courtesy of IBM Corporation; Figure 1-39, © Peter Beck/CORBIS; Figure 1-40a, © AP/WIDE WORLD PHOTOS; Figure 1-0c, © Gabe Palmer/CORBIS; Figure 1-42, © EPA/Ulrich Perrey/Landov; Figure 1-43, © Charles O'Rear/CORBIS; Career Corner, © Jana Birchum/Getty Images; Technology Trailblazer 1, © Justin Sullivan/Getty Images; Technology Trailblazer 2, Photo by Business Wire via Getty Images; **Special Feature 1 Timeline:** 1937, Courtesy of Iowa State University; 1937, Courtesy of Iowa State University; 1937, Courtesy of Iowa State University; 1943, Photo courtesy of The Computer History Museum; 1943, Photo courtesy of The Computer History Museum; 1945, Courtesy of the Archives of the Institute for Advanced Study; 1946, From the Collections of the University of Pennsylvania Archives; 1947, © IBM Corporate Archives.; 1947, © IBM Corporate Archives.; 1951, Courtesy Unisys Corporation; 1952, Courtesy of Hagley Museum and Library; 1953, © IBM Corporate Archives; 1957, © IBM Corporate Archives; 1957, © IBM Corporate Archives; 1957, Courtesy of the Department of the Navy; 1958, Courtesy of Texas Instruments; 1958, Courtesy of Texas Instruments; 1958, Courtesy of Texas Instruments; 1959, © IBM Corporate Archives; 1960, Courtesy of Hagley Museum and Library; 1964, © IBM Corporate Archives; 1964, © IBM Corporate Archives; 1964, © IBM Corporate Archives; 1965, Courtesy of Dartmouth College; 1965, Courtesy of Digital Equipment Corporation; 1969, Courtesy of IBM Corporation. Unauthorized use not permitted; 1970, © IBM Corporate Archives; 1971, Courtesy of Intel Corporation; 1971, Courtesy of Intel Corporation; 1975, Photo courtesy of Computer History Museum; 1975, Courtesy of InfoWorld; 1976, Courtesy of Apple Computer, Inc.; 1976, © Bettmann/CORBIS; 1979, Photo courtesy of Computer History Museum; 1980, Courtesy of Microsoft® Corporation; 1981, © IBM Corporate Archives; 1982, Courtesy of Zoom Telephonics, Inc.; 1983, © Time Life Pictures/Getty Images; 1983, © IBM Corporate Archives; 1984, Courtesy of Apple Computer, Inc.; 1984, Courtesy of Hewlett-Packard Company; 1989, © 1997-1998W3C (MIT, INRIA, Keio); 1989, Courtesy of Intel Corporation; 1992, Courtesy of Microsoft® Corporation; 1993, Courtesy of Intel Corporation; 1993, Courtesy of Microsoft® Corporation; 1993, © Costa Cruise Lines/Getty Images; 1994, Courtesy of Netscape Communications Corporation; 1995, Courtesy of Sun Microsystems, Inc.; 1995, Box shot reprinted with permission from Microsoft® Corporation; 1996, Box shot reprinted with permission from Microsoft Corporation; 1996, Courtesy of palm, Inc. Palm, Treo, Tungsten, Zire, LifeDrive, VersaMail, Blazer, Addit, Handspring, "T" stylized, "Z" stylized, stylizations and design marks associated with all the preceding, and trade dress associated with Palm, Inc.'s products, are among the trademarks or registered trademarks owned by or licensed to Palm, Inc.; 1997, Motion Picture & Television Archives; 1997, Courtesy of Denon Electronics; 1997, Courtesy of Intel Corporation; 1998, © Andersen Ross/Getty Images; 1998, Courtesy of Apple Computer, Inc.; 1998, Box shot reprinted with permission from Microsoft® Corporation.; 1999, Box shot reprinted with permission from Microsoft® Corporation; 2000, Box shot reprinted with permission from Microsoft® Corporation; 2000, Box shot reprinted with permission from Microsoft® Corporation; 2000, © B Busco/Getty Images; 2000, Courtesy of Intel Corporation; 2001, Box shot reprinted with permission from Microsoft® Corporation; 2001, Box shot reprinted with permission from Microsoft® Corporation; 2002, Courtesy of RCA/Thomson Consumer Electronics; 2002, Courtesy of Sharp Electronics; 2002, Courtesy of Intel Corporation; 2003, Courtesy of ViewSonic® Corporation; 2002, Courtesy of Intel Corporation; 2002, © Scott Goodwin Photography; 2002, Courtesy of Handspring, Inc.; 2003, ©LWA- JDC/CORBIS; 2003, © Royalty-Free/CORBIS; 2003, © Jim Cummins/CORBIS; 2003, © Ed Bock/CORBIS; 2003, © Koichi Kamoshida/Getty Images; 2003, Box shot reprinted with permission from Microsoft® Corporation; 2003, © Getty Images; 2003, © REUTERS/Mannie Garcia; 2004, Courtesy of Sony Electronics Inc.; 2004, Courtesy of ViewSonic® Corporation. All rights reserved.; 2004, © Transcend Information Inc. All rights reserved.; 2004, Courtesy of Sandisk Corporation; 2004, Siemens AG Press Picture; 2004, Courtesy of Apple Computer, Inc.; 2004, Courtesy of Apple Computer, Inc.; 2005, Courtesy of The Mozilla Foundation; 2005, Courtesy of Microsoft Corporation; 2005, Courtesy of Apple Computer Inc.; 2005, © PRNewsFoto/Microsoft Corp.; 2005, Courtesy of palm, Inc. Palm, Treo, Tungsten, Zire, LifeDrive, VersaMail, Blazer, Addit, Handspring, "T" stylized, "Z" stylized, stylizations and design marks associated with all the preceding, and trade dress associated with Palm, Inc.'s products, are among the trademarks or registered trademarks owned by or licensed to Palm, Inc.; 2006, Photo by Nintendo via Getty Images; 2006, © PRNewsFoto/Sony; 2006, Courtesy of Intel Corporation; 2006, Courtesy of Microsoft Corporation; 2006, © Kim Blaxland/Getty Images; 2006, Courtesy of Microsoft Corporation; **Chapter 2:** Picture Yourself, © Freitag/zefa/Corbis; Picture Yourself, © Juan Silva/Getty Images; Picture Yourself, © GDT/Getty Images; Picture Yourself, © Rubberball/Getty Images; Picture Yourself, © Ross Durant/FoodPix; Picture Yourself, © Mark Sykes/Alamy; Picture Yourself, © Mark Sykes/Alamy; Picture Yourself, © Mark Sykes/Alamy; Picture Yourself, Courtesy of Logitech, Inc.; 2-1, Copyright ©David Young-Wolff/Photo Edit — All rights reserved.; Looking Ahead 2-1, Courtesy of Internet2; Figure 2-2a, Siemens press picture; Figure 2-2c, © Royalty-Free/Corbis; Figure 2-2d, ©LWA-Dann Tardif/CORBIS; Figure 2-2e, ©LWA-Dann Tardif/CORBIS; Figure 2-2f, © Paul C. Chauncey/CORBIS; Figure 2-2g, © Rob Lewine/CORBIS; Figure 2-3 Step 2, Courtesy of Motorola, Inc.; Figure 2-3 Step 3, Courtesy of Terayon Communication Systems, Inc.; Figure 2-3 Step 4, © Stephen Chernin/Getty Images; Figure 2-3 Step 6, Courtesy of Fujitsu Siemens

Figure 10a, Courtesy of Sony Electronics Inc.; Figure 10b, Courtesy of Matsushita Electric Corporation of America; Figure 10c, Courtesy of Logitech; Figure 11a, Courtesy of Sony Electronics Inc.; Figure 11b, © Art Vandalay/Getty Images; Figure 12a, Courtesy of JVC Company of America; Figure 12b, Courtesy of Pinnacle Systems, Inc.; Figure 12c, Courtesy of Matsushita Electric Corporation of America; Figure 12d, © Meeke/zefa/Corbis; Figure 13, Courtesy of Adobe Systems Incorporated; Figure 16, Courtesy of Adobe Systems Incorporated; Figure 17, Courtesy of Microsoft Corporation; Figure 18, Courtesy of Microsoft Corporation; Figure 19, Courtesy of Mediachance; **Chapter 7:** Picture Yourself, © Ken Welsh/Alamy; Picture Yourself, © Leslie Garland Picture Library/Alamy; Picture Yourself, © Alex Mares-Manton/Getty Images; Picture Yourself, © Cale Merege/Bloomberg News /Landov; Picture Yourself, © John Froschauer/Bloomberg News /Landov; Picture Yourself, © Steve Allen/Alamy; Picture Yourself, © Mark Wilson/Getty Images; Picture Yourself, Courtesy of Iomega; Picture Yourself, Courtesy of SanDisk Corporation; Figure 7-1a, © Masterfile (Royalty Free Div.) www.masterfile.com; Figure 7-1b, Photo Courtesy of Iomega Corporation. Copyright © 2003 Iomega; Corporation. All Rights Reserved. Zip is a registered trademark in the United States and/or other countries. Iomega, the stylized "i" logo and product images; are property of Iomega Corporation in the United States and/or other countries.; Figure 7-1c, Courtesy of Seagate Technology; Figure 7-1d, Courtesy of Toshiba America Information Systems, Inc.; Figure 7-1e, Courtesy of Western Digital; Figure 7-1f, Courtesy of Fujitsu Siemens Computers; Figure 7-1g, Courtesy of Quantum Corporation; Figure 7-1h, Courtesy of Kingston Technology Company, Inc.; Figure 7-1i, Courtesy of Sandisk Corporation; Figure 7-1j, Courtesy of Lexar Media, Inc.; Figure 7-1k, © Aaron Flaum/Alamy; Figure 7-6a, © Gary Herrington Photography; Figure 7-6b, Courtesy of Western Digital; Figure 7-8, Courtesy of Maxtor Corporation; Figure 7-11, Courtesy of Intel Corporation; Figure 7-13a, Courtesy of Maxtor Corporation; Figure 7-13b, Photo Courtesy of Iomega Corporation. Copyright © 2005 Iomega; Corporation. All Rights Reserved. Zip is a registered trademark in the United States and/or other countries. Iomega, the stylized "i" logo and product images; are property of Iomega Corporation in the United States and/or other countries.; Figure 7-14a, Courtesy of Quantum Corp.; Figure 7-14b,c, Photo Courtesy of Iomega Corporation. Copyright © 2005 Iomega; Corporation. All Rights Reserved. Zip is a registered trademark in the United States and/or other countries. Iomega, the stylized "i" logo and product images; are property of Iomega Corporation in the United States and/or other countries; Figure 7-15a, b, Photo Courtesy of Iomega Corporation. Copyright © 2005 Iomega; Corporation. All Rights Reserved. Zip is a registered trademark in the United States and/or other countries. Iomega, the stylized "i" logo and product images; are property of Iomega Corporation in the United States and/or other countries.; Looking Ahead 7-1, Courtesy of IBM Corporation; Figure 7-17, © Gary Herrington Photography; Figure 7-21a, Courtesy of Merriam-Webster Inc.; Figure 7-21b, c, Courtesy of Memorex Products, Inc.; Figure 7-21d, Coutesy of DeLorme; Figure 7-21e, f, Courtesy of Memorex Products, Inc.; Figure 7-22a, Courtesy of Encyclopædia Britannica, Inc.; Figure 7-22b, Courtesy of Microsoft Corporation; Figure 7-22c, © Gary Herrington Photography; Figure 7-23c, Courtesy of NEC Solutions (America), Inc.; Figure 7-23d, Courtesy of Ulead Systems, Inc.; Figure 7-23e, © Steven Brahms/Bloomberg News /Landov; Figure 7-24a, © 2005 Dell Inc. All Rights Reserved.; Figure 7-24b, Courtesy of DeLorme; Figure 7-26, Courtesy of Sony DADC; Looking Ahead 7-2, Courtesy of Blu-ray Disc Association; Looking Ahead 7-2, HD DVD logo is a Trademark of DVD Format/Logo Licensing Corporation.; Figure 7-27, Courtesy of Sony Electronics Inc.; Figure 7-28a, Courtesy of Toshiba America Information Systems, Inc.; Figure 7-28b, Courtesy of Toshiba America Information Systems, Inc.; Figure 7-30a, ©Sonda Dawes/The Image Works; Figure 7-30b, Courtesy of Delkin Devices, Inc.; Figure 7-30c, Courtesy of Lexar Media, Inc.; Figure 7-31, Courtesy of Sandisk Corporation; Figure 7-32, Courtesy of Delkin Devices, Inc.; Figure 7-33, Toshiba America Information Systems, Inc.; Figure 7-34, © Jean-Yves Bruel/Masterfile; Figure 7-35a, Copyright ©Bill Aron/Photo Edit — All rights reserved.; Figure 7-35b, Copyright ©Bill Aron/Photo Edit — All rights reserved.; Figure 7-37, © Wes Thompson/CORBIS; Figure 7-38a, © Comstock Images; Figure 7-38b, © Paul Barton/CORBIS; Figure 7-38c, © C. Görling/zefa/Corbis; Figure 7-38d, © Mark Harmel/Alamy; Figure 7-38e, © Dynamic Graphics Group/ IT Stock Free/Alamy; Career Corner, © Noel Hendrickson/Masterfile; Technology Trailblazer 1, Courtesy of Al Shugart International; Technology Trailblazer 2, Courtesy of IBM Research; **Chapter 8:** Picture Yourself, © Daisuke Morita/Getty Images; Picture Yourself, © Masterfile (Royalty-Free Division); Picture Yourself, Courtesy of Microsoft Corporation; Picture Yourself, Courtesy of Symantec Corporation; Picture Yourself, © Royalty-Free/Corbis; Picture Yourself, © David Young-Wolff/Alamy; Picture Yourself, © Koopman/CORBIS; Picture Yourself, Courtesy of Microsoft Corporation; Picture Yourself, Courtesy of Sony Ericsson Mobile Communications AB. All Rights Reserved.; Figure 8-1a,; Figure 8-1b, Courtesy of Kingston Technology; Figure 8-1c, Courtesy of Lexmark; Figure 8-1d, Courtesy of Acer America Corp.; Figure 8-1e, Courtesy of Hewlett-Packard Company; Figure 8-3, Step 7, Courtesy of Hewlett-Packard Company; Figure 8-5, Courtesy of Fujitsu Siemens Computers; Figure 8-7a, Courtesy of Kingston Technology; Figure 8-7b, Courtesy of Seagate Technology; Figure 8-8a, Courtesy of IBM Corporation; Figure 8-8b, Courtesy of Seagate Technology; Figure 8-8c, Courtesy of Lexmark; Figure 8-25a, © Getty Images; Figure 8-25b, Courtesy of Microsoft Corporation; Figure 8-26, Courtesy of Microsoft Corporation; Figure 8-28, Courtesy of Apple Computer, Inc.; Figure 8-29, Courtesy of K Desktop Environment, KDE.org; Figure 8-30, Courtesy of Red Hat; Looking Ahead 8-1, Courtesy of The Gimp, ewing@isc.tamu.edu; Figure 8-31, Courtesy of BERNINA® of America, Inc.; Figure 8-32a, © 2005 Dell Inc. All Rights Reserved.; Figure 8-32b, Courtesy of Audiovox; Figure 8-33a, Courtesy of palm, Inc. Palm, Treo, Tungsten, Zire, LifeDrive, VersaMail, Blazer, Addit, Handspring, "T" stylized, "Z" stylized, stylizations and design marks associated with all the preceding, and trade dress associated with; Palm, Inc.'s products, are among the trademarks or registered trademarks owned by or licensed to Palm, Inc.; Figure 8-33b, Courtesy of Kyocera; Figure 8-34, Courtesy of Sharp Electronics; Figure 8-35a, Courtesy of UIQ Technology; Figure 8-35b, Courtesy of Sony Ericsson Mobile Communications AB. All Rights Reserved.; Figure 8-37, Courtesy of Symantec Corporation; Figure 8-38, Courtesy of WinZip International L LC. WinZip is a registered trademark of; WinZip International LLC. All rights reserved. Figure 8-39, Courtesy of Nero Inc.; Figure 8-40, Courtesy of Symatec Corporation; Career Corner; Career Corner, © MTPA Stock/Masterfile; Technology Trailblazer 1, © AP/WIDE WORLD PHOTOS; Technology Trailblazer 2, © Kim Kulish/CORBIS; **Special Feature 8 Buyer's Guide:** Opener 1, Courtesy of Acer America, Inc.; Opener 2, Courtesy of Apple Computer; Opener 3, Courtesy of Acer America, Inc.; Figure 1a, Courtesy of Acer America, Inc.; Figure 1b1, Courtesy of Acer America, Inc.; Figure 1b2, Courtesy of ViewSonic; Figure 1b3, Courtesy of UTStarcom Personal Communications, a division of UTStarcom,; Inc.; Figure 1b4, Courtesy of palm, Inc. Palm, Treo, Tungsten, Zire, LifeDrive, VersaMail,; Blazer, Addit, Handspring, "T" stylized, "Z" stylized, stylizations and design marks associated with all the preceding, and trade dress associated with; Palm, Inc.'s products, are among the trademarks or registered trademarks owned by or licensed to Palm, Inc.; Figure 1c, © White Packert/Getty Images; Figure 4a, Courtesy of JVC; Figure 4b, Courtesy of Sandisk; Figure 4c, PRNewsFoto/SANYO Fisher Company; Figure 4d, Copyright © 2000-2005 Avid Technology, Inc. All Rights Reserved; Figure 4f, Courtesy of Seagate; Figure 4g, Courtesy of Logitech; Figure 4h, Courtesy of Microsoft; Figure 4j, Courtesy of Zoom Technologies Inc.; Figure 4k, Courtesy of ViewSonic Corporation; Figure 4l, Courtesy of Logitech; Figure 4m, Courtesy of 3Com Corporation; Figure 4n, Courtesy of EPSON America, Inc.; Figure 4o, Courtesy of Intel Corporation; Figure 4p, Courtesy of Kingston Technology; Figure 4q, Courtesy of UMAX; Figure 4s, Courtesy of Logitech; Figure 4t, Courtesy of Logitech; Figure 4u, Courtesy of Sandisk; Figure 4v, Courtesy of 3Com Corporation; Figure 4w, Courtesy of D-Link Corporation/D-Link Systems, Inc; Figure 4x, Courtesy of Iomega; Figure 12, PRNewsFoto/Mindjet LLC; Figure 13, Courtesy of Toshiba America Information Systems, Inc.; Figure 14, Courtesy of InFocus Corporation; Figure 15, Courtesy of IBM Corporation; Figure 16, Copyright ©Patrick Olear/Photo Edit — All rights reserved.; Figure 19, © 2005 by Electrovaya Inc. www.electrovaya.com; Figure 21, Courtesy of ViewSonic Corporation.